Annual Review of Information Science and Technology

Volume 4

1969

Z
699
A1
A65
v. 4

AMERICAN
SOCIETY FOR
INFORMATION
SCIENCE

Volume
4 Annual Review of
1969 Information Science
and Technology

CARLOS A. CUADRA, Editor
ANN W. LUKE, Assistant Editor

Encyclopædia Britannica, Inc. Chicago
William Benton, Publisher

**ASIS Advisory Committee
For the
Annual Review**
Pauline Atherton
Phyllis B. Baxendale
W. Douglas Climenson
Robert M. Hayes
Joseph H. Kuney
Richard H. Orr
William J. Paisley

**SDC Editorial and
Support Staff**
Donald V. Black, Technical Advisor
Harold Borko, Technical Advisor
Jules Mersel, Technical Advisor
Everett M. Wallace, Technical Advisor
Eileen Sever, Bibliographic Advisor
Cynthia A. Hudson, Staff Secretary

Major support for the initiation of the ASIS Annual Review series and the development of this volume was provided by the National Science Foundation through a grant to the ASIS. Additional support was contributed by the System Development Corporation and by Encyclopædia Britannica.

Copyright © 1969 by Encyclopædia Britannica, Inc.
All rights reserved. This book or any part thereof must not be reproduced in any form without the written permission of the publisher.

Library of Congress Catalog Card Number: 66-25096
Standard Book Number: 85229 147 7
Printed in the United States of America

List of Contributors

Thomas J. Allen
Massachusetts Institute of Technology,
Cambridge, Massachusetts

Lawrence H. Berul
Auerbach Corporation,
Philadelphia, Pennsylvania

Evelyn Daniel
University of Maryland,
College Park, Maryland

Robert A. Fairthorne
Hampshire, England

Robert V. Katter
System Development Corporation,
Santa Monica, California

Ruth M. Katz
System Development Corporation,
Falls Church, Virginia

Stella Keenan
National Federation of Science Abstracting
 & Indexing Services,
Philadelphia, Pennsylvania

Frederick G. Kilgour
The Ohio College Library Center,
Columbus, Ohio

Herbert B. Landau
Auerbach Corporation
Philadelphia, Pennsylvania

John G. Lorenz
Library of Congress, Washington, D.C.

Anne S. McFarland
Case Western Reserve University,
Cleveland, Ohio

Christine A. Montgomery
Bunker-Ramo Corporation,
Canoga Park, California

Carl F. J. Overhage
Massachusetts Institute of Technology,
Cambridge, Massachusetts

M. E. Senko
IBM Corporation, San Jose, California

Jesse H. Shera
Case Western Reserve University,
Cleveland, Ohio

Allen B. Veaner
Stanford University,
Stanford, California

Paul Wasserman
University of Maryland,
College Park, Maryland

Preface

This, the fourth volume of the *Annual Review of Information Science and Technology*, is both like and unlike its predecessors. The basic objective — to provide the most comprehensive and technically sound progress review ever prepared in the information science field — remains the same, as do the basic areas of interest and coverage. Too, the primary emphasis continues to be on published literature and reports, to permit the reader to identify, locate, and examine interesting and important sources of information about various aspects of our technical progress.

Some new areas of growing importance are introduced this year. For the first time, a chapter on reprography and microform technology and one on the international aspects of information transfer have been included. Also, the topics of document dissemination and the secondary services, usually covered in parts of other chapters, have full and separate chapters this year. Another change, made in response to suggestions from readers for better signposts within each volume, is the division of the book into several major segments, each introduced by a short description of the contents of the section, the relationships among the chapters within it, and, in some instances, one or two highlights of the year's technical progress.

Regular readers of the *Annual Review* will also notice that Volume 4 is considerably larger than prior volumes. It has 14 chapters, each somewhat longer than the average in past years, and this year's authors have had somewhat more space in which to analyze and report on the significant developments in their areas.

No longer new, since it was initiated in Volume 3, is the use of photocomposition techniques to publish this book. It seems altogether appropriate that the primary review tool in the information sciences should itself take effective advantage of the advanced techniques of the field, and ASIS is fortunate to have in Encyclopædia Britannica a publisher with a serious interest in information technology, as well as in annual reviews. We hope and plan to explore, for subsequent volumes, other uses of information technology—for example, the semi-automatic preparation of indexes to the *Annual Review* from the tapes used for photocomposition.

As with puddings, the success of an annual review is measured by consumption. Last year we mentioned preliminary findings from a survey of the impact of the *Annual Review of Information Science and Technology* on professional communication within our field. The survey, conducted with the help of the Stanford Institute of Communication Research, covered members of ASIS, SLA, ALA, and other organizations, and identified the characteristics of *Annual Review* users and non-users. The findings (discussed in Chapters 1 and 14) seem to confirm the general impression that annual review series have very broad usefulness; they also provide retrospective justification for the hope, on which the establishment of this series was based, that it could significantly improve the quality of professional communication in library and information science.

As there has been a programmed decline in the extent of financial support of the National Science Foundation, without whom this series could not have been started, other sources of support have begun to assume greater importance. In addition to income generated from sales, support for the present volume has been shared by the Foundation (again), the U.S. Office of Education, Encyclopædia Britannica, System Development Corporation, and the sponsoring organization, ASIS. The main technical contribution, as in previous years, has come from a group of talented specialists who have been willing to study carefully an enormous amount of current literature and to prepare comprehensive analyses of progress. Previous authors have testified that the effort, painful and time-consuming as it may be, is, in the end, its own reward. Be that as it may, we feel compelled to express also our admiration and gratitude for a difficult job very well done.

Carlos A. Cuadra
Santa Monica, California

Contents

I
Planning Information Systems and Services — 1

1 Information Needs and Uses — 3
Thomas J. Allen

2 Design and Evaluation of Information Systems — 31
Robert V. Katter

II
Basic Techniques and Tools — 71

3 Content Analysis, Specification, and Control — 73
Robert A. Fairthorne

4 File Organization and Management Information Systems — 111
Michael E. Senko

5 Automated Language Processing — 145
Christine A. Montgomery

6 Reprography and Microform Technology — 175
Allen B. Veaner

7 Document Retrieval — 203
Lawrence H. Berul

8 Document Dissemination — 229
Herbert B. Landau

III
Applications — 271

9 Abstracting and Indexing Services in Science and Technology — 273
Stella Keenan

10 Library Automation — 305
Frederick G. Kilgour

11	Information Networks Carl F. J. Overhage	339
12	International Transfer of Information John G. Lorenz	379

IV

	The Profession	403
13	Library and Information Center Management Paul Wasserman and Evelyn Daniel	405
14	Professional Aspects of Information Science and Technology Jesse H. Shera and Anne S. McFarland	439
	Index: Ruth M. Katz	473
	Combined Index	500

I

Planning Information Systems and Services

All aspects of information systems involve planning. This section describes recent progress in two of the major aspects: identifying the needs for information and the uses to which the information will be put, and designing and evaluating the systems themselves.

This is the fourth year in which the topic of user information needs and information-seeking behavior has been the subject of a chapter in the *Annual Review*. Like its predecessors, Chapter 1, "Information Needs and Uses," discusses the more generally useful and valid research in the field and reflects the many improvements in scope and methodology that have been characteristic of the past year's work. Indeed, a comparison of current work with that of several years ago shows clearly that even more knowledge, sophistication, and skill are being applied to this area of inquiry than were applied in the earlier years.

Allen's chapter marks something of a shift in emphasis toward the matter of *impact* of information upon the productivity of scientists and technologists. This emphasis runs counter to the view, current several years ago and still strongly held by some, that the concerns of information science are (or should be) limited largely to the "marking and parking" of documents. As more attention is given to the end result of information use — increased productivity — information science is moving away from exclusive concern with records and toward the broader issues of human communication.

Methodological and conceptual problems are still with us, as Allen points out. One salient fault to be found with the present work, as well as that of the past, is the failure to make a clear distinction between the scientist and the technologist. Allen deals with that difficulty, as well as with the several problems of developing a community of researchers in an interdisciplinary area, and suggests means of solving or alleviating these difficulties.

The second chapter considers the design and evaluation of systems as a cyclical process, in which new systems represent improvements to existing systems and evolve from evaluations of existing systems. Katter follows through the steps of system development—or "redevelopment," as he prefers to call it—from requirements analysis through design, evaluation, and cost/effectiveness analysis. Because he treats the subject more generally and comprehensively than is traditionally done, he provides an enlarged setting in which to consider associated problems and approaches that are not usually discussed in information science literature.

Katter discusses the assessment of the needs, demands, and goals of the system in terms of planning and designing the information system, and analyzes the problems of estimating, justifying, and obtaining the necessary financial support for the system. He also examines such operational constraints as copyright restrictions, data file security, standardization, and functional overlap. Because, as he suggests, interactive systems and their attendant technological advances have focused more attention on the interface between man and machine, Katter also gives coverage to the human factors analysis of this interface.

Research on document relevance, and "precision" and "recall" scores are still of considerable interest and concern in the literature. Yet there seems to be a growing recognition that measures of system value need to be much broader than retrieval performance, and that the measures of system performance that are the most useful are those that help us to decide what to do next in system redesign.

1 Information Needs and Uses

THOMAS J. ALLEN
Massachusetts Institute of Technology

INTRODUCTION

Previous authors in this series, writing on this subject, have usually felt it necessary to begin with a statement concerning the state of the methodology of "user" studies. They have, for the most part, found it improved over the past, and this year is no exception in that regard. There remains, however, the tendency on the part of many who are untrained in social science methodology to assume that the art of questionnaire design and administration is a very simple one that anyone with intelligence can master in a single attempt. One never realizes how truly wrong this view is until he finds himself the author of a review chapter and is then confronted with the sort of trivia that many authors submit as research reports.

The Approach

There is, on the other hand, a strong corpus of good research in the field, and the intent of this review will be not so much to point out what is wrong with the "bad," as to hold the "good" up as an example to be followed.

This approach should economize on the reader's time and sacrifice little in meeting his needs. In addition to excluding many of the very poor studies from review, we will also exclude any study that does not have general implications beyond the need of a single organization. There are many good studies performed for single organizations or libraries, and many of these studies contain implications or findings that can be generalized to other situations. Others, however, are so involved with local circumstances that any generalization is questionable. It is very doubtful that such local studies will be of interest to many readers of the review, and they will be excluded for that reason.

In addition to stating the ground rules for inclusion or exclusion of material, there are two conceptual points that should be made at the outset as well. First, looking back at last year's review, we find that Paisley (46) attempted to develop a conceptual framework for the field, placing the user in a series of concentric systems. This framework will be followed more or less in the present review since, as we will discover, the field does appear to be developing along the suggested lines. Furthermore, viewing the field through this framework reveals a striking alignment and relationship with several mainstreams of behavioral science research. The further development of these relations with other areas cannot help but be beneficial to the field in the future.

The second conceptual point is a simple one. It has, however, plagued much of the "research on research" literature for many years. We are concerned with the information needs and uses of scientists and technologists. Yet, in far too many reports, it is unclear which of the two was studied. In others, the sample includes both, but they are called "scientists." A major work reviewed last year was entitled *Scientists in Organizations* (50), but the majority of the subjects in the study were clearly technologists. The argument that "scientist" is a more generic term that covers both scientists and technologists merely evades the fundamental issue. The two populations are very different in their behavior, perhaps most particularly in their communication behavior. (See, for example, Allen, 3.)

The differences between these two populations and the difficulties that can be encountered by ignoring these differences have been pointed out quite clearly by Kaplan (36). Several studies have shown the very marked differences in motivation and social enculturation of scientists and technologists that underlie their differences in information needs and uses. (See, for example, Krulee & Nadler, 38; and Pelz & Andrews, 50.) Of course, this is not the place to explore in very great detail the nature of these differences or the implications thereof. Let us merely enter a plea for better indentification of the subject populations in future work.

Framework of the Review

Paisley (46), in last year's review, developed a conceptual framework in which he progressed outward from the individual scientist (or technologist) through a series of concentric systems in which the individual operated. We will follow the same scheme this year, with only some minor changes in the titles given to the several systems, and some adaptation to fit the nature of the past year's work. We will begin with the individual as an information processor and then work in sequence through his behavior in his research group, his organization, his professional society, and his "invisible college." We will conclude with a consideration of the individual within a formal information system. We have reduced Paisley's original list of ten concentric systems to six. This does not mean that any of the ten should be eliminated. They have merely been collapsed and joined again to better fit the material in this year's review.

THE YEAR IN REVIEW

The Scientist or Engineer as an Information Processor

This is the level of analysis that Paisley (46) labeled "The Scientist Within His Own Head." In the present treatment, we will broaden the category to include not only the decision involved in the selection of an information channel, but also the actual process of using the information as well. Few studies have attempted to pursue information beyond its consumption by a user, and yet the evidence that is available shows that the information needs of an individual vary greatly as he progresses with a project (Allen et al., 6). At least part of this variation can be attributed to the fact that different information channels better serve different problem-solving functions (Allen, 4).

The Relations Between Information Source and Problem-Solving Function. The year 1968 saw publication of three studies that further illumine this area. The first, reported by Frischmuth & Allen (19), is an elaboration of an earlier work (Allen, 4) and develops a model of the technological process that isolates several key functions of an information system. This model, which describes the actual process of using technological information, should aid future research in conceptualizing problems and in analyzing observed patterns of information use. The principal contribution of this model is to differentiate between those functions associated with *idea generation* and those associated with *problem definition*. The two processes, although far from independent, can be separated through analysis, and, as the next two studies show, rely upon quite different sources for their needed information.

Baker et al. (13) make this same distinction, and, for three "idea generating groups" in a division of a "major United States corporation," compare the sources used during *need events* (problem definition) with those used during *means events* (idea generation). They find that "thinking by self" and interaction within one's immediate group were important for both need and means events. Interaction with colleagues outside the group (but within the company) was more frequently associated with need events, while the use of the library was cited only for means events.

Utterback, in a well-conceived investigation of the innovative process (57), gathered protocols of the process leading to 15 award-winning industrial innovations. He differentiates — in a manner similar to the first two studies — between the functions of problem definition and idea generation.

Considering, first of all, the initial stimulus for an innovation, he contrasts innovations that were "means stimulated" with those that were "need stimulated," and finds that

> Need events were most often initiated by someone other than the person who initiated the idea for the innovation (63.4%), while means events were most often initiated by the innovator himself (58.5%). Means inputs came mainly from three sources: discussion outside the firm (31.0%), literature (24.2%) and analysis and experiment (24.2%); while the overwhelming majority of need inputs (73.4%) came from discussion, most from outside the firm (56.7%). While both types of stimuli came most frequently from external discussion, the source was most often a customer or potential customer for need events and most often a vendor or other source of technical information for means events.

The Utterback (57) and Baker et al. (13) studies clearly agree in emphasizing the importance of literature for idea-generating functions and of discussion for problem-definition functions. They differ only in that the principal locus of discussion in the Utterback case was *outside* the organization, while in the Baker et al. case it was *inside*.

These studies represent a start toward relating information source to problem-solving function. There is much more to be done, however. The functions to be served by an information system can be subdivided much further and, to some extent, can be arranged along a time dimension. Once this has been done, it will become possible to program information services and discussion contacts in a more optimal manner.

The Channel Selection Process. Last year's *Annual Review* reports two studies, by Rosenberg (53) and by Gerstberger & Allen (22), of the channel selection process; these have now been amplified and further supported by two 1968 studies (Allen et al., 8; Utterback, 57). The 1967 studies found that engineers turn first to the most accessible information channel, independent of the expected value of the information it will provide, and use more accessible channels more frequently. In his study of innovation, Utterback (57) provides data supporting this conclusion.

> In sum, search for information is more highly ordered following problem identification than before, and search proceeds in a hierarchical order from more to less easily accessible information sources.

Utterback shows that the search for information proceeds from literature and experience to discussion, and finally, to analysis and experiment, although the finding is not significant statistically. He goes on to rationalize the apparent conflict between his high placement of the literature and the Gerstberger & Allen (22) finding that literature was viewed as less accessible than discussion partners on the basis that his subjects were functioning as "technological gatekeepers" (Allen & Cohen, 7), and were, thereby, more exposed to the literature. This rationalization is not really necessary. The correlations between accessibility, frequency of use, and search order are far from perfect (magnitudes are of the order of 0.40 to 0.70). Another study by Allen et al. (8), drawing upon the same set of data as the earlier Gerstberger study, shows that engineers consult written channels first with a frequency far above that expected by chance, while discussion channels are found more frequently to be the last source consulted (the information-producing one).

Allen et al. (8) explain the tendency to use the literature more frequently as a first source in the following way:

> ... literature is sometimes employed to obtain background for oral communication, or to avoid oral communication completely in certain situations.

They point out a strategy by which engineers prepare themselves for oral communication by first gaining some background through the literature. In summary, it still appears that accessibility is the overriding determinant in channel selection and that even the apparent exception to this can be understood in terms of a second-order effect, the use of one information channel to make another more accessible.

The Context of the Work Team

Several of this year's studies view the individual in the context of his work team. These studies, in the case of technologists employed in organizations, differentiate between teams on the basis of whether they are composed of people who are all working on the same project and teams of people who all share the same functional or disciplinary interests. The importance of this distinction has been recognized for many years by organizational practitioners, but only recently has it received any attention from researchers.

Baker et al. (13), in the same study mentioned earlier, looked at a particular project that was concerned with a specific phase of the problem-solving process: idea generation. They studied three "idea-generating groups" in a division of a "major United States corporation." One or more members of their research team attended each of the idea-generating sessions held by the three groups, and took "notes summarizing all interactions which took place during the . . . meeting." In total, 303 ideas were submitted by 17 participants during the course of the sessions that were observed. Of these, the researchers were able through interview to determine the origins of 285 of the ideas. Each idea was later evaluated by each of the participants in the group and by two members of management to establish the performance criterion for the study. A further distinction was made between those ideas that had originated before the group meeting and those that originated during the meeting.

Of the "before" ideas, 28% of the total of 39 and 33% of those judged "best" came from interaction between group members and other members of the laboratory technical staff not assigned to the group. Six% of the total and 8% of the "best" ideas came from interaction outside of the company; 6% of the total and none of the "best" ideas came from the library. The remaining 60% of the ideas were attributed to "thinking alone."

Even after the groups were convened, members continued to receive many of their ideas from outside the group. Of 232 ideas, 16% came from interaction with colleagues within the company, but outside the group, and 16% from interaction with colleagues outside the company. Colleagues within the company contributed 20% of the "best" ideas; those outside were responsible for only 8.6% of the "best" ideas. Interaction within the group contributed 29% of the total number of ideas and 31% of the "best" ideas. The high contribution from within the groups should be expected in this instance, since the generation of ideas through interaction was the goal of the *idea-generating groups*. The high proportion of ideas that entered from outside is quite striking and illustrates the great dependence of technical groups upon the social system in which they are embedded.

A second 1968 study reinforces this point. Allen, Gerstenfeld, & Gerstberger (8) studied six parallel research and development projects[1] in which independent teams in different organizations worked on identical problems. The high-performing teams, in this case, made more extensive use of consultants from within their own organization. This was true both when a project member consulted with a colleague in his own area of specialty, and when he consulted with people in other specialties. The relation with performance is especially pronounced in the latter case.

Consulting within the project team, surprisingly, showed no relation to performance. Both high- and low-performing teams displayed a very high level of interaction within the projects themselves.

---

[1]This particular research method was reviewed by Menzel (42).

The Individual in an Organization

The formal structure of an organization, the structure normally depicted on an organization chart, is, of course, an important determinant of communication patterns and information flow. That is what it is intended to be. The purpose of formal organization is to determine lines of reporting, chains of command, direction of control, and coordination. These are all communication functions in the organization. Only recently, however, have we become fully aware of its importance in determining the patterns of technical information flow. Allen & Cohen (7), in a study of two Research and Development (R and D) laboratories, demonstrate this point quite clearly. They show that formal organization exerts a significant influence over both technical discussion patterns and the flow of critical information influencing the conduct of research projects.

Industrial and governmental organizations have experimented for years with numerous organizational structures (functional, project, matrix, etc.) for R and D laboratories. This was done primarily to improve the effectiveness of coordination and control of work, although to some extent it was done with the hope of keeping the technical staff more closely in touch with their field. Only in the past few years has any research been directed toward determining the effectiveness of the numerous organizational forms that have been developed.

Marquis & Straight (41) first compared R and D organizational structures in terms of their effectiveness in relation to the accomplishment of major projects. Their principal conclusion was that a functional form of organization, in which individuals are located both physically and organizationally with colleagues sharing the same technical specialty, was the more effective form for technical personnel. Higher technical performance was found in those instances in which this form of organization was used. On the other hand, project organization in which individuals report directly to and are located near a project manager, who is directly responsible for their work, was found to be the best form for administrative personnel. Use of this form of organization for contract administration and accounting personnel resulted in much tighter control over costs and schedules.

The authors make no attempt to explain this result in terms of the different communication patterns that result from the two forms of organization, but the present reviewer would like to speculate that communication lies at the heart of their results. Technologies can be roughly ordered in terms of their rate of change: the degree to which their "state of the art" is advancing. If we were to do this for R and D projects we could all agree that the technical people in the Marquis & Straight study were all involved in technologies that lie somewhat nearer the dynamic end of this continuum than do the administrative "technologies." Cost accounting and contract administration have not undergone any very rapid growth periods recently. It is, therefore, not as essential that accountants and contract lawyers maintain themselves in close contact with disciplinary colleagues. By contrast, technologists in rapidly changing fields do have to maintain close contact with colleagues, or the field may pass them by. Perhaps we can even generalize from this extreme example and suggest that functional organization is most essential for the more dynamic of physical technologies, while, for the older, more stable, physical technologies, we may find that engineers can afford to be cut off for a period of time from colleague interaction and that, in such cases, the project form of management may produce superior results through its capability of greater direct control and responsibility.

The Informal Organization. Informal organization is defined by one of this year's authors (Conrath, 14) as:

> ... an organization that arises without conscious planning, initially to meet personal and/or organizational needs that are not met within the framework of the formally recognized structure.

Allen & Cohen (7) find that this informal organization (measured by them in terms of social interactions) has a strong influence over communication structure. Moreover, to some degree this influence operates independently of the formal organization. Allen et al. (8) go on from here to show some of the dynamics through which informal organization operates. Friendships, or even acquaintanceships, can do wonders to reduce the "psychological cost" of consulting with colleagues within one's organization. Many of these acquaintanceships are developed through such "neutral social interactions" as noon-hour bridge and chess games, as well as transfers of personnel within the organization.

Conrath (14) provides anecdotal evidence of the ability of informal organization to influence administrative decisions on technical subjects. He confuses this informal organization with something like an invisible college and calls his subjects "scientists," although they are clearly technologists. Beyond this, however, he does argue quite effectively that the informal organization, by controlling the flow of technical information to management, can significantly influence managerial decisions. Conrath also goes on to show that informal organization, spontaneous though it may be, can be dealt with to some extent, and possibly controlled, by management.

Architecture: A Neglected Factor in Communication. In addition to formal and informal organization, a third factor exerting a significant influence over the communication network in a technical organization is the architectural layout of the facilities. The influence of spatial location upon interactions among people is a subject that has received a great amount of attention over the years (Festinger et al., 18; Gullahorn, 24; Kennedy, 37; and Maissoneuve, 40). This year, and to this reviewer's knowledge for the first time, this line of research has been extended into the realm of science and technology. O'Gara (44), in a study of an academic department and two industrial R and D laboratories, demonstrates the relationship between the physical distance separating people and their probability of technical communication. Communication probability declines very greatly as the distance separating people is increased. As a matter of fact, communication probability decreases with the square of distance and, in all three of the cases cited by O'Gara, reaches its asymptotic level within 25 yards. This asymptotic level, it should be added, was quite low—less than 0.05 in all cases. The use of the term "probability" to describe past events might be criticized by a purist; nevertheless, the results remain, and they have very profound implications for laboratory architecture. One would certainly want to avoid long, narrow corridors that maximize the separation between people. In addition, the dropoff in communication with increasing distance may apply to interaction with such nonhuman communication points as computer consoles and bookshelves. A study by Frohman (20), on the use of library facilities by technological groups at differing distances from the library, provides results similar to those on interpersonal communication.

For the most part, the architectural profession seems to have ignored these considerations. The present reviewer was recently shown architectural plans for a new industrial research laboratory. The structure was to be a very beautiful one. Both internally and externally, its aesthetic qualities were quite pleasing. At the same time, its impact upon communications in the organization that it was to house would have been disastrous. The offices were laid along three long corridors that together formed a "Z" shape! The net effect was that the distance separating people was maximized.

This is not at all an isolated case. Now that researchers have some knowledge of the communication behavior of scientists and engineers in organizations, they have the concomitant responsibility to make architects aware of the impact that their designs will have on this behavior. Communication patterns, or organizational information flow, will eventually have to become one of the more important criteria of architectural design.

In the meantime, this area appears to be quite fruitful for research. We are fortunate this year in having a review by Patterson (49) of the spatial determinants of social interaction. Hopefully, this review will be helpful in stimulating more work on the part of those who are concerned with communications.

The Individual in a Professional Society

This year saw studies of two major international scientific congresses and a comparison between the two. The Eighteenth International Congress of Psychology was analyzed by study teams from the United States, Russia, and Europe. The United States study was reported by both the American Psychological Association's (APA) Project on Information Exchange in Psychology (11) and the Johns Hopkins Center for Research in Scientific Communication (33). The bodies of the reports are identical, although some of the conclusions and recommendations differ in their emphasis. In addition, the Johns Hopkins report includes a study of the Sixth World Congress of Sociology, with an interesting comparison between the two meetings.

Both Johns Hopkins studies provide some interesting insights into the transfer of scientific information across national boundaries, and the value of international meetings in accomplishing this goal. They challenge, for example, the image that such meetings provide "mainly a rehash of older work." While, at both meetings, a substantial proportion of the papers (psychology, 53%; sociology, 39%) were reviews or syntheses derived from a series of studies, there was a slight tendency for the reviews to contain material of a more current nature than is found in the reports of single studies and experiments. Although this seems surprising at first, it is reasonable to expect that an author would be willing to add to a review some additional material that might be too premature or speculative to stand by itself.

It was the authors who were the principal beneficiaries of interaction at the two congresses. This was also found to be true in earlier studies of national meetings in the United States, but at international meetings, the effect is more pronounced:

> ... it appears that interaction resulting from making a presentation at an international meeting has a greater effect upon an author's work than is true of such interaction at a national one in either (psychology or sociology).

Probably a more important function of international meetings is that of developing and extending informal communication networks on a worldwide basis.

> Three-fourths of the authors reported that they had established or planned to establish some continuing information-exchange relationship with other participants. . . .

Of course, we have no knowledge of how enduring these links will be, and it would be of value to follow up these studies to see how long they persist. In this regard, it would be interesting to learn whether the authors and attendants at such international conferences form a stable community, or whether there is a substantial turnover in conference attendance. Informal relationships are almost certain to expire with time unless there is some direct contact to rejuvenate them.

Once we have some idea of the duration of relationships established by an international conference, we can begin to think about optimum periods between attendance. Perhaps a small core of key scientists should attend every conference; or perhaps we should vary an individual's attendance by financing attendance at only one out of every three or five conferences. On the other hand, it is entirely possible that international conferences should be held less than annually. These are all problems for further research, and it is hoped that the results from the first two studies will stimulate further work in this area—perhaps, now, in additional scientific fields.

Two replications of APA's experiment in publishing a *Proceedings* prior to its convention are reported in APA Report Number 18 (12). The original experiment was reviewed by Paisley (46). The replications are more realistic, in that members were asked to pay for the *Proceedings*. In the original experiment, the *Proceedings* was distributed free of charge to 6,700 members. When asked to pay for a preconvention copy, only 2,000 members responded in 1966 and 3,500 in 1967. Even at this disappointing level of distribution, the preconvention *Proceedings* was found to have essentially the same impact as was found in the original experiment. When the preconvention *Proceedings* is coupled with discussion sessions at the conference, it stimulates greater interaction between author and attendant and leads to many modifications in attendants' work.

Garvey and his team at the Johns Hopkins Center for Research in Scientific Communication are continuing their work with a wide range of technological and scientific societies. This work apparently began with the idea of transferring the proven methodology of the APA studies to the study of other societies. The Hopkins team concentrated at first on the study of society meetings. Working outward from this focus, they are now beginning to consider other communication media of the societies and informal communication among the membership.

Using a major conference as an initial reference point in time, the Johns Hopkins team has initiated a series of longitudinal studies. They first work back through questionnaire and interview to the inception of a research idea and initiation of the project. Then they follow the work forward, sampling at one or more subsequent points in time to determine the eventual publication fate of the material presented at the conference. The detailed content of the ten reports produced in 1968 is far too rich to attempt to summarize in a few paragraphs, but we can comment on the general approach.

In essence, the Hopkins people have developed, in nine disciplines, panels of scientists and technologists whose work they can now follow over a period of time. Thus far, they have pursued seven of these panels from their initial conference presentation to a point one year later to determine such things as:

> ... the current state of the manuscript (derived from the conference presentation); the *inclusion* in the manuscript of work additional to that presented at the meeting; instances and results of submissions of manuscripts to journals other than those by which they were accepted and published; reasons for not publishing in journals of such prior submissions and additional dissemination plans. (30)

This set of nine parallel, longitudinal studies should greatly increase our understanding of the social systems and communication patterns, both formal and informal, in science and technology. One hopes that they will pursue at least some of these panels, to determine more about the way in which future work develops.

We also look forward to comparisons among the nine disciplines. Such comparisons will certainly shed more light on the differences among social and physical sciences and technologies. Garvey et al. (21) whet our appetite in this regard with a report directed principally to a comparison of educational researchers with researchers in the eight other fields. In the process of comparing educational research, which they classify as a social science, with other social and physical sciences and physical technologies, they reveal several very interesting differences among these fields of activity.

Educational research resembles the physical technologies in several very important aspects. Researchers in this area make high use of technical reports as a medium for dissemination of research results. This is also true for the physical technologies, but is found far less in the other social sciences or the physical sciences. Attendants at meetings of the American Educational Research Association resemble physical technologists in being far less familiar with the work of presentation authors than is typical in the physical and social sciences. In line with this, the educational researchers show relatively low use of informal distribution of preprints prior to journal publication. This again is true of physical technologists but not of scientists.

On the other hand, educational researchers behave like scientists in general, in that a large proportion of presentations at meetings are based on theses or dissertations. They also regard the meeting as an interim report mechanism and seek the final publication of their work elsewhere. Furthermore, they display their kinship to social scientists by spreading their publication over a very large number of journals and by eventually publishing in journals other than the one to which the work had been originally submitted.

In the view of the present author, these comparisons have very interesting implications for comparisons between the communication activities of scientists and technologists, both physical and social. Garvey et al. (21) admit in their paper that their division of the nine disciplines into social science, physical science, and technology is only an approximation, and that they are currently attempting to refine their basis for classification. However, even this first attempt has produced very promising results, and their work should eventually lead to an empirically derived classification scheme that will finally resolve the old problem of determining into which category a specific activity should fall.

Even without resolving this dilemma, however, the Johns Hopkins studies will be of enormous value simply because they demonstrate the differences in communication needs that exist among disciplines. This will be particularly important to the professional engineering societies, who presently know little more than the names and mailing addresses of their membership, and who have no idea of the relative merits of the various communication media that they sponsor. It is conceivable that the professional engineering societies might discontinue the publication of journals entirely and concentrate their efforts on conferences and meetings. The Hopkins studies will provide the necessary information for such major policy changes by the societies.

There will, of course, be no single answer for all fields within either science or technology. Fields differ greatly in their needs, and the comparative approach that is being pursued is eminently suited to clarifying these differences.

As an example of some interesting differences that have already appeared among disciplines, the Hopkins comparison of psychologists with sociologists (30) shows a greater tendency among the latter to publish their work in books rather than journals. Thirty-two % of the authors at the Sixth World Congress of Sociology planned final publication in book form; this compared with 19% of the psychologists at the Eighteenth International Congress of Psychology. It will be valuable to learn more about the reasons for these differences (variations in the reward systems of the disciplines, perhaps) as well as their consequences.

16 THOMAS J. ALLEN

The Invisible College

The "invisible college" hypothesis has been an appealing but elusive one. The past year, however, marks a considerable increase in our understanding of this phenomenon. Studies by Crane (15, 16), by the APA team (10), and by the Stanford Institute for Communication Research (39, 48) are major contributions to this improved understanding.

Crane (16) surveyed authors listed in Rogers's (52) exhaustive bibliography of research on the diffusion of agricultural innovations. The survey obtained data on six types of relationship (informal communication, current collaboration, thesis direction, thesis influence, influence on selection of problems, influence on selection of techniques) that might exist among authors, and to this was added the additional relation, "published collaboration." Crane then performed a sociometric analysis on these data, grouping individuals on the basis of their productivity and continuity in the area of research. She found that, "Respondents chose scientists who had not published in the area almost as often as they chose scientists within the area." She refused to accept this as sufficient evidence for the absence of a social structure in the research area, and moved on to a second level of analysis. Grouping members on the basis of their productivity and continuity in the area, she found that the more productive scientists who had remained in the research area were the most usually chosen. She argues that these scientists provide a gravitational force, holding the field together and providing it with a structure that differentiates it from other research areas. This is a conclusion that finds reinforcement from similar discoveries by the APA research team (10) and Lingwood (39). These findings not only provide the first really convincing empirical support for the invisible college hypothesis, but also take us a long way toward a better understanding of the manner in which such social systems function.

Crane went on to compare five subgroups within the agricultural diffusion area. The five subgroups are determined on the basis of productivity and continuity in the area. Unfortunately, at this point, she introduces into the analysis the concept of "indirect choice." An indirect choice exists between scientists A and C when A says that he communicates with B, and B says that he communicates with C. Of course, the number of intermediaries between the terminal points in the communication path can be increased indefinitely by the simple device of raising the original sociometric choice matrix to the nth power; Crane does just this and never lets the reader know just how high n became before the analysis terminated itself. Her analysis, using indirect choices, should therefore be approached with some skepticism. To infer that information passes from A to C because A talks to B, who talks to C, is very risky, but once the number of intermediaries becomes greater than one, the analysis becomes merely an interesting game with little chance of any relation to reality. The existence of a citation, first of all, does not guarantee that any information was transferred between two authors. Authors, as Whitley (58) so clearly demonstrates, cite for many reasons other than to acknowledge the receipt of information. Furthermore, the probability that separate links in a citation chain all deal with the same kind of information, let alone the same message, is very small. Scientist B may cite C's work for its methodology, scientist A then cites B's results, or the mismatch between A and C may be due to the fact that many scientists are active in several research areas. To infer from the indirect citation of C by A that any communication or social relation exists between the two is a very chancy business. Of course, as the number of indirect links increases, the risk increases, too. If nothing else, perhaps the conceptual difficulties encountered through the use of indirect citation will serve to make us all more aware of the assumptions and risks implicit in the methodology of citation network analysis.

Apart from the indirect citation problem, the Crane study is a good one. She attempts to analyze the social dynamics in the field as it developed over 25 years, and she concludes that the invisible college is akin to a "social circle." This is a loosely structured social system in which "members come together on the basis of their interests rather than propinquity or acquired statuses." Furthermore, "Each member is usually aware of some but not all members. The exact boundaries of the social circle are difficult to locate." This description of the social circle certainly fits what we know thus far about the invisible college.

In a second study based on the same survey, Crane (15) compares groups of formal collaborators on the basis of group size. Groups in this case are based on the existence of direct or indirect citation links among members. She finds that members of large groups of collaborators were more frequently named as persons with whom scientists in the area discussed their ongoing research and named as having influenced the selection of research problems. Members of large groups had more indirect (as defined above) communication ties, but certain members of medium-sized groups who had been more productive in the early phase of growth of the area had considerable indirect influence upon the selection of research problems in the field. Their ideas were transmitted to other scientists in the area through members of large groups. Large groups were also more productive.

Size of group also appears to influence communication patterns. The number of reciprocated choices per member was nearly twice as large for large groups as for small groups and isolates. Furthermore, members of large groups have more communication ties with each other, with members of smaller groups, and with scientists outside the area as well.

Following in this vein, the most recent of the APA studies (10) analyzes informal communication linkages and degree of social organization for five research areas in psychology. Groups of psychologists (averaging about nine per group) were selected in each of 12 areas of research. Group membership was based on high productivity as determined from *Psychological Abstracts* for a five-year period. The groups were surveyed to determine the informal communication practices. Two important considerations emerge at this point. First, four of the 12 fields showed such little contact among members that they had to be eliminated from the analysis. It might prove as interesting to learn more about these four fields and the reasons for their low interaction as it was to study the remaining eight fields, which were later collapsed into five. Second, an attempt to estimate group structure through *Science Citation Index* proved futile, because ". . . checks of reciprocal citation by persons in each of (three) groups, within the three most recent *S.C.I.* volumes, showed so few links among researchers as to be of little assistance in estimating structure." This is particularly important because, as we shall see later, there was a considerable degree of structure to be found in some of these groups.

Informal links among scientists, determined by both the original survey and selected follow-up interviews, were analyzed sociometrically. The analyses show a wide variation in degree of organization among groups. Some areas are highly organized with a great deal of informal contact among researchers and a great amount of influence from certain key members. Other areas show scarcely any organization, and one of these was found to be primarily a secondary area of research for its members who pursued it as more of a "hobby." High degree of organization was found to be associated with situations in which a limited number of institutions had the necessary research facilities; or a specialized professional organization existed for the field; or many student-teacher relationships had developed. Informal information exchange can, apparently, occur independent of social organization. This was the case in one field. In the view of the authors, the absence of both communication and organization can occur only in a field that most researchers regard as a subsidiary interest.

According to the report, "Conferences and committees and the Center for Advanced Study in the Behavioral Sciences may contribute to the creation of short-lived interactive groups" (10, p. 253). Unfortunately, in the one case studied, the group very soon became fractionated. It may be that such devices are effective in forcing structure on a field, but their effect is transitory unless the field is viable on other bases. Probably the most important message for the scientific societies lies in the finding that the research literature had no consistent relation to social structure or informal communication. Whether anything can be done about this, and, if so, whether it is necessary or desirable, is a question that now must be addressed.

The phenomenon of highly influential scientists who hold the system together is found once again in this study. These key people, as Crane found, are generally senior people who, over the years, have developed a large alumni of former thesis students. The Crane and APA studies cover a great deal of common ground with generally consistent findings that, combined, take us a long way toward understanding the way in which social organization mediates informal communication in science.

In another study that focuses on a research specialty, Parker et al. (48) examine the field of communications research. In last year's *Annual Review*, Paisley (46) justifiably criticized one of the 1967 studies for inadequate problem conceptualization and data analysis. This year, he and his two colleagues set an excellent example to follow in this regard. Beginning with a survey of research workers in several fields related to the study of communications, they conduct good, sound, data analysis. Realizing, first, that intercorrelating a large number of variables necessarily produces a large number of spuriously significant results, they split their sample in half, randomly analyze each half separately, and accept only those results that are significant in both halves.

They then wend their way through a mass of data, discovering trends and determining structure in a very artful manner. They begin with a large number of zero order correlations that produce little, if any, sense. Then, using factor analysis, they isolate several components among the data, which they then use as variables in further analysis. They conclude with a series of multiple regression analyses, moving variables in and out, one at a time, to determine their effect on the amount of variance explained in the dependent variable. About the only criticism that can be made of their data analysis concerns their presentation, which might have been a little clearer if it had included more of their partial correlations.

Unfortunately, after all of this, the analysts were able to explain only "22% to 31%" of the variance in productivity. This is perhaps due to the very mixed nature of their sample (researchers and teachers in education, general semantics, journalism, public opinion, health, and documentation). They might improve the explanatory power of their results by looking at some of these subdivisions separately.

The information input variables again (cf. Parker et al.) turn out to be the strongest predictors of output: "amount of information the respondent inputs is the strongest predictor of how much he produces."

If anyone still needs assurance of the value of communication to the scientist or engineer, here it is. Both the amount and variety of information consumed are strong determinants of scientific or technological output.

Here we can refer back to the Allen et al. (8) study of organizational consulting. For the engineers in that sample, both the amount and diversity of consulting showed strong correlations with technological performance. Thus, in quite independent studies, we find confirmation of the need for both amount and variety in information consumption.

As for the means used in acquiring information, Parker et al. find the single strongest predictor of output to be "the utilization of interpersonal contact with other researchers as a primary source of scientific information input." They say that

> ... it is not so much total information consumed by the individual that predicts his productivity, but rather, integration within *inter*personal communication channels. More productive researchers do not use *im*personal channels significantly more than less productive researchers.[2]

This is not an isolated finding (cf. 3, 5, and 13), but it is one to which far too little attention has been paid. It contains an important message for those investigators and research-sponsoring agencies that have focused their attention much too heavily on improving the operation of impersonal channels.

In still a fourth investigation of the invisible college, Lingwood (39) begins with externally defined groupings of attitude researchers and educational researchers. An individual was included in one of the groupings if he indicated it to be his specialty in any of a number of ways, e.g., joining a specialty group in a professional society. The initial samples were then "snowballed" by including anyone mentioned as a colleague by two or more members of the original sets.

Following the methodology of Parker et al. (48), Lingwood factor analyzes information inputs and derives four input factors in each case. He then performs a multiple regression analysis with number of authorships in the past five years as the dependent variable, and as independent variables he uses demographic factors first, then information inputs, and finally a quantity that he labels "sociometric prestige." This quantity uses a measure of the centrality of an individual in a sociometric network weighted by the number of other individuals with whom he has either direct or indirect sociometric relations. In both cases, the addition of sociometric prestige to the analysis explains an additional 3 to 4% of the variance in output. Demographic information input and sociometric factors together account

---

[2]Emphasis added.

for 21% of the output variance in the case of attitude researchers and 19.3% in the case of educational researchers.

Lingwood then attempts to locate invisible college groups among his educational researchers. He compares the number of observed sociometric connections among individuals who indicated the same research interest with the number that could be expected at random. The expected values are based upon a formula "which estimates how many choices a random subgroup should receive from a group of respondents, each making a certain number of unduplicated choices." There are all sorts of problems of classification and definition that could be raised here, but Lingwood appears well aware of them and claims that this is merely a first try at analysis, and a very promising first try it is. Six of the 14 research areas show a significantly higher proportion of internal choices than would be expected by chance. Four do not show significant results, and four more show significantly *fewer* internal choices than expected. Research fields as the APA study also showed us, display a very wide variance in the propensity to form invisible colleges. Some appear to have no cohesion at all. It will be interesting to see what investigators like Lingwood are able to determine about the reasons behind these differences among research areas.

Another 1968 investigation that set out to explore "oral/informal technical communications behavior" is reported by Graham et al. (23). It is based upon tape-recorded telephone interviews with 326 scientists and engineers in a broad range of specialties. With a sample this size and the amount of effort that must have gone into the study, it is extremely unfortunate that the methodology was so poor. Participants were asked to reply to such questions as: "In what way are informal communications essential to the transfer of scientific and technical information?", "Please give an example of how informal communications contribute to research motivation.", and "What would help to improve scientific and technical communications within your organization?" Researchers in the field of information needs and uses gave up the approach of asking scientists and technologists for their opinions at least ten years ago, after it had been shown to produce poor and often entirely misleading results (Menzel, 42). Fortunately, the authors do not apply a very sophisticated analysis to these very unreliable data; they merely tabulate the frequency of responses. We could dwell at length on the further shortcomings of this study; suffice it to say that it is an interesting catalog of the *stated* opinions of the respondents, but is of questionable value in predicting their behavior.

Before we leave the topic of the invisible college, one further inclusion should be made. Last year's review commented on James Watson's autobiographical study of the discovery of the structure of the DNA molecule,

The Double Helix. In reviewing this year's work, we would be particularly remiss if we failed to mention Merton's (43) review of that book. The review is a separate analysis in itself, and should be of enormous value to readers of the original book.

The Formal Information System

The Slater & Keenan (54) work continues. Following their initial survey of methods used by physicists in maintaining current awareness (reviewed by Paisley), they have constituted three panels comprising all United Kingdom respondents to their first questionnaire; those United States respondents who indicated a willingness to continue; and a new set of all United States subscribers (n = 527) to *Current Papers in Physics.* It must be remembered that, in considering the first two panels formed out of first questionnaire respondents, the initial response rate was only about 30%. Any biases introduced because of this will continue to influence results and may be strengthened by a continually diminishing response. The response to the second-phase survey continued at a disappointingly low level. Only the United Kingdom sample remained essentially intact (90%). Both United States samples produced disappointing response rates (47 and 58%, respectively).

The Slater & Keenan study is extremely well conceived and executed, and it is terribly frustrating to see such poor response rates. The difference in response between the second United Kingdom and United States samples may provide a methodological clue. In the United Kingdom case, subscriptions to *Current Papers in Physics* were awarded free of charge to the panel, which may have committed the panel to the study, whereas in the United States, physicists had to pay their subscription. This point may be worth investigation to find a way to avoid poor response in the future.

The second survey showed respondents to be generally satisfied with *Current Papers in Physics.* The degree of coverage that was preferred was "the same as *Physics Abstracts.*" Respondents had been given a choice between core journals, journals peripheral to the field, and fairly complete coverage as in *Physics Abstracts.* Furthermore, there did not appear to be any bias toward a particular area of physics.

The third survey was based entirely on use of one particular issue of *Current Papers in Physics.* Participants were asked first to number the sections in the order in which they scanned them and then to mark all items of interest, indicating whether an abstract or the full paper was desired. They then returned the entire issue to the American Institute of Physics. This idea of requesting the return of a marked-up version of the publication is a creative one and carries potential for future work. Unfortunately, in this case, respondents were asked only to indicate the order in which they scanned topics. This resulted in the finding that slightly more than half of the respondents followed a "sequential scan" strategy, beginning at the front and working their way through the entire issue. The rest sequenced their scan in order of their degree of interest in each of the sections. Where one goes from here is not entirely clear. It is thus disappointing that Slater & Keenan did not push for more information from their respondents. Still more could be done with what they have, however. The most important aspect of the data lies in the relation between subject field of the user and his range of interests among the subject specialties within *Current Papers in Physics*. This analysis could be fruitfully pursued much further.

In addition, a more direct test of the effectiveness of *Current Papers in Physics* would assess its effect on the current awareness practices of physicists. A repetition of the initial survey questionnaire would provide a comparative basis for determining this.

Cuadra et al. (17) this year report a first study of the impact of the *Annual Review of Information Science and Technology*. The study was performed after the publication of the 1966 edition and employed survey questionnaires administered to 3,000 individuals, about evenly divided among those who had previously reported (by an initial postcard survey) using the *Annual Review*, those who had only seen or heard of it, and others who had neither seen nor heard of it. The sample was chosen on the basis of membership in one of four professional societies concerned with information science. Comparison of the three categories of exposure produced some interesting results, which will help in determining whether the *Annual Review* is reaching its intended audience and what strategies are most effective in bringing it to this audience. Far more important than this is the demonstration of the *Annual Review*'s impact upon its audience. The authors wisely differentiate between measurements of what they call "effectiveness" of a medium, its comprehensiveness, clarity, etc., and its "impact," its effect on behavior. While admitting the limitations of survey methods in determining impact, they nevertheless muster some convincing arguments that the *Annual Review* did modify its users' communication behavior. It would be interesting to go on from this initial study and examine the impact and value of annual reviews in several fields, using more sensitive methods than the survey questionnaire. It will be interesting also to see what effect the organization of an annual review has upon the formation and continuance of invisible colleges in the fields it covers.

THE PRESENT AND FUTURE STATE OF THE FIELD

As the Parker et al. study (48) shows, there is little unity within the field of communication research. It is undoubtedly more difficult for an interdisciplinary area to develop any structure of its own, given the opposing, and often competing, attractions of the scientists' home disciplines. Within that subset of communication researchers who are interested in the use of information by scientists and technologists, this situation continues to hold true. Many studies are still performed by individuals who are primarily concerned with a limited and very local problem, but these are usually of poor quality and provide little contribution to the field in general. However, there has developed a very loosely structured invisible college, whose members are almost entirely located within four or five institutions. The possibility that this nucleus of researchers will ever develop a social structure that even approaches that of Crane's agricultural sociologists remains a dim one, because the members are divided among several disciplines and must look to these disciplines for reward and recognition. This introduces a divisive force that external measures can offset only temporarily. It is rather tempting at this point to speculate on the reasons why so little work of any value has come out of the university schools of communication and information science that have been established for the study of communications. Perhaps it is because they cannot compete with the disciplinary departments for talent and their output reflects this shortage of talent.

On the positive side, there is much that can be said for the present state of the field. Three or four groups have developed that are performing research of very high quality. Moreover, the divided nature of the field may be more of an asset than a liability. The split allegiance of the researchers allows them to draw from already established streams of scientific investigation. There now appear to be at least three of these. First of all, the view of an individual scientist or technologist as an information processor ties the field directly to cognitive psychology and should provide a mutually beneficial interaction at that point. Second, the introduction of bureaucratic organization as an important determinant of information flow among technologists brings much of the work directly into the mainstreams of organizational psychology and sociology. There is certainly a great deal to be gained by both sides in this transaction. Virtually nothing is known at the present time concerning the nature of communications in organizations, yet communications is the keystone of organizational functioning. We may see this important general area of organization theory opened through studies of laboratory organizations. The resulting activity will definitely feed back information upon which improvements in laboratory communications can be based.

The third point of contact is with the sociology of science. This is a new and rapidly developing area. Yet we have only to look at Crane's work to see major contributions emanating from it. This is perhaps the point at which "user studies" overlap an established field to the greatest extent, and the resulting interaction bodes fruitful.

In sum, we appear to be in much the same divided condition as the psycholinguists of APA report number 21 (10). Researchers enter the field of user studies from several different bases and for a variety of reasons. Unlike the psycholinguists, however, they seem at the present time to have a reasonably effective degree of interaction among themselves. Perhaps this is due to the small size of the field, and that may be the best of all situations: an interdisciplinary group with high interaction, but with strong ties to their present disciplines. This should provide for a high degree of creative symbiosis in the years to come.

One final word of caution should be added. It was only four years ago that Paisley (45) first attempted a review of the flow of information in *behavioral* science. He quickly concluded that there existed no literature to review and then attempted to extrapolate from the findings in physical science. Judging from the contents of the present review, such an extrapolation would no longer be necessary. The number of studies concerned with social and behavioral scientists has become quite large in the past three years and is growing at a prodigious rate. The reasons for this can be found quite easily. First of all, studies of information needs and uses have now become a recognized area of activity for behavioral scientists. This legitimization of the field has attracted a greater number of competent behavioral researchers to it. At the same time, these very competent behavioral scientists have little understanding, and perhaps even some fear, of the more established physical sciences. For very good reasons, they prefer to study the behavior of scientists whom they can understand. There is a fair amount of truth in the adage that familiarity and some subjective understanding of an activity are a prerequisite for interpreting research results. A withdrawal strategy, however, is seldom an effective way of dealing with unpleasant situations. Behavioral scientists must be encouraged not to neglect the physical sciences and technologies. After all, that is still where most of society's research funds are spent. To the extent possible, they will have to develop greater understanding of these areas themselves. Perhaps a more suitable long-range solution would be to attract more competent physical scientists and engineers into the behavioral sciences *and to provide them with proper training.* In the interim, perhaps the best solution will lie in fostering effective collaboration among well-trained behavioral scientists and physical scientists, or former physical scientists and engineers who have a genuine concern for the problem and a sympathetic understanding of behavioral science methods.

REFERENCES

(1) ABRAMS, R. A. Residential propinquity as a factor in marriage selections. American Sociological Review, 8 (1943).
(2) ALLEN, THOMAS J. Communications in the research and development laboratory. Technology Review, 69 (1967).
(3) ALLEN, THOMAS J. Managing the flow of scientific and technological information. Doctoral thesis. Alfred P. Sloan School of Management, Massachusetts Institute of Technology, Cambridge, Mass., 1966.
(4) ALLEN, THOMAS J. Studies of the problem-solving process in engineering design. IEEE Transactions on Engineering Management, 13 (1966).
(5) ALLEN, THOMAS J. The utilization of information sources during R and D proposal preparation. Report no. 97-64. Research program on the organization and management of R and D, Massachusetts Institute of Technology, Cambridge, Mass., October 1964.
(6) ALLEN, THOMAS J.; ANDRIEN, M.; GERSTENFELD, A. Time allocation among three technical information channels by R and D engineers. Massachusetts Institute of Technology, Cambridge, Mass., 1966. (Alfred P. Sloan School of Management. Working paper no. 184-66)
(7) ALLEN, THOMAS J.; COHEN, S. I. Information flow in two R and D laboratories. Administrative Science Quarterly (March 1969).
(8) ALLEN, THOMAS J.; GERSTENFELD, A.; GERSTBERGER, P. G. The problem of internal consulting in an R and D laboratory. Massachusetts Institute of Technology, Cambridge, Mass., 1968. (Alfred P. Sloan School of Management. Working paper no. 319-68)
(9) AMERICAN PSYCHOLOGICAL ASSOCIATION. PROJECT ON SCIENTIFIC INFORMATION EXCHANGE IN PSYCHOLOGY. Information exchange activities involved in psychological work. Report no. 19. Washington, D.C., 1968.
(10) AMERICAN PSYCHOLOGICAL ASSOCIATION. PROJECT ON SCIENTIFIC INFORMATION EXCHANGE IN PSYCHOLOGY. Networks of informal communication among scientifically productive psychologists: an explanatory study. Report no. 21. Washington, D.C., 1969.
(11) AMERICAN PSYCHOLOGICAL ASSOCIATION. PROJECT ON SCIENTIFIC INFORMATION EXCHANGE IN PSYCHOLOGY. Scientific communication at the XVIII International Congress of Psychology, Moscow, 1966, and some implications for the design and operation of international meetings. Report no. 20. Washington, D.C., 1968.
(12) AMERICAN PSYCHOLOGICAL ASSOCIATION. PROJECT ON SCIENTIFIC INFORMATION EXCHANGE IN PSYCHOLOGY. A study of innovation in the context of a large scientific meeting. Report no. 18. Washington, D.C., 1968.
(13) BAKER, N. R.; SIEGMANN, J.; RUBENSTEIN, A. H. The effects of perceived needs and means on the generation of ideas for industrial research and development projects. IEEE Transactions on Engineering Management, 14 (1968).
(14) CONRATH, D. W. The role of the informal organization in decision making on R and D. IEEE Transactions on Engineering Management, 14 (1968).
(15) CRANE, DIANA. Collaboration: communication and influence. A study of the effects of formal and informal collaboration among scientists. Johns Hopkins University, Baltimore, Md., 1968.
(16) CRANE, DIANA. Social structure in a group of scientists: test of the "invisible college" hypothesis. Johns Hopkins University, Baltimore, Md., 1968.
(17) CUADRA, CARLOS; HARRIS, LINDA; KATTER, ROBERT. Impact study of the "Annual review of information science and technology." Final report. System Development Corp., Santa Monica, Calif., 15 November 1968, 114 p. (TM-4135)
(18) FESTINGER, L.; SCHACHTER, D.; BACK, K. Social pressures in informal groups: a study of human factors in housing. Harper, New York, 1955.
(19) FRISCHMUTH, D. S.; ALLEN, THOMAS J. A model for the description and

evaluation of technical problem solving. IEEE Transactions on Engineering Management (in press).
(20) FROHMAN, A. Determinants of library use in an industrial firm. Term paper. Alfred P. Sloan School of Management, Massachusetts Institute of Technology, Cambridge, Mass., 1968.
(21) GARVEY, W. D.; NELSON, C.; LIN, N. A preliminary description of scientific information exchange in educational research. American Educational Research Association, Washington, D.C., 1968. Paper read at the Colloquium on Improving the Social and Communication Mechanisms of Educational Research.
(22) GERSTBERGER, P. G.; ALLEN, THOMAS J. Criteria used by R and D engineers in the selection of an information source. Journal of Applied Psychology, 52 (1968).
(23) GRAHAM, W. R.; WAGNER, C. P.; GLOEGE, W. P.; ZAVALA, ALBERT. Exploration of oral/informal technical communications behavior. American Institutes for Research, Washington, D.C., 1967.
(24) GULLAHORN, J. T. Distance and friendship as factors in the gross interaction matrix. Sociometry, 15 (1952).
(25) JOHNS HOPKINS UNIVERSITY. CENTER FOR RESEARCH IN SCIENTIFIC COMMUNICATION. The dissemination of scientific information, informal interaction, and the impact of information received at the annual meeting of the American Educational Research Association. Baltimore, Md., October 1968. (Preliminary Report 4)
(26) JOHNS HOPKINS UNIVERSITY. CENTER FOR RESEARCH IN SCIENTIFIC COMMUNICATION. The dissemination of the program material from two meetings of the American Institute of Aeronautics and Astronautics. Baltimore, Md., March 1968. (Technical Note 2)
(27) JOHNS HOPKINS UNIVERSITY. CENTER FOR RESEARCH IN SCIENTIFIC COMMUNICATION. The journal publication fate of work reported at two 1967 meetings of the American Meteorological Society. Baltimore, Md., June 1968. (Technical Note 5)
(28) JOHNS HOPKINS UNIVERSITY. CENTER FOR RESEARCH IN SCIENTIFIC COMMUNICATION. Journal publication of material presented at the 1967 annual meeting of the American Geophysical Union during the year following the meeting. Baltimore, Md., June 1968. (Technical Note 6)
(29) JOHNS HOPKINS UNIVERSITY. CENTER FOR RESEARCH IN SCIENTIFIC COMMUNICATION. Journal publication of material presented at the 1967 annual meeting of the Association of American Geographers. Baltimore, Md., June 1968. (Technical Note 7)
(30) JOHNS HOPKINS UNIVERSITY. CENTER FOR RESEARCH IN SCIENTIFIC COMMUNICATION. The 1966 International Congresses of Psychology and Sociology: a study of information exchange and meeting effectiveness. Baltimore, Md., February 1968, 82 p. (Series 2, report 1)
(31) JOHNS HOPKINS UNIVERSITY. CENTER FOR RESEARCH IN SCIENTIFIC COMMUNICATION. The publication efforts of authors of presentations at the 1966 annual meeting of the American Sociological Association during the year following the meeting. Baltimore, Md., April 1968. (Technical Note 3)
(32) JOHNS HOPKINS UNIVERSITY. CENTER FOR RESEARCH IN SCIENTIFIC COMMUNICATION. The publication fate of material presented at the October 1966 annual meeting of the Optical Society of America. Baltimore, Md., February 1968. (Technical Note 1)
(33) JOHNS HOPKINS UNIVERSITY. CENTER FOR RESEARCH IN SCIENTIFIC COMMUNICATION. A study of the scientific and technical information exchange at the 1968 annual meeting of the American Society of Heating, Refrigerating and Air-conditioning Engineers. Baltimore, Md., May 1968. (Series 1, report 8)
(34) JOHNS HOPKINS UNIVERSITY. CENTER FOR RESEARCH IN SCIENTIFIC COMMUNICATION. The subsequent dissemination of material presented in sessions of the Metallurgical Society at the 96th AIME annual meeting. Baltimore, Md.,

April 1968. (Technical Note 4)
(35) JOHNS HOPKINS UNIVERSITY. CENTER FOR RESEARCH IN SCIENTIFIC COMMUNICATION. A survey of authors on the publication practices in meteorology. Baltimore, Md., June 1968. (Preliminary Report 3)
(36) KAPLAN, NORMAN. Professional scientists in industry: an essay review. Social Problems, 13 (1965).
(37) KENNEDY, R. Premarital residential propinquity. American Journal of Sociology, 18 (1943).
(38) KRULEE, G. K.; NADLER, E. B. Studies of education for science and engineering: student values and curriculum choice. IEEE Transactions on Engineering Management (December 1960).
(39) LINGWOOD, D. A. Interpersonal communication, scientific productivity, and invisible colleges: studies of two behavioral science research areas. American Educational Research Association, Washington, D.C., 1968. Paper read at the Colloquium on Improving the Social and Communication Mechanisms of Educational Research.
(40) MAISSONEUVE, J. Selective choices and propinquity. Sociometry, 15 (1952).
(41) MARQUIS, D. G.; STRAIGHT, D. M. Organizational factors in project performance. In: Yovits, M. C., et al. Research program effectiveness. Gordon and Breach, New York, 1966, p. 441–458.
(42) MENZEL, HERBERT. Information needs and uses in science and technology. In: Annual review of information science and technology, Carlos A. Cuadra, ed. Interscience, New York, 1966, vol. 1, p. 41–69.
(43) MERTON, R. K. Making it scientifically. New York Times Book Review (25 February 1968).
(44) O'GARA, P. W. Physical location as a determinant of communication possibility among R and D engineers. S. M. thesis. Alfred P. Sloan School of Management, Massachusetts Institute of Technology, Cambridge, Mass., 1968.
(45) PAISLEY, WILLIAM J. The flow of (behavioral) science information — a review of the research literature. Institute for Communication Research, Stanford University, Stanford, Calif., November 1965.
(46) PAISLEY, WILLIAM J. Information needs and uses. In: Annual review of information science and technology. Carlos A. Cuadra, ed. Encyclopaedia Britannica, Chicago, 1968, vol. 3, p. 1–30.
(47) PAISLEY, WILLIAM J.; PARKER, E. B. The AAPOR conference as a communication medium. Public Opinion Quarterly, 32 (1968).
(48) PARKER, E. B.; LINGWOOD, D. A.; PAISLEY, W. J. Communication and research productivity in an interdisciplinary behavioral science research area. Institute for Communication Research, Stanford University, Stanford, Calif., 1968.
(49) PATTERSON, MILES. Spatial factors in social interactions. Human Relations, 21:4 (November 1968).
(50) PELZ, D. C.; ANDREWS, F. M. Scientists in organizations: productive climates for research and development. Wiley, New York, 1966.
(51) RITTI, RICHARD. Work goals of engineers and scientists. Industrial Relations, 7 (1968).
(52) ROGERS, E. M. Bibliography on the diffusion of innovations. Research report no. 4. Michigan State University, East Lansing, Mich., 1966.
(53) ROSENBERG, VICTOR. Studies in the man-system interface in libraries. Report no. 2: The application of psychometric techniques to determine the attitudes of individuals toward information seeking. Center for the Information Sciences, Lehigh University, Bethlehem, Pa., July 1966, 46 p. (AD-637 713)
(54) SLATER, MARGARET; KEENAN, STELLA. Current papers in physics user study — coverage, arrangement and format. American Institute of Physics, New York, May 1968, 61 p. (Report no. AIP/CPP 2)
(55) SLATER, MARGARET; KEENAN, STELLA. Results of a questionnaire on current awareness methods used by physicists prior to publication of "Current Papers in Physics." American Institute of Physics, New York, 1967.

(56) SLATER, MARGARET; KEENAN, STELLA. Use made of "Current Papers in Physics." American Institute of Physics, New York, July 1968, 67 p. (Report no. AIP/CPP 3)
(57) UTTERBACK, J. M. The process of technical innovation in industrial firms. Doctoral thesis. Alfred P. Sloan School of Management, Massachusetts Institute of Technology, Cambridge, Mass., 1969.
(58) WHITLEY, RICHARD. Communication networks in science: status and citation patterns in annual physiology. Sociological Review (in press).

2 Design and Evaluation of Information Systems

ROBERT V. KATTER
System Development Corporation

INTRODUCTION

In corresponding chapters of earlier volumes of this review—Bourne (16), Borko (14), Rees (128), and King (86)—may be discerned a trend toward progressive broadening of content coverage. The initial emphasis was on design and evaluation concepts and on techniques that were rather closely —and narrowly—connected with information storage and retrieval systems. It is becoming increasingly clear, however, that there are many activities and ideas outside of this context that have, or can have, a very important bearing on the work of systems analysts, designers, and evaluators working on library and documentation systems. This chapter attempts to continue enlarging our perception of the range of reported activities that can help to improve the kinds of systems in which our readers are chiefly interested.

Design activities are often based on information obtained in prior evaluative activities, and evaluative activities are often motivated by design goals and requirements. Thus, these activities are usually very much interrelated with each other and with several other kinds of activities normally carried out in what we will call "the system redevelopment cycle." We choose to say *re*development because most system development activities are associated not with a brand-new system totally divorced from any previous system but with the replacement of an older system by one that is newer, usually more expensive, and presumably more effective. The literature of design and evaluation is probably best understood if presented in the context of the system redevelopment cycle. This chapter will attempt such a presentation.

The usual redevelopment cycle consists of several kinds of activities, each distributed throughout the redevelopment process, but each concentrating or peaking at its special point in the process, with much interleaving and iteration of activities. A typical sequence of such activities might be: discover and state needs; derive and state system objectives; and canvass and describe available system resources and constraints. Using the previous three, produce system operating concept; using operating concept as basis, do functional phase, and task analyses; from the results of these, produce detailed design requirement specifications; on basis of requirement specifications, depict alternative system configurations; for each alternative configuration, do cost-effectiveness analyses of each element, component, and procedure; apply tradeoff analyses to cost-effectiveness data to select best alternative; produce detailed design specifications for the alternative selected; use these design specifications to produce preliminary operating version of system; do shake-down and sensitivity testing and evaluation; use test results to modify the system; do final acceptance testing; produce, deploy, and install the system.

In reviewing the literature of 1968, we have tried to assume the working systems analyst's perspective, which asks, "How can reading this article help me perform redevelopment activities better?" For the systems analyst, an article can contribute three kinds of information: (*1*) It can inform, or provide a checklist, about procedures, viewpoints, techniques, considerations, philosophies, value judgments, etc., that are relevant to the redevelopment process; (*2*) it can provide empirical data values and results that may be used directly in the redevelopment task facing the individual, *provided* that his situation is comparable to the one depicted in the article; and (*3*) it can describe means by which he may obtain necessary empirical facts and data values for use in his particular task, hopefully providing some idea of the costs and procedures involved in getting that information for himself. For this chapter, articles were selected on the basis that they contained one or more of these three kinds of information. Of approximately 750 items scanned, more than 200 were judged relevant enough to include in citations, and approximately half of these are discussed. The chapter is organized into seven sections, as follows: Introduction, The System Redevelopment Process, The System's Demand Environment, The System's Support Resources, The System's Operational Constraints, Achieving Cost-Effectiveness, and Conclusions.

THE SYSTEM REDEVELOPMENT PROCESS

Perspective

It was suggested earlier that a more balanced appreciation of design and evaluation might be gained by considering them in the total redevelopment context. Similarly, the redevelopment process may also be considered in its broader context. Gaining a broad view may have value to the extent that the effects demonstrated for scientific and technological idea borrowing and analogy also operate for cross-fertilization of ideas in systems analysis, evaluation, and design. How, then, do systems analysis and development activities fit into the intellectual, scientific, technological, and cultural endeavors of our society, and how should they fit? With which disciplinary fields does systems analysis trade? What is its overall value-orientation and posture in human affairs, and where is it going? A good place to start this inquiry is with two books by Churchman (26, 27). His book on the systems approach is an examination of its place and value for society, and his perspective is wide and balanced. There is no attempt to "sell" systems analysis, but rather an attempt to see past the concept and its techniques to the social, behavioral, technical, cultural, and personal realities that condition its justification and use. Several standard concepts of systems analysis are treated from this view; among them are efficiency, input-output, budgeting, time, and planning. Churchman's other book, *Challenge to Reason*, is a collection of essays from the years prior to his writing the volume just reviewed, and provides deeper insight into the development of many of his views on the systems approach.

Fisher (48) comments on the current state of systems analysis, with a primary focus on the kind of large military systems that have provided much of the impetus to applied work in systems analysis and to broadening its conception. He emphasizes that the time frame for such systems is the reasonably distant future (five to ten years), the environment one of great uncertainty, and the context of analysis *very* broad; he notes that many variables are not amenable to adequate quantification or even conceptualization. Simple, straightforward solutions are therefore the exception, and analysis is never complete. In long-range planning, he sees systems analysis as a tool used simply to sharpen intuition and judgment; the results of the analysis rarely "make" the decision. He considers that more study needs to be done to decide whether the money a system will cost is the most adequate indicator of the costs in lost alternative opportunities incurred by society as a whole in choosing the system.

Milsum (107) discusses the problem of optimizing the cost-benefit balances between the "technosphere," the "biosphere," and the "sociosphere," three broad areas of concern in planning and designing complex, socially embedded systems for modern society. He identifies a main problem as one of establishing quantitative measures for social aspects and values, and analyzes this problem in relation to dynamic changes in the three spheres.

Sackman (140) considers it essential to develop a public philosophy for real-time information systems. The real-time information system is one that gathers, processes, organizes, and transmits information about changing events rapidly enough that the recipients of the information are able to intervene effectively in those events. How rapid the system must be to provide effective intervention depends on the time scale of the events being monitored. Sackman notes that the power of information creates a new dilemma in our fast-moving society. He asks questions: When is information a public or a private commodity? Should it be freely distributed or metered like electricity? Should information activities be publicly supported, privately supported, or should there be a cooperative arrangement? He sees a public philosophy regarding such issues as vital and long overdue.

Planning Aids

For most kinds of systems, the redevelopment cycle, whether accomplished with efficiency and precision or in a haphazard manner, costs considerable calendar time. Thus, the object of redevelopment activity is always some future state of affairs, and the requirement to project or envision that future is ever present. Such projections are embodied mainly in planning activities. The concepts of "future" and of "planning" themselves, as well as the various models and systematizations of these ideas, can be of conceptual aid to most kinds of redevelopment tasks.

Rescher (130) writes on the future as an object of research. The future, he notes, has recently come into fashion as a worthy object of scientific study. He reviews recent future-study literature, distinguishes between explanation and prediction in science, advances the opinion that the former cannot substitute for the latter, and centers the remainder of his paper on the problem of predictive methodology. He distinguishes between the predictive methods of historical extrapolation, use of analytic models, and use of experts and forecasters.

Rosove (132, 133) presents a description of contextual mapping, a "methodology of conjecturing about the future." He defines a contextual map as a "graphic display of the logical and causal dependencies of functionally related phenomena," and cites reviews of 21 methods used in the study of the future. In the earlier document, he describes the structure and content of a contextual map aimed at educational policymaking, and indicates how such a map can aid in generating alternative futures, exploring alternative pathways to selected futures, exploring alternative consequences of selected pathways, and several other forms of aid. In the later document, he presents the results of applying contextual mapping to the prediction of possible future roles for educators in the late 1980's.

Helmer (72, 73, 74) discusses the use of the "Delphi" technique in formulating policies and plans. The technique is a "method for the systematic solicitation and collation of expert opinions." This method of arriving at a consensus replaces direct debate by a program of sequential individual interrogations, interspersed with information and opinion feedback derived by computed consensus from earlier parts of the program. It eliminates committee activity, reducing the effects of specious persuasion, unwillingness to abandon publicly expressed opinions, and the bandwagon effect of majority opinion. In the earliest paper, he describes an application of the Delphi technique to problems of educational innovations. In his second paper, on the future of science, he identifies trends such as the rising social consciousness among scientists, an increasing weight on the pragmatist's "science for society's sake," and a decline of fatalism with the increased recognition of science's ability to do something about the future. In his third paper, he carries this analysis to an optimistic conclusion about the potential progress of social technology that lies within the grasp of the next generation, and suggests some of the paths along which such progress may be accomplished.

McKenney (102) proposes guidelines for a planning simulation model. He emphasizes the model as an aid to the planning process, discusses the relation of the model to the planning process, and assesses the role of the model in improving the planner's intuition and generating alternatives. Cetron (23) discusses methodological and administrative problems of technological forecasting. Anderson (6) has edited a very useful collection of 16 papers resulting from a conference on "possible futures and their relations to the man-controlled environment." The conference was sponsored by groups concerned primarily with architecture, education, and the fine arts, but the range of the contributed papers is broader than this might suggest, and the topic of planning itself is treated in a general manner and with sophistication.

Still another planning aid is the planning information system—an information system designed specifically to aid the functions of planning. A view of a representative sample of one such type of planning information system can be obtained from a collection of papers on information systems for urban planning published by the American Society of Planning Officials (5).

Another kind of article useful as a conceptual aid for planning and prediction purposes is the "visionary" piece, especially when it is well focused on the range of matters for which the author has recognized competence. Hays et al. (68) examine the concept of a billion books for education in America and the world. The authors are careful to note that the paper, although the result of extensive data-gathering and deliberations by a large and competent staff, should not be considered the product of a maximum, exhaustive, in-depth project. The paper is offered as a kind of preliminary planning concept document and illustrates the transition from planning activities to later stages of analysis in the thinking of experienced systems analysts.

In a somewhat more broadly oriented and less formal visionary piece, Doebler & Tewlow (44) attempt to identify some of the concepts now emerging for applying technological innovations to the publishing industry, and to chart their future impact. Their paper is organized around the concept of a new kind of "total communications" or "knowledge" industry. The implications of using the emerging new communications technology for such an industry are examined.

Simon (155) presents a sober view of the future of information processing technology:

> We must not expect that technological progress will produce Utopia; it is reasonable to hope that it will bring relief to acute hardship and acute pain. . . . The information that nature presents to us is unimaginably redundant. When we find the right way to summarize and characterize that information—when we find the pattern hidden in it—its vast bulk compresses into succinct equations, each one enormously informative . . . in the period ahead of us, more important than advances in computer design will be the advances we can make in our understanding of human information processing—of thinking, problem solving, and decision making.

Modeling Aids

Many different kinds of systems share large numbers of general features and problems in common, and most specific applications of systems design and evaluation are enhanced by being based on clear, unambiguous descriptions of such aspects of the environment and system being considered. The language of mathematics can be used as the medium for constructing descriptive metaphors (models), of varying accuracy and exhaustiveness, for many such empirical phenomena. There is a range of highly general models, deeply mathematical in their exposition and treatment, contained in various journals and texts. For these, the present reviewer claims below-minimum competence and has omitted them for this reason, as well as the possibility (perhaps self-comforting) that the bulk of his readers will also be unequipped to understand highly mathematical expositions. Selected tutorial and introductory material for the general case will be cited, and applications particularly germane to redevelopment of document-handling systems will be included.

Two closely related streams of work have been concerned with the mathematical modeling or description of human choice and decision. These are statistical decision theory and utility theory. Statistical decision theory has concentrated on modeling the concept of the decision maker's *uncertainty* about the outcomes of different courses of action he might take. It attempts to formulate ways in which his limited information about the probable outcomes of decisions can be most effectively (rationally) used so that his decision takes account of all the information available about probable outcomes. Utility theory has concentrated on modeling the concept of the decision maker's preferences or values relating to the different costs and benefits that are simultaneously available in a choice situation. The aim has been to depict accurately the satisfaction-substitutability (value-tradeoff) relations between various costs and benefits, so that, in situations in which the gain of one benefit must be at the cost of losing another, a choice can be made based on all the information about preferences. Since most complex decision situations involve not only uncertainty about outcomes but also the potential availability of mutually antagonistic or exclusive benefits, both lines of thinking have come to be represented in many mathematical models of choice and decision making.

Copeland (35) provides a readable, short introduction to statistical decision theory. He discusses, among others, the concepts of goal, uncertainty, value judgment, and outcomes. Quantitative concepts such as maximum absolute gain and maximum expected net value are defined. Fishburn (47) presents a somewhat more mathematical, far-ranging, introductory tutorial account of utility theory. His paper discusses the utility concept and why it is of interest, sketches a number of alternative theories of utility, and discusses certain technical problems common to several theories.

North (115) provides an excellent tutorial introduction to decision theory that treats both the utility and statistical aspects in a balanced and unified framework. Mathematical notation is introduced gradually and in a reasonably clear, though not always explicit, explanatory context. This article is the first in a special journal issue devoted to decision analysis. The issue contains 16 articles on the current state of the art in various aspects of decision analysis, written for the most part by recognized contributors; it is a must for the aspiring decision theorist. Kaufmann (84) has authored a compact, introductory book (which has been translated from the French) on the science of decision-making, or "praxeology." The book has good illustrations and covers a wide range of topics in the mathematical modeling of decision phenomena.

Marschak (104, 105) has published two working papers concerned more directly with applications of decision theory to systems for the collection, processing, and use of information. In the first, he considers the economics of inquiring, communicating, and deciding, bringing to bear a decision-theoretic approach flavored with concepts from economics and presented without mathematical notation. He discusses the demand price of various informational services in the light of expected payoffs for their users. The second paper is a slightly more mathematical exposition of decision theory as it applies to efficient choice of information services. The information system is modeled as a chain of processes—inquiring, data-storing, encoding, etc.—each being represented by a stochastic matrix and a cost function. He describes the conditions under which an optimal system can be determined with all elements of the chain being considered.

The other main line of application of mathematics that is of interest here is the modeling of system structures, relations, and flows. When a mathematical model is constructed so that it can be exercised by a computer program, the model can be used as a simulation device to estimate the effects of various patterns of inputs, operating policies, and alternative system configurations. Only a sample of available papers on this topic will be covered.

The structures and flow relations represented in mathematical models of systems correspond to those depicted in the logical flow-charting of a system, a well-standardized graphical technique described in a tutorial paper by Gull (62), in which library and information center examples are used. Homer (78) presents a mathematical model of the quantitative flow of data in a management information system and employs matrix algebra for the modeling. He provides a brief but understandable introduction to his topic, but the description of his model requires a solid knowledge of matrix theory to be understood and appreciated. Models such as Homer's can attain substantial applied usefulness when embodied in computer programs by which they can be exercised. Caras (18) provides an illustrative example of computer simulation of a small information system. He discusses the conditions under which computer simulation is useful for system redevelopment work. Kiviat (87) presents a lengthy and very readable discussion of the process of analyzing a system and designing a computer program that allows a system's operations to be reproduced and studied. Fishman (49) describes, in mathematical terms, a method for choosing sample sizes as inputs to computer simulation models to optimize the allocation of computer time in comparing results from the simulation of different experimental conditions.

Textbooks

Several texts on systems analysis, systems engineering, and systems development appeared this year. Chestnut (25) has written a well-organized text with the emphasis on engineering. Some discussion is also provided on social, economic, and political aspects. Heany (70) has written a book on information systems development aimed at familiarizing the interested layman and the manager with the main concepts of systems analysis, with representative configurations and examples of equipment systems and computer programming "software," with a typical electronic data-processing installation, and with some of the considerations for managing a system development effort.

Hare (66) has authored a most impressive intermediate text on the emerging diagnostic approach to systems analysis. The book concentrates on conceptual aids to systems diagnosis, presenting these in a way aimed at fostering new insights and invention, rather than as cookbook methods. Many different kinds of systems applications are used for examples, and a full panoply of the comparatively new mathematical-conceptual tools available to systems analysis is covered in a clear and interesting fashion.

Two other books discuss systems analysis in the context of a particular type of application. Quade & Boucher (127) have edited a multi-authored book on systems analysis and policy planning. The application examples are from the national defense establishment, but the approaches to analyzing policy issues are generalizable. Sackman's book (139) tackles the issues of large-scale computer systems, systems science, and their applications to our evolving society. A main theme is that society should use such systems, rather than be used by them. The orientation is one of extensive firsthand experience with the analysis, design, and development of several of the larger man-computer systems in existence. He does not presume to guess whether such systems will cure very many of society's ills, but he does envision them as an almost inevitable and powerfully evolving central factor for this phase of our social evolution.

Managing the Redevelopment Cycle

Systems analysis, design, evaluation, and implementation are not activities improved by a preponderance of solitary, uncoordinated efforts from various individuals. Time for creative deliberation must be balanced with time for confronting the raw environment-system complex to be redeveloped, and must be interleaved with time for repeatedly exchanging and sharing the emerging results of the ongoing activities between the members of the redevelopment team. Duplication of effort must be avoided, the process must be kept within time and budgetary constraints, and the shock and resistance effects of innovation and change on the existent system and environment must be accurately anticipated and effectively dealt with. This is system redevelopment management, still more an art than a technology, now emerging through hard experience as a prime factor in the success or failure of system redevelopment efforts, and clearly moving toward well-defined and recognized professional roles.

Holt (77) provides an insightful discussion of the progression of a practitioner in science or technology, through the role of managing a scientific or technical information service, facility, or publication channel, to the role of manager of the innovative process of redeveloping that system. The impression is that for the "first generation" manager there usually occurs a rather predictable series of stages and events (including mistakes), and the attendant deepening of sophistication follows a reasonably standard pattern. Whittenburg & Schumacher (175) developed and pretested an information system planning guide. Three specialized information retrieval systems were employed as objects of the pretest. The guide was found to be particularly useful for the component and concept planning stages, somewhat less for the configuration stage, and least helpful for function allocation.

At the interface between management concepts and systems analysis concepts, the management of systems analysis and the systems analysis of management prove to be mutually facilitating and profitably redundant; a man thoroughly fitted to do either one of these is probably well on the road to achieving capability in the other. Two thoughtful papers that treat these concepts are those by Feigenbaum (46) and Young (181). Both papers describe and recommend a systems approach to organizational management problems, and both provide critiques of problems and pitfalls to be encountered in achieving this approach.

A systems-oriented manager of an organization would be likely to consider the possible utility of a management information system. Couger (37) uses data gathered at 43 firms regarding the management practices used in developing their management information systems. He discovered seven main inhibitors to development of a successful management information system: incomplete identification of managerial information needs; design of independent systems for interdependent activities; system priorities not in accordance with their importance to the firm; inadequate feasibility studies; lack of post-implementation audits; failure to include external information requirements; and use of unsophisticated systems analysis and design techniques. Conway (32) discusses the information system audit as a control technique for managers to avoid many of these inhibitors, and Moore (111) does the same for the planning of Electronic Data Processing (EDP) installations.

Two points of special concern appear repeatedly in the literature on managing a system redevelopment effort. First is the necessity of maintaining close communication between the managers and systems analysts of the redevelopment effort on the one hand, and the managers and sponsors of the system being redeveloped on the other. Second is the need for early and extensive involvement of the personnel of the system being redeveloped. Such involvement will reduce their resistance, help cushion the shock of innovative change, and gain the use of their knowledge of unique situational factors that might otherwise be overlooked in analysis and design.

Discussing communication between system redevelopers and system management and sponsors, Cloot (29) and Keller (85) present convincing arguments that the communications gap must be closed by the innovators who are redeveloping the system. Gleason (55), in Chapter III of his excellent paper on the role of the period of transition in the implementation of information systems, provides a comprehensive and readable account of the details of personnel communication problems, especially problems of communicating with management, during the transition period. Turoff (166) describes a decision-theory model for locating a decision point to be used by the analyst in communicating with the decision maker (manager) about conflicting measures of value.

Proper documentation for all aspects and products of the system redevelopment process is important because of the necessity for maintaining close and detailed communication between the diverse persons and interests concerned with the outcomes. Discussions on system documentation are included in the general methodological sources cited earlier, and examples of good articles specifically addressed to this topic are those by Billups & Gordon (12) and Wuelfing (180). Regarding the second point of special concern, Wolk (178) provides a nicely rounded account of the general phenomena of employees' resistance to change in their work environment and job patterns, covering symptoms, reasons, and remedies. Putnam (126) presents detailed and interesting results of a survey of 20 firms, each of which attempted installation of an integrated business system. Examples of the kinds of implicit questions arising when employees were asked to cooperate during a time of change in their own routines were: "Shouldn't I get credit for all or part of a modified new proposal?" "Why should I do the extra work when the new and old systems run in parallel?" "If new information highlights problems that I know exist so that they become visible to my boss, will he blame me?" Putnam analyzes relative degree of cooperation by type of function in the organization, and discusses techniques for helping to achieve the proper attitude toward change during innovation.

Three other articles also deal with failure of innovation due to employee resistance—these, with employees in hospital settings. Coe & Barnhill (30) report the results of a longitudinal sociological study conducted in a hospital among nurses who were to learn to use a new medications system. Runck (138) discusses ways that nurses in a large hospital are being involved in the work of defining data and work flows in preparation for an automated patient-record system. Cooke (33) discusses theories of employee motivation and indicates their application to the computerized hospital for gaining employee cooperation. Essays by Graziano (59) and

Gummere (63) treat a similar, though perhaps more complex, problem in discussions of the impact of computers, systems analysis, and systems science on the work patterns, role conceptions, and skill and knowledge requirements of librarians, all from the point of view of producing more effective responses toward innovations.

Whether the systems innovator is attempting to gain the cooperation of management, employees, sponsors, or potential users of the system, continuing cooperation will depend partly on taking the mystery out of systems analysis and redevelopment activities. Clear, nontechnical descriptions and explanations are needed. Krueger (91) presents a broadbrush survey of systems analysis firms and services that are available, and discusses their future role. Simms (154) considers the question, "What is a systems analyst?" He gives a brief definitional description, followed by a view of the analyst's behavior "from the outside," and concludes with a list of ten steps involving do's and don'ts to be used as advice by a hypothetical "novice systems analyst." Herner (75, 76) provides an easily understood, step-by-step, actual case study of design, evaluation, and costing done for a small-scale system for selective dissemination of information. The paper provides good coverage of many relevant details in down-to-earth language. Carter (21) compares the mystique with the reality of a systems approach to education in a highly readable and penetrating paper. He gives two step-by-step examples of applying systems analysis techniques to the analysis of educational requirements. One example is of a very large-scale air defense training program involving thousands of pupils, many sites, and a wide range of educational objectives. The other is that of developing an introduction to the reading of English for problem readers among Mexican-American children. By noting the contrasts and similarities between these two extreme examples, Carter demonstrates the abstractness, general applicability, and power of properly applied systems analysis concepts.

THE SYSTEM'S DEMAND ENVIRONMENT

For information systems, the problem of the system's demand environment is mainly one of predicting the pattern of near-future information needs, whose satisfaction will be used to justify the system's operation. The study of information needs and uses is a technical specialty in its own right—much like statistical decision theory or psychological scaling. The point of view taken in many papers on information needs and uses is heavily methodological and discipline-oriented, as it should be. One might ask how the information needs of a systems analyst would tend to orient him in considering the material on information needs and uses. To this reviewer, it appears that besides an interest in this year's problems and findings, as covered in the appropriate chapter, the analyst might also have four other partial orientations: articulation of discovered information needs and uses with *planning* activities; interest in study *methodologies* especially calibrated and tuned to unique applications; articulation of discovered information needs and uses with *design* activities; and wide, evenly distributed *sensitivities* (as distinguished from uneven, highly focused sensitivities) for the underlying social-psychological, technical, organizational, and other factors that affect information needs and uses.

Papers depicting relations between described information needs and uses and systems planning activities are those by Wooster (179), Lawson (96), and Bill (11). A series of papers by Orr et al. (117, 118, 119) provides an excellent example of a study aimed at developing methodological tools for designing a specific type of system to gather and articulate data on system capabilities and usage patterns with system redevelopment planning and design activities. A document by Lister (101) describes a methodology for designing storage allocation arrangements to match information category use statistics. Finally, an extensive literature survey by Voos (169) on studies of intra- and intergroup communication illustrates the kind of document that can help the analyst to achieve broad, evenly distributed sensitivities to factors that he may need to consider in trying to anticipate the system's demand environment.

THE SYSTEM'S SUPPORT RESOURCES

No one doubts that redevelopment plans must be based on realistic estimates of the resources to be made available. Nevertheless, there are numerous instances of redevelopment efforts that have failed in this respect, and many resultant examples of badly degraded compromise systems— essentially "unfinished symphonies" for which some considerable portion of the original redevelopment effort has been wasted because funds ran out or didn't materialize. Less frequently, a redevelopment manager is caught with unanticipated excess funds that have to be "spent during the fiscal year." This creates another kind of wastefulness. A concrete grasp of the overall support level of the planned system is a necessary condition for a clear conception of most other aspects of the plan; the promise (and the threat) of having one's plans carried out makes a realistic approach seem essential.

How does the redeveloper deal with the problem of attaining realistic funding and support projections? For one thing, he treats funding and funders conceptually as part of the system problem. For another, he recognizes that the best techniques for obtaining adequate and predictable funding are different for different kinds of system applications. Baker & Nance (9) present simulation models for the "system-user-funder-complex" for library and information retrieval systems, and show how the two models can lead to different conclusions about obtaining funding for the two kinds of systems. Also on the topic of different patterns of funding, Humphrey (79) outlines the changing patterns of library support and describes survey tools for accurately estimating such support. Hamblen (64) surveys expenditures, sources of funds, and utilization of digital computers in higher education.

With respect to stable, predictable funding, there are the two problems that must be clearly distinguished. One concerns funds for system redevelopment and the other concerns funds for operation of the system. Regarding the former, one problem is that of justifying systems analysis and redevelopment to a customer set including Federal, State, and local governments. It is almost tautological to note that governmental views of system redevelopment are heavily conditioned by political considerations. Schlesinger (150) evaluates the role of systems analysis as it functions in a highly political environment. After detailing many kinds of apprehensions about systems analysis in this setting, he concludes that while he is hopeful and moderately enthusiastic about such applications, systems analysis "cannot transmute the dross of politics into the fine gold of Platonic decision-making." Adams (2) depicts the changing mood in the view from Washington regarding systems studies. He depicts the growth of positive attitudes of members of Congress toward the potential value of such studies for helping to solve some national problems. Titus (165) gives an account and analysis of a very important focal point of systems analysis in governmental politics—the efforts and techniques of lobbyists. Grant (58) discusses gamesmanship and the "total" systems concept used in obtaining Federal funding grants for some large regional information systems. Mohrhardt (109) outlines certain interactions between technical, bureaucratic, and political considerations in planning for Federal information systems. Finally, Hyslop (80) details a "we were there" case history of the attempt of one professional society to use Federal funds to help the society upgrade its information systems and services and at the same time move toward self-sufficiency.

The maintenance of stable and predictable funding for the *system itself* may involve selling and re-selling the system's services to users. In support of such sales activities, users needs for service may be discovered, invented, created, and more or less carefully evaluated for their differential strengths. Moreland (112) reports an interesting experiment in a county library system to discover the "saturation points" for numbers of copies required of each paperback title to provide immediate response to user needs that had been stimulated and focused by the experiment itself. Dickson (43) describes the National Aeronautics and Space Administration's (NASA) "hard-sell" approach to both discovering and heightening needs for the products and services of NASA information systems. Wellisch (172) discusses the concept of the "adoption diffusion process," and reports findings on the effectiveness of an experimental direct-mailing information program aimed at gaining adoption of fall-out shelter features for new building construction.

Green et al. (60) offer a book describing experiments on the value of information in simulated marketing environments, in which Bayesian decision analysis is the central conceptual tool. Finally, Bjorge et al. (13) report an excellent study done for the Clearinghouse for Federal Scientific and Technical Information (CFSTI). The study used an adaptation of the survey methods of advertising research to assess the effectiveness of various forms of CFSTI announcement media on the sales of CFSTI products and services. Definitive results were obtained for planning CFSTI announcement media to be more effective in stimulating demand for CFSTI products.

THE SYSTEM'S OPERATIONAL CONSTRAINTS

Two general classes of factors are often referred to as constraints in the systems analysis literature—fiscal and operational. In this chapter, the former have already been considered in the section on system resources. An operational constraint is a factor or condition that, by the fact of its existence, should alter the system's requirement specifications in ways not predictable from a consideration of environmental demands and system resources. Four kinds of possible operational constraints to be briefly considered are: copyright, data file security, standardization, and functional overlap.

Copyright

Clapp (28) has prepared a description of a librarian's view on copyright for the National Advisory Commission on Libraries. He discusses authors' rights versus public interest, the "for profit" principle, mass-dissemination versus normal use, and the rights of use. He further analyzes the history of formal and informal agreements in library copying and photocopying. Lazowska (97) also addresses the problem of copyright. Aines (45) reports the results of a study of the copyright law as it relates to national information systems and national programs, done by an *Ad Hoc* COSATI task group on legal aspects involved in national information systems. The basic issue is that of drawing the line between the claims of various conflicting financial interests, particularly as this line applies to the narrowness or broadness of certain kinds of exemptions. Heilprin (71) considers the future of the copyright principle in the light of several extrapolated trends in information needs and use, and in information technology. A short bibliography (125) provides selected recent citations on legal protection for computer program "software."

Data File Security

There are both technical and legal considerations in protecting the contents of files—especially computer-stored files—from unauthorized disclosure and use. Graham (57) discusses this problem from the technical point of view, offering an example of a computer programming arrangement aimed at protecting file contents. Freed (50) presents a case study of legislation for computer technology, in which the object was to ensure that records *not* readable by visual means would be made readable for authorized inspections, and to permit the use of legible counterparts of such records for legal evidence. Harrison's extensive bibliography on personal privacy and protection of publicly held files of personal information (67) was cited in last year's review, but should be mentioned again.

Standardization

Standardization is a type of system constraint that has implications for the sharing and exchange of information between systems, and for personnel job mobility between systems as a result of possible transfer of training in skills required for working in different systems. Lohse (168) provides the results of deliberations on U.S. standards for keyboard arrangements and symbols for automated information systems. Problems and implications for personnel training, ease of conversion between systems, and for compatibility with international standards are discussed, and standards are suggested.

Mooers (110) makes a plea for standardization of the command language vocabulary and grammar used in computer-based, on-line information retrieval systems, outlines the problems and considerations, and provides extensive examples of what he thinks the standards should look like. Salton (145) provides a thoughtful article on the reasons for, and problems connected with, standardizing the unit record format for information retrieval systems.

Functional Overlap

Another class of factors that can be thought of as posing potential operational constraints on the design of any particular system are those having to do with overlap or duplication among the functions of various systems and subsystems. While these constraints are perhaps more nebulous than those previously described, their overall importance may be just as great. Friedman (53) presents and defends the interesting proposition that, in order for an organization to maintain its desired and already established configuration after acquiring a computerized management information system, the information system should have a configuration just the opposite of the organization (either centralized or decentralized, depending on the configuration of the organization). Nugent (116) and Reitz (129) describe data-collection and cost-and-effectiveness factors affecting centralization-decentralization decisions for classification and serials-handling problems in libraries.

Moving the discussion of functional overlap and centralization-decentralization to the level of networks, Information Dynamics Corporation (81) discusses the relative economics of regional information networks and provides a checklist for developing a network model. Aines (3) concentrates on the range of factors that argue for the early advent of large-scale national information systems networks. Dammers (41) provides detailed analyses of several issues, including functional overlap, viewed from the point of cost-effectiveness analysis for large networks. Grant (58) examines the interrelated problems of functional overlap and the apportioning of resource support requirements for various sectors of information networks.

To this point, we have covered material on the redevelopment process and on the system's demand environment, support resources, and operational constraints. Still to be considered is the topic of achieving cost-effectiveness, but first, the reader's attention is called to a very incomplete sample of reports and papers authored by individuals operating essentially as managers for early (and in some cases intermediate) stages of system redevelopment efforts. These papers constitute planning and status documents with varying degrees of detail and exhaustiveness; most are taken up with aspects of the redevelopment process and its planning and management, as well as with problems of predicting the system's demand environment, support resources, and operational constraints. As accounts of the real experiences encountered in efforts at system redevelopment, they serve as a sample of applications of some of the concepts discussed to this point; relevant papers are by Koch (89); Smith (156); Aitchison et al. (4); CONSAD (31); Schumacher (152); CONLIS (1); Wixon & Housman (176); Chartrand et al. (24); Lilly (100); and Wall (170).

ACHIEVING COST-EFFECTIVENESS

In the system redevelopment cycle, cost-effectiveness analysis activities peak at a point just prior to selection from among the feasible alternative system design configurations, since it is usually through cost-effectiveness analysis (CEA) that the selections are made. A somewhat idealized and simplified description of cost-effectiveness analysis would be as follows. For each subsystem and major component and procedure of each alternative system configuration being considered, various cost aspects are estimated from experience, from the literature, or occasionally, by direct tests. Also, for each such element, possible benefits are identified and described, criteria for quantifying the effectiveness of delivery of each benefit are specified, and the effectiveness of the element in delivering each benefit is estimated from experience, from the literature, or occasionally, by direct test and measurement. Next, the cost and effectiveness data are used in a tradeoff analysis. The tradeoff analysis can be accomplished in a number of ways, but usually tends to include the following activities in one form or another: value arbiters or judges are identified whose opinions regarding the negative and positive values of the various costs and benefits will carry weight in the final decisions; the value functions (opinions regarding the values) of these judges for each benefit are gathered in a more or less formal and systematic way, usually by comparing the perceived substitutability and/or compensatory relations (tradeoffs) between different benefits and costs; where there is disagreement between judges, the weight to be assigned to each judge's opinion is determined by force of debate, by fiat, or by the social and organizational power relations existing between judges (i.e., by the judge's degree of control over the system and the system redevelopment process); finally, the decisions are made and formalized.

The above sketch suggests that there is indeed a very wide range of information that might be valuable to the analyst confronted with the problem of conducting CEA. This section will review articles touching on topics in the following sequence: general discussions of CEA; examples of applications of CEA; measures of information-retrieval effectiveness; judgmental and other factors perturbing retrieval-effectiveness measures; results from retrieval-effectiveness studies; effectiveness and cost considerations for the man-system interface arrangement, primarily in machine-based information retrieval systems; and C-E considerations for computer display hardware, computer hardware, and computer programming software.

General Discussions of CEA

Sutherland (161) provides an introductory "primer of cost effectiveness" in the form of a programmed text. He covers the general purpose of cost-effectiveness studies, five essentials of a cost-effectiveness study, costing procedures, and analysis techniques. The text is organized in page-long discussions, each followed by a question, and the reader is directed to another page depending on which answer he selects. Jestes (82) presents a tutorial example of systems analysis in the process of locating a book in the library reference room. Logical flow-charting, cost-time estimates, and alternative systems are considered. Laut (95) describes a highly engineering-oriented method for conducting a tradeoff study, aimed at generating more ideas about measures of effectiveness. Two hypothetical spacecraft subsystems are analyzed and the results displayed by block diagrams, tabulations, and graphs.

One problem of tradeoff analysis is that of displaying to the judge the large amount of data represented by cost and effectiveness estimates of numerous system elements and the relations between them. Gregg (61) describes the uses of one of the customary solutions to this problem, i.e., decision tables. His examples are very simple and easy to follow. Addressing the same problem, Sadacca & Root (142) offer a method for the evaluation of large numbers of system alternatives by large numbers of judges. The method provides for the combining of alternatives for each factor bearing on a decision, and the rank-ordering of all possible configurations of alternatives. The rankings can be based on the judgments of judges with diverse points of view. The method used is an adaptation of analysis of variance techniques to multifactor scaling problems. An example of an application is provided, and a test showed the method to be quite successful.

Another problem of tradeoff analysis is that of including calendar time expenditures and savings in the various comparisons. Schriever (151), former commander of the Air Force Systems Command, notes that many new system configurations potentially available today represent radical innovations, with benefit and effectiveness levels far exceeding those of the systems they may replace. He points out that, at the same time, the development time period requirements associated with such radically innovative systems and the possible magnitudes of error in estimating their development time requirements are both large. The large but uncertain development time, representing a large risk factor, becomes even more important as a result of rapid and accelerating rates of technological obsolescence and the need to keep many such systems current and competitive. Thus, the projected active-use life of even a highly innovative system must be carefully estimated, if possible, and its development costs as well as its other costs amortized over the predicted useful life period. The complexities of tradeoff analyses are magnified for costly, highly innovative systems.

Specific Applications of CEA

The system applications of special interest to readers of this chapter are information retrieval and dissemination. Among the items reviewed this year, two companion documents by Bryant et al., of Westat Research, Inc. (174) undoubtedly provide the most comprehensive, sophisticated, and useful treatment of cost-effectiveness analysis for such systems. The first document contains a paper providing a perspective on evaluation of retrieval effectiveness of document retrieval systems, a general paper on the application of measurement theory and methodology to retrieval system evaluation, and five technical papers on theoretical mathematical and statistical topics that support the general measurement paper. The second document is a procedural guide for evaluation of document retrieval systems; it discusses many of the applied procedural ramifications of the concepts covered in the companion document. Two strengths of these documents are the explicit way in which they put retrieval effectiveness into a more general framework of cost-effectiveness analysis, and the treatment of microevaluation (diagnostic as distinguished from overall figure-of-merit measurement) procedures for the retrieval function.

Herner's foreword to Lancaster's (93) textbook on information retrieval systems and their evaluation accurately characterizes it as free from unexplained and unnecessary jargon. Lancaster provides the student with brief but clear treatments of the historical background, the conceptual and mathematical bases, and examples of applications of most currently viable and widely applicable procedural features of information retrieval systems. The descriptive emphasis in approximately half the book is on human-performed procedural aspects of information retrieval (IR) processing, and the last half is devoted to system evaluation using methods and concepts from the Cranfield and Medical Literature and Retrieval System (MEDLARS) evaluation projects, with which Lancaster was associated. He distinguishes between the operational and economic efficiency of a system. The former centers around search accuracy considerations and is not taken up with cost. The latter considers search accuracy as well as other benefit and effectiveness criteria, together with cost data, in the light of tradeoff analysis.

Rothenberg (134) presents an efficiency model and a performance function for information retrieval systems. The mathematical model follows a systems-engineering descriptive approach with overtones of economic analysis. Porter & Rudwick (123) describe a conceptual approach for evaluating and selecting among alternative proposed electronic data processing systems designed to meet a set of user needs. They note that the question, "Which is the better system to buy?" can be restated as, "Is the additional amount of effectiveness worth the added amount of cost?" Two different selection strategies may be used to resolve the problem: in "pivoting on constant effectiveness," one specifies a level of effectiveness that all systems must meet to be considered, and then selects from these the system with the lowest total cost; in "pivoting on constant cost," all systems considered must not exceed a specified total cost, and the one among these that provides the highest level of effectiveness is selected.

Packer's article (120) investigates ways in which concepts of model building and cost-effectiveness can be applied to the health planning process. This excellent paper provides a clear exposition of decision-theory modeling applied to a complex problem of cost-effectiveness analysis. Criterion measures are discussed, such as the statistically expected value of the weighted sum of the population's expected duration of stay in each of several disability states.

Schieber & Shoffner (149) report a well-conceptualized and well-conducted experimental study of the *cost* effectiveness of a system. They studied facsimile transmission and analyzed its implications for interlibrary loan systems. User expectations and habits regarding tolerable delays were examined, and rather wide disparities between voiced needs and user behavior were recorded. The authors conclude that users, despite their intentions and aspirations, do not take time to actually adapt to the availability of high-speed service.

Measures of Retrieval Effectiveness

There are several different components of effectiveness for information retrieval systems, such as exhaustiveness, accuracy, and appropriateness of the information collection, convenience of user access, ease and brevity of user transactions required to obtain a system response, and rapidity of that response. Nevertheless, retrieval system effectiveness has become almost synonymous with retrieval system "accuracy" (i.e., the delivery of all and only those information items that the user would have selected for himself by direct inspection). Perhaps this emphasis occurs because, without reasonable accuracy, other possible system benefits pale to relative insignificance; perhaps it occurs because other effectiveness variables seem comparatively easier to conceptualize and measure, and thus need less attention.

Brookes (17) briefly sketches recent retrieval accuracy formulas and thinking, especially that of Swets's paper (162), which was described in King's chapter last year (86). He clarifies the intended usefulness of the kind of formula developed by Swets, that is, to reduce the effort required for evaluating retrieval accuracy by reducing the number of sampling points required for a stable and accurate result. He provides a modification of Swets's formula that has known distribution properties so that tests can be made of the statistical significance of differences obtained between accuracy values.

Pollock (122) provides good verbal sketches of some accuracy measures in current use and indicates the main disadvantages of each. He summarizes the problem as that of treating the lists of items produced by a retrieval system in ways having no direct relation to the manner in which the recipient might be expected to use the lists. He then develops several formulas. One is a weighted rank-order formula that gives higher weights to correspondences between high-ranking relevance values (as determined both by the system and by the user) than to correspondence between low-ranking values. Another formula is a "browser's statistic," whose aim is to depict the expected number of documents it will take for the requester to be satisfied, given a particular ranked list of documents which he examines in that order. A third formula adapts the precision/recall-ratio type of measure for use with relevance values other than 0 and 1. Finally, there is a decision-theory model for expressing the cost and/or utility associated with various degrees of rank-matching of requests to documents having a known utility value. Pollock's paper is a relatively brief but effective stimulus for opening a reader's thinking to the range of conceptual treatments that might profitably be applied to retrieval accuracy measurement problems, and it provides a vivid treatment of some sequential characteristics of the user's response to the system output.

Cooper (34) also addresses himself to the problem of the user's sequential response to system output. He sets himself the goal of providing an accuracy measure that meets four criteria: it can be expressed as a single value, can compare the obtained performance with that of a random search, takes account of the amount of material the user wants, and operates on the not-unrealistic assumption that the system will provide a "weak ordering" of its output by computed relevance, and that the user will scan and judge the output in that order (weak ordering is defined by the relation, "Document X has at least as great an overlap with the search question as document Y," so that ties are allowed). The formula he offers for "expected search length" appears to satisfy all the criteria.

Wiederkehr, in Bryant et al. (174), carries on the line of thinking presented by Cooper and generalizes the concept of expected search length in a function called the "search characteristic curve." This curve shows the plotted relationship between search *return* as measured in number of relevant documents, and search *effort* as measured in number of documents examined. Wiederkehr derives the relationships between the search characteristic curve and recall-precision ratios and Swets's operating characteristic curve. The presentation is quite mathematical, however, and the unprepared reader can perhaps increase his understanding of the discussion by consulting Brookes's (17) description of the Swets model of an IR system, where much the same ground is covered in a more tutorial fashion.

King and Bryant, in Bryant et al. (174), describe a diagnostic model for evaluating accuracy of retrospective searching, the model being in the form of a finite Markov chain with absorbing states. The model contains processing stages such as the verbalized request, the coder's interpretation, the encoded request, the system's response, and the screener's judgment. Each stage is treated as a source of possible information loss in transmitting the description of the document contents, the error properties being expressed in the form of conditional probability values inserted in the Markov chain. The authors' discussion neatly ties in this model with measures such as search characteristic curves and with more detailed and exhaustive schematic conceptual models for cost-effectiveness analysis and evaluation of searching and retrieval functions. On the latter topic, Stanfel (159) provides an example of a linear-programming model approach to the problem of modifying retrieval system performance by utilizing user-provided feedback information. He points out that the strategies and tactics used in reacting to such feedback information are crucial, in that under-reaction can waste the value of the feedback, and over-reaction can create new problems of reactive oscillation.

Error Sources in Search Accuracy Measurement

The preceding chapters in the *Annual Review* by Rees (128) and by King (86) each made a point of emphasizing papers concerned with factors that can reduce the validity of measures of retrieval accuracy. In particular, retrieval measures are largely based on judgments of relevance, and the previous two years had seen a number of analyses, discussions, and empirical studies aimed at identifying the weightier factors that might contribute to spurious variability of relevance judgments. Salton & Lesk (146) set out to obtain an empirical answer to the question, "Are recall and precision results unreliable because relevance judgments are unstable?" Their well-controlled experiment used care in the criterion definition of relevance, in selection of relatively uniformly knowledgeable judges, in homogeneity of the document set, in strict control of the query-generation process, and in control of inter-judge communication. Within these strict conditions, four very similar (but distinct) experimental treatments of relevance judgments were tested: relevance asserted by query author, relevance asserted by another subject expert, relevance asserted by either query author *or* another subject expert, and relevance asserted by both query author and the other expert. Eight judges were used in all. Judgments were on a two-point scale of "relevant" and "not relevant."

Using these judgment data, three retrieval methods were evaluated by the SMART system paradigm, and the experimental question was, "Would the four relevance treatments preserve the same ranking order of effectiveness among the three retrieval methods?" The answer was an emphatic "Yes." Salton & Lesk analyzed the results further to explain the findings; there was better discrimination performance for those documents showing higher agreement between judges and higher relevance to the queries. Also, these documents were retrieved earlier in the search process, and the recall and precision measures were more sensitive to documents retrieved early in the search. This study demonstrates that the recall-precision ratio is sensitive enough to make reliable gross distinctions between performances of various retrieval procedures under conditions in which factors that may perturb relevance judgments are well controlled. The results are, in fact, a model argument for the persuasive power that can be achieved by careful design, proper controls, and the right choice of dependent variable measures.

Saracevic et al. (22) provide a three-part report of an extensive research effort in constructing and testing a model information-retrieval system using medical literature in their Comparative Systems Laboratory. They concentrate on factors introducing variability into component functions of the system, such as acquisitions, input sources, and indexing language—especially variability attributable to human performance. In pages 72–108 of their first volume, they discuss the kinds of factors studied, and in pages 214–237 they provide a wide-ranging discussion of factors affecting relevance judgments that they encountered in their experimental situations.

Gifford & Baumanis (54) report an investigation of the role of documents in relevance judgments. Their results suggest that the textual bases of user relevance judgments are expressible largely as meaningful co-occurrences of terms closely related to the question. Streufert & Castore (160) studied the effects of increasing success and failure on perceived information quality and the relationship of this to information search and information utilization. It was found that estimates of quality initially increase and do not differ until success and failure levels are quite high. At a certain point, failure-treated subjects do not increase their estimates of quality further, while success-treated subjects continue to increase their estimates of quality. The authors suggest that decision makers operating in complex environments may be easily misled by favorable information, and that some corrective procedures, such as the introduction of an occasional failure, might contribute to a more reasonable assessment of the environment. The implications of this idea for providing feedback to delegated searchers is worth pondering. Jordan (83) describes a model for comparing Source Data Information (SDI) systems, in which two critical variables that are controlled (taken account of in analysis) are the interest levels of users and the number of documents provided to them. Romerio & Cavara (131) develop mathematical models for a number of factors that need to be considered and controlled both in searching activities and in evaluation of searching activities: query size, search size, an aperture factor, and two parameters which they call "focusing" and "efficiency." Finally, returning to the matter of instability of human judgment processes, Tversky (167) provides a good bibliography on experimental studies of the topic, gives a clear and concise exposition of the concept of intransitivity of preferences, and provides experimental evidence for the conditions under which intransitivity of preferences is likely to occur. Smith (157) proposes a consistent procedure for deriving subjective probability distributions by the use of statistical ranking techniques. Concepts in these last two cited papers have relevance to the judgmental processes involved in the tradeoff analyses discussed earlier, as well as to judgments of relevance involved in measuring retrieval accuracy considered in this section.

Some Search Accuracy Studies

Salton (36, 143, 144, 145) and Lesk (98, 99) report on the SMART experimental computer-based automatic information retrieval system, its recent evolution, and recent research products. Salton (143) provides a well-organized, clearly-written book on automatic information organization and retrieval. The weight of attention in this book, as in the current SMART system applications, is on automatic retrieval procedures, techniques, and considerations, and on measuring retrieval accuracy. The latest report in the series by Salton (36) sketches earlier results and conclusions and details more recent ones. Of special interest for computer-based systems is the work on interactive search and retrieval methods. The effects of relevance feedback techniques are considered in several aspects: positive and negative feedback, dynamically evolving document spaces, query splitting, document-defined queries, and feedback-based indexing.

The thrust of Lancaster's work in evaluating an actually operating retrieval system is in two very profitable directions: cost-effectiveness tradeoff analysis of retrieval functions, and detailed diagnosis ("microevaluation," in King's and Bryant's terms) of the reasons for true and false positives and negatives in document retrieval. Lancaster & Climenson (94) discuss obtainable precision and recall ratios in the context of such considerations as the professional skill and consequent salary requirements of personnel doing various technical jobs in the system. They present a "system parameter network" relating many cost and effectiveness factors, some of which they discuss. To them, the question to be answered is not, "Is the system operating efficiently?" but rather, "Is the system worthwhile?"

Lancaster (92) reports the results of a major evaluation study conducted on the operating MEDLARS demand-search service. He presents effectiveness and cost results of interest from both a data and a methodological point of view (these are also discussed in the procedure guide of Bryant et al. (174, p. 61). Of special importance are the results he reports for the diagnostic analysis of retrieval failures. Failure sources are grouped by indexing practices, indexing language, formulation of searches, and interaction between user and system. On the basis of the results of these analyses, he concludes that the greatest potential for improvement of

MEDLARS exists at the interface between user and system, specifically, in the improvement of the statement of requests.

Saracevic reached a similar conclusion in the study reviewed earlier (22), and in another paper (148) he reports results from an experimental study of the effects of narrowing and expanding the search formulation by a procedure of formalized analysis. When terms from the question were used without elaboration, about 35% of the relevant documents were retrieved and about half the documents retrieved were not relevant. With the best question-elaboration procedure, about 70% of the relevant documents were retrieved and about three-fourths of the documents retrieved were not relevant.

Freeman (51) describes a study that analyzed and evaluated the results of running 25 search questions against a file of about 9000 UDC-classified records of documents in metallurgy. He concludes that no insoluble problems were found and that the results are encouraging for those considering UDC for use in computer-based retrieval systems. Exhaustive attention is given to the range of variables and conditions impinging on the study. Freeman & Atherton (52) give a well-rounded account of the development and characteristics of AUDACIOUS, an on-line interactive retrieval system employing UDC as the content-coding scheme. Atherton et al. (7) present the results of an experiment using the above-described facility and another data base of 2800 items from the field of nuclear science. Perhaps the most important and, to the reviewer, most interesting part of the results concerns the diagnostic failure analysis. Ten precisely specified different reasons for retrieval failure are identified, and the frequencies with which each contributed to search failures are presented in tabular form. Query formulation was the biggest source of failure, with individual differences between search analysts being noted. Failure of the indexers to index a topic specifically mentioned in the title or in the abstract was the next largest source.

Price & Schiminovich (124) describe an experiment evaluating computer clustering of a collection of 240 articles in high-energy physics; the articles were clustered by a measure of bibliographic couplings. The authors conclude that the resulting subject headings produced a better classification system than that provided by the *Physical Review*, but, unfortunately, they do not provide a clear explanation of how they arrived at this conclusion. Borko et al. (15) performed an experiment to test how five variables (type of indexing, depth of indexing, classification algorithm, order of data input, and homogeneity of document collection) would affect the stability of clusters produced by a computerized hierarchical grouping program. Statistically significant instability of clusters was obtained only for variations in the order of input of data to be clustered.

Man-System Interface Arrangements

Man-system interfaces rank high as sources of nonrandom noise introduced into the system and as focal points for transmission loss. As this fact has begun to emerge more clearly to a wider range of system designers, conceptual and experimental work on interfaces has quickened. The generality and usefulness of the concept of "interface" is well represented in a report by Taylor (163), who analyzes interfaces in a library between the inquirer and the intermediary, the intermediary and the files, and the inquirer and the files. Recommendations are made for improving the information displays at the interface between inquirer and system.

Samuelson (147) introduces the idea of "performance-oriented sequential structuring" of the information to be displayed at the interface, restricting his attention to "complex-deterministic systems where man is not 'left alone in the woods on a random walk,' but instead can be sure to arrive at the destination if a goal-directed performance structure is followed." The steps of the decision sequence in his system, called **RAPIDS**, appear adaptable to fields such as business, management, military, medical, and service applications. Thompson et al. (164), interested in similar problems, investigate user search times obtained when information is displayed in two hierarchical forms: a "table of contents" or indentation form, and a "decision tree" form. A visual search-time formula is derived and an optimal shape for display structures suggested (three to five information items selectable at each successive level of the structure).

Man-system interface problems, ordinarily not so severe for batch-processing computer systems, become potent forces in on-line interactive systems. Smith et al. (158), describing a transition from batch-processed to on-line information and reference retrieval, summarize their experimental findings and observations by noting that full benefits of the on-line concept require system redesign rather than extension of existing procedures. Sackman & Gold (141) experimentally compared human problem-solving performance when supported by the time-sharing versus the batch-processing mode. Time-sharing used more computer time but showed greater effectiveness in fewer dropouts, faster initial and terminal decision times, better pacing, and more positive attitudes toward computer-aided problem solving.

Human factors analysis of man-machine interface characteristics for time-shared on-line interactive textual information systems is just now gathering momentum. Nickerson et al. (114) describe the economics of this change. Earlier, the cost of computer time was high relative to the cost of the user's time, and users constituted a select, highly skilled and highly motivated group of specialists. Now, however, time-sharing promises drastic reductions in costs of computer time to the individual user and also promises large-scale availability of on-line computer facilities to many individuals untrained in any area of computer technology. Mitchell et al. (108) present similar arguments and provide a quite extensive list of human factors and other considerations that may need careful attention and experimental study if optimum performance is to be achieved.

One such factor is operator-machine pacing. If machine response were always instantaneous, the operator would never have to take his attention from the machine except to attend to his part of the mutual problem-solving process. In this case both machine-time and operator-time would be utilized with maximum efficiency, since the machine would only wait for the operator when necessary, and the operator would never wait for the machine. The fact is, however, that machine-response times are rarely instantaneous. Carbonell (19) and Carbonell et al. (20) give an excellent analysis of this problem and report results of experiments showing that for an intermediate part of the range of possible machine delay periods, there is a value-tradeoff function for the operator between invariability and shortness of the machine delay period. Solutions to the problem are also discussed. The current state of the design art with respect to on-line man-machine interfaces can be sensed from a survey of five on-line retrieval systems by Welch (171).

With a large number of on-line consoles operating from one computer in the time-shared mode, there is the problem of designing the computer programs to optimize the distribution and use of computer time. How should the program designer conceive of the computer-time requirements of the console? Denning (42) presents a statistical model for input-output operating system design based on the concept of a hypothetical "virtual console" —a model of the collective characteristics of the actual consoles. The problem of evaluating the cost-effectiveness of such time-shared computer systems is even more complex. Gold (56) offers a detailed account of a method for such evaluation, which has been successfully tested.

Interface Display Hardware

Detailed cost-effectiveness evaluation of hardware is a book-length topic, and involves exhaustive comparisons of manufacturers' documented specifications and claims. Survey articles perform the useful functions of alerting readers to the range of equipments available and the range of considerations involved in evaluating them. Cropper & Evans (38) consider the application of ergonomics—the combined application of human sciences such as anatomy, physiology, and psychology to human performance improvement in different physical environments—to computer display design.

Curry (39), in a series of status surveys, provides examples of a range of applications of cathode ray tubes (CRTs), and lists CRT manufacturers. In another paper (40), Curry offers a well-written and comparatively complete introductory account of CRT display fundamentals, with a technical glossary and schematic diagrams of circuitry and tube anatomy and a sketch of cost data. Kleiman (88) describes various information display devices, including CRTs and several other electrically driven applications. He provides a tabulation of 25 equipment models from 20 manufacturers, covering for each about three dozen points of information, including costs. A good survey done for NASA by Auerbach Corporation (8) on visual information display systems is nontechnical and intended as an introduction for middle-management personnel.

System Hardware

Berul (10), in a survey of equipment for information storage and retrieval systems, points out that until recently two competing approaches to IS&R system equipment problems were both failing—the approach involving expensive, special-purpose microfilm equipment, and the approach of trying to use computer systems to automate the entire IS&R process, including indexing, abstracting, and vocabulary control. The advent of third-generation computers has provided the basis for a compromise between the two approaches. He discusses examples of compromise equipment configurations. Melcher (106) compares the rosy prospects with the cold facts of past automation development projects in the publishing industry, providing examples of disparities between promised and actual cost-effectiveness characteristics of various automated components and subsystems for publishing practices. His candid article portrays a cautious approach obviously attained at some expense. Schwartz (153) provides a short, readable, but quite thorough, procedural checklist for doing cost-effectiveness comparisons between computers, and Kriebel (90) takes a somewhat deeper and more extended look at the need for determining company computer-usage strategy for purposes of computer system planning and computer cost-effectiveness evaluations.

Computer Programming Software

Assuring the performance of proper cost-effectiveness analysis for computer hardware is no small task, but at least relatively "hard" data and knowledge are available concerning more elements of this problem. The situation is less clear for computer program software technology. The software problem, moreover, cannot be dismissed lightly because most estimates are that programming software costs will become a larger proportion of the costs of computer-based systems, exceeding hardware procurement and maintenance costs many times, over the long run, in some kinds of systems. This is the context within which the systems analyst and designer must formulate procedures for evaluating alternative decisions. Can off-the-shelf items be purchased and used as is? What parts of the software programming can or should be done in-house? How will the inevitable requirements for software program maintenance be handled?

Head & Linick (69) discuss acquisition of software packages, touching on sources, make-or-buy decisions, and cost and effectiveness considerations. Hammersmith (65) provides a listing and description of considerations for selecting a vendor of time-shared computer services. He discusses how appearances can be deceiving. West et al. (173) present some principles of software procurement management and concentrate on systematically evaluating the proposed management of the software development effort.

The importance of good management for software program development efforts is at present receiving much attention. Nelson (113) describes the application of general management principles to this task. Pietransanta (121) focuses on estimation of resources available for computer program development and indicates why considerations of quality of programming talent are more important than quantity. Wofsey (177), in a wide-ranging book on management of automatic data processing, also concentrates on the problems of maintaining quality programmer performance. McLamore (103) describes an approach to program production strategy called "recursive product development," using cybernetically well-designed check and feedback loops to control software production. Finally, Rothery provides short, readable, introductory discussions of some general issues at the working programmer level that have obvious ramifications for managing programming efforts: software standardization (135), program model changes (136), and the problem of validity of data input to programming systems (137).

CONCLUSIONS

As applied to systems for document information, the concepts of design and evaluation have, in the past, been linked most closely with large-scale systems and with the trends toward automation, and this emphasis continues in the literature. Viewed from the perspective of finding solutions to the problems of large-scale automated applications for document information systems, the impact of the past year's literature might be characterized as producing a sense of an emerging overall orchestration of thoughts and efforts that is accompanying a maturing discipline. A sharpening of judgment is also evident. There are fewer starkly oversimplified solutions to problems generalized out of their context. Earlier literature contained many instances of glowingly optimistic projections of almost effortless achievement of large-scale automated systems, and equally despairing accounts of the discovery of insurmountable problems on the critical path. Both kinds of articles are being replaced by perhaps less emotionally stimulating (but likely more motion-producing) step-by-step analyses of whether and how various details can or cannot be accomplished, how well, how soon, and for what costs.

Specific accomplishments this year include a growing consensus on the desirable characteristics of measures of retrieval accuracy and the presentation of several refined measures. The need for control of variables affecting relevance judgments has been recognized and dealt with in several evaluation studies. Measures of retrieval accuracy have been conceptually embedded in more general cost-effectiveness analyses of retrieval systems. There seems to be a growing recognition of competent design and evaluation as necessary but not sufficient for achieving effective systems, and of the additional necessities of technically well-informed management of the entire process within which design and evaluation efforts are either well-utilized or wasted. The long-felt concerns of a few for the human performance aspects of the man-machine interface in projected on-line computerized systems are now starting to receive wider attention. In sum, this appears to have been a good year; while time has moved projected large-scale automated information systems one year closer to the "moment of truth" of their operational tests, a more-than-average year's worth of progress toward successfully meeting these tests has also been recorded.

REFERENCES

(1) AD HOC JOINT COMMITTEE ON NATIONAL LIBRARY INFORMATION SYSTEMS (CONLIS). A national library agency . . . a proposal. ALA Bulletin, 62:3 (March 1968) 255–265.
(2) ADAMS, T. W. Systems studies: views from Washington. In: International Technical Communications Conference, 15th, Los Angeles, Calif., 8–11 May 1968. Proceedings. Society of Technical Writers and Publishers, Washington, D.C., 1968, paper W-18 (7 p.).
(3) AINES, ANDREW A. The promise of national information systems. Library Trends, 16:3 (January 1968) 410–418.
(4) AITCHISON, T. M.; MARTIN, M. D.; SMITH, J. R. Developments towards a computer-based information service in physics, electrotechnology and control. Information Storage and Retrieval, 4:2 (June 1968) 177–186. Presented at the First Cranfield International Conference on Mechanized Information Storage and Retrieval Systems, College of Aeronautics, Cranfield, England, 29–31 August 1967.
(5) AMERICAN SOCIETY OF PLANNING OFFICIALS NATIONAL PLANNING CONFERENCE. Houston, Tex., April 1967. Threshold of planning information systems. Selected papers presented at the ADP workshops. American Society of Planning Officials, Chicago, Ill., 1967, 108 p.
(6) ANDERSON, STANFORD, ed. Planning for diversity and choice. MIT Press, Cambridge, Mass., 1968, 340 p.
(7) ATHERTON, P.; KING, D. W.; FREEMAN, R. R. Evaluation of the retrieval of nuclear science document references using the universal decimal classification as the

indexing language for a computer-based system. American Institute of Physics, New York, 1 May 1968. (AIP/UDC-8)
(8) AUERBACH CORPORATION. Visual information display systems: a survey. Philadelphia, Pa., 1968, 95 p. (NASA SP-5049)
(9) BAKER, NORMAN R.; NANCE, RICHARD E. The use of simulation in studying information storage and retrieval systems. American Documentation, 19:4 (October 1968) 363–370. Presented at Thirty-second National Meeting of the Operations Research Society of America, Chicago, Ill., 1–3 November 1967.
(10) BERUL, LAWRENCE H. Survey of IS&R equipment. Datamation, 14:3 (March 1968) 27–32.
(11) BILL, EDWARD S. Managing NASA data requirements with specifications. In: International Technical Communications Conference, 15th, Los Angeles, Calif., 8–11 May 1968. Proceedings. Society of Technical Writers and Publishers, Washington, D.C., 1968, paper I-19 (7 p.).
(12) BILLUPS, RODERICK C.; GORDON, LOUIS. A logical approach to documenting the internal logic of a programming system. In: International Technical Communications Conference, 15th, Los Angeles, Calif., 8–11 May 1968. Proceedings. Society of Technical Writers and Publishers, Washington, D.C., 1968, paper I-20 (8 p.).
(13) BJORGE, S. E.; URBACH, P. F.; EARL, P. H.; KING, D. W.; WIEDERKEHR, R. R. V. An experiment to determine the effectiveness of various announcement media on CFSTI sales. In: American Society for Information Science Annual Meeting, Columbus, Ohio, 20–24 October 1968. Proceedings, Vol. 5. Greenwood Publishing Corp., New York, 1968, p. 327–329.
(14) BORKO, HAROLD. Design of information systems and services. In: Annual review of information science and technology. Carlos A. Cuadra, ed. Interscience, New York, 1967, vol. 2, p. 35–61.
(15) BORKO, HAROLD; BLANKENSHIP, D. A.; BURKET, R. C. On-line information retrieval using associative indexing. System Development Corp., Santa Monica, Calif., May 1968, 124 p. (RADC-TR-68-100) (TM-(L)-3851)
(16) BOURNE, CHARLES P. Evaluation of indexing systems. In: Annual review of information science and technology. Carlos A. Cuadra, ed. Interscience, New York, 1966, vol. 1, p. 171–190.
(17) BROOKES, B. C. The measures of information retrieval effectiveness proposed by Swets. Journal of Documentation, 24:1 (March 1968) 41–54.
(18) CARAS, G. J. Computer simulation of a small information system. American Documentation, 19:2 (April 1968) 120–122.
(19) CARBONELL, JAIME R. On man-computer interaction: a model and some related issues. Bolt, Beranek and Newman, Inc. Cambridge, Mass., 15 September 1967, 34 p. (Report nos. Scientific-1, BBN-1593) (AFCRL-68-0053) (AD-666 666)
(20) CARBONELL, JAIME R.; ELKIND, JEROME I.; NICKERSON, RAYMOND S. On the psychological importance of time in a time sharing system. Bolt, Beranek and Newman, Inc., Cambridge, Mass., 14 September 1967, 30 p. (Report no. Scientific-6, BBN-1687, AFCRL-68-0120) (AD-670 604)
(21) CARTER, L. F. The systems approach to education—the mystique and the reality. System Development Corp., Santa Monica, Calif., 27 January 1969. (SP-3291)
(22) CASE WESTERN RESERVE UNIVERSITY. CENTER FOR DOCUMENTATION AND COMMUNICATION RESEARCH. An inquiry into testing of information retrieval systems. Part I: Objectives, methodology, design, and controls. Part II: Analysis of results. Part III: CSL related studies. Tefko Saracevic, Manager. A. J. Goldwyn, Principal Investigator. (Comparative Systems Laboratory Final Technical Report) Cleveland, Ohio, 1968.
(23) CETRON, M. J. Using technical forecasts. Science & Technology, No. 79 (July 1968) 57–63.
(24) CHARTRAND, ROBERT L.; JANDA, KENNETH; HUGO, MICHAEL, eds. Information support, program budgeting, and the Congress. Spartan Books, New York, 1968, 231 p.

DESIGN AND EVALUATION OF INFORMATION SYSTEMS

(25) CHESTNUT, HAROLD. Systems engineering methods. Wiley, New York, 1967, 392 p.
(26) CHURCHMAN, C. WEST. Challenge to reason. McGraw-Hill, New York, 1968, 223 p.
(27) CHURCHMAN, C. WEST. The systems approach. Delacorte Press, New York, 1968, 243 p.
(28) CLAPP, VERNER W. Copyright—a librarian's view. Prepared for the National Advisory Commission on Libraries. Copyright Committee, Association of Research Libraries, Washington, D.C., August 1968, 40 p.
(29) CLOOT, P. L. Management information systems—can computers help? Computer Bulletin, 11:4 (March 1968) 276–281.
(30) COE, R. M.; BARNHILL, E. A. Social dimensions of failure in innovation. Human Organization, 26:3 (Fall 1967) 149–156.
(31) CONSAD RESEARCH CORPORATION. An information system development program. Pittsburgh, Pa., 15 January 1968, 78 p. (PB-177 809) Prepared in cooperation with Regional Planning Council, Baltimore, Md., and Department of Housing and Urban Development, Washington, D.C.
(32) CONWAY, BENJAMIN. The information system audit. Management Review, 57:3 (March 1968) 37–48.
(33) COOKE, J. E. Needs of the employee in the computerized hospital. Canadian Hospital, 45 (March 1968) 50–53.
(34) COOPER, W. S. Expected search length: a single measure of retrieval effectiveness based on the weak ordering action of retrieval systems. American Documentation, 19:1 (January 1968) 30–41.
(35) COPELAND, B. R. Statistical decision theory. Management Services, 5:2 (May–June 1968) 45–51.
(36) CORNELL UNIVERSITY. DEPARTMENT OF COMPUTER SCIENCE. Information storage and retrieval. Scientific report no. ISR-14 to the National Science Foundation. Reports on analysis, search and iterative retrieval. Gerard Salton, Project Director. Ithaca, N.Y., October 1968, 1 vol. (various pagings)
(37) COUGER, J. DANIEL. Seven inhibitors to a successful management information system. Systems & Procedures Journal, 19:1 (January–February 1968) 16–18.
(38) CROPPER, ANN G.; EVANS, S. J. W. Ergonomics and computer. Computer Bulletin, 12:3 (July 1968) 94–98.
(39) CURRY, WILLIAM C. Technology profile: CRT displays. Part 2. Modern Data, 1:6 (August 1968) 47–52.
(40) CURRY, WILLIAM C. Technology profile: CRT displays. Part 3. Modern Data, 1:7 (September 1968) 24–36.
(41) DAMMERS, H. F. Integrated information processing and the case for a national network. Information Storage and Retrieval, 4:2 (June 1968) 113–131. Presented at the First Cranfield International Conference on Mechanized Information Storage and Retrieval Systems, College of Aeronautics, Cranfield, England, 29–31 August 1967.
(42) DENNING, PETER J. A statistical model for console behavior in multiuser computers. Communications of the ACM, 11:9 (September 1968) 605–612.
(43) DICKSON, P. A. Hard selling technology. [Information centers] Electronics, 41 (22 January 1968) 111–115.
(44) DOEBLER, PAUL D.; TEWLOW, JULES S. The shape of the future, II. Book Production Industry (January 1967) 35–62.
(45) FEDERAL COUNCIL FOR SCIENCE AND TECHNOLOGY. COMMITTEE ON SCIENTIFIC AND TECHNICAL INFORMATION. The Copyright Law as it relates to national information systems and national programs: a study by the *ad hoc* task group on legal aspects involved in national information systems. Washington, D.C., July 1967, 82 p. (PB-175 618)
(46) FEIGENBAUM, DONALD S. The engineering and management of an effective system. Management Science, 14:12 (August 1968) B-721–B-730.
(47) FISHBURN, P. C. Utility theory. Management Science, 14:5 (January 1968)

335–378.
(48) FISHER, C. H. Some comments on systems analysis. RAND Corp., Santa Monica, Calif., September 1967, 18 p. (P-3677) Prepared for presentation at the "Systems Analysis and Cost-Effectiveness" session of a MORS Symposium, Washington, D.C., October 1967. (AD-658 426)
(49) FISHMAN, G. S. Digital computer simulation: the allocation of computer time in comparing simulation experiments. RAND Corp., Santa Monica, Calif., October 1967, 31 p. (RM-5288-1-PR) (AD-662 592)
(50) FREED, ROY N. Providing by statute for inspection of corporate computer and other records not legible visually: a case study on legislating for computer technology. Law and Computer Technology, 1:5 (May 1968) 6–10.
(51) FREEMAN, ROBERT R. Evaluation of the retrieval of metallurgical document references using the universal decimal classification in a computer-based system. American Institute of Physics, New York, 1 April 1968, 1 v. (AIP/UDC-6)
(52) FREEMAN, R. R.; ATHERTON, P. AUDACIOUS—an experiment with an on-line, interactive reference retrieval system using the universal decimal classification as the index language in the field of nuclear science. American Institute of Physics, New York, 25 April 1968. (AIP/UDC-7)
(53) FRIEDMAN, L. Designing management functions in man/computer systems. System Development Corp., Santa Monica, Calif., 28 August 1967, 23 p. (SP-2872)
(54) GIFFORD, G.; BAUMANIS, G. J. On understanding user choices: textual correlates of relevance judgments. American Documentation, 20:1 (January 1969) 21–26.
(55) GLEASON, EDWARD MICHAEL. The role of the period of transition in the implementation of information systems. Final report. Army Logistics Management Center, Fort Lee, Va., June 1968, 62 p. (AD-672 838)
(56) GOLD, MICHAEL M. A methodology for evaluating time-shared computer system usage. Carnegie-Mellon University, Pittsburgh, Pa., August 1967, 78. (AD-668 084)
(57) GRAHAM, ROBERT M. Protection in an information processing utility. In: ACM Symposium on Operating System Principles, Gatlinburg, Tenn., 1–4 October 1967. Proceedings. Communications of the ACM, 11:5 (May 1968) 365–369.
(58) GRANT, C. B. S. Federal grants encourage regional centers, total systems. (Education and Data Processing) Data Processing Magazine, 10:7 (July 1968) 36–37.
(59) GRAZIANO, EUGENE E. "Machine-men" and librarians: an essay. College & Research Libraries, 28:6 (November 1967) 403–406.
(60) GREEN, PAUL E.; ROBINSON, PATRICK J.; FITZROY, PETER T. Experiments on the value of information in simulated marketing environments. Allyn and Bacon, Boston, 1967, 194 p.
(61) GREGG, H. R. Decision tables for documentation and system analysis. Union Carbide Corp., Computing Technology Center, Oak Ridge, Tenn., 3 October 1967, 21 p. (K-1718)
(62) GULL, C. D. Logical flow charts and other new techniques for the administration of libraries and information centers. Library Resources & Technical Services, 12:1 (Winter 1968) 47–66.
(63) GUMMERE, RICHARD M., JR. Toward a new breed of librarians. Wilson Library Bulletin, 41 (April 1967) 810–813.
(64) HAMBLEN, JOHN W. Expenditures, sources of funds, and utilization of digital computers for research and instruction in higher education, 1964–65, with projections for 1968–69. Communications of the ACM, 11:4 (April 1968) 257–262.
(65) HAMMERSMITH, ALAN G. Selecting a vendor of time-shared computer services. Computers and Automation, 17:10 (October 1968) 16–22.
(66) HARE, VAN COURT, JR. Systems analysis: a diagnostic approach. Harcourt Brace, New York, 1967, 554 p.
(67) HARRISON, ANNETTE. The problem of privacy in the computer age: an annotated bibliography. RAND Corp., Santa Monica, Calif., December 1967, 125 p. (RM-5495-PR/RC)
(68) HAYS, DAVID G. et al. A billion books for education in America and the world: a

DESIGN AND EVALUATION OF INFORMATION SYSTEMS 65

proposal. RAND Corp., Santa Monica, Calif., April 1968, 79 p. (RM-5574-RC)
(69) HEAD, ROBERT V.; LINICK, EVAN F. Software package acquisition. Datamation, 14:10 (October 1968) 22–27.
(70) HEANY, DONALD F. Development of information systems: what management needs to know. Ronald Press, New York, 1968, 421 p.
(71) HEILPRIN, LAURENCE B. Technology and the future of the copyright principle. American Documentation, 19:1 (January 1968) 6–11. Reprinted from: Phi Delta Kappan, January 1967.
(72) HELMER, OLAF. The future of science. RAND Corp., Santa Monica, Calif., May 1967, 17 p. (Report no. P-3607) Also published under title "Science" in Science Journal, 3:10 (October 1967) 49–53.
(73) HELMER, OLAF. Prospects of technological progress. RAND Corp., Santa Monica, Calif., August 1967, 14 p. (P-3643)
(74) HELMER, OLAF. The use of the Delphi technique in problems of educational innovations. RAND Corp., Santa Monica, Calif., December 1966, 22 p. (P-3499)
(75) HERNER, SAUL. System design, evaluation, and costing. Special Libraries, 58:8 (October 1967) 576–579.
(76) HERNER, SAUL. System design, evaluation and costing—in plain English. Herner and Co., Washington, D.C., 1 March 1967, 15 p. (AFOSR-67-1998) (AD-657 788)
(77) HOLT, ARTHUR LEE. Design and test of a sponsor's measure of effectiveness for scientific and technical information centers. University Microfilms, Ann Arbor, Mich., 1967, 316 p.
(78) HOMER, EUGENE D. A mathematical model of the flow of data in a management information system. Vol. 1. Doctoral thesis. New York University, Dept. of Industrial Engineering and Operations Research, New York, May 1968, 160 p. (AFOSR-68-0095-Vol-1) (AD-671 949)
(79) HUMPHREY, JOHN A. Survey of library administration: budget and finance. In: Tauber, Maurice F.; Stephens, Irlene R., eds. Library surveys. Columbia Press, New York, 1967.
(80) HYSLOP, MARJORIE R. The economics of information systems: observations of development costs and nature of the market. In: American Society for Information Science Annual Meeting, Columbus, Ohio, 20–24 October 1968. Proceedings, vol. 5. Greenwood Publishing Corp., New York, 1968, p. 301–306.
(81) INFORMATION DYNAMICS CORPORATION. A method for systems design and analysis. Wakefield, Mass., [n.d.] 16 p. (PB-176 191)
(82) JESTES, EDWARD C. An example of systems analysis: locating a book in a reference room. Special Libraries, 59:9 (November 1968) 722–728.
(83) JORDAN, JOHN R. A framework for comparing SDI [Selective Dissemination of Information] Systems. American Documentation, 19:3 (July 1968) 221–222.
(84) KAUFMANN, ARNOLD. The science of decision-making: an introduction to praxeology. Translated from the French by Rex Audley. McGraw-Hill, New York, 1968, 256 p.
(85) KELLER, A. E. Putting systems into management. In: Business automation, 15:7 (July 1968) 40–45.
(86) KING, DONALD W. Design and evaluation of information systems. In: Annual review of information science and technology. Carlos A. Cuadra, ed. Encyclopaedia Britannica, Chicago, 1968, vol. 3, p. 61–103.
(87) KIVIAT, P. J. Digital computer simulation: modeling concepts. RAND Corp., Santa Monica, Calif., August 1967, 62 p. (RM-5378-PR) (AD-658 429)
(88) KLEIMAN, ELLIOT B. A survey of various information display devices. Naval Training Device Center, Orlando, Fla., May 1967, 19 p. (Technical report no. NAVTRADEVCEN-IH-74) (AD-653 867)
(89) KOCH, H. WILLIAM; HERSCHMAN, ARTHUR. A network for physics information. American Institute of Physics, Information Division, New York, October 1968, 16 p. (ID 68-13)
(90) KRIEBEL, C. H. The strategic dimensions of computer systems planning. Carnegie-

Mellon University, Pittsburgh, Pa., January 1968, 22 p. (AD-665 319)
(91) KRUEGER, R. W. Systems analysis, computers, and the future of professional services. Computers and Automation, 17:7 (July 1968) 34–36.
(92) LANCASTER, F. WILFRED. Evaluation of the MEDLARS demand search service. National Library of Medicine, Bethesda, Md., January 1968, 276 p.
(93) LANCASTER, F. WILFRED. Information retrieval systems: characteristics, testing, and evaluation. Wiley, New York, 1968, 222 p.
(94) LANCASTER, F. WILFRED; CLIMENSON, W. D. Evaluating the economic efficiency of a document retrieval system. Journal of Documentation, 24:1 (March 1968) 16–40.
(95) LAUT, STANLEY. Subsystem optimization effectiveness improvement by the option tradeoff analysis process. IEEE Transactions on Systems Science and Cybernetics, SSC-4:2 (July 1968) 133–137.
(96) LAWSON, H. B. Defense Documentation Center reports user needs study results. Defense Industry Bulletin, 4:7 (July 1968) 9–12.
(97) LAZOWSKA, (Mrs.) EDWARD S. Photocopying, copyright, and the librarian. American Documentation, 19:2 (April 1968) 123–130.
(98) LESK, MICHAEL E. Performance of automatic information systems. Information Storage and Retrieval, 4:2 (June 1968) 201–218. Presented at the First Cranfield International Conference on Mechanized Information Storage and Retrieval Systems, College of Aeronautics, Cranfield, England, 29–31 August 1967.
(99) LESK, MICHAEL E. Word-word associations in document retrieval systems. American Documentation, 20:1 (January 1969) 27–38.
(100) LILLY, ROGER M. The test and evaluation of large-scale information processing systems in the army. In: Donald E. Walker, ed. Information system science and technology. Thompson, Washington, D.C., 1967, p. 35–38.
(101) LISTER, W. C. Cost decision rules for the selection of library material for compact storage. Ph.D. thesis. Purdue University, Lafayette, Ind., 1967. (PB-174 441)
(102) McKENNEY, JAMES L. Guidelines for simulation model development. In: Donald E. Walker, ed. Information system science and technology. Thompson, Washington, D.C., 1967, p. 169–173.
(103) McLAMORE, HILLIARD. Recursive product development. Journal of Data Management, 6:1 (January 1968) 28–31, 64.
(104) MARSCHAK, JACOB. Efficient choice of information services. Western Management Institute, University of California, Los Angeles, May 1968, 30 p. (Report No. WMSI Working paper-136) (AD-670 734)
(105) MARSCHAK, JACOB. Economics of inquiring, communications, deciding. University of California, Western Management Science Institute, Los Angeles, January 1968, 36 p. (WMSI-Working paper-134) (AD-668 496) "Based on the Richard T. Ely Lecture delivered at the American Economic Association session of 28 December 1967."
(106) MELCHER, DANIEL. Automation: rosy prospects and cold facts. Library Journal, 93:6 (15 March 1968) 1105–1109.
(107) MILSUM, J. H. The technosphere, the biosphere, the sociosphere. IEEE Spectrum, 5:6 (June 1968) 76–82.
(108) MITCHELL, M. B. et al. Technique for establishing personnel performance standards (TEPPS): procedural guide. 2d ed. Dunlap and Associates, Santa Monica, Calif. January 1968, 71 p. (AD-665 689)
(109) MOHRHARDT, FOSTER E. Planning for Federal information systems. In: International Technical Communications Conference, 15th, Los Angeles, Calif., 8–11 May 1968. Proceedings. Society of Technical Writers and Publishers, Washington, D.C., 1968, paper I-2 (3 p.).
(110) MOOERS, CALVIN N. Standards for user procedures and data formats in automated information systems and networks. Zator Co., Cambridge, Mass., 1967.
Part I: The need for standardization and the manner in which standardization can be accomplished.
5 July 1967, 45 p. (PB-177 550)

Part II: The standardizable elements of user control procedures and unified system model.
10 August 1967, 39 p. (PB-177 551)
Part III: A suggested standard keyboard assignment for the elemental user control actions.
1 August 1967, 21 p. (PB-177 552)
Part IV: A standard method for the description of external data formats.
28 August 1967, 32 p. (PB-177 553)

(111) MOORE, MICHAEL R. Pitfalls in planning an EDP installation. Management Services, 5:5 (September–October 1968) 25–32.
(112) MORELAND, GEORGE B. Operation saturation. Using paperbacks: branch libraries in Maryland conduct an experiment to equate book supply with patron demand. Library Journal, 93:10 (15 May 1968) 1975–1979.
(113) NELSON, EDWARD A. Managing the economics of computer programming: current methodological research. In: National Conference of the Association for Computing Machinery, 23rd, Las Vegas, Nev., 27–29 August 1968. Proceedings. Brandon/Systems Press, Princeton, N.J., 1968, p. 346–349.
(114) NICKERSON, R. S.; ELKIND, J. I.; CARBONELL, J. R. Human factors and the design of time sharing computer systems. Bolt, Beranek and Newman, Inc., Cambridge, Mass., 15 November 1967, 25 p. (Report no. Scientific-2) (AFCRL-68-0054) (AD-666 443)
(115) NORTH, D. W. A tutorial introduction to decision theory. IEEE Transactions on Systems Science and Cybernetics, September 1968, No. 3, vol. SSC-4, p. 200.
(116) NUGENT, WILLIAM R. Statistics of collection overlap at the libraries of the six New England State universities. Library Resources & Technical Services, 12:1 (Winter 1968) 31–36.
(117) ORR, RICHARD H.; PINGS, VERN M.; PIZER, IRWIN H.; OLSON, EDWIN E. Development of methodologic tools for planning and managing library services. I: Project goals and approach. Bulletin of the Medical Library Association, 56:3 (July 1968) 235–240.
(118) ORR, RICHARD H.; PINGS, VERN M.; PIZER, IRWIN H.; OLSON, EDWIN E. Development of methodologic tools for planning and managing library services. III: Standardized inventories of library services. Bulletin of the Medical Library Association, 56:4 (October 1968) 380–403.
(119) ORR, RICHARD H.; PINGS, VERN M.; PIZER, IRWIN H.; OLSON, EDWIN E.; SPENCER, CAROL C. Development of methodologic tools for planning and managing library services. II: Measuring a library's capability for providing documents. Bulletin of the Medical Library Association, 56:3 (July 1968) 241–267.
(120) PACKER, A. H. Applying cost-effectiveness concepts to the community health system. Operations Research, 16:2 (March–April 1968) 227–253.
(121) PIETRANSANTA, ALFRED M. Managing the economics of computer programming: current methodological research. In: National Conference of the Association for Computing Machinery, 23rd, Las Vegas, Nev., 27–29 August 1968. Proceedings. Brandon/Systems Press, Princeton, N.J., 1968, p. 341–346.
(122) POLLOCK, S. M. Measures for the comparison of information retrieval systems. American Documentation, 19:4 (October 1968) 387–397.
(123) PORTER, J. D.; RUDWICK, B. H. Application of cost-effectiveness analysis to EDP system selection. MITRE Corp., Bedford, Mass., March 1968, 33 p. (AD-667 522)
(124) PRICE, NANCY; SCHIMINOVICH, SAMUEL. A clustering experiment: first step towards a computer-generated classification scheme. Information Storage and Retrieval, 4:3 (August 1968) 271–280.
(125) Protection of computer programs—bibliography. Communications of the ACM, 11:1 (January 1968) 67.
(126) PUTNAM, ARNOLD O. The human side of management systems. Business Automation, 15:11 (November 1968) 42–48.

(127) QUADE, E. S.; BOUCHER, W. I., eds. System analysis and policy planning: applications in defense. RAND Corp., Santa Monica, Calif., June 1968, 453 p. (R-439-PR abridged)
(128) REES, ALAN M. Evaluation of information systems and services. In: Annual review of information science and technology, Vol. 2, p. 63–86. Carlos A. Cuadra, ed. Interscience, New York, 1967.
(129) REITZ, CONRAD. Organizing the acquisition of serials for greater efficiency. Ontario Library Review, 51 (September 1967) 158–161.
(130) RESCHER, NICHOLAS. The future as an object of research. RAND Corp., Santa Monica, Calif., April 1967, 12 p. (P-3593) (AD-651 425)
(131) ROMERIO, G. F.; CAVARA, L. Assessment studies of documentation systems. Information Storage and Retrieval, 4:3 (August 1968) 309–325.
(132) ROSOVE, PERRY E. An analysis of possible future roles of educators as derived from a contextual map. System Development Corp., Santa Monica, Calif., 8 March 1968, 82 p. (SP-3088)
(133) ROSOVE, PERRY E. The use of contextual mapping to support long-range educational policy making. System Development Corp., Santa Monica, Calif., 14 December 1967, 36 p. (SP-3026)
(134) ROTHENBERG, DOUGLAS H. An efficiency model and a performance function for an information retrieval system. Center for Documentation and Communication Research, School of Library Science, Case Western Reserve University, Cleveland, Ohio, November 1967, 26 p. (Comparative Systems Laboratory. Technical Report No. 13)
(135) ROTHERY, BRIAN. Compatibility and order. Data Processing Magazine, 10:4 (April 1968) 56–57.
(136) ROTHERY, BRIAN. The problems of program change. Data Processing Magazine, 10:3 (March 1968) 68–69.
(137) ROTHERY, BRIAN. Resolutions, restraints, and reality. Data Processing Magazine, 10:2 (February 1968) 40–41.
(138) RUNCK, HOWARD. Information systems need nurses. Datamation, 14:9 (September 1968) 56–59.
(139) SACKMAN, HAROLD. Computers, system science, and evolving society. System Development Corp., Santa Monica, Calif., 1967, 638 p.
(140) SACKMAN, H. A public philosophy for real time information systems. System Development Corp., Santa Monica, Calif., 19 July 1968, 27 p. (SP-3126)
(141) SACKMAN, H.; GOLD, MICHAEL M. Time-sharing versus batch processing: an experimental inquiry into human problem-solving. System Development Corp., Santa Monica, Calif., 14 June 1968, 103 p. (SP-3110)
(142) SADACCA, ROBERT; ROOT R. T. A method of evaluating large numbers of system alternatives. Human Factors, 10:1 (1968) 5–10.
(143) SALTON, GERARD. Automatic information organization and retrieval. McGraw-Hill, New York, 1968, 514 p. (Computer Science Series)
(144) SALTON, GERARD. A comparison between manual and automatic indexing methods. American Documentation, 20:1 (January 1969) 61–71.
(145) SALTON, GERARD. The use of standardized documentary data in automatic information dissemination. IEEE Transactions on Engineering Writing and Speech, EWS-11:2 (August 1968) Advance abstract in: IEEE Spectrum, 5:7 (July 1968) 117.
(146) SALTON, GERARD; LESK, M. E. Relevance assessments and retrieval system evaluation. Cornell University, Department of Computer Science, Ithaca, N.Y., September 1968, 35 p. (Technical Report No. 68–25)
(147) SAMUELSON, KJELL. Information structure and decision sequence. In: FID/IFIP Joint Conference, Rome, Italy, 14–17 June 1967. Proceedings: Mechanized information storage, retrieval and dissemination. Edited by Kjell Samuelson. North-Holland Publishing Co., Amsterdam, 1968, p. 622–636.
(148) SARACEVIC, TEFKO. The effect of question analysis and searching strategy on performance of retrieval systems: selected results from an experimental study. Center for Documentation and Communication Research, School of Library Science, Case

Western Reserve University, Cleveland, Ohio, May 1968, 10 p. (Comparative Systems Laboratory. Technical report no. 15)
(149) SCHIEBER, WILLIAM D.; SHOFFNER, RALPH M. Telefacsimile in libraries: a report of an experiment in facsimile transmission and an analysis of implications for interlibrary loan systems. Institute of Library Research, University of California, [Berkeley] February 1968, 137 p.
(150) SCHLESINGER, J. R. Systems analysis and the political process. RAND Corp., Santa Monica, Calif., June 1967, 31 p. (P-3464)
(151) SCHRIEVER, G. A. Systems analysis: useful, yes—but scarcely a panacea. Space Digest (May 1968) 57–60.
(152) SCHUMACHER, ANNE W. A small college information system: an analysis and recommendations. Whittenburg, Vaughan Associates, Inc., Alexandria, Va., April 1968. (W/V-RR-68/2-Tn) (NSF Grant GN-624)
(153) SCHWARTZ, E. S. Computer evaluation and selection. Data Management, 6:6 (June 1968) 58–62.
(154) SIMMS, DANIEL M. What is a systems analyst? Special Libraries, 59:9 (November 1968) 718–721.
(155) SIMON, HERBERT A. The future of information processing technology. Management Science, 14:9 (May 1968) 619–624. "A slightly adapted version of a speech presented at the TIMS International Meeting in Mexico City, August 24, 1967."
(156) SMITH, FOSTER D., JR.; CREAGER, WILLIAM A. Developing a coordinated information program for geological scientists in the United States. American Geological Institute, Washington, D.C., December 1967, 56 p. (PB-177 290)
(157) SMITH, L. H. Ranking procedures and subjective probability distributions. Management Science, 14:4 (December 1967) B-236–B-249.
(158) SMITH, WILLIAM A., JR.; ANDERSON, RONALD R.; JENNINGS, MICHAEL A. Experimental retrieval systems studies. Report no. 4. Transition to on-line information and reference retrieval. Final summary report. 1 June 1966–31 May 1968. Lehigh University, Center for the Information Sciences, Bethlehem, Pa., August 1968, 65 p. (AD-674 954)
(159) STANFEL, LARRY E. On a quantitative approach to improving document retrieval performance. Information Storage and Retrieval, 4:3 (August 1968) 281–286.
(160) STREUFERT, SIEGFRIED; CASTORE, C. H. An implication for the information search concept: effects of increasing success and failure on perceived information quality. Purdue University, Lafayette, Ind., in cooperation with Rutgers–The State University, New Brunswick, N.J., February 1968, 11 p. (Technical Report No. 9) (AD-668 529)
(161) SUTHERLAND, WILLIAM H. A primer of cost effectiveness. Research Analysis Corp., McLean, Va., March 1967, 95 p. (Economics and Costing Department Technical Paper RAC-TP-250)
(162) SWETS, JOHN A. Effectiveness of information retrieval methods. American Documentation, 20:1 (January 1969) 72.
(163) TAYLOR, ROBERT S. Studies in the man-system interface in libraries. Lehigh University, Bethlehem, Pa., July 1967, 99 p. (AD-659 468)
(164) THOMPSON, D. A.; BENNIGSON, L. A.; WHITMAN, D. A proposed structure for displayed information to minimize search time through a data base. American Documentation, 19:1 (January 1968) 80–84.
(165) TITUS, JAMES P. Lobbying in Washington. (Washington Commentary) Communications of the ACM, 11:1 (January 1968) 54.
(166) TUROFF, MURRAY. A heuristic compromise between probability of success and limited resources. Institute for Defense Analysis, Arlington, Va., August 1967, 41 p. (Research paper P-338) (AD-657 168)
(167) TVERSKY, AMOS. Intransitivity of preferences. Psychological Review, 76:1 (January 1969) 31–48.
(168) UNITED STATES OF AMERICA STANDARDS INSTITUTE. General purpose alphanumeric keyboard arrangement for information interchange. (Proposed USA

Standard) Communications of the ACM, 11:2 (February 1968) 126–129.
(169) VOOS, HENRY. Organizational communication: a bibliography. Rutgers University, New Brunswick, N.J., 1967, 132 p. (AD-657 647)
(170) WALL, EUGENE. Possibilities of articulation of information systems into a network. American Documentation, 19:2 (April 1968) 181–187.
(171) WELCH, NOREEN O. A survey of five on-line retrieval systems. MITRE Corp., Washington, D.C., August 1968, 53 p. (MTP-322)
(172) WELLISCH, DR. JEAN B. Adoption diffusion processes in the direct mail shelter development system—DMSDS: some previous research, and where it leads us. System Development Corp., Santa Monica, Calif., 17 January 1969, 27 p. (SP-3285)
(173) WEST, G. P.; HUDSON, G. R.; REGAN, E. D. Principles of software procurement management. System Development Corp., Santa Monica, Calif. 23 April 1968, 9 p. (SP-3127)
(174) WESTAT RESEARCH, INC. Evaluation of document retrieval systems: literature perspective, measurement, technical papers. Procedural guide for the evaluation of document retrieval systems. (E. C. Bryant, Project Director.) Bethesda, Md., 31 December 1968, 2 vols.
(175) WHITTENBURG, JOHN A.; SCHUMACHER, ANNE W. An information system planning guide: preliminary development and checkout. Interim report. Whittenburg, Vaughan Associates, Inc., Alexandria, Va. February 1968, 262 p. (W/V-RR-68/1-Wd) (PB-177 601)
(176) WIXON, D. W.; HOUSMAN, E. M. Development and evaluation of a large-scale system for selective dissemination of information (SDI). Army Electronics Command, Fort Monmouth, N.J., August 1968, 38 p. (Research and development technical no. ECOM-3001) (AD-674 661)
(177) WOFSEY, MARVIN M. Management of automatic data processing. Thompson, Washington, D.C., 1968, 213 p.
(178) WOLK, STUART. Resistance to EDP: an employee-management dilemma. Data Management, 6: 9 (September 1968) 44–46, 74–76.
(179) WOOSTER, HAROLD. Policy planning for technical information in industry. Air Force Office of Scientific Research, Directorate of Information Sciences, Arlington, Va., 29 November 1967, 19 p. (AFOSR-67-2588) (AD-661 589) Proceedings presented at the FID/DC Symposium, Bad Godesberg, Germany, 29 November 1967.
(180) WUELFING, RON A. Information systems documentation—a functional approach. In: International Technical Communications Conference, 15th, Los Angeles, Calif., 8–11 May 1968. Proceedings. Society of Technical Writers and Publishers, Washington, D.C., 1968, paper I-17 (4 p.)
(181) YOUNG, STANLEY. Organization as a total system. California Management Review, X:3 (Spring 1968) 21–32.

II

Basic Techniques and Tools

The core problem of information science is still that of determining what documents are about and deciding what to call this "aboutness." Chapter 3 identifies the major elements of progress in this difficult area. Fairthorne asserts that one of the impediments to progress has been the careless use of terminology, the effect of which has been to mask important issues, such as whether indexers should be concerned with the verity of statements in documents or simply with the fact that the statements are about something. The chapter helps to show the current and likely limitations of computer science in solving problems of analyzing and describing document content.

Once documents have been described, and the descriptions coded for entry into a computer store, attention turns to the problems of organizing and managing the files. In Chapter 4, Senko discusses a major technical thrust in the area of file organization: converting from several special-purpose file-manipulation programs to highly generalized programs capable of integrating many special-purpose data files into one organization-wide system. He gives examples of such systems in medicine, education, government, and business. Senko describes four primary accessing techniques, discusses secondary key-accessing techniques, and outlines some considerations governing selection of primary and secondary techniques for tailoring file access to particular conditions. He then reviews papers applying various approaches to the problem of using use-statistics to improve file structure design.

Automated Language Processing, the subject of Chapter 5, is closely allied to that of content analysis; the system for content analysis and representation provides the medium of communication between the user and the information store in natural-language information systems. Systems for automatic content analysis and representation cover a wide range of complexity. Miss Montgomery points out that, though the approaches and techniques described are promising, most of them involve fairly small data bases, and it seems questionable whether the techniques can be extrapolated easily to large-volume systems. Nonetheless there are grounds for cautious optimism about the future of automated language processing, if only because the two groups on whom progress depends—the linguists and the data-oriented computer people—are beginning to share some common perspectives on the useful means of semantic representation.

Chapter 6 contains the *Annual Review*'s first full treatment of reprography. Veaner first deals with fundamental definitions of terms and scope, and then discusses the field of reprography in terms of eight topics ranging from the impact of software to applications of microform technology to engineering drawing. He indicates that full-sized reprography has reached a high state of technical perfection. In contrast, microform technology shows a lack of compatible equipments and quality standards, although Veaner sees much promise in microforms as a high-density storage medium when coupled with advanced software now under development.

The next chapter, "Document Retrieval," concentrates primarily on techniques for computerized retrieval. A review of system models shows general agreement on system functions but not on how the functions should be performed. Most of the contention centers on the degree of mechanization that is desirable. Berul discusses the results of experiments with interactive systems, the advantages of interactive over batch-processing systems, and the important role of query languages. An underlying theme in discussion of search strategies is the use of feedback to improve search results. Berul notes that future document retrieval advances will require improved on-line hardware and software, and better cost/effectiveness data.

In the final chapter in this section, Landau treats document dissemination as one aspect of scientific communication. He discusses the increasing participation of the Federal Government in dissemination efforts and the general dissatisfaction with inefficient operations resulting from lack of standards and coordination. The dissemination activities of the three national libraries receive a more favorable review. The growth of information analysis centers and their functions as dissemination establishments are discussed, with heavy emphasis being given to SDI systems. Dissemination by microform, facsimile, and magnetic tapes are treated briefly, and speculations about the future interplay of data processing technology and the publishing industry are included. The interchange of machine-readable records among the members of the information community is discussed as a fitting piece of the information transfer puzzle.

3

Content Analysis, Specification, and Control

ROBERT A. FAIRTHORNE

INTRODUCTION

Readers go to libraries to find out what people have had to say. Librarians and their tools exist just to help readers do this. Therefore, however much the scope of the words "librarian" and "reader" and "say" may have been widened by technical and social change, librarians must be able to supply records or replications of what people have said, or at least facilitate access to these. They must also devise methods both to allow readers to prescribe the type of discourse they require, and to provide for labeling discourse to anticipate such prescription. These are necessary, though not sufficient, for any activities based upon communication through discourse.

Systems of labeling based upon the circumstances of production of the discourse and of its record, and the physical characteristics of the record, include what are known as Bibliographic and Descriptive Cataloguing. They are essential, because with them even partial or imperfect knowledge of a title, author, publisher, date and place of publication, size, shape, typography, color, and so forth, of the record can lead to its immediate or eventual retrieval. However, retrieval does demand some bibliographic knowledge, particularly of arbitrary matters such as the formats of proper names. This knowledge may not be available, especially when the reader requires discourse that is "about" some topic or topics, but does not know even if any exists; or if he is uncertain (though not completely ignorant) of the terms in which it may be talked about.

System Goals and Limitations

Many systems have been devised that label discourse according to its "content," in the sense of what it is about, and provide the reader with a corresponding prescriptive language, adequate in scope and refinement for the anticipated demands. In considering such systems, we must keep in mind that there are two targets at least that they cannot achieve, even ideally. First, no "informational" activity or system can deal with knowledge as such. The only knowledge within its competence is knowledge of (recorded) discourse, not of what the discourse is about. This fundamental distinction is often overlooked. In medicine, for instance, Lancaster (100) assesses the content ("aboutness") of retrieved items by their value when applied by their requester. Confusion of "book knowledge" with knowledge, or even with truth, is quite widespread also among those who devise classification schemes (structures of discourse), though usually this confusion is not overt.

The second unattainable target is for the librarian or system to substitute for the individual reader in the selection of documents. Could he do so, he would have to be the reader himself, in heredity, history, emotions, interests, intellect, and what he ate for breakfast. A librarian or library system is not a substitute for the reader, but is his delegate. [For a discussion of this view, which is not unanimous, see O'Connor v. Lancaster (122). The latter argues for a deontic function of librarians.] A delegate not only must be able to do what he is told, but must also be able to be told what to do. Most habitual readers acquire a flair for picking out what they want from the shelves, shortcircuiting the need for analysis of what it is about and the expression—even mentally—of what it is about. They do not know how they do this, let alone how to tell others how to do it for them. Librarians and retrieval systems can do only what they are told to do; they can be told to do only what the characteristics of the prescriptive language, its user, and its interpreter allow them to be told.

Terminology

I follow reviewers in preceding volumes by having to report widespread slovenly, misleading, vague, and inconsistent terminology that clogs thought and action. Too often, "terms," "descriptors," "key words," and variants thereof are used interchangeably for words in the text, assigned words, index terms, and concepts of any kind.

The matter of terminology is important not only *within* library and retrieval systems but also in discussing such systems in a meaningful way. A well-chosen terminology can do much to clarify and differentiate fundamental notions. An ill-chosen one will mislead by evoking erroneous mental images or provoking false assumptions. This is particularly true of discussion about content analysis and its ramifications, for this topic has to deal with all levels of language, from the physical representation to relations between concepts.

Too often, no distinction is made between use and mention of words; between type and token; between name and what is named; between representation, the thing represented, and interpretations of it. Far more serious are the bad terminological habits of those who have much to say that is worth saying well. Not all follow the example of Bohnert (21) who declares, and observes, the self-denying ordinance:

> No new terminology is introduced. Instead, a few generally known and accepted words have been sharpened up a little, and then used as consistently as possible . . . a limitation is the use of as precise and as concrete words as possible. For instance, 1. the word "document" instead of "information", . . . 4. the word "retrieval" instead of "information storage and retrieval. . . .

She develops her arguments from mutually consistent and carefully considered definitions of essential terms such as "data," "document," and "retrieval."

Definitions often seem to be afterthoughts or ornamental embellishments. Even when given early and careful consideration, too many definitions in the literature are defective. Some are circular, others confuse definitions with a mere listing of examples, and far too many define *ignotum per ignotius*. For example, Saracevic et al. (26), otherwise exemplary in both matter and manner, define their use of the word "knowledge" and other words in terms of "information." This leaves the term not only undefined, but used in more than one sense—both as "message" (conceptual) and "document" (verbal record)—in the text.

This particular offence is widespread at rather high levels. Indeed, many humbler offenders are the victims of organizations that should know better. For example, in the making of the Office of Naval Research's *Thesaurus of Engineering and Scientific Terms* (123), the term "information retrieval" occurred in twenty-three contributed vocabularies. One said that the term must not be used for "manual" techniques (i.e., those involving intellectual judgments), and another put it generically under "data processing"; yet another equated it with "data processing."

Authors must necessarily pay some attention to the verbal habits of their readers and the occasional conditioned reflexes of their editors, but they must not be servile. Nowadays, many authors feel obliged to use the word "relevance," but they usually make it clear whether they refer to a relation between request and response or to a relation between one topic and another. Lancaster (101), for example, conforms to custom but sterilizes it to some extent by giving good reasons to deplore the debasement of "descriptor," the malapropism of "fact" retrieval, the inflation of "look up" to "data retrieval," and other lapses from semantic hygiene. Artandi (7) also helps her exposition, and her readers, with linguistic good manners.

Terminology can be uncouth, but otherwise unobjectionable. The important things are whether it refers to anything at all; whether it refers to matters that need to be raised or differentiated without lengthy circumlocution; or whether it refers in terms with misleading connotations. Much of the near-invective invoked by terms coined by Perreault, Richmond, Farradane, and others [see, e.g., Perreault (85) for relations in classification structures, and Jolley (88) for relations occurring particularly in "feature card" (joint-attribute) indexing and retrieval] was not objection to unworthy words, but objection to unfamiliar ideas.

Though future reviewers certainly will have cause to deplore deplorable terminology and careless writing, there are signs of uneasy conscience, at least, and of definite improvement, at best. These, professional bodies and editors should encourage.

Scope and Environment of Content Analysis

Content analysis centers on those aspects of "aboutness" that can be used for retrieving records according to readers' prescriptions. For this end, "content" has two aspects:

1. What a record or prescription mentions.
2. The circumstances of its expected uses:
    a. with respect to a particular task or problem,
    b. with respect to a particular user or agent,
    c. with respect to a requirement as expressed by the reader.

Judgments of content are based on evidence of the text of the document or request and are made against a background—implicit or explicit—of social experience. Four primary methods for making such judgments are:

1. matching of text marks by rule,
2. conceptual matching of textual interpretations,
3. construction and matching of conceptual elements,
4. "classification rules" embodying elements and relations expressed in systematic notation and vocabulary.

Even in its narrowest retrieval function, the subject of content analysis clearly extends into and draws upon other fields of activity covered by other chapters. For instance, "matching of text marks by rule" involves, at least, linguistics, automatic language processing, file organization, and automation procedures. This chapter will comment primarily upon the conceptual aspects of content analysis, not upon its managerial, clerical, or computational realization. Nor will it deal with testing, assessment, or evaluation as such. But, because any well-considered studies of these matters must decide what responses and requests are about, or whether they are about the same thing, some reference will be made to them.

Even within the restraints suggested above, some hundreds of papers and books have appeared this year. Adequate discussion of, and justice to, all of them cannot be done. However, the chapter will try to identify major trends and to illustrate them with a discussion of typical contributions.

Content analysis, specification, and control are functions necessary but not sufficient for retrieval. Treatments of them as embedded in this larger activity are given by Bohnert (21), from the managerial and procedural point of view; Lancaster (101), from that of concepts and human agents; Artandi (7), from that of functional automation; Salton (142), from that of automatic organization and language processing; and Jolley (88), from that of joint-attribute ("feature card") retrieval systems.

CONTENT DETECTION, IDENTIFICATION, AND ATTRIBUTION

A reader uses a document to find out what someone has said. An indexer uses it to find out how what has been said will interest the kinds of readers he serves. He then comments upon this in terms of these interests, and in some standard language. The range and structure of the standard language reflect the range and structure of the interests considered by the indexer, and conversely. An indexer does not and cannot index all the ways in which a document will interest all kinds of readers, present and future. Nor can he index only matters of interest that are referred to in the document. For a document can be of interest for reasons that appear only when it is judged against the background of its expected environment of use; in short, by the criteria of that rather neglected form of Information Retrieval called "acquisition policy." See, for instance, Ranganathan (135).

Thus, indexing is an extremely complex activity, inextricable from the classification—that is, structure—of the field of discourse concerned, the verbal expression of this structure, methods for presenting the index and rules for its use to readers, and methods and languages and codes for matching it to the retrieval processes. Landry & Rush (103) outline a theory of indexing. Indexing as a total activity is described and discussed by Bernier (20), Bohnert (21), Harbeck & Lutterbeck (74), Vickery (166), and, within the environment of automatic text-processing methods, Salton (143) and Williams (171). Bernier and Vickery seemingly differ in the number of operations performed by the indexer, but this apparent discrepancy arises from different conventions about distinct operations by human indexers. The word "read" can refer to the recognition of printed words or to their recognition and interpretation. The difference is trivial when all agents are very literate humans, but not when some of the tasks are delegated to symbol-handling devices, human and mechanical, with specialized skills and sharply constrained types of understanding.

Vickery (166) makes a comment on the nature of "understanding" required of an indexer as opposed to that of a reader, which goes some way towards a definition of "book knowledge," to wit, "their understanding being shown, perhaps, by their ability to formulate its (the text's) subject in words that differ from those used by the author." By taking the paraphrase as the objective rather than the effects of the text on the world outside, Vickery not only clarifies the conventional indexing position but shows the common ground that supports both conventional indexing and the standpoint of linguistic semantics. Broadly, the linguistic approach holds that the structure of language has a weak relation to the structure of meaning. Thus, through study of enough text, a reader will detect, though not identify, something of its meaning (e.g., Garvin et al., 64). Because of the weakness of the relation, explicit rules for paraphrasing textual statements into a reasonable number of equivalent statements, even within the restricted field of "question-answering," raise formidable problems (Watt, 167; O'Connor, 121). These cannot be solved by consideration of the text alone. Detection of what a document is "about" in terms of reader interests necessarily depends on what kind of reader and what kind of interest.

Characteristics of "Aboutness"

"Aboutness" is a property of some kinds of discourse. It has been studied by logicians and linguists for a long time because it is a special aspect of meaning. Special topics can be treated as isolated topics only at the risk of sterility; therefore, some acquaintance with the general problems of language and meaning is essential. Among recent writings on these themes that bear also upon content analysis are Bar-Hillel (13), Carroll (24, 25), Rubenstein (139), and Werner & Kaplan (169). In his book about William James and phenomenology, Wilshire (172, pages 86f, 99f) discusses "about," "interest," and "importance." Graziano (70) also uses the phenomenological approach. Hays (76) examines the linguistic foundations of content analysis.

Much discussion of meaning, sense, and denotation has no direct bearing on documentary applications. Existence or nonexistence of named entities, and the truth or falsehood of propositions are not properties that can be used in indexing, since an indexer has no way of verifying the statements made by authors and has no guarantee that readers will be interested in nonfictions alone. From the indexer's point of view, proper names, nouns, and substantival clauses refer, not to what the author may have had in mind, but to reader interests. Similarly, when readers request documents about this and that, they do not know what the author has to say about these things; that is why they want to see the document. So the aboutness of a statement (which is of direct concern to the indexer/requester) must be the same as for its contradiction. Similar considerations apply to attributive statements. In short, indexers are concerned with the appearance of things as exhibited by author and reader behaviour and thus follow, consciously or unconsciously, the outlook of the logician Nelson Goodman.

These comments summarize briefly the case for taking a document as being "about" what it mentions; *Moby Dick* is about a whale; *Othello* about a handkerchief, and about other things. At one extreme, this is done by newspaper indexes of the names of people, places, and dates; at the other, by the designatory theory of Hillman and his school. The difficulties are to identify which of the things mentioned refer to relevant topics, and how to deal with topics of the document that are not mentioned explicitly. Fairthorne (56) points out, as have others before him, that parts of a document are not always about what the entire document is about, nor is a document usually about the sum of the things it mentions. A document is a unit of discourse, and its component statements must be considered in the light of why this unit has been acquired or requested. This may be called its "intensional" aboutness, while the aboutness of its components is its "extensional" aboutness. Intensional aboutness cannot be derived from the text alone, because one cannot infer a question from its answer; if so, one could dispense with an experiment by listing all outcomes, and with calculation by consulting a long enough sequence of random numbers. Bohnert (21), clarifying the confusion surrounding "data" (i.e., parts of a document that, in the given environment, will be read in isolation from the rest of the text), points out that retrieval of data must begin with retrieval of the correct document (i.e., one with the correct intensional aboutness).

The difference between intensional and extensional aboutness parallels the difference between the syntagmatic and paradigmatic in linguistics. Usually, the intensional aboutness is masked in the acquisition policy because the item is assumed to be about what the collection is about, or what the journal that contains it is about. It is masked also by the rules of indexing, which are embedded in the wider environment.

Thus, both Watt (167) and O'Connor (121) discuss the problems of "question-answering" from documents, "question" and "answer" being used in their dictionary senses, not as genteel synonyms for "request" and "response." Watt is concerned more with general linguistic problems arising from direct invocation of computers. In his summary, he points out, *inter alia*, that ". . . besides having differences of form, utterances are partly interpreted and disambiguated on the basis of the situation of usage." O'Connor's careful analysis of retrieval of "answer-providing" documents also illuminates the problem of documentary (extensional) aboutness. He is concerned with retrieval of documents, in response to a question, from which answers to that question may be inferred. Without reference to permissible rules of inference, a retrieved document can answer a question only if it contains the answer *as* an answer to that question, not as a coincidental sequence of letters and digits. To retrieve this answer, we use look-up ("data retrieval") methods. But whether an answer can be inferred from a document depends upon an "inference specification," which must approximate common habits of inference in the particular field.

O'Connor suggests ways of dealing with the problem of extensional aboutness, i.e., that a statement mentioning all things mentioned by the question is not necessarily an answer to that question. He also suggests ways of dealing with "House that Jack built" structures that arise from an inference specification that allows a wide background knowledge, i.e., offers a choice of intensional aboutnesses. Clearly, O'Connor's ideas apply to ordinary retrieval as a special case.

The distinction between intensional and extensional aboutness must be considered not only when considering the document as such, as opposed to the aggregate of sentences it contains, but also when considering a particular collection as such, as opposed to the separate documents that compose it, and a corpus of recorded discourse as opposed to the particular collections that form it. At each level, one depends upon the environment defined by the other, and content analysis must be conducted in this light. One method is to find how aboutness is altered by contradictions.

These considerations throw light on some of the vexed questions about abstracts, which are often used to indicate the aboutness of the original document, i.e., as document substitutes when indexing (e.g., Caras, 23; Hagerty, 73; and Bernier, 19). To this end, an abstract is usually either a set of extracts or a paraphrased abridgement, together with the original title. Only the title will, in general, indicate the author's views on the intensional aboutness. The intensional aboutness of the abstract is indicated by the policy of the abstract journal, and the abstractor will select those parts of the original that are compatible with this. Thus, an abstract is an unreliable index source unless author, abstract journal, abstractor, and the anticipated reader all have the same interests. If the abstract is a genuine linguistic "condensation" in the sense of being the original wording, coded to remove orthographical and linguistic redundancy (Deese, 51), it is equivalent to the original, provided that the process is reversible. But in general, the original cannot be recovered from an abstract.

Making Judgments of Aboutness

Indexers and others can and do make judgments of aboutness without knowing how they make them. Because making judgments is a social action, we have to study not only the algorithmic "how" they are made, but also the psychological "why." Cuadra (43) emphasizes that the latter concern lies at the root of all library activities. In particular, the "why" affects the consistency of judgments by indexers and searchers.

Two kinds of aboutness judgment are important in retrieval. The first is that discussed above, where an indexer must express in a given language his views on how a document will interest a given type of reader. The other is a judgment on whether or how much a document matches a request that, itself, may be viewed as a document, in the sense that it is about the topics requested. This interpretation of "relevance" is not to be confused with the relevance of one topic to another topic within a given field of discourse. Topics are not documents.

Judgments can be inconsistent for reasons other than incorrect assignment of aboutness. Because of its professional, practical, and commercial, as well as theoretic importance, indexer consistency has a large literature, which is reviewed by St. Laurent (140). Tinker (164) has experimented on imprecision of expression, imprecision of matching, and imprecision of meaning in identifying the aboutness of indexed abstracts. The last, he displays in graphs showing the deviation from unanimity of assignment or nonassignment of terms denoting broad interests well understood by the indexers. This imprecision is unaltered by relaxing or restricting the choice of indexing terms. From his studies of MEDLARS, Lancaster (100) also reports some wide variations in assigning certain indexing terms. This reviewer suggests that this indicates lack of guidance about assignment of broad categories that, being concerned with intensional aboutness, cannot be determined from the textual evidence alone.

The Case Western Reserve enquiry (26) devoted much time to indexing consistency and produced a number of detailed conclusions. Among them was the conclusion that inconsistencies were due to indexers rather than to indexing languages. Though technical terms, used as index tags, were assigned fairly consistently, variation in their assignment was still the major cause of indexing inconsistency.

In recent years, there has been more work on criteria for matching of two documents than on criteria for detecting and identifying the aboutness of one. (This is because indexers are most often concerned with the problem of assigning a new document to an existing collection with established categories.) Moreover, the major attention has been on criteria for matching the system response to the expressed request in the retrieval environment. Without such criteria, it is impossible to tell what the system is supposed to do, let alone telling whether it is doing well or poorly. Henderson (78) summarizes each of about 150 papers on retrieval testing published from 1953 through mid-1965 and gives a bibliography through 1967. King (96) reviews the literature for 1967. The first, in particular, reveals the rather baroque development from original unclear notions. The second brings this up to date, but shows also some prophylactic self-criticism within this field.

Most reports on retrieval systems and their performance now treat as fundamental the operational and theoretical criteria for saying that request and response are "about the same thing," and how consistently these criteria are applied. For example, Saracevic and his colleagues at Case Western Reserve (26, Chapter 8) state that they reject "relevance" as an inherent property of a document but take it as a relation between a document or its representation and a request, which is an expression for a "need" to be told something about something. To assess this, they used a consensus of experts. On the other hand, Lancaster (100) stalwartly asserts that, for evaluating an entire system, "a 'relevant' document is . . . a document of some value to the user in relation to the information need that prompted his request. . . . In other words, in a real operating situation, a 'relevance assessment' is a value judgment made on a retrieved document" (100, page 16). Here, Lancaster states clearly a widespread but usually unclear view and openly shows that "information need" is undefined. Three possible interpretations of an information need are made by O'Connor (122). First, the request as it would have been expressed if the requester were as adept in invoking the system as is the library staff or, stated otherwise, the request as arrived at by negotiation with the staff. O'Connor points out that this definition can be circular, because the system aims to reflect the "need." Second, a request for something that will help the requester's work. The question here is, "Help his work according to whom?" Anything can help anybody's work if the anybody knows how to use it. Third, what the requester is glad to get. The question here is, "Apart from being a poor way of expressing the first interpretation, does this interpretation give any guide as to whether the gladness will persist?" In this reviewer's opinion, neither the second nor the third interpretation provides targets attainable by any human institution.

Clearly, no kind of "content analysis" and system based upon it can provide, except by accident, a fulfillment of "need." Nor, for that matter, can librarians. The claim that they know other people's business better than other people do lacks humility. Worse, it is silly, especially as the tangle arises from poor terminology—a confusion of "need" with "want," or "information" with "what people have had to say." What people want or request is by no means the same as what they need, and what they need is scarcely within the power of librarians to pronounce, let alone to satisfy; they are not oracles.

Turning our backs on this mirage, we are faced with the difficult but attainable target of how to assess to what extent two documents are about the same things. The last four words still have many meanings, even after removal of those leading to absurdities. Many people, especially Cuadra, Katter, and Rees, have shown that the assessment of "sameness" depends upon many things other than those connected with the document and its retrieval environment. Though studies to separate, identify, and control these influences fall within the scope of retrieval testing and evaluation, rather than that of content analysis, the results are essential to any applications of content analysis that depend on stable judgments.

Fundamental to the matter of stability is consideration of what types of scale are appropriate to measure stability and show its influence upon matching retrieval systems (Katter, 92). In a general discussion of measurement scales, Stevens (154) tabulates them and their appropriate statistics, according to different kinds of invariance in the observed phenomena, i.e., according to the kinds of change that leave unaltered measured values of characteristics. The weakest is the nominal, identification, or labelling scale, measured in terms of the mode, and a measure of dispersion such as Shannon's uncertainty measure of "information." Clearly, both of these are unaltered by reversible translation of assigned labels into fresh labels. So also are unaltered judgments of aboutness, for the aboutness of a document is independent of the language in which it is expressed.

Stronger is the ordinal scale, measured by the median and percentile deviation. These are unaltered by any changes that leave the original rankings in the same order. Because it is easier to compare the relative aboutness of two documents than it is to detect and identify the aboutnesses of one, the stronger ordinal scale type may be justified for comparisons. The stronger the scale the better, so long as it means something; otherwise, the stronger the worse. Salton (143) gives his own evidence, and cites the evidence of others, for accepting the stability of individual judgments on the rank of aboutness matches, provided that we take the average of several individual judgments. He used the SMART collection of 1200 documents on library science and documentation. Even if stability of average ranking judgments be valid only for small specialist collections, it remains important and useful. Among other things, it would allow use of some kind of "standard test documents" for control of indexing quality.

Validity of an ordinal scale for comparisons of aboutness or "relevance" does not in any way imply the validity of interval or distance measures, and still less of ratio measures. On the other hand, invalidity of the ordinal scale would certainly invalidate interval and ratio scales.

STRUCTURING THE RESULTS OF CONTENT ANALYSIS

The Need for Structure

As indicated earlier, what a document is about depends upon what its reader will use it for as well as upon what the author says. Anybody can write anything about anything, and any reader in the future can use it for anything else. But the indexer is not a seer, or an oracle, or immortal, nor is the intended reader. This difficulty cannot be evaded merely by saying that a document is, for example, "about rabbits," because rabbit-centered discourse must deal with "rabbitness" in relation to other notions. The interest may be in rabbits as pets, pests, or for the pot; in the training of pet rabbits, the reproductive system of *oryctolagus cunniculus*, or in rabbits' feet as locomotory organs, or as amulets. In short, there is no isolated concept of "rabbitness," with the tag "Rabbit" slung round its neck. "Rabbitness" can be a part of many concepts, according to its topical neighborhood in the kind of discourse at issue.

The only solution is to decide in what kind or kinds of discourse a given concept is likely to be used, the topics of the likely kinds of discourse, how these topics are related to each other, and how they are usually expressed. The reader should have to know only the last but be able to rely on the others to guide him—or his delegates, the librarian or retrieval system—to any properly indexed document. Thus, the structure of the indexing or classification schema should, to some extent, reflect or, better, be coded to reflect, expected search techniques and reader use. Hence, it must first reflect the structure and expression of the discourse as they are and may reasonably be expected to be, not as they might be or should be. This does not prohibit comments and recommendations, but the purpose of a schema or classification is to serve as a guide to the retrieval of documents based upon knowledge of how, and in what contexts, the subject matter is usually talked about.

Construction of useful guides to the structure, expressions, and notations of recorded discourse demands massive intellectual, sociological, lexicographical, managerial, and financial effort, from individuals to international organizations. Historically, these classifications (I use the word in the European sense of taxonomies, not in the restricted sense of shelf arrangement of books) have commenced with individuals thinking out types of primitive topics and methods for the synthesis and organization, together with notations for display of the schema and for search. These notations may be applied by institutions or organizations to particular subject fields. The surviving systems of general applicability are published, extended, and mutated by use and adaptation. Those few that cross state, national, and linguistic frontiers are, after a fashion, maintained, revised, and stabilized by international organizations.

Means of Providing Structure

In the past two decades, classification (subject matter taxonomy) systems of a sort have evolved from the lexicographical, not the conceptual, level, though they are usually not called classifications. This psittacine exercise continues, for survival, as a confluence of thesaurus, dictionary, and alphabetical subject index, with the topical structure concealed in references and cross-references. The entries can be terms used in discourse, or the names of topics of discourse, and often no distinction is made between them. Thus many "word choosing" methods (such as that of Shaw & Rothman, 149) that claim to dispense with indexing and classification, just as did "Uniterms" in the early 1950s, depend entirely upon some classificatory structure and terminology common to the word choosers. Whether these judgments are put into their minds as a by-product of their professional education, or as habits acquired in using specialist libraries, is not important. What is important is that, ostensibly, "nonindexing" or "nonclassification" methods are essentially parasitic on indexing and classification, or they must embody these in arrangement, rules of use, and cross-referencing of the entries. Kochen & Tagliacozzo (97) discuss some graph-theoretical and linguistic aspects of cross-referencing structure.

Too many purely verbal approaches to retrieval spring from the union of otherwise decidedly immature notions about language and semantics. But text-processing methods in general must not be dismissed out of hand. If it is plausible to believe that *what* people talk about and ask for is to some extent reflected in *how* they talk about and ask for it, then one should study how and to what extent it is reflected. Knowledgeable attacks on aspects of this formidable subject are under way.

Although text processing as such lies outside the scope of this chapter, one should note that controversy about whether text-processing methods provide quality indexing or classification are beside the point. They are not substitutes for content analysis, but alternatives to be used instead, where they can be used. Certainly in very restricted and temporary semantic environments, it is good enough to request documents that contain certain words in certain parts of the format. It is not so certain that lexical statistics of request and response are usefully correlated, but it is worth finding out. Wheels are sometimes better than legs. A succession of different, if blunt, tools rapidly applied may sometimes be more effective than a very sharp one used only once. But tools must be different from each other. Iterated use of the same retrieval tool, sharp or blunt, will not lead to better response.

Text-processing methods are already indispensable as ancillary aids to the preparation of classificatory schema and their associated lexical displays. The development of such methods also brings to light problems coped with unconsciously by human agents.

Sparck Jones & Needham (151) describe the evolution of procedures for "clumping" index terms and for using the resulting term categorizations for retrieval. They frankly lay bare the difficulties and defects of existing methods. Jardine & Sibson (87) show also that most cluster or clump methods fail to satisfy the condition theoretically necessary for both hierarchical and nonhierarchical classification. Williams (171) makes clear that three distinct processes are involved in classification: defining the structure of categories, determining criteria for classification decisions, and classifying documents into categories. He discusses in detail various approaches to the last two processes that use the statistics of word occurrence in the document text. These are discussed in other papers also, such as that of Stone (155).

"Association" techniques, which hinge on co-occurrence of words in the text at different levels of inter-word distance, are discussed by Lesk (107), Tague (161), and Curtice et al. (44). The last paper deals more with computer techniques for inverting large, sparse matrices as power series than with the appropriateness of the techniques to retrieval.

Computer methods are suggested or described in action for structuring, revising, and testing indexing vocabularies and subject heading lists by, for instance, Ginsberg et al. (65), Way (168), and Gotlieb & Kumar (68). Construction of dictionaries of various types for linguistic analysis is described by Keen (94, 95), and of permuted (rotated) title and keyword indexes by Aagard (1) and Chonez (33).

Among special applications of computer-aided recognition, that of chemical data naturally has a very extensive literature. Representative of this are the papers of Gallagher (63) and Lynch (110). The latter reviews methods of storing chemical structures and points out the difficulties in retrieving substructures. Documentation of chemical reactions is even more difficult because there is no widely accepted nomenclature. Computer applications of the International Union of Pure and Applied Chemistry (IUPAC) linear notation are discussed thoroughly by Dammers & Polton (47). Artandi & Baxendale (8) report on the procedures of Project Medico, an experiment in automatic indexing of drug literature, which uses word statistics of the full texts.

Classification

Subject classification assumes that recorded discourse can be adequately described and prescribed for retrieval in terms of appropriately selected topics and their interrelations. Topics are conceptual aspects of discourse and therefore are independent of language, though to talk about them one must necessarily use language, and to retrieve with them, one must use a notation. The language will depend upon who uses the classification, the notation upon the facilities available for retrieval, and the topics and their structure upon the particular interests of the particular public who will be reading the documents. In a well-balanced scheme, all these will be harmonized, but they must not be confused with one another.

The number and nature of topics of discourse and their interrelations have changed much and rapidly in this century. Existing classificatory systems have been and are being modified in scope and depth and, more recently on the notational level, to exploit symbol-manipulative and reprographic techniques. Also, there is much work on principles of, and methods for increasing the flexibility and precision of, document classifications. Here the search is for principles required to construct or modify classifications as need arises, not for *a priori* classificatory edifices of permanent utility. The ghosts of Wilkins and Leibniz are not completely laid—the allure of unique factorization into a set of eternal semantic atoms is too strong for newcomers from the mathematically-based sciences—but their haunts have shifted to the more naive and less literate fringes of retrieval.

The general reader will find a clear and concise history of classification, from Plato and Aristotle to the present day, in an address by Foskett (61) to the Classification Society (United Kingdom). Mills (114), in another address on the same occasion, and for the general reader, described current and chronic problems of application involving classification concepts in information retrieval. Mayne (112), in an individual approach based on Shera's views on the general organization of knowledge, emphasizes the attack from the top down, rather than from the bottom up. The latter is the more favoured at present, largely because the upper structure is already established in accepted classification systems. As do many others, Mayne pursues the idea of a map, in some sense, of knowledge. How far this is more than a metaphor is questionable. In particular stable situations there may be a local and contemporary topology but, in general, topical neighborhoods are not preserved under changes of point of view. Thus, they cannot satisfy conditions necessary even for topological spaces. Most "maps" of subject matter are maps of educational curricula in a particular field, and their metric is of classrooms rather than of classes.

For those acquainted with the ideas and terminology, Ranganathan (134) admirably analyses the origins and aims of classification of subject matter.

Choice of a suitable classification is a complex matter (e.g., Ranganathan, 132, 133). Still more is the decision to change (e.g., Perreault, 38, 127). But though a good classification can be wrecked by poor realization, a poor conceptual foundation cannot be shored up by notational or mechanical ingenuity, nor even by hard work.

Selection of topics for document classification, whether as general categories, subtopics, or component topics, varies widely. The Library of Congress and the Sears schemes (Corrigan, 39) are the most enumerative. That is, they tend to the extreme of listing separately each and every thing that is talked about, however conceptually complex, provided that it has a name. This has the advantages and disadvantages of the telephone directory. If you know the correct name, and it is in the directory, everything is fine. Otherwise, this dictionary type of classification raises difficulties.

At the other extreme are those parts of most current classifications that permit composition of novel and more specific topics from other topics and various kinds of relations. The problem of displaying topics so synthesized is acute, unless one allows an enormous multiplicity of class entries.

When dealing with disciplined discourse within a narrow field, one finds that the choice of suitable topics and their aspects is usually fairly unambiguous. Most of the problems arise at the most specific and most general levels, involving the choice of entities and relations for synthesizing new combinations of interest as they arise in the literature. The classification of general collections that have to satisfy readers with different points of view presents great difficulties, which are not adequately resolved by developing a sheaf of special classifications, each of which is generally based on the common usage and practice for that subject.

To deal with this, the Classification Research Group (CRG) of London (35) is applying the notion of "integrative levels," familiar in other contexts. Generally speaking, this notion corresponds to the theory of types in logic, and to the distinction between sets and classes in mathematics; i.e., sets are classes that are members of other classes, but classes are not necessarily members of anything and, if they are, they are members of a higher type or level of aggregate. The CRG assumed that distinct levels are characteristic of distinct subject areas, and hoped that this would allow a uniquely definable place for every entity, which also could be incorporated at appropriate levels in different contexts. For instance, particular rocks placed as geological entities could be used also in the context of materials for buildings or sculptures.

The bulletin cited above (35) describes the work of the CRG and its difficulties in trying to construct a general classification. Universally applicable principles do not exist, so the CRG work clarifies many problems, and solves some at the price of raising others. For instance, the relations between properties, activities, and levels prove unhelpful in general application. Discussion of these and cognate matters are reported upon in the bulletin, which also prints extracts from the minutes of CRG meetings.

Neelameghan (120) and Gopinath (67), in two distinct papers published together, also discuss general and special classifications. The former states the problem of interaction between a topic and its environment of topics, and the effects of this on classificatory schema. The latter, in a report on Indian classification research, describes some high-definition classifications in special subjects within medicine and engineering, varying from rigidly faceted to freely faceted. [Facets, developed by Ranganathan in the 1930s, are the principal categories appropriate to a particular activity, whose combinations can synthesize the specialist subject matter sought. Independent re-inventions of facet principles were Mooers's "descriptors" and the "roles" of Perry and others, usually for synthesis by the searcher at time of search rather than pre-combined in the index to the classification. In other words, the term "facet" is used mainly for "pre-coordinated" classifications, and "descriptor" or "role" for "post-coordinated." Compared with facets, roles are very loosely thought out and carelessly applied (Lancaster, 102, though Lancaster is more charitable than is this reviewer)].

Summaries of principles and applications of faceted classification, the Universal Decimal Classification (UDC), and some word-based retrieval methods are presented in the proceedings, edited by Bakewell (12), of an intensive course on classification for retrieval held at the School of Librarianship, Liverpool, England, in September 1968.

All classificatory systems must use relations between their elements. All search methods based upon them attempt to reflect these relations in procedures, and conversely. To choose the relations most appropriate to a given purpose is difficult, both in practice and in theory. The balance of elements to relations is, to some extent, arbitrary. If the topic of, say, "green-lizards-licking-northwestern-table-legs-on-Fridays-if-it-rains" is of wide concern to sauro-sociologists, they will give it a name and treat it as a unit in normal discourse with their fellows. If the topic is not that much assimilated, or if not yet discussed, a system should provide some way of synthesizing it and other fresh notions as the need arises. Relations between existing notions will permit this synthesis.

Relations, the syntax of classifications, should be independent of the meanings of the elements they relate. In fact, few types of relation are universally applicable. They tend, naturally and properly, to reflect the relations inherent in the topic of discourse or, if originating from the searching end, of the search facilities available. There is always the danger of confusing the relations of the topic with the syntax of the natural language in which the classification and its rules are expressed. The crudest and most expensive manifestation of this is the endemic identification of word matching with coordination of concepts.

Such confusions lie in successful ambush even for the wary, because relational aspects of classification involve ideas, language, notation, and procedures as a whole. Moreover, they must be discussed and expressed in language. So even the International Symposium on Relational Factors in

Classification, edited by Perreault (85), sometimes resembles a get-together of normally disjunct Robinson Crusoes. The resemblance is but superficial; the problem is in fact a sheaf of problems, each demanding specialist-level competence in at least one field, ranging from linguistics to philosophy. The proceedings of this symposium provide a convenient collection of contemporary aspects and attitudes, from fundamental considerations to day-to-day applications. They also contain valuable summaries, such as the initial survey of Perreault (126), the summing up of de Grolier (50), and Soergel's (150) forty-four-page tabulation of comparative structural data of various systems, useful if only to be argued about—as indeed it was. The nonspecialist reader might do best to begin by reading the discussions alone. These make important points colloquially and vigorously. However, beyond a certain limit, one cannot present technical matters without technical language, even with great effort and good will. Topics such as linguistics and library science and technology are as much technical matters as are, say, computer programming and design. Because most people can read, and more talk, they sometimes forget this.

Representative contemporary attacks on relations for retrieval, rather than on linguistics or philosophical structure of knowledge in its widest sense, are those of Farradane, Perreault, and Gardin. The SYNTOL model, associated with Gardin, is described by Levy (108). Here the elements are organized within a hierarchical structure by four types of relations between pairs (i.e., binary or dyadic relations): coordinative, consecutive, associative, and attributive. Farradane (59) bases his relations on Guilford's (72) psychological factorization, on the plausible grounds that we must consider how people relate notions, not on mathematical, logical, or empirical relationships; these are valid only for mathematical, logical, or empirical objects, not for discourse. Therefore, he uses nine relations formed by combining three degrees of increasing association—awareness, temporary and fixed—with three degrees of increasing perception—concurrent, not distinct, and distinct. Thus, the weakest relation is mere concurrence, and the strongest is functional dependence. A concise account appears in the CRG Bulletin (35). Perreault (126, 128) also favours relational trichotomy: subsumptive, determinative, and ordinal. Trichotomies and compounds of trichotomies, resulting in 3 x 3 matrices and the like, are certainly precise enough for many purposes and certainly are computationally convenient. Also, because they correspond to basic differentiations such as positive, negative, zero, and backwards, forwards, stationary, they crop up in the first stages of refining anything. Whether there is any deeper magic to 3 x 3, as Santiago (144) seems to imply, is irrelevant here. Some authors fail to distinguish between three levels of binary relations, such as those just mentioned, and a single ternary relation between three elements. The latter cannot always be reduced to binary relations between pairs of its elements, as de Grolier (50) incautiously asserts. For instance, "between" is irreducible; three elements are essential.

As a part of his examination of the relations used in the Universal Decimal Classification (UDC), Perreault (128) tabulates those used by classificationists from Aristotle through Lull to contemporaries such as Braffort and Pagés. Wesseling (128) in the same reference, examines the principles used for this tabulation. In a later paper, Perreault (38) analyzes some examples of Library of Congress Classification (LC) and Decimal Classification (DC) code assignments and compares their structures with those of the corresponding UDC formations with respect to reclassification. For retrieval of discourse by subject matter, rather than for the pure taxonomy of "knowledge," past, present, and future, the crude but fundamental relations are co-occurrence and inclusion. From these, one can refine and compound syntagmatic and paradigmatic relations according to need or inclination. They are fundamental to retrieval because they correspond to both conceptual and procedural realizations, to wit, co-occurrence of attributes or joint membership of sets, more specific attribute, or set inclusion. Thus one can contrive descriptions in terms of topics to be at the same time addresses of or prescriptions for retrieving discourse about these topics. This demands, among other things, strict correspondence between set memberships and topics. It does not happen automatically simply by associating set memberships with assorted linguistic fragments of some of the ways in which the topics may be expressed, even within one ethnic language.

In the initial stages of retrieval of anything, one must use inclusion, implicitly or explicitly, to get hold of or into the most likely part of the most likely collection. Thus, even in "post-coordinated" systems, in which the reader synthesizes his requirement rather than finding it ready-made in the index or schema, hierarchical structure is used in the "shelf-arrangement" of optical-coincidence and other "coordinate indexing" cards (Perry, 129; Delany & Neville, 52). In other words, the accepted structure of discourse is used to arrive at a level of specificity where the subject matter has no accepted *structure* of discourse, and probably precious little *discourse*. Similarly, in the opposite direction, for novel combinations of hitherto disjunct major topics. At both these levels, co-occurrence of appropriate characteristics of the required topic can be entirely adequate at the start. Subsequently, refinements and elaborations are needed, and one is back in the so-called "traditional" classification theory and practice. Conceptually, these cannot be distinguished from "nonconventional" methods such as "coordinate indexing." The differences lie in procedures and points of view. The librarian classificationist has to consider all kinds of readers and work down to special interests; the "nonconventional" works upward from his immediate and contemporary interests to wider and more permanent ones. Whether one applies the conceptual principles at the time of individual search, or beforehand on behalf of a variety of individual searchers, the procedures vary but the principles are the same.

These two different approaches to the same problem have had twenty years in which to enrich each other. Unfortunately, after a promising start around 1950, they have been regarded as mutually incompatible, if not antagonistic. Thus, when more powerful procedures became possible, they tended to be identified with the classification and detection of topics, rather than with the exploitation of these conceptual matters in new ways. Things are improving, and the road is being cleared of sleepwalkers and hucksters. Certainly too much of what still goes on under the label of "coordinate indexing," as under the label of "information retrieval," is unnecessary random scratching and clawing at unnecessary expense. Some random scratching and clawing is essential, but it is often best done at the readers' end.

A fair sample of the full range of activities coming under these vague labels is given by Dammers (46) in his report on the Aslib Coordinate Indexing Group.

Presentation and Control

The preceding sections considered approaches to topical structures and categories starting from the conceptual end, independent of the languages and facilities in which and with which they will be expressed and exploited in use. Another approach is from the language of discourse to the topics discussed. This is usual when preparing glossaries for specialists using a single language. Words and phrases in current use are collected, grouped into broad subject categories, and then defined in relation to the category into which they fall, with the general topic as background. The hierarchical structure is usually less complex than in topic-based classifications.

The approaches are different but the principles are the same. Therefore, the products should differ only inasmuch as they are devised for different ranges of readers and are to last for different ranges of time between revisions.

They differ also in distribution of effort. The total effort demanded to produce any topical classification is huge, but the verbal approach demands, at the beginning, an extensive lexicographical campaign. The principles and organization of that campaign can either smother or be mistaken for the principles of topical classification.

Barhydt & Schmidt (14), in their thesaurus of educational terms and concepts, emphasize the necessity of underlying principles and use those of hierarchical and faceted classification. The Federal Council for Science and Technology Committee on Scientific and Technical Information (COSATI) (60) gives some general advice. Angell (5), in two papers on thesaurus construction, compares and discusses, first, the relations used by ten thesauri and subject authority lists to differentiate acceptable from unacceptable terms; and second, their specific-to-general *see* references. Heald (77), describing the making of TEST, the Engineers' Joint Council's Thesaurus of Engineering and Scientific Terms (123), shows in detail the many administrative, clerical, lexical, and conceptual problems that must arise and must be solved. TEST was based on 145 vocabularies drawn from 330 specialist word lists of one kind or another, yielding 145,000 terms, apart from syntactical words to be considered by panels of specialists. Their decisions had to be compared, harmonized, edited, and then presented to display structure and category, with auxiliary aids. These were a subject category list, a permuted index of compound terms, and a hierarchical index of families of terms.

Other recent thesauri and subject-arranged vocabularies include the multi-coordinate vocabularies of the American Institute of Physics, derived from the terminology of primary journals, to cover chemical physics, plasma physics, and lasers and masers. The vocabularies were compiled, respectively, by Lerner (104), Chu (34), and Pariser (124). Their construction is described by Lerner (104, 105, 106). Tancredi & Nichols (162) arranged 1,300 terms alphabetically within categories, and more specific terms alphabetically under their generic terms, for use with an optical coincidence system covering the effects of atmospheric pollution. The Association for Computing Machinery (27) uses a classified subject heading list for computing science and applications for articles in their publications. They also use uncontrolled words and phrases assigned by the author and optimistically called "keywords." Gordon (69) and Jacobs (86) discuss the retrieval of medical and biomedical literature through natural language; that is, through the particular language natural to medicine.

The strengths of the lexical approach are the weaknesses of the conceptual approach. Given the necessary finances and effort, subject headings can be far more up-to-date in specialist fields, and can be changed more easily when needed, which is often too often. They are journalistic, so they cannot avoid reflecting verbal fashions rather than the ideas blurred or masked by vogue words. They are also parochial, being tied to one natural language. Even in specialist fields, subject headings in one language do not always correspond directly with subject headings in another, nor do even the simpler hierarchical and collateral relations. Coates (36) met typical difficulties when collaborating on the Intermediate Lexicon Project (CRG, 35) for interconversion between French and English lists of terms, alphabetical and classified, used to index documentation and library science literature. There are thirty known indexing systems for this field. In 1965, J. C. Gardin and F. Levy of the Groupe d'Etude sur l'Information Scientifique proposed and initiated an intermediate lexicon as a first step towards interconversion. The difficulties of the subject itself were reinforced by differing but implicit points of view, due, in Coates's words, "to a diet of professional reading exclusively in one's native tongue." The French-English dictionary of the twenty-five main groups, with definitions, is expected in 1969.

Whether the approach be conceptual or lexical, the complete final presentation must have a display of the topical structure, i.e., the verbal expressions and notations arranged according to subject matter. It must also have the inverse, or dictionary, in which subject matter expressions or notations are arranged by convention, usually alphabetical. The notation reflects the topical structure and the label, or address, or search prescription for the subject matter. Because topics will be referred to in more ways than can be predicted, let alone listed, there must also be scope notes to constrain requests to the language of the system.

This constraint is not the hardship or tyranny that some people make it out to be. All social situations demand and receive the sublanguages appropriate to them because it is convenient to conform. Similarly, the constraints on retrieval languages are reasonable if their relaxation would involve readers in even greater inconvenience. These constraints must be made explicit somewhere. Mulvihill (118) points out that many current "thesauri" (the word by now is battered almost senseless) omit constraints on individual use of language and rely entirely and vainly upon term interrelations to do the job instead. He recalls Mooers's insistence that the terms for his "descriptors"—which were concepts, not words—must be defined before addition to the system. Mulvihill prefers notes on usage to definitions and gives reasoned examples. His arguments would be clearer if words were distinguished more sharply from concepts, but the paper is useful in giving a much-needed warning.

Another muddle is caused by using one of the terms in a group as the name of that group, a practice exemplified by the remark about the naming of a male infant: "These days, every Tom, Dick, and Harry is called John." In a short note, Davis (49) recommends that retrieval vocabularies should use classification numbers—LC, DC, or UDC—for the referents of the entries. The only surprising thing about this suggestion is that many retrieval experts will find it surprising.

All of the elements comprising a classification need not be displayed separately and explicitly. Some may be implicit, others abbreviated, and still others combined to do double duty. What simplifications are suitable depends upon whether the classification is to be translated into other languages, used with other search techniques, or used for other particular purposes. Structure and notation are affected least by translation and most by the search methods. Thus, a subject classification for monoglot users who will select what they want by recognizing the label, or the label of the shelf where the requested item may lie, can be represented just as a dictionary, provided that there is not too much structure—that is, provided that most subjects have a direct entry. An obvious example is a catalogue using Library of Congress subject headings. Dewey (53) discusses these in relation to reclassification. Alphabetical indexing is discussed by Bernier (18) in all its aspects, with an extensive bibliography.

Statistical and linguistic methods for transforming natural language phrases into substantival phrases are not proper parts of this chapter, but their purpose is. Therefore they should not be ignored, but sought elsewhere in this volume (see Chapter 5). A careful attack on part of the problem is made by Armitage & Lynch (6). They refer to Crestadoro's treatise, published in 1856, on the art of indexing library catalogs. Developing a blend of algorithm with human linguistic judgments, they produce index entries from natural language indexing phrases, and a sorting procedure to select entries that lead to better organization of the index display.

Statistical methods for selecting technical words for vocabularies or indexes continue to be studied. A brief, clear account of one method is given by Stone & Rubinoff (156). Their hypothesis, a variation on a long-established one, is that speciality words will cluster in a few documents, while nonspeciality words will be more uniformly distributed over the whole collection. Examining 70,000 word occurrences in 217 reviews of papers on computer programming, they found speciality words to be discriminated best by the variance to total frequency ratio. This may be due to a roughly Poisson distribution of nonspeciality words within documents. They refer to other workers with a similar approach.

From the point of view of content analysis, this is interesting as indicating the way in which statistical and algorithmic methods can approximate linguistic experience in narrow situations. Linguistic experience does not, of course, necessarily imply high intelligence or understanding; it implies only experience. All such methods to select "keywords" from text or title are attempts to simulate the method given by Mooers many years ago: take someone of average schooling and get him to underline words he does not understand.

Compatibility, Cooperation, Standards, and Special Classifications

Comparison between classifications is more important than competition. Increasing contact and cooperation between libraries, which are growing in number and size, raise problems of compatibility and reclassification. Angell (4) studies the hierarchical and collateral relations between index terms as exhibited in five U.S.A. vocabularies. He concludes that these could have been merged only if they had used common principles for relating terms.

The University of Maryland held a conference in April 1968 on the rationale and problems of reclassification. The proceedings, edited by Perreault (38), touched on the planning, finance, work flow, and mechanization of reclassification, as well as on the characteristics of the Library of Congress (LC), Decimal (DC), and Universal Decimal (UDC) Classifications, and the Library of Congress subject headings. Mølgaard-Hansen (116) describes a small experiment comparing LC, DC, and UDC, in the new Danish University Library at Odense, on 225 books dealing with history of religion, archaeology, and philology. On the whole, even in this nonscientific sample, UDC was preferred. It was felt that the others were handicapped by being designed originally for shelf arrangement rather than for retrieval.

Compatibility of mechanization with classification systems is important also. Though mechanization should conform to the classification, it is unreasonable to devise classifications that demand storage and retrieval facilities that do not yet exist. Fortunately, hierarchical classification, whether scattered saplings or senior sequoias, can be enhanced by mechanical aids, provided that certain essentials are dealt with. Most important, as Schneider (146, 147) emphasizes, is thorough conceptual analysis and organization before input to the mechanized part of the system. He uses a FORTRAN program on an IBM 360/50 to carry out selective dissemination of information (SDI) on biomedical aspects of cancer research, whose literature had been analyzed and organized hierarchically.

Mechanized retrieval of documents classified according to the UDC is widespread. The American Institute of Physics is carrying out an extensive programme, with the literature of metallurgy and nuclear science, in conjunction with the Classification Research Committee of the International Federation for Documentation (FID/CR), and aided by a grant from the National Science Foundation. Freeman (3) assesses the retrieval of metallurgical references; Atherton et al. (9) and Freeman & Atherton (62) describe and assess interactive retrieval of references to nuclear science, through a system called AUDACIOUS. Schneider (148) summarizes recent work in West Germany. In September 1968, FID/CR held an International Seminar on the UDC in Mechanized Retrieval Systems.

These are a few of the current attempts to mechanize the retrieval of literature indexed according to established and developing classifications. The effort is not, of course, confined to UDC, though this, in conjunction with complementary methods such as faceted classification, is the more common because it is the more widespread. Editions, either complete or abridged, and covering many subjects, are available in many languages. These are published under the control of the FID Central Classification Committee (FID/CCC) at The Hague, on which seventeen countries are represented. Complete English-language editions of all sections of UDC should be available by the end of 1969 from the British Standards Institution, London.

The FID/CR is concerned with all classifications and problems, such as the standardization of classification terms in which to talk about classification. It also cooperates with the Bibliographic Systems Center in Cleveland, Ohio, in operating an international collection of classification systems and thesauri. Nor is the FID wholly concerned with classification. It has committees concerned with various documentation matters that range from fundamental theory and linguistics in documentation, through machine techniques and information for industry, to training of documentalists and the needs of developing countries. Sviridov (160) describes these and other international projects, including cooperation with UNESCO and the international standardizing bodies.

Documentation standards deal mainly with physical aspects, formats, and procedures, from paper sizes to transliterations. Of direct bearing on the matters of this chapter are standard terminology and glossaries and, even more important, standards for terminology and glossaries. The International Standards Organization (ISO) has a technical committee, TC 37, on the principles and coordination of terminology. Also, there are draft ISO recommendations on Naming Principles DR 676; Vocabulary of Terminology, DR 781; and the International Unification of Concepts and Terms, DR 1187. Hudson (83) surveys the current activities in international standardization of documentation.

Too many special classifications have appeared in 1968 to be listed here in full, even if the list were confined only to those in English. Among those not already mentioned, and not concerned with science, technology, or medicine, is that by Croghan (42), who has prepared a faceted classification of the performing arts and discussed its literature. He omits music, already covered in other classifications, and the circus. The structure is of entity terms subdivided according to activity terms. Moys (117) has designed a classification scheme for law books that will fit into the Library of Congress, Class K, and has also an alternative arrangement to fit Decimal Classification, Class 340. The price of these conveniences is an uneasy compromise between classification principles and the LC notation. Mitchell (115) summarizes the current NATO and British Ministry of Technology classifications and coding of commodities.

CONCLUSIONS

In many ways, the state of content analysis is good and the outlook bright. There has been much more work worthy of mention than could be mentioned here and, presumably, much more that the reviewer did not come across, or could not have assimilated if he had. The work has been on many levels—conceptual, procedural, linguistic, lexical, and symbol-manipulative. International cooperation is now much more extensive than what was once achieved by the backbreaking efforts of a few enthusiasts alone, though, as always, backbreaking efforts of a few enthusiasts are still necessary. But they are not sufficient without some backing by paid secretariats and funds. These have been forthcoming and the effort, thought, and some public money has been expended to good purpose.

Whatever the effort, thought, and public money expended to good purpose, even more effort and money, but not thought, has been expended to no purpose at all. Much work was not mentioned here because there was no room to mention it. More was not mentioned because it was unmentionable, exhibiting an invincible ignorance about the difference between manipulating labeled objects, and the design and assignment of the labels for various social ends. Huge sums are expended in the belief, not that the problem of indexing (content analysis) is solved, but that it does not exist. The symbol is believed to be the sense, so that all you need for information retrieval is to play unprincipled word games on a computer. This belief is widespread in management circles, because they have been told by computer experts that it is true. Though the latter may believe that the principles of computer science are the principles of library science, it is distressing, and potentially disastrous, that others should be infected by them. It should be clear to management that the principles of computer science are not the principles of managerial science any more than they are of medical science, or indeed, of anything but computer science. However, it is obviously not clear, and clarity will come only through expensive failure, as has happened before.

Unhappily, the good work in this field, considerable in quantity and quality, is sharply confined to those actively concerned with library science and librarianship, together with some very welcome resident aliens from linguistics and logic. Also there is a minority—small comparatively, yet growing in number—who understand that the objects of attention and the principles of library science (documentation) are not those of computer science and technology. But this view does not seem to inform, in any sense, the official and usual attitude of the computing profession and industry toward what they think is information retrieval. So long as words like "information," "translation," "language," "thesaurus," "key word," and "descriptor" are used in public with private meanings, the public will be misled. So long as articles in computer journals discuss retrieval systems without any reference to concept analysis or indexing, and set questions in qualifying examinations that cannot be answered adequately outside a library school, the computing profession will be misled.

Also the Information Sciences will be, indeed are, confused and distorted. The librarian or documentalist and the computer scientist and technologist have much to teach to and learn from each other. The principles of librarianship are essential to the management of the discourse of the computer sciences. The principles of computer science are essential to the carrying out of symbol manipulation and organization demanded by librarians and linguists. Similar considerations apply to the needs of the customers of librarians and computer folk. Without such professional cooperation, there will continue to be expensive bungling and unnecessary amateurism.

REFERENCES

(1) AAGARD, JAMES S.   BIDAP: a bibliographic data processing program for keyword indexing. American Behavioral Scientist, 10:2   (February 1967) 24–27.
(2) ACKERMANN, H. J.; HAGLIND, J. B.; LINDWALL, H. G.; MAIZELL, R. E. SWIFT: Computerized storage and retrieval of technical information. Journal of Chemical Documentation, 8:1   (February 1968) 14–19.
(3) AMERICAN INSTITUTE OF PHYSICS.   UDC PROJECT. Evaluation of the retrieval of metallurgical document references using the Universal Decimal Classification in a computerband system. New York, 1968. (AIP-UDC 6)
(4) ANGELL, RICHARD S.   Compatibility in subject access vocabularies: the role of relations between index terms. Library of Congress, Washington, D.C., 1968. (Preprint, 22 p.) Prepared for presentation at the International Congress on Scientific Information, Moscow, September 1968. To be published in a volume of the Congress papers, by VINITI.
(5) ANGELL, RICHARD S.   Two papers on thesaurus construction. 1: The language of term relation designations in subject access vocabularies. 2: The specific-to-general "see" reference in thesaurus construction. Originally presented at the 33rd International Conference of FID and International Congress on Documentation in Tokyo, September 1967. (Preprint, 30 August 1967, revised January 1968, 27 p.) Published in the FID/CR report series no. 8.
(6) ARMITAGE, JANET E.; LYNCH, MICHAEL F.   Some structural characteristics of articulated subject indexes. Information Storage and Retrieval, 4:2   (June 1968) 101–111. Presented at the First Cranfield International Conference on Mechanized Information Storage and Retrieval Systems, College of Aeronautics, Cranfield, England, 29–31 August 1967.
(7) ARTANDI, SUSAN.   An introduction to computers in information science. Scarecrow, Metuchen, N.J., 1968, 145 p.
(8) ARTANDI, SUSAN; BAXENDALE, STANLEY.   Project MEDICO (Model Experiment in Drug Indexing by Computer) First progress report. Graduate School of Library Service, Rutgers, The State University, New Brunswick, N.J., January 1968, 108 p. (LM-94 grant)
(9) ATHERTON, PAULINE; KING, DONALD W.; FREEMAN, ROBERT R. Evaluation of the retrieval of nuclear science document references using the Universal Decimal Classification as the indexing language for a computer-based system. American Institute of Physics UDC Project, New York, 1 May 1968, 33 p.+ appendices.

(Report no. AIP/UDC-8) (NSF Grant GN-433)
(10) ATLIS WORKSHOP, 1st, Redstone Arsenal, Ala., 15–17 November 1966. Automation in libraries. Redstone Scientific Information Center, Redstone Arsenal, Ala., June 1967, 185 p. (Army technical library improvement studies, ATLIS-13) (Report no. RSIC-625) (AD-654 766)
(11) BAILLE, A.; ROUAULT, J. Un essai de formalisation de la sémantique des langues naturelles. [A study of the formalization of natural language semantics] T. A. Informations, no. 1 (1967) 1–7.
(12) BAKEWELL, K. G. B., ed. Classification for information retrieval. Papers presented at an intensive course held in September 1967 at the School of Librarianship, Liverpool College of Commerce. Archon, Hamden, Conn.; Bingley, London, 1968, 100 p.
(13) BAR-HILLEL, YEHOSHUA. Dictionaries and meaning rules. Foundations of Language, 3:4 (November 1967) 409–414.
(14) BARHYDT, G. C.; SCHMIDT, C. T. Information retrieval thesaurus of education terms. Case Western Reserve Press, Cleveland, Ohio, 1968.
(15) BATTEN, W. E. Ghillying for science—rod or net? [discriminating power or gathering power?] ASLIB Proceedings, 20:3 (March 1968) 157–161.
(16) BATTEN, W. E. The duality of the chemist's language. ASLIB Proceedings, 20:5 (May 1968) 246–253; discussion, 253.
(17) BELL, COLIN J. Implicit information retrieval. Information Storage and Retrieval, 4:2 (June 1968) 139–160. Presented at the First Cranfield International Conference on Mechanized Information Storage and Retrieval Systems, College of Aeronautics, Cranfield, England, 29–31 August 1967.
(18) BERNIER, CHARLES L. Alphabetic indexes. In: Encyclopedia of Library and Information Science, vol. 1. Dekker, New York, 1968, p. 169–201.
(19) BERNIER, CHARLES L. Abstracts and abstracting. In: Encyclopedia of Library and Information Science, vol. 1. Dekker, New York, 1968, p. 16–38.
(20) BERNIER, CHARLES L. Indexing and thesauri. Special Libraries, 59:2 (February 1968) 98–103.
(21) BOHNERT, LEA M. Retrieval of technical documents. Final technical report, no. CEIR-70-0219-27. (AFOSR-68-0244) (AD-664 596)
(22) BREGZIS, RITVARS. Query language for the reactive catalogue. In: National Colloquium on Information Retrieval, 4th, 3–4 May 1967, Philadelphia. Proceedings, edited by Albert B. Tonik. International Information Incorporated, Philadelphia, 1967, p. 77–90, discussion, p. 90–91.
(23) CARAS, GUS J. Indexing from abstracts of documents. Journal of Chemical Documentation, 8:1 (February 1968) 20–22.
(24) CARROLL, JOHN B. Words, meanings, and concepts. Part I: Their nature. In: De Cecco, John P., ed. The psychology of language, thought and instruction. Readings. Holt, Rinehart and Winston, New York, 1967, p. 219–228.
(25) CARROLL, JOHN B. Words, meanings, and concepts. Part II: Concept teaching and learning. In: De Cecco, John P., ed. The psychology of language, thought and instruction. Readings. Holt, Rinehart and Winston, New York 1967, p. 385–394.
(26) CASE WESTERN RESERVE UNIVERSITY. CENTER FOR DOCUMENTATION AND COMMUNICATION RESEARCH. An inquiry into testing of information retrieval systems. Part I: Objectives, methodology, design, and controls. Tefko Saracevic, Manager. A. J. Goldwyn, Principal Investigator. (Comparative Systems Laboratory final technical report CSL: TR-FINAL-1) Cleveland, Ohio, 1968, 256 p.
(27) Categories of the computing sciences. Classification system for Computing Reviews. Communications of the ACM, 11:2 (February 1968) 133.
(28) CECCATO, SILVIO. Concepts for a new systematics. Information Storage and Retrieval, 3:4 (December 1967) 193–214; Critique, by Ritvars Bregzis, p. 215–216; Critique, by Donald E. Walker, p. 216–217; Discussion, p. 217–218. Presented at International Symposium on Relational Factors in Classification, University of Maryland, College Park, 8–11 June 1966.
(29) CHARNEY, ELINOR. Structural semantics: theory of sentential meaning. In: Con-

ference on Computer-related Semantic Analysis, Las Vegas, Nev., 3–5 December 1965. Proceedings. Wayne State University, Detroit, June 1966, p. III/1–25. (AD-655 073)
(30) CHERNYI, A. I.   A criterion for the semantic conformity of a document retrieval system. Translated from: Nauchno-Tekhnicheskaya Informatsiya, series 2, no. 9 (1967) 17–25.
(31) CHERNYI, A. I.   Obshchaya metodika postroeniya tezaurusov. [General methods of IR thesaurus compilation] Nauchno-Tekhnicheskaya Informatsiya, series 2, no. 5 (1968) 9–32.
(32) CHERNYI, A. I.   Sintagmaticheskie otnosheniya mezhdu deskriptorami. [Syntagmatic relations between descriptors] Nauchno-Tekhnicheskaya Informatsiya, series 2, no. 4 (1968) 6–16.
(33) CHONEZ, NICOLE.   Permuted title or key-phrase indexes and the limiting of documentalist work needs. Information Storage and Retrieval, 4:2   (June 1968) 161–166. Presented at the First Cranfield International Conference on Mechanized Information Storage and Retrieval Systems, College of Aeronautics, Cranfield, England, 29–31 August 1967.
(34) CHU, C. K.   Multi-coordinate vocabulary: plasma physics. In: Lerner, Rita G. Development of multi-coordinate vocabulary: plasma physics. Information Division, American Institute of Physics, New York, March 1968, Appendix A (4 p.)
(35) CLASSIFICATION RESEARCH GROUP.   Classification Research Group Bulletin no. 9. Journal of Documentation, 24:4   (December 1968) 273–298.
(36) COATES, E. J.   Library science and documentation literature: a new development in international cooperation. Library Association Record, 70 (July 1968) 178–179.
(37) COLBY, KENNETH MARK; ENEA, HORACE.   Machine utilization of the natural language word "good." Stanford University, Computer Science Department, Stanford, Calif., 25 September 1967, 6 p. (Technical report no. CS 78) (PB-176 771)
(38) CONFERENCE ON RECLASSIFICATION, University of Maryland, College Park, 4–6 April 1968. Proceedings: Reclassification; rationale and problems. Edited by Jean M. Perreault. University of Maryland, School of Library and Information Services, College Park, 1968, 191 p.
(39) CORRIGAN, PHILIP.   An introduction to "Sears list of subject headings." Archon Books, Hamden, Conn.; Clive Bingley, London, 1968, 94 p.
(40) COYAUD, M.; DECAUVILLE, N. SIOT.   L'analyse automatique des documents. [Automatic analysis of documents] Mouton, Paris/La Haye, 1967, 148 p. (Informatique 1)
(41) CRANFIELD INTERNATIONAL CONFERENCE ON MECHANIZED INFORMATION STORAGE AND RETRIEVAL SYSTEMS,   1st, College of Aeronautics, Cranfield, England, 29–31 August 1967. Proceedings. Edited by C. W. Cleverdon. Information Storage and Retrieval, 4:2   (June 1968) 85–256.
(42) CROGHAN, A.   A faceted classification for and an essay on the literature of the performing arts. London, 1968, 120 p.
(43) CUADRA, CARLOS A.   The implications of relevance research for library operations and training. (Abstracts of [59th SLA] Conference papers; abstract 5) Special Libraries, 59:3   (March 1968) 177–178.
(44) CURTICE, R. M.; GIULIANO, V. E.; JONES, P. E.; SHERRY, M. E.   Application of statistical association techniques for the NASA document collection. Arthur D. Little, Inc., Cambridge, Mass., February 1968, 111 p. (NASA-CR-1020) (N68-17154)
(45) DALE, ALFRED G.   Indexing and classification for interactive retrieval systems. Information Storage and Retrieval, 3:4   (December 1967) 377–380. Critique, by T. M. Williams, p. 380–381; Critique, by F. W. Lancaster, p. 381–383; discussion, p. 383. Presented at International Symposium on Relational Factors in Classification, University of Maryland, College Park, 8–11 June 1966.
(46) DAMMERS, H. F.   ASLIB CIG [Coordinate Indexing Group] Research Project: Progress report I. ASLIB Proceedings. 20:4   (April 1968) 218–232.
(47) DAMMERS, H. F.; POLTON, D. J.   Use of the IUPAC [International Union of

Pure and Applied Chemistry] notation in computer processing of information on chemical structures. Journal of Chemical Documentation, 8:3 (August 1968) 150–160. Presented at Division of Chemical Literature, 155th Meeting, ACS, San Francisco, 4 April 1968.

(48) DATTOLA, R. T.; MURRAY, D. M. An experiment in automatic thesaurus construction. In: Cornell University. Department of Computer Science. Information storage and retrieval. Scientific report no. ISR-13 to the National Science Foundation. Reports on evaluation procedures and results 1965–1967. Gerard Salton, Project Director. Ithaca, N.Y., December 1967, Sec. 8 (26 p.).

(49) DAVIS, CHARLES H. Integrating vocabularies with a classification scheme. [Brief communication] American Documentation, 19:1 (January 1968) 101.

(50) DE GROLIER, ERIC. Synoptic critique. Information Storage and Retrieval, 3:4 (December 1967) 385–396; discussion, 396–397. Presented at International Symposium on Relational Factors in Classification, University of Maryland, College Park, 8–11 June 1966.

(51) DEESE, JAMES. Content analysis: paraphrase or coding. Presented at National Conference on Content Analysis, Annenberg School of Communications, University of Pennsylvania, Philadelphia, 16–18 November 1967.

(52) DELANY, D. P.; NEVILLE, H. H. "Grouped" coordinate index. [Letter] Journal of Documentation, 23:2 (June 1967) 153–154.

(53) DEWEY, H. The relationship between the headings in the subject catalog and the classification numbers of the books. In: Conference on Reclassification, University of Maryland, College Park, 4–6 April 1968. Proceedings: Reclassification; rationale and problems. Edited by Jean M. Perreault. University of Maryland, School of Library and Information Services, College Park, 1968, p. 57–74.

(54) DITTRICH, WOLFGANG. Einige Gedanken und Vorschläge zur Wissensordnung und Wissensvermittlung. [Some thoughts and suggestions on the classification and conveyance of knowledge] Nachrichten für Dokumentation, 19:3 (April/May 1968) 62–66.

(55) EARL, L. L.; BHIMANI, B. L.; MITCHELL, R. P. Statistics of operationally defined homonyms of elementary words. MT (Mechanical Translation and Computational Linguistics), 10:1 & 2 (March & June 1967) 18–25.

(56) FAIRTHORNE, ROBERT A. Functional analysis of information retrieval. Final report. School of Library Science, State University of New York, August 1968.

(57) FAIRTHORNE, ROBERT A. The limits of information retrieval. [Critique, by J. Z. Nitecki] Journal of Library History, Philosophy and Comparative Librarianship, 3 (October 1968) 363–374.

(58) FAIRTHORNE, ROBERT A. The scope and aims of the information sciences and technologies. (Preprint). Prepared for presentation at the International Congress on Scientific Information, Moscow, September 1968. To be published in a volume of the Congress papers, by VINITI.

(59) FARRADANE, J. Concept organization for information retrieval. Information Storage and Retrieval, 3:4 (December 1967) 297–311. Critique, by Pauline Atherton, p. 312; Critique, by Harold Borko, p. 312–313; discussion, p. 313–314. Presented at International Symposium on Relational Factors in Classification, University of Maryland, College Park, 8–11 June 1966.

(60) FEDERAL COUNCIL FOR SCIENCE AND TECHNOLOGY. COMMITTEE ON SCIENTIFIC AND TECHNICAL INFORMATION. Guidelines for the development of information retrieval thesauri. 1st ed. Washington, D.C., 1 September 1967, 8 p.

(61) FOSKETT, D. J. Some historical aspects of the classification of knowledge. Classification Society Bulletin, 1:4 (1968) 2–11.

(62) FREEMAN, ROBERT R.; ATHERTON, PAULINE. AUDACIOUS—an experiment with an on-line, interactive reference retrieval system using the Universal Decimal Classification as the index language in the field of nuclear science. American Institute of Physics, UDC Project, New York, 25 April 1968, 59 p. (AIP/UDC-7)

(PB-178 374). Shorter version published in: American Society for Information Science Annual Meeting, Columbus, Ohio, 20–24 October 1968. Proceedings, vol. 5. Greenwood Publishing Corp., New York, 1968, p. 193–199.
(63) GALLAGHER, P. J. Storage and retrieval of chemical structure data. ASLIB Proceedings, 20:2 (February 1968) 107–117; discussion, p. 117.
(64) GARVIN, P. L.; BREWER, JOCELYN; MATHIOT, MADELEINE. Predication-typing: a pilot study in semantic analysis. Language, 43:2, part 2 (June 1967) supplement, 116 p.
(65) GINSBERG, HELEN F.; SCHMITZ, RICHARD F.; HOLMAN, K.; HALL, MICHAEL D. Computer aids in the evaluation of indexing terminology. Journal of Chemical Documentation, 7:4 (November 1967) 237–239. Abstract in: American Chemical Society. Abstracts of papers, 154th Meeting, Chicago, Sept. 10–15, 1967. Washington, D.C., 1967. (Sec. G-Division of Chemical Literature, paper 10)
(66) GOLDHAMMER, DONALD. Toward a more general inquirer: convergence of structure and context on meaning. Presented at National Conference on Content Analysis, Annenberg School of Communications, University of Pennsylvania, Philadelphia, 16–18 November 1967.
(67) GOPINATH, M. A. Classification research; trend report (India). Danish Centre for Documentation, Copenhagen, 1967. (FID Publication No. 405)
(68) GOTLIEB, C. C.; KUMAR, S. Semantic clustering of index terms. Journal of the Association for Computing Machinery, 15:4 (October 1968) 493–513.
(69) GORDON, B. L. Biomedical language and format for manual and computer applications. Methods of Information in Medicine [Methodik der Information in der Medizin], 7:1 (January 1968) 5–7.
(70) GRAZIANO, EUGENE E. On a theory of documentation. American Documentation, 19:1 (January 1968) 85–89.
(71) GRUNWALD, WILHELM. Klassifikationstheorie [Classification theory] Zeitschrift für Bibliothekswesen und Bibliographie, 15:1 (1968) 17–34.
(72) GUILFORD, J. P. The nature of human intelligence. McGraw-Hill, New York, 1967.
(73) HAGERTY, KATHERINE. Abstracts as a basis for relevance judgment. M.A. thesis. University of Chicago, Graduate Library School, February 1967, 36 p. (Report on a project—Studies in Indexing Depth and Retrieval Effectiveness) (Working paper 380-5) (PB-174 394)
(74) HARBECK, RUDOLF; LUTTERBECK, ERNST. Inhaltsangaben in der Dokumentation. [Contents indication in documentation] Nachrichten für Dokumentation, 19:1-2 (February/March 1968) 15–18.
(75) HAYES INTERNATIONAL CORPORATION. Automated literature processing handling and analysis system—first generation. Huntsville, Alabama, 23 June 1967, 491 p. (Army technical library improvement studies, no. 17) (RSIC-549) (AD-658 081)
(76) HAYS, DAVID G. Linguistic foundations for a theory of content analysis. Presented at National Conference on Content Analysis, Annenberg School of Communications, University of Pennsylvania, Philadelphia, 16–18 November 1967.
(77) HEALD, J. HESTON. The making of TEST: thesaurus of engineering and scientific terms. Final report, October 1965–November 1967. Office of Naval Research, Project LEX, Washington, D.C., 1967, 162 p. (ONR-26) (AD-661 001)
(78) HENDERSON, MADELINE M. Evaluation of information systems: a selected bibliography with informative abstracts. Technical Information Exchange, Center for Computer Sciences and Technology, National Bureau of Standards, Washington, D.C., December 1967, 209 p. (NBS Technical note 297)
(79) HERNER, SAUL. Study of documentation procedures and mechanisms. Final technical report. Herner and Co., Washington, D.C., 9 August 1967, 10 p. (AFOSR-67-2248) (AD-659 625)
(80) HILLMAN, DONALD J. Negotiation of inquiries in an on-line retrieval system. Information Storage and Retrieval, 4:2 (June 1968) 219–238. Presented at the First Cranfield International Conference on Mechanized Information Storage and Retrieval

Systems, College of Aeronautics, Cranfield, England, 29–31 August 1967.
(81) HIRST, NORMAN F.; HIRST, CAROLINE PERKINS. Prolegomena to an organismic theory of questions. TRACOR, Inc., Austin, Tex., December 1967, 53 p. (TRACOR-67-1130-U) (AD-665 447)
(82) HOLST, WILHELM. Ein Versuch zur Anpassung des Präkoordinierungsindexes an die individuellen Informationsprofile des betriebseigenen Informationssystems durch Facettierung und Kategorisierung. [An attempt at adjusting the precoordination index to the individual information profiles of the company information system by means of faceting and categorizing] Nachrichten für Dokumentation, 19:3 (April/May 1968) 77–80.
(83) HUDSON, S. International documentation standards. ASLIB Proceedings, 20:12 (December 1968) 553–564.
(84) IKER, HOWARD P.; HARWAY, NORMAN. A computer systems approach towards the recognition and analysis of content—methods and illustrative results. Presented at National Conference on Content Analysis, Annenberg School of Communications, University of Pennsylvania, Philadelphia, 16–18 November 1967. (Preprint)
(85) INTERNATIONAL SYMPOSIUM ON RELATIONAL FACTORS IN CLASSIFICATION, Center of Adult Education, University of Maryland, College Park, 8–11 June 1966. Proceedings. Edited by Jean M. Perreault. Held under the sponsorship of the National Science Foundation. Information Storage and Retrieval, 3:4 (December 1967) 177–410.
(86) JACOBS, H. A natural language information retrieval system. Methods of Information in Medicine [Methodik der Information in der Medizin], 7:1 (January 1968) 8–16.
(87) JARDINE, N.; SIBSON, R. The construction of hierarchic and non-hierarchic classifications. Computer Journal, 11:2 (August 1968) 177–184.
(88) JOLLEY, J. L. Data study. Weidenfeld and Nicholson, London, 1968.
(89) JONES, RONALD D. User-designed retrieval indices: a case study. In: National Colloquium on Information Retrieval, 4th, 3–4 May 1967, Philadelphia. Proceedings, edited by Albert B. Tonik. International Information Incorporated, Philadelphia, 1967, p. 155–163.
(90) KARTTUNEN, LAURI. The identity of noun phrases. RAND Corp., Santa Monica, Calif., December 1967, 23 p. (P-3756). Presented at Annual Meeting of Linguistic Society of America, 42nd, Chicago, 28 December 1967.
(91) KASARDA, J. J. A syntactically oriented natural language document retrieval system with a browsability feature. Center for the Information Sciences, Lehigh University, Bethlehem, Pa., April 1967. (Experimental retrieval systems studies. Report no. 3)
(92) KATTER, ROBERT V. The influence of scale form on relevance judgments. Information Storage and Retrieval, 4:1 (March 1968) 1–11.
(93) KEEN, E. MICHAEL. An analysis of the documentation requests. In: Cornell University. Department of Computer Science. Information storage and retrieval. Scientific report no. ISR-13 to the National Science Foundation. Reports on evaluation procedures and results 1965–1967. Gerard Salton, Project Director. Ithaca, N.Y., December 1967, Sec. 10 (41 p.).
(94) KEEN, E. MICHAEL. Suffix dictionaries. In: Cornell University. Department of Computer Science. Information storage and retrieval. Scientific report no. ISR-13 to the National Science Foundation. Reports on evaluation procedures and results 1965–1967. Gerard Salton, Project Director. Ithaca, N.Y., December 1967, Sec. 6 (22 p.).
(95) KEEN, E. MICHAEL. Thesaurus, phrase and hierarchy dictionaries. In: Cornell University. Department of Computer Science. Information storage and retrieval. Scientific report no. ISR-13 to the National Science Foundation. Reports on evaluation procedures and results 1965–1967. Gerard Salton, Project Director. Ithaca, N.Y., December 1967, Sec. 7 (59 p.).
(96) KING, DONALD W. Design and evaluation of information systems. In: Annual

review of information science and technology, vol. 3. Carlos A. Cuadra, ed. Encyclopaedia Britannica, Chicago, 1968.
(97) KOCHEN, MANFRED; TAGLIACOZZO, RENATA. A study of cross-referencing. Journal of Documentation, 24:3 (September 1968) 173–191.
(98) KOSOLAPOV, V. V.; BERNSHTEIN, E. S. Analysis of information requirements and processing for scientific research. Joint Publications Research Service, Washington, D.C., 30 October 1967, 28 p. Translation of: Nauchno-Tekhnicheskaya Informatsiya, Senya 2, Informatsionnye Protsessy i Sistemy (USSR) n6 p3–11 1967. (JPRS-43173)
(99) LAFFAL, JULIUS. Contextual similarities as a basis for inference. Presented at National Conference on Content Analysis, Annenberg School of Communications, University of Pennsylvania, Philadelphia, 16–18 November 1967.
(100) LANCASTER, F. WILFRED. Evaluation of the MEDLARS demand search service. U.S. Department of Health, Education, and Welfare, Public Health Service, National Library of Medicine, Bethesda, Md., January 1968, 276 p.
(101) LANCASTER, F. WILFRED. Information retrieval systems: characteristics, testing, and evaluation. Wiley, New York, 1968, 222 p.
(102) LANCASTER, F. WILFRED. On the need for role indicators in postcoordinate retrieval systems. American Documentation, 19:1 (January 1968) 42–46.
(103) LANDRY, B. CLOVIS; RUSH, JAMES E. Toward a theory of indexing. In: American Society for Information Science Annual Meeting, Columbus, Ohio, 20–24 October 1968. Proceedings, vol. 5. Greenwood Publishing Corp., New York, 1968, p. 59–64.
(104) LERNER, RITA G. Development of a multi-coordinate vocabulary: chemical physics. American Institute of Physics, Information Division, New York, March 1968, 1 vol. (various pagings) (ID-68-3)
(105) LERNER, RITA G. Development of multi-coordinate vocabulary: plasma physics. American Institute of Physics, Information Division, New York, March 1968, 1 vol. (various pagings) (ID-68-4)
(106) LERNER, RITA G. Progress report on the development of a laser/maser vocabulary. American Institute of Physics, Information Division, New York, March 1968, 1 vol. (various pagings) (ID-68-5)
(107) LESK, M. E. Word-word association in document retrieval systems. In: Cornell University. Department of Computer Science. Information storage and retrieval. Scientific report no. ISR-13 to the National Science Foundation. Reports on evaluation procedures and results 1965–1967. Gerard Salton, Project Director. Ithaca, N.Y., December 1967, Sec. 9 (52 p.).
(108) LEVY, FRANCIS. On the relative nature of relational factors in classifications. Information Storage and Retrieval, 3:4 (December 1967) 315–325. Critique, by Phyllis A. Richmond, p. 325–327; Critique, by Harold Borko, p. 327–328; discussion, p. 328–329. Presented at International Symposium on Relational Factors in Classification, University of Maryland, College Park, 8–11 June 1966.
(109) LOCKHEED MISSILES AND SPACE COMPANY. ELECTRONIC SCIENCES LABORATORY. Automatic indexing and abstracting. Annual progress report. Palo Alto, Calif., March 1967, 118 p. (Report no. LMSC-M-21-67-1) (AD-659 057)
(110) LYNCH, M. F. Storage and retrieval of information on chemical structures by computer. Endeavour, 27 (May 1968) 68–73.
(111) MARTINEZ, SAMUEL J.; HELANDER, DONALD P. The development and maintenance of a specialized, controlled-vocabulary thesaurus. In: American Society for Information Science Annual Meeting, Columbus, Ohio, 20–24 October 1968. Proceedings, vol. 5. Greenwood Publishing Corp., New York, 1968, p. 279–287.
(112) MAYNE, A. J. Some modern approaches to the classification of knowledge. Classification Society Bulletin, 1:4 (1968) 13–17.
(113) MENDEN, WERNER; LEVY, BERT. Multiple test of ABC method. Part III: Mathematical model. Harry Diamond Laboratories, Washington, D.C., May 1967, 39 p. (Report no. HDL-TR-1334) (ATLIS-18) (AD-658 668)
(114) MILLS, J. Some current problems of classification for information retrieval. Classifi-

cation Society Bulletin, 1:4 (1968) 18–27.
(115) MITCHELL, H. S. Commodity classification and coding. Industrial Electronics, 6:5 (May 1968) 199–200.
(116) MØLGAARD-HANSEN, RASMUS. UDC, DC, and LC in competition on the domain of the university library. Tidskrift für Dokumentation, 24:1 (1968) 1–7.
(117) MOYS, ELIZABETH M. A classification scheme for law books. Butterworth, London, 1968.
(118) MULVIHILL, JOHN G. Supplementing thesaural relationships with usage notes. Presented at Author Panel no. 3, 1968 Annual Meeting of the American Society for Information Science in Columbus, Ohio, October 1968. (Preprint, 5 p.)
(119) NATIONAL CONFERENCE ON CONTENT ANALYSIS. Annenberg School of Communications, University of Pennsylvania, Philadelphia, 16–18 November 1967. Conference Chairman: George Gerbner, Dean.
(120) NEELAMEGHAN, A. Classification and the study of structure, and the development of the universe of subjects. Danish Centre for Documentation, Copenhagen, 1967. (F.I.D. Publication No. 405)
(121) O'CONNOR, JOHN. Retrieval of answer-providing documents. American Documentation, 19:4 (October 1968) 381–386.
(122) O'CONNOR, JOHN. Some questions concerning "Information Need." [Opinion paper] American Documentation, 19:2 (April 1968) 200–203. Letter on above paper, by F. W. Lancaster, same issue, p. 206.
(123) OFFICE OF NAVAL RESEARCH. PROJECT LEX. Thesaurus of engineering and scientific terms. Washington, D.C., 1967, 690 p. (AD-672 000)
(124) PARISER, BERTRAM. LASER/MASER vocabulary. In: Lerner, Rita G. Progress report on the development of a laser/maser vocabulary. Information Division, American Institute of Physics, New York, March 1968, Appendix A (9 p.) (ID 68-5)
(125) PENDERGRAFT, EUGENE D. Semantic self-organization. In: Conference on Computer-Related Semantic Analysis, Las Vegas, Nev., 3–5 December 1965. Proceedings. Wayne State University, Detroit, Mich., June 1966, p. XI/1-16. (AD-655 073)
(126) PERREAULT, JEAN M. On the articulation of surrogates: An attempt at an epistemological foundation. Information Storage and Retrieval, 3:4 (December 1967) 177–189. Critique, by Phyllis A. Richmond, p. 189–191; discussion, p. 191–192. Presented at International Symposium on Relational Factors in Classification, University of Maryland, College Park, 8–11 June 1966.
(127) PERREAULT, JEAN M. Re-classification: some warnings and a proposal. University of Illinois, Graduate School of Library Science, Urbana, September 1967. (Occasional Papers No. 87)
(128) PERREAULT, JEAN M.; WESSELING, J. C. G. On the Perreault scheme of relators. Danish Centre for Documentation, Copenhagen, (FID/CR Report No. 4)
(129) PERRY, PETER. Combined grouping for coordinate indexes. American Documentation, 19:2 (April 1968) 142–145.
(130) PRATT, ALLAN D. Objectives and performance evaluation of information systems. In: American Society for Information Science Annual Meeting, Columbus, Ohio, 20–24 October 1968. Proceedings, vol. 5. Greenwood Publishing Corp., New York, 1968, p. 323–325.
(131) PRICE, NANCY; SCHIMINOVICH, SAMUEL. A clustering experiment: First step towards a computer-generated classification scheme. Information Storage and Retrieval, 4:3 (August 1968) 271–280.
(132) RANGANATHAN, S. R. Basic subjects and their kinds. (Classification problems, 27) Library Science with a Slant to Documentation, 5:2 (June 1968) 97–133. (Paper C)
(133) RANGANATHAN, S. R. Choice of scheme for classification. (Classification problems, 26) Library Science with a Slant to Documentation, 5:1 (March 1968) 1–69.
(134) RANGANATHAN, S. R. Hidden roots of classification. Information Storage and Retrieval, 3:4 (December 1967) 399–410. Presented at International Symposium on Relational Factors in Classification, University of Maryland, College Park, 8–11 June

1966.
(135) RANGANATHAN, S. R. Specialist library versus generalist library: document selection. (Teaching in library science, 20) Library Science with a Slant to Documentation, 5:2 (June 1968) 182–192. (Paper G)
(136) RAYWARD, W. B.; SVENONIUS, ELAINE. Consistency, consensus sets and random deletion. University of Chicago, Graduate Library School, Chicago, February, 1967. (Studies of indexing depth and retrieval effectiveness. Progress report no. 2) (NSF GN-380)
(137) ROMNEY, A. KIMBALL. Multidimensional scaling and semantic domain. In: Conference on Computer-Related Semantic Analysis, Las Vegas, Nev., 3–5 December 1965. Proceedings. Wayne State University, Detroit, June 1966, p. IX/1–19. (AD-655 073)
(138) ROSTRON, R. M. The construction of a thesaurus. ASLIB Proceedings, 20:3 (March 1968) 181–187.
(139) RUBENSTEIN, HERBERT. Some problems of meaning in natural languages. Center for the Information Sciences, Lehigh University, Bethlehem, Pa., January 1968.
(140) ST. LAURENT, M. C. Studies in indexing depth and retrieval effectiveness: a review of the literature of indexer consistency. University of Chicago, Graduate Library School, February 1967. (PB-174 395)
(141) SALTON, GERARD. Automatic content analysis in information retrieval. Presented at National Conference on Content Analysis, Annenberg School of Communications, University of Pennsylvania, Philadelphia, November 1967.
(142) SALTON, GERARD. Automatic information organization and retrieval. McGraw-Hill, New York, 1968, 480 p.
(143) SALTON, GERARD. Relevance assessments and retrieval system evaluation. Department of Computer Science, Cornell University, Ithaca, N.Y., September 1968. (Technical Report No. 68-25)
(144) SANTIAGO, ANTONY. Systematics of knowledge with enneametry and data processing machines. American Documentation, 19:2 (April 1968) 158–162.
(145) SCHANK, ROGER. The use of conceptual relations in content analysis and data base storage. TRACOR, Inc., Austin, Tex., January 1968. (TRACOR 68-347-U)
(146) SCHNEIDER, JOHN H. Experimental trial of selective dissemination of biomedical information in an automated system based on a linear hierarchical decimal classification. In: American Society for Information Science Annual Meeting, Columbus, Ohio, 20–24 October 1968. Proceedings, vol. 5. Greenwood Publishing Corp., New York, 1968, p. 243–245.
(147) SCHNEIDER, JOHN H. Hierarchical decimal classification of information related to cancer research. National Cancer Institute, Bethesda, Md., 2 February 1968, 124 p. (PB-177 209)
(148) SCHNEIDER, KLAUS. Maschinelle Dokumentation in der Bundesrepublik Deutschland. Dritte zusammensstellung: Stand vom 1 Januar 1968. Zentralstelle für Maschinelle Dokumentation (ZMD), Frankfurt a/M, (ZMD-A-15).
(149) SHAW, T. N.; ROTHMAN, H. An experiment in indexing by word choosing. Journal of Documentation, 24:3 (September 1968) 159–172.
(150) SOERGEL, DAGOBERT. Some remarks on information languages, their analysis and comparison. Information Storage and Retrieval, 3:4 (December 1967) 219–293. Critique, by Pauline Atherton, p. 293; Critique, by Robert A. Fairthorne, p. 293–294; discussion, p. 295–296. Presented at International Symposium on Relational Factors in Classification, University of Maryland, College Park, 8–11 June 1966.
(151) SPARCK JONES, KAREN; NEEDHAM, ROGER M. Automatic term classifications and retrieval. Information Storage and Retrieval, 4:2 (June 1968) 91–100. Presented at the First Cranfield International Conference on Mechanized Information Storage and Retrieval Systems, College of Aeronautics, Cranfield, England, 29–31 August 1967.
(152) SPARCK JONES, KAREN. Semantic classes and semantic message forms. In: Conference on Computer-Related Semantic Analysis, Las Vegas, Nev., 3–5 December

1965. Proceedings. Wayne State University, Detroit, June 1966, p. X/1-20. (AD-655 073)
(153) STARKWEATHER, JOHN. Computer aids to content recognition. Presented at National Conference on Content Analysis, Annenberg School of Communications, University of Pennsylvania, Philadelphia, 16-18 November 1967.
(154) STEVENS, S. S. Measurements, statistics, and the schemapiric view. Science, 161:3844 (30 August 1968) 849-861.
(155) STONE, DON CHARLES. Word statistics in the generation of semantic tools for information systems. Moore School of Electrical Engineering, University of Pennsylvania, Philadelphia, December 1967, 87 p. (Report 68-23) (AFOSR 68-0237) (AD-664 915)
(156) STONE, DON C.; RUBINOFF, MORRIS. Statistical generation of a technical vocabulary. [Brief communication] American Documentation, 19:4 (October 1968) 411-412.
(157) STONE, PHILIP J. Computer-aided content analysis. In: International Technical Communications Conference, 15th, Los Angeles, 8-11 May 1968. Proceedings. Society of Technical Writers and Publishers, Washington, D.C., 1968, paper I-21 (6 p.).
(158) STONE, PHILIP J. Improved quality of content analysis categories. Computerized disambiguation rules for high frequency words in the English language. Presented at National Conference on Content Analysis, Annenberg School of Communications, University of Pennsylvania, 16-18 November 1967.
(159) SUGA, T. Document retrieval system with concept hierarchy tree. [M. S. dissertation] Kyoto University, Japan, March 1968.
(160) SVIRIDOV, F. A. International projects sponsored by FID (International Federation for Documentation). ASLIB Proceedings, 20:12 (December 1968) 565-573.
(161) TAGUE, JEAN MARY. Statistical measures of term association in information retrieval. Thesis—Western Reserve University. University Microfilms, Ann Arbor, Mich., 1967, 108 p.
(162) TANCREDI, SAMUEL A.; NICHOLS, OWEN D. Air pollution technical information processing—the microthesaurus approach. American Documentation, 19:1 (January 1968) 66-70.
(163) TAULBEE, ORRIN E. Content analysis, specification and control. In: Annual review of information science and technology, vol. 3. Carlos A. Cuadra, ed. Encyclopaedia Britannica, Chicago, 1968.
(164) TINKER, JOHN F. Imprecision in indexing. Part II. American Documentation, 19:3 (July 1968) 322-330.
(165) ULLMANN, STEPHEN. Some quantitative problems in semantics and lexicology. In: Conference on Computer-Related Semantic Analysis, Las Vegas, Nev., 3-5 December 1965. Proceedings. Wayne State University, Detroit, June 1966, p. V/1-19. (AD-655 073)
(166) VICKERY, B. C. Analysis of information. In: Encyclopedia of Library and Information Science, vol. 1. Dekker, New York, 1968, p. 355-384.
(167) WATT, W. C. Habitability. American Documentation, 19:3 (July 1968) 338-351.
(168) WAY, WILLIAM. "Subject Heading Authority List," computer prepared. American Documentation, 19:2 (April 1968) 188-199.
(169) WERNER, HEINZ; KAPLAN, EDITH. Development of word meaning through verbal context: an experimental study. In: De Cecco, John P., ed. The psychology of language, thought and instruction. Readings. Holt, Rinehart and Winston, New York, 1967, p. 291-295.
(170) WESSEL, ANDREW E. Some thoughts on machine indexing. RAND Corp., Santa Monica, Calif., June 1968, 12 p. (Report no. P-3869) (AD-671 989)
(171) WILLIAMS, J. H., JR. Computer classification of documents. Annual progress report. IBM Federal Systems Division, Gaithersburg, Md., 1967, 25 p. (AD-663 178) Prepared for presentation at the FID/IFIP Conference, Rome, Italy, 15 June 1967.
(172) WILSHIRE, BRUCE. William James and phenomenology. Indiana University Press, Bloomington, 1968, p. 86+; p. 99+.

(173) ZHOGOLEV, E. A. Algorithm of the selection of concepts with the help of a syntactic table. Foreign Technology Division, Wright-Patterson AFB, Ohio, 9 June 1967, 22 p. (Report no. FTD-MT-67-76) Edited machine translation of: Zhurnal Vychislitelnoi Matematiki i Matematicheskoi Fiziki (USSR) 5:4 (1965) 689–698.

4 File Organization and Management Information Systems

MICHAEL E. SENKO
IBM Research Laboratory

INTRODUCTION

File organization technology is in a period of major renaissance. This new interest is the result of two events: the appearance of large-scale Management Information Systems (MIS) requiring capabilities for handling billion-character data bases in real time, and the appearance of hardware capable of fulfilling economically this MIS requirement. In this chapter, we shall cover the various functions of Management Information Systems and devote special attention to the organization and design of their central component, the system for handling information files.

In reviewing the literature, the author has encountered three types of contributions. First, there are tutorial papers intended primarily for management personnel. Possible titles might include: "Management Information Systems: The Wave of the Future," and "Understanding Management Information Systems." These papers present an author's personal conceptual structure of MIS and normally are of little technical interest to the information scientist. One of the best, by a computer-oriented writer, is that of Head (59). This review will devote no further consideration to these essentially introductory papers.

Typical titles for the second class of papers include: "The Management Information System at ABC Hospital" and "The XYZ Corporation's Production Control System." These papers generally provide very little new technical information, but they do list and describe implemented applications, usually providing valuable quantitative data on computing systems, data base size, numbers of terminals and transactions, etc. In the section on MIS Applications, the reviewer will list and describe a sampling of the literature from four major economic areas.

The third type of paper describes particular widely usable functions for the technical audience. In the section on MIS Structure, the author will discuss each of these functions separately.

Many functions such as simulation, decision making, and display generation are major fields of specialization for large groups of scientists and are peripheral to our central concern, the file-handling systems. Papers on these functions have been accorded treatment similar to that of the applications papers. It is important for information scientists to understand the state of development of these functions, but a comprehension of the technical details is not necessary. In the areas of direct interest to the information scientist, an in-depth evaluation of the literature and the state of the art is provided, along with the author's opinion on the useful future directions.

In the selection of papers, the primary consideration has been the paper's possibility (or danger) of technically influencing the reader—a criterion that has led to the rejection of many essay-like papers. Of the selected papers, many have the predominant characteristic of being recent informative examples of specific functions. They will be mentioned with little further comment at the appropriate position within the structure of the chapter. Only unique features deserving the reader's special attention (or caution) will be highlighted in detail.

While it may seem that, by this process of elimination, the in-depth evaluation has been confined to a rather small area, the area is extremely important in terms of economics and technical progress. File processing and maintenance alone are the objects of probably more than three-quarters of the productive computer time used today.

It is not surprising that other disciplines are beginning to take an interest in a field of such economic importance and new promise. In particular, systems programmers are especially active in the design and coding of file-handling systems. They bring a passion for detail and a point of view to the data management system field that differ dramatically from those of the information scientist. It will be extremely important for the information scientist to comprehend their standards, accomplishments, and terminology if he wishes to contribute effectively to the field in the next few years. This review, therefore, will discuss the literature with both points of view in mind.

MIS APPLICATIONS

In large, modern organizations, standards for efficiency and response time can no longer be met by batch processing of small, fragmented, and dispersed files. Instead, files must be integrated and processed in a more systematic, real-time fashion. In addition, information must be derived from these files to support both machine-made and man-made decisions.

FILE ORGANIZATION AND MANAGEMENT INFORMATION SYSTEMS

The total system that implements these processes to provide information for management, whether in a traditional batch-processing manner or in a new integrated, fast-response mode, is termed a Management Information System.

Many authors appear to believe that Management Information Systems are mystic creations, different in kind from any previously existing systems. In fact, there are few, if any, that meet such criteria. A detailed reading of the technical literature will reveal that they have evolved directly from, and encompass many of the functions of, earlier administrative data processing systems.

This section will describe areas of application in medicine, education, government, and business.

Medical Systems

In Volume 3 of the *Annual Review*, Levy & Cammarn (86) present an excellent analytical chapter on medical information systems. We shall provide a guide only to the more recent literature.

The hospital information system area continues to be very active. Both Baruch (6) and Poliski (111) present general reviews of the state of the art. Poliski quotes estimates of 250 hospital computers in 1965 and 500 in 1968. While computers are engaged primarily in accounting procedures, the trend is toward greater support of professional duties.

For example, one of the more recent areas of impact is the real-time computer handling of laboratory and pharmaceutical services where schedules are set, results correlated by patient, and billings prepared. Fontana et al. (44) and Lamson et al. (79) describe systems operating at the University of Alabama and UCLA, respectively. The Lamson paper includes cost comparisons with a manual system.

Several papers deal with scheduling of resources, which is a new development since the writing of the Levy & Cammarn chapter. Cronkhite (28) describes the real-time room-scheduling system of the 350-bed Boston Children's Hospital. Dunn & Howell (36) and Leighton & Headly (83) describe, in addition, how this system's data base can be analyzed for better resource allocation. Finally, Rosenbaum (119) and Erat et al. (38) describe systems for out-patient scheduling. Siegel (126) describes a similar system that also accounts for in-hospital services in real time.

The Rosenbaum system also includes maintenance of the patient's medical record. Other papers on medical records include those of Gelblat (49) and Hall et al. (57). The latter paper supports an argument of the reviewer, that a medical information system does not differ significantly from a general information system.

The largest reported medical records system handles more than 125,000 examination records. Input is by questionnaires prepared by the patient, the laboratory, and the physician, and the system checks for abnormal responses (Davis et al., 29). At the same time, plans are being made at another hospital for interviewing of patients via console (Slack & Van Cura, 129).

The basic data for an individual could, of course, be stored in a national data bank for transmission to any part of the country. Implementation of such a system is relatively far in the future, but Freed (46) and Davis (30) have anticipated several of the problems. Extracts from the records can also be used [as discussed by Vransky et al. (142)] for early detection of epidemics and other analyses of the general health picture. Finally, administrative data can be extracted for high-level management control as in the Veterans Administration system of 166 hospitals (Rosen, 118).

Management Information Systems have a wide range of proven application in the medical field, but implementations are at present confined to only a few institutions.

Education Systems

Volume 3 of the *Annual Review* contains a chapter on computers in education (Silberman and Filep, 127), and a short review by Forsythe (45) has appeared even more recently. Computer-assisted instruction, the primary topic of both reviews, is not appropriate for this chapter; we shall, therefore, list only the more recent literature on instructional management, educational data processing, and administrative planning.

Tondow (140) discusses the implementation of a multifunction system covering pupils, staff, and instructional materials for the 16,000-student Palo Alto school districts, and Grossman (55) discusses the much larger California Educational Information System. These systems show a trend toward integration of multiple functions that was not indicated in the Silberman review.

Finally, there is considerable interest in more than simple report generation. In particular, much work is being done on class scheduling (Hall & Acton, 56; Stewart & Clark, 132; Lions, 88; Johnston & Wolfenden, 70). This problem is so challenging that only specialized, heuristic algorithms are reported.

Government Systems

In this section, we shall discuss motor vehicle, law enforcement, criminal justice, legislative, and urban planning and control applications.

The motor vehicle application appears in a paper by Montijo (98). He discusses the real-time system to be completed by California in 1970. The system will have hundreds of terminals for inquiry by courts and law enforcement and insurance agencies to thirty million records on drivers and motor vehicles.

The Alameda County (California) Police Information Network, which serves 93 law enforcement agencies in the San Francisco Bay area, provides real-time inquiry to 200,000 warrants for arrest, with thirty-second response for officers interested in violations associated with motor vehicle licenses. This type of service is also available on a national basis from the National Crime Information Center (42). Another interesting application uses data bases of local crime statistics to provide input to a police beat allocation program (Gass, 48).

The police information network is one part of the criminal justice system described by Finkler (43). The other component is the court system. Stinnett (133) provides details on the area of court records, and Taylor & Navarro (136) use court records in a resource-allocation simulation of the court decision system. A few pioneering implementations have been made in the courts, but activity is not widespread.

Chartrand has presented several papers, including (19) and (20), on a proposed legislative information system for the Congress. He notes that during each session Congress must know the status of approximately 25,000 bills.

State and local information systems have recently been reviewed by Dueker (35). The range of data that they might store is indicated by an inventory for the Greenville-Pickens region of South Carolina (54). This document lists 1,700 separate data collections, including a directory of all county roads and streets. This sample data collection introduces a file organization problem of particular interest to government systems—that of storage and retrieval on the basis of geographic location. This problem plays an important part in the papers of Black & Shaw (8), CONSAD (27), Richter (116), Stanley & Cranshaw (131), and Willis (148). As in other areas, a wide range of applications is being automated, but no truly integrated system exists at this time.

Business Systems

In the area of large real-time information systems, the initiative for advancement of the art may well be passing from military to business systems. The literature is now almost completely dominated by descriptions of business applications. If anything, the literature vastly underrepresents the size and number of business systems.

Insurance and utility customer files fall at the lowest level of complexity. Each customer record is essentially a separate entity. In the insurance area, real-time systems for maintenance and analysis of policy records are well described by Allen (3) and Cueto (2). The real-time maintenance and query of utility customer records are described by Kamman & Saxton (74) and Thompson (139). The system described in the latter paper has some parallel to urban systems in that it includes the use of retrieval by geographical location.

Systems used for railroad records appear at a slightly more complex level. Day (31) presents an excellent description of the Denver and Rio Grande Western Railroad system for monitoring the positions of its freight cars and trains. Two other papers (Nakanishi et al., 103; Leddon, 82) indicate the utility of simulation in the railroad environment.

At the next level are the order-inventory systems where the products can be considered to be monolithic units. That is, the system does not need to know the component parts of an ordered item. Cohen (26), Menkhaus (96), and Kronenberg (77) describe systems for wholesale inventory control of electronic parts, food, and lumber, respectively.

At the most complex level are files representing products composed of assemblies of assemblies. In this class are the production control systems described by Brown & Nordyke (14), Barnett & Lightfoot (5), Bird & Hedley (7), Lambert & Ruffels (78) and White (146). These systems for both bills of material describing the final assemblies and routing files describing manufacture and assembly must be capable of representing trees with thousands of branches. As we shall see later, the search and processing of these files requires extremely complex algorithms.

Books by Heany (60) and Li (87) present excellent summaries of the business application area for investigators not having a detailed background in programming. Several case studies make the books especially interesting. The chapters by Heath (61), Powell (113), and Cheek (21) in the Business Equipment Manufacturers Association (BEMA) Management Conference proceedings are also of particular value.

MIS STRUCTURE

In the MIS field, publications and reviews tend to emphasize, or even exaggerate, the uniqueness of each contribution (often by personalized terminology). In this review, we shall attempt to create a basis for more systematic understanding by interrelating the contributions within an MIS functional structure.

The initial sections will deal with MIS file-handling components. We shall then devote particularly close attention to the complete technical literature on file-access techniques and file design. The next set of MIS functions discussed will be those that place the data in a better form to aid management decisions or actually to make certain straightforward decisions. The final sections will review the literature of system design and total information systems.

FILE ORGANIZATION AND MANAGEMENT INFORMATION SYSTEMS

File Handling Systems

At the central core of all Management Information Systems are the programs that maintain and access the data files. At first, programs were all written specially in machine language for each file. This occurred, in part, because little knowledge of the generalizable functions of file handling existed. The programs were constrained to sequential batch processing by the lack of existing alternatives to magnetic tape storage.

Even in tape systems, more and more useful generalizable functions were discovered and made available to the user. The trend toward generalization has, however, been given major impetus by the appearance of hundred-million-character random-access files. These files provide new dimensions of flexibility to the user (especially in fast-response systems), but at the expense of more complex, detailed programming. The use of generalized routines, compiler language functions, or even complete generalized file-handling systems, depending on the application, provides means for avoiding the detailed programming, usually at a smaller total expense for the application.

In the next few sections, we shall examine the literature on file handling with respect to various levels of program generalization and flexibility.

Record-Keeping Systems. The first file-handling systems that appeared were those for providing operational control of accounting records. They almost certainly still dominate the file-handling environment. Many are still written in assembly-type languages, although higher-level languages such as COBOL are well accepted. The files normally have relatively simple record formats, although in some applications records can contain five hundred or more data items. A more important characteristic is that each record describes a separate entity and has no complex relationships with the remainder of the file.

Examples include most programs for personnel records, library records, accounts receivable, merchandise control, mortgage accounting, public utility customer accounts, parts inventory, insurance policy accounting, etc. In this year's literature, papers by Cronkhite (28), Dunn & Howell (36), and Hall (57) describe medical systems at this level of flexibility. Papers by Cueto (2) and Thayer (137) describe systems in the insurance and utility areas.

Generally, because of their extremely rigid limits, these systems provide little in the way of condensed management information. Nonetheless, they are handling files that could provide the basis for more flexible management information systems.

Record-Keeping with Exception Reporting. These are the first systems specifically designed to provide management information. They check values of data items against standards of performance. Data items that show unusually good or poor performance can be flagged and reported for subsequent management attention. The exceptional conditions include overdrawn accounts, late orders, sales quotas exceeded, etc. Systems operating at this level are still inflexible in the sense that they check only anticipated conditions.

Record-Keeping with Query Capability. These systems are distinguished from the previous ones by the ease that they afford the user in obtaining answers to unanticipated questions. The systems attempt to remove much of the detailed housekeeping burden from the user. The report program generators (RPG's) described by Friedberg (47), Leslie (85), and McLaurin & Traister (93) are intermediate steps in this direction. As the authors note, even this intermediate step produces great savings in programmer time and time to obtain results.

These generator programs are able to reduce the program specification effort because they are dealing with complex but rather well-defined file-handling processes. From a multitude of possible techniques of performing these processes, the program selects one. If the user is satisfied with the selected method (in most cases, it is marginally different from competing methods), he need only describe "what" he wants done (in nonprocedural language). He need not indicate in detail "how" to do it in some procedural language, which allows programming of any of the multitude of possibilities. Olle (107, 108) is especially perceptive in describing the differences between the nonprocedural and the procedural file-handling systems.

The final level of flexibility contains systems for update and maintenance that allow questions to be phrased in English-like languages. Two early versions, the Formatted File Systems (32, 33) and INFOL (Olle, 107), were tape-oriented. Under "Systems" we shall discuss more recent versions, GIS and TDMS.

Complex File Handling. There are many applications, particularly in the manufacturing area, where complex relationships occur between records in the file. For example, a file describing an automobile can be related to a hierarchic tree structure, where each node of the tree is a record that describes a particular assembly (i.e., engine) of smaller assemblies (pistons, valves, etc.). In this type of file, much of the information is contained in the branches interrelating the various nodes, and the file-handling program must be capable of acting on this information. Bills-of-material and plant-routing files are adequately represented by tree structures; in Program Evaluation and Review Technique (PERT) charts, the nodes (records of equivalent format) are interrelated in graph-like structures (Gerdel, 50; Cloot & Sutton-Smith, 25; and Noble, 106).

The reviewer is not aware of any generalized, nonprocedural systems for handling these files. There are, however, three existing methods of processing complex files. The first is an application-specific program; PERT programs are typical examples. The second is a generalization of existing procedural programs [for example, IDS—Integrated Data Store—as described by Jones (72)]. Programs of this type require considerable knowledge of the file structure to be embedded in the program. This characteristic tends to run counter to the concept of "data structure independence," which we shall discuss later.

The third possibility is the use of list-processing languages (Evans, 40; Rovner, 120). These languages are implemented for lists normally contained in core storage and, therefore, not directly applicable to large data files. However, they do provide functions generally required for the processing of trees and certain other types of graph structures.

In effect, none of the existing approaches is ideally complete, but each has certain characteristics to contribute to the desired system.

More Sophisticated Report Generators. Exception reporting and special queries certainly decrease the amount of information presented to a manager, but they do little to make the information that he does receive meaningful. (It is extremely difficult to see the interrelationships between one hundred pairs of ten-digit numbers.) Desirable further processing may include statistical analyses (standard deviations, variance, regression), or it may involve plotting the numbers in two-dimensional displays. Since many of these functions are generalizable, we should in the future see them as integral parts of information systems.

In the recent literature, the papers of Lawrence (80) and Pyle (114) discuss uses of an automated plotting table. Ninke (105) provides a description of similar facilities for a CRT display. Bowman & Lickhalter (12) present the most interesting paper. It describes an interactive CRT graphical system that interfaces directly with TSS-LUCID, a predecessor of the data-management system TDMS.

In our discussion of CRT displays, it should be noted that they can also be extremely useful as input devices. The papers of Uber et al. (141), Cloot & Sutton-Smith (25) and Morton & Stephens (102) describe interactive input of data on medical tests, PERT diagrams, and production planning, respectively.

File Organization. Before we discuss literature on MIS functions that the file-handling system must support, we shall look in some depth at file organization for both document retrieval and MIS systems. We shall attempt to maintain terminology that is consistent with the excellent earlier *Annual Review* chapters of Climenson (24), Minker & Sable (97) and Shoffner (125).

File organization can be separated into two parts—file-accessing techniques and file design. In reviewing the literature on the first area, the author has found a disturbing lack of structure and a tendency to treat accessing techniques in an overly abstract fashion. File-access techniques must work in an environment of agonizingly slow mechanical motions and must provide adequate performance for mundane file-maintenance processing as well as for more glamorous file query. Those techniques that ignore this environment are not likely to be very useful for processing large files on hardware whose implementation is now forseeable. In the next section, we shall present a state-of-the-art structure for evaluating the literature on this more realistic basis.

File-Accessing Techniques. There are essentially four primitive methods of accessing a record with a given primary identifier (for example, the automobile record with license number XYZ 123).

All peripheral storage devices provide for a specific physical ordering of data. In the first and most used method, *sequential access*, the program starts reading at the beginning of the file and compares the primary identifier of each record with the desired identifier. When a job must access a sizable number of the records in the file on one pass, then sequential access is the most efficient method. Since the next record is physically the nearest one, mechanical access time is minimized and usually averages only a few milliseconds. The method has two major drawbacks. First, if a job requires access to only one record, one-half the file, on the average, must be searched; for a large file, the access time for one useful record might range from five minutes to an hour. Second, if one wishes to add records between existing records, the entire file must be rewritten—a process that may take minutes or even hours.

In *direct access*, there is a direct mathematical relationship between the arithmetic magnitude of the identifier and the device address at which the record is located. Given the identifier, the access program in the central processing unit mathematically converts it to the desired address and uses the address to access the correct file location. This is the fastest method of obtaining a single desired record, since no intermediate records need be accessed. In files in which all possible identifiers occur, direct access is probably preferred. Unfortunately, few existing files have this characteristic. Usually, only a small number of the possible identifiers occur. For example, only a fraction of the (27^{20}) possible names of twenty letters or less appear in a telephone book. Since the (27^{20}) address space required is clearly not available in real-world devices, recourse is taken to transforming mathematically the long identifier into a realistically small address space that is still capable of storing all the names that do occur. There are several ways of dealing with two or more names transforming to the same address, but they all involve further searching, thereby diluting the original single-access advantage of the method.

Since key (identifier)-to-address transforms have been an exceedingly popular field, it is pertinent to discuss their principal characteristics. Clearly, if one does not use knowledge of the key distribution, he cannot guarantee freedom from duplicates. Maurer (95) essentially proposes division by a prime number and use of the remainder as the device address. If this produces a duplicate, a quadratic equation is used to produce further addresses until an open space is found. Many transforms like this one are designed to break up certain types of clusters in identifier space. None of the methods guarantees anything about duplicates produced by identifiers from different clusters.

The other method of attack is to scan and make some use of the knowledge of the data. One may store tables of duplicates, but then he must access two or more places; or he may, by iterative processes, construct complex mathematical equations which ensure that no duplicate appears. The problem with this approach is that many scans of the data (perhaps thousands) must be made to produce the equations, and these processes will probably result in a coefficient matrix that cannot be maintained in core storage. In effect, all methods pay some type of time penalty for avoiding duplicates.

A recent paper by Morris (100) reviews transformation techniques. Unfortunately, it is primarily concerned with files small enough to fit into core storage. It is the reviewer's opinion that relatively simple techniques should be used and monitored to see if they produce excessive numbers of duplicates. If the selected specific technique is unsatisfactory, an analysis of the duplicates will almost certainly lead to a slight, but effective, modification of the technique. The user should always leave a reasonable amount of free space (10–20%) and increase the size of the space allotted to an address (i.e., create multiple-record buckets).

A key-to-address transform normally randomizes the order of the records in physical store. While the nearest sequential record is only a millisecond distant, a record position accessed at random in large files is normally one hundred milliseconds away. For this reason, the loading of a large file will generally require twenty to one hundred times longer for direct access than for sequential access. Kaiman's (73) conclusion that direct access is the best random-access method ignores the file-creation problem and also the problem of update with large numbers of batched transactions. When one considers these and other factors, the applicability and the desirability of random access for even moderately active large files become extremely restricted.

The third method, *chained access* (or list processing), utilizes an address (or identifier) stored in the present record to indicate the location of the next record. In effect, it amounts to a sequential access method in which the next record may be placed anywhere on peripheral storage. This property makes the method particularly useful for dealing with record insertion. One address modification allows the record to be placed in an available empty location (the total process requiring about two hundred milliseconds) and still be at the correct search point in the logical chain. Search speeds vary from fast sequential access (1–5 milliseconds average per record) to slow random access (100 milliseconds average per record), depending on how much care is taken to maintain physical proximity of the next record. Systems like the Integrated Data Store (Jones, 72) attempt, to some extent, to maintain this contiguity on at least one key field.

A major consideration in the use of chained access is that neither machines nor programmers perform perfectly to specification. An error that breaks a primary identifier chain essentially renders a significant portion, if not most, of the data base inaccessible. However, breakage of a short chain affects much less and therefore can often be tolerated.

If a file is sorted on the basis of primary identifier, then one can perform binary search on the file. The number of random accesses (~25–100 milliseconds) required in an average search is $\log_2 n$, where n is the number of records in the file. While one could use hybrid access methods to improve its performance slightly, the method is not very useful for accessing peripheral device files. A more useful access method utilizes a hierarchic set of indexes created by extracting, for example, every tenth identifier from the sorted file, placing it in the next-higher-level file. When the program wishes to access the file for a specific key, it goes to the highest-level index and searches down to the data. This process normally takes only one to three random accesses per record (100–300 milliseconds). The fourth access method, *indexed sequential*, provides a very attractive compromise between direct access and sequential access for most nontrivial MIS files. For random access, it is normally two to three times slower than direct access and orders of magnitude faster than sequential access. In file creation and sequential processing, it is one to two orders of magnitude faster than direct access and marginally slower than sequential access. A paper by Brewer (13) provides a short survey on the above primitive access methods in somewhat different terminology.

In most practical situations, only the sequential- and chained-access methods can be used in primitive form. Because of a general need for insertion of new records and a requirement for realistic storage space, practical direct- and indexed-access methods are generally hybrids of a set of primitive methods. A practical direct-access method will use either sequential search or chaining to deal with duplicates, and a practical indexed-access method will use direct and sequential searching in its indexes, and possibly chaining for handling new inserts.

FILE ORGANIZATION AND MANAGEMENT INFORMATION SYSTEMS

While there is little more to be learned or said about the primitive access methods, a similar situation does not occur with the hybrids. There exists a large, if not infinite, variety of hybrids, and they can be written in semi-general form so that the user also has several options (blocking factor, index buffering, data buffering, data packing factor, etc.) as to the final specific file structure.

At this point, we can relate the systems in this year's literature on the basis of their dominant characteristic, the primary access method.

With regard to examples, several systems are tape-oriented and, therefore, are limited to *sequential access*. These include systems discussed by Erskine (39), McLaurin & Traister (93), and Olle (107). The Report Program Generators (Leslie, 85; Friedberg, 47) also generally operate in the sequential mode, although modifications allow some systems to use indexed files. MARK IV (Postley, 112) has similar sequential and indexed-sequential characteristics.

Some examples of *direct access* have already been presented. The insurance system described by Cueto (2) uses a typical hybrid access method. Direct access is an initial step to select a tape strip. Sequential search of an index on the strip is then used to obtain direct access to a track that is scanned sequentially for the data.

Examples of *chained access* occur in papers by Evans (40) and Rovner (120) describing list-processing systems designed primarily for core storage. The paper by Jones (72) on DATA FILE TWO also describes the use of chains for primary identifier access to large random-access files.

Finally, the systems described by Allen (3), Brown & Nordyke (14), Barnett & Lightfoot (5), Borsei & Bos (11) and Bleier & Vorhaus (9) use *indexes* for accessing on the basis of primary identifier.

Often, one wishes to access and process records on the basis of secondary identifiers (age equal to 27, or job title equal to manager, rather than man number equal to 2079630). If no auxiliary access aids are provided, then one must access each record and examine the secondary identifier field for each. While most of the systems in existence must perform this time-consuming complete file scan, there are certain means of avoiding or ameliorating this problem, at a cost in file maintenance and storage space.

Descriptor search is the simplest form of secondary-key access. The descriptors that appear in document retrieval are instances of repeated fields of the same type in a single record. They could, for example, be considered detail records under a master record. There have been several proposals to encode these fields and superimpose them into one field that hopefully, can be tested more quickly than can the multiple fields. Chow (23) proposes a geometric coding method for this purpose. This method, like its predecessors, still requires a sequential search of the file and, therefore, cannot be expected to produce qualitative improvements in descriptor search speed.

Another unique file organization paper (Morrison, 101) is presented on PATRICIA, a text-string retrieval system utilizing a binary tree-structured index. The presentation, using uniquely coined mathematical terminology, makes for unnecessarily difficult reading. The file organization presents numerous difficulties, including problems of providing access to descriptors which apply to several documents. Minimal storage and search time occur only in a selected mathematical sense because, for actual large data bases, index size will far exceed inverted file structures (partly because the index must address to the bit level rather than to the word level in the text string), and tree-search times become prohibitive when the file exceeds core storage.

Salton (121) discusses file organizations for document retrieval. His conclusions are based on core storage characteristics and would have to be significantly modified for large files requiring mechanical device storage.

The two most used methods of accessing secondary keys are *chains* and *secondary indexes*. In the *index methods*, a separate file is created for each field selected for indexing. The file contains each value appearing in the selected field, followed by the direct addresses or identifiers of all records containing the value. Higher levels of index can be created to provide for fast access to a particular field value.

In *chained methods*, a chain for each field starts with the record having an extreme field value, and passes in field-value order through all records containing that field. While this type of organization is feasible, it is unsatisfactory from a practical standpoint because accessing even the median value in a twenty-thousand-record file (at fifty milliseconds per random access) would take about ten minutes. One can, of course, create index levels that point to the beginning of chains for sets of field values. For a single field qualification, this method results in access times that may, in special cases, be as low as pure index methods. These hybrids cannot, however, approach pure indexes for multiple-field qualification. In the index case, the qualifications can be performed on tightly packed strings with random accesses required only to obtain qualified records. In the case of chains, the field with the shortest chain would be selected for search. Even then, the program must make random accesses to all records that contain the field value, not just to the qualified records.

A major consideration with regard to both methods is whether pointers should be direct addresses or identifiers. The use of direct addresses speeds up retrieval by circumventing a search on the primary index, but a tradeoff exists because, at file reorganization time, changing direct addresses invalidates chain pointers or secondary indexes for all indexed fields. When primary identifiers are used, the pointers or indexes retain their fidelity.

In the literature this year, the papers of Allen (3), Evans (40), Gelblat (49), Hsiao (66), Jones (72), and Rovner (120) use chains for secondary key access. The Jones paper describes a structure based on the Integrated Data Store, in which extreme fragmentation of the record leads to an overhead of about ten times the size of the data. Other IDS organizations require much less overhead for chains.

Papers discussing systems using indexes include Bleier & Vorhaus (9), Morenoff & McLean (99), Childs (22), Sheldon & Backer (124), and Warheit (143). GIS (67) originally specified indexes but they do not appear in most recent announcements.

The paper by Warheit discusses a single-index system, CFSS. This index contains some ambiguity as to whether the record containing the desired value contains it in the correct property field.

The paper of Childs is a useful, exploratory effort to bring the power of set theory directly to bear on retrieval languages, but the underlying implementation uses a slight extension of standard index techniques. Fast retrieval speeds are, in part, due to the small record size and to a partial prestoring of answers to anticipated queries. Storage requirements are greater than for sequential storage of the data and minimal only in an author-prescribed sense.

There are, finally, two other papers on multiple-key retrieval: one by Ghosh (51) on a unique technique that has many properties similar to direct access, and one by Kisylia (75) on associative memory hardware.

After the system has located the primary identifier, it still must access the pertinent information associated with the identifier. The fields that contain the basic units of information are usually concatenated into segments that contain all fields related to a particular event or entity. In the most general form, these segments may be superior to, subordinate to, or at the same level as other segments of like or different format. There may be many-to-many relationships between the various segments, and related segments need not even be in the same file as the segment of interest.

The list-processing languages allow the ultimate in flexibility; they even allow the segments to be broken into separate fields connected by relationships. DATA FILE TWO (Jones, 72) exemplifies this possibility. McGee (91) presents a terminology for this level of flexibility. Yet, if one wishes to go to this ultimate of physical flexibility, he must pay a penalty in both time and space. In particular, each field must have one or more pointers to connect it to the correct logical format (more than doubling the size of physical store required). Access time is also lengthened because at least one iteration of pointer decode and item access must be performed for every field. This penalty is moderate for fields in core storage, but it becomes as much as 100,000 times larger for mechanical device accesses.

It is possible to reduce these penalties significantly by representing certain relations using physical contiguity, type identifiers, or counts. In particular, most systems (with essentially no loss of flexibility) physically concatenate all fields of a segment using a system-known ordering. IDS, TDMS, GIS, OMNIBUS, IMS, Multilist, RPG, etc. are all systems that allow and normally use this option.

A further improvement might be attained by limiting the system to tree-structured records, with the entire structure in physically contiguous storage. IDS does not have this limitation, but does attempt to achieve physical contiguity when properly instructed. The TDMS language, which requires it, maintains the segment pointer table in a separate area. In GIS, counts are used and the hierarchic format is the standard language assumption; however, special language involving procedurally accessed and maintained pointers may be used to provide certain types of chains. OMNIBUS and IMS use identifiers. In general, there is a tradeoff between physical contiguity (with its associated logical constraints), storage cost, and access time. We shall discuss work on this and other tradeoffs in the file design section.

One of the major goals of file organization is to minimize the mechanical access motion time required to obtain the qualified records. In theory, this could be accomplished by clustering records physically.

Most of the work on clustering has been done on descriptor-based files rather than on formatted numeric files, but similar techniques are applicable to both. The difficulty with clustering techniques is that they require an enormous number of comparisons, and the number increases faster than linearly with the number of documents. There also appears to be a tradeoff between clustering speed and the control the user has over cluster quality. The faster methods provide essentially no guarantee of quality, relative sizes, or numbers of clusters; therefore, processing may have to be repeated several times to achieve a satisfactory layout.

The fastest methods appear to be those of Hill (63) and Williams (147); both methods have times probably proportional to $C \times N$, where C is the number of clusters and N is the number of records. Cluster sizes are not very well controlled, and there exists the unresolved question of cluster quality in the case of the single-pass Hill method. Hill does indicate that 5,000 documents required only three minutes of computer time in one run.

It is difficult to determine whether the method proposed by Rocchio (117) and used by Salton (121) increases in time as N^2 or $C \times N$ (the latter case becomes proportional to N^2 if cluster size is kept constant as the number of records increases). Multiple passes provide means for systematically improving cluster quality. If we extrapolate results on a set of 17 clusters derived from 82 documents taking about seven minutes (53), we obtain, for a single pass, 200 clusters, and 20,000 documents (a small collection), at least 320 hours of machine time.

Borko et al. (10) present a study of a clustering algorithm suggested by Doyle. He believes that the increase in the number of iterative steps only as log N represents a breakthrough. Unfortunately, the size of each step increases as $C \times N$ so the total time actually increases as $(C \times N) \log N$.

It appears that the clustering process described by Jones & Jackson (71) would best control clustering, but it also appears to be both more complex and slower than its competitors.

It would be very useful if researchers in this field extrapolated their techniques to a realistic standard data base—for example, 20,000 documents, 20 descriptors per document, and 200 clusters.

It is also appropriate to include here a discussion of the work on file organizations for two-dimensional information (geo-coding). The proposals occupy a spectrum from the use of no grid to the use of a very fine one. Jacobsen (69) provides a search procedure for determining whether a point lies within an arbitrary polygon. The procedure requires that all entries in the file be tested. Hanel (58) mentions large-scale automatic translation of addresses to census tracts, ZIP codes, etc., but does not describe methodology. Thompson (139) uses a grid whose smallest area is a district of many square miles. Richter's (116) smallest grid square is 1,250 feet and Horwood (65) discusses grids down to ten feet on a side. Slivinski & Lum (130) present the only paper that discusses quantitative optimization of grid size. It also discusses several possible file structures for geographic retrieval.

File Design

As we have seen, there are a limited number of primitive primary- and secondary-key access methods. Initially, it might seem that the file design problem is not very challenging. However, we have also seen that there is available an almost infinite variety of combinations of primitive access methods, file and record formats, devices, etc. Each combination has its strong and weak points, and no one combination is best on all possible application parameters. Furthermore, the total time for query and maintenance is a very strong, discontinuous function of the content of the fields being processed, the physical layout, and the access methods used, etc. It is possible to conceive of examples in which the addition of one character to a thousand-character record will double the application processing time. A paper by Senko et al. (122) illustrates the complexity of the more difficult file-design problems. Even though they used an extremely condensed application description, an example simulation contained about 6,000 unique parameters.

The area of challenge is, therefore, shifting from the relatively mature field of file-accessing techniques toward the extremely complex problem of optimization of files. During the past year, there has been only a modest amount of work in file design; there should be much more in the future.

We have already mentioned the file-design aspects of the paper of Slivinski & Lum (130). In discussing the other papers, we shall progress from the detailed-device level to the general-systems level.

The paper of Abate et al. (1) presents a relatively standard queueing-theory determination of the delays encountered by a stream of simple transactions directed to a multipack disk unit. Mattson & Jacob (94) present an analytical optimization model for a storage hierarchy. Several assumptions are required to make the problem tractable. Borsei & Bos (11) present an analytical queueing model for terminal transactions and a model of the CPU storage hierarchy. This latter model appears to use time-clock simulation techniques; that is, rather than describe the total processing of all transactions in terms of analytical equations, the model calculates completion times for very primitive transactions. The transactions are placed on various queues and processed further only when the time clock has advanced to their calculated completion time. Models of this type usually run at speeds slower than real-time, but are much easier to construct than exact analytical models.

The models up to this point are pertinent only for random accesses to the files. The next series of models begins to consider patterns of access. In this area are the models of Sharma (123) and Weingarten (145). Sharma's paper on the optimization of a semibatched message-processing system is particularly excellent.

Proceeding one level further, we have the paper of Thompson et al. (138) on the optimization of a hierarchic structure for an interactive display system. Scan time of a number of entries in a level is traded off against time to move from level to level.

A paper by Lowe (90) looks at descriptor type files. The first part discusses a tradeoff involving number of entries per physical block in inverted file lists. The second part compares linked-list and inverted-file organizations. For an example using simplified organizations, linked lists appear to be two orders of magnitude slower on retrieval. This conclusion agrees with an earlier conclusion stated by Minker & Sable (97).

Leimkuhler (84) discusses optimization of the physical storage structure of a literature collection. The assumption of sequential search at each level probably restricts the range of application of this model.

Finally, at this level, Stogniy & Afanassiev (134) mention an interesting proposal for optimizing file structure on the basis of query population. The paper does not present enough details for evaluation.

FILE ORGANIZATION AND MANAGEMENT INFORMATION SYSTEMS

At a more general level is a paper on FOREM by Senko et al. (122). This model provides a complete, semianalytical structure for simulating complex queries and file organization, such as those encountered in GIS, TDMS, or DM-1. In this sense, the model meets many of the goals set for a file-design paper by Shoffner (125). The earlier, proprietary SCERT system (Herman, 62) is apparently limited to very simple access methods and application descriptions.

While there is much work to be done in the file-design area, there remains a crucial lack of quantitative application description statistics (number and kind of queries and updates, file content, etc.). Statistics on four files have been collected for use in the FOREM model, but they are clearly not representative of Management Information Systems in general. Since it will be very difficult to perform adequate evaluations of design proposals in the file-organization area until this information is available, steps should be taken to encourage wide dissemination of quantitative application descriptions. We now return to the discussion of MIS functions.

Operating Decisions

The major deterrent to the use of computers for making certain human-monitored, straightforward decisions is the cost of assembling the required data base. In the past, special translation and file-handling programs were constructed for each application that had high economic significance. In the future, decision-making programs should be supported directly by the generalized file-handling programs that maintain corporate accounts. To achieve this desirable situation, information in the files must be accessible through an easily usable, efficient user interface.

Simple Decision by Computer. Once the inventory history records of a company are being maintained by a generalized file-handling system, it is relatively simple to add a program that prints orders when stocks fall below specific thresholds. Cohen (26) and Menkhaus (96) describe implementations of this function.

Given maintenance of order, bill of material, production routing, and inventory files, it becomes much less troublesome to do the priority loading of orders on equipment (White, 146 and Lambert & Ruffels, 78).

Given files describing student course requirements, the task of automated scheduling (Johnston & Wolfenden, 70; Lions, 88; and Stewart & Clark, 132) becomes much less burdensome.

Optimum Solutions. Much of the code written for linear programming systems really deals with file handling and report generation (Orchard-Hays, 110). Running an optimization of a refinery usually requires agonizing extraction and translation of information from order and inventory files, because they are not in the linear programming system formats.

Planning Decisions. Similar situations occur in the use of simulation for planning. The papers of CONSAD Research Corporation (27), LeBoulanger & Gourio (81), Horwood (65), Stanley & Cranshaw (131), and Willis (148) all point out that the first step in a large-scale simulation is collection and maintenance of a large data base. Noble (106) indicates the same need in the case of a cost-accounting model of a large corporation.

This above list of functions is not a survey of the decision-making field; it is presented to indicate that information systems have impact far beyond that of file maintenance and report generation. Management science techniques are an integral part of MIS, and their application will become significantly less expensive when they can be interfaced directly to existing integrated data banks.

Systems

Going beyond the area of file organization, we come to consideration of the design and implementation of total Management Information Systems.

Design. The central computer, its files, and its programs are not the only considerations in the design of a Management Information System. A total system includes people; their characteristics and requirements for information are, in a sense, the reason for existence of the computer and its programs. There is a vast body of systems and procedures literature devoted to these latter considerations. In this section, we will, however, review only the more limited information sciences literature on system analysis and design.

One useful tool would be an abstract description of information flow that could be manipulated to produce design information for the systems analyst. Chapin (18) and Namian (104) both propose new descriptive terminology for this purpose.

New terminology, of itself, may have a negative effect, because it adds to the existing terminological confusion and becomes valuable only when it leads to new results. Neither terminology had led to new results at the time of the presentation of Chapin's and Namian's papers. Homer (64), on the other hand, has produced a matrix formulation of data flow that can be manipulated to uncover data redundancies. Lack of a necessary distinction between an "attribute" and its "value" may, however, limit the validity of some results.

It is also possible to simulate the behavior of the total system. Both Caras (17) and Kiviat (76) present simple illustrative simulations. Finally, a paper by Information Dynamics (68) reviews excellent earlier work on an analytical model of a national document retrieval and dissemination network.

MIS Programming. The excellence of a generalized file-handling system depends on many interrelated considerations. They include ease of programming; speed of maintenance; speed of retrieval; flexibility of data structures; ability to detect and recover from hardware, software, and input errors; ability to maintain data security; etc. There exist strong interactions between each of these considerations and, therefore, none of them (for example, data structure flexibility) can be considered predominant. A recent Booz Allen study (37) indicated that systems planning and programming accounted for 29 percent of total computer costs; equipment rental, 38 percent; and other operating costs, 33 percent. When one considers, in addition, that 50 percent of the computer time, or more, can be spent on compilation, debugging, and maintenance of programs, one can understand that programming ease is probably the most significant of the many factors in total system evaluation. Essentially, the motivation for the construction of generalized file-handling systems is the hope and belief that they will ease the problems of programming complex data management systems in the same fashion as FORTRAN eased the programming of scientific problems. Strangely enough, there is also some hope that, by providing more sophisticated data structures and data searches, they will also be more efficient in terms of application speed.

Perhaps the most striking and important concept that has appeared in this year's literature is that of "data independence" or "data structure independence." It is mentioned by Morenoff & McLean (99) and Liu (89), and its importance is clearly recognized by many investigators. The concept is concerned with making application programs as independent of changes in the structure of the data as is possible. These include changes in field size, number of fields, hierarchic record structure, search and accessing organization, physical device allocation, etc. To achieve data independence, the application program should contain as little information as possible about data structure. This knowledge should be maintained separately in a data description table. The table can be accessed by the file-handling system, when the source code is entered, to tailor the code to the existing data structure. In the spectrum of data base systems from procedural language extensions to nonprocedural languages as described by Olle (108), the nonprocedural languages tend to achieve more data independence. However, all languages fall short of the ultimate in data independence. The contents, and the compiler usage, of the data description table provide a key to improvements and should be more thoroughly studied.

It is a fact of life that computers, programmers, and operators of terminals commit errors. These errors are not very critical in the case of small, batch-processed files. In billion-character, real-time systems, however, errors create catastrophes. While error control was, in the past, an afterthought, it is now of as great a significance as the processing language or the file organization. Oppenheimer & Clancy (109) excellently summarize error recovery procedures directed at hardware failures. Although many software systems contain features for checking input, code, or data, there appears to be no equivalent software summary paper available.

Encoding, another consideration, is a relatively straightforward process that can make a considerable difference in the amount of file storage. TDMS dictates certain types of field encoding and decoding; GIS offers them as an option. The paper by Liu (89) describes several types of compaction. Much of the high percentage of compaction achieved in his example, however, is due to the use of variable-length records. This type of compaction is common in most file-handling systems.

Finally, there is the consideration of security. Most papers such as that of Fano (41) dealing with on-line programming systems discuss only password security for complete files. For many integrated data bases, nothing less than security to the field level will be adequate. Only few systems like GIS provide the facility at the present time. It will eventually be desirable to perform a full procedural check on user-requested data before they are made available. For example, a manager might be allowed to see only the salaries of persons in Department 476 earning less than seven hundred dollars per month. Security checks of this complexity must be well-designed to avoid a major impact on system performance.

Finally, we come to the state of implementation of various data base systems. Much of the recent discussion has been devoted to new extensions of procedural languages. Their interfacing philosophy is exemplified by the Integrated Data System (IDS) (Bachman & Williams, 4); a fixed-format segment is passed between the data controller and the procedural program.

IDS itself is rather data-structure-dependent because of the embedding of knowledge of segment relationships in the program. DM-1, while providing faster access through the use of secondary indexes, encounters data independence limitations, particularly when accessing more than one field in a segment.

Other extensions of procedural systems also provide real-time support for terminals. The XIMS-TCS pair (Borsei & Bos, 11) provides support only at the record level; it is the user's responsibility to format and access fields. The system used for Rio Grande message switching (Day, 31) and the California Department of Motor Vehicles System (98) all apparently provide support at this level. Other functions are performed completely by procedural programs. The well-publicized on-line programming or time-sharing systems also provide this minimal type of support to data base systems.

FILE ORGANIZATION AND MANAGEMENT INFORMATION SYSTEMS

The programs described by Allen (3), Barnett & Lightfoot (5) and Liu (89) provide assistance in handling both terminals and files. They also provide assistance in the storage and handling of variable-format records. The Allen system, OMNIBUS, has some very interesting data integrity features, but takes advantage of certain characteristics of insurance records and, therefore, is somewhat specialized. The Barnett system provides a more general record structure hierarchy. The Liu paper provides an excellent description of the various facets of data independence, data management, data security, application program format, etc., that produce an information system with high transaction rates.

The procedural language extension systems all provide significant improvements in data-base-handling capability over those of pure procedural languages, but the improvements evolve along certain programmer-oriented, constrained lines. In particular, the systems are usable only by programmers and are not very responsive to unanticipated, complex queries. For these queries and other processing, the procedural language application programs require unnecessarily complex instruction.

The nonprocedural systems start with the fundamentally better basis of the interface to the nonprogrammer-user as a primary consideration. In this case, one is more concerned with developing a coherent total system than with incremental improvements to languages biased by primary attention to nonsecure, fixed arrays and extensive arithmetic computation.

Qualitative advances in large-scale programming systems are, however, extremely difficult to achieve, and the nonprocedural systems have experienced these difficulties. In particular, systems like TDMS, GIS, and IMRADS, which have been discussed for over two years, were not released for extensive operational use during 1968.

As aids to evaluating nonprocedural information systems, three papers (Informatics, Inc., 34; Sundeen, 135; and Ziehe, 150) provide useful lists of qualitative parameters. However, before quantitative comparisons can be made, we must have better descriptions of the typical application load for information systems.

At the first level of system capability lie the Report Program Generators (RPG's) (Leslie, 85; Friedberg, 47; and Ziegler, 149). These systems tend to be nonprocedural programs for handling tape representations of punched-card files. As the papers note, even simple RPG's provide a considerable saving in programmer time over procedural languages.

At the same level are a set of papers on less conventional systems. In particular, the papers of Buckerfield (16), Erskine (39), and Warren (144) describe decision-table, questionnaire, and model-concept languages for file handling. These systems can be excellent for simple problems, but it is extremely difficult to code complex problems in their rigid languages.

At the next level are the systems described by Gould & Mosior (52) and Sinowitz (128) that provide flexible response, but only for one specific application file. It is difficult to determine the effort required to apply their desirable capabilities to other files.

At the third level are the INFOL and MARK IV systems (Olle, 107; Postley, 112), which handle hierarchic structure records. Both systems are oriented to sequential processing and have seen operational use.

It is difficult to classify and evaluate the work of McIntosh & Griffel (92). Their paper contains much in the way of unexplained figures and unique terminology. Their system, however, apparently provides for very flexible data structures. DATA FILE TWO (Jones, 72) also provides extremely flexible data structures. The paper contains a listing of a nonprocedural query, but gives little indication of the properties of the language. A similar problem exists in the report on INSCAN, a generalized language compiler for DM-1 (Resnick & Sable, 115).

Another class of systems is described in the documentation on GIS (67) and the most recent in a series of papers on TDMS (Bleier & Vorhaus, 9). Both systems have described the use of secondary indexes to access the data. TDMS has the most attractive nonprocedural language, but its complex pointer structure will probably be time-consuming to create and maintain.

At the present time, none of the nonprocedural languages provides a very satisfactory interface to programs for algorithm processing. It is expected, however, that progress will be made in this area.

CONCLUSION

The field of Management Information Systems is of major economic importance to computer users, computer programmers, and computer manufacturers. For this reason, the study of these systems (whose primary characteristic is the integration of large data files) is entering a period of particular interest. In the case of file accessing, the focus of work should shift away from the relatively mature field of file-accessing techniques to the field of file design. To make progress, however, it will be necessary to obtain considerably more information on how files are used.

In the area of languages, much work is being done on both procedural and nonprocedural approaches. Of these, nonprocedural programming appears to be fundamentally the best way of minimizing the total cost of programming, operating, and using a Management Information System.

REFERENCES

(1) ABATE, J.; DUBNER, H.; WEINBERG, S. B. Queueing analysis of the IBM 2314 disk storage facility. Journal of the Association for Computing Machinery, 15:4 (October 1968) 577–589.
(2) ADI Proceedings, Vol. 4, 1967 Annual Meeting. Special Supplement. Levels of interaction between man and information. American Documentation, 19:3 (July 1968) 263–310.
(3) ALLEN, R. P. OMNIBUS: A large data base management system. In: American Federation of Information Processing Societies. AFIPS conference proceedings, vol. 33, part 1; 1968 Fall Joint Computer Conference, San Francisco, 9–11 December 1968. Thompson, Washington, D.C., 1968, p. 157–169.
(4) BACHMAN, C. W.; WILLIAMS, S. B. A general purpose programming system for random access memories. In: American Federation of Information Processing Societies. AFIPS conference proceedings, vol. 26, part 1; 1964 Fall Joint Computer Conference, San Francisco, 27–29 October 1964. Spartan, Baltimore, 1964, p. 411–422.
(5) BARNETT, A. J.; LIGHTFOOT, J. A. A S/360 on-line production order location and reporting system using the Information Management System (IMS). In: Congress of the International Federation for Information Processing (IFIP), 4th, Edinburgh, 5–10 August 1968. Proceedings. North-Holland Publishing Co., Amsterdam, 1968, p. I104–I108.
(6) BARUCH, J. J. The generalized medical information facility. In: Congress of the International Federation for Information Processing (IFIP), 4th, Edinburgh, 5–10 August 1968. Proceedings. North-Holland Publishing Co., Amsterdam, 1968, p. 19–23.
(7) BIRD, R.; HEDLEY, W. W. An integrated production management system. In: Congress of the International Federation for Information Processing (IFIP), 4th, Edinburgh, 5–10 August 1968. Proceedings. North-Holland Publishing Co., Amsterdam, 1968, p. F56–F62.
(8) BLACK, H.; SHAW, E. Detroit's data banks. Datamation, 13:3 (March 1967) 25–27.
(9) BLEIER, R. E.; VORHAUS, A. H. File organization in the SDC Time-Shared Data Management System (TDMS). In: Congress of the International Federation for Information Processing (IFIP), 4th, Edinburgh, 5–10 August 1968. Proceedings. North-Holland Publishing Co., Amsterdam, 1968, p. F92–F97.
(10) BORKO, H.; BLANKENSHIP, D. A.; BURKET, R. C. On-line information retrieval using associative indexing. Final report. System Development Corp., Santa Monica, Calif., May 1968, 133 p. (SDC-TM-L-3851) (RADC-TR-68-100) (AD-670 195)
(11) BORSEI, A. A.; BOS, A. C. Real-time information management design criteria for system efficiency. In: Congress of the International Federation for Information Processing (IFIP), 4th, Edinburgh, 5–10 August 1968. Proceedings. North-Holland Publishing Co., Amsterdam, 1968, p. 40–58.
(12) BOWMAN, S.; LICKHALTER, R. A. Graphical data management in time-shared environment. In: American Federation of Information Processing Societies. AFIPS conference proceedings, vol. 32; 1968 Spring Joint Computer Conference, Atlantic City, 30 April–2 May 1968. Thompson, Washington, D.C., 1968, p. 353–362.
(13) BREWER, S. Data base or data maze? An exploration of entry points. In: National Conference of the Association for Computing Machinery, 23rd, Las Vegas, Nev., 27–29 August 1968. Proceedings. Brandon/Systems Press, Princeton, N.J., 1968, p. 623–630.
(14) BROWN, R. R.; NORDYKE, P., JR. ICS: An Information Control System. In: FID/IFIP Joint Conference, Rome, Italy, 14–17 June 1967. Proceedings [title]: Mechanized information storage, retrieval and dissemination. Edited by Kjell Samuelson. North-Holland Publishing Co., Amsterdam, 1968, p. 312–325.
(15) BRYANT, J. H.; SEMPLE, P., JR. GIS and file management. In: National Conference of the Association for Computing Machinery, 21st, Los Angeles, 30 August–1 September 1966. Proceedings. Thompson, Washington, D.C., 1966, p. 97–107.

(16) BUCKERFIELD, P. S. T. A technique for the construction and use of a generalized information table. In: Congress of the International Federation for Information Processing (IFIP), 4th, Edinburgh, 5–10 August 1968. Proceedings. North-Holland Publishing Co., Amsterdam, 1968, p. B61–B68.
(17) CARAS, G. J. Computer simulation of a small information system. American Documentation, 19:2 (April 1968) 120–122.
(18) CHAPIN, N. A deeper look at data. In: National Conference of the Association for Computing Machinery, 23rd, Las Vegas, Nev., 27–29 August 1968. Proceedings. Brandon/Systems Press, Princeton, N.J., 1968, p. 631–638.
(19) CHARTRAND, R. L. Computer-oriented information for the U.S. Congress. Law and Computer Technology, 1:2 (February 1968) 2–7.
(20) CHARTRAND, R. L. Congress seeks a systems approach. Datamation, 14:5 (May 1968) 46–49.
(21) CHEEK, R. C. TOPS: the Westinghouse teletype order processing and inventory control system. In: Business Equipment Manufacturers Association. The computer: tool for management. Business Press, Elmhurst, Ill., 1968, p. 78–90.
(22) CHILDS, D. L. Feasibility of a set-theoretical data structure—a general structure based on a reconstituted definition of relation. In: Congress of the International Federation for Information Processing (IFIP), 4th, Edinburgh, 5–10 August 1968. Proceedings. North-Holland Publishing Co., Amsterdam, 1968, p. 162–172.
(23) CHOW, D. K. A geometric approach to coding theory with application to information retrieval. University of Illinois, Coordinated Science Laboratory, Urbana, October 1967, 89 p. (Report no. R-368) (AD-663 806)
(24) CLIMENSON, W. D. File organization and search techniques. In: Annual review of information science and technology, vol. 1. Carlos A. Cuadra, ed. Wiley, Interscience, New York, 1966, p. 107–135.
(25) CLOOT, P. L.; SUTTON-SMITH, C. N. Management use of displays in critical path analysis. In: Congress of the International Federation for Information Processing (IFIP), 4th, Edinburgh, 5–10 August 1968. Proceedings. North-Holland Publishing Co., Amsterdam, 1968, p. F27–F31.
(26) COHEN, H. M. A MIS that scores as a decision-maker. Business Automation, 14:11 (November 1967) 44–48.
(27) CONSAD RESEARCH CORPORATION. An information system development program. Pittsburgh, Pa., 15 January 1968, 78 p. (PB-177 809) Prepared in cooperation with Regional Planning Council, Baltimore, and Department of Housing and Urban Development, Washington, D.C.
(28) CRONKHITE, L. W., JR. Patient location control as a first step toward a total information system. Hospitals, 41 (1 May 1967) 107–112.
(29) DAVIS, L. S.; COLLEN, M. F.; RUBIN, L.; VAN BRUNT, E. E. Computer-stored medical record. Computers and Biomedical Research, 1:5 (May 1968) 452–469.
(30) DAVIS, R. J. Information transfer in a universal health information bank by use of the social security number. In: American Society for Information Science Annual Meeting, Columbus, Ohio, 20–24 October 1968. Proceedings, vol. 5. Greenwood Publishing Corp., New York, 1968, p. 249–253.
(31) DAY, W. J. Rio Grande Message Switching/Transportation System. In: National Conference of the Association for Computing Machinery, 23rd, Las Vegas, Nev., 27–29 August 1968. Proceedings. Brandon/Systems Press, Princeton, N.J., 1968, p. 307–319.
(32) DEFENSE INTELLIGENCE AGENCY. IDHS 1410 formatted file system: File maintenance and file generation manual. Revised ed. Washington, D.C., 1 August 1966, 256 p. (DIAM-65-9-1) (AD-637 017)
(33) DEFENSE INTELLIGENCE AGENCY. IDHS 1410 formatted file system: Retrieval and output manual. Washington, D.C., 1 August 1966, 229 p. (DIAM-65-9-2) (AD-637 018)
(34) DOWKONT, A. J. A methodology for comparison of generalized data management systems. Informatics, Inc., Sherman Oaks, Calif., March 1967. (AD-811 682L)

(35) DUEKER, K. J.   A look at state and local information systems efforts. In: National Conference of the Association for Computing Machinery, 23rd, Las Vegas, Nev., 27–29 August 1968. Proceedings. Brandon/Systems Press, Princeton, N.J., 1968, p. 133–142.
(36) DUNN, R. G.; HOWELL, J. T.   An admissions scheduling program. Henry Ford Hospital Medical Bulletin, 15 (Winter 1967) 319–324.
(37) EDP's new management man.   Business Automation, 15:2 (February 1968) 44–45.
(38) ERAT, K.; JESSIMAN, A. G.; WALKER, J. E. C.   Application of a time-shared computer to the appointment system of a hospital outpatient department. In: Congress of the International Federation for Information Processing (IFIP), 4th, Edinburgh, 5–10 August 1968. Proceedings. North-Holland Publishing Co., Amsterdam, 1968, p. I141–I145.
(39) ERSKINE, R.   Exception programming—the model concept. In: Congress of the International Federation for Information Processing (IFIP), 4th, Edinburgh, 5–10 August 1968. Proceedings. North-Holland Publishing Co., Amsterdam, 1968, p. B50–B54.
(40) EVANS, D.   Data structure programming system. In: Congress of the International Federation for Information Processing (IFIP), 4th, Edinburgh, 5–10 August 1968. Proceedings. North-Holland Publishing Co., Amsterdam, 1968, p. C67–C72.
(41) FANO, R. M.   The computer utility and the community. In: Institute of Electrical and Electronics Engineers. 1967 IEEE international convention record. New York, 1967, Part 12, p. 30–37.
(42) FBI opens computer center: states, cities to tie in. Datamation, 13:5   (May 1967) 82–83.
(43) FINKLER, R.   Some information retrieval problems in the criminal justice system. In: National Colloquium on Information Retrieval, 4th, Philadelphia, 3–4 May 1967. Proceedings, edited by Albert B. Tonik. International Information Incorporated, Philadelphia, 1967, p. 213–223.
(44) FONTANA, J. M.; SHEPARD, R. B.; HILL, S. R., JR.   Computer applications at the University of Alabama Medical Center. Alabama Journal of Medical Sciences, 5 (January 1968) 98–106.
(45) FORSYTHE, G. E.   Computer science and education. In: Congress of the International Federation for Information Processing (IFIP), 4th, Edinburgh, 5–10 August 1968. Proceedings. North-Holland Publishing Co., Amsterdam, 1968, p. 92–106.
(46) FREED, R. N.   A legal structure for a national medical data center. In: American Federation of Information Processing Societies. AFIPS conference proceedings, vol. 33, part 1; 1968 Fall Joint Computer Conference, San Francisco, 9–11 December 1968. Thompson, Washington, D.C., 1968, p. 387–394.
(47) FRIEDBERG, L. M.   RPG: the coming of age. Datamation, 13:6 (June 1967) 29–31.
(48) GASS, S. I.   On the division of police districts into patrol beats. In: National Conference of the Association for Computing Machinery, 23rd, Las Vegas, Nev., 27–29 August 1968. Proceedings. Brandon/Systems Press, Princeton, N.J., 1968, p. 459–473.
(49) GELBLAT, M.   Computerized storage and retrieval of cardiac catheterization and pathology data. Moore School of Electrical Engineering, University of Pennsylvania, Philadelphia, June 1968, 79 p. (Report no. 68–38) (AD-671 912)
(50) GERDEL, J. K.   Integrated data system for project management. Office, 67 (March 1968) 59–62.
(51) GHOSH, S. P.   On the problem of query-oriented filing schemes using discrete mathematics. In: Congress of the International Federation for Information Processing (IFIP), 4th, Edinburgh, 5–10 August 1968. Proceedings. North-Holland Publishing Co., Amsterdam, 1968, p. F74–F79.
(52) GOULD, E. P.; MOSIOR, J. W.   TELPORT: time-shared information systems. Bell Laboratories Record, 46:6 (June 1968) 197–202.
(53) GRAUER, ROBERT T.; MESSIER, MICHEL.   An evaluation of Rocchio's clustering algorithm. In: Cornell University. Department of Computer Science. Information storage and retrieval. Report no. ISR-12 to NSF. Gerard Salton, Director. Ithaca,

N.Y., June 1967, sec.-6 (39 p.)
(54) GREENVILLE-PICKENS REGIONAL PLANNING BOARD. Data inventory, Greenville-Pickens region. Greenville, S.C., February 1968, 123 p. (PB-178 038). Prepared in cooperation with the Department of Housing and Urban Development, Washington, D.C.
(55) GROSSMAN, A. The California educational information system. Datamation, 13:3 (March 1967) 32–37.
(56) HALL, A. D., JR.; ACTON, FORMAN S. Scheduling university course exams by computer. Communications of the ACM, 10 (April 1967) 235–238.
(57) HALL, P.; MELLNER, C.; DANIELSON, T. J-5: A data processing system for medical information. Methods of Information in Medicine, 6 (January 1967) 1–6.
(58) HANEL, R. S. Handling small area data with computers. Computers and Automation, 17 (December 1968) 16–19.
(59) HEAD, R. B. Management information systems: a critical appraisal. Datamation, 13:5 (May 1967) 22–27.
(60) HEANY, DONALD F. Development of information systems: what management needs to know. Ronald Press, New York, 1968, 421 p.
(61) HEATH, F. R. Will today's concepts of managing become obsolete? In: Business Equipment Manufacturers Association. The computer: tool for management. Business Press, Elmhurst, Ill., 1968, p. 1–10.
(62) HERMAN, D. J. SCERT: A computer evaluation tool. Datamation, 13:2 (February 1967) 26–28.
(63) HILL, D. R. A vector clustering technique. In: FID/IFIP Joint Conference, Rome, Italy, 14–17 June 1967. Proceedings [title]: Mechanized information storage, retrieval and dissemination. Edited by Kjell Samuelson. North-Holland Publishing Co., Amsterdam, 1968, p. 225–234.
(64) HOMER, E. D. A mathematical model of the flow of data in a management information system. Vol. 1. Doctoral thesis. New York University, Dept. of Industrial Engineering and Operations Research, New York, May 1968, 160 p. (AFOSR-68-0095-Vol-1) (AD-671 949)
(65) HORWOOD, E. M. Computer applications to urban planning and analysis. In: Congress of the International Federation for Information Processing (IFIP), 4th, Edinburgh, 5–10 August 1968. Proceedings. North-Holland Publishing Co., Amsterdam, 1968, p. 118–130.
(66) HSIAO, D. K-M. A file system for a problem solving facility. Doctoral thesis. Moore School of Electrical Engineering, University of Pennsylvania, Philadelphia, 1968, 180 p. (Report no. 68-33) (AD-671 826)
(67) IBM CORPORATION. GIS (Generalized Information System) applications description manual. White Plains, N.Y., 1965, 42 p. (H20-0574)
(68) INFORMATION DYNAMICS CORPORATION. Parameter requirements for description of alternative LINC systems. Final report. Bethesda, Md., 20 March 1968, 54 p. (PB-178 218)
(69) JACOBSEN, J. D. Interactive graphics in data processing geometric relationships for retrieval of geographic information. IBM Systems Journal, nos. 3 & 4 (1968) 331–341.
(70) JOHNSTON, H. C.; WOLFENDEN, K. Computer-aided construction of school timetables. In: Congress of the International Federation for Information Processing (IFIP), 4th, Edinburgh, 5–10 August 1968. Proceedings. North-Holland Publishing Co., Amsterdam, 1968, p. G73–G80.
(71) JONES, K. S.; JACKSON, D. Some experiments in the use of automatically obtained term clusters for retrieval. In: FID/IFIP Joint Conference, Rome, Italy, 14–17 June 1967. Proceedings [title]: Mechanized information storage, retrieval and dissemination. Edited by Kjell Samuelson. North-Holland Publishing Co., Amsterdam, 1968, p. 203–212.
(72) JONES, R. S. Data File Two—a storage and retrieval system. In: American Federation of Information Processing Societies. AFIPS conference proceedings, vol. 32; 1968 Spring Joint Computer Conference, Atlantic City, 30 April–2 May 1968. Thompson,

FILE ORGANIZATION AND MANAGEMENT INFORMATION SYSTEMS 139

Washington, D.C., 1968, p. 171–181.
(73) KAIMAN, R. A.   Entry to the file, randomize on index. Part II. Data Processing Magazine, 10:12   (December 1968) 24–27.
(74) KAMMAN, A. B.; SAXTON, D. R.   Anatomy of a real-time trial — Bell Telephone's centralized records business office. In: American Federation of Information Processing Societies. AFIPS conference proceedings, vol. 32; 1968 Spring Joint Computer Conference, Atlantic City, 30 April–2 May 1968. Thompson, Washington, D.C., 1968, p. 415–422.
(75) KISYLIA, A. P.   An association processor for information retrieval. University of Illinois, Coordinated Science Laboratory, Urbana, August 1968, 56 p. (Report no. R-390) (AD-675 310)
(76) KIVIAT, P. J.   Digital computer simulation: modeling concepts. RAND Corp., Santa Monica, Calif., August 1967, 62 p. (RM-5378-PR) (AD-658 429)
(77) KRONENBERG, R. A.   Weyerhaeuser's management information system. Datamation, 13:5   (May 1967) 28–30.
(78) LAMBERT, W. M.; RUFFELS, W. R.   The ISCOR real-time industrial data processing system. In: American Federation of Information Processing Societies. AFIPS conference proceedings, vol. 32; 1968 Spring Joint Computer Conference, Atlantic City, 30 April–2 May 1968. Thompson, Washington, D.C., 1968, p. 193–196.
(79) LAMSON, B. G.; RUSSELL, W. S.; GLINSKI, B. C.; MARTZ, P.   A hospitalwide system for handling medical data. Hospitals, 41   (1 May 1967) 67–68.
(80) LAWRENCE, D.   Digital plotting with punched card input. Datamation, 13:7   (July 1967) 27–30.
(81) Le BOULANGER, H.; GOURIO, H.   Operations research: slave or master of the computer. In: Congress of the International Federation for Information Processing (IFIP), 4th, Edinburgh, 5–10 August 1968. Proceedings. North-Holland Publishing Co., Amsterdam, 1968, p. 59–65.
(82) LEDDON, C. D.   Management science: a simulation example. Systems & Procedures Journal, 19:2   (March–April 1968) 23–27.
(83) LEIGHTON, E.; HEADLY, P.   Computer analysis of length of stay. Hospital Progress, 49   (April 1968) 67–70.
(84) LEIMKUHLER, F. F.   A literature search and file organization model. American Documentation, 19:2   (April 1968) 131–136.
(85) LESLIE, H.   The report program generator. Datamation, 13:6   (June 1967) 26–28.
(86) LEVY, P. P.; CAMMARN, M. R.   Information systems applications in medicine. In: Annual review of information science and technology, vol. 3. Carlos A. Cuadra, ed. Encyclopaedia Britannica, Chicago, 1968, p. 397–428.
(87) LI, D. H.   Accounting/computers/management information systems. McGraw-Hill, New York, 1968, 416 p.
(88) LIONS, J.   A generalization of a method for the construction of class/teacher timetables. In: Congress of the International Federation for Information Processing (IFIP), 4th, Edinburgh, 5–10 August 1968. Proceedings. North-Holland Publishing Co., Amsterdam, 1968, p. G68–G72.
(89) LIU, H.   A file management system for a large corporate information system data bank. In: American Federation of Information Processing Societies. AFIPS conference proceedings, vol. 33, part 1; 1968 Fall Joint Computer Conference, San Francisco, 9–11 December 1968. Thompson, Washington, D.C., 1968, p. 145–156.
(90) LOWE, T. C.   The influence of data base characteristics and usage on direct access file organization. Journal of the Association for Computing Machinery, 15:4   (October 1968) 535–548.
(91) McGEE, W. C.   File structures for generalized data management. In: Congress of the International Federation for Information Processing (IFIP), 4th, Edinburgh, 5–10 August 1968. Proceedings. North-Holland Publishing Co., Amsterdam, 1968, F68–F73.
(92) McINTOSH, S.; GRIFFEL, D.   Admins from Mark III to Mark V. In: Congress of the International Federation for Information Processing (IFIP), 4th, Edinburgh, 5–10 August 1968. Proceedings. North-Holland Publishing Co., Amsterdam, 1968,

p. 1109-1114.
(93) McLAURIN, M. J.; TRAISTER, W. A. Martin Orlando reporting environment. In: American Federation of Information Processing Societies. AFIPS conference proceedings, vol. 32; 1968 Spring Joint Computer Conference, Atlantic City, 30 April-2 May 1968. Thompson, Washington, D.C., 1968, p. 197-208.
(94) MATTSON, R. L.; JACOB, J. P. Optimization studies for computer systems with virtual memory. In: Congress of the International Federation for Information Processing (IFIP), 4th, Edinburgh, 5-10 August 1968. Proceedings. North-Holland Publishing Co., Amsterdam, 1968, p. 189-193.
(95) MAURER, W. D. An improved hash code for scatter storage. Communications of the ACM, 11:1 (January 1968) 35-38.
(96) MENKHAUS, E. J. Data bank grows in the valley. Business Automation, 15:3 (March 1968) 46-49, 56.
(97) MINKER, J.; SABLE, J. File organization and data management. In: Annual review of information science and technology, vol. 2. Carlos A. Cuadra, ed. Wiley, Interscience, New York, 1967, p. 123-160.
(98) MONTIJO, R. E., JR. California DMV goes on-line. Datamation, 13:5 (May 1967) 31-36.
(99) MORENOFF, E.; McLEAN, J. B. On the design of a general purpose data management system. In: National Colloquium on Information Retrieval, 4th, Philadelphia, 3-4 May 1967. Proceedings, edited by Albert B. Tonik. International Information Incorporated, Philadelphia, 1967, p. 19-29.
(100) MORRIS, R. Scatter storage techniques. Communications of the ACM, 11:1 (January 1968) 38-44.
(101) MORRISON, D. R.   PATRICIA: Practical algorithm to retrieve information coded in alphanumeric. Journal of the Association for Computing Machinery, 15:4 (October 1968) 514-534.
(102) MORTON, M. S. S.; STEPHENS, J. A. The impact of interactive visual display systems on the management planning process. In: Congress of the International Federation for Information Processing (IFIP), 4th, Edinburgh, 5-10 August 1968. Proceedings. North-Holland Publishing Co., Amsterdam, 1968, p. 198-1103.
(103) NAKANISHI, T.; SATO, A.; ITO, Y. Development of a system simulator for railway marshalling yard. In: Congress of the International Federation for Information Processing (IFIP), 4th, Edinburgh, 5-10 August 1968. Proceedings. North-Holland Publishing Co., Amsterdam, 1968, p. F11-F15.
(104) NAMIAN, P. Algebra of management information. In: Congress of the International Federation for Information Processing (IFIP), 4th, Edinburgh, 5-10 August 1968. Proceedings. North-Holland Publishing Co., Amsterdam, 1968, p. F63-F67.
(105) NINKE, W. H. The growth of computer graphics at Bell Laboratories. Bell Laboratories Record, 46 (June 1968) 180-188.
(106) NOBLE, A. S. Input-output cost models and their uses for financial planning and control. In: Congress of the International Federation for Information Processing (IFIP), 4th, Edinburgh, 5-10 August 1968. Proceedings. North-Holland Publishing Co., Amsterdam, 1968, p. F32-F37.
(107) OLLE, T. W. Generalized systems for storing structured variable length data and retrieving information. In: FID/IFIP Joint Conference, Rome, Italy, 14-17 June 1967. Proceedings [title]: Mechanized information storage, retrieval and dissemination. Edited by Kjell Samuelson. North-Holland Publishing Co., Amsterdam, 1968, p. 192-202.
(108) OLLE, T. W. A non-procedural language for retrieving information from data bases. In: Congress of the International Federation for Information Processing (IFIP), 4th, Edinburgh, 5-10 August 1968. Proceedings. North-Holland Publishing Co., Amsterdam, 1968, p. C60-C66.
(109) OPPENHEIMER, G.; CLANCY, K. P. Considerations for software protection and recovery from hardware failures in a multiaccess, multiprogramming, single processor system. In: American Federation of Information Processing Societies. AFIPS conference proceedings, vol. 33, part 1; 1968 Fall Joint Computer Conference, San Francisco,

FILE ORGANIZATION AND MANAGEMENT INFORMATION SYSTEMS 141

9–11 December 1968. Thompson, Washington, D.C., 1968, p. 29–37.
(110) ORCHARD-HAYS, W.   Structure of mathematical programming systems. In: National Conference of the Association for Computing Machinery, 23rd, Las Vegas, Nev., 27–29 August 1968. Proceedings. Brandon/Systems Press, Princeton, N.J., 1968, p. 439–458.
(111) POLISKI, I. M.   EDP: first aid for hospitals. Business Automation, 15:7 (July 1968) 34–39.
(112) POSTLEY, J. A.   The MARK IV system. Datamation, 14:1 (January 1968) 28–30.
(113) POWELL, H. W.   Developing a data base for production, inventory, and marketing. In: Business Equipment Manufacturers Association. The computer: tool for management. Business Press, Elmhurst, Ill., 1968, p. 48–56.
(114) PYLE, J. L.   Digital plotting in business. Datamation, 13:7 (July 1967) 31–33.
(115) RESNICK, M.; SABLE, J.   INSCAN: A syntax-directed language processor. In: National Conference of the Association for Computing Machinery, 23rd, Las Vegas, Nev., 27–29 August 1968. Proceedings. Brandon/Systems Press, Princeton, N.J., 1968, p. 423–432.
(116) RICHTER, A. C.   GEO-CODING: an application in a local governmental information system. In: National Conference of the Association for Computing Machinery, 23rd, Las Vegas, Nev., 27–29 August 1968. Proceedings. Brandon/Systems Press, Princeton, N.J., 1968, p. 117–131.
(117) ROCCHIO, J. J., JR.   Document retrieval systems—optimization and evaluation. Doctoral thesis. Harvard University, Cambridge, Mass., March 1966.
(118) ROSEN, D.   Medical care information system of the Veterans' Administration. Public Health Reports, 83 (May 1968) 363–371.
(119) ROSENBAUM, C. P.   Computer simplifies record-keeping and review in psychiatric clinic. Hospitals, 42 (16 April 1968) 70–73.
(120) ROVNER, P. D.   The leap language and data structure. In: Congress of the International Federation for Information Processing (IFIP), 4th, Edinburgh, 5–10 August 1968. Proceedings. North-Holland Publishing Co., Amsterdam, 1968, p. C73–C77.
(121) SALTON, GERARD.   Automatic information organization and retrieval. McGraw-Hill, New York, 1968, 480 p.
(122) SENKO, M. E.; LUM, V. Y.; OWENS, P. J.   A File Organization Evaluation Model (FOREM). In: Congress of the International Federation for Information Processing (IFIP), 4th, Edinburgh, 5–10 August 1968. Proceedings. North-Holland Publishing Co., Amsterdam, 1968, p. C19–C23.
(123) SHARMA, R. L.   Analysis of a scheme for information organization and retrieval from a disc file. In: Congress of the International Federation for Information Processing (IFIP), 4th, Edinburgh, 5–10 August 1968. Proceedings. North-Holland Publishing Co., Amsterdam, 1968, p. D126–D130.
(124) SHELDON, R. C.; BACKER, S.   Development of a time-shared storage and retrieval system. Master's thesis. MIT, Dept. of Mechanical Engineering, Cambridge, Mass., 13 January 1967, 158 p. (Design of information storage and retrieval system, Part 3) (PB-176 551)
(125) SHOFFNER, R. M.   The organization, maintenance and search of machine files. In: Annual review of information science and technology, vol. 3. Carlos A. Cuadra, ed. Encyclopaedia Britannica, Chicago, 1968, p. 137–167.
(126) SIEGEL, S. J.   Developing an information system for a hospital. Public Health Reports, 83 (May 1968) 359–362.
(127) SILBERMAN, H. F.; FILEP, R. T.   Information systems applications in education. In: Annual review of information science and technology, vol. 3. Carlos A. Cuadra, ed. Encyclopaedia Britannica, Chicago, 1968, p. 357–395.
(128) SINOWITZ, N. R.   DATAPLUS—a language for real time information retrieval from hierarchical data bases. In: American Federation of Information Processing Societies. AFIPS conference proceedings, vol. 32; 1968 Spring Joint Computer Conference, Atlantic City, 30 April–2 May 1968. Thompson, Washington, D.C., 1968, p. 395–401.
(129) SLACK, W.; VAN CURA, L. J.   Patient reaction to computer-based medical inter-

viewing. Computers and Biomedical Research, 1:5 (May 1968) 527–531.
(130) SLIVINSKI, T. A.; LUM, V. Y. File organization for aerial photography. In: National Conference of the Association for Computing Machinery, 23rd, Las Vegas, Nev., 27–29 August 1968. Proceedings. Brandon/Systems Press, Princeton, N.J., 1968, p. 639–648.
(131) STANLEY, W. J.; CRANSHAW, D. D. Use of a computer-based total management information system to support an air resource management program. Journal of the Air Pollution Control Association, 18 (March 1968) 158–159.
(132) STEWART, J.; CLARK, R. L. University of Maryland student scheduling algorithm. In: National Conference of the Association for Computing Machinery, 23rd, Las Vegas, Nev., 27–29 August 1968. Proceedings. Brandon/Systems Press, Princeton, N.J., 1968, p. 555–562.
(133) STINNETT, B. R. Practical application of E.D.P. in the court system. Law and Computer Technology, 1:7 (July 1968) 2–5.
(134) STOGNIY, A. A.; AFANASSIEV, V. N. Some design problems for automatic fact information retrieval and storage systems. In: FID/IFIP Joint Conference, Rome, Italy, 14–17 June 1967. Proceedings [title]: Mechanized information storage, retrieval and dissemination. Edited by Kjell Samuelson. North-Holland Publishing Co., Amsterdam, 1968, p. 289–299.
(135) SUNDEEN, D. H. General purpose software. Datamation, 14:1 (January 1968) 22–27.
(136) TAYLOR, J. G.; NAVARRO, J. A. Simulation of a court system for the processing of criminal cases. Simulation, 10:5 (May 1968) 235–240.
(137) THAYER, G. N. BIS in the Bell System. Bell Laboratories Record, 46:11 (December 1968) 354–361.
(138) THOMPSON, D. A.; BENNINGSON, L. A.; WHITMAN, D. A. A proposed structure for displayed information to minimize search time through a data base. American Documentation, 19:1 (January 1968) 80–84.
(139) THOMPSON, K. C. The utilization of direct access facilities for electricity board customer accounting purposes. In: Congress of the International Federation for Information Processing (IFIP), 4th, Edinburgh, 5–10 August 1968. Proceedings. North-Holland Publishing Co., Amsterdam, 1968, p. F16–F19.
(140) TONDOW, M. Computers in the schools: Palo Alto. Datamation, 14:6 (June 1968) 57–62.
(141) UBER, G. T.; WILLIAMS, P. E.; HISEY, B. L. The organization and formatting of hierarchical displays for the on-line input of data. In: American Federation of Information Processing Societies. AFIPS conference proceedings, vol. 33, part 1; 1968 Fall Joint Computer Conference, San Francisco, 9–11 December 1968. Thompson, Washington, D.C., 1968, p. 219–226.
(142) VRANSKY, V. K.; PASCALEV, T. G.; BAYKUSHEV, B. P.; BOROV, G. I. A country-wide system for automatic health data processing. Methods of Information in Medicine [Methodik der Information in der Medizin], 7:2 (April 1968) 92–96.
(143) WARHEIT, I. A. File organization for information retrieval. In: FID/IFIP Joint Conference, Rome, Italy, 14–17 June 1967. Proceedings [title]: Mechanized information storage, retrieval and dissemination. Edited by Kjell Samuelson. North-Holland Publishing Co., Amsterdam, 1968, p. 259–268.
(144) WARREN, M. E. E. Program generation by questionnaire. In: Congress of the International Federation for Information Processing (IFIP), 4th, Edinburgh, 5–10 August 1968. Proceedings. North-Holland Publishing Co., Amsterdam, 1968, p. B55–B60.
(145) WEINGARTEN, A. The analytical design of real-time systems. In: Congress of the International Federation for Information Processing (IFIP), 4th, Edinburgh, 5–10 August 1968. Proceedings. North-Holland Publishing Co., Amsterdam, 1968, p. D131–D137.
(146) WHITE, C. Production control in the U.K. Datamation, 13:12 (December 1967) 32–34.
(147) WILLIAMS, J. H., JR. Computer classification of documents. In: FID/IFIP Joint

Conference, Rome, Italy, 14–17 June 1967. Proceedings [title]: Mechanized information storage, retrieval and dissemination. Edited by Kjell Samuelson. North-Holland Publishing Co., Amsterdam, 1968, p. 235–246.
(148) WILLIS, B. H.   The software challenge: urban planning and computer technology. Software Age, 1:2   (November 1967) 18–24.
(149) ZIEGLER, J. R.   Program generators: How good are they? Computers and Automation, 17:7   (July 1968) 18–20.
(150) ZIEHE, T. W.   Data Management: a comparison of system features. TRACOR, Inc., Austin, Tex., October 1967, 43 p. (AD-661 861)

5

Automated Language Processing[1]

CHRISTINE A. MONTGOMERY
The Bunker-Ramo Corporation

INTRODUCTION

This review discusses recent developments in automated language processing as well as developments in linguistic theory which have some relevance to automated language processing. The rather substantial treatment of linguistic theory is included because of the significance of current research on (*1*) the theory of grammar (see below under "Syntax and Semantics") and on (*2*) the role of grammar in speech production and recognition (see below under "Psycholinguistics").

In the first case, important convergences of opinion among linguists, logicians, and information scientists concerning the nature of semantic representation may have far-reaching effects in the area of automated language processing. In the second, recent experiments suggest the significance of heuristics in the recognition process, thus providing new insights for the construction of recognition devices in automated language processing applications.

The theoretical discussion presupposes some knowledge of and interest in linguistics. Readers who are interested in the applicability of these notions rather than in their substance may prefer to omit the majority of the section on linguistic theory and begin reading with the subsection entitled "Linguistic Theory: Concluding Remarks."

---

[1] I am indebted to J. L. Kuhns for reviewing an earlier version of this chapter.

RECENT DEVELOPMENTS IN LINGUISTIC THEORY

Syntax and Semantics

Two of the major linguistic publications in 1968 deal with phonology rather than syntax or semantics. *The Sound Pattern of English* by Chomsky & Halle (21) presents a formal description of English phonology, while Postal's *Aspects of Phonological Theory* (86) is essentially a discussion aimed at disconfirming traditional or "autonomous" phonology rather than an explication of phonological theory. His arguments include specific rebuttals of Lamb's stratificational approach[2] and of Hockett's position on sound change.

Meanwhile, Hockett (55) has restated his position, and has specifically challenged Chomsky's notion of the set of sentences of a natural language as well defined. This observation is also made in Harris's *Mathematical Structures of Language* (51), which the author describes as an attempt to discover a model suitable for precisely characterizing natural language by examining language data to determine the relations necessary and sufficient for describing language structure. The book is essentially a distillation of Harris's earlier works, reformulated in a quasi-mathematical style which requires a great deal of intellectual stamina to decipher.

A recent paper by Sakai (95) also examines the formal properties of language as a prerequisite to the construction of an appropriate model for grammatical description. His discussion is in some respects a synthesis of the stratificational and generative approaches.

Some other mathematical approaches to linguistics are described in *Mathematical Linguistics in Eastern Europe* by Kiefer (66). Unlike Harris, whose stated objective is to construct a model based on a precise mathematical formulation of the relations necessary and sufficient for characterizing the structure of natural language—thus going from the data to the model—the theoreticians discussed by Kiefer characteristically proceed from the model to the data. Kiefer evaluates each theory in terms of a set of questions, ranging from whether the model is satisfactorily motivated from a linguistic point of view to whether it can be considered linguistically relevant in any way. The major portion of the book is devoted to description and evaluation of the set-theoretic model of Kulagina and the generative model of Šaumjan; however, he also treats some aspects of the work of Bierwisch, himself and Abraham, Marcus, Revzin, Čulik, and Sgall.

A fairly complete catalog of European and American publications in the various areas related to computational linguistics is provided annually by the RAND bibliography (53).

---

[2] For the other side of the controversy, see the annotated bibliography of stratificational theory (Fleming, 31).

For a presentation of the various linguistic theories of the United States and Western Europe, Lyons's *Introduction to Theoretical Linguistics* (77) is quite valuable. Although the book is primarily oriented toward formal theory, the coverage of traditional and modern linguistics is in some respects more thorough than in other existing introductory texts. The book contains a substantial treatment of semantics, in which the author introduces his own theory of "meaningfulness." In addition, Lyons points out the rapprochement between formal grammar and traditional "notional" grammar, in terms of their similar views on the existence of linguistic universals.

The adherents of a formal descriptive approach to linguistic analysis are currently engaged in a deep-seated controversy involving the logical and psychological primacy of syntax versus semantics in a generative model of a speaker's competence. Inasmuch as many of the automatic language processing projects described below are based on generative grammar, the issues involved in this debate are worth noting.

The theory of linguistic description proposed by Chomsky in *Aspects of the Theory of Syntax* (19) (as well as in a number of earlier publications) defines a grammar as a system of rules which are capable of iteration in order to generate the infinitely many sentences of natural language. Such a grammar is characterized by three basic sets of rules, which constitute the syntactic, semantic, and phonological components, respectively. The syntactic component is described by Chomsky as generative. It specifies "for each sentence, a *deep structure* that determines its semantic interpretation and a *surface structure* that determines its phonetic interpretation." The semantic and phonological components are "purely interpretive"; their role is to correlate semantic and phonological representations with the structures generated by the syntactic component. The base of the syntactic component (sometimes called the "base component") consists of the categorial component—a system of rewrite rules which generate a set of "basic strings" with their associated structural descriptions or "base Phrase-markers"—and a lexicon, which is an unordered set of lexical entries, each of which contains a distinctive feature matrix giving the phonologic shape of the particular lexical items, and a complex symbol specifying the syntactic features of the lexical item. Insertion of the lexical items produces the terminal string which is input to the transformational rules. [Some refinements of this formulation are introduced in Chomsky & Halle (21), primarily involving the interface between the surface structure representations and the phonological representations.]

Aspects had hardly appeared before some of Chomsky's followers were beginning to question the sequence of lexical insertion and the operation of the transformational rules. In many instances—especially in the case of idioms—it appears that lexical items should not undergo some of the transformations, but should themselves be introduced by transformation (Rosenbaum, 90; Bach, 2; McCawley, 79). A related problem concerns the placement of word-derivation rules, which may possibly constitute a morphological subcomponent of the transformational component (Chapin, 18).

Difficulties with lexical insertion as well as problems with deep structure representation have led some disciples of Chomsky to challenge his notion of the generative nature of the syntactic component, maintaining that it is rather the semantic component which is the creative element and the syntactic component which is interpretive.

Although the "surface structure" of the controversy reveals a concern with the generative/interpretive status of the syntactic and semantic components, the basic issue is whether the linguistic universals postulated in Chomsky (19), Katz & Fodor (63), and Katz & Postal (64) are in fact universal enough. More specifically, are the previously postulated linguistic universals sufficient to account for the common—and therefore the essential—features of all natural languages? The general feeling, especially with regard to the notion of deep structure, is that they are not.

In *Aspects*, Chomsky defines two types of linguistic universals: formal and substantive. Substantive universals denote the fixed classes of items from which the elements of individual languages are drawn; they constitute "the vocabulary for the description of language." Examples of substantive universals presented in Chomsky are phonological distinctive features. Katz & Postal present, in addition, some syntactic examples of substantive universals—noun phrase, modifier, question, *wh*—and the semantic concepts of "(Male), (Physical Object), (Process), (Selector)." Formal universals are specifications of the form of the linguistic description itself; i.e., the types of rules characteristic of the different components which constitute a linguistic description.

In a later discussion of semantic theory, Katz (60) adds the concept of "organizational universals," which define the notion "semantic component" by specifying the structure of its subcomponents (a dictionary and a set of projection rules) and their interrelations.

That the fundamental issue is deeper than the generative/interpretive controversy is suggested in Fillmore's introduction to the first report of the Ohio State Lexicology Project (30). In this report, he discusses the impact of a generative versus an interpretive view of syntax on lexicology; but he is obviously most seriously concerned with the problem of semantic representation and with the "formal universals" of current semantic theory—specifically the one-term predicate approach to semantic properties, which he characterizes as "quite wrong."

Although the existence of a level of syntactic deep structure has been questioned in a number of unpublished papers, in 1968 it surfaced in an article by Lakoff (71) and in a volume containing a series of papers presented at a University of Texas symposium in 1967 (Bach & Harms, 3). Although the symposium participants were not in agreement on all points, the general consensus was that the notion of "deep structure" as currently formulated is not sufficiently removed from its "surface structure" representation to be capable of characterizing all languages. Three of the papers (Fillmore, 29; Bach, 2; McCawley, 79) reflect the participants' views of how deep structure should be modified. Noting the parallels between the assignment of case forms in inflected languages and the assignment of prepositions in English and postpositions in Japanese, Fillmore argues that the notion of case is basic, and should be substituted for the less general deep structure syntactic relations "subject of," "object of." Postulating that "each case relationship can occur only once in a simple sentence," he develops the concept of "case grammar," in which the basic structure of a sentence is represented as a "proposition" and a "modality" constituent. The "modality" includes the notions of tense, mood, and negation of the whole sentence, while the "proposition" can be rewritten as a verb and a non-empty set of distinct case categories.

Fillmore objects to the subject/predicate dichotomy of "formal [presumably Aristotelian] logic" as obscuring "the many structural parallels between 'subjects' and 'objects.'" This objection is sustained by Bach's appeal for a base component resembling the systems of symbolic logic in which subject and object are both designated as arguments of a given predicate and are thus logically equal. The details of his hypothesis include the derivation of nouns from underlying relative clauses and the postulation of a "linguistic analogue" to the logical system of operators and variables as a replacement for referential indices. [A similar suggestion is presented in Karttunen (58), while Hiż points out some differences between natural language referentials and logical variables (54).] In proposing a base component of this type, Bach intends it as a universal of linguistic description; he asserts that the rules of the base are the same for every language and that the idiosyncratic elements are introduced by the lexicon and the transformational rules.

Although Fillmore describes case as an "underlying syntactic-semantic relationship" and Bach speaks of the base component as developing "the sets of semantic and syntactic features," it is McCawley (79) who stresses the interdependence of syntax and semantics, taking specific exception to the Katz-Fodor (63) notion that "linguistic description minus grammar equals semantics." In discussing the notion of a lexical item, McCawley supports Weinreich's view (110) that each particular sense of a word should be listed as a separate item in the lexicon in order that terminal nodes of deep structure would have a single semantic reading (or word sense) attached. McCawley illustrates the utility of this formulation by demonstrating that determinations of anomaly or non-anomaly could be based on the entire deep structure rather than on combinations of constituents, as proposed by Katz & Fodor.

Although the paper was presented in the context of Chomsky's concept of generative grammar, McCawley states in a "postscript" that he no longer feels that Chomsky's notion of a level of deep structure is valid. Instead, he sees the replacement of the syntactic and semantic components by a single system of rules which will derive the surface syntactic representation from a base semantic representation in terms of symbolic logic.

In a later paper, McCawley (78) further develops the notion of a generative semantics, asserting that it is possible to derive surface syntactic representations from semantic representations by a system of transformations involving lexical insertions as well as syntactic reordering, because both types of representation are formally similar. The units and categories involved in syntactic transformations of the type described in *Aspects* are largely the same as the units and categories of symbolic logic, which he proposes as a system for representing meaning. This proposal, however, is subject to the qualification that symbolic logic be enriched by "certain devices."[3]

On the other hand, Gruber (50) does not expect formal logic to provide a satisfactory representation for natural language. The keystone of the model he proposes is the lexicon; this permits him to interpret the system of base trees (generated by the phrase-structure base component) without lexical items attached (these are supplied subsequently from the lexicon) as a "semantic language," which underlies all syntactic structures.

In the light of McCawley's proposals and Langendoen's mention of formal logic as "perhaps the single most important tool" for semantic investigations (73), it is interesting to survey the recent history of projected symbolic logic solutions for linguistic problems of meaning.

Although Bar-Hillel made such a suggestion in 1954 (4), Chomsky's negative rejoinder (20) seemed to close the issue until it was resurrected by Weinreich (111), who characterized the study of language in the context of logic as "one of the most important frontiers of linguistics for the decades ahead" and described the linguistic counterparts of the various logical signs and categories as universals of language. In a later article (110), Weinreich reintroduced some of these notions in a programmatic discus-

---

[3] J. L. Kuhns has observed that McCawley is apparently unfamiliar with the extended predicate calculus, and with Russell's theory of descriptions, as presented in Chapter XVI of his *Introduction to Mathematical Philosophy* (94) and, more technically, in *Principia Mathematica* (112).

sion of a semantic theory which he proposed as an alternative to Katz-Fodor (63). Weinreich's linguistic criticisms were subsequently rebutted by Katz (60), who was simultaneously advertising the power of his theory in defining analyticity (61) and defending it against the philosophical criticism of Quine and Wilson (in 62). Since these articles are essentially defenses of Katz's theory of semantic representation against those of formal logic, it is instructive to examine his arguments. If valid, they provide evidence of the unfeasibility of McCawley's proposals as well as of the logic-based automated language processing activities described below.

Katz's main contention is that his theory provides a natural means of defining semantic concepts and relations, whereas the symbolic logic system of Carnap requires "such *ad hoc* devices as meaning postulates and semantic rules" (61), and Quine relies on behavioral criteria (62). The current controversy over the generative/interpretive nature of the semantic component affects the validity of Katz's claim, as his semantic theory is syntax-based (63). Moreover—although he expressly rejects behavioral criteria as a means of defining terms—he asserts a requirement for such criteria to confirm the empirical adequacy of his "theoretical" definitions (59, 61, 62). The postulation of such a requirement is equivalent to opening Pandora's box, as psycholinguists are discovering.

Psycholinguistics

In this connection, a brief excursion into the area of psycholinguistics is a worthwhile endeavor. For a general background, de Cecco's textbook for educational psychology contains many of the classic articles in traditional and generative linguistic theory as well as in the psychology of verbal behavior (24). A substantive review of the field is presented in Diebold (97), and Fraser & Klatt's bibliography (34) contains references to recent (as well as earlier) developments, of which many are hard-to-come-by citations of the journal literature.

In an article entitled "Mentalism in Linguistics," Katz (59) is concerned with defending the theoretical constructs of "mentalistic" or generative linguistics as necessarily psychologically real. He further stipulates that linguistic theory must "harmonize" with psychological and physiological theories, such that a linguistic theory is refutable on the basis of inconsistencies which may emerge between it and the other disciplines. Since this article, work in psycholinguistics by followers of Chomsky seems to have concentrated unequally on attempts to confirm the psychological reality of the generative model (Fodor & Bever, 32; Fodor & Garrett, 33) and efforts to disconfirm psychological methodologies and theories which are incompatible with the theory of generative grammar (Garrett & Fodor, 39; Bever, Fodor & Garrett, 5; Bever, Fodor, & Weksel, 7; Bever, Fodor, & Weksel,

6). Although initial experiments on the former met with some success, later experimental results were inconclusive or negative with respect to the psychological reality of the model itself; however, some evidence for the psychological reality of the structural descriptions produced by the model did emerge (Fodor & Garrett, 33). The basic difficulty appears to reside in the Chomskyan dichotomy of linguistic competence versus performance, a useful concept in the tradition of de Saussure's *langue-parole* distinction (Godel, 43), which in theory allows the distillation of the competence of an "ideal" speaker from the "adulterations of the ideal" (Katz, 61) represented by the performance of individual speakers in producing and understanding utterances. In practice, however, it is extremely difficult to sort out the evidence for linguistic competence from the facts of linguistic performance —both in constructing a model of a speaker's competence in a particular language and in evaluating that model through experimental testing.

A further complication arises from the fact that the competence/performance distinction has more than one interpretation in the literature, as Fodor & Garrett have pointed out (33). The expectations of Chomsky (19), Katz (59), and others, that a competence model would constitute a subcomponent of a performance model (as an abstraction of the psychological mechanisms underlying language use, in the second sense of the competence/performance distinction) are not substantiated by the later experiments mentioned above. As a result of these experiments, the relation between a grammar and a performance model is seen as increasingly abstract. It now appears that a speaker's use of his competence in producing and understanding utterances is in no way analogous to the operations of formal models for synthesizing and analyzing sentences. In fact, the picture that is beginning to emerge from these experiments reveals that the most significant elements of a performance model are analogs of the strategies and heuristics actually used by speakers in processing sentences.

Linguistic Theory: Concluding Remarks

In summary, there are two recent developments in theoretical linguistics which are especially significant for automated language processing. The first of these is the reassessment of the role of semantics in formal descriptive linguistics. It is an unfortunate fact that linguistics has previously had little to offer in the area of semantic analysis, with the result that researchers in automated language processing have depended on lexicography, formal logic, or their own ingenuity for an approach to semantics. Recognition of the centrality of semantics in a theory of grammar is a first step toward the explicit semantics which is required for automation. A further step in this direction is the specification of formal logic as a means of semantic representation; this development is particularly encouraging, since linguists, logicians, and information scientists seem to be thinking along the same lines.

The elaboration of the notion of a "performance model" is a second development of major significance in linguistic theory. Although the full explication of such a model may be unrealizable, the recent evidence for the importance of heuristics and strategies is of considerable value in the design of automated analogs of human understanding.

A further development of major significance in linguistic theory would be the application of computers and automated language processing techniques to problems involving the analysis and synthesis of linguistic data. Conversely, the field of automated language processing (in the broadest sense of the term) has much to gain from the involvement of linguists in all areas. Unhappily, these events have not yet occurred.

Now it is an incontrovertible fact that linguists and persons engaged in automated language processing are two sets of people whose primary interest is natural language. Although there is some intersection of the sets, it is insufficient to insure that linguists have a proper perspective on automated language processing,[4] or that researchers in automated language processing have a proper perspective on linguistics. It is therefore not surprising that these two sets of people have quite different views on the nature of language; these views will be summarized following the discussion of automated language processing.

APPLICABILITY OF RECENT DEVELOPMENTS IN AUTOMATED LANGUAGE PROCESSING TO INFORMATION SYSTEMS

Language is the primary vehicle for communicating information in human society. The processing of natural language data in its various forms is thus the basic function of an information system. In the following sections, we present a simple model of an information system and discuss current research in automated language processing in terms of the model.

A Model of an Information System

An information system can be defined very simply in terms of two key elements and two basic operations, any one of which may involve language processing. The elements are the information records comprising the system and the information requirements of the user or users; if either or both

---

[4]This is abundantly clear from a recently published collection of papers presented at a conference on information in the language sciences (Freeman et al., 35). In spite of Gardin's urging that linguistics provide the frame of reference for document processing studies, and that new forms of information meeting "linguistic criteria of adequacy" should be introduced in linguistics "for a theoretical, if for no other, motivation," the recommendations of the conference with regard to linguistic information read no differently from the recommendations of, say, the IEEE.

of these elements involve natural language data, the system is called a natural language information system. The basic operations are those of content analysis and representation, and information request and retrieval. The system for content analysis and representation provides the medium of communication between the user and the information store, while the system for request and retrieval determines the specific mode of interaction between the user and the information store.

The information store consists of information records which have undergone content analysis and representation; they may thus be documents or document surrogates, or natural language statements reduced to some atomic form.

Similarly, the user's information requirement may be specific or general. It may consist of a request made at a particular time, it may be a request which remains in effect over a long period of time—in the form of a standing requirement or user interest profile—or it may take the form of a continuous interaction with the system in an on-line mode. Like the information records, the user requirements undergo content analysis and representation before they are matched against the information store.

Other operations of an information system which are less germane to the present discussion are covered elsewhere in this volume. Moreover, space does not permit coverage of important aspects of natural language information processing concerning computer representation and manipulation. For programming languages especially suited to manipulation of natural language data, see Bobrow (9); for storage schemes, see the individual automated language processing articles referenced below.

Content Analysis and Representation

Broadly speaking, content analysis and representation can be seen as encompassing a variety of operations, ranging from the activities of indexers analyzing the content of documents and representing it in terms of a particular scheme of content categorization (e.g., the Universal Decimal Classification) to the activities of translators analyzing the entire content of a document in one language and representing it in another language. However, in this review, we will limit the discussion to automated systems of content analysis and representation, and primarily to those in which the analysis of content is not restricted to the compilation of concordances (or word indexes to the text) and frequency statistics. Some exceptions to this limitation will be treated in the section on language processing research in anthropological linguistics and the humanities; moreover, it will be convenient to discuss automatic translation activities in a separate section.

Even within the limited scope of this definition, systems for automatic content analysis and representation range in complexity from dictionary look-up to intricate systems involving the recognition and specification of both syntactic and semantic categories and relations. The module which controls content analysis and representation is the core of an information system and, ideally, contains both syntactic and semantic subcomponents, the functions of which may be interdependent to such a degree as to preclude separate discussion. Since several of the question-answering systems are structured in this way, question-answering systems will be treated under information retrieval. Other systems falling within the range of this definition will be discussed below under the separate headings of automatic syntactic analysis and automatic semantic analysis.

Automatic Syntactic Analysis. Of the several computer systems which are primarily or exclusively oriented toward syntactic analysis, perhaps the most interesting are those designed as vehicles for rule testing in the construction of transformational grammars. Friedman has built an off-line batch system of this type, which is an extension and refinement of the MITRE transformational grammar. Friedman has described the system in a series of publications, all of which are abstracted in (37); (36) contains a general description of the system.

The system may be initiated either by the user inputting a base tree, or by the "directed random" generation of base trees from the phrase structure grammar on the basis of a user-specified "skeleton." Unlike other systems of this type, the Friedman grammar provides a lexical insertion algorithm which follows the phrase structure generation of the base tree. Although Friedman foresees handling of idioms as trees in the lexicon, it would still appear that this solution presents problems for the subsequent operation of the transformational component, as discussed by Rosenbaum (90) and others.

One of the advantages of this system is the amount of control which can be exercised by the user. Although all the grammar testers allow user specification of the traffic rules governing the sequencing of the transformations and the point at which they are applied, Friedman provides the user with further options to solve a problem aptly described elsewhere as "theoretical slack" (Rosenbaum, 90). The problem derives from the fact that even the most explicit theory is in many instances insufficiently specific for a computer implementation, so the required specifications must be supplied by the designer. Where possible—as in the case of the traffic rules—Friedman leaves the choice up to the user. Where some specification must be selected, she opts for the most general solution, and allows the user the full power of the system if desired; otherwise, the metalanguage (a modified version of Backus Naur Form) permits the definition of a subset of the full syntax. For example, the syntax for analyses (which appear in the structural description of transformations or as contextual features) is fully recursive in that the terms are "structures" which may optionally specify additional analyses. This represents a significant generalization of the definition given in Chomsky (19), which characterizes the terms of an analysis as a string of nodes occurring from left to right in a particular tree.

Other developments of grammar testers based on the MITRE system are described in Gross & Walker (49) and Gross (48). The first discusses an on-line implementation for a cathode-ray tube (CRT), while the second is essentially a subset of the first developed for use with an on-line typewriter under the MIT time-sharing system. The CRT implementation allows generation of base trees by cycling through a set of phrase structure rules displaying alternative expansions; the desired expansion is then selected with a lightgun. Both systems provide a capability for specifying and applying transformations to produce surface trees; in addition, the CRT system supplies algorithms for recovering the base trees of an input sentence, based on the MITRE Syntactic Analysis Procedure.

An on-line interactive transformational grammar tester (TGT) has been implemented by Londe & Schoene (76), primarily to aid the Air Force UCLA English Syntax Project (AFESP), whose objective is the integration of transformational analyses of English. Input/Output (I/O) is by means of a teletype or CRT, but each user may maintain files of trees and rules on magnetic tape, permitting the simultaneous testing of several distinct grammars, or subparts of a single grammar. A test run is initiated by calling a tree and a set of transformational rules from the file, or by inputting a complete new tree, or by modifying one of the existing trees. New transformation rules are input to the system by the command RULE: phrase structure rules require the label PS and a different rule format. Unlike Friedman's option of producing base trees from PS rules by the "directed random" generation algorithm, Londe & Schoene's TGT optionally uses PS rules to verify whether a particular tree could have been generated by the given set of PS rules. Like the on-line MITRE grammar testers, TGT is primarily aimed at syntax checking; thus no lexicon or lexical insertion algorithm is currently included in the system.

Although the goal of the IBM transformational grammar project was not to build a grammar tester, but to provide a computer with the competence of a speaker of English, the necessity of a sentence-synthesizing program to deal with "the mind-warping properties of complex transformational grammars" was recognized. A first approximation to the ultimate goal was English Grammar I [the IBM Core Grammar, discussed in Rosenbaum & Blair (91); described in detail in Rosenbaum & Lochak (92)]. Recent research has concentrated on the development of English Grammar II (Rosenbaum, 90) which is noteworthy in several respects. In the first place, the IBM group—unlike Friedman—postulates that the operation of lexical insertion is not limited to the output of the phrase structure rules, but includes the output of the transformational rules as well; therefore, Grammar II will include at least two lexical passes. Another interesting feature of Grammar II is the treatment of prepositions, which are introduced into the base trees through subcategorization rules on nouns, permitting the selection of verb-preposition combinations on the same basis as verb-object or verb-subject combinations—that is to say, in terms of context-sensitive selectional subcategorization rules. [In a certain sense, this is an application of Fillmore's case hypothesis (29).] Moreover, an attempt has been made to determine the potential utility of English II as a subset of English (see below). Also included in Rosenbaum (90) is Postal's scheme for coordination reduction (87) and Robinson's discussion of dependency rules equivalent to the phrase structure rules of English II (89). A further development in the area of grammar testers is the on-line phonological rule tester reported by Bobrow & Fraser (10).

Sager's string analysis project is represented by the publication of a voluminous report containing computer printouts of sentences processed by the string decomposition program (Bookchin, 13). The basic principle of string theory is that sentences are constructed of strings of strings; atomic strings are word classes. To decompose a sentence according to this theory, it is necessary to recognize an elementary sentence which is the grammatical center (more or less equivalent to a kernel) and to which all other strings are joined directly or indirectly. The report consists mainly of printouts of a great number and variety of decomposed sentences from scientific text; to aid in evaluating the output, Sager supplies an explanation of format and Bookchin provides explanatory notes on many of the parsings.

In addition to the above-mentioned projects, which are primarily or exclusively oriented toward automatic syntactic analysis and synthesis, there are a number of automated language processing systems containing syntactic analysis modules. Some of these are rather primitive systems which parse text into chunks: Briner's SYNTRAN (15) is an analyzer of this type. Using suffixes, a small dictionary of stems and suffixes, and various empirical criteria, SYNTRAN attempts recognition of word groups corresponding to subjects, objects, and predicates. Other automated language processing systems use well-known algorithms for syntactic analysis: for example, the SMART system (Salton, 96) includes the Kuno-Oettinger multiple-path syntactic analyzer and several others use versions of the Cocke algorithm.

A novel modification of the basic Cocke algorithm is described by Martins & Smith (81), who introduce the concept of a complex symbol: the "vector-symbol." The characteristic feature of the vector-symbol approach is the division of intermediate and terminal symbols into constant and variable parts, permitting greater economy and flexibility in the writing of grammar rules. This concept was adopted as a basis for the automatic syntactic analysis module of a large-volume natural language processing system which accepts input from a multifont optical character reader for automatic content analysis and representation (Montgomery et al., 83).

Although the suggestion was made some time ago that computational linguistics should be interpreted not only as computation in linguistics but also as linguistics in computation, it is only recently that the latter aspect has been considered seriously. In comparing the programming languages Formula Translator (FORTRAN) and Programming Language #1 (PL/1) with Algorithmic Language (ALGOL), Goodenough (44) uses the Chomskyan notion of deep and surface structure, in conjunction with his own levels of surface string, semantic interpretation, and effective interpretation to characterize the structure of statements in the different languages. In a state-of-the-art survey of translator-writing systems, Feldman & Gries (28) note that the syntactic theory of translator-writing systems is based on Chomsky's formal statement on automata and on the properties of context-free, context-sensitive, and unrestricted rewriting systems, and thus is parallel in some respects to computational linguistics developments (at least to those based on formal descriptive theory; the authors are apparently unaware that some work in computational linguistics has other theoretical bases). Another article of interest in this connection is a substantive survey of the use of linguistic techniques in computer graphics and digital pattern recognition (Miller & Shaw, 82).

Automatic Semantic Analysis. Most systems of content analysis currently in existence use some sort of indexing vocabulary—a subject authority list, key word list, or thesaurus—for the representation of semantic information. For automatic language processing applications—as well as for manual ones—the generation and maintenance of a dynamic system of semantic categories is a formidable undertaking. The projects described below have attempted various solutions of the problem, or have ignored it, at least at the present state of the research.

A promising approach to vocabulary generation is presented in Stone (103) and Stone & Rubinoff (104). Using a data base of some 70,000 words culled from the section on computer programming in *Computer Reviews* for the years 1962, 1964, and 1966, the authors investigated the possibility of compiling a technical vocabulary based on word distributions throughout the document collection. They postulated that words characteristic of a particular specialty (i.e., terms which would form the basis of a technical vocabulary) would typically have a distribution distinctively different from that of "non-specialty" words. The authors found that the variance of the within-document frequency distribution of a word divided by the total frequency in the collection did in fact provide a measure for discriminating between specialty and non-specialty words.

Other statistical approaches of interest in natural language processing include several studies of word associations. Jones et al. (57) discuss a retrieval system based on association by co-occurrence in a coordinate indexing scheme, which is similar in some respects to the work reported by Sparck-Jones & Needham (102), although the latter authors also generate "clumps" of maximally associated properties by various formulae. Other approaches to word association are techniques based on co-occurrence in bibliographic citations (Garfield, 38) and co-occurrence in a hierarchically structured indexing vocabulary (Gotlieb & Kumar, 45). Rubenstein (93) also outlines an interesting approach in which *Roget's Thesaurus* groupings are used as an index of semantic similarity.

A large-volume automatic indexing system is the core of the natural language processing system described in Montgomery et al. (83). In addition to the parsing algorithm discussed above, the content analysis module includes an extensive thesaurus and a complex indexing algorithm. Because of the relatively small amount of high-value information in the voluminous data base and the consequent requirement for considerable discriminatory power, the thesaurus and indexing algorithm are necessarily complex. The thesaurus is sorted in dictionary form for the indexing operation. In this form, the entries are in the form of semantic trees, where the words which constitute cues for the search algorithm form the apex of the tree and the nodes represent the various levels of modifying words and phrases. Each node contains one or more grammatical labels indicating the grammatical category or categories of the word or phrase, and nodes which are terminal with respect to some semantic category or categories are also given a code to represent the category or categories. The code is hierarchically structured, such that the thesaurus format is obtained by sorting on the successive positions. As in the SMART system (96), the assignment of semantic category codes or index terms to the particular sentence is subject to verification by the parsing algorithm, which determines whether the constituents of phrases identified as cues to the semantic categories are in fact syntactically related. The SMART system performs the additional step of looking up the resulting syntactic structures in a dictionary of "criterion trees" to determine whether the particular structures are acceptable for the given concepts. Salton has stated that syntactic phrases as content indicators are too specific for document retrieval. In this connection, two observations might be made. In the first place, the extra step of verification with "criterion trees" could certainly cause rejection of otherwise acceptable phrases if (and this is clearly conceivable) all possible acceptable syntactic representations of the concept were not included in the dictionary of "criterion trees." Secondly, it should be noted that Salton's experiments were carried out on a small data base of presumably high-value information. In extremely large data bases, where the amount of high-value information may be small, a more powerful discriminatory capability would certainly be an advantage, if not a requirement.

Unlike SMART, and the system discussed in Montgomery et al. (83), the semantic analyzer proposed by Wilks (113) does not include a syntactic analysis module. Instead, Wilks breaks sentences into "fragments"—single words, elementary sentences, noun phrases, or clauses—and concatenates all fragments of a single paragraph, ignoring sentence boundaries. The words occurring in the fragments are looked up in the main dictionary, and a subdictionary is formed for each paragraph. The dictionary entries consist of a list of pairs, one for each sense of the given word, ordered as in a standard dictionary. One element of each pair is a "semantic formula" and the other, a natural language phrase describing the meaning of the particular formula. A semantic formula is a classification of the particular sense of the word in terms of semantic primitives (existence, cause, action, etc.). The system of semantic analysis then uses the formulae to construct a number of "frames" or formula strings for each fragment, taking one sense of each word of the fragment at a time until all possible combinations are exhausted. Each frame is then rewritten as a number of "templates"—the semantic structures forming the basic repertoire of the system. The objective of the semantic analysis is to reduce the original paragraph to a single string of templates, rejecting all but one template for each fragment on the basis of incompatibility of semantic formulae within the fragment or of incompatibility between fragments. Wilks's approach is certainly unique and—quite aside from its obvious applicability to the analysis of discourse—could be promising for handling the ungrammatical sentences often produced by native speakers, since syntactic well-formedness is not a requirement for acceptability. On the other hand, Wilks notes that ideally the system should include a fallback position whereby, in the event that no single string of templates is obtainable on a first pass, the fragments could be reformulated differently as input to a second pass. This suggests that it might be more feasible to require syntactic well-formedness on the first pass, and use the "fragmenting" approach as a fallback device.

"Correlational Grammar" (CG) as developed by von Glasersfeld and others in the tradition of Ceccato falls between content analysis systems which include a capability for syntactic analysis—those described in Salton (96) and Montgomery et al. (83)—and those which are exclusively devoted to semantic analysis, like that of Wilks. The correlational approach is defined as "a system based on the relations created between individual lexical items and their constructed constituents" (Dutton, 27). The fact that the fundamental structure of the system derives from the "relations between individual lexical items" indicates that CG is semantically based; however, the reference to "constructed constituents" is evidence of the significance of syntax. In fact, the network of correlations begins with semantic relations and ends with syntactic relations, but there is no identifiable boundary between semantic correlators and syntactic correlators.

Correlational analysis thus begins by looking up words in the master table of correlations to determine the various applicable indices. The correlational analysis proceeds by "reclassifying" the correlations; the "reclassification" rules essentially rewrite a pair of constituents of a correlation as a single correlation. The order of application of the reclassification rules is not clear from any of the discussions currently available and is probably undecided at this stage. A lucid presentation of correlational grammar is given in Dutton (27); however, since this discussion is largely limited to syntactic correlations, the interested reader should also see von Glasersfeld & Notamarco (106) for a treatment of semantic classes of adjectives.

Information Request and Retrieval Systems

The following discussion is limited to question-answering systems—to those systems in which information is stored and retrieved in the form of concepts and their interrelations. (Document retrieval and document dissemination are discussed in Chapters 7 and 8, respectively.) Since characteristics of existing question-answering systems have been covered in some detail in previous volumes of the *Annual Review*, they will be treated summarily below. REL (Dostert et al., 26) is not discussed since information currently available is insufficient to characterize the system.

Question-answering systems which have been described in the literature can be conveniently grouped in terms of the two operations defined as basic in the model of an information system previously presented—that is, the operations of content analysis and representation, and request and retrieval. The first group consists of question-answering systems which include some capability for all aspects of both operations; that is to say, these systems include capabilities for the analysis and representation of syntactic as well as semantic content of both data-base inputs and question inputs. Systems described by Simmons et al. (101), Schwarcz et al. (98), and by Kellogg (65) are the only ones which appear to fall into this group. The former system includes transformational rules which substantially improve content analysis performance over earlier versions of the system. Simmons's model, which includes inference-making ability as well as the properties mentioned above, has more of the types of capabilities required by a question-answerer than any of the other systems currently under development; however, it should be noted that some of the modules of the system have been tested only on a single paragraph of text. Kellogg's CONVERSE performs some of the same operations (e.g., syntactic and semantic analysis) in a less elegant manner than Simmons's model, but has specific strengths in the areas of file search and storage, since it is intended primarily as an on-line system for data management.

A second group of approaches is characterized by a content analysis operation in which syntactic and semantic analysis procedures are simultaneously accomplished. The systems of Bohnert & Backer (12), Kochen (68), and Coles (22) can be characterized as similar in this respect, although dissimilar in others. Bohnert is not concerned with the request and retrieval operation at this stage of development, but rather with the content analysis of a subset of English (English II—not to be confused with the English II of Rosenbaum) and the representation of it in the first order predicate calculus; his method of content analysis is thus biased in favor of the semantic representation he uses. While Bohnert discusses an implemented system for automatic English to logic translation, Kochen describes the design of a system for analysis of questions concerning the various geometric figures contained in single diagrams (each such diagram is considered a data base). His method of content analysis involves a bottom-to-top parser which uses formation and transformation rules to translate questions into a formal language and produce a flow diagram specifying the search procedure for answering the question. The model proposed by Coles is limited to the universe of discourse represented by graphics which can be displayed on a CRT. He uses a syntax-directed compilation technique to analyze the content of natural language sentences and to represent it in terms of the predicate calculus. The truth value of the sentences is then assessed by verifying them with respect to the graphic display they describe.

A third class of question-answering systems assumes a separate syntactic analysis component that produces the input; processing thus begins with semantic analysis. The system reported in Woods (114) presently falls into this category, as his semantic interpretation procedure operates on two types of nodes (S nodes and NP nodes) in a tree which constitutes the output of the assumed syntactic analysis. The tree or subtree dominated by the S or NP node is matched against the tree or subtree required by the pattern portion of the semantic rule. If the match is successful, the output of the rule is an operation for specifying the semantic interpretation of the input subtree.

A final class of systems includes those which perform no syntactic or semantic analysis on natural language sentences, but require input in the form of statements of the predicate calculus. Systems which fall into this category are the QA1 and QA2 models of Raphael (88) and the system described in Levien & Maron (75), and in Kuhns (70). Both of these systems place a high priority on inferential capability and a relatively low priority on the manipulation of natural language (although Kuhns has devoted some attention to analysis of questions and Raphael plans to couple his QA2 model with Coles's language processor). Raphael's QA2 was designed to exploit the power of existing theorem-proving systems to specify a strategy for answering queries. This approach requires the determination of which facts are relevant to the question (or theorem) at which point in the answering (or proof) procedure. While Raphael is currently operating on small data sets, Levien & Maron stress the importance of an extremely large file in the construction of nontrivial inferences. Rather than building a great deal of inferential power into the system, they feel that it is more realistic to allow the user to specify inferences, which then can be executed automatically. Other types of inferences, however, are derived by referencing a file containing data about the relations in the system. A separate study by Kuhns deals with the problem of calculating the value set of a particular question, assuming it has been translated into symbolic form.

In summary, although many promising approaches to question-answering are currently being pursued, it is unlikely that any of the present implementations will form the core of an ultimate operational capability. A particular problem is the very small amount of material which has typically been processed by such systems; the last system mentioned is apparently the only one which operates on a large data base and may thus have relevance in an operational context. Because of the complexity of the individual modules of a question-answering system—as well as of the interactions between modules—it seems improbable that techniques developed for extremely limited data bases can be extrapolated to large-volume systems.

The Information System and the User: "Habitability"

In order to achieve realistic objectives in some identifiable time frame, automatic language processing activities are necessarily restricted to subsets of some natural language, leaving the linguists to speculate on the full set, whatever that may be. Although the subsets defined thus far are many and varied, the fact remains that they are subsets; in using them as a means of communication, the user must suspend his normal language habits. This raises the very important question of whether a user can in fact express himself without resorting to utterances which are not included in the subset; as Watt (109) inquires, ". . . will people find that sublanguage 'habitable'?"

In his thoughtful article, Watt also raises a second and related question in regard to Chomsky's distinction of competence versus performance. The computerized information systems now in existence have based their grammars on some subset of the set of sentences representing the competence of an ideal speaker; but in reality, the computer system will have to deal with the individual instances of language use or performance. As we saw under "Psycholinguistics," the notion of performance—the actual use a speaker makes of his linguistic competence in producing and recognizing utterances—is still inexplicit, and may never be fully understood. Yet in order to be "habitable," the sublanguage of the computer system will necessarily constitute a subset of the unexplicated "performative sentences"; this will require some criterion for deciding what to leave in and what to leave out. Apart from this problem of determining probability of submission of sentences by users and the corresponding requirement for inclusion in the subset, there is the further difficulty of insuring the "processability" of those sentences by the computer. Because they are sentences of performance, their interpretation is to a great extent dependent on context, which must be simulated in some way.

Since the particular question-answering system Watt discusses is one based on the *Official Airline Guide* (see Woods, 114), he makes the reasonable assumption that the opportunity for adapting to the subset through successive performances will not be available. Rosenbaum (90, Section II) takes the opposite tack and presents a somewhat more optimistic picture for the builders of question-answering systems. He inquires whether existing subsets can in fact be used in particular applications, and most crucially, whether a user can learn to express himself solely in terms of the subset. In other words, can the subset become "habitable" for a user through a learning experience? Rosenbaum supplies a positive answer to this question, as well as to the first one, in recounting an experience in which English II was learned by a psychologist and used by him to record observations of parent-child interactions in a structured situation.

OTHER LANGUAGE PROCESSING ACTIVITIES

Machine Translation

The publication of the Automatic Language Processing Advisory Committee (ALPAC) report in 1966 (84) cast somewhat of a pall over machine translation activities in the United States. There are, however, a number of reports dealing with MT research in 1966 and 1967 which have not been previously discussed in the literature; these will be covered briefly here.

A possible successor to the IBM Mark II translation system is described in Plath et al. (85). The Combinatorial Syntactic Analysis (CSA) system uses what appears to be a modified version of the Sakai-Cocke algorithm to parse input text. The parser is described as "exhaustive," a characteristic of the Sakai-Cocke algorithm, which is not necessarily applicable to the table of grammar rules used by the algorithm. At present the system is limited to analysis of Russian sentences; no English synthesis or translation algorithm is included.

An experimental system which also includes a version of the Cocke algorithm in its analysis module is described in Martins & Smith (81); the modification of the Cocke algorithm involves the development of more powerful rule symbols (the "vector-symbols" discussed above). The output of the analysis program serves as one of the inputs to the Basic Translator, which maps source language grammar rules into target language grammar rules and synthesizes a target language sentence translating the source language original. Since the experimental translation system is implemented for a small computer, procedures which are well understood—i.e., dictionary creation and look-up—are simulated in the model. An application of essentially the same model to Chinese, however, uses a larger computer and therefore includes a small dictionary and dictionary look-up subroutine (Chai, 17).

A Russian-English machine translation program implemented at the National Physical Laboratory in Teddington, England, is described in McDaniel et al. (80). The analysis algorithm employs multiple passes through a sentence to construct a unified tree. In certain respects, this approach is similar to the multiple-pass analysis of Garvin's fulcrum technique (41, 42). However, the search items for particular passes do not always coincide with the fulcra specified by Garvin. For example, the fulcrum for Garvin's nominal blocking pass is the noun, while in the Teddington system, the analysis of a nominal structure is initiated when a potential "starter" (adjective, participle, or numeral) is encountered. The report includes sample translations produced by the program, as well as the results of a generally favorable formal evaluation of translation output, the consensus being that "there is a real demand for translations of this quality." Other work at Teddington includes error correction techniques reported in Szanser (105); in this connection, see also Cornew (23).

A 1966 article by Birnbaum (8) discusses analysis of the Russian predicative infinitive and reviews various approaches to the problem in machine translation applications.

Recent developments in the United States have concentrated on machine-aided translation, rather than on a fully automatic procedure. A substantive article by See (100) discusses and evaluates various types of possible machine aids. Automatic aids to editors of Chinese-English translations and translators of Chinese-English mathematical texts are treated in Walker et al. (108). Software aids include concordances and parallel text comparisons; hardware aids include use of a CRT and light pen to create input in the form of Chinese characters and use of the SC4020 plotter as an output device. A related article (Hayashi et al., 52) contains somewhat more detail on use of the RAND tablet as an input device.

Other Research in Linguistics and the Humanities

In addition to the computational projects in formal linguistics (discussed mainly in the section on automatic syntactic analysis), there are many possibilities for the use of the computer in traditional linguistics. Some of these—including data manipulation operations, cryptanalytic procedures, pattern recognition operations, and the like—are discussed by Yngve (115). Grimes et al. (47) presented a method for analyzing phoneme distributions in unexplored languages by computer, based on tentative assumptions concerning segmentation and bounded contexts.

One of the few language processing projects based on a heuristic—rather than an algorithmic—approach is described in Garvin (40). This research involves a simulation of the heuristics employed by a linguist in eliciting and analyzing the responses of a native speaker of some language unknown to the investigator. In the course of this research, Garvin proposes to isolate two types of linguistic universals: "absolute" and "potential." Potential universals correspond approximately to the notion of "substantive" universals in generative theory, but the adjective "potential" indicates that Garvin is making a much weaker claim about their universality. Absolute universals, on the other hand, constitute the defining criteria of a language, e.g., the fact that every linguistic form has a meaning. The means of investigating these notions is a computerized simulation of informant work, in which a display console is used to elicit and record informant responses; these are then sent to a morphological analysis subroutine for segmentation and analysis.

In the humanities, most automatic language processing applications in some sense involve the analysis of literary style, which Sedelow et al. (99) defines as "the patterns formed in the linguistic encoding of information." On the other hand, Milic (in 14) points out that "one limiting factor in the study of literary style is the question of what inferences can be drawn from the facts gathered." At present, however, there seems to be more concern with collecting facts and developing tools to collect facts than with interpreting them, although there are some exceptions.

Sedelow is concerned with establishing stylistic criteria for distinguishing authors and speakers, and with the construction of tools to facilitate the identification of patterns characteristic of different styles. Two automatic aids to stylistic analysis reported in Sedelow are a program which produces "text-specific" thesauri and a display program which exhibits the patterns of occurrence of words in a given text.

The journal *Computers and the Humanities* has thus far followed the laudable custom of presenting a series of survey articles each September. The most recent surveys include Burton's review of computational stylistics (16), in which she echoes Milic's complaint. Thus the number of concordances she reports exceeds the number of more substantive studies such as an automatic syntactic analysis (IC) of the prose of Thomas Carlyle and a transformational analysis of the style of Wilfred Owen. In the same survey volume of the journal, Waite reviews work in the classics (107), which in general shows more originality than does computational work in the humanities, including metrical studies of both Greek and Latin poetry.

Allais & Allais (1) report a "structural" study of *Les liaisons dangereuses*, in which the text consists of letters exchanged by the six main characters. A set of variables is constructed to represent each pair of the six who exchange letters; the novel is then segmented into two-week periods, and the structure of patterns of exchange is examined for each period.

In addition to these specific language processing projects, a great deal of useful language data has recently been converted to machine-readable form for use in automated language processing applications. These data include *Webster's Seventh New Collegiate Dictionary* and the *New Merriam Webster Pocket Dictionary* (prepared by the System Development Corporation); *The Random House Dictionary of the English Language* (created by Random House); Kenyon and Knott's *A Pronouncing Dictionary of American English* (prepared by the Speech Communications Research Laboratory); *The English Word Speculum* (compiled by Dolby & Resnikoff (25); and a large corpus of 1,014,232 words representing various types of "Present-Day American English," compiled and analyzed by Kučera & Francis (69).

CONCLUSIONS

In evaluating the work in automated language processing for the past year, it is useful to inquire what progress has been made toward a more explicit definition of natural language and of the operations involved in processing natural language, whether by people or by machines.

Concerning the explication of natural language, it appears that some new insights have emerged in the area of semantic representation, where both linguists and persons engaged in automated language processing have made substantial contributions. In the case of developing a more explicit notion of the operations involved in language processing, the evidence adduced by psycholinguists for a complex heuristics as basic to a speaker's performance is a significant discovery. In terms of language processing by machines, the most notable advances have been made in the area of on-line interactive applications, where more flexible and powerful systems for manipulating a variety of data structures are under development. It is interesting to note that these advances resulted from the activities of two groups of people with two quite different views of natural language.

Linguists (most particularly those of the formal descriptive school) are theory-oriented; researchers in automated language processing are data-oriented. The first group thinks in terms of counter-examples; the second, in terms of probability of occurrence. The first group is concerned with the ideal of competence, while the second must deal with the facts of performance. Linguists speculate on the entire set of a natural language; researchers in automated language processing concentrate on subsets.

Do these attitudes represent irreconcilable differences in views of what language is, or can they be regarded as complementary perspectives on the nature of language? A further question—one most crucial to the advancement of both linguistic science and automated language processing—is whether the two perspectives are parallel in the Euclidean sense, or whether there exists a possibility of convergence. In other words, can the two approaches be combined in some way to provide a balanced attack on problems of natural language description?

It appears that this question can be answered in the affirmative. The potential for convergence is already evident in the similarity of views on semantic representation in terms of formal logic. Hopefully, this trend will continue.

REFERENCES

(1) ALLAIS, CHRISTIANE; ALLAIS, CLAUDE. A method of structural analysis with an application to "Les liaisons dangereuses." In: Revue, vol. 2. International Organization for Ancient Languages Analysis by Computer, 110 Boulevard de la Sauvenière, Liège, Belgium, p. 13–33.
(2) BACH, EMMON. Nouns and noun phrases. In: Bach, Emmon; Harms, Robert T., eds. Universals in linguistic theory. Holt, Rinehart and Winston, New York, 1968, p. 90–122.
(3) BACH, EMMON; HARMS, ROBERT T., eds. Universals in linguistic theory. Holt, Rinehart and Winston, New York, 1968, 210 p.
(4) BAR-HILLEL, YEHOSHUA. Logical syntax and semantics. Language, 30 (1954) 230–237.
(5) BEVER, THOMAS G.; FODOR, JERRY A.; GARRETT, MERRILL. A formal limitation of associationism. In: Dixon, Theodore R.; Horton, David L., eds. Verbal behavior and general behavior theory. Prentice-Hall, Englewood Cliffs, N.J., 1968, p. 582–585.
(6) BEVER, T. G.; FODOR, J. A.; WEKSEL, W. Is linguistics empirical? In: Jakobovits, Leon A.; Miron, Murray S., eds. Readings in the psychology of language. Prentice-Hall, Englewood Cliffs, N.J., 1967, p. 285–293.
(7) BEVER, T. G.; FODOR, J. A.; WEKSEL, W. On the acquisition of syntax: a critique of "contextual generalization." In: Jakobovits, Leon A.; Miron, Murray S., eds. Readings in the psychology of language. Prentice-Hall, Englewood Cliffs, N.J., 1967, p. 257–273.
(8) BIRNBAUM, HENRIK. Some notes on Russian predicative infinitives in automatic

translation. MT (Mechanical Translation and Computational Linguistics), 10:1 & 2 (March & June 1967) 11–17.
(9) BOBROW, DANIEL G., ed. Symbol manipulation languages and techniques. Proceedings of the IFIP Working Conference on Symbol Manipulation Languages, Pisa, Italy, 5–9 September 1966. North-Holland Publishing Co., Amsterdam, 1968, 487 p.
(10) BOBROW, DANIEL G.; FRASER, J. BRUCE. A phonological rule tester. Communications of the ACM, 11:11 (November 1968) 766–772.
(11) BOBROW, DANIEL G.; FRASER, J. BRUCE; QUILLIAN, M. R. Automated language processing. In: Annual review of information science and technology, vol. 2. Carlos A. Cuadra, ed. Interscience, New York, 1967, p. 161–186.
(12) BOHNERT, HERBERT G.; BACKER, PAUL O. Automatic English-to-logic translation in a simplified model. A study in the logic of grammar. Final report, 1961–1966, IBM Watson Research Center, Yorktown Heights, N.Y., March 1966, 117 p. (AD-637 227)
(13) BOOKCHIN, BEATRICE. Computer outputs for sentence decomposition of scientific texts. New York University, Institute for Computer Research in the Humanities, Linguistic String Project, New York, March 1968. 403 p. (String program reports, no. 3)
(14) BOWLES, EDMUND A., ed. Computers in humanistic research—readings and perspectives. Prentice-Hall, Englewood Cliffs, N.J., 1967, 264 p.
(15) BRINER, L. L.; CARNEY, G. J. SYNTRAN/360, a natural language processing system for preparing text references and retrieving text information. IBM Corp., Gaithersburg, Md., 1968. (Preprint)
(16) BURTON, DOLORES M. "Respice finem" and the "tantum quantum"—an essay review of computational stylistics for 1967–1968. Computers and the Humanities, 3:1 (September 1968) 41–48.
(17) CHAI, D. T. Chinese-English machine translation. Law and Computer Technology, 1:8 (August 1968) 10–16.
(18) CHAPIN, PAUL G. On the syntax of word-derivation in English. MITRE Corp., Bedford, Mass., September 1967, 191 p. (Information system language studies, no. 16) (MTP-68) (MITRE Project 1117)
(19) CHOMSKY, NOAM. Aspects of the theory of syntax. MIT Press, Cambridge, Mass., 1965, 251 p.
(20) CHOMSKY, NOAM. Logical syntax and semantics: their linguistic relevance. Language, 31:1, part 1 (January–March 1955) 36–45.
(21) CHOMSKY, NOAM; HALLE, MORRIS. The sound pattern of English. Harper and Row, New York, 1968, 470 p.
(22) COLES, L. STEPHEN. An on-line question-answering system with natural language and pictorial input. In: National Conference of the Association for Computing Machinery, 23rd, Las Vegas, Nev., 27–29 August 1968. Proceedings. Brandon/Systems Press, Princeton, N.J., 1968, p. 157–167.
(23) CORNEW, RONALD W. A statistical method of spelling correction. Information and Control, 12:2 (February 1968) 79–93.
(24) DE CECCO, JOHN P., ed. The psychology of language, thought, and instruction. Readings. Holt, Rinehart and Winston, New York, 1967, 446 p.
(25) DOLBY, J. L.; RESNIKOFF, H. L. The English word speculum. Mouton, The Hague, 1967, vols. 1–5.
(26) DOSTERT, BOZENA H.; LOCKEMANN, PETER C.; THOMPSON, FREDERICK B. A brief description of REL. California Institute of Technology, Pasadena, Calif., July 1968.
(27) DUTTON, BRIAN. An introduction to the theory and practice of correlational grammar. Georgia Institute for Research, Athens, October 1968, 114 p. (Informal scientific report CG2)
(28) FELDMAN, JEROME; GRIES, DAVID. Translator writing systems. Communications of the ACM, 11:2 (February 1968) 77–113.
(29) FILLMORE, CHARLES J. The case for case. In: Bach, Emmon; Harms, Robert T.,

eds. Universals in linguistic theory. Holt, Rinehart and Winston, New York, 1968, p. 1-90.
(30) FILLMORE, CHARLES J. First report of the Ohio State Lexicology Project. In: Working papers in linguistics. Ohio State University Research Foundation, Columbus, December 1967, p. 1-8.
(31) FLEMING, ILAH. Stratificational theory: an annotated bibliography. Linguistic Automation Project, Yale University, New Haven, Conn., June 1968. (Preprint, 51 p.)
(32) FODOR, J. A.; BEVER, T. G. The psychological reality of linguistic segments. In: Jakobovits, Leon A.; Miron, Murray S., eds. Readings in the psychology of language. Prentice-Hall, Englewood Cliffs, N.J., 1967, p. 325-332.
(33) FODOR, J. A.; GARRETT, M. Some reflections on competence and performance. In: Lyons, J.; Wales, R. J., eds. Psycholinguistics papers. Chicago, 1967, p. 135-154.
(34) FRASER, BRUCE; KLATT, MARY M. A selected psycholinguistic bibliography. Bolt, Beranek and Newman, Cambridge, Mass., November 1968, 80 p. (Scientific report no. 9)
(35) FREEMAN, ROBERT R.; PIETRZYK, ALFRED; ROBERTS, A. HOOD. Information in the language sciences. American Elsevier, New York, 1968, 247 p. (Mathematical linguistics and automatic language processing, vol. 5)
(36) FRIEDMAN, JOYCE. A computer system for transformational grammar. Stanford University, Department of Computer Science, Stanford, Calif., January 1968, 31 p. (CS-84) (AD-665 827)
(37) FRIEDMAN, JOYCE. A computer system for writing and testing transformational grammars. Final report. Stanford University, Department of Computer Science, Stanford, Calif., September 1968, 14 p. (CS-109)
(38) GARFIELD, EUGENE. Primordial concepts, citation indexing, and historiobibliography. Journal of Library History, 2:3 (1967) 235-249.
(39) GARRETT, M.; FODOR, J. A. Psychological theories and linguistic constructs. In: Dixon, Theodore R.; Horton, David L., eds. Verbal behavior and general behavior theory. Prentice-Hall, Englewood Cliffs, N.J., 1968, p. 451-477.
(40) GARVIN, PAUL L. Computer-based research on linguistic universals. Quarterly progress reports, September 1967-December 1968: G096-8U1, 15 December 1967, 8 p.; G096-8U3, 1 April 1968, 39 p.; G096-8U7, 1 July 1968, 25 p.; G096-8U8, 1 October 1968, 9 p.; G096-9U1, 1 January 1969, 32 p. Bunker-Ramo Corp., Canoga Park, Calif.
(41) GARVIN, PAUL L. The place of heuristics in the fulcrum approach to machine translation. Lingua, 21 (1968) 162-182.
(42) GARVIN, PAUL L.; WORTHY, R. M.; MONTGOMERY, C. A.; SMITH, S. B.; AGNEW, I. Adaptation of advanced fulcrum techniques to MT production system (Russian-English). Vol 1. Final report. Rome Air Development Center, Griffiss Air Force Base, N.Y., October 1967. (RADC-TR-67-416)
(43) GODEL, ROBERT. F. de Saussure's theory of language. In: Seboek, Thomas, ed. Current trends in linguistics. Vol. 3: Theoretical foundations. Mouton, The Hague, 1966, p. 479-493.
(44) GOODENOUGH, JOHN B. The comparison of programming languages: a linguistic approach. In: National Conference of the Association for Computing Machinery, 23rd, Las Vegas, Nev., 27-29 August 1968. Proceedings. Brandon/Systems Press, Princeton, N.J., 1968, p. 765-785.
(45) GOTLIEB, C. C.; KUMAR, S. Semantic clustering of index terms. Journal of the Association for Computing Machinery, 15:4 (October 1968) 493-513.
(46) GREEN, C. CORDELL; RAPHAEL, BERTRAM. The use of theorem-proving techniques in question-answering systems. In: National Conference of the Association for Computing Machinery, 23rd, Las Vegas, Nev., 27-29 August 1968. Proceedings. Brandon/Systems Press, Princeton, N.J., 1968, p. 169-181.
(47) GRIMES, JOSEPH; ALSOP, JOHN R.; WARES, ALAN. Computer backup for field work in phonology. Presentation at Sixth Annual Meeting, Association for Machine Translation and Computational Linguistics, University of Illinois, 24-25 July 1968.

(48) GROSS, LOUIS N. A computer program for testing grammars on-line. MITRE Corp., Bedford, Mass., July 1968, 63 p.
(49) GROSS, LOUIS N.; WALKER, DONALD E. On-line computer aids for research in linguistics. To appear in Proceedings of the IFIP Congress, Edinburgh, 1968. North-Holland Publishing Co., Amsterdam. In press.
(50) GRUBER, JEFFREY. Functions of the lexicon in formal descriptive grammars. System Development Corp., Santa Monica, Calif., 3 December 1967, 148 p. (TM-3770)
(51) HARRIS, ZELLIG. Mathematical structures of language. Wiley, New York, 1968, 216 p.
(52) HAYASHI, HIDEYUKI; DUNCAN, SHEILA; KUNO, SUSUMU. Graphical input/output of nonstandard characters. Communications of the ACM, 11:9 (September 1968) 613-618.
(53) HAYS, DAVID G. ; HENISZ-DOSTERT, BOZENA; HOUSTON, JEAN I. Computational linguistics: bibliography, 1967. RAND Corp., Santa Monica, Calif., July 1968, 68 p. (RM-5733-PR)
(54) HIŻ, HENRY. Referentials. University of Pennsylvania, Philadelphia, 1968, 37 p. (Transformations and discourse analysis papers, no. 76)
(55) HOCKETT, CHARLES F. The state of the art. Mouton, The Hague, 1968, 123 p.
(56) JAKOBOVITS, LEON A.; MIRON, MURRAY S., eds. Readings in the psychology of language. Prentice-Hall, Englewood Cliffs, N.J., 1967, 636 p.
(57) JONES, PAUL E.; CURTICE, ROBERT M.; GIULIANO, VINCENT E.; SHERRY, MURRAY E. Application of statistical association techniques for the NASA document collection. Arthur D. Little, Cambridge, Mass., February 1968, 104 p. (NASA CR-1020)
(58) KARTTUNEN, LAURI. What do referential indices refer to? RAND Corp., Santa Monica, Calif., May 1968, 31 p. (P-3854)
(59) KATZ, JERROLD, J. Mentalism in linguistics. In: Jakobovits, Leon A.; Miron, Murray S., eds. Readings in the psychology of language. Prentice-Hall, Englewood Cliffs, N.J., 1967, p. 73-84.
(60) KATZ, JERROLD J. Recent issues in semantic theory. Massachusetts Institute of Technology, Research Laboratory of Electronics, Cambridge, 1967, 72 p.
(61) KATZ, JERROLD J. Some remarks on Quine on analyticity. Journal of Philosophy, 64 (February 1967) 35-52.
(62) KATZ, JERROLD J. Unpalatable recipes for buttering parsnips. Journal of Philosophy, 65:2 (January 1968) 29-44.
(63) KATZ, JERROLD J.; FODOR JERRY A. The structure of a semantic theory. In: Jakobovits, Leon A.; Miron, Murray S., eds. Readings in the psychology of language. Prentice-Hall, Englewood Cliffs, N.J., 1967, p. 398-431.
(64) KATZ, JERROLD, J.; POSTAL, PAUL M. An integrated theory of linguistic descriptions. MIT Press, Cambridge, Mass., 1964, 178 p.
(65) KELLOGG, CHARLES H. A natural language compiler for on-line data management. System Development Corp., Santa Monica, Calif., 30 August 1968, 51 p. (SP-3160) For presentation at the 1968 Fall Joint Computer Conference, San Francisco, 9-11 December 1968.
(66) KIEFER, FERENC. Mathematical linguistics in eastern Europe. American Elsevier, New York, 1968, 180 p. (Mathematical linguistics and automatic language processing, no. 3)
(67) KIPARSKY, PAUL. Linguistic universals and linguistic change. In: Bach, Emmon; Harms, Robert T., eds. Universals in linguistic theory. Holt, Rinehart and Winston, New York, 1968, p. 171-202.
(68) KOCHEN, MANFRED. Automatic question-answering of English-like questions about simple diagrams. Journal of the Association for Computing Machinery, 16:1 (January 1969) 26-48. (AD-670 545)
(69) KUČERA, HENRY; FRANCIS, W. NELSON. Computational analysis of present-day American English. Brown University Press, Providence, R.I., 1967, 424 p.
(70) KUHNS, J. L. Answering questions by computer: a logical study. RAND Corp.,

Santa Monica, Calif., December 1967, 192 p. (RM-5428-PR)
(71) LAKOFF, GEORGE. Instrumental adverbs and the concept of deep structure. Foundations of Language, 4:1 (February 1968) 4–29.
(72) LAKOFF, GEORGE. Pronominalization and the analysis of adverbs. In: Kuno, Susumu. Mathematical linguistics and automatic translation. Harvard University, Computational Laboratory, Cambridge, Mass., May 1968, part 2, p. 1–19.
(73) LANGENDOEN, D. TERENCE. The accessability of deep (semantic) structures. In: Working papers in linguistics. Ohio State University Research Foundation, Columbus, December 1967, p. 118–127.
(74) LANGENDOEN, D. TERENCE. On selection, projection, meaning, and semantic content. In: Working papers in linguistics. Ohio State University Research Foundation, Columbus, December 1967, p. 100–109.
(75) LEVIEN, R. E.; MARON, M. E. A computer system for inference execution and data retrieval. Communications of the ACM, 10:11 (November 1967) 715–721.
(76) LONDE, DAVE L.; SCHOENE, WILLIAM J. TGT: Transformational grammar tester. In: AFIPS conference proceedings, vol. 32, 1968 Spring Joint Computer Conference. Thompson, Washington, D.C., p. 385–393.
(77) LYONS, JOHN. Introduction to theoretical linguistics. Cambridge at the University Press, Cambridge, England, 1968, 519 p.
(78) McCAWLEY, JAMES D. Meaning and the description of languages. Kotoba No Uchū (Tokyo), 2:9 (1967) 10–18, 2:10 (1967) 38–49, 2:11 (1967) 52–57.
(79) McCAWLEY, JAMES D. The role of semantics in a grammar. In: Bach, Emmon; Harms, Robert T., eds. Universals in linguistic theory. Holt, Rinehart and Winston, New York, 1968, p. 124–169.
(80) McDANIEL, J.; DAY, A. M.; PRICE, W. L.; SZANSER, A. J. M.; WHELAN, S.; YATES, D. N. Translation of Russian scientific texts into English by computer—a final report. Autonetics Division, National Physical Laboratory, Teddington, England, July 1967.
(81) MARTINS, GARY R.; SMITH, STEVEN B. Adaptation of advanced fulcrum techniques to MT production system (Russian-English). Vol. 2: BEAST (The Basic Experimental Automatic Syntactic Translator system). Final report. Rome Air Development Center, Griffiss Air Force Base, N.Y., October 1967, 118 p. (RADC-TR-67-416)
(82) MILLER, W.; SHAW, A. Linguistic methods in picture processing: a survey. In: AFIPS conference proceedings, vol. 33, part 1, 1968 Fall Joint Computer Conference. Thompson, Washington, D.C., p. 279–290.
(83) MONTGOMERY, C. A.; WORTHY, R. M.; REITZ, G. Optical character reader applications study. Final technical report covering period Jan. 24, 1967–Aug. 24, 1968. Rome Air Development Center, Griffiss Air Force Base, N.Y., August 1968, 480 p.
(84) NATIONAL ACADEMY OF SCIENCES—NATIONAL RESEARCH COUNCIL. AUTOMATIC LANGUAGE PROCESSING ADVISORY COMMITTEE. Language and machines: computers in translation and linguistics. National Academy of Sciences—National Research Council, Washington, D.C., 1966, 124 p. (Publication 1416)
(85) PLATH, WARREN J.; ANDREYEWSKY, A.; STROM, R. E. Syntactic analysis of the Russian sentence. IBM Watson Research Center, Yorktown Heights, N.Y., October 1967, 157 p. (Technical report no. RADC-TR-67-484) (AD-824 057)
(86) POSTAL, PAUL M. Aspects of phonological theory. Harper and Row, New York, 1968, 326 p.
(87) POSTAL, PAUL M. Coordination reduction. In: Rosenbaum, Peter S. Specification and utilization of a transformational grammar. Scientific report no. 2, October 1966–September 1967. IBM Watson Research Center, Yorktown Heights, N.Y. October 1967, Section 3.
(88) RAPHAEL, BERTRAM. Research on intelligent question-answering systems. Final report. 15 April 1966–14 May 1968. Stanford Research Institute, Menlo Park, Calif., May 1968, 13 p. (AFCRL-68-0266) (AD-671 970)
(89) ROBINSON, JANE J. On some alternative sets of dependency rules equivalent to

the rewriting rules of grammar II. In: Rosenbaum, Peter S., ed. Specification and utilization of a transformational grammar. Scientific report no. 2, October 1966–September 1967. IBM Watson Research Center, Yorktown Heights, N.Y., October 1967, Section 4.

(90) ROSENBAUM, PETER S., ed. Specification and utilization of a transformational grammar. Scientific report no. 2, October 1966–September 1967. IBM Watson Research Center, Yorktown Heights, N.Y., October 1967, 272 p. (AFCRL-68-0070) (AD-667 800)

(91) ROSENBAUM, PETER S.; BLAIR, FRED. Specification and utilization of a transformational grammar. Final report, July 1965–September 1966. IBM Watson Research Center, Yorktown Heights, N.Y., October 1966. (AD-643 203)

(92) ROSENBAUM, P.; LOCHAK, K. The IBM core grammar of English. In: Lieberman, D., ed. Specification and utilization of a transformational grammar. Scientific report no. 1. IBM Watson Research Center, Yorktown Heights, N.Y., March 1966, Section 1.

(93) RUBENSTEIN, HERBERT. Some problems of meaning in natural languages. Center for the Information Sciences, Lehigh University, Bethlehem, Pa., January 1968, 39 p.

(94) RUSSELL, BERTRAND. Introduction to Mathematical philosophy. George Allen & Unwin, London, 1919, 208 p.

(95) SAKAI, ITIROO. Some mathematical aspects of syntactic description. First Research Center, Defense Agency, 2-2-1 Makamegura, Megura, Tokyo, Japan, June 1968. Privately circulated paper.

(96) SALTON, GERARD. Automated language processing. In: Annual review of information science and technology, vol. 3. Carlos A. Cuadra, ed. Encyclopaedia Britannica, Chicago, 1968, p. 169–192.

(97) SAPORTA, SOL, ed. Psycholinguistics: a book of readings. Holt, Rinehart and Winston, New York, 1961, 551 p. Reviewed by A. Richard Diebold, Jr. In: Language, 40:2 (April–June 1964) 197–259.

(98) SCHWARCZ, ROBERT M.; BURGER, JOHN F.; SIMMONS, ROBERT F. A deductive question answerer for natural language inference. System Development Corp., Santa Monica, Calif. 15 November 1968, 51 p. (SP-3272)

(99) SEDELOW, SALLY Y.; SEDELOW, WALTER A.; SMITH, WALTER L.; BARDEZ, JOAN N.; BUTTELMANN, H. WILLIAM; HICKOK, WILLIAM G.; PETERS, JOAN; RUGGLES, TERRY. Automated language analysis, 1967–1968. Report on research for the period March 1, 1967–February 29, 1968. Department of Information Science, University of North Carolina, Chapel Hill, 1968, 137 p.

(100) SEE, RICHARD. Machine-aided translation and information retrieval. In: Kent, Allen; Taulbee, Orrin E.; Belzer, Jack; Goldstein, Gordon D., eds. Electronic handling of information: testing and evaluation. Thompson, Washington, D.C.; Academic Press, London, 1967, p. 89–107.

(101) SIMMONS, ROBERT F.; BURGER, JOHN F.; SCHWARCZ, ROBERT M. A computational model of verbal understanding. System Development Corp., Santa Monica, Calif. 30 April 1968, 52 p. (SP-3132)

(102) SPARCK-JONES, K.; NEEDHAM, R. M. Automatic term classification and retrieval. Information Storage and Retrieval, 4:2 (June 1968) 91–100.

(103) STONE, DON CHARLES. Word statistics in the generation of semantic tools for information systems. Moore School of Electrical Engineering, University of Pennsylvania, Philadelphia, December 1967, 87 p. (Report 68-23) (AFOSR 68-0237) (AD-664 915)

(104) STONE, DON CHARLES; RUBINOFF, MORRIS. Statistical generation of a technical vocabulary. American Documentation, 19:4 (October 1968) 411–412.

(105) SZANSER, A. J. M. Error-correcting methods in natural language processing. I: Optimum letter sequence for longest strings in English. National Physical Laboratory, Division of Computer Science, Teddington, England, 1963.

(106) VON GLASERSFELD, ERNST; NOTAMARCO, BRUNELLA. Some adjective

classes derived from correlational grammar. Georgia Institute for Research, Athens, October 1968, 12 p. (Informal scientific report CG 1)
(107) WAITE, STEPHEN V. F. Computers and the classics. Computers and the Humanities, 3:1 (September 1968) 25–29.
(108) WALKER, G. L.; KUNO, S.; SMITH, B. N.; HOLT, R. B. Chinese mathematical text analysis. IEEE Transactions on Engineering Writing and Speech, EWS-11:2 (August 1968) 118–128.
(109) WATT, W. C. Habitability. American Documentation, 19:3 (July 1968) 338–351.
(110) WEINREICH, URIEL. Explorations in semantic theory. In: Sebeok, Thomas A. Current trends in linguistics. Vol. 3: Theoretical foundations. Mouton, The Hague, 1966, p. 395–477.
(111) WEINREICH, URIEL. On the semantic structure of language. In: Greenberg, Joseph H., ed. Universals of language. MIT Press, Cambridge, Mass., 1966, p. 114–171.
(112) WHITEHEAD, ALFRED N.; RUSSELL, BERTRAND. Principia mathematica, vol. 1. 2d ed. Cambridge at the University Press, Cambridge, England, 1950, 674 p.
(113) WILKS, YORICK. Computable semantic derivations. System Development Corp., Santa Monica, Calif., 15 January 1968, 160 p. (SP-3017)
(114) WOODS, W. A. Procedural semantics for a question-answering machine. In: AFIPS conference proceedings, vol. 33, part 1, 1968 Fall Joint Computer Conference. Thompson, Washington, D C., p. 457–471.
(115) YNGVE, VICTOR H. Some applications of computers in linguistics. Reprinted from: Languages and areas: studies presented to George V. Bobrinskoy, 1967. Division of the Humanities, University of Chicago, 1967, p. 172–179.

6 Reprography and Microform Technology

ALLEN B. VEANER
Stanford University

INTRODUCTION

We propose to begin this chapter with definitions, followed by a brief characterization of the reprographic industry, emphasizing the past ten to twelve years, and briefly summarizing basic literature on the subject. Hardware will be reviewed wherever a description or evaluation of it serves to illustrate a process, an application, or a trend. The following subjects will be excluded: technology of graphic arts and its companion industry, large-scale printing and publishing, phototypesetting, patents, and copyright.

Reprography is the class of processes whose purpose is to replicate by optical or photomechanical means previously created graphic or coded messages. The ability of optical systems to change the scale of a subject is one of the most powerful features of reprography, and, accordingly, in its most generic sense, "reprography" is a term that is independent of image size. Unfortunately, in popular usage reprography connotes full-size reproduction. Hence, almost all literature dealing with images sufficiently reduced to require optical aid for viewing incorporates the prefix "micro-" as an explicit warning to the reader. In this chapter, the term "reprography" will be employed in its *generic* sense, and "micro-" will indicate reduced images. The reader is advised that, while reprography subsumes microphotography, it does not follow that the technology of full-scale reproduction can be extrapolated to microreproduction. It is particularly essential to be aware of this distinction because of differences in the way photographic systems respond to optical enlargement and reduction. Extreme reduction of scale introduces many nonlinear phenomena, and it is wise to avoid the error of believing that the problems of microreproduction are merely those of full-size copying "writ small."

While reprography is almost entirely concerned with analog or graphic material, it does not exclude digitized data from its domain. It includes all methods using a portion of the electromagnetic spectrum to reproduce documents, where document is defined as some modulated two-dimensional medium. All photographic and nonphotographic processes whose variables range over space and time can generate data suitable for inputs for reprography. In fact, there appears to be no scheme of modulating a medium that cannot find expression by reprography.

Another useful characteristic of reprography is its ability to apply images to a variety of supports. Film and paper are the most common supports, but it is also possible to imprint images on glass, plastic, cloth, and metal.

The word "reprography" was coined by the Germans about a decade ago to provide a concise and generic term comprehending all aspects of document reproduction and to combat the imprecision arising from the application of trade names to generic methods. Reprography embraces all methods, materials, equipments, kinds, and sizes of originals and reproductions. It provides the technology for "near print" publication as well as for copying. The International Congress on Reprography was held in Cologne, Germany in 1963 and again in 1967; a third Congress meets in London in 1971.

Full-size reproduction can be divided into four major categories: (*1*) reproduction of engineering drawings, (*2*) office and library copying, (*3*) plate-making for printing, and (*4*) specialized industrial applications, such as the making of templates for ship and aircraft assemblies. The last two categories will not be treated in this chapter, but interested readers are referred to Denstman & Schultz (21).

For full-size copying, the chief successful commercial methods are those based on silver-halide photography, electrophotography, diazotypy, thermography, and electrolysis. In microreproduction, only silver-halide and diazo technology have enjoyed wide success, although experiments have been conducted using electrophotography and photochromism. A host of equipments and processing variations have been built around these methods, and nearly all are described exhaustively in Hawken (29). The document, a manual of copying methods published by the American Library Association, includes descriptions of some methods that are still developmental as well as those that are declining in popularity.

For tasks requiring full-size copies at or near a one-to-one reproduction scale, reprography has reached a very high state of technical perfection, mainly owing to the user's requirement for rapid turnaround time. Consider the users of full-size reproduction systems: architects, executives, engineers, the military, printers, manufacturers. Wherever the user required quick use of the finished product, competition motivated technical achievement. Today, there is practically no full-scale reproduction requirement for which some excellent reprographic technique or equipment does not exist. The existence of professional organizations, such as the Society of Reproduction Engineers, and annual trade shows, such as the Visual Communication Congress, is strong evidence that in its application to full-size replication, reprography has reached maturity.

The successes of full-size reprography have not, unfortunately, been so nearly well matched in microreproduction, for reasons that will be enumerated. We shall interpose here a brief review of how the reprographic industry has developed during the past decade.

THE REPROGRAPHIC INDUSTRY

Continuum of Reprographic Processes

Until recently, a sharp dividing line separated processes that created an original document and those that furnished copies. It is difficult to maintain this distinction, and in place of a graded series of separate processes, a continuum is emerging. Similarly, the once-important distinction between processes that produced one copy and those that produced many is no longer tenable. The development of such continua is attributable to the rapid introduction of cheap, automated electrophotographic copiers about a decade ago. Today, the courtship of reprographic and computer technology is further uniting two partners that must eventually merge into a single graphic communication facility. Combinations of magnetic storage, text-editing programs, soft copy, hard copy, and other reprographic techniques enable a collection of keystrokes, or their coded representation, to pass through a comprehensive series of steps capable of producing any desired number of copies of a given document.

Decade of Rapid Change

Reprographic techniques have only recently emerged from the era of craft operation to systematic management. As long as the physics and chemistry of photographic processes remained imperfectly understood by much of the user community, and available knowledge was not communicated to management, photographers and reproduction personnel were gladly left alone in their wet, messy darkrooms with their chemical odors and livid lights. About a dozen years ago, however, all this began to change radically. The primary impetus for change came from a Government decision to require all Department of Defense (DoD) contractors to submit complete sets of microfilmed drawings as part of their contract obligations. The design, manufacture, and maintenance of complex weapons systems virtually ruled out the traditional method of using full-size blueprints and schematics, which would have aggregated tons of paper at every facility. Indeed, the very creation of complex weapons systems would have been impossible without suitably compact means of recording and communicating graphic information. Furthermore, updating of conventional drawings would have required a staggering number of draftsmen and file maintenance personnel in the field.

At the end of World War II, it was still common for industrial and commercial reprographic installations to mix their own processing solutions from bulk chemicals, a practice that has virtually disappeared in favor of prepackaged mixes prepared under careful process control. Ten years ago it was common for reprographic technicians to "eyeball" exposure and development. However, today there is widespread use of automatic devices for determining optimum exposure, and, invariably, a fully automatic, highly mechanized processing apparatus is employed for all types and sizes of sensitized materials. Both in full-size reproduction and in microphotography, the decade saw a switch from simple step-and-repeat to continuous processing; this change occurred mainly in the silver-halide and electrophotographic processes, but to no great extent in diazotypy or thermography, because the latter processes cater mostly to plan and office copying—applications that deal with very large originals and relatively few copies, respectively, and hence are unsuitable for continuous processing.

A social change has occurred, too. Old-style reprographers not only mixed their own "soup," but they also made their own work schedules, exerted their best efforts for their favorite customers, and varied their productivity widely. As mechanization took over, the reprographic technician no longer interacted directly with his customer. He was replaced by the reprographic professional, knowledgeable in chemistry, mechanics, electronics, and cost accounting. Those who could not adapt remained as machine operators or left to take other jobs. In response to the rapid application of newer techniques, trade schools and industrial training institutions established curricula to promote education and training for professional reprography. The most well-known school is the Hatfield College of Technology, which also hosts the British National Reprographic Centre for Documentation (9), an agency charged with gathering information on microrecording, evaluating equipment, and conducting research.

New Processes and Methods

During the past dozen years, a number of new processes have reached commercial success, owing to the stimulus of the DoD and the National Aeronautics and Space Administration (NASA). Among them are thermography, xerography, and other electrophotographic processes; vesicular films,[1] thermoplastic recording, various methods of "dry" processing, nonreversing silver-halide materials; and reversible diazo materials. Some older processes, such as photochromism and ultrahigh reduction, have been rediscovered and subjected to intensive research, while some newer ones, such as holography and laser-beam recording, are still in the laboratory. However, in reprography, application lags far behind research.

Within this same period, manufacturers developed and marketed more refined instrumentation, which permitted reprography to benefit from the experience of the process control industry. These instruments included sensitometers; densitometers and microdensitometers to replace former instruments relying on visual comparison; focussing meters—again, to remove the subjective element of human vision; and film inspection stations for finished products. The National Bureau of Standards (56) issued improved resolution charts for measuring the performance of the complete reprographic system. Chemical testing setups were marketed to encourage consistent, repeatable results in tests for archival permanence, a responsibility that had been neglected or performed in hit-or-miss fashion.

Thus, until quite recently, the reprographic industry presented a paradox: the one thing it lacked was reproducibility of results from one laboratory to another, given the same tasks, equipment, materials, and methods. Responsible for the radical changes that occurred in this short time was the realization by Government and industry that reprography is part of a larger communication facility. Once designers and users began to understand this, the same techniques of analysis, design, and standardization that worked so well in electronic communication could be applied to reprography.

Characteristics of Reprographic Literature

Software is only beginning to make an impact upon reprography, an industry that has heretofore been exclusively hardware oriented. Hence, reprographic literature is represented almost entirely by trade publications rather than research journals. In fact, the vast majority of reprographic literature is frankly promotional. More than a dozen different periodicals are sent each month, without charge, to managers and technicians, service companies, and educational institutions. Advertising pays for these subscriptions, and advertising income is directly related to the consumption of supplies, which generates far more profits than hardware. Articles in such journals often tend to trumpet the virtues of a particular method, material, or piece of equipment because they are usually written by sales-oriented persons, or "tech reps," whose main responsibility is promotion. Despite

---

[1] Vesicular films form images by light scattering rather than absorption; a detailed functional description of vesicular imaging materials and systems may be found in Nieset (58).

this bias, the literature of reprography does not lack outstanding titles of research interest. Imprints prior to 1967 have been described in a bibliography by Veaner (72), and currently published research works are described in the next section.

BASIC WORKS IN REPROGRAPHY AND MICROFORM TECHNOLOGY

Monographs

A handful of monographs constitutes the basic library of reprographic literature. All are modern works, none bearing an imprint prior to 1965, so recently has reprography emerged as a distinct discipline. In fact, when Stevens's (67) book was first issued, in 1957, some colleagues doubted that there was enough material to justify a volume on microphotography and that more than a few people would buy such a book. Extensive reviews of these basic works cannot be attempted, but each will be briefly described.

Stevens's book is the most comprehensive textbook in microphotography. He expended much effort in delineating the features that distinguish microreproduction from all other branches of photography. By stating that in microphotography "matters of convenience cannot be permitted the priority they doubtless deserve in other photographic activities," Stevens has articulated the basic rule for success in microreproduction work. The main focus of Stevens's volume is on scientific, laboratory, and photofabrication applications, particularly microcircuits and reticles. It is by no means a handbook for those whose main concern is the microreproduction of documents, although he does devote one excellent chapter to that subject. Containing over 450 references, it is not only the best-documented work on microphotography in English, but also an excellent antidote to the popular fallacy that other established photographic techniques are applicable to microreproduction.

Nelson (54) has written a book concerned almost exclusively with the application of microphotography to the storage and dissemination of engineering drawings. His text is richly illustrated and is presented with great clarity. It is ideally suited for reading by students, managers of reprographic facilities, and scientists. Verry (78) has published a recent work that is less successful. It retains many errors from an earlier edition and includes a few new ones. In addition to offering an erroneous explanation of resolution, it also claims that there is one reader that has condensor lenses that "automatically separate when the film is moved" to protect film from scratching. This appears to indicate confusion with the movable glass flats present on a number of readers. In a table illustrating the causes of various processing faults, "exhausted solution" is cited as a cause and "poor quality microfilm" as the result. A brief handbook issued by the British Government's Interdepartmental Group in Microcopying (36) is intended to educate administrators in various branches of the British civil service. By carefully emphasizing the problems, disadvantages, and hidden costs associated with microcopying, the handbook offers an admirably balanced view of a subject that has frequently been distorted in many directions.

Hawken (29) has published the only work dealing with the reprographic problems of a special and voluminous class of subjects typically found in research libraries: the nonstandard input documents ranging from cuneiform and hieroglyphs through printing, photography, and all graphic-recording media. Both full-size reprography and microreproduction are treated. A beginner's booklet issued by the Eastman Kodak Company (23) in 1968 is available for a dollar in most camera stores. The Kodak booklet, while elementary, convinces the reader that copying is far from a casual activity.

None of these monographs deals with the problems of staffing, supervision, and personnel training that are peculiar to the reprographic industry. Errors of judgment in reprography either perpetuate themselves through many generations of copies or are responsible for increased costs through unnecessary equipment maintenance, work needlessly done over, or undesirably rapid staff turnover. The personnel requirements for machine operators in the reprographic industry are somewhat contradictory; a condition of constant alertness for changes in the input, coupled with the ability to withstand repetitive work. The authors of these basic texts would do well to incorporate a chapter on personnel management in revised editions of these works.

There are two indispensable works to aid in the selection of microphotographic equipment. They are the equipment guide edited by Ballou (5) for equipment manufactured in the United States and a companion guide edited by Rubin (62) for equipment manufactured abroad.

Journals and Bibliographies

The principal technical journals devoted entirely to microreproduction are both official organs of the National Microfilm Association. They are the *NMA Journal* (59) and the *Proceedings* (53) of the annual convention. In Great Britain, the chief journals are those issued by the Microfilm Association of Great Britain (48) and the Institute of Reprographic Technology (61).

Besides the fundamental texts and journals, Kiersky (39) and Veaner (74) have regularly published annual bibliographies and review articles. A comprehensive bibliography by Veaner (72) is contained in Hawken (29). Another useful bibliography has been issued by the Defense Documentation Center (20).

IMPACT OF SOFTWARE ON REPROGRAPHY AND MICROPHOTOGRAPHY

The Optical-Electronic Communication Model

There are numerous analogies between photographic and electronic systems. A lens may be compared to a wideband channel that transmits large quantities of data in parallel; the behavior of chemically processed photographic materials can be compared to families of fixed-gain amplifiers functioning without feedback. Craig (18) has published an excellent, detailed account of these analogies, an understanding of which is essential to full comprehension of the merger of computer and reprographic technologies.

Actually, in conventional chemical processing, some limited manual feedback can be provided by the experienced darkroom technician. Photographers who develop film by inspection, or "dodge" or "burn it," prints are making themselves part of the feedback loop in a subjective, nonrepeatable way. They are varying the amplitude response (gain) of the system. The absence of feedback, however, has been one of the characteristics distinguishing photo-optical from electronic information processing systems. (Another distinguishing characteristic has been the time delay inherent in photographic processing, an area in which considerable progress has recently been made.) About a decade ago, two equipments incorporating feedback were introduced, marking the earliest impact of software upon reprography: the LogEtronic SP10/70 contact printer and the Stromberg-Carlson computer output microfilm (COM) recorder.

A brief discussion of photographic system characteristics will assist readers in understanding the significance of software for reprography. Unlike systems that handle data serially, reprographic information systems process large quantities of data—up to half a billion bits per second—in parallel. Conventional methods and equipments do not permit differential amplification of portions of the message or signal, however. Conventionally, an input signal (image) is subjected to a first stage of fixed-gain amplification by parallel transmission (exposure through the lens) onto some photographic material manufactured to be uniformly responsive across its surface. A second stage of amplification occurs when the exposed material is subjected to development, another process where uniformity of action is the goal. But in the LogEtronic SP10/70 contact printer, an image is projected by a flying spot scanner, its brightness is detected, and through negative feedback, immediate correction is applied to the flying spot. The result, equivalent to *programmed* dodging, is piece-by-piece management of the data in a photographic record. For the first time, it has become possible to provide for reprography the same variable amplification facility long known in electronic systems.

Computer Output Microfilm Recorder

The SC-4020 computer output microfilm recorder, the first commercially available device of its kind, was introduced in 1959 by Stromberg-Carlson. For a long time, Stromberg-Carlson dominated the field, but within the past few years, more than half a dozen manufacturers have entered the market with competing COM recorders, and as the devices really began to catch on, dozens of service companies were established. COM devices have successfully solved a major problem for computer users, namely, the inability of mechanical line printers to keep pace with computer output. Additionally, the COM recorders can act as programmed film plotters, generating vector representations, schematic illustrations, and synthetic motion pictures. COM devices have already been used to provide motion-picture representations of equipotential surface contours and even worldwide weather projections. Models of many physical phenomena, including galaxy formation, are now for the first time being seen through this new "window."[2] COM recorders also can be programmed to generate any kind of graphic symbol or non-Roman alphabetic characters. An excellent anonymous article (33) surveys current COM equipment and applications to scientific and business problems.

One of the best-documented cost and application studies on the computer-output microfilm recorder is that issued by the Army Materiel Command (22). Designated NIPP, for Non-Impact Printing Project, the study details how a conventional report-generating system in seven computer installations was replaced by a system in which reports are disseminated on microfilm cartridges. The itemized lists of cost factors in this report are an excellent model. Computer time and supplies, freight, space, and minor office supplies are included; only the cost of utilities is omitted.

Programmed Film Readers and Plotters

Jackson et al. (38) reported on the development of Automated Microfilm Aperture Card Update System, (AMACUS), a device that permits a microfilm aperture card to become the primary unit of storage in an engineering drawing system. It is said to afford complete independence from original drawings, once the first-generation microcopy has been made. A high-resolution scanner converts information in a given aperture card into analog data, which in turn are digitized and stored on a drum, from which they are displayed to an operator seated at a control console. The operator can use teletypewriter and light pen to modify the displayed image with new alphabetic and graphic information. Modifications are stored, and,

---

[2] For arranging a demonstration of COM films, I am indebted to Professor Oscar Buneman, Department of Electrical Engineering, Stanford University.

upon command, are recorded directly upon an unexposed aperture card that is immediately processed by a self-contained film processor supplied by the 3M Company. Complete cycle time is five minutes, including film processing. The over 25 million bits stored on the drum are derived from 4,096 lines of 6,144 discrete points each. There is no character generator for alphanumeric data; a prepared aperture card with a complete character set is scanned at the beginning of a session and internally stored.

A great advantage of the AMACUS lies in the redundancy afforded by the digitized storage of graphic images. It is well known that progressive information loss occurs during conventional iterative copying of photographic images, and it would be interesting to know how many generations the AMACUS system could take a given graphic image through before degradation sets in. In other words, how many update cycles does this expensive digital system buy? Unfortunately, the report does not touch upon this subject. Also not described is the delicate and sensitive nature of the system. Special cycles, not unlike those needed for computer operations, are required for startup and shutdown if catastrophe is to be avoided, and these are detailed in the manufacturer's operator training manual (25). The AMACUS has been delivered to the Rock Island Arsenal of the U.S. Army Weapons Command at Rock Island, Illinois. Silkiner (65) has published a popular article on the AMACUS.

Gray (26) reported on studies aimed at employing microfilm as an intermediate input to a developmental OCR (Optical Character Recognition) device suited for reading line and text material. To assess the information content of a given document, he introduces the concept of "document resolution," which is defined as the ratio of the diagonal of a document to the width of the narrowest significant line on the document. Typewritten documents, then, are characterized by a document resolution of about 2,800, and engineering drawings reach about 3,800. The author goes on to suggest that optimum results require a scanner resolution about twice the document resolution, and suggests that this capability is already at hand because a CRT 4.25″ in diameter can display a spot half a mil in diameter. "Points in text or line drawings," he goes on to say, "are scannable at the rate of 3 million per second." Gray's calculations indicate about 24 million bits in a typical engineering drawing, assuming 130 linear bits per inch and a line width of .015″. This checks well with Jackson et al. (38). Gray suggests that a typical engineering drawing might be scanned in less than 10 seconds. He rejects the notion that it might be possible to enhance images by working on them one point at a time. Instead, he indicates the need for an extremely complex array of software that examines the density of each image point in relation to its neighbors, the geometric characteristics of a given line, its length, thickness, and so forth.

Continuous vs. Step-and-Repeat Systems

Despite the great amount of research still remaining to make programmable film readers commonplace, reliable devices, the task is worthwhile because mircofilm has the advantage not only of increasing the contrast of many input documents, but also of substituting continuous reading for step-and-repeat reading. (Manufacturers and service companies prefer continuous equipment over step-and-repeat devices, not necessarily because of greater instantaneous throughput rates, but because of greater reliability, which is achieved by employing a large number of rotary components in the equipment, rather than reciprocating components.) The microfilm industry has well-established systems for recording different kinds and sizes of documents. Camera systems can integrate into a standard, continuous format (16mm or 35mm film) a variety of original documents, somewhat as punched cards are integrated into a continuous medium by copying onto magnetic tape. (The analogy is imperfect, because the punched card is a highly standardized input document.) Once a continuous strip of film is formed, it can be read—even reread—under program control much more easily than discrete paper documents that require complex feeding devices.

HIGH-REDUCTION MICROFORM SYSTEMS

Background

Although ultrahigh reductions have been known for more than a century, their commercial possibilities have not been exploited, owing to the extremely severe demands they place upon materials, methods, equipment, and environment. Photochromic materials, for instance, must be refrigerated to 0°C to maintain their sensitivity and their recorded data. All dust particles larger than one-third of a micron must be excluded from the refrigeration chamber. Dust or dirt within a high-reduction optical system is a much more serious problem than with conventional reductions. No manufacturer has yet met the challenge of manufacturing, for sale to the mass market, inexpensive reading devices for ultrahigh reduction images.

The production of ultrahigh reduction images requires special care and considerable investment in the master copy. Usually, the master copy is produced in two steps of reduction rather than one. There are several reasons for this: (*1*) except for reversed microscopes, there are no commercial lenses capable of achieving an ultrahigh reduction in a single step, and (*2*) the need to avoid catastrophic loss of thousands of exposures because of some accident that occurs while the master is being processed. To achieve the final image successfully, a carefully controlled primary film is required. This is created at a rather low reduction (on the order of 8X to 28X) by means of refined versions of conventional microfilm cameras. Perforated film is sometimes used for the primary film to assist with accurate image registration when the second reduction is taken. Two major techniques are currently in use, a photochromic system and a silver-halide system.

Carlson & Ives (15) have described some highly refined laboratory techniques for recording microimages by means of a laser beam. Energy absorbed by the recording medium from the laser beam raises the temperature of the recording medium to the point where some detectable physical change takes place, i.e., change of color or formation of troughs or ridges. A threshold-effect characteristic of certain recording media enables the system to record a spot considerably smaller than the diameter of the recording beam. Despite the fact that the experimental system here described was developed from highly adjustable, off-the-shelf components, it is apparent that the technology of laser beam recording is still in the laboratory stage and some distance from achieving commercial success. Beiser (7) has published a mathematical treatment of the mechanical-optical criteria for designing high-resolution scanning systems employing laser beams.

Ver Hulst & Belok (77) reported a series of mathematical simulation techniques for preparing camera operator instructions to optimize exposure techniques when creating ultrafiche from a variety of input materials. To develop their simulation technique, data were gathered on 60 different type faces, ranging in size from 4 to 14 points. The net effect is to translate heuristic document-sorting operations, empirical choice of exposure, and variation of processing parameters into a series of carefully controlled, algorithm-like steps essential for production of high-quality primary film. Muller (50) has described in popular language the work of Ver Hulst & Belok, who originally developed this silver-halide system for the Republic Aviation Division of Fairchild-Hiller. All rights to the system have recently been acquired by Microform Data Systems, Inc., of Palo Alto, Calif.

Problems and Potentials of Ultrahigh Reduction Systems

The possibility of condensing vast stores of text in ultrareduced form has fascinated men for a long time. Over a century ago, Sir John Herschel (34) and his brother-in-law, John Stewart, corresponded about the possibility of "preserving public records in a concentrated form on microscopic negatives." They even mentioned the need for creating enlarged positive copies. Although today's advanced technology has brought closer the realization of this dream, many obstacles still remain. Hays et al. (30) have suggested creation of a thousand libraries which would have a million books each in ultrafiche form to distribute in this country and abroad, especially among the developing nations. A somewhat similar proposal has been suggested by Teplitz (68, 69). Both proposals are based on an idea promoted by Heilprin (31) that libraries should consider distributing, rather than circulating, material. Major technical problems remain to be solved before this idea can be implemented. For instance, Hays et al. suggest a system of diagonal stripes and manual filing to maintain file integrity, despite strong contrary evidence from users that lack of fully automated handling is the most exasperating aspect of using fiche (35).[3] They also suggest providing a wall projector for classroom use. However, they do not point out that there are substantial optical and heat transfer problems associated with transmitting sufficient light flux through an image only a few millimeters square. Another critical problem, which appears to have been ignored, is that of contamination of the high-resolution glass plates used to make masters in the silver-halide process. Levine (43) describes *in extenso* the removal of glass chips by ultrasonic cleaning (which must be done in darkness prior to exposure) and the need for ultrapure water and filtration of processing solutions. Even after the most elaborate precautions, selected plates may still contain an irreducible minimum of 30 to 50 defects per square inch—clearly a limiting factor for choice of reduction ratio.

Neither Hays et al. nor Teplitz deals with the problem of recording original material that varies widely in size, format, and type font. The whole advantage of the ultrafiche is built around creation of a new, artificially standardized document from a multiplicity of unstandardized source documents. If the source material varies widely and the output terminal can deal with only a single magnification, then either some documents must be eliminated from the collection or alternate systems must be devised. How, for example, will an ultrafiche system record and display newspapers, broadsides, maps, folios, and quarto books? This remains one of the unsolved problems of the proposed ultrafiche systems.

Despite the manifold problems of bringing ultrafiche to practical, everyday use, Encyclopaedia Britannica issued a brochure in 1968 (24) announcing plans to publish a library of 20,000 volumes in ultrafiche by 1970. Since the books to be filmed have not yet been selected and will aggregate millions of pages—all of which will require low-reduction primary films of the highest quality—and no low-cost commercially available readers exist, it seems unlikely that this program can be achieved within the time frame specified.

A major problem with the ultrafiche is lack of standards. With the aid of a grant from the Office of Education, the Denver Research Institute is

---

[3]Donald C. Holmes, Principal Investigator of the Association of Research Libraries' Microform Technology Study (4), has indicated to the author that a large number of interviewees in his study pointed to handling as their chief objection to the major difficulty with sheet microforms. The need for constant refiling has often led to misfiling and loss. Dirt from the fingers of users also contributed to surface contamination and attendant scratching and loss of legibility. Holmes concludes that effective use of microforms is dependent upon development of some non-manual system for handling them. Results of this study, which is funded by the Office of Education, will be published, probably in 1969.

studying ultrafiche technology. A first goal of this project is to determine to what degree image legibility is dependent upon reduction ratio. From this and related studies, the Institute expects to formulate recommendations that could be considered for adoption as standards.

Teplitz (68, 69) has suggested adoption of an intermediate reduction ratio, on the order of 50X or 60X, for library materials, based upon an assumed average book length of 300 to 400 pages. Reference is made to an Eastman Kodak 45X lens, but no documentation is provided about this lens. In general, the higher-reduction camera lenses and their companion higher-magnification reader lenses do not represent the manufacturer's best efforts in lens design, because they are usually created for business systems centering around cancelled checks or invoices—applications where low-grade components are acceptable and devices must be built to sell at low prices. Held (32) points to lens *quality* as the most important factor in ultramicrofilming. He also indicates that the manufacturing precision required for ultramicro optics is about ten times that required for normal lenses. In a long and detailed technical paper, Buzawa et al. (14) support this contention by specifying the fabrication tolerances for microphotographic objectives. For example, surface finishing must be perfect to within one-eighth of a wave length, centering of lens elements accurate within ± 10 microradians, and interelement spacing precise within 0.0001 inch. Similar results are reported by Tibbetts & Wilczynski (70), who have developed a large number of low-reduction lenses for two-step production of microcircuits. They maintain that to avoid image degradation, each lens must be used only at its designed reduction. Even a 10% departure from the design center makes it impossible to produce usable microcircuits.

Teplitz (69) has also written a cost-benefit analysis of the proposed intermediate reduction microfiche. In it, he claims that fiche generated from a computer output microfilm printer, such as the Stromberg-Carlson SC-4060, can result in more economical dissemination of a given number of copies of a document than conventional offset printing or the COSATI microfiche. However, in suggesting that these same cost benefits accrue to microfiche of retrospective documents, Teplitz's analysis is seriously misleading. He asserts that:

> because of the relatively low cost of Book Fiche, it is possible to make available to a country . . . a university . . . an individual . . . all of the available knowledge and collections of books and information that is now not available because of costs. Historians, economists, social scientists, hard scientists can collect books from Harvard University Library and have them available in Tel Aviv, and London, and Rome, and Tokyo, at a cost of 15 cents per book.

The flaw in this argument lies in the fact that retrospective collections must still be optically copied by conventional microphotographic equipment because they possess all the physical problems so well described by Hawken (29). These materials will continue to require conventional cameras, lenses, and films until some OCR equipment or digitizing devices are perfected that will, by making source data independent of the medium, free microphotography from its dependence upon the format and type font characteristics of the original. It appears that such a development will not be forthcoming soon, and any claim that the book fiche or ultrafiche represents the ultimate solution to the storage and dissemination of research materials must be judged unwarranted and premature.

REMOTE STORAGE AND ACCESS DEVICES

Conway (17) describes a new, computer-controlled aperture card management system in use at Westinghouse Electric Corporation. The new facility extends a previously installed system by utilizing touch-tone telephones and the Mosler Selectriever storage unit. For each drawing required by a user, the identification number and number of copies are keyed into a touch-tone instrument. Inventory and status information on each drawing are maintained on a disc file, along with a series of canned messages on a voice-response unit. Each request is automatically followed by an appropriate voice response, and each of these responses also causes an activity record for each drawing to be posted. Simultaneously, a message is sent to the Selectriever unit, and this causes the requested aperture card to be extracted, copied onto diazo film, and then restored to the file. The diazo copy is used to generate the desired prints by means of an electrostatic printer. The operation of the Selectriever itself is described in two separate reports (10, 80).

Halsey (27) proposed a similar but much more elaborate and versatile system to serve the needs of secondary schools and public libraries in the St. Louis area. Under Title III of the Elementary and Secondary Education Act, a planning project was designed to incorporate nearly every known microstorage and micropublication medium in a resources center having access to a computer, remote terminals, a central file access mechanism, facsimile transmission facilities, and a complete microreproduction laboratory. An interesting facet of this proposal is an idea that goes contrary to current practises in academic microfilm repositories, namely, that microfilm should be used not for rarely storing consulted research materials, but for providing storage of and access to those study resources that are most heavily in demand. To this observer, it seems that substantial advances in standards, methods, and hardware are prerequisite to the success of this ambitious proposal.

The Mosler Selectriever described by Conway (17) is one of several devices now reaching the commercial market. Most are descended from earlier, multimillion dollar, one-of-a-kind equipments such as Walnut, Cypress, Dare, Magnacard, and others. These devices preceded the widespread use of large-scale computer systems with high-speed graphic display terminals. A variety of lower-priced microstorage equipments, some under $100,000, were exhibited at the 1968 convention of the National Microfilm Association. Included were Sperry Rand's Remstar, HF Image Systems' CARD, and the SD-500 Automatic Microimage Retrieval System, a joint venture of Sanders Associates and Diebold, Inc. Except for CARD, none of these equipments has as yet been described in the literature, but all are now being marketed. All except CARD depend upon a centralized file and remote display terminals. In the CARD system, each station is a self-contained, decentralized storage and display unit employing microfiche in magazines. CARD terminals are being effectively used by MIT's Project INTREX (44) as the storage devices in text access experiments.

The remote display of microfilmed images presents substantial optical and electronic challenges that have been detailed in a study by Knudson et al. (40). A major contribution of the Knudson study lies in its employment of the optical system/linear network analogy. Knudson utilizes a concept similar to Gray's (26) "document resolution," and he concurs with Gray's contention that the number of scan lines for transmission should be twice the document resolution. However, Knudson also states that higher scan rates may be required under certain conditions. Knudson's thorough work is an excellent model that illustrates well the hazards that might follow if simplistic assumptions are made in dealing with systems combining film, optics, electronics, and screen phosphors.

APPLICATIONS OF MICROFORM TECHNOLOGY TO ENGINEERING DRAWING

An obvious candidate for the application of microphotographic systems is the engineering drawing. However, many formidable obstacles have stood in the way of such applications, and, owing to limitations of equipment and originals, the candidate has proved quite refractory in early implementations. There were four major problems that had to be solved: (*1*) development of drafting standards for new drawings, (*2*) how to record both line and halftone copy on high-contrast materials, (*3*) how to record reproducible images of low-contrast drawings, and (*4*) how to control illumination of the subject. Actually, the illumination problem is common to all systems employing high-contrast materials. Ten years ago, no solution existed for the first three problems, although the illumination problem could be solved with much patience and difficulty. Impetus from several Government agencies, notably the Department of Defense, the Atomic Energy Commission, and NASA, provided the solutions.

Drafting Standards

NASA (51) has issued a detailed handbook specifying that agency's microfilming requirements for engineering drawings and supporting data. Nelson's (55) book on drafting is an excellent primer and self-education manual for experienced microphotographers unfamiliar with newer technical terms, such as "line spread function," "edge gradient," and "acutance." Of special interest is the "microfont" type style created by the National Microfilm Association's Standards Committee and recommended for drawings that might be subject to future microfilming. The effects of variations in line density, line width, and spacing (spatial frequency) are carefully documented, and examples are reproduced in the text to illustrate how such variations affect output. A table details the characteristics of engineering drawings and the corresponding specifications required by DoD, Canadian, British, and NMA standards. Davis (19) presented a paper on drafting for microfilming, but it contains little not already said more effectively by Nelson (55). Davis's paper lacks illustrations—a serious defect in any presentation on graphic communication.

Mixed Line and Halftone Copy

High-contrast materials typically used in microfilming do not accept an admixture of continuous tone, halftone, and line copy. Jackman (37) reported use of a straight-line screen to microfilm mixed copy for the production of photodrawings. A 62-line screen consisting of 50% lines and 50% spaces is used to break up a continuous-tone or halftone image into a line-like image, which is then exposed to form a positive transparency. The film transparency, now resembling a television raster, is superimposed upon line copy, and the combination is microfilmed. Because photodrawings closely resemble a finished product, they are widely used to speed assembly operations in manufacturing.

Maps and Old, Soiled Drawings

Topographic maps and old, soiled engineering drawings are not amenable to direct, one-step copying on 35mm film. The very thin lines and near halftones in topographic maps do not hold up well at the high reductions that would normally be required to film these large originals in one step. A report issued by the National Reprographic Centre for Documentation (52) indicated the suitability of 70mm film with moderate reduction ratios for copying these materials, and 105mm film has long been used for this purpose in the United States.

Old and worn engineering drawings constitute an interesting reprographic problem. Manufacturers of long-established products that change slowly, frequently need to replicate some very old drawings. If the number of such drawings is large, redrafting to modern standards would be prohibitively expensive. The nonlinearity of the exposure-development mechanism militates against effective recording of low-contrast data or halftone dots. A unique solution to this problem is found in a two-step microreproduction process described by Barrett (6) and Morgan (49), who developed the apparatus, and by Buckley (10), who recounts successful applications. A first step requires use of 105mm film. Very low reductions of large drawings on 105mm film are quite successful because the exposed images do not trespass into the "forbidden" range where the nonlinearity effects occur. Morgan points out that successful further reduction to 35mm film is possible by direct projection onto diazo microfilm, a grainless material that produces a dye image. It is thus possible to obtain in two reduction steps an image quality not achievable in one step.

Illumination

The illumination of the original document to be copied has been subject to much misconception, misinformation, and persistent error. Experienced reprographers have long recognized that to compensate for nonlinear light losses in the optical system, it is necessary to illuminate the subject *unevenly*. The larger the original to be copied, the more difficult it is to control illumination; hence, the problem is most critical with large drawings. Varden (71) has thoroughly detailed the facts of proper illumination technique, but practically despairs of exploding the persistent fallacies, many of which have crept into established textbooks, including two U.S. Navy handbooks on lithography (12, 13). Varden's despair is understandable when one observes the "even lighting" fallacy in two 1968 publications. Ollerenshaw (60) erroneously asserts that "the whole of the copy must be evenly illuminated," and Matthews (45) repeats the fiction. (Matthews devotes a whole chapter to copying flat subjects, but his work is of little practical value because he includes no technical data on films. Instead, he characterizes sensitized materials with imprecise terms that fell out of use decades ago, such as "process," "ordinary," and "medium-speed panchromatic." It is quite meaningless to suggest lens apertures and shutter speeds in the light of this sparse information.) Kramer (41) has devised a unique and highly ingenious technique to assure proper illumination of the subject. Recognizing that the purpose of uneven copyboard illumination is to secure even illumination in the focal plane, he describes a probe that is inserted into the film plane. The probe contains 13 CdS cells and is used in conjunction with a test subject containing 13 test patches in corresponding positions on the copyboard. When the lighting is adjusted so that equal readings are obtained from each cell, one can feel sure that illumination of the original is satisfactory. This technique should be a useful replacement for its predecessor, which required a time-consuming series of actual exposures, each of which had to be developed and examined with a densitometer, until a final exposure with even density was obtained.

MICROPUBLISHING

Need for Micropublication Systems

With the advent of a variety of 16mm cartridges and recent adoption of the 105mm-by-148mm microfiche, micropublication has been widely promoted. Prior to this time, only a few commercial firms, such as Micro Photo and University Microfilms, and Government services, e.g., the Library of Congress and the National Archives, accounted for most of the nation's micropublication efforts. Through long experience, these organizations established high standards of bibliographic control and technical performance, and users needed worry only over the inferior output of a few marginal producers. The recent proliferation of micropublication has radically changed this situation. Entrepreneurs, inexperienced in microreproduction and lacking bibliographic or technical competence or knowledge of user requirements, have entered the field.

Although 16mm cartridge and fiche systems are working well in current awareness applications (technical reports, parts catalogs, company reports, etc.), micropublication has never been popular in the academic community, where use has centered primarily on archival materials. Actually, with the sole exception of newspapers, micropublication has been a failure in academe. Veaner (73, 74, 76) attributes the problem to a clash between a system that demands optimization of the input and the actual input, which consists of uncontrolled, archival material, such as manuscripts and poorly printed originals. Even the relatively simple and obvious requirement of file completeness has been ignored by some micropublishers who do not even attempt to locate a nearly complete file or to fill in gaps. The completeness problem is compounded by inadequate bibliographic control, the use of hardware designed for other purposes, the lack of standards for filming such materials, and the failure to observe existing guidelines such as those established by the Library of Congress (63) and the American Library Association (2). The latter organization has set up a reviewing mechanism to assist librarians in evaluating films, and has issued a technical review of the microfilm edition of *The New York Times* (57), based upon United States of America Standards Institute (USASI), Library of Congress, and ALA standards. Veaner (75) has detailed USASI and other standards applicable to micropublication.

Harris (28) suggests that offset printing is now cheap enough that micropublication may have outlived its usefulness as a means of disseminating doctoral dissertations, but she does not mention the disadvantage of stockpiling hard copies, a requirement that on-demand micropublication eliminates. The narrow scope of many theses may still point to on-demand generation of hard copies from a master microfilm as the best means of disseminating dissertations.

In an invited paper given before the 1968 meeting of NMA, Burchinal (11) outlined the U.S. Office of Education's interests in furthering new technologies, particularly through micropublication, to upgrade and enrich education at all levels, but specifically in primary and secondary schools. He stressed the hope that the "systems approach" through the medium of individually accessible, micropublished learning materials would facilitate the attempts of educators to make it possible for students to move ahead at their own pace. A valuable feature of Burchinal's paper is his review of the microfilm industry's apparent lack of initiative in providing equipment for, or even in assessing, the needs of the educational market. His critique comes very close to being an indictment of the industry for undue pessimism and lack of imagination. In this connection, the Office of Education has recently commissioned the Association of Research Libraries (4) to undertake a study of user requirements as a prerequisite for successful implementation of micropublication systems in schools and libraries. Preliminary evidence within this study, in which this writer is participating, indicates that micropublication has a long way to go before it can claim to provide a "systems approach" to recording and disseminating archival and library data.

Microfilm Cartridges and Standardization in General

Cartridges in the microfilm industry have developed parallel to a similar standardized device in the motion picture industry, the 8mm film loop. However, in the flurry to gain a competitive lead, major microfilm manufacturers have made sure that none of their products would be compatible with another maker's system. Five manufacturers now offer cartridges for three different film sizes: 8mm, 16mm, and 35mm. Recordak, 3M, and Micro Photo all offer magazines designed for 16mm film; each is locked into the manufacturer's specific output hardware. The model ID-101 35mm cartridge marketed by Information Design, Incorporated, an independent company, can be adapted to several makes of readers, but it is costly and does not result in fully automated operation. Persistent rumors indicate that a revolutionary new and cheap 35mm cartridge may soon be marketed. Such a device, if inexpensive and efficient, could permit ready conversion of extensive libraries of roll film to systems more suitable to user requirements than conventional reels. The 8mm cartridge is part of a product-information system, one of whose objectives was a mailable cartridge. A recent article (16) effectively describes the optical and film-drive problems of the 8mm reader. Smitzer (66) has analyzed a variety of roll-film storage and lookup systems, including cartridges, and has analyzed their performance in terms of cost, speed, skill required for use, and operator fatigue.

The cartridge offers the possibility of improving the exploitation of roll film's greatest advantage—file integrity—while also removing the irritant of hand threading. Cartridge users suffer not only from system incompatibility, but also from lack of performance standards for cartridges. There is no repeatable way of testing how film is affected by drive systems, rapid acceleration and deceleration, and the subtle frictional forces present during high-speed rewinding. Archard (3) has described efforts by the British Standards Institution to work with industry to standardize 16mm cartridges. In the absence of internal agreement by the industry in the United States, it is possible that some type of standardization may be externally imposed. There is precedent for this in the choice of the 105mm x 148mm size for microfiche by DoD, NASA, the Atomic Energy Commission (AEC), and the Office of Technical Services (OTS). Wooster (79) claims that even this standard needs revision because it does not solve the image registration problem. He suggests use of perforated microfiche with a compact reader. McCamy (46) recounts the historical development of photographic standards, with particular emphasis on the workings of USASI.

CONCLUSION

If full-size reprography is healthy, then microform technology is not well. It is a field riddled with unsystematic, disconnected collections of "gimmicks" masquerading as systems. A communication system that requires a mechanical device between the sender and receiver—whether the device is an electronic or optical terminal—is completely dependent upon standards for its efficacy. Insofar as human perception is concerned, microforms in their "raw" state are as much an invisible product as are digitized data, and their effective use also requires rigorous adherence to standards. Up to now, the main impetus for standards development has come from outside the industry. This has been the case with systems designed to disseminate current information, such as engineering drawings and technical reports. Undue dependence upon the external motivations for standards development creates a default condition that permits proliferation of incompatible equipment and dissemination of microreproductions that lack technical excellence. Widespread use of microforms, so necessary for reduction of unit costs, is likewise inhibited. Beyond the limited domain of current information systems lie both the future, in the form of computer output microfilm (where standards work is already underway), and the past, in the form of retrospective document collections. Today, if a light bulb did not fit a socket, one would know it at once and something would be done about it. But if millions of pages of microreproductions are issued, who will certify their legibility, archival permanence, and suitability to output equipment? A vigorous program of standards development and product inspection and certification is particularly needed in the micropublication area; the less the control over the input, the greater the need. The aggressive development of standards is the industry's most pressing need. It would also be useful to form a national testing or certifying institute under the auspices of manufacturers, service companies, users, and professional societies. Without these steps, microform technology is in danger of repeating the past century's characteristic pattern of developing fascinating and potentially useful hardware without ever creating a true information system.

Notably absent in the literature are studies of failures. Where are the systems that have been implemented and rejected? Why did they fail? How can future mistakes be prevented? One has a right to suspect an endeavor that records only its successes.

The lack of rational, thoughtful innovation in equipment design has been particularly disheartening. Some equipments have been on the market for decades, virtually unchanged (except for price increases). Almost universal is the practice of attempting to use in one application a device that was developed for some quite different, unrelated use. From the human engineering standpoint, some devices are so poorly designed that one might suppose they were made to intentionally frustrate the user. With the sales force acting as insulator, users and designers are practically held incommunicado. Manufacturers explain that they undertake little development work because market research indicates little sales potential. No wonder the literature of reprography and microforms is so filled with the desperate voice of the "tech rep," proclaiming that his piece of equipment is *the* answer. A program of industry-wide basic research, perhaps coordinated by NMA, might aid the user, enhance the commercial prospects of microforms, and, as a by-product, upgrade the literature.

When coupled with advanced software now under development, microfilm may rapidly achieve dominance as the high-density storage medium; not just for static data, but also for dynamic data if turnaround times of a few minutes or longer can be tolerated. The accommodation of a complete engineering drawing in an aperture card created by the AMACUS represents a storage density of about sixteen million bits per square inch, far short of the billion-bit-per-square-inch capacity of high-resolution film calculated by McCamy (47), but well above the practical limit of 250,000 bits cited only a few years ago by Scott (64). A major recent achievement pointing towards future, high-density photographic storage devices is the IBM 1360 photo-digital store, which holds over 3×10^{11} bits. The IBM 1360 has been described in considerable technical detail by Kuehler & Kerby (42). Since it seems likely that magnetic storage devices will not get much more capacious or compact, nor overcome the problems associated with complex electromechanical and electrohydraulic systems, microfilm appears to have a bright future as a medium for input, output, storage, and dissemination. But the challenge of standardization must be met before its ultimate potential can be realized.

REFERENCES

(1) AMERICAN CHEMICAL SOCIETY JOURNAL ON MICROFILM. Scientific Information Notes, 10:3 (June–July 1968) 25.
(2) AMERICAN LIBRARY ASSOCIATION. RESOURCES AND TECHNICAL SERVICES DIVISION. Microfilm norms. Chicago, 1966, 49 p.
(3) ARCHARD, T. N. J. Microfilm standards. In: A technical appraisal of the 70mm format for map reproduction; papers of a symposium held at Hatfield Technical College on 10 January 1968, under the chairmanship of G. H. Wright. Technical Library Service, Hertfordshire County Council, Hertford, England, 1968, p. 43–44.
(4) THE ASSOCIATION OF RESEARCH LIBRARIES STUDIES MICROFORM TECHNOLOGY. Scientific Information Notes, 10:5–6 (October–December, 1968) 11.
(5) BALLOU, HUBBARD W. Guide to microreproduction equipment. 3d ed. National Microfilm Association, Annapolis, Md., 1965, 552 p. (4th ed. in press)
(6) BARRETT, WILLIAM. Criteria for a 105mm Engineering Micrographics System. Reproduction Methods, 8:5 (May 1968) 36–37.
(7) BEISER, LEO. Laser beam scanning for data storage and retrieval. In: Murray, Richard D., ed. Applications of lasers to photography and information handling. Society of Photographic Scientists and Engineers, Washington, D.C., 1968, p. 235–246.
(8) BIOSCIENCES INFORMATION SERVICE OF BIOLOGICAL ABSTRACTS MICROFILM FILE CONTAINING 2,000,000 RESEARCH REFERENCES. Scientific Information Notes, 10:3 (June–July 1968) 24.
(9) BRITISH NATIONAL REPROGRAPHIC CENTRE FOR DOCUMENTATION [established at Hatfield College of Technology] Information Retrieval & Library Automation, 4:3 (August 1968) 3.
(10) BUCKLEY, CLAY W. The 105-35mm microminiature film system for engineering drawings for the Pacific Gas and Electric Company. NMA Journal, 1:4 (Summer 1968) 131–145.
(11) BURCHINAL, LEE. Microform technology and education. In: Tate, Vernon D., ed. Proceedings of the 17th Annual Meeting and Convention, National Microfilm Association. The Association, Annapolis, Md., 1969, p. 355-364.
(12) BUREAU OF NAVAL PERSONNEL. Lithographer 1 & C. Revised 1966. Washington, D.C., 1966, 305 p. (NAVPERS 10454-A)
(13) BUREAU OF NAVAL PERSONNEL. Lithographer 3 & 2. Revised 1963. Washington, D.C., 1963, 503 p. (NAVPERS 10452-A)
(14) BUZAWA, M. JOHN; MILNE, GORDON G.; SMITH, ABBOTT M. Optical systems for direct projection on photoresists. In: Hance, C.R., ed. Ultra-microminiaturization: precision photography for electronic circuitry. [Proceedings of a two-day seminar held on November 6–7, 1968, in Palo Alto, Calif.] Society of Photographic Scientists and Engineers, Washington, D.C., 1968, p. 41–68.

(15) CARLSON, C. O.; IVES, H. D. Some consideration in the design of a laser thermal microimage recorder. National Cash Register Company, Electronics Division, Hawthorne, Calif. June 1968, 8 p. (NCR-ED Technical Document 31417) Shorter version published in: Science, 154:3756 (23 December 1966) 1550–1551.

(16) Catalog file puts 5,000 pages in one microfilm cartridge. Product Engineering, 39:6 (11 March 1968) 80–81.

(17) CONWAY, EDWARD F. WESTAR: an improved system for data retrieval with or without the computer. In: Tate, Vernon D., ed. Proceedings of the 17th Annual Meeting and Convention, National Microfilm Association. The Association, Annapolis, Md., 1969, p. 11–20.

(18) CRAIG, DWIN R. Billions of bits/minute. Photogrammetric Engineering, 27:3 (June 1961) 394–406.

(19) DAVIS, ARTHUR I. Value drafting for the sake of microfilm and reduced cost. In: Tate, Vernon D., ed. Proceedings of the 17th Annual Meeting and Convention, National Microfilm Association. The Association, Annapolis, Md., 1969, p. 42–54.

(20) DEFENSE DOCUMENTATION CENTER. A DDC bibliography on microfiche, microfilm and related equipment. Alexandria, Va., 1968, 2 vols. (AD-675 300; AD-838 400)

(21) DENSTMAN, HAROLD; SCHULTZ, MORTON J. Photographic reproduction; methods, techniques, and applications for engineering and the graphic arts. McGraw-Hill, New York, 1963, 187 p.

(22) DORAN, THOMAS G. Report on Non Impact Printing Project (NIPP). Prepared for the Chief of Staff, U.S. Army. Army Materiel Command, Directorate of Management Systems and Data Automation, Washington, D.C., January 1968, 80 p. (AD-671 611)

(23) EASTMAN KODAK. Copying. 7th ed. Rochester, N.Y., 1968, 44 p. (Kodak Professional Data Book, M-1)

(24) ENCYCLOPAEDIA BRITANNICA. Encyclopaedia Britannica announces a program to develop a series of resources and research libraries in ultramicrofiche beginning with the Library of American Civilization. Chicago, 1968, 16 p.

(25) GENERAL PRECISION SYSTEMS. ADVANCED PRODUCTS DIVISION. LINK GROUP. AMACUS, automated microfilm aperture card updating system. Prepared for U.S. Army Weapons Command, Rock Island Arsenal, Rock Island, Illinois. Sunnyvale, Calif., 1968, 41 p. (Operation Training Manual APD-52)

(26) GRAY, S. B. Aspects of the computer-microfilm interface. In: Tate, Vernon D., ed. Proceedings of the 17th Annual Meeting and Convention, National Microfilm Association. The Association, Annapolis, Md., 1969, p. 87–92.

(27) HALSEY, RICHARD S. A microform cooperative for St. Louis area secondary schools and public libraries. (An ESEA Title III, P.L. 89-10, Planning Project) In: Tate, Vernon D., ed. Proceedings of the 17th Annual Meeting and Convention, National Microfilm Association. The Association, Annapolis, Md., 1969, p. 21–33.

(28) HARRIS, JESSICA L. Offset printing from typescript as a substitute for microfilming of dissertations. American Documentation, 19:1 (January 1968) 60–65.

(29) HAWKEN, WILLIAM R. Copying methods manual. Library Technology Program, American Library Association, Chicago, Ill., 1967. 375 p. (LTP Publications, no. 11)

(30) HAYS, DAVID G., et al. A billion books for education in America and the world: a proposal. RAND Corp., Santa Monica, Calif., April 1968, 79 p. (RM-5574-RC)

(31) HEILPRIN, L. B. The economics of "on demand" library copying. In: Tate, Vernon D., ed. Proceedings of the 11th Annual Meeting and Convention, National Microfilm Association. The Association, Annapolis, Md., 1962, p. 311–339.

(32) HELD, STUART. Developments in Japan in commercial optics. Part II. In: Hance, C. R., ed. Ultra-microminiaturization: precision photography for electronic circuitry. [Proceedings of a two-day seminar held on November 6–7, 1968, in Palo Alto, Calif.] Society of Photographic Scientists and Engineers, Washington, D.C., 1968, p. 195–203.

(33) Here comes the COM Information and Records Management, 2:7 (October/November 1968) 45–57.

(34) HERSCHEL, J. F. W. New photographic process. Athenaeum, 1341 (9 July 1853) 831.
(35) HOADLEY, HOWARD W. Microfiche publishing techniques, use in automated systems. Plan and Print, N41:10 (October 1968) 37–41, 79.
(36) INTERDEPARTMENTAL GROUP IN MICROCOPYING. Methods in miniature; an introduction to microcopying. Her Majesty's Stationery Office, London, 1968, 30 p.
(37) JACKMAN, CHESTER I. The microreproduction of photodrawings. In: Tate, Vernon D., ed. Proceedings of the 17th Annual Meeting and Convention, National Microfilm Association. The Association, Annapolis, Md., 1969, p. 74–86.
(38) JACKSON, B. F.; JACKSON, D. G.; LaRIVIERE, F. D. AMACUS II. [Automated Microfilm Aperture Card Updating System] In: Tate, Vernon D., ed. Proceedings of the 17th Annual Meeting and Convention, National Microfilm Association. The Association, Annapolis, Md., 1969, p. 93–105.
(39) KIERSKY, LORETTA J. Developments in photoreproduction. Special Libraries, 59:4 (April 1968) 261–264.
(40) KNUDSON, D. R.; TEICHER, S. N.; REINTJES, J. F.; GRONEMANN, U. F. Experimental evaluation of the resolution capabilities of image-transmission systems. Information Display, 5:5 (September/October 1968) 31–43.
(41) KRAMER, D. R. An improved engineering microfilm system. Graphic Science, 10:7 (July 1968) 18–23.
(42) KUEHLER, J. D.; KERBY, H. R. A photo-digital mass storage system. In: AFIPS Conference Proceedings, vol. 29; 1966 Fall Joint Computer Conference, San Francisco, Calif. Spartan Books, Washington, D.C., 1966, p. 735–742.
(43) LEVINE, JOSEPH E. Cleaning and processing of high resolution plates, and techniques for evaluating their quality for critical applications. In: Hance, C. R., ed. Ultraminiaturization: precision photography for electronic circuitry. [Proceedings of a two-day seminar held on November 6–7, 1968, in Palo Alto, Calif.] Society of Photographic Scientists and Engineers, Washington, D.C., 1968, p. 83–110.
(44) MASSACHUSETTS INSTITUTE OF TECHNOLOGY. PROJECT INTREX. Semiannual activity report, 15 September 1967 to 15 March 1968. Cambridge, Mass., 1968, 56 p.
(45) MATTHEWS, S. K. Photography in archaeology and art. John Baker, London 1968, 161 p.
(46) McCAMY, C. S. A half century of photographic standardization in the United States. Photographic Science and Engineering, 12:6 (November–December 1968) 308–312.
(47) McCAMY, C. S. On the information in a microphotograph. Applied Optics, 4:4 (April 1965) 405–411.
(48) MICRODOC. (Quarterly) Microfilm Association of Great Britain, Cambridge, 1962–
(49) MORGAN, ROBERT A. Microfilm conversion; two size systems in one. Plan and Print, N40:5 (May 1967) 26–28.
(50) MULLER, JEROME K. Ultrafiche: how to put 9,801 pages on a single 4 x 5 inch sheet of film. Reproductions Review, 18 (May 1968) 18–22.
(51) NATIONAL AERONAUTICS AND SPACE ADMINISTRATION. Specifications for NASA Engineering Data Microreproduction Systems. Washington, D.C., 1968 (various pagings) (NHB 1440.4A)
(52) NATIONAL REPROGRAPHIC CENTRE FOR DOCUMENTATION. A technical appraisal of the 70mm format for map reproduction; the papers of a symposium held at Hatfield Technical College on 10 January 1968, under the chairmanship of G. H. Wright. Technical Library Service, Hertfordshire County Council, Hertford, England, 1968, 44 p. (SBN 85267-004-4)
(53) NATIONAL MICROFILM ASSOCIATION. Proceedings of the annual convention. Annapolis, Md., 1952–
(54) NELSON, CARL E. Microfilm technology, engineering and related fields. McGraw-Hill, New York, 1965, 397 p.
(55) NELSON, CARL E. Modern drafting techniques for quality microreproductions.

National Microfilm Association, Annapolis, Md., 1968, 38 p. (NMA Information Monographs, no. 3)
(56) NEW NBS MICROCOPY RESOLUTION TEST CHARTS HAVE HIGHER FREQUENCIES. NMA Journal, 1:2 (Winter 1968) 37-38.
(57) NEW YORK TIMES ON MICROFILM. Choice, 5:10 (December 1968) 1276-1279.
(58) NIESET, ROBERT T. The basis of the Kalvar system of photography. In: National Microfilm Association Convention, 10th, Chicago, 1961. The Association, Annapolis, Md., 1961, p. 177-191.
(59) NMA JOURNAL. (Quarterly) National Microfilm Association, Annapolis, Md., Vol. 1, 1968.
(60) OLLERENSHAW, R. Photographic copying. In: Engel, Charles E., ed. Photography for the scientist. Academic Press, New York, 1968, p. 513-551.
(61) REPRO. (Quarterly) Institute of Reprographic Technology, London, 1963-
(62) RUBIN, JACK, ed. International directory of micrographic equipment. 1st ed. International Micrographic Congress, Saratoga, Calif., 1967, 519 p.
(63) SALMON, STEPHEN R. Specifications for Library of Congress microfilming. Library of Congress, Washington, D.C., 1964, 21 p.
(64) SCOTT, PETER R. Graphic aids for information retrieval. In: Simonton, Wesley, ed. Information retrieval today; Papers presented at the Institute conducted by the Library School and the Center for Continuation Study, University of Minnesota, September 19-22, 1962, p. 71-87.
(65) SILKINER, M. D. Revising microfilm documents. Plan and Print, N41:11 (November 1968) 23-25.
(66) SMITZER, L. A. The art of roll film look-up. In: Tate, Vernon D., ed. Proceedings of the 17th Annual Meeting and Convention, National Microfilm Association. The Association, Annapolis, Md., 1969, p. 57-73.
(67) STEVENS, G. W. W. Microphotography; photography and photofabrication at extreme resolution. 2nd ed., rev. Chapman & Hall, London, 1968, 510 p.
(68) TEPLITZ, ARTHUR. Library fiche: an introduction and explanation. In: Tate, Vernon D., ed. Proceedings of the 17th Annual Meeting and Convention, National Microfilm Association. The Association, Annapolis, Md., 1969, p. 125-132.
(69) TEPLITZ, ARTHUR. Microfiche for technical information dissemination: a cost-benefit analysis. System Development Corporation, Santa Monica, Calif., 4 September 1968. (SP-3223)
(70) TIBBETTS, RAYMOND E.; WILCZYNSKI, JANUSZ S. A series of high-performance reduction lenses for the production of microelectronics. In: Hance, C. R., ed. Ultra-microminiaturization: precision photography for electronic circuitry. [Proceedings of a two-day seminar held on November 6-7, 1968, in Palo Alto, Calif.] Society of Photographic Scientists and Engineers, Washington, D.C., 1968, p. 69-82.
(71) VARDEN, LLOYD E. Copyboard Lighting. Reproduction Methods, 8:12 (December 1968) 40-41, 46.
(72) VEANER, ALLEN B. Annotated Bibliography. In: Hawken, W. R. Copying methods manual. American Library Association, Chicago, Ill., 1966, p. 322-339.
(73) VEANER, ALLEN B. The crisis in micropublication. Choice, 5:4 (June 1968) 448-453.
(74) VEANER, ALLEN B. Developments in reproduction of library materials and graphic communication, 1967. Library Resources and Technical Services, 12:2 (Spring 1968) 203-214.
(75) VEANER, ALLEN B. Microreproduction and micropublication standards—what they mean to you, the user. Choice, 5:7 (September 1968) 739-744.
(76) VEANER, ALLEN B. On the need for improved communication between producers and users of research microfilm. In: Proceedings of the Second International Congress on Reprography, Cologne, 17-24 October 1968. Helwich Verlag, Darmstadt, Germany. (In press.)
(77) VER HULST, J.; BELOK, A. The use of mathematical simulation techniques in the

application of ultrafiche information systems. In: Tate, Vernon D., ed. Proceedings of the 17th Annual Meeting and Convention, National Microfilm Association. The Association, Annapolis, Md., 1969, p. 106–114.
(78) VERRY, H. R. Microcopying methods. Revised by Gordon H. Wright. Focal Press, London, 1967, 183 p.
(79) WOOSTER, H. Towards a uniform federal report numbering system and a cuddly microfiche reader—two modest proposals. Air Force Office of Scientific Research, Arlington, Va., May 1968, 18 p. (AFOSR-68-0772) (AD-669 204) Presented at Third Annual Northeastern DDC/Industry Users Conference, Waltham, Mass., 17 April 1968.
(80) ZENNER, PHILLIP. A hybrid computer/microfilm engineering information system. In: Tate, Vernon D., ed. Proceedings of the 17th Annual Meeting and Convention, National Microfilm Association. The Association, Annapolis, Md., 1969, p. 115–122.

7 Document Retrieval

LAWRENCE H. BERUL
Auerbach Corporation

INTRODUCTION

Scope of the Chapter

Document retrieval involves the searching of a collection and the delivery of relevant documents or references that answer the user's search request. A document retrieval system encompasses such functions as query formulation, indexing and vocabulary control, file maintenance, index searching, and delivery of search products. The end product of most automated systems is a list of references to documents, rather than the documents themselves. Hence, this chapter is concerned with means for identifying and searching for document attributes rather than with the physical means for storing, fetching, copying, or transmitting documents.

This chapter deals primarily with the tools and techniques of computerized document retrieval. Articles primarily discussing the application of document retrieval to a particular field are not reviewed unless they also present a unique or otherwise relevant technique. Content analysis, techniques of design and evaluation of information systems, and document dissemination are each the subject of a separate chapter.

The literature of 1968 has seen a major shift in emphasis to interactive computer-based document retrieval systems. Of particular importance are search strategies that take user relevance reactions to initial search outputs and feed them back to the computer to refine the original search question automatically. The significance of these user-controlled search strategies and dialogue-mode query languages is that computer-based document retrieval systems are finally beginning to provide facilities that allow a user to interact directly with the index. Such interaction has always been the standard *modus operandi* with manual card catalogs and book-form indexes. Another development noted this year is the increased availability of proprietary software packages for document retrieval. These packages, which are marketed for a fraction of what it would cost a user to develop his own tailor-made programs, should significantly accelerate the use of computers in document retrieval. The major topics covered in this year's review of document retrieval are: functional models of document retrieval systems; noncomputer retrieval techniques; and computerized retrieval systems, including batch-processing systems, interactive systems, search strategies, text searching, and document retrieval software; and conclusions.

FUNCTIONAL MODELS OF DOCUMENT RETRIEVAL SYSTEMS

Document retrieval is typically only part of a larger document storage, retrieval and dissemination system, which may provide such additional services as initial document dissemination (primary publication), announcement (secondary publication), information analysis (critical reviews, state of the art syntheses), and document loan or replication. Some of these services are performed by documentation centers and libraries, while others are primarily within the province of information centers (e.g., the information analysis function). The subject of document dissemination *per se* is covered by Landau in Chapter 8.

Many of the system functions involved in providing dissemination and retrieval services are common. For example, the acquisition, indexing and abstracting, vocabulary control, and index file maintenance functions are required for both retrieval and dissemination. In document retrieval, the surrogate data are searched against a query, whereas, in dissemination they may be used to print out an announcement journal or to be matched against a user profile and then print out a selective dissemination of information (SDI) notice.

Freeman & Atherton, of the American Institute of Physics, present a model of contemporary mechanized retrieval systems (20). They group processing functions into five major categories: analysis and control, surrogation, physical transformation, file processing, and display. The experimental system (which is described later) demonstrates that the Universal Decimal Classification (UDC) code can be used as an indexing language in a mechanized document retrieval system.

Judge (35) presents a useful conceptual model of the relationship between a user and various components of the document system and shows evolving patterns of international cooperation. A much more substantive model of a document retrieval system is provided in a paper by Lancaster

& Climenson (41). Their model presents parameters of user needs, e.g., coverage, usability, recall, precision, response time, presentation, and user effort. The authors also show how various tradeoffs and interrelationships can be effected between the various functions in order to optimize user satisfaction at a minimum cost. A more complete discussion is contained in Lancaster's new book (40).

Degree of Mechanization

There is surprising agreement on the general functions of a document retrieval and dissemination system. Much more controversial are such subjects as the techniques applied to performing these functions, the extent to which any function can be automated, and the relative importance of one function compared to another—for example, indexing, vocabulary control or search strategies. Rolling & Piette (56) discuss the tradeoffs between manual, semiautomatic, and automatic operation. They present a so-called "optimum" balance for the EURATOM system, which involves manual indexing together with computer storage and retrieval of index and citation data rather than of abstracts or full text. Unfortunately, some of their conclusions are not supported by empirical data. For example, they claim that a batch-search technique on magnetic tape is the most economical. This reviewer would challenge that statement today because it does not take into account the availability of interchangeable disk files that can eliminate the need to search entire files, and further, because it ignores the essential need for user-system interaction in a search process. What good is efficiency if the system is not effective? On the other hand, Rolling & Piette do point out that "every time improved hardware appears on the market, the optimum (balance) goes in the direction of automation."

Dammers (15) describes the retrieval activities at Shell Research, Ltd., and provides insight into system economics. In contrast to EURATOM, Shell appears to be moving more quickly into a highly automated system, placing less dependence on manual indexing and providing (early) on-line search capabilities. It is noteworthy that personnel costs are dropping as a percentage of Shell's total system costs, while computer costs are rising.

A major work of 1968 on the general subject of document retrieval was Salton's book *Automatic Information Organization and Retrieval* (60). Chapter 1 presents simple functional models of both information dissemination and information search and retrieval. Chapter 6 presents a number of abstract models of the retrieval process itself, in which "retrieval" is considered as a mapping between the "space" of all keyword sets and the "space" of all retrievable document sets. He discusses set and lattice theory, set-theoretical models of retrieval with partially ordered sets, systems based on classification, and the special problems in the use of negation, i.e., the NOT operator. Chapter 7 is of more practical value in that it describes actual retrieval methods including various file organizations and search strategies. The balance of the book is devoted mostly to the various methods (statistical, syntactical, and associative) of indexing, information analysis, and dictionary construction, and to evaluation methodology. It is clearly written and, in spite of the complex subject matter, is relatively easy to comprehend. It is recommended for the experienced designer as well as for the student.

Vickery (75) provides an excellent analysis of the process of matching queries against documents. He demonstrates that even a word-by-word, full-text search does not assure effective retrieval, aside from questions of efficiency or cost. He analyzes various modes of document representation, ranging from words in the title through rather complex representations using a combination of techniques. He provides an example of the complex surrogate used in the *National Aeronautics and Space Administration* (NASA) information system—which includes the title, author, selectively extracted terms or descriptors, corporate source, author, contract number, and a number of assigned "base" codes. He concludes by raising the following question:

> From representations of this kind we can construct subfiles and we can amplify queries. Whether or not this apparatus is more efficient and economical than whole-text matching, it is certainly far from simple, presenting many problems of record and file organization and of search strategy. Is this completely justified by the service it enables us to give? Documents are complex entities, but perhaps the crucial question that they pose is, what are the simplest means by which we can represent them and still satisfy user needs? In all our discussions of retrieval, we must not lose sight of its goal. User requirements must determine system design.

NONCOMPUTER RETRIEVAL TECHNIQUES

Our definition of a noncomputer system or technique is similar to that employed by Brown & Jones (9) in Volume 3 of the *Annual Review*. A system is termed noncomputer if it uses searching devices such as uniterm cards, edge-notched cards, optical coincidence techniques, or microfilm search and display methods.

The literature devoted to noncomputer retrieval systems in 1968 was not as extensive as that devoted to the more glamorous "automated" systems, though undoubtedly there are more noncomputer systems than computerized ones.

Two papers by Berul (4, 5) present a comprehensive analysis of equipment used in computer as well as noncomputer retrieval systems—card picking devices, computer output microfilming, microfilm retrieval units, and so on. The respective role of each type of equipment is clearly outlined and the state of the art summarized. A paper by Schless et al. (62) presents an interesting evaluative comparison of two manual coordinate indexing systems (edge-notched cards and optical coincidence) and a computer-based retrieval system. On the basis of their evaluation, they chose the optical coincidence method.

Several papers discussed applications of the TERMATREX system. This optical coincidence technique appears to be firmly established in situations where coordinate indexing of items in a small or moderate-sized file is required. Baker & Hoshovsky (1) describe an Air Force Office of Aerospace Research TERMATREX System for retrieving graphic arts materials. A Montreal General Hospital peek-a-boo system for indexing and retrieval of nephrological literature is reported on by Kaye & Nyeky (36). Another recent article (17) discusses two interesting applications of TERMATREX: one at the U.S. Coast Guard Personnel Office, and the other at the Washington, D.C. Civil Disorder Information System. Shank (64) summarizes the design features of two Sandia Laboratories optical coincidence retrieval systems using 80-column internally punched cards— the Environmental Laboratories Information Retrieval Technique (ELIRT) and the Supplier Capability Information Retrieval Technique (SCIRT).

The application of a Miracode microfilm storage and retrieval system to the handling of information on political parties is described in an article by Janda (34) and also in a book on information retrieval applications to political science by Janda (33). This system also employs a computer-produced bibliography.

Conway, in two reports (11, 12), describes the WESTAR (Westinghouse Telephone Aperture Retrieval) system, which can use touch-telephones as terminals and is designed to be used with or without a computer.

COMPUTERIZED RETRIEVAL SYSTEMS

Although the majority of operational systems use batch processing, the bulk of the 1968 literature is devoted to on-line systems and techniques for user-system interaction. In particular, extensive treatment is given to adaptive or heuristic algorithms for utilizing user feedback dynamically to produce more effective search strategies. This section of the review begins with a brief discussion of batch-processing systems. Our main emphasis, however, is on on-line facilities including query languages, dialog facilities, and user-controlled search strategies.

Batch-Processing Systems

A lucid presentation of a batch-processing computer retrieval system is given by Freeman & Atherton (20). The system was developed as an experiment in the use of the Universal Decimal Classification (UDC) as an indexing language. The basic system software is the IBM Combined File Search System, which includes both a linear (or serial) document file and an inverted descriptor file (Warheit, 76). Queries are translated into descriptors connected by AND, OR, or NOT operators. Batches of queries are read into the computer. The descriptors for each query in the batch are sorted into UDC numeric sequence and matched against the inverted descriptor file to pull off all document numbers satisfying the initial batch. The full query is then compared to each item in the linear file for which a tentative match has been identified. For each "hit," the logical record is written onto a working file. The hits are sorted back by query number and printed out, if the requester desires.

Salton (60) explains the preponderance of batch-processing applications by observing that a real-time procedure normally requires all of the data to be in random-access storage. He argues that the expense of the random-access devices is usually not warranted for the small volume of requests typical of a document retrieval application. Instead, cheaper bulk-storage devices (tapes) are used and a batch of requests is processed against the whole file or a major portion thereof. He notes that today batch processing may be cheaper to perform with random-access devices than with conventional tape-oriented systems, when the activity is low. This assumes that the random-access devices (e.g., disk packs) are removable and hence are not tying up the drive when not in use. Various file organizations — the direct or serial file, the inverted file, the combined file (i.e., inverted index and serial citation), the multilist system, and multilevel search methods — are also reviewed by Salton.

Interactive Systems

Advantages of Interactive Systems. An interactive retrieval system is one in which the user can interact with the computer at various stages in the process. The system can help him choose relevant search terms by presenting displays of the classification schedule or indexing vocabulary, and frequency counts. By means of a dialogue, the system can help the user phrase the query in the proper logical form. To help the user broaden or narrow the search, the system can print out counts of items retrieved and also a sample for him to review. Finally, the system can allow the user to express relevance judgments and automatically adjust the original search strategy to retrieve more highly relevant items. This is potentially the most important value of an on-line system, in that a user is rarely so articulate as to phrase his question precisely right the first time. In a batch-processing environment, the response times are typically so long (several hours to several weeks) that the user is rarely motivated to rephrase his query and make a second or third try. Freeman & Atherton (20) extrapolated their experiences with an experimental batch-processing system and concluded that an on-line retrieval system provides a closer analogue to the man-system interaction that takes place in a conventional manual library or information center than does a computer batch-processing system. They add:

> ... at the same time this interaction helps to overcome some of the physical access problems of manual systems such as the need to manipulate large books and card files. In short, the interactive retrieval system appears to be a reasonable prototype for future systems, at least in concept.

In a later paper, Freeman & Atherton (19) describe their actual experience with an experimental on-line system named AUDACIOUS.

Borko (6) sees the principal advantage of on-line retrieval as allowing the user to interact with the collections and modify his query based on feedback, thereby guiding the retrieval process. This, he says, serves to overcome these four basic weaknesses of batch processing:

1. The need for intermediaries which tend to distort or misinterpret the user's intention;
2. the rigidity of the system in that it is difficult to modify queries;
3. the unacceptably long interval between the time the request is entered and the responses received; and
4. a lack of user confidence, since the result received may not contain certain relevant material the requester believes to be available.

Examples of Interactive Systems. One of the most useful reports of on-line systems was an evaluation study of the NASA RECON system by Meister & Sullivan (47). Actual user reactions to an on-line system were obtained over a seven-week period. The order of importance placed by users on various search strategies was: (*1*) subject, (*2*) author, (*3*) report number, (*4*) corporate source, and (*5*) contract number. They also considered titles and index terms associated with retrieved items as desirable components of the feedback display, and they found the frequency count to be useful. Deficiencies in indexing became more obvious to the knowledgeable user through the display facilities. It is interesting to observe that, whereas off-line users were usually willing to wait more than 24 hours for a response, the user at a console became impatient if more than a minute transpired.

Bennett of IBM (3) describes an experimental facility to aid indexers in making better indexing decisions through on-line access to a thesaurus as well as to the data base. This system allows the user to enter data, operate on them, save them for future reference, and search the thesaurus or the data base by various search keys. Two key features of the system are the display of the vocabulary and the capability to view how related documents have been indexed.

Hillman (25) describes a prototype interactive retrieval system at Lehigh University that is being designed to accept queries as free-form text. The system is being implemented for an IBM 2741 communications terminal using DATATEXT (29) and QUICKTRAN (30) which are both IBM time-sharing languages. DATATEXT operates on an IBM 1460 computer system, whereas QUICKTRAN utilizes an IBM 7040/7044. The data base deals with information science. The objectives of query negotiation are elegantly stated by Hillman:

> . . . a characteristic feature of this process is that the scientist's original inquiry or interest is invariably modified and restructured on the basis of the information presented to him. . . . Most experimental work today looks upon both the inquiry and the relevance of the answers as single events. We think that this is a mistake and that an inquiry is merely a micro-event in a shifting, adaptive process. It is not a command, as in conventional search strategy, but rather a description of an area of doubt in which the question is open ended, negotiable and dynamic.

Additional examples of on-line systems are discussed later in this chapter under the topic "document retrieval software."

Query Languages. An important component of any interactive retrieval system is the language, usually known as a query language, in which the user communicates with the system. Query languages range from natural English used on an interactive typewriter to a highly structured form to be filled in by the user and then keyed in or encoded with field numbers or appropriate punctuation. The literature of 1968 describes a number of attempts at building query languages using natural English with relatively few restrictions on syntax.

Researchers at the University of Pennsylvania have reported considerable activity in connection with the systems known as "Easy English" (Rubinoff et al., 57, 58) and "Real English" (Cautin & Regan, 10). "Easy English" is a part of the Moore School Information Systems Laboratory

Retrieval System. While the system requests can be stated in English, they must be formulated in the following syntactical form:

(Introductory Clause), (Document Clause), (Data Clause)

The system scans a message, breaks it down into the three types of clauses, and searches through dictionaries for each clause type for acceptable words. The query is further assembled into the symbolic command language of the retrieval system.

The paper by Cautin & Regan (10) on "Real English" discusses the requirements for an information retrieval language that apparently is intended to go further than "Easy English." A flow chart of the system shows how the user is required to resolve ambiguities and rephrase requests as required. The system provides assistance to the user in the form of counts of items retrieved, printouts, and frequency of term usage (both in indexing and in request usage).

Another project described by Bregzis (7) is likely to have more practical results in the early future. This is the Reactive Catalog query language for the Pilot I system being developed at the University of Toronto library. It operates on systematically structured bibliographic records and uses an IBM 360/50 computer with disk storage and a keyboard-CRT terminal device. There are four major access data categories: TITLE, NAME, CLASS symbol, and CODEN symbol; and six minor access data categories: TOPICAL TERM, PUBLISHER, DATE OF PUBLICATION, PLACE OF PUBLICATION, LANGUAGE and LOCATION. The other principal elements of the query language are the functions or verbs that express commands to the system, such as "FIND NAME/SMITH, JOHN." The emphasis on the bibliographic structure of the record will provide greater retrieval power within the major and minor access categories. To accomplish this, the language must compromise somewhat by not using free-form English language statements. As Bregzis demonstrates, the nature of the query language depends on the type of information to be retrieved, e.g., descriptive bibliographic data, whereas the University of Pennsylvania "Real English" system emphasizes retrieval of document references. The structured bibliographic information is similar to a structured management information system or data retrieval application, such as inventory control. Sinowitz (66) describes DATAPLUS, which is a retrieval language developed for the GE 265. DATAPLUS is also a restricted set of English words with a highly formal syntax.

Query languages for highly specific "fact retrieval" systems are beyond the scope of this paper, but will inevitably have an impact on document retrieval query languages. Descriptions of fact retrieval query languages using natural English are provided by Kellogg (38, 39); Vallee et al. (74); Stogniy & Afanassiev (69); and Green & Raphael (22).

For further information on query languages, the user is referred to the chapter on Automated Language Processing.

Search Strategies

The choice of search strategies is one of the major decisions facing the designer. It will determine both the efficiency and effectiveness of the total system. This section deals with such techniques as multistage search in a batch system, which primarily improves efficiency; multistage search in an interactive environment using user relevance reactions, which improves effectiveness; and weighting schemes, which also improve effectiveness.

Multistage Search—Batch. One concept that appeared a number of times this year is that of multistage search, wherein files are organized to allow a quick and inexpensive initial search to determine whether an item or class of items is probably relevant to a particular search, followed by a second-stage search of only those items (in most cases) passing the first test. Two theoretical papers by Leimkuhler (42, 43) suggest that files could be organized in decreasing order of an item's probability of being sought. This theory, of course, assumes that sufficient prior information is available to make possible a ranking of all items in the file according to their probable utility. The conclusion reached is that a good two-stage search plan for scientific literature is one in which from 15 to 20% of the most useful documents are examined first. In only about 1/3 of the searches would the remainder of the file have to be examined, which assumes that the user does not want to examine all possibly relevant items. The concept of multistage searching is also used in Salton's SMART system, where the items are grouped into clusters or centroid vectors, which are examined first (13, 60). Hoffman (26) describes a chemical storage and retrieval system at E. I. duPont deNemours & Company that involves a three-stage search: a series of screens, e.g., a requirement that both chlorine and nitrogen atoms must be present; a chemical substructure search, which generates a registry number; and a document retrieval search using Boolean logic.

Two other systems using multistage search techniques for serial searching are the PEEKABIT system for atomic energy literature, described by Hutton of Union Carbide (27) and the German GREMAS system, discussed by Meyer (48). Both of these systems utilize highly condensed superimposed random coding to represent an item as a screen within a linear file. In the first stage of the query, a selected item, or screen, is compared to a compact superimposed code representing the query. The random superimposed coding systems resemble Calvin Mooers' Zatacoding system (49). If the item does not pass the initial screening, the record is not "unpacked"; this preliminary screening saves considerable computer processing time otherwise used in the formatting and reformatting of data. Meyer estimates a reduction in search costs by as much as 95%. Most of the multistage search techniques for batch processing improve efficiency and reduce costs but have little bearing on recall or relevance. Of course, if the file is segmented into two or three portions that have presumed relevance values, and some segments are never searched, this will also affect performance.

Multistage Search—Interactive. With the advent of on-line interactive systems, information retrieval researchers have turned their attention to means of utilizing user feedback in improving search results.

Wilde (79) states the user relevance judgments problem rather clearly:

> After completion of the first search attempt, three sets of information remain. First, there is the original search strategy; second, there are the retrieved document records, each of which includes the terms used to index that document; third, there is a list of "relevant" retrieved documents as determined by the strategy designer. Why not feed those three data sets back into the computer and ask it to devise the retrieval strategy for the next search iteration?

The selection of index terms can be facilitated by use of a thesaurus; this approach generally puts the burden on the user to choose initial terms related to his concept. A second method uses statistical association techniques based on the co-occurrence of, or correlation between, all terms in the file. In the system described by Wilde (79), the computer calculates cross-correlations between the terms of the original strategy and the terms of relevant documents selected by the user in response to his first query. The computer then presents the searcher with an ordered list of index terms from which he selects the terms to use next. Instead of using a pure Boolean representation of the relationships between terms, Wilde uses a threshold logic gate model that is a form of weighted index term logic.

Stanfel (67) presents a theoretical mathematical model that might be applied to employing user feedback in an iterative manner to improve retrieval. A very useful point made by Stanfel with respect to user feedback is that the user may not properly articulate his interest to the system and may, instead, pass his judgment on the basis of what he thought he said, rather than on what he actually did say. The system would alter the initial query expressed by the user, possibly giving too much emphasis to terms that were not those responsible for retrieving the items first presented to the user.

A rather sophisticated "browsing game" is described by Treu (73). The objective of this game is to find a compromise between, on the one hand, requiring the user or his intermediary to state a query precisely and, on the other, requiring him to browse personally through the entire document file for items of interest. Once a query is formulated, the system computes an association function between the terms in the query and all other terms in the vocabulary. The system then displays candidate term pairs having a high association level because of their co-occurrence. The user then decides whether to add these terms to his query, and the query continually is modified by computation of the association factor, and by user decisions such as to enter or accept additional pairs or single terms.

The work by Salton, Keen, Lesk, and others on the SMART system represents one of the most promising research efforts in the field (13, 37, 60, 61). In addition to their excellent research in automatic indexing and natural language searching, they have expended considerable effort on employing user feedback in the search strategy design.

Lesk (44) shows how a user request in the SMART system can be augmented by the use of several types of dictionaries, including a computer-generated dictionary or term list, a manually compiled thesaurus, and a manually prepared dictionary of statistical phrases that uses words frequently co-occurring with related concepts. The SMART system, using the previously constructed dictionaries, analyzes the words in the request. The result of this process is a list of content indicators and associated weights, which together are called the "concept vector." This concept vector is then matched against the concept vectors of the document collection.

Salton identifies two significant problems in the use of time-sharing for on-line searching of full text or automatically indexed collections (61):

a) The small amount of internal storage which can normally be allocated to any given user (users must compete for memory space with many other users);

b) The rudimentary nature of the input/output console equipment likely to be made available to each user, which permits the introduction or withdrawal of only limited amounts of information.

This project is contrasted to the earlier work in which batch searches were carried out with each search request being compared against each analyzed document. Salton describes how the limitations of time-sharing can be overcome by interaction with the users and by fast-search algorithms confined to small subsets of the file. Salton's basic solution to these problems is a two-stage search strategy. Clusters of documents are grouped and a representative element, known as a centroid vector, is chosen for each group. First the query is compared to the centroids of all document groups, and the individual documents located in groups with highly matching centroids are then compared against the search request.

Another useful point discussed by Keen (37) is the fact that in SMART a variety of search strategies can be applied either singly or in combination, according to the user's own requirements. For example, the user may desire particularly high recall, which calls for a search of the full file of document vectors as well as a search of document clusters. In addition, the relevance feedback by the user can be combined with both cluster searching and vector searching.

The experimental system at Lehigh, as described by Hillman (25), utilizes a user-controlled search strategy wherein the user ranks phrases presented by the system rather than accepting or rejecting them. He may also rank pertinent documents to provide feedback to the system. The system then retains phrases associated with satisfactory documents, inhibits phrases associated with rejected documents, and returns to the browsing portion of the retrieval operation.

Weighting Schemes. A project reported by Curtice et al. (14) uses statistical associative techniques for query term expansion and term weights for ranking. The authors conclude that statistical association should be used in conjunction with, and not as a replacement for, human query renegotiation, particularly in a time-sharing environment, where users can define their search strategies iteratively. Several other papers (50, 24) discuss the use of term weights as an element of user-designed search strategy.

Mulvihill & Brenner, of the American Petroleum Institute (50), describe a very simple technique for obtaining ranked output of a Boolean search. This data base provides indexes to approximately 80,000 abstracts on petroleum. Each document was indexed with approximately 35 terms, with three terms being flagged for use in a printed alphabetical subject index. The ranking scheme begins with the premise that these three "flagged" terms best express the subject of the abstract and that, as such, they can be considered a weighting factor. The searcher is asked to underline those terms in his request that most closely match the concept of his request, scan the abstract bulletin, and select the three categories that might contain pertinent documents. Using these two rating factors assigned by the searcher, the system ranks the documents into nine groups. Within each group, the documents are then ranked by the original indexer's weights. The result of one experiment showed that 90% of the documents judged pertinent by two judges ranked in the upper 30% of the 255 documents retrieved by the search.

Haygarth Jackson & Matthews (24) describe a second weighted search technique, applied to the Uniterm Index to U.S. Chemical Patents. The procedure requires the searcher to list all terms in the search query relating to each concept, rank the concepts in order of their importance, and rank the terms within each concept in order of importance.

Text Searching

More and more computer retrieval systems provide natural language text-searching facilities for use on titles, abstracts, or full text. As might well be expected, much of the impetus for this activity comes from IBM. The procession started over ten years ago with the KWIC indexing scheme conceived by the late Hans Peter Luhn. In 1968, we still see references to KWIC and KWOC systems, but we also see new systems such as SYNTRAN/360, (Briner & Carney, 8), Document Processing System (DPS) (28), ITIRC (Magnino, 45), and several systems specially developed by IBM (Bell, 2; Jacobs, 32). On the commercial software side is DATA CENTRAL (16), a powerful generalized information retrieval system with text-searching facilities; this system will be discussed in the next section. Much meaningful experimental work is continuing at Cornell by Salton and his associates on project SMART (13, 37, 60, 61) and at Lehigh by Hillman (25). The major technical problem areas in text searching still revolve around content analysis and linguistics, treated separately in Chapters 3 and 5.

The encouraging aspect of text-searching systems is that they do, in fact, work. This performance compares favorably with other methods of automated retrieval. As might be expected, full-text search tends to produce higher recall at the expense of lower relevance. This was the experience reported by Haibt et al. (23), with a full-text data base of 5,000 stories from *Time* magazine. The system was relatively unsophisticated, but contained a few refinements, such as a root word-form dictionary of regularly inflected forms of words—the singulars, plurals, and possessives of nouns, and the present tense forms, participles, and past tense forms of verbs. The system automatically equates (as synonyms) words in the text with those found in the dictionary. Two factors are relevant to the reported "success" of this experiment. First, the query words were primarily proper names (thus, the semantic problems were minimized), and second, the criterion for "success" was rather soft, i.e.,

> To measure performance we used the notion "satisfactorily answered query", defined as a query in which at least one relevant reference is found, and in which there are no more than thirty answers. One answer out of every ten must be relevant. . . .

On the basis of the above criteria, 1,980 of 2,180 queries, or 91%, were deemed satisfactorily answered. The actual performance was far better than the minimum standard.

IBM's Internal Technical Information Retrieval Center (ITIRC) uses an interesting combination of text processing and intellectually assigned tags (Magnino, 45). The authors of IBM reports are required to assign category terms, and one to four subject terms selected from an IBM thesaurus, to each report. These terms are used in the computer compilation of current-awareness bulletins and cumulative indexes. On the retrieval side, an information retrieval specialist translates the user's profile (for SDI) or query into a search formulation, which is searched against the full-text abstract file, that has been arranged alphabetically by word and sorted by word length with indicators showing the position of the word, and other useful identifiers.

SYNTRAN/360, described by Briner & Carney (8), is a completely automated natural language processing system for retrieval or indexing. In contrast to ITIRC, the query is a textual statement in natural English. SYNTRAN uses a computer-generated thesaurus, based on the text being processed, to augment query words. The query logic includes the use of automatically assigned weights to individual query words as computed by an association factor. The same automatic indexing algorithms are used for extracting or abstracting (which is simply a compilation of the statistically most significant extracted sentences).

Another IBM natural language retrieval system, this one dealing with surgical and pathological medical records, is reported on by Jacobs (32). The heart of the system is a thesaurus processor that allows for the grouping of descriptors into clusters of synonyms as well as for storing the relations among synonym classes. It was noted that this thesaurus process required approximately 21 man-months of effort, or 75% of the total programming effort for the retrieval and updating system. The thesaurus expands the query for searching the text of the medical record file.

While the results of the full-text and automatic indexing systems appear promising, as reported by Salton (13, 60, 61), Keen (37), Haibt et al. (23), Hillman (25), Jacobs (32), and Magnino (45), there are others who offer warnings against expending too much effort in the attempt to achieve fully automatic text processing. Wessel (78) cites the homograph problem as a major deterrent to fully automatic indexing. He states:

> This should cause some deep soul searching on the part of those who hope to instruct computers to index raw text without significant human participation. If humans, using the most powerful tools available, are unable to develop acceptably rigorous explication of the language of the scientists, I think it rather optimistic that with the relatively weaker logical tools available for computer analysis, machine indexing can be achieved for material far less precise and rigor-

ously structured than the language of physics. . . . The text required for our data banks will be in languages for which a rigorous and formal syntax cannot be developed and for which a formal and rigorous semantic interpretation does not exist. The fact that computers can "count" very rapidly does not seem to help us very much in this case.

Wessel argues instead for machine-aided intellectual indexing, which can provide on-line error checking and error correction guidance, consistency checks, indexer training, and probably more thorough indexing by human indexers than is possible by purely manual methods. It is possible, however, that full-text searching may overcome the logical weaknesses of automatic indexing, by considering every word an index term. This then would put the burden on the search strategy, and, of course, require much greater storage capacities.

Document Retrieval Software

Rationale for Software Packages. With the growing importance of computer-based information retrieval systems, it is not surprising to find a significant number of attempts to build "packaged" systems. In view of the magnitude of the programming effort required for an information retrieval system, it is appropriate that this chapter consider the impact of software packages. The effort involved in an information retrieval program with updating facilities might range anywhere from one man-year to 20 man-years. If the developer of a new retrieval application has control of the data formats, it is quite likely that he can use existing packages to great advantage. The need for general-purpose software is analyzed by Sundeen (71) in terms of the increasing shortage of skilled programmers. He estimates that, with general-purpose information management systems for file creation and maintenance, information retrieval, and report generation, at least 80% of the applications encountered in data processing can be implemented without any formal programming being required. Obviously, general-purpose information management systems have a very broad application in data processing beyond document retrieval and dissemination.

Document Retrieval Packages vs. Generalized Data Management Systems. It is useful for the purpose of this review to distinguish between simple data-oriented retrieval systems, data or information management systems, and document retrieval systems. The data retrieval system may simply be an extension of the report generator concept; such software allows the user to describe the structure of his file and specify queries to it in a restricted language or on a structured form. Samples of this type of system include IBM's 9-PAC and CDC's INFOL (Sundeen, 71). On the other hand, generalized information or data management systems, such as AUERBACH's DM-1, or SDC's TS/CDMS (formerly TDMS), take over the majority of file creation, maintenance, restructuring, security and retrieval functions for the entire data processing installation. This subject was covered in last year's *Annual Review* by Shoffner (65) and is treated in this volume by Senko in Chapter 4.

Document retrieval software is much more specialized and less flexible than the generalized data management system. A document retrieval package has a fixed file structure and, typically, only involves a single file of citations or abstracts. The file structure of the package is usually designed to be able to accommodate a large variety of document collections. However, the buyer of the package must adjust his system to the internal structure of the software package. The document retrieval system also depends on an external vocabulary, such as a dictionary or thesaurus, whereas data retrieval and data management systems normally use internal vocabularies based on the context and structure of the record.

Bibliographies, Surveys, and Reviews. A number of useful survey papers were published in 1968 on the subject of retrieval and file management software. The most complete bibliography this reviewer has seen was prepared by Pietrzyk et al. (54); it contains 216 references. Three surveys provided comparative analysis of data management systems (59, 68, 80). The survey by Ziehe (80) covers TS/CDMS by System Development Corporation, RFMS by the University of Texas, DM-1 by AUERBACH Corporation, GIS by IBM, and CATALOGS by the RAND Corporation. Stefferud (68) reviews and compares TDMS, DM-1, GIS, IMS, COGENT II, AEGIS, MADAM, MARK IV, QWICK QUERY, and SPAN. Sable & Cochrane (59) provide a review and comparative analysis of eight data management systems: TDMS, GIS, ICS, DM-1, TSS/360, BTSS, MULTICS, and INTIPS.

Sundeen (71) provides a historical perspective of general-purpose software systems and capsule summaries of GIS, MANAGE, INFOL, IMRADS, BEST, TDMS, and ASI-ST. Another extensive survey by Reilly (55) gives a detailed description and analysis of four systems, CFSS, INFOL, MARK IV, and GIS. Of considerable interest to document retrieval applications is a recent survey of five on-line retrieval systems by Welch (77). The survey covers DATA CENTRAL, CCA 103, DIALOG, LUCID, and TDMS. All five of these systems are available off the shelf, all have interactive capabilities, and all can handle bibliographic data and index terms.

Fry et al. (21), of MITRE Corporation, review DM-1, FORGE, COGENT II, RAPID, IDS, MARK IV, National Military Command System Support Center's NIPS, DL-1 (also known as IMS), MANAGE, and TDMS.

Examples of Software Packages. IBM's Combined File Search System (CFSS), a batch-oriented package, has been used in a number of retrieval systems, including the American Institute of Physics experimental system using UDC (20), the Engineering Index CITE tape service (18, 53), and Food and Drug Administration retrieval systems (63). CFSS, as described by Warheit (76), is a general-purpose information storage and retrieval system that operates on an IBM 1401 computer. It consists of three basic files: the master file, the descriptor file, and the dictionary. The master file is arranged by item or record number and can accommodate a MARC catalog record, a MEDLARS compressed citation record, or any other similar record up to 2,200 characters. Additional text can be added to the 2,200 characters but would not be searchable. The descriptor file is arranged in inverted order: record numbers are filed behind descriptors. Each descriptor can also have attached to it a subdescriptor, a role, and a line or value entry. The dictionary file allows for control over the terminology and acts as an authority list with provision for synonyms. The major advantages of CFSS are that it is available without charge and that it can operate on a relatively small second-generation computer system. Its disadvantages are that it operates only in the batch-processing mode, has no text-processing capabilities, and cannot take appropriate advantage of direct-access storage devices.

IBM's more recent offering in the document retrieval area is its Document Processing System (DPS), which operates on an IBM 360/40 or larger (28). DPS is currently supported for operation in the batch mode, although one installation, the Bio-Medical Center of the State University of New York (SUNY), has developed a special monitor that uses nine remote on-line consoles under the MFT version of OS/360.

DPS has substantial text-processing capabilities and can operate either on formatted or natural-language records. Two types of index search logic are allowed: AND/OR logic and weighted key words. Further specificity in the search is provided by using the formatted data (author, title, etc.) or by limiting the search to a range of document numbers. Additional search features include root word capability, expansion of query to synonym and/ or to an equivalence list, and context specification in terms of differences between words, word order, same sentence context, or same paragraph context.

Data Corporation provides a commercial software package that has both text-processing capabilities and on-line remote access. The system known as DATA CENTRAL operates on an IBM 360/30 or 40 with F memory under DOS. The system accommodates structured data as well as textual data and can search on all elements (16). When processing full-text material, it automatically develops a key-word dictionary for the data base from the information used to build the file. All terms, except certain articles and common words possessing no retrieval value, are entered into the key-word dictionary. The search logic includes standard logical operators, standard arithmetic operators, and a "universal character" for truncation or root-word purposes. DATA CENTRAL is also capable of generating permuted title indexes.

Another proprietary on-line retrieval system is dubbed INQUIRE (31), produced by InfoData Systems, Inc. INQUIRE is written in Programming Language No. 1 (PL/1) and operates on an IBM 360/40 or larger, under OS/360. Like DATA CENTRAL, INQUIRE maintains a separate key-word file (which is called Index File), a search file, and an item file containing various segmented fields. The basic retrieval logic utilizes key words and a chaining technique. Each key word is looked up in the index file, which has an indexed sequential organization. The outputs of this lookup are a key-word code, a frequency count of the number of items described by that key word, and an address pointer to the first occurrence of the key word in the search file. The search file is a direct-access file containing one record for each item in the data base.

ORBIT is an on-line retrieval system designed primarily for retrieval of bibliographic text. Produced by System Development Corporation, ORBIT currently operates on IBM 360/65 and 360/50 computers in conjunction with a time-sharing executive system (46; Nance & Lathrop, 51). ORBIT operates in an instructional mode with either a long or short form of dialog. The dialog provides the user with a list of qualifiers by which the search can be narrowed, e.g., country of information, type of document, subject area or date. The current operational system accommodates 21 remote terminals and can accommodate 525,000 documents. The system can search on any bibliographic element that contains fewer than 36 characters, e.g., subject descriptors, authors' names, or subject codes.

Lockheed's DIALOG is another proprietary on-line retrieval system that can be used with bibliographic information (Summit, 70). In DIALOG, the user may invoke commands at a remote terminal, which is a keyboard/display device with a printer, connected to the central computer by a data communications facility. The system operates on a relatively small computer (IBM 360/30). Other on-line systems that have potential application for document retrieval include Generalized Information Management (GIM), by TRW Systems (Nelson, 52), and CCA 103, by Computer Corporation of America, described by Welch (77).

With the exception of the several surveys of data management and data retrieval systems described earlier, the literature of 1968 was relatively barren on the subject of generalized document retrieval software. It is hoped that 1969 will see objective reporting on the usefulness and difficulties of applying generalized packages for document retrieval and dissemination.

CONCLUSIONS

The literature of 1968 dealt primarily with advanced techniques for retrieval, such as the multistage user-controlled search strategy. While a number of advanced systems are in experimental use, most of the systems in operation today employ much simpler equipment and techniques; either they do not employ computers at all or they use batch-processing methods. The importance of the new interactive search strategies is not to be understated; however, several conditions must be met before they will receive widespread operational use. First, hardware and software facilities for on-line data base operations must be greatly improved so that each installation is not faced with an extremely expensive communications software development effort. Second, carefully controlled experiments utilizing these search techniques should be conducted and the failures as well as the successes reported. This will serve to assure that the algorithms described herein do, in fact, work.

There was a dearth of analytical reporting on such subjects as the relative cost/effectiveness of non-computer vs. computer retrieval systems and of batch vs. on-line retrieval. Much more cost information is needed to aid the designers of tomorrow's systems to make intelligent choices. It was noted that at least one observer (Salton, 60) reported on the economies that can be gained by the application of interchangeable random-access storage devices even in a batch-processing environment. However, a European article (Rolling & Piette, 56) reached an opposite conclusion, perhaps because of a lack of awareness of the changes that have taken place in equipment technology.

A respectable number of interactive retrieval systems are now operational, and at least five of these are commercially available as packaged software systems. This reviewer believes this to be a major milestone in the evolution of retrieval system technology. The cost of software development has always been a major budget item for every computer-based retrieval center. Now, essentially all of the software required can be purchased for a small fraction of what it would cost an installation to build its own. This fact, coupled with the possibility of using a time-sharing service, where the information center does not have a computer available, should increase substantially the number of computer-based retrieval systems in use. It is also believed that only an on-line interactive system can provide the responsiveness required by the user. The majority of users who have access to batch-processing retrieval systems still utilize the published book-form indexes for their retrospective searching. While the computer file is more deeply indexed and can make a more complete search, the user apparently feels a need to interact directly with the index during the search process. It is this one feature, the interactive mode of operation, that provides the major promise for tomorrow's document retrieval systems.

REFERENCES

(1) BAKER, WALTER S.; HOSHOVSKY, ALEXANDER G. The storage and retrieval of "visuals." Graphic Science, (March 1968) 22, 24, 26, 27.
(2) BELL, COLIN J. Implicit information retrieval. Information Storage and Retrieval, 4:2 (June 1968) 139–160. Presented at the First Cranfield International Conference on Mechanized Information Storage and Retrieval Systems, College of Aeronautics, Cranfield, 29–31 August 1967.
(3) BENNETT, JOHN L. On-line computer aids for the indexer. Presented at the 31st Annual Meeting of the American Society for Information Science, Columbus, Ohio, 24 October 1968, User Discussion Group VIII: Interactive Language Processing for the Working Information Scientist.
(4) BERUL, LAWRENCE H. Survey of equipment developments in the information storage and retrieval field. In: F.I.D./I.F.I.P. Joint Conference, Rome, Italy, 14–17 June 1967. Proceedings [title]: Mechanized information storage, retrieval and dissemination. Edited by Kjell Samuelson. North-Holland Publishing Co., Amsterdam, 1968, p. 26–29.
(5) BERUL, LAWRENCE H. Survey of IS&R equipment. Datamation, 14:3 (March 1968) 27–32.
(6) BORKO, H. Interactive document storage and retrieval system-design concepts. In: F.I.D./I.F.I.P. Joint Conference, Rome, Italy, 14–17 June 1967. Proceedings [title]: Mechanized information storage, retrieval and dissemination. Edited by Kjell Samuelson. North-Holland Publishing Co., Amsterdam, 1968, p. 591–599.
(7) BREGZIS, RITVARS. Query language for the reactive catalogue. In: National Colloquium on Information Retrieval, 4th, 3–4 May 1967, Philadelphia, Pa. Proceedings, edited by Albert B. Tonik. International Information Incorporated, Philadelphia, Pa., 1967, p. 77–90, discussion, p. 90–91.
(8) BRINER, L. L.; CARNEY, G. J. SYNTRAN/360, a natural language processing system for preparing text references and retrieving text information. IBM Corp., Gaithersburg, Md., 1968. (Preprint)
(9) BROWN, PATRICIA L.; JONES, SHIRLI O. Document retrieval and dissemination in libraries and information centers. In: Annual review of information science and technology, vol. 3. Carlos A. Cuadra, ed. Encyclopaedia Britannica, Chicago, 1968.
(10) CAUTIN, HARVEY; REGAN, EDWARD. Real English project report. Moore School of Electrical Engineering, University of Pennsylvania, Philadelphia, November 1967, 16 p. (AD-673 899)
(11) CONWAY, EDWARD F. WESTAR: an improved system for data retrieval with or without the computer. In: National Microfilm Association Convention, 17th, Chicago, 21–24 May 1968. Preprint of general session papers and seminar materials. The Association, Annapolis, Md., 1968, p. 11–20.
(12) CONWAY, EDWARD F. WESTAR microfilm retrieval system. Office, 67:5 (May 1968) 65–67.
(13) CORNELL UNIVERSITY. DEPARTMENT OF COMPUTER SCIENCE. Information storage and retrieval. Scientific report no. ISR-13 to the National Science Foundation. Reports on evaluation procedures and results 1965–1967. Gerard Salton, Project Director. Ithaca, N.Y., January 1968, 1 vol. (various pagings) including Appendix A: Recall-precision tables.

(14) CURTICE, R. M.; GIULIANO, V. E.; JONES, P. E.; SHERRI, M. E. Application of statistical association techniques for the NASA document collection. Arthur D. Little, Inc., Cambridge, Mass., February 1968, 111 p. (NASA-CR-1020) (N68-17154)
(15) DAMMERS, H. F. Phased transition from non-mechanized information storage and retrieval to on-line computer operation. In: F.I.D./I.F.I.P. Joint Conference, Rome, Italy, 14–17 June 1967. Proceedings [title]: Mechanized information storage, retrieval and dissemination. Edited by Kjell Samuelson. North-Holland Publishing Co., Amsterdam, 1968, p. 415–436.
(16) DATA CORP. This is Data Central: an automated general purpose information storage and retrieval system. Dayton, Ohio, 1968, 6 p.
(17) Data search technique lights up the subject. Data Systems News, 9:16 (November 1968) 6, 11–12.
(18) ENGINEERING INDEX, INC. CITE. New York. (Brochure, 4 p.)
(19) FREEMAN, ROBERT R.; ATHERTON, PAULINE. AUDACIOUS—an experiment with an on-line, interactive reference retrieval system using the Universal Decimal Classification as the index language in the field of nuclear science. American Institute of Physics, UDC Project, New York, 25 April 1968, 59 p. (AIP/UDC-7) (PB-178 374) Shorter version published in: American Society for Information Science Annual Meeting, Columbus, Ohio, 20–24 October 1968. Proceedings, vol. 5. Greenwood Publishing Corp., New York, 1968, p. 193–199.
(20) FREEMAN, ROBERT R.; ATHERTON, PAULINE. File organization and search strategy using UDC in mechanized reference retrieval systems. In: F.I.D./I.F.I.P. Joint Conference, Rome, Italy, 14–17 June 1967. Proceedings [title]: Mechanized information storage, retrieval and dissemination. Edited by Kjell Samuelson. North-Holland Publishing Co., Amsterdam, 1968, p. 122–152.
(21) FRY, J. P. et al. A survey of data management systems. MITRE Corp., Washington, D.C., 7 March 1968, 119 p. (MTR 5036)
(22) GREEN, CLAUDE CORDELL; RAPHAEL, BERTRAM. Research on intelligent question-answering system. Stanford Research Institute, Menlo Park, Calif., May 1967, 52 p. (Report no. Scientific-1) (AFCRL-67-0370) (AD-656 789)
(23) HAIBT, LUTHER; FISCHER, MARGARET; KASTNER, MARGARET; KETELHUT, ROBERT; OGG, JAY; WOOLLEY, JON H. Retrieving 4,000 references without indexing. In: National Colloquium on Information Retrieval, 4th, 3–4 May 1967, Philadelphia, Pa. Proceedings, edited by Albert B. Tonik. International Information Incorporated, Philadelphia, Pa., 1967, p. 127–132; discussion, p. 132–133.
(24) HAYGARTH JACKSON, A. R.; MATTHEWS, F. W. A case study of the "Uniterm Index to U.S. Chemical Patents" using a weighted term search technique. Aslib Proceedings, 20:2 (February 1968) 118–128; discussion, p. 128.
(25) HILLMAN, DONALD J. Negotiation of inquiries in an on-line retrieval system. Information Storage and Retrieval, 4:2 (June 1968) 219–238. Information Storage and Retrieval, 4:2 (June 1968) 218–239. Presented at the First Cranfield International Conference on Mechanized Information Storage and Retrieval Systems, College of Aeronautics, Cranfield, England, 29–31 August 1967.
(26) HOFFMAN, WARREN S. An integrated chemical structure storage and search system operating at Du Pont. Journal of Chemical Documentation, 8:1 (February 1968) 3–13.
(27) HUTTON, FRED C. PEEKABIT, computer offspring of punched card PEEKABOO, for natural language searching. Communications of the ACM, 11:9 (September 1968) 595–598.
(28) IBM CORPORATION. IBM System/360 document processing system (360A-CX-12X) program description and operations manual. White Plains, N.Y., 1967, 282 p. (H20-0477-0)
(29) IBM CORPORATION. Introduction to DATATEXT. IBM, White Plains, N.Y., 1968, 29 p. (J20-0011-1)
(30) IBM CORPORATION. QUICKTRAN user's guide. IBM, White Plains, N.Y., 1966, 90 p. (E20-0240-0)

(31) INFODATA SYSTEMS. INQUIRE user's guide 1968. Rochester, N.Y., October 1968, 38 p.
(32) JACOBS, H. A natural language information retrieval system. Methods of Information in Medicine [Methodik der Information in der Medizin], 7:1 (January 1968) 8–16.
(33) JANDA, KENNETH. Information retrieval; applications to political science. Bobbs-Merrill, Indianapolis, Ind., 1968, 230 p.
(34) JANDA, KENNETH. A microfilm-and-computer system for analyzing comparative politics literature. Presented at National Conference on Content Analysis, Annenberg School of Communications, University of Pennsylvania, Philadelphia, 16–18 November 1967.
(35) JUDGE, P. J. The user-system interface today—national and international information systems. In: De Reuck, Anthony; Knight, Julie, eds. Communication in science. Little, Brown, Boston, 1967, p. 37–51; discussion, p. 52–56.
(36) KAYE, M.; NYEKY, R. A reprint retrieval system for nephrology using Termatrex cards. Canadian Medical Association Journal, 98 (20 April 1968) 781–784.
(37) KEEN, E. MICHAEL. User controlled search strategies. In: National Colloquium on Information Retrieval, 4th, 3–4 May 1967, Philadelphia, Pa. Proceedings, edited by Albert B. Tonik. International Information Incorporated, Philadelphia, Pa., 1967, p. 141–154; discussion, p. 154.
(38) KELLOGG, CHARLES H. CONVERSE: a system for the on-line description and retrieval of structured data using natural language. In: F.I.D./I.F.I.P. Joint Conference, Rome, Italy, 14–17 June 1967. Proceedings [title]: Mechanized information storage, retrieval and dissemination. Edited by Kjell Samuelson. North-Holland Publishing Co., Amsterdam, 1968, p. 600–607.
(39) KELLOGG, CHARLES H. On-line translation of natural language questions into artificial language queries. Information Storage and Retrieval, 4:3 (August 1968) 287–307.
(40) LANCASTER, F. WILFRED. Information retrieval systems: characteristics, testing, and evaluation. Wiley, New York, 1968, 222 p.
(41) LANCASTER, F. WILFRED; CLIMENSON, W. D. Evaluating the economic efficiency of a document retrieval system. Journal of Documentation, 24:1 (March 1968) 16–40.
(42) LEIMKUHLER, FERDINAND F. A literature search and file organization model. American Documentation, 19:2 (April 1968) 131–136. [Letter, p. 206–207]
(43) LEIMKUHLER, FERDINAND F. Mathematical models for library systems analysis. Purdue University, School of Industrial Engineering, Lafayette, Ind., 4 October 1967, 17 p. Presented at Drexel Institute of Technology, 17–20 September 1967. (PB-176 113)
(44) LESK, MICHAEL E. Performance of automatic information systems. Information Storage and Retrieval, 4:2 (June 1968) 201–218. Presented at the First Cranfield International Conference on Mechanized Information Storage and Retrieval Systems, College of Aeronautics, Cranfield, England, 29–31 August 1967.
(45) MAGNINO, JOSEPH J., JR. IBM's unique but operational international industrial textual documentation system—ITIRC. Presented at 33rd Conference of FID and International Congress of Documentation, Tokyo, 12–22 September 1967. (Preprint, 9 p. and appendix)
(46) Man/machine—a contemporary dialogue. SDC Magazine, 10 (September 1967) 13–14.
(47) MEISTER, D.; SULLIVAN, D. J. Evaluation of user reactions to a prototype on-line information retrieval system. Bunker-Ramo Corp., Canoga Park, October 1967, 62 p. (NASA-CR-918) (N-67-40083)
(48) MEYER, E. Superimposed screens for the GREMAS system. In: F.I.D./I.F.I.P. Joint Conference, Rome, Italy, 14–17 June 1967. Proceedings [title]: Mechanized information storage, retrieval and dissemination. Edited by Kjell Samuelson. North-Holland Publishing Co., Amsterdam, 1968, p. 280–288.
(49) MOOERS, C. N. The application of simple pattern inclusion selection to large scale

information retrieval systems. Zator Co., Cambridge, Mass., April 1959. (Technical bulletin no. 131) (AD-215 434)
(50) MULVIHILL, JOHN; BRENNER, EVERETT H.   Ranking Boolean search output. [Brief Communication] American Documentation, 19:2   (April 1968) 204–205.
(51) NANCE, J. W.; LATHROP, J. W.   System design specifications, general purpose ORBIT. System Development Corporation, Santa Monica, Calif., 15 September 1968, 31 p. (TM-DA-20/000/00)
(52) NELSON, DONALD B.   Generalized information management. TRW Systems, Redondo Beach, Calif., 13 p. Presented to the 4th Annual Engineering Graphics Seminar, University of Southern California, Los Angeles.
(53) New CITE service offered by Engineering Index. Scientific Information Notes, 10 (October–November–December 1968) 7.
(54) PIETRZYK, ALFRED; LAMBERTS, FRANCES; FREEMAN, ROBERT R: File-management techniques and systems with applications to information retrieval—a selective bibliography. Center for Applied Linguistics, Washington, D.C., June 1968, 31 p. (PB-178 792)
(55) REILLY, KEVIN D.   Evaluation of generalized file management systems. In: University of California, Los Angeles. Institute of Library Research. Mechanized information services in the university library. Phase I: Planning. Los Angeles, 15 December 1967, Vol. 1, part 6. (PB-178 441)
(56) ROLLING, L.; PIETTE, J.   Interaction of economics and automation in a large size retrieval system. In: F.I.D./I.F.I.P. Joint Conference, Rome, Italy, 14–17 June 1967. Proceedings [title] : Mechanized information storage, retrieval and dissemination. Edited by Kjell Samuelson. North-Holland Publishing Co., Amsterdam, 1968, p. 367–390.
(57) RUBINOFF, MORRIS; BERGMAN, S.; CAUTIN, H., RAPP, F.   Easy English, a language for information retrieval through a remote typewriter console. Moore School of Electrical Engineering, University of Pennsylvania, Philadelphia, Pa., April 1967, 15 p. Prepared in cooperation with Pennsylvania Research Associates, Inc., Philadelphia. (AD-660 081)
(58) RUBINOFF, M.; BERGMAN, S.; CAUTIN, H.; RAPP, F.   Easy English, a language for information retrieval through a remote typewriter console. Communications of the ACM, 11:10   (October 1968) 693–696.
(59) SABLE, JEROME D.; COCHRANE, JAMES.   Data management system study: final report. Auerbach Corp.; Philadelphia, Pa., 1 April 1968, 1 vol. (Report no. 1469-TR-4) (NASA CR-86057) (N68-26292)
(60) SALTON, GERARD.   Automatic information organization and retrieval. McGraw-Hill, New York, 1968, 480 p.
(61) SALTON, GERARD.   Search strategy and the optimization of retrieval effectiveness. In: F.I.D./I.F.I.P. Joint Conference, Rome, Italy, 14–17 June 1967. Proceedings [title] : Mechanized information storage, retrieval and dissemination. Edited by Kjell Samuelson. North-Holland Publishing Co., Amsterdam, 1968, p. 73–107.
(62) SCHLESS, ARTHUR P.; PURDY, MARIE E.; STEVENSON, ROBERT E.   Reading guide and index to the cancer-virology literature. American Documentation, 19:2 (April 1968) 163–167.
(63) SERVICE BUREAU CORPORATION.   Food and drug administration information retrieval system.   Phase I.   Palo Alto, Calif., 1968, 193 p.
(64) SHANK, R. D.   Information retrieval of supplier evaluation data. Systems and Procedures Journal, 18   (November–December 1967) 16+.
(65) SHOFFNER, RALPH M.   Organization, maintenance and search of machine files. In: Annual review of information science and technology, vol. 3. Carlos A. Cuadra, ed. Encyclopaedia Britannica, Chicago, 1968.
(66) SINOWITZ, NORMAN R.   DATAPLUS—a language for real time information retrieval from hierarchical data bases. In: AFIPS Conference Proceedings, vol. 32; 1968 Spring Joint Computer Conference. Thompson, Washington, D.C., p. 395–401.
(67) STANFEL, LARRY E.   On a quantitative approach to improving document retrieval performance. Information Storage and Retrieval, 4:3   (August 1968) 281–286.

(68) STEFFERUD, EINAR A. New software for data management. System Development Corp., Santa Monica, Calif., 6 September 1968. (Sp–3221) Presented at the 15th International Meeting of the Institute of Management Sciences, Cleveland, Ohio, 11–13 September 1968.
(69) STOGNIY, A. A.; AFANASSIEV, V. N. Some design problems for automatic fact information retrieval and storage systems. In: F.I.D./I.F.I.P. Joint Conference, Rome, Italy, 14–17 June 1967. Proceedings [title] : Mechanized information storage, retrieval and dissemination. Edited by Kjell Samuelson. North-Holland Publishing Co., Amsterdam, 1968, p. 289–299.
(70) SUMMIT, ROGER K. On-line information retrieval comes of age. In: Joint Engineering Management Conference, Philadelphia, Pa., 30 September–1 October 1968. Computer impact on engineering management [Proceedings] Instrument Society of America, Pittsburgh, Pa., 1968, p. 49–51.
(71) SUNDEEN, DONALD H. General purpose software. Datamation, (January 1968) 22–27.
(72) SWANSON, ROWENA W. Information services for small-scale industry. [Brief communication on several papers presented at Puerto Rico Conference on Technology and Resources held in San Juan on 20–21 June 1968] American Documentation, 19:4 (October 1968) 412–413.
(73) TREU, SIEGFRIED. The browser's retrieval game. American Documentation, 19:4 (October 1968) 404–410.
(74) VALLEE, JACQUES F.; KRULEE, GILBERT K.; GRAU, ALBERT A. Retrieval formulae for inquiry systems. Information Storage and Retrieval, 4:1 (March 1968) 13–26.
(75) VICKERY, B. C. The raw material of retrieval. In: F.I.D./I.F.I.P. Joint Conference, Rome, Italy, 14–17 June 1967. Proceedings [title] : Mechanized information storage, retrieval and dissemination. Edited by Kjell Samuelson. North-Holland Publishing Co., Amsterdam, 1968, p. 15–25.
(76) WARHEIT, I. A. File organization for information retrieval. In: F.I.D./I.F.I.P. Joint Conference, Rome, Italy, 14–17 June 1967. Proceedings [title] : Mechanized information storage, retrieval and dissemination. Edited by Kjell Samuelson. North-Holland Publishing Co., Amsterdam, 1968, p. 259–268.
(77) WELCH, NOREEN O. A survey of five on-line retrieval systems. MITRE Corp., Washington, D.C. Operations, August 1968, 53 p. (MTP-322) The work reported herein was undertaken by the MITRE Corp. in support of Panel 2 of the Committee on Scientific and Technical Information (COSATI) of the Federal Council for Science and Technology.
(78) WESSEL, ANDREW E. Some thoughts on machine indexing. RAND Corp., Santa Monica, Calif., June 1968, 12 p. (Report no. P-3869) (AD-671 989)
(79) WILDE, DANIEL U. Computer-aided strategy design using adaptive and associative techniques. In: American Society for Information Science Annual Meeting, Columbus, Ohio, 20–24 October 1968. Proceedings, vol. 5. Greenwood Publishing Corp., New York, 1968, p. 175–178.
(80) ZIEHE, THEODORE W. Data management: a comparison of system features. TRACOR, Austin, Tex., October 1967, 43 p. (TRACOR-67-904-U) (AD-661 861)

8 Document Dissemination

HERBERT B. LANDAU
Auerbach Corporation

INTRODUCTION

This chapter is a review of the issues, concepts, and techniques of document dissemination, as represented in the literature of 1968. As Brown & Jones (28) pointed out in Volume 3 of the *Annual Review*, document dissemination often overlaps document retrieval. The coverage of document dissemination in this year's *Annual Review* may also bridge subjects covered in other chapters, such as Secondary Services, Information Networks, and Library Automation. While this reviewer has sought to eliminate unnecessary overlap, a certain amount still exists. It should help the reader to identify the close relationship between dissemination and other aspects of information systems.

This chapter is directed to those whose vocation (or avocation) is information. While we may call ourselves librarians, information scientists or technologists, abstractors and indexers, documentalists, IS&R specialists, literature searchers, and so forth, we all have one thing in common: We are either directly or indirectly involved in the dissemination of information. As disseminators, we are interested in far more than the techniques for transmission of information from one point to another. Despite McLuhan's (93) statement that "the medium is the message," we must concern ourselves with not only the means of document dissemination, but also the content and value of the documents we disseminate. This idea is prevalent throughout most of the papers reviewed in this chapter. A disseminator should think of himself as a selective switching center, inputting data, evaluating them, selecting worthy items, and directing and controlling their transmission to a target: the reader.

It has become trite to say that information is a valuable commodity. It is valuable only if it is cogent and relevant in the eyes of the beholder, and only if it is presented to him in the right form, at the right time, and at the right place. Technology gives us the tools to achieve both relevance and proper presentation. Many of these tools and techniques have been discussed in the literature of 1968, and they are reviewed below. In selecting items for this chapter, preference was given to papers that clearly illustrated both novel and conventional techniques for disseminating and delivering documents and document surrogates to the information consumer.

The emphasis of this review has been on techniques, rather than on applications in a particular subject field. This will facilitate comparison and evaluation and will demonstrate that many aspects of document dissemination are nearly universal and can be found in all dissemination systems, regardless of subject orientation or audience.

In this chapter, we first discuss current dissemination issues and trends, such as Federal Government dissemination activities, the role of the national libraries in document dissemination, dissemination of surrogates versus that of full text, and the trend towards information analysis centers. We then survey the range of document dissemination techniques in current use, including the issue of system input (i.e., the nature of the primary source literature) as a dissemination problem, and specific means of dissemination, such as personal contact, information exchange groups, critical reviews, newsletters, preprints, reading guides, and Selective Dissemination Information (SDI) systems. A brief discussion of document delivery techniques, such as microfiche, facsimile, and digital techniques, is presented, with a final section on the magnetic tape distribution of document surrogates.

DISSEMINATION ISSUES AND TRENDS

The Federal Government and Document Dissemination

The increasing role of the Government in information dissemination activities is demonstrated by the relatively large number of papers on the subject. Simpson (127), for example, predicts that management of scientific and technical information will tend to become the responsibility of the Federal Government. This reviewer believes that this Federal control is rapidly becoming a reality in the area of document dissemination. Lowry (91) points out the "vast increase in Federal funds poured into information services" and Holzbauer (66) states that "many privately generated abstracting and indexing tools are in part supported by Federal funds, as the Federal and private research efforts are interwoven."

An article by Holzbauer presents a broad overview of Federal Government announcement, searching, and retrieval services (66). He points out that the very laws that create new departments and agencies almost invariably include responsibility for making available information pertinent to the agency's work. Discussing the information dissemination techniques now used in Government, Holzbauer points out that automated and semiautomated equipment is playing an increasingly important role. This fact is illustrated in the COSATI directory (Ockerman et al., 104), which describes 13 operational computer-based systems designed for the analysis, storage, retrieval, and secondary distribution of technical reports.

Swanson (130) reports on a conference that looked at large-scale Federal information systems (such as the Science Information Exchange, National Referral Center, Clearinghouse for Scientific and Technical Information, and NASA) from a small-scale industry point of view. She reports that NASA not only disseminates technical documents but, through its Computer Software and Management Information Center (COSMIC) at the University of Georgia, also distributes computer programs at an average cost of $75 each.

Through the State Technical Services Act, technical information from national and State governments to industry is disseminated as presented in the papers of Grogan (58), Heintz (61), Levesque (87), and Stevenson (128).

Several authors discussed the flow of information both within and outside the Federal Government. Klempner (80) studied the distribution patterns for four Government abstracting and indexing services: *Nuclear Science Abstracts, Scientific and Technical Aerospace Reports, Technical Abstract Bulletin*, and *U.S. Government Research and Development Reports*. Toward this end, he tested the hypotheses that the abstracting and indexing services of the national documentation centers are inadequately utilized, that an economically undesirable pattern exists in the distribution of the services, and that there is a correlation between the utilization of these services and the geographic regions and industries of the users. He concluded that:

> Inadequate distribution of abstracting and indexing services and other federally produced documents, the parsimonious and generally sporadic support of the information dissemination function and information management decisions which often work at cross purposes, are in no small measure attributable to the lack of a formalized national policy for information dissemination.

Klempner's findings on the inadequacy of Federal information dissemination programs parallel those derived by others. A report by the Intergovernmental Task Force on Information Systems (71) finds that information flow within and among Federal, State, and local governments is unreliable, uneconomical, difficult to control, and fraught with duplication. A principal cause of this situation is the lack of strong central coordination at all levels of government over the development and operation of internal information systems. Another cause is the absence of effective information controls and standards within Federal and State agencies. Lowry (91) identifies these same problems in his assessment of science information problems in Government.

The remarks of Toll (131), who discusses technical report dissemination problems encountered by the Air Force Avionics Laboratory, are more poignant. He states:

> Unlike virtue, research is not its own reward. Technical data dissemination must not rely on a passive program to spread the word. ... The distribution of reports deserves a better fate than it now has. ... The hard cold facts are that the bulk of R&D effort may be very well languishing in the originator's bottom drawer or in a library file as a direct result of poor and inadequate distribution.

Toll reports that the Avionics Laboratory, rather than using standard Government channels, such as the Defense Documentation Center (DDC), set up its own document dissemination program, known as the Technical Objective Document Release Program and directed at R&D organizations.

Budington (29) comes to a similar conclusion concerning the inefficient dissemination of Federal R&D information to the public. He comments:

> Except for holders of defense contracts, it is a difficult and slow process for the general public to (i) learn what usable technology results from Department of Defense-sponsored research, and (ii) ... examine or obtain copies of potentially interesting reports.

Perhaps the COSATI Task Group on Dissemination of Information (54), formed in 1967, will solve some of the Federal dissemination problems. This group is charged with making recommendations to COSATI on improving present dissemination procedures and policies and on establishing uniform guidelines for handling unclassified scientific and technical information.

The activities of the Department of Commerce Clearinghouse for Scientific and Technical Information (CFSTI) were discussed in several publications in 1968. The CFSTI serves as a focal point for the collection, announcement, and dissemination of unclassified, Government-sponsored R&D reports and translations. A report by King et al. (79) discussed the experimentation, modeling, and analysis that went into the establishment of the new CFSTI pricing policy. A document by Bjorge et al. (22) outlined an experiment that determined the effectiveness of various announcement media on CFSTI sales. Results showed the Fast Announcement Service (FAS) to be the most effective single announcement medium. A series of CFSTI user-needs studies were described by Urbach (136). These studies measured the habits, needs, and preferences of users to determine the effectiveness of different announcement media and to estimate the impact on sales of changes in pricing policy. Boylan (26), in her "History of the Dissemination of PB Reports," provided a chronology of report-distribution techniques used by the Clearinghouse's predecessor agencies. The Clearinghouse announced its new CAST (Clearinghouse Announcements in Science and Technology) service in 1968 (35, 101), and a complete guide to CFSTI products and services was also issued at about the same time (34).

The National Libraries and Document Dissemination

The three national libraries—the Library of Congress (LC), the National Library of Medicine (NLM), and the National Agricultural Library (NAL)—have demonstrated their increasing impact on the document dissemination and retrieval scene in 1968. An article by Dickson (46) discusses the potential impact of the national libraries' automation programs on the electronic hardware market.

As demonstrated in the literature, U.S. national libraries now have three basic functions: document surrogate dissemination (e.g., MEDLARS, MARC); service as a document depository (the traditional library role); and the operation of information-switching centers to identify, collect, and distribute literature in specific subject areas (e.g., the NAL project on the secondary literature of agriculture). These examples are discussed in more depth below.

Of particular significance was the announcement that LC would implement a full-scale operational MARC (Machine-Readable Cataloging) subscription service in 1968 (Avram, 11). This service will distribute weekly magnetic tapes containing LC cataloging data on English-language monographs. As planned, this service will utilize the new MARC II communication format (Avram et al., 12), which was developed through the experiences of the MARC Pilot Project. The results of this pilot project are presented in informal summary form by an LC report (89) and the papers of Avram (10, 11) and Leach (86). It was found that the MARC tapes could save time and labor in cataloging operations. Of interest are the findings that the best results were obtained with locally produced (as opposed to LC-supplied) programs and that computer size was not a factor in successful use of the tapes. The problem of libraries not having access to the computer programs required to process this machine-readable bibliographic data was a major topic of discussion at the Fourth Conference on Machine-Readable Cataloging Copy in December 1967 (37). One possible solution for libraries with compatible computers is a software package for MARC processing, such as the one developed by five cooperating libraries in the NELINET Project, described by Nugent (103). In addition to MARC, the LC is also seeking to automate the production and distribution of its printed catalog cards through its CARDS (Card Automated Reproduction and Distribution System) project (108).

One of the first organizations to disseminate machine-readable bibliographic material was the National Library of Medicine, which began its computer-based MEDLARS (Medical Literature Analysis and Retrieval System) in 1963. The first four years of this magnetic-tape dissemination program are described in *MEDLARS 1963–1967* (Austin, 9).

In another project (69), the NLM cooperated with the Food and Drug Administration and Chemical Abstracts Service to prepare an index to chemical substances known as the *Desktop Analysis Tool (DAT)*.

Two recent projects of the National Agricultural Library (NAL) involve an analysis of the Library's role in agricultural document dissemination as related to secondary information services. One project (98) will evaluate the NAL's *Bibliography of Agriculture* as it compares to other abstracting and indexing services. The other study (97) will plan for the utilization of existing bibliographic data banks by the NAL.

All three national libraries are also participating in the U.S. National Libraries Task Force, as described by Lazerow (85). This group has as its purpose the coordination of automation efforts among the three libraries. A significant step was made when these libraries agreed to accept MARC II as their standard communication format for machine-readable bibliographic information.

Dissemination of Document Surrogates vs. Dissemination of Full Text

It is quite common for papers on document dissemination to concern themselves with only the delivery of a reference, an abstract, or a condensation or extract of the document. Indeed, the numerous papers on sophisticated document surrogate retrieval and dissemination systems often completely omit any mention of facilities or systems for providing a user with an actual document (as opposed to a surrogate). One might ask, "Is the traditional librarian's concern with putting a document into a reader's hand old-fashioned? Of what use is a surrogate without access to the full text?"

Toll (131) is justifiably critical of information systems that do not pay adequate attention to the dissemination and retrieval of actual documents on a timely basis. He declares:

Most computer operated information programs are announcement programs only. They always identify reports by titles, authors, key words, and they frequently supply abstracts of the report. . . . (the reader) must order the reports he wants to read in order to learn whether they actually are of technical interest. Finally after what the impatient requestor always considers an excessive period of time, the full text of the reports is retrieved in one half the original size to assure difficult reading. By this time he couldn't care less. He has completed the project or he has gone into something else. What he receives is interesting in a historical or academic sense, but, no longer pertinent.

Dammers (42) also addresses the problem of timeliness in document delivery. He suggests the mass storage of all current literature in digital form at a central location from which it could be digitally transmitted over high-speed voice-grade lines to remote libraries or regional computer centers for local dissemination. However, as Berul (21) suggests, our present telephone systems are not geared to handle large-scale full-text transmissions.

The report of the Committee on Scientific and Technical Communication (SATCOM) (16) defines the paradox associated with the advent of more efficient announcement techniques: As secondary services become more effective in identifying relevant literature, they also cause the user the problem of locating and obtaining copies of the publications to which he has been alerted. On-demand document delivery systems, reports SATCOM, are now operated in coordination with such secondary publications as *U.S. Government Research and Development Reports (USGRDR), Index Medicus, Bibliography of Agriculture, Chemical Abstracts, Biological Abstracts, Current Contents, NASA Fast Announcements, GPO Monthly Catalog,* and *Engineering Index.* SATCOM recommends the establishment of document delivery systems or depots to which a user might conveniently turn in order to obtain an original publication.

The Information Analysis Center (IAC)

Salton (113), in his textbook *Automatic Information Organization and Retrieval*, states that at least three types of dissemination centers take part in the dissemination process: abstracting and indexing services, libraries (or document depots), and information analysis centers. In this section the newest of these three types of dissemination establishments, the information analysis center (IAC), is discussed. The other two types of dissemination centers are discussed in Chapters 9 and 10, respectively.

Definition and Rationale of the IAC. The Weinberg Report of 1963

(109) predicted that the specialized information analysis center would ultimately become the accepted retailer of information to the scientific community, supplanting the technical library. A more recent study of System Development Corporation (SDC) on technology and libraries (Lanham, 84) echoes the sentiment of the Weinberg Report when it states:

> (Specialized) users need and are demanding more and better technical information support. They do not always find it in the conventional library, and this has given rise to a multitude of specialized information facilities . . . a technological force that the libraries must contend with.

In the face of such predictions, special librarians have observed the continuing growth of the IAC with a certain amount of awe. This growth has certainly been rapid; a recent *selective* directory of Federally supported IAC's (53) lists 113 centers, none of which existed prior to 1946.

The COSATI Panel 6 on Information Analysis Centers defines the IAC as follows (53):

> An information analysis center is a formally structured organizational unit specifically (but not necessarily exclusively) established for the purpose of acquiring, selecting, storing, retrieving, evaluating, analyzing, and synthesizing a body of information and/or data in a clearly defined specialized field or pertaining to a specified mission with the intent of compiling, digesting, repackaging, or otherwise organizing and presenting pertinent information and/or data in a form most authoritative, timely, and useful to a society of peers and management.

Simpson (127) defines the role of the IAC more simply and clearly. The IAC, he states, will be able to give the specialist answers to such important questions as, "Who is doing what, where, and how?", "What is going on in a technical speciality?", and "What should be done to advance the state of the art?" Simpson identifies two types of IAC's: those dealing with highly specialized and significant problems, generally of relatively short range, and those (called data analysis centers) dealing with areas of critical data having a long time importance and high use rates. Both types of IAC's exist only as long as R&D is being conducted in their areas of interest. Simpson states that, as soon as this interest ceases to exist, the IAC should cease operation. This is a commendable philosophy, which we hope will be adopted by Government and private IAC's alike.

The IAC vs. the Special Library. One might ask, "Just how does the

IAC differ from the special library?" This reviewer believes that the difference between the traditional technical library and the IAC is one of degree, not of kind. The information services that the IAC offers are more direct, more concentrated, and more selective than those normally offered by a library. Many special libraries, especially those of R&D establishments, offer all of the services of the IAC, including evaluation, analysis, and synthesis of information.

But unfortunately, not all special libraries provide the required depth of service to their clientele. Darby (43) points out that the traditional information system does not supply information; it only indexes the documents that may contain information. Too often, designers of information systems have lost sight of the fact that users of the system do not want mere citations; they want *actual information*. Salton (113) emphasizes the basic distinction between a library and an information analysis center: the library disseminates abstracts and bibliographies, the IAC supplies factual answers to technical questions and prepares and disseminates analytical studies. A further distinction, pointed out by Mount (95), is that the IAC staff is usually composed of scientists and engineers who have had several years of technical experience before entering the information dissemination field. Their subject training allows them to relate better to the interests and needs of their clientele, and, as Kershaw & Davis (77) indicate, it also allows the IAC staff to communicate better with their computer programmers.

Klempner (81) correctly postulates that IAC's were created to meet information needs within our society that libraries were not fulfilling. This need for critically evaluated and synthesized information represents a natural extension of library service, still unfulfilled because of deficiencies in the education of librarians. The path recommended by Klempner is clear; libraries must intensify their staff training and services. If they do not, the situation predicted in the SDC report *Technology and Libraries* (described by Lanham, 84) may very well become reality:

> ... these functions are going to take place; and if the library does not bring them about, some other type of agency will. That agency will then occupy the central role in the information business—the role that was occupied by the library.

Established Information Analysis Centers. Mount (95) estimates that there are now 200 IAC's in operation. The COSATI-sponsored *Directory of Federally Supported Information Analysis Centers* (53) provides brief, though well-organized, descriptions of some 113 centers, along with indexes of center directors, locations, sponsoring organizations, and subject interests. Information covered by this directory includes, for each center, the date started, mission, scope, services, staff, and user qualifications. As reported by this directory, typical information services offered by the IAC include SDI; preparation of abstract bulletins, critical reviews, bibliographies, handbooks, compendia, and analytical studies; distribution of reprints; consultation; and reference question-answering.

One of the centers listed in the directory should be of prime interest to the readers of this review, even though it does not yet meet all of the COSATI criteria for IAC's. This is the ERIC Clearinghouse on Library and Information Sciences (ERIC CLIS) located at the University of Minnesota. Started in 1967, ERIC CLIS disseminates information on the operation of libraries and information centers, the technology used to improve their operations, and the education and training of librarians and information specialists. A more detailed description of ERIC CLIS and its plans is given by Simonton (126).

Several papers reviewed the activities of specific IAC's. For example, Darby (43) discusses the IAC's of the Department of Defense, the Atomic Energy Commission, NASA, the National Institute of Neurological Diseases and Blindness, and the National Bureau of Standards. Darby's paper includes a bibliography of directories of specialized information centers and services. Other papers discussing the work of IAC's were those of Roberts & Woyna (ERIC Clearinghouse for Linguistics, 112); Johnson (Cryogenic Data Center, 72); Kokoropoulos (High Polymer Science and Technology Center, 82); Cottrell (Nuclear Safety Information Center, 39); and Turnbull (U.S. Department of Agriculture Current Research Information System, 133). Hoffer (65) proposes that a network of social welfare IAC's be established to disseminate information on innovations in social work.

The IAC was born because the traditional special library had not adapted itself to serve the expanded needs of the sophisticated information consumer. The knowledgeable user will no longer be content with a "signpost" information service that merely directs him to potential information sources that he must laboriously analyze and evaluate himself. Users should expect and demand from all special libraries the level of service now offered by the IAC.

The information analysis center simply reflects the needs of the user, needs often overlooked by conventional libraries. Furman, as reported by Swanson (130), in describing the State Technical Services Act in Ohio, concisely sums up some basic needs:

1. Information must be packaged in a variety of ways to make it acceptable to different types of clients.

2. Industry users do not want information about information (for example, bibliographies); they want data useful in decision making.
3. Effective information transfer requires that information specialists play an active role in educating potential users to information resources rather than a passive role of merely disseminating printed materials to them.

If more librarians had recognized these basic requirements in 1946, there might not have been a trend towards information analysis centers in 1968. It is doubtful that the special library is doomed to extinction, but its true function and level of service must be redefined and expanded.

OVERVIEW OF DISSEMINATION TECHNIQUES

The search for improved dissemination techniques is aptly characterized by Bernier (20) when he states:

> Whether it is called continuing education, adult education, keeping up with the literature, preventing functional obsolescence or upgrading technical personnel, there is tremendous interest and importance in the new and valuable techniques for painless, perfect learning as a way of keeping abreast.

This interest in more effective and efficient techniques for document dissemination is widespread. The literature describes a range of dissemination problems and an even greater array of proposed solutions to these problems. A number of these are presented below.

System Input as a Dissemination Problem

A number of observers have found that keeping up with the literature is somewhat less than painless. While dissemination of documents or document surrogates may at first glance appear to be an output problem, some persons feel the problem lies more with the input, i.e., the primary source document itself.

London (90) condemns the overproduction and distribution of "psuedo-communications" and predicts that the input of these questionable documents to automated systems, without proper selection and filtering, may well result in a bibliography of "irrelevant, duplicate, obsolete, inadequate, and unreliable information" that will require a lifetime to read and study. Jones (73) describes, somewhat humorously, the perils of the "re-hash" paper and the "bland generalizations abstract." Bond (25) warns:

> ... the proportion of new information to the amount of communication used to disseminate it is small. We have generated, in some

respects, a sophisticated rumoring process. One bit of original information is multiplied by many hundreds of second-, third-, and fourth-generation bits of information to produce thousands of items so contaminated and polluted as to be more a communication function than an information one

However, things may not be so bleak after all, according to Sarett (114). He states that information retrieval and dissemination systems, in addition to satisfying the psychic need for the scientist "to leave immortal thumbprints behind him," tend to bury older literature—a fact that provides no great inconvenience for most scientists.

Specific Dissemination Techniques

Schless et al. (119) outlined some basic tools the user can employ to keep afloat in a flood of automation:

1. Personal contacts and conferences
2. Information exchange groups
3. Review articles
4. SDI
5. Conventional indexes
6. Serial listings of publications, such as *Current Contents*
7. Specialized indexes and collections of abstracts
8. Indexes of Government-supported research
9. Annotated bibliographies and various collections of abstracts.

Several of these techniques have been covered in the literature of 1968 along with others, such as manuscript distribution, newsletters, and reading guides. Those that fall within the scope of this chapter are discussed below. These are personal contacts, information exchange groups, critical reviews, newsletters, manuscript services, reading guides, and SDI.

Personal Contact. Herring (63) remarks that ". . . one institution that has been and is continuing to be, remarkably effective at making information available, is the grapevine—i.e. the whole complex of informal communication whereby scientists tell one another about interesting things, exchange preprints, and so on." Herring concludes that while grapevine effectiveness varies from field to field, his own experience indicates that in most fields of physics, and in many fields of chemistry, a great deal of valuable information would be missed if one relied on the grapevine at the expense of systematic perusal of the published literature.

Information Exchange Groups. Cooper (38) reviews the now-defunct National Institutes of Health Information Exchange Group Experiment.

This experiment disseminated memoranda among researchers within seven subject groups and without reviewers or referees. Cooper analyzes the pros and cons of this experiment and concludes that the study successfully ascertained how invisible colleges function, and highlighted the basic question of the relationship between informal communication and the formal literature.

Critical Reviews. At a recent meeting of the American Chemical Society's Division of Chemical Literature, several papers examined the role of the critical review in the dissemination of scientific information. Henderson (62) defined this tool as follows:

> Critical reviews, evaluations, or appraisals, are a distillation, so to speak, of a large volume of research literature into a more compact, accessible form. Reviews should emphasize new ideas, and should provide both synthesis and prediction.

Herring (63) discusses the critical review from the user's viewpoint, emphasizing the need for improved quality, quantity, and accessibility of reviews. From the sponsor's point of view, as presented by Bering (18), major items of consideration are: subject and scope of the review, method of production, audience, and distribution of the product. Townsend (132) gives an outline for critical review authors to follow. Review editors, asserts Hart (60), must exercise discretion in the choice of subjects and authors.

Bernier (19) contends that "the approach to the primary literature through indexed abstracts is unsatisfactory because the primary literature retrieved is just as large as before." His proposed solution to the problem is a technical literature condensate consisting of a terse sentence or aphorism representing the most important conclusions in a paper. These "microreviews" (Bernier, 20) could be collected and published as a daily newspaper.

The communications impact of the first volume of the *Annual Review of Information Science and Technology* was studied by System Development Corporation (Cuadra et al., 41; Harris & Katter, 59). Results of a mail survey suggested the importance of the *Annual Review* for continuing-education functions, such as current awareness, checking on particular items, and learning and identifying areas requiring further research. The SDC study found that annual reviews have great potential as tools for summarizing and critically evaluating many fields of inquiry and should be encouraged and supported.

Newsletters. Wyatt (139), notes the utility of the informal newsletter in the biological sciences. Though the research newsletter often contains social information such as addresses, personnel notes, and appointments, it always contains current-research information that may consist of short accounts of research in progress, information about the research material, and a select bibliography of recent and forthcoming publications. The informal newsletter usually has very limited circulation and is, in Wyatt's opinion, more effective than the information exchange group. It should be noted that three newsletters were introduced to the library-information field in 1968. These are the American Library Association's *Libraries in International Development* (4), the University of Leicester's *Information Usage* (70), and the University of Minnesota's *ERIC Clearinghouse for Library and Information Sciences Newsletter* (50).

Manuscript Announcement Services. Three professional society services that announce and disseminate papers prior to publication are summarized by Cooper (38). The American Chemical Society (ACS) publication, *Industrial and Engineering Chemistry*, has a regular "Research Results" feature, which announces papers that have been submitted for publication to four ACS journals. This service is aimed at the rapid dissemination of information, with the exclusion of refereeing and indexing, and covers about 600 papers a year. The American Psychological Association's *Manuscripts Accepted for Publication* service announces papers to appear in five psychological journals, as much as six months prior to actual publication. The Institute of Electrical and Electronic Engineers, in an experiment similar to that of the ACS system, announces papers being considered for publication in IEEE journals through their "Computer Group Repository" section of the publication, *Computer Group News*.

Reading Guides. A reading guide is a selective collection of documents or their surrogates chosen by a specific group of specialists for a specific group in the same field. An interesting cooperative alerting service provided by the National Cancer Institute for cancer virology literature is presented by Schless et al. (119). This service uses a system of cooperative reviewing whereby 200 scientists, who are also users of the service, regularly review journals and submit informative abstracts to a central office. These abstracts (which the authors call "reviews") are then published in the form of a *Reading Guide to Cancer Virology Literature*.

In another attempt to provide information services to a specific user group, the Library Automation Research Consultants (LARC) Association has initiated a service to disseminate reports on planned and implemented library automation projects (88).

Selective Dissemination of Information (SDI). The comments of Brown & Jones (28) and McKenna (6) on the relative profusion of SDI papers in 1967 may accurately be applied to 1968 as well. As in 1967, many of the papers discuss experimental systems; however, it is important to note the increasing number of articles that speak of SDI with a sophistication bred of long association with operational systems. Good examples are the contributions of Wente & Young (137) and Brown (27). Other indications that automated SDI has truly graduated from potentiality to practicality are found in the recent announcements of commercially available SDI services in various fields, and in the expanding capabilities of major abstracting and indexing services to supply machine-readable outputs that readily lend themselves to SDI processing. SDI systems are discussed in detail in the next section.

SDI Systems

In both concept and practice, the function that is now known as SDI is not new. Although the concept is, in fact, at least as old as libraries, the goal of supplying individuals with current items of relevant information remained to a large degree unattainable until the application of the computer to document dissemination. Studer (129) pinpoints the shortcomings of manual SDI systems when he states:

> . . . although the practice of SDI is not new, its application in libraries has been generally irregular, informal, and very limited, depending variously upon the memory, willingness and free time of the librarian and contingent on the desire and ability of the patron to make his interest known.

SDI, as commonly known, represents a formal and continuing technique for disseminating current information *selectively*—a "rifle" approach as opposed to the "shotgun" approach found in most secondary publications.

Evaluation of SDI Systems

While Katter (Chapter 2) provides an in-depth analysis of information system evaluation, a brief discussion of evaluation techniques commonly used for SDI systems is presented here. This reviewer doubts that there is a great difference in technique between the evaluation of SDI and that of other types of information systems, though Anthony et al. (7) state that "one of the difficulties in evaluating operating SDI systems is that the measures used for retrospective systems are not strictly applicable, mainly because of the introduction of two additional variables, namely time and number of users."

Cost Evaluation of SDI Systems. To establish the true worth of an SDI system, we must evaluate it on the basis of cost and effectiveness (quality of output). Unfortunately, the matter of cost-benefit or cost-justification of SDI systems is virtually ignored in the literature. While there is a large amount of data on operational costs and cost per subscriber, one finds relatively little on the cost-benefit justification for a particular system and, in any case, the reporting techniques are rarely comparable. For example, a recent study (Anthony et al., 7) compares a computer SDI system with a corresponding manual system. While the costs were found to be equivalent, the computer system achieved a significant saving in clerical and professional manpower. Unfortunately, this report omits mention of programming costs, which, of course, can be sizeable. In attempting to justify their SDI system, Housman & Wixon (68, 138) utilize a more traditional justification technique. They report that one item of information supplied to a subscriber resulted in a saving of $42,000 and 750 man-hours, equivalent to 1.5 years of the SDI system's operating costs.

The reports of Studer (129) and Luginbyhl & Downie (92) both sidestep the difficult issue of cost-benefit justification by relying on a somewhat subjective form of cost evaluation. Both studies pass the burden of cost justification to the user, who is asked how much SDI is worth to him. It is interesting to note that, in both cases, the former at Indiana University and the latter at the U.S. Air Force research establishment, the value of the SDI program to the user was calculated to be $150 to $200 per year, which is, coincidentally, the reported upper limit of operational costs for internal SDI systems. (See the table.)

Several papers approach the question of operational costs in a definitive manner. Bloch & Offer (24) identify SDI operating costs as falling into three major areas: (*1*) manpower, (*2*) cost of obtaining the input in machine-readable form, and (*3*) computer time. They report that obtaining the machine-readable input presents the greatest expense in their system's operation, because of the cost of keypunching titles and abstracts. As they indicate, SDI input costs can be significantly decreased through the use of available machine-readable data bases, a practice that is now being adopted by a great many systems. Anthony et al. (7) also advocate use of available magnetic-tape data bases to achieve what they call "minimum input" systems at a local level. Artandi (8) suggests that the use of available data bases may tend to expand SDI coverage at decreased costs, though duplication would be a problem here (unless one had an effective algorithm for checking duplicates). In addition to the cost advantage of obtaining machine-readable input, costs can be further reduced if the source of the input also provides the SDI software, such as Chemical Abstracts Service did in their SDI experiment (Diesing et al., 47).

The literature of information retrieval is noted for its dearth of detailed objective data on system costs. The literature of SDI appears to be a bit better in this respect. Most authors present at least the cost per subscriber, though in most cases we are given little indication as to how these costs

REPORTED OPERATING COSTS/CHARGES OF SDI SYSTEMS

SDI System	Cost/Charge	Source of Data
U. S. Air Force (Experimental)	$15/user/year	Luginbyhl & Downie (92)
NASA/SCAN (Operational)	$18.60/user/year	Wente & Young (137)
U. S. Army ECOM (Operational)	$58/user/year	Wixon & Housman (68, 138)
Dow Chemical (Operational)	$65/user/year	Brown (27)
Indiana University (Experimental)	$145-$206/user/year	Studer (129)
Ames Lab., USAEC (Operational)	$150/user/year	Jordan & Watkins (75)
PANDEX (Operational)	$150/user/year or $6500 for tapes and software	Cooper (38) and PANDEX Literature (105, 106)
SUNY-TIDB (Operational)	$225/user/year	Cooper (38)
CBAC Custom Searches (Operational)	$1750/yr and computer charges	CAS literature (31)
Chemical Titles Custom Searches (Operational)	$1750/yr and computer charges	CAS literature (31)
POST Custom Searches (Operational)	$3400/yr and computer charges	CAS literature (31)
CA Basic Journal Abstracts/ Custom Searches (Operational)	$4000/yr and computer charges	CAS literature (31)
CA Condensates Custom Searches (Operational)	$4000/yr and computer charges	CAS literature (31)
CITE Plastics (Planned)	$2300/yr for tapes and software	Engineering Index Literature (49)
CITE Electrical/Electronics (Planned)	$2800/yr for tapes and software	Engineering Index Literature (49)
Scientific Documentation Centre (Operational)	$.05 per reference	Davison (44)
National Cancer Institute (Experimental)	$.088 per match	Schneider (121)
Mathematical Offprint Service (Planned)	$30 per 100 offprints	Cooper (38)

were derived. Studer (129) and Wixon & Housman (138) both give fairly good cost breakdowns for their SDI systems, a practice that is not, unfortunately, followed by the vast majority of authors.

A summary of SDI costs per subscriber, as reported in the literature, is presented in the table. It should be noted that costs are not directly comparable from organization to organization, due to variations in accounting practices, overhead rates, depth of indexing, and user populations (in addition to the intentional or accidental omission of certain cost factors). Most costs listed in the table are operating costs; little information is available on implementation costs, such as cost of programming or of initial profile preparation.

Wente & Young (137) draw upon the five years of SDI experience at NASA to formulate a set of valid, and possibly surprising, conclusions with respect to SDI system costs. They say, for example, that SDI is relatively expensive in comparison with simple awareness methods such as the circulation of secondary journals or primary documents, and they state that SDI costs are unattractive for large user populations because of their approximately linear increase with additional users.

Savage (115) disputes the first conclusion, claiming SDI to be the "... least expensive, most effective, and most easily evaluated system to use as a base of information services." With regard to the second conclusion, Wente & Young fail to note that the assumption is valid only for operational costs such as those of profile construction, input preparation, data processing, and printout. Studer (129) recognizes this when he indicates that development costs, such as those for computer programming, are very nearly fixed and, therefore, would decrease on a per capita basis as more users were added to the system. Bloch & Offer (24) go even further to indicate that the incremental computer time per additional client is only a marginal cost. (The reviewer feels that this conclusion is somewhat questionable for a large-scale system, and in this context Wente & Young's conclusion is probably more accurate.)

Wente & Young (137) also report that one can decrease SDI output costs by allowing many users to share one output (thereby decreasing the number of profiles per user population) and by shifting production of user notifications from linearly expensive computer printout to reproduction methods in which unit costs will decrease with volume.

Day (45), also of NASA, approaches the matter of SDI system costs from the point of view of the output. He indicates that costs for a large-scale SDI system using cards as an announcement medium range between $100 to $150 per user annually, and that computer-printed listings of selected references are less expensive than cards.

Quality Evaluation of SDI Systems. Quality evaluation of SDI has been approached on two separate, though not unrelated, planes. The conceptual school develops generalized mechanisms for choosing between many SDI systems via evaluative comparison. The pragmatic school devises methods for evaluating only the systems that they operate. The truth, we believe, is that a valid evaluation technique may be reasonably applicable to either of the above cases. Unfortunately, as Hoshovsky & Downie (67) point out, evaluation of SDI is still subjective.

While Savage (115) believes SDI to be the most easily evaluated of information services, he believes that the development of broad-based evaluative and comparative techniques has been given insufficient attention. He contends that recall and relevance (or "precision")[1] are inappropriate to SDI evaluation and promulgates use of the mutually reciprocal terms "miss" and "trash." These measures seem disconcertingly similar to the reciprocals "recall" and "relevance." He makes the valuable point that these evaluative parameters are comparative and not metric. Is this not true of most measures applied to information storage and retrieval systems? Jordan (74) addresses the introduction of Savage's concept of "miss" into a numerically oriented framework for comparing SDI systems and emphasizes the effect of the document collection's quality, or "*a priori* match," on system performance.

Artandi (8) reminds us that a hit in an SDI system is the result of a "satisfactory match," and the definition of what is satisfactory is influenced by the combined effect of a number of variables (such as *a priori* match, collection size, search strategy, vocabulary, and so forth). The fact that the definition of "satisfactory match" is variable from system to system demonstrates the true difficulty in evaluating SDI operations.

Recent reports on the evaluation of operational SDI systems reflect a marked degree of similarity in the systems' general reliance on concepts of relevance or precision, de-emphasis of recall, and use of user feedback techniques.

Studer (129), in his experimental SDI system at Indiana University, relies upon relevance as a measure of system performance, while he intentionally avoids arriving at a value for recall. In justifying the technique of using relevance without recall, he discounts the standard practice of sending randomly generated notices to SDI system users in order to obtain a statistical estimate of recall.

Studer intuitively concludes that while this technique may be sound for a document collection fairly homogeneous in subject content, it is highly questionable for a heterogeneous file such as the MARC tapes.

---

[1]Some authors use the term "relevance," others use the term "precision." While this reviewer prefers "relevance," this chapter will use the term specified in the paper being reviewed.

Apparently, Housman & Wixon (68, 138) have similar feelings. They also employ relevance measures in their U.S. Army system while making no attempt to establish a recall ratio. On the other hand, the Culham laboratory system, described by Anthony et al. (7), employs a user sampling technique to get measures of relevance, recall, and timeliness. Timeliness is determined on the basis of whether or not the user has already seen the paper. Aitchison et al. (3) allow the user to specify document relevancy, but use a control technique of periodically comparing requests from a bulletin containing all documents with the individual SDI notices.

A recent account of an Israeli SDI system (Bloch & Offer, 24) indicates a rather novel evaluative feature, which is described by the authors as being "theoretically quite worthless" although it "has proved itself in practice" (a paradox with which anyone engaged in information storage and retrieval work is familiar). This interesting feature is know as "Virginia," a psuedo-client to whom notifications of all papers that do not drop on any profile are sent. These "orphan" papers are then analyzed to determine if anything has gone awry in the system.

Evaluation of SDI by User Feedback

Virtually all SDI systems employ some form of user-feedback questionnaire to evaluate the system performance, usually on the basis of a percentage rating of recall and precision. Some people (Housman & Wixon, 68, 138) also judge a system by the percentage of documents requested from the SDI notices. Most reports give evaluation statistics based on returned SDI notices but ignore an important point made by Studer (129) that statistics based on only a partial return of evaluated notices can be inaccurate and misleading. Schneider (121), together with Wixon & Housman, reports that about 80% of the evaluation slips were returned for their respective systems, leaving a question as to the 20% of the user population who did not respond. Brown (27) reports an even worse response of only about 50%, some of which arrived weeks or months late. The response-rate problem is inherent in all mail questionnaire surveys, and casts some doubt on the traditional method of SDI system evaluation by user feedback.

The relevance and precision ratios reported for SDI systems show a moderate degree of variation. Studer (129) reports that his literature survey showed the interest (or relevance) rating to be normally between 50–70% for operating SDI systems. This interest average of 60% appears to be generally valid for SDI systems. For example, Studer reports 73% interest and Housman & Wixon (68, 138) report 40% relevance. Wente & Young (137) aim a bit higher, at 80% relevance for their system, while they achieve 75%. Day (45) and Anthony et al. (7) report 85% precision for their systems. Brown (27) reports an interest ratio of only 18–28%, which appears to be quite low for the SDI literature.

An interesting semantic point is made by Schneider (121) with respect to relevance or interest measurement. He questions the widespread practice of evaluating an SDI system in terms of a document's "interest" to the user. Instead, he feels that the document should be rated as "useful" to current work rather than just "of interest." In his National Cancer Institute SDI evaluation form, he allows the user to determine the relative degrees of interest, work relatedness, and usefulness of each SDI-announced paper. Schneider reports a combined "very useful/of definite but limited use" ratio of 54%, but unfortunately does not give the corresponding "of interest" and "work relatedness" ratios that would test his hypothesis.

Kerr-Waller (76) reports a method of establishing recall that must surely be time consuming if nothing else. He has a group of indexer-engineers manually scan the entire document file in order to establish a recall ratio for his SDI system, Standard Telecommunications, Ltd. Precision is determined by another group using a performance control test. This test employs four acceptance criteria that indicate the number of term hits required for a document to drop out. Kerr-Waller reports an experimental recall ratio of about 73% and a precision ratio of 58–67%. He expresses the belief that it would actually be possible to obtain a figure of 100% for both recall and precision (an optimistic view not supported by the figures reported in the majority of the SDI literature). He admits that the high cost of programming and the human processing could not be justified. However, "figures between 80% and 90% are well within the practical reach."

Aitchison et al. (3) seek to supplement the more subjective assessments of SDI service with more objective measurements, such as rate of withdrawal from the service, number of announced documents the user sought to obtain, and what proportion of papers found most useful had been announced by the SDI service.

SDI System Characteristics

The utility of the SDI concept is demonstrated by the fact that it can be found in each of the five organizational environments that comprise the spectrum of information storage and retrieval application. These are (*1*) private industrial firms, (*2*) academic institutions, (*3*) government agencies, (*4*) professional societies, and (*5*) commercial profit-making organizations.

A timely, though unfortunately nonanalytical, survey of 17 SDI or SDI-like systems is presented by Cooper (38). The systems described fall within all of the five areas mentioned above. A comparison table showing system differences and similarities is also presented and proves to be quite helpful.

For the sake of expediency, the discussion of SDI system characteristics that follows will treat SDI systems as they fall into the five organizational environments mentioned above. It is admitted that these are artificial divisions for, as Cooper points out, there is a growing tendency to undertake joint SDI experiments. A good example of this trend is the cooperative experiment of Chemical Abstracts Service (CAS) and 24 industrial, academic, government, and professional society groups (Cooper, 38; Diesing et al., 47).

Industry-Based SDI Systems. Of the relatively few industrial systems reported on in 1968, one of the most interesting is the Dow Chemical Company system, discussed by Brown (27). This SDI system uses all the magnetic-tape services supplied by Chemical Abstracts Service as its machine-readable input. *Chemical Titles (CT), Chemical Biological Activities (CBAC), Basic Journal Abstracts,* and *Polymer Science and Technology (POST-J&P)* are reformatted and searched using Dow-produced programs run on a Burroughs 5500 computer. The system uses a combined weighted vocabulary of title key words, journal CODEN, and authors' names. An interesting feature of this Dow system is that a user can frame his profile using an unlimited number of terms. The largest profile has 652 terms. The biweekly output is issued within five days of receipt of the CAS tape. Dow users are encouraged to revise their profiles as frequently as necessary.

Dammers (42) also discusses an SDI system using CT and CBAC tapes at Shell Research, Ltd. The Sandia SDI system (Paxton et al., 107), the B. F. Goodrich system (Cooper, 38) and the Sulzer system (Becker, 17) all use a basic machine-readable library document record as their input. Sandia uses the IBM 1401-CR-01X package, modified for a CDC 3600 computer, to print notices containing citations and matched terms.

The Sulzer Brothers' SULIS SDI system, described by Becker (17), matches on a vocabulary of 12-digit UDC codes (two precoordinated six-digit numbers) on a CDC 3300 computer. Goodrich's plans (Cooper, 38) call for the use of a system similar to the IBM SDI-4 and -5 systems to match weighted terms from a thesaurus, using a 16K GE 235 computer. A potentially valuable byproduct of the Goodrich system will be a skills inventory produced by combining and then inverting the user profiles.

University-Based SDI Systems. With the thought of offsetting the virtual monopoly of technical services on automated academic library operations, Studer (129) undertook his well-documented SDI experiment at the University of Indiana. His approach is quite novel, in that his input consisted of Library of Congress (LC) catalog card data provided on the weekly MARC Pilot Project magnetic tapes. Using a vocabulary of weighted LC subject headings and class numbers, Studer generated biweekly SDI notices for 40 faculty members in the social sciences and humanities. His dual profiling technique assigned an average of 136 subject headings and 375 class numbers per user. Matching was accomplished on a 64K CDC 3400/3600 using three FORTRAN programs.

This experiment demonstrates how the availability of low-cost machine-readable records, such as the MARC tapes, serves to stimulate SDI research and development.

The University of Chicago system discussed by Farkas (52) is an interesting application of the SDI concept to medical records. Patient records containing clinical data, tests, and charts were searched selectively by medical department profiles. This system represents systems for disseminating specialized data as opposed to documents.

The system of the State University of New York Technical Information Dissemination Bureau (TIDB), described by Cooper (38), represents an ambitious attempt to provide current awareness services to the scientific community of western New York. Using Institute for Scientific Information (ISI) Source Index Tapes, PANDEX tapes, and its own input of Clearinghouse for Scientific and Technical Information (CFSTI) reports and journal literature, TIDB supplies biweekly notices to over 200 scientists and engineers in universities and industry. TIDB's search strategy employs an uncontrolled vocabulary of subject terms along with Boolean logic, term weights, and term negation. SDI matching is accomplished via a 128K IBM 360/40 computer.

Government-Affiliated SDI Systems. The concept of SDI appears firmly established within the Federal Government. Indeed, most of the SDI literature, representing a wide range of operational and experimental systems, emanates from Government and Government-financed organizations. Holzbauer (66) states that there now exist over 50 operating SDI systems within the U.S. Government.

One of the largest, and best known, of the Federal SDI systems is the National Aeronautics and Space Administration's Selected Current Aerospace Notices service, commonly known as NASA/SCAN. This system achieves low-cost, large-scale SDI by providing a compromise between the individual user profile and the conventional abstract and index announcement bulletin.

Two recent reports (Wente & Young, 96, 137) and a paper by Day (45) describe this new low-cost ($18.60 per user per year) group SDI service. NASA/SCAN, first initiated in 1966, achieved large-scale operation in 1968. It draws upon five years of experience accumulated in the operation of the NASA SDI system. NASA/SCAN achieves its economy through the offset reproduction of computer-printed notices in each of 189 subject areas. These notices are distributed to intermediate information centers for final distribution to the individual user. As of December 1968, 360 NASA centers and contractors participated in the distribution of over 20,000 SDI notices to over 6,500 individual subscribers. Profiles are submitted by participating organizations on a form indicating the number of copies of output (i.e., number of local subscribers) required for each subject topic. Biweekly output is compiled on an IBM 360/40 computer, which matches the group profiles against the subject terms assigned to the open-literature documents. The sources of document surrogates are *Scientific and Technical Aerospace Reports (STAR)* and *International Aerospace Abstracts (IAA)*. A Boolean form of search strategy is employed and resulting output is manually scanned to ensure relevance. User surveys have been employed to optimize the set of topics and the structure of the selection profiles. It has been reported (96) that NASA/SCAN is successful and that it will be expanded.

Similar to NASA/SCAN is the NASA-supported Aerospace Research Application Center (ARAC) (1) Standard Interest Profile approach to group SDI (Counts, 40). ARAC (2) employs a set of 56 standard interest profiles as part of its selective dissemination service. By subscribing to one or more of these profiles, a client will receive either a semimonthly or a monthly collection of literature abstracts relative to his subject interests. The system employs both computer and manual processing and uses as its input both machine-readable and hard-copy versions of *STAR*, *IAA*, *U.S. Government Research and Development Reports (USGRDR)*, *Nuclear Science Abstracts*, and *Aerospace Medicine and Biology*. Additional services include customized interest profiles and retrospective searching.

Two reports by Schneider (120, 121) and a summary by Cooper (38) outline a trial of an experimental SDI system by the National Cancer Institute. This system employs a linear hierarchical decimal classification scheme (Schneider, 122) to perform selective dissemination of biomedical information to 103 research scientists. The system uses no Boolean logic and no coordination or weighting of terms to identify a match. Instead, matching of any one category assigned to a user with any one category assigned to a document is sufficient to generate a hit. Use of a hierarchical classification scheme allows a user choosing a broad category to receive items indexed under all subcategories of that number. The system is programmed in FORTRAN IV and implemented on an IBM 360/50 computer. Trial input consists of 1,389 articles selected from 12 leading cancer research journals. Output takes the form of a listing showing matches between articles and scientists along with a set of mailing labels. To this output is appended a photocopy of the document title page containing the citation and author abstract. An evaluation form designed to determine the degree of interest, usefulness, and work-relatedness is also supplied.

Schneider's work, along with that reported by Studer (129) and Becker

(17), demonstrates the feasibility of using classification schemes as SDI system matching factors.

The operational U.S. Army Electronics Command (ECOM) SDI System, described by Housman & Wixon (68, 138), also keeps its input costs down by making use of available machine-readable bibliographic records on magnetic tape. Using a series of COBOL programs on a Burroughs 5500 computer, the system reformats semimonthly magnetic tape issues of the Defense Documentation Center's (DDC) *Technical Abstract Bulletin (TAB)* and compares these with the profiles of 500 technical personnel. A controlled vocabulary, in the form of the DDC Thesaurus, is used as the source of profile descriptors, with profile terms automatically validated against a digitally stored word list. Search logic allows for flagging of certain terms that must be matched in order for a document to drop out. Negative terms may also be used. The output consists of a semimonthly booklet of about 20 citations and abstracts, known to users as "a personalized TAB." The accounting capabilities of the ECOM system are impressive. Regular and cumulative data are compiled on the number of citations per subscriber, the number of hits per profile, the number of hits per descriptor, and the number of documents ordered by each subscriber. A byproduct of the system is a current interest profile roster. It is interesting to note that Wixon & Housman (138) are contemplating the introduction of other magnetic tape services into their system, such as those of *Chemical Abstracts, Index Medicus, Engineering Index,* Institute for Scientific Information, and PANDEX.

The SDI experiment outlined by Luginbyhl & Downie (92) was jointly sponsored by the U.S. Air Force Office of Air Space Research and CFSTI. This trial sought to test the feasibility of a "subjournal," a hybrid of the true SDI system and the traditional announcement journal. The reader should compare this system with that described by Wente & Young in their NASA/ SCAN report (137). Using a set of 65 subject categories, derived from the 188 COSATI field groups, this system re-sorted complete entries from *USGRDR* into subject-oriented subjournals. Recipients of this service included 1,300 Air Force, National Bureau of Standards, and nongovernment research personnel. This experiment showed that the concept of a subjournal is valid and that it compares favorably with normal machine-based SDI, while providing an improved cost-benefit ratio. These findings led the Clearinghouse to announce a new subjournal service in July 1968, known as CAST (Clearinghouse Announcements in Science and Technology) (35, 101).

The Ames Laboratory SDI system has been serving 60 U.S. Atomic Energy Commission scientists since 1964. A recent paper by Jordan & Watkins (75) discusses the application of a KWOC (Key Word Out of

Context) index as an adjunct to the SDI system. A survey of SDI service users at Ames indicated that a majority tended to accumulate SDI notices that were of interest to them. To assist these individuals, a KWOC indexing feature was added to the SDI system, and a personal index of papers was produced for each SDI user. This index contained only citations that had been indicated on the returned feedback cards as being "of interest" to the user. The additional cost of KWOC indexing was $14.50 per user per year, or about 10% more than SDI without KWOC indexing.

SDI systems are also being implemented by agencies of other governments. Bloch & Offer (24) describe an Israeli Ministry of Defense Operation that disseminates citations and abstracts from 50 journals in the field of electronics. They utilize a Philco 212 computer, programmed in the ALTAC language, to perform Boolean searches on titles, abstracts, and journal CODEN. An intermediary information specialist is employed at the input stage to ensure that optimal profile techniques are applied by the users. A stopword list and term truncation algorithm are other features of this system.

The small-scale SDI system reported by Anthony et al. (7) serves 100 researchers at the United Kingdom Atomic Energy Authority Culham Laboratory. Users' interests are mapped by means of a "profile matrix" used to facilitate various term coordinations. Weekly matching runs on a KDF 9 computer compare profiles with enriched titles and authors' names taken from journal articles and reports. While originally developed to keep plasma physicists up to date, the Culham SDI system has recently found quite a different application, as reported in *Datamation* (57). It is now being used to provide group SDI services to members of Parliament. Newspaper articles, journals, books, government reports, and pamphlets are indexed at the Parliamentary Library with the document surrogates sent to Culham for SDI processing. Output takes the form of a series of 36 bulletins broken down by such subjects as agriculture, defense, international trade, health services, social problems, transport, taxation, and so forth. Members of Parliament subscribe to the particular bulletins that best suit their interests. This reviewer believes that this legislative information experiment is worthy of scrutiny by various groups in the United States, particularly by the Library of Congress and by the State legislative libraries.

Professional Society-Affiliated SDI Systems. The professional society is assuming an increasingly active role in making SDI services available to the professional community, especially in science and technology. However, some analysts, such as Lowry (91), question the capability of the professional society to plan, design, and operate computer information systems. He states:

... most (societies) are inexperienced in information system work. Despite this, the bandwagon effect will cause many to jump in where experts fear to tread.

The Chemical Abstracts Service (CAS) appears to be an exception; they have studied the matter of providing a machine-based SDI service in a relatively cautious and scientific manner. In June 1968, CAS concluded a one-year experiment to "explore the potential of computer based SDI" (Diesing et al., 47; Cooper, 38). This cooperative project involved 24 educational, Governmental, and industrial organizations, which shared the cost of the experiment with CAS. The CAS SDI experiment supplied one of two types of magnetic-tape data bases to the participants on a weekly basis: a tape containing author, title, and journal references in addition to a full text abstract; or a tape containing a "condensate" that included the bibliographic references and human-assigned keywords.

Computer SDI programs and flowcharts were supplied by CAS for either the IBM 360/40 or 50 or the IBM 1401 configurations. In the "condensates" experiment, all the participants used the CAS programs at their own installation. In the "abstracts" experiment, some participants performed their own searches, while others asked CAS to search the tapes for them. Profiles were prepared by the user's own technical library or information center using CAS-supplied user aids such as a thesaurus-like search guide (32) and a profile preparation manual (33). The SDI search strategy employed word-match techniques coupled with free-text abstract searching, term truncation, term weights, and use of Boolean operators. The experiences of the Dow Chemical Company in this SDI experiment are described by Brown in the paper mentioned earlier (27).

In late 1968, CAS announced two SDI-oriented tape services similar to those employed in the SDI experiment: *Basic Journal Abstracts* and *CA Condensates* (31). Custom SDI computer searches of these and other CAS magnetic tapes are also available. The guide for the preparation of the search profiles (32) used in the CAS SDI experiment also contains instructions for the use of *Chemical Biological Activities, Chemical Titles*, and *Polymer Science and Technology* tapes in an SDI system.

Engineering Index (EI) is now offering a new computerized SDI tape package known as CITE (Current Information Tapes for Engineers) (49, 100). CITE subscribers receive the monthly *EI* tape data bases on plastics and electrical electronics, the *EI* thesaurus on tape, and a source-deck program tape containing an Autocoder Program for the IBM 1401. SDI matching is done on user interest profiles. Output is in the form of an interest profile printout, lists of documents selected along with their index terms, and a summary showing the number of hits by document number.

An SDI service planned by the American Mathematical Society is reviewed by Cooper (38). Known as the Mathematical Offprint Service (MOS), this project will allow a user to profile his interests according to four parameters: subject, author, journal title, and language. Subject interest will be indicated by means of a special classification scheme available in English, French, German, Italian, or Russian. A "special interests" category, employing Boolean equations, will allow for exceptions to the general rules. Input to the MOS system will be 60 high-priority mathematics journals selected from among those reviewed in *Mathematical Reviews.* Output will be either article offprints or article citations, as determined by the number of hits for each paper. A Honeywell H-200 computer will be used for matching profiles with documents.

In reviewing this service, Cooper (38) implies some doubt:

> It seems that the project will be operational without going through a pilot stage. Also it seems that the membership (of the American Mathematical Society) was not surveyed on their need or desire for such a service . . .

The MOS SDI project should be watched closely to see whether it is indeed responsive to the true needs of the American Mathematical Society or is just another manifestation of Lowry's (91) "bandwagon effect."

In April 1968, the British Institution of Electrical Engineers (IEE) began a one-and-one-half year SDI investigation as part of its INSPEC (Information Service in Physics, Electrotechnology and Control) research program. This experiment appears to be particularly well planned and should serve as a model to others. Recent reports (Aitchison et al., 3; Blee, 23; and Cooper, 38) state that the goal of this pilot project is to "assess the value, economics, efficiency and acceptability to users of the SDI system." Serving 600 participants from government, industry, and education, this system disseminates references from English-language technical journals supplied by *Science Abstracts.* Profiles are based on participant-expressed interests, which are reviewed and translated into descriptors by trained information staff members. Subject terms are selected from a vocabulary based on the Engineers Joint Council *Thesaurus of Engineering Terms.* Matching, performed on an ICT 1901 computer, involves three levels: (*1*) simple descriptor match, (*2*) descriptor matching where one or more terms are considered essential, and (*3*) descriptor matching employing Boolean logic. Weekly output is about 240 citations per user. In addition to use of relevance feedback forms, recall is determined by supplying each user every eighth week with a printed subject heading index containing total weekly output. Feedback from this complete catalog can then be matched against the feedback on individual notices for that week to determine recall. Additional plans call for a test of various SDI output formats.

Two other nonprofit organizations now planning SDI services are the American Institute of Physics, which is considering SDI using group profiles (Herschman, 64) and the Excerpta Medica Foundation (51).

Commercial SDI Services. In 1968, PANDEX (Cooper, 38; Richmond, 111) offered interdisciplinary SDI service on two levels: direct "SPOT-CARD" SDI service to individuals or groups (106); or machine-searchable tapes along with an SDI computer program for organizations desiring to provide in-house SDI to their users. Both options employ the same book, journal, and report data base and the same IBM 360/40 COBOL programs. The PANDEX profiling technique uses weighted terms, negation, and uncontrolled input terms, screened against an internally stored vocabulary.

Share Research Corporation (125) has also announced the availability of a direct SDI service for subscribers, using document surrogates taken from *Nuclear Science Abstracts, Scientific and Technical Aerospace Reports,* and *U.S. Government Research and Development Reports.* Profiles employ an open vocabulary of weighted terms. Matching is done on an IBM 360/65 computer using two COBOL programs, which are also available from Share as proprietary software packages for in-house SDI. Worth noting is the feature that allows for automatic profile adjustment on the basis of user responses toward a document. Output consists of citations and abstracts and quarterly personal bibliographies in KWOC format. This KWOC output feature is remarkably similar to the Ames Laboratory System described by Jordan & Watkins (75).

Started in May 1967, the Automation Instrument Data Service of London, England, provides commercial SDI services relating to new products in the electronics, instrumentation, and automation fields. As reported by Barlow (14, 15), this system employs an IBM 360/40 assembly language program to match engineering specifications with users' profiles. Specifications are disseminated on preprinted punched cards, which are matched to profiles using terms derived from the Scientific Instrument Research Association classification scheme.

Davison (44) describes a British commercial SDI service offered by the Scientific Documentation Centre. Started in 1963, this SDI service covers 2,350 technical journals and claims to have "the most extensive coverage of any comparable service in the world."

Further Sources of Information on SDI

Readers desiring to dig deeper into the literature of SDI are directed to the excellent review of SDI in Chapter 1 of Studer's report (129); the timely survey of Cooper (38); and Savage's bibliography (116), which covers the literature of SDI through December 1967. Those wishing to delve into the history of SDI and into the personality of H. T. Luhn, the man acknowledged to be the "father" of the concept, would do well to consult the significant collection of Luhn's papers assembled by Schultz (123).

Trends in SDI

The SDI systems discussed in the literature of 1968 cover a wide variety of applications using an even wider range of techniques. Increasing use of available machine-readable bibliographic information, such as the magnetic-tape services supplied by many organizations, is a distinct trend in SDI operations. It appears clear that the expansion of SDI will be directly proportional to the degree of availability of low-cost, machine-readable bibliographic material—what Anthony et al. (7) call "minimum input" information.

The use of standard group profiles is also becoming a popular technique to offset some of the high cost associated with personal SDI service. Another interesting development is found in the contract SDI services now offered by several service organizations.

Machine-based SDI has come of age, but, as is true of any relatively novel technique, there are still a number of unanswered questions, especially with respect to the extent to which SDI can be truly perfected in order to satisfy the real information needs of its users. In this respect, the motivation behind the SDI investigation of Aitchison et al. (3) merits serious consideration. This motivation is stated simply and directly as follows:

> Since SDI is a relatively new and different dissemination system, it will be of interest and value to discover what changes, if any, it produces in the information gathering habits of users and in their general approach to information.

Though SDI has been around for many years, the question posed by this statement still remains to be answered. This reviewer believes that the increasing number of objective and evaluative studies of SDI will help us to reach this goal.

DOCUMENT DELIVERY SYSTEMS

A number of papers address the technology for providing a full-text document to a reader. Microfiche has become an accepted, if not preferred, document dissemination medium in some Government agencies. Koppa (83), NCR Administrator for the ERIC Document Reproduction Service, discusses the merits of the fiche and states: "Microfiche for distribution of technical report literature is here to stay." In a summary of the microfiche program of the Atomic Energy Commission, Shannon (124) asserts "this medium (microfiche) fills a critical need in that it makes possible circulation of information which should be disseminated but which has no other practical means of issuance." While praise of this sort will definitely assure the place of microfiche in document dissemination, another development provided probably the most significant boost for microforms to date. This was the Defense Documentation Center (DDC) notice (110) that, as of 1 July 1968, "the majority of requests for hard copies of technical reports in the DDC collection will be subject to a $3.00 service charge. Full text on microform will be available to all users without charge . . ."

King (78) proposes another microform, high-density microfiche created through the Photo Chromic Micro Image (PCMI) system, as a means for bulk dissemination of information to multiple locations.

Another technique of full-text document dissemination is facsimile transmission. An excellent nontechnical review of facsimile applications is presented in the state-of-the-art survey by Schatz (117). She begins with general characteristics of facsimile as it applies to libraries and presents a review of experimental library facsimile networks, such as those at the University of Nevada, the University of California, the Houston Research Institute, Project INTREX, and the New York State Library Facts Network. (A more detailed account of the University of California experiment is given by Schieber & Shoffner, 118.) Schatz identifies a major roadblock to the library use of facsimile: currently available machines lack the ability to scan directly from the pages of a bound book. She concludes that the facsimile technique has now reached the point, in terms of development, technical competence, period of experimentation, and low costs, to warrant a thorough investigation of the feasibility of its use in a library document dissemination environment.

Berul (21) is somewhat less optimistic. He reports that use of the high-speed devices that efficiently handle large volumes of information is limited because of the high cost of the broad-band transmission lines required. Only when communication costs can be reduced will facsimile gain widespread use in document distribution systems. Another survey, by Manning (94), covers facsimile installations at the University of Hawaii, the University of Nevada, and the New York State Library. Axner (13) provides a technical view of 18 currently available facsimile devices, including both high-speed and low-speed models.

The matter of storage and dissemination of full-text documents in digital form was brought up at a recent EDUCOM conference (48). A provocative point made at this conference was the statement by John Markus of McGraw-Hill that the cost of storing a book on magnetic tape (about $30.00 per year) is competitive with that of storing the bound volume (about $25.00 per year) when one considers the space-saving and machine-searchable features of magnetic tape. This reviewer believes, however, that until a means of low-cost conversion of text to machine-readable form is available, and until the use of inexpensive interactive "browseable" machine systems becomes widespread, the use of magnetic tape as a medium for full-text document distribution and storage will not be seriously considered.

Two papers (Friedlander, 55; Furth, 56) discuss the implications of modern data processing technology to the publishing industry. Friedlander, after presenting the current state of the art of automated publication techniques, speculates on the future of distribution systems. He predicts that within 20 years the establishment of a new concept in publishing, which he calls the "first distribute then manufacture" concept, will be upon us. Publishers would convert their publications immediately to digital form, with hard copy used only for archival records and facsimile transmission. These digital documents would then be transmitted for storage to a central communication exchange from which they would be transmitted, on demand, to satellite printing plants for publication as documents. It is not too difficult to imagine that, through a system of this sort, using the interactive techniques described by Furth, an author might be able to input his paper on his own console directly to the central communication exchange, from which it could then be selectively retrieved by an interested reader for output on his own personal communication device. The publisher would assume the role of bibliographic communication exchange operator, in addition to his all-important editorial function.

MAGNETIC TAPE DISTRIBUTION OF SURROGATES

While it may be some time before full-text documents are widely disseminated in digital form, the dissemination of digitally encoded document surrogates is now becoming common, with the advent of the magnetic tape service. With libraries and information centers having greater access to computing equipment, an increasing number of organizations are offering or are planning to offer machine-language copies of their standard printed files for use by their subscribers. The SATCOM Report (102) presents a tabulation of 23 private and Government organizations now regularly supplying the bibliographic records in machine-readable form. Information on a great many other organizations maintaining machine-readable data bases, some of which are available for dissemination, is presented in the *Directory of Computerized Information in Science and Technology*, edited by Cohan (36).

The advantages to be derived from the use of these readily available machine records, such as the use of computer search services; automatic preparation of current awareness bulletins; and elimination of redundancy, cost and effort in processing bibliographic records, have prompted at least two investigations into the matter of reprocessing these magnetic tape data bases at a central information center. A National Agricultural Library study (97), begun in 1968, will determine the most effective and efficient methods of utilizing available bibliographic index data in machine-readable form.

Another project, completed at the Institute of Library Research at the University of California at Los Angeles (UCLA), investigated the use of magnetic-tape data bases in a university library. The well-documented results of this study (135) include an inventory of available data bases and a semitechnical evaluation of several generalized or task-oriented file management software systems that appear to be adaptable to library applications. Various administrative considerations for automatic information processing centers are also presented. This document should prove valuable to anyone planning the utilization of magnetic-tape bibliographic data bases.

Though having bibliographic information on magnetic tape offers many advantages to libraries and information centers that have facilities to process it, there are still several significant problems. With book-form indexes, a human inquirer may intellectually bridge the gap formed by inconsistencies in form, sequence, and indexing terminology. The advent of machine records imposes new problems (especially with the variation in format among various tape services) that must be solved by different means. Attempts to solve machine format problems have taken two approaches. One, a UCLA study (135), involves a software solution using a generalized file or data management system to resolve inconsistencies of format and vocabulary. This is a short-range solution. The second approach appears to be the only logical long-range alternative. This requires the promulgation of bibliographic standards for machine-readable records. Various efforts, such as the establishment of the MARC standard communications format (Avram et al., 12) and the work of the United States of America Standards Institute (USASI), Committee Z39, Sub-Committee SC2 on Machine Input Records (134), hold promise in the area of standardized tape formats. The matter of incompatibility among subject indexing vocabularies still remains basically unsolved, although we believe more attention will be devoted to vocabulary conversion techniques in the future. Standardization is necessary and it must be accepted by the information community.

While the future of dissemination and exchange of machine-readable bibliographic records seems assured, we recommend that those involved in these efforts heed the caution of Amey (5):

The time is ripe for universal coding of data in machine-readable form for transmission between the various hierarchies of information systems. When this is achieved, we will not have solved the information problem, of course, and any system manager who has assumed otherwise will find vast quantities of material being spewed out of his printers, which require more information specialists than before to evaluate, while his interactive consoles seem to provide more frustration to the user than ever.

CONCLUSION

Surveying the literature leads this reviewer to observe that 1968 was truly a year of evolution, if not revolution, in document dissemination. Many concepts, techniques, and trends reached an advanced state of development in 1968.

The Federal Government went even further towards achieving its role as the major document disseminator in the United States. The professional societies have also become more active in this area. However, the rapid expansion of Government information activities has brought with it a fair degree of disorganization and inadequate planning, which must be resolved if progress is to keep pace with expenditure. On the positive side, the increase of Government R & D dollars being spent to develop automated retrieval and dissemination methods will ultimately provide the information community with a variety of new techniques adaptable to many other environments.

Increased concern for the needs of the information consumer has led to an expansion of Information Analysis Center (IAC) activity. It is hoped that the rapid growth of IAC's, along with other developments such as the machine-readable data base, will serve as an inducement for a total reappraisal of the role of the special library.

Large-scale SDI has made the transition from drawing board to operational system. The marketability of SDI is evidenced by the rapid increase in commercial and noncommercial SDI services.

A significant increase in the number of organizations disseminating machine-readable bibliographic data has served as a stimulus to libraries and information centers to develop more sophisticated information systems. To enable users to fully exploit these services, functional standards must be developed and adopted by the disseminators of machine-readable data. The MARC II format (Avram et al., 12) is a step in the right direction, but we still have a long way to go.

New products and new techniques are rapidly appearing on the dissemination scene. The dissemination specialist will have to develop a sophisticated and broad awareness of these emerging products and techniques if he is to be able to select and utilize those most appropriate to his needs, which are, ultimately, the needs of the user.

REFERENCES

(1) AEROSPACE RESEARCH APPLICATIONS CENTER (ARAC). ARAC operating manual. 6th ed. Bloomington, Ind. April 1967, 16 p.
(2) AEROSPACE RESEARCH APPLICATIONS CENTER (ARAC). 1968 guide to ARAC standard interest profiles. Bloomington, Ind., 31 January 1968, 88 p.
(3) AITCHISON, T. M.; MARTIN, M. D.; SMITH, J. R. Developments towards a computer-based information service in physics, electrotechnology and control. Information Storage and Retrieval, 4:2 (June 1968) 177-186. Presented at the First Cranfield International Conference on Mechanized Information Storage and Retrieval Systems, College of Aeronautics, Cranfield, England, 29–31 August 1967.
(4) American Library Association issues new library newsletter. Scientific Information Notes, 10:3 (June-July 1968) 25.
(5) AMEY, GERALD X. Channel hierarchies for matching information sources to users' needs. In: American Society for Information Science Annual Meeting, Columbus, Ohio, 20–24 October 1968. Proceedings, vol. 5. Greenwood Publishing Corp., New York, 1968, p. 11–14.
(6) Annual Review of Information Science and Technology, Vol. 3. Carlos A. Cuadra, ed. Reviewed by F. E. McKenna in: Special Libraries, 59:9 (November 1968) 739–743.
(7) ANTHONY, L. J.; CHENEY, A. G.; WHELAN, E. K. Some experiments in the selective dissemination of information in the field of plasma physics. Information Storage and Retrieval, 4:2 (June 1968) 187–200. Presented at the First Cranfield International Conference on Mechanized Information Storage and Retrieval Systems, College of Aeronautics, Cranfield, England, 29–31 August 1967.
(8) ARTANDI, SUSAN. An introduction to computers in information science. Scarecrow Press, Metuchen, N.J., 145 p.
(9) AUSTIN, CHARLES J. MEDLARS 1963–1967. National Library of Medicine, Bethesda, Md., 1968, 76 p. Available through the U.S. Government Printing Office, Washington, D.C.
(10) AVRAM, HENRIETTE D. MARC—the first two years. Library Resources & Technical Services, 12:3 (Summer 1968) 245–250.
(11) AVRAM, HENRIETTE D. MARC is a four-letter word—a report on the first year and a half of LC's Machine-Readable Cataloging Pilot Project. Library Journal, 93:13 (July 1968) 2601–2605.
(12) AVRAM, HENRIETTE D.; KNAPP, JOHN F.; RATHER, LUCIA J. The MARC II format: a communications format for bibliographic data. Information Systems Office, Library of Congress, Washington, D.C., January 1968, 167 p. Supplement One, 1968, 7 p.
(13) AXNER, DAVID H. The facts about facsimile. (Auerbach on computer technology) Data Processing, 10:5 (May 1968) 42–44, 46, 48–49, 52–53.
(14) BARLOW, D. H. Computer-based information service. Data Processing, 10:2 (March-April 1968) 102–110.
(15) BARLOW, D. H. Designing a commercial SDI product awareness service. In: F.I.D./I.F.I.P. Joint Conference, Rome, Italy, 14–17 June 1967. Proceedings [title]: Mechanized information storage, retrieval and dissemination. Edited by Kjell Samuelson. North-Holland Publishing Co., Amsterdam, 1968, p. 349–363.
(16) The basic access services: document availability, bibliographic control, abstracting and indexing. In: National Academy of Sciences. National Academy of Engineering. Committee on Scientific and Technical Communication (SATCOM). Scientific and technical communication. A pressing national problem and recommendations for its solution. National Academy of Sciences, Washington, D.C., 1969, p. 130–175.

(17) BECKER, A. M. Documentation and electronic data processing. American Documentation, 19:3 (July 1968) 311–316.
(18) BERING, EDGAR A., JR. Critical reviews – the sponsor's point of view. Journal of Chemical Documentation, 8:4 (November 1968) 236–238. Presented before the Division of Chemical Literature, 155th National Meeting, ACS, San Francisco, April 1968.
(19) BERNIER, CHARLES L. Condensed technical literatures. Journal of Chemical Documentation, 8:4 (November 1968) 195–197. Presented before the Division of Chemical Literature, Symposium on Redesign of the Technical Literature, 156th Meeting, ACS, Atlantic City, September 1968.
(20) BERNIER, CHARLES L. Symposium on Redesign of the Technical Literature – introductory remarks. Journal of Chemical Documentation, 8:4 (November 1968) 194–195. Presented before the Division of Chemical Literature, Symposium on Redesign of the Technical Literature, 156th Meeting, ACS, Atlantic City, September 1968.
(21) BERUL, LAWRENCE H. Survey of IS & R equipment. Datamation, 14:3 (March 1968) 27–32.
(22) BJORGE, S. E.; URBACH, P. F.; EARL, P. H.; KING, D. W.; WIEDERKEHR, R. R. V. An experiment to determine the effectiveness of various announcement media on CFSTI [Clearinghouse for Federal Scientific and Technical Information] sales. In: American Society for Information Science Annual Meeting, Columbus, Ohio, 20–24 October 1968. Proceedings, vol. 5. Greenwood Publishing Corp., New York, 1968, p. 327–329.
(23) BLEE, MICHAEL. Keeping the scientist informed. Data Systems (April 1968) 38–40.
(24) BLOCH, U.; OFFER, K. D. Experiments with an SDI system. In: F.I.D./I.F.I.P. Joint Conference, Rome, Italy, 14–17 June 1967. Proceedings [title]: Mechanized information storage, retrieval and dissemination. Edited by Kjell Samuelson. North-Holland Publishing Co., Amsterdam, 1968, p. 739–743.
(25) BOND, SELAH, JR. Information as a product. Datamation, 14:12 (December 1968) 217–218.
(26) BOYLAN, NANCY. A history of the dissemination of PB reports. Journal of Library History, 3:2 (April 1968) 156–162.
(27) BROWN, MARILYN T. A computerized current awareness system using Chemical Abstracts tape services. Dow Chemical Corp., Midland, Mich. (Preprint, 11 p.) Presented at 59th Annual Conference of the Special Libraries Association, Los Angeles, 4 June 1968.
(28) BROWN, PATRICIA L.; JONES, SHIRLI O. Document retrieval and dissemination in libraries and information centers. In: Annual review of information science and technology, vol. 3. Carlos A. Cuadra, ed. Encyclopaedia Britannica, Chicago, 1968.
(29) BUDINGTON, W. S. Information distribution: a plea for efficiency. Science, 158 (20 October 1967) 320–321.
(30) CARAS, GUS J. Computer simulation of a small information system. American Documentation, 19:2 (April 1968) 120–122.
(31) CHEMICAL ABSTRACTS SERVICE. CAS computer-based services – 1969. Columbus, Ohio, 1968, 20 p.
(32) CHEMICAL ABSTRACTS SERVICE. Chemical Abstracts Service search guide. Columbus, Ohio, 1967, 468 p.
(33) CHEMICAL ABSTRACTS SERVICE. Preparation of search profiles: A guide to the effective use of CAS search services on magnetic tape. Columbus, Ohio, 1967, 41 p.
(34) CLEARINGHOUSE FOR FEDERAL SCIENTIFIC AND TECHNICAL INFORMATION. Clearinghouse for Federal Scientific and Technical Information: a guide to its products and services. Springfield, Va., 1968, 16 p.
(35) Clearinghouse offers new announcement service. [CAST – Clearinghouse Announcements in Science and Technology] Scientific Information Notes, 10:3 (June-July 1968) 23.
(36) COHAN, LEONARD, ed. Directory of computerized information in science and technology. Preface by Margaret R. Fox. [A continuing service publication] Science

Associates/International, Inc., New York, May 1968. (The international information network series)
(37) CONFERENCE ON MACHINE-READABLE CATALOG COPY, 4th, Washington, D.C., 4 December 1967. Proceedings. Library of Congress, Washington, D.C., 1968, 11 p.
(38) COOPER, MARIANNE. Current information dissemination—ideas and practices. Journal of Chemical Documentation, 8:4   (November 1968) 207–218.
(39) COTTRELL, WILLIAM B.   Evaluation and compression of scientific and technical information at the Nuclear Safety Information Center. American Documentation, 19:4 (October 1968) 375–380.
(40) COUNTS, RICHARD W.   Information services and operations of the Aerospace Research Applications Center (ARAC). In: Clinic on Library Applications of Data Processing, 5th, Urbana Campus, University of Illinois, 30 April-3 May 1967. Proceedings of the 1967 Clinic. Edited by D. E. Carroll. University of Illinois, Graduate School of Library Science, Urbana, 1967, p. 41–54.
(41) CUADRA, CARLOS; HARRIS, LINDA; KATTER, ROBERT.   Impact study of the "Annual review of information science and technology." Final report. System Development Corp., Santa Monica, Calif., 15 November 1968. 114 p. (TM 4125)
(42) DAMMERS, H. F.   Integrated information processing and the case for a national network. Information Storage and Retrieval, 4:2   (June 1968) 113–131. Presented at the First Cranfield International Conference on Mechanized Information Storage and Retrieval Systems, College of Aeronautics, Cranfield, England, 29–31 August 1967.
(43) DARBY, RALPH L. Information analysis centers as a source for information and data. Special Libraries, 59:2   (February 1968) 91–97.
(44) DAVISON, P. S.   Letter to the Editor. American Documentation, 19:1 (January 1968) 104–105.
(45) DAY, MELVIN S.   Selective dissemination of information. In: Advisory Group for Aerospace Research and Development. Storage and retrieval of information: a user-supplier dialogue. Paris, June 1968, p. x111/1-x111/5. (AD-674 168)
(46) DICKSON, PAUL A.   Federal libraries cast a long shadow. Electronics, 41:14 (8 July 1968) 123–128.
(47) DIESING, ARTHUR C.; TERRANT, SHELDON W., JR.; TATE, FRED A. Cooperative experiments on selective dissemination of information. Presented at the 153rd Meeting of the American Chemical Society, Division of Chemical Literature, Miami, Fla., 19 April 1967.
(48) Document vs. digital storage of textual materials for network operations.   EDUCOM, 2   (December 1967) 1–5.
(49) ENGINEERING INDEX, INC.   CITE. New York. (Brochure, 4 p.)
(50) ERIC Clearinghouse for Library and Information Sciences. Newsletter, no. 1. University of Minnesota, Minneapolis, September 1968, 4 p.
(51) EXCERPTA MEDICA FOUNDATION.   A brief outline of the Excerpta Medica Foundation program for the automated storage and retrieval of medical information. Amsterdam, 1968, 29 p.   (PB-179 815)
(52) FARKAS, IRENE S. Selective dissemination of information from medical records. In: American Society for Information Science Annual Meeting, Columbus, Ohio, 20–24 October 1968. Proceedings, vol. 5. Greenwood Publishing Corp., New York, 1968, p. 263–265.
(53) FEDERAL COUNCIL FOR SCIENCE AND TECHNOLOGY. COMMITTEE ON SCIENTIFIC AND TECHNICAL INFORMATION.   Directory of federally supported information analysis centers. Washington, D.C., April 1968, 196 p.   (PB-177 050)
(54) FEDERAL COUNCIL FOR SCIENCE AND TECHNOLOGY. COMMITTEE ON SCIENTIFIC AND TECHNICAL INFORMATION.   Progress of the United States Government in scientific and technical communications 1967. Washington, D.C., 1968, 91 p.
(55) FRIEDLANDER, GORDON D.   Automation comes to the printing and publishing

industry. IEEE Spectrum, 5:5 (May 1968) 53–62.
(56) FURTH, STEPHEN E. Man-machine interaction in publishing technical literature. Journal of Chemical Documentation, 8:4 (November 1968) 202–203. Presented before the Division of Chemical Literature, Symposium on Redesign of Technical Literature, 156th Meeting, ACS, Atlantic City, September 1968.
(57) Government data banks to go commercial. Datamation, 15:1 (January 1969) 175.
(58) GROGAN, PAUL J. The State Technical Services Program at the national level. Special Libraries, 59:3 (March 1968) 186–191.
(59) HARRIS, LINDA; KATTER, ROBERT V. Impact of the "Annual review of information science and technology." In: American Society for Information Science Annual Meeting, Columbus, Ohio, 20–24 October 1968. Proceedings, vol. 5. Greenwood Publishing Corp., New York, 1968, p. 331–333.
(60) HART, HAROLD. Critical reviews—the editor's point of view. Journal of Chemical Documentation, 8:4 (November 1968) 241–244. Presented before Division of Chemical Literature, 155th National Meeting of ACS, San Francisco, 1 April 1968.
(61) HEINTZ, H. F. The state technical services program at the state level. Special Libraries, 59:3 (March 1968) 192–194.
(62) HENDERSON, MADELINE M. Critical reviews: introductory remarks. Journal of Chemical Documentation, 8:4 (November 1968) 231. Presented before the Division of Chemical Literature, 155th National Meeting, ACS, San Francisco, April 1968.
(63) HERRING, CONYERS. Critical reviews—the user's point of view. Journal of Chemical Documentation, 8:4 (November 1968) 232–236. Presented before the Division of Chemical Literature, 155th Meeting, ACS, San Francisco, April 1968.
(64) HERSCHMAN, ARTHUR. Information retrieval in physics. American Institute of Physics, Information Analysis and Retrieval Division, New York, October 1967, 13 p. (IARD 67-1)
(65) HOFFER, JOE R. The communication of innovations in social welfare—the role of the specialized information centers. In: American Society for Information Science Annual Meeting, Columbus, Ohio, 20–24 October 1968. Proceedings, vol. 5. Greenwood Publishing Corp., New York, 1968, p. 25–27.
(66) HOLZBAUER, HERBERT. Trends in announcement, searching, and retrieval services. Special Libraries, 59:2 (February 1968) 104–106.
(67) HOSHOVSKY, A. G.; DOWNIE, C. S. Selective dissemination of information in practice: Survey of operational and experimental SDI systems. Office of Aerospace Research, Arlington, Va., 21 September 1967, 19 p. (Report no. OAR-67-0012) (AD-668 072) Presented at the Congress of the International Federation on Documentation (FID), Tokyo, 21 September 1967.
(68) HOUSMAN, EDWARD M.; WIXON, DARVEY W. Impact of a large-scale computerized SDI system on an R & D installation. In: American Society for Information Science Annual Meeting, Columbus, Ohio, 20–24 October 1968. Proceedings, vol. 5. Greenwood Publishing Corp., New York, 1968, p. 223–226.
(69) Index to common data base linking information systems of Food and Drug Administration and National Library of Medicine with Chemical Abstracts Service Chemical Compound Registry System published. Scientific Information Notes, 10:4 (August-September 1968) 20.
(70) Information newsletter [entitled Information Usage] initiated in England. Scientific Information Notes, 10:3 (June-July 1968) 12.
(71) INTERGOVERNMENTAL TASK FORCE ON INFORMATION SYSTEMS. The dynamics of information flow: Recommendations to improve the flow of information within and among federal, state and local governments. Washington, D.C., April 1968, 37 p. (PB-178 307)
(72) JOHNSON, VICTOR J. Development and operation of a specialized technical information and data center (The Cryogenic Data Center). Journal of Chemical Documentation, 8:4 (November 1968) 219–224. Presented before the Division of Chemical Literature, 155th Meeting, ACS, San Francisco, 3 April 1968.
(73) JONES, DAVID M. Presenting papers for pleasure and profit. Datamation, 14:11

(November 1968) 84, 89-91.
(74) JORDAN, JOHN R. A framework for comparing SDI [Selective Dissemination of Information] Systems. American Documentation, 19:3 (July 1968) 221-222.
(75) JORDAN, JOHN R.; WATKINS, W. J. KWOC index as an automatic by-product of SDI. In: American Society for Information Science Annual Meeting, Columbus, Ohio, 20-24 October 1968. Proceedings, vol. 5. Greenwood Publishing Corp., New York, 1968, p. 211-215.
(76) KERR-WALLER, R. D. Automated Information Dissemination System (AIDS) data processing procedure. In: F.I.D./I.F.I.P. Joint Conference, Rome, Italy, 14-17 June 1967. Proceedings [title]: Mechanized information storage, retrieval and dissemination. Edited by Kjell Samuelson. North-Holland Publishing Co., Amsterdam, 1968, p. 333-348.
(77) KERSHAW, GEORGE; DAVIS, J. EUGENE. Mechanization in defense libraries. Datamation, 14:1 (January 1968) 48-53.
(78) KING, D. E. A new data publishing medium. Medical and Biological Illustration, 18 (January 1968) 51-53.
(79) KING, D. W.; WIEDERKEHR; R. R. V.; BJORGE, S. E.; URBACH, P. F. Experimentation, modeling, and analysis to establish a new pricing policy at the Clearinghouse for Federal Scientific and Technical Information. In: American Society for Information Science Annual Meeting, Columbus, Ohio, 20-24 October 1968. Proceedings, vol. 5. Greenwood Publishing Corp., New York, 1968, p. 311-313.
(80) KLEMPNER, IRVING M. Diffusion of abstracting and indexing services for government-sponsored research. Final report. Scarecrow, Metuchen, N.J., 1968, 336 p. (AFOSR-68-0437) (AD-666 091)
(81) KLEMPNER, IRVING M. Information centers and continuing education for librarianship. Special Libraries, 59:9 (November 1968) 729-732. Based on his talk presented at the Annual Meeting of SLA's Upstate New York Chapter on 6 April 1968.
(82) KOKOROPOULOS, PANOS. An information center for high polymer science and technology. In: American Society for Information Science Annual Meeting, Columbus, Ohio, 20-24 October 1968. Proceedings, vol. 5. Greenwood Publishing Corp., New York, 1968, p. 43-46.
(83) KOPPA, C. J. Microfiche: a fad or here to stay. Interview. Newsletter of the ERIC Clearinghouse on Educational Media and Technology at Stanford University, 1:2 (Winter 1968/69).
(84) LANHAM, RICHARD. Marian the technologist. SDC Magazine, 11:10 (November 1968) 2-9.
(85) LAZEROW, SAMUEL. The U.S. National Libraries Task Force—an instrument for national library cooperation. Special Libraries, 59:9 (November 1968) 698-703. This review of the work of the Task Force was presented at the Second Annual Session of SLA's 59th Annual Conference in Los Angeles on 3 June 1968.
(86) LEACH, THEODORE EDWARD. A compendium of the MARC system. Library Resources & Technical Services, 12:3 (Summer 1968) 250-275.
(87) LEVESQUE, ROBERT. The state technical services program—an interface with industry. Special Libraries, 59:3 (March 1968) 195-200.
(88) LIBRARY AUTOMATION RESEARCH AND CONSULTING (LARC). Library automation research and consulting services. Newport Beach, Calif., 1968, 4 p.
(89) LIBRARY OF CONGRESS. INFORMATION SYSTEMS OFFICE. The MARC pilot experience, an informal summary. Washington, D.C., June 1968, 15 p.
(90) LONDON, GERTRUDE. The publication inflation. American Documentation, 19:2 (April 1968) 137-141.
(91) LOWRY, W. KENNETH. Science information problems needing solution. [Opinion paper] American Documentation, 19:3 (July 1968) 352-354.
(92) LUGINBYHL, T. T.; DOWNIE, C. S. The poor man's SDI. In: American Society for Information Science Annual Meeting, Columbus, Ohio, 20-24 October 1968. Proceedings, vol. 5. Greenwood Publishing Corp., New York, 1968, p. 227-230.
(93) McLUHAN, MARSHALL. Understanding media: the extensions of man. McGraw-

Hill, New York, 1964, 364 p.
(94) MANNING, JOSEPHINE. Facsimile transmission—problems and potential. Library Journal, 93:19 (1 November 1968) 4102–4104.
(95) MOUNT, ELLIS. Conference on information engineering. Special Libraries, 59:2 (February 1968) 107.
(96) NASA/SCAN: Large-scale selective aerospace information service. Scientific Information Notes, 10:5 and 6 (October–November–December 1968) 9.
(97) National Agricultural Library plans for effective use of existing data bases. Scientific Information Notes 10:5 and 6 (October–November–December 1968) 11.
(98) National Agricultural Library studies bibliography of agriculture. Scientific Information Notes, 10:5 and 6 (October–November–December 1968) 12.
(99) NELSON, DONALD B. Generalized information management. TRW Systems, Redondo Beach, Calif., [n.d.] 13 p. Presented at the 4th Annual Engineering Graphics Seminar, University of Southern California, Los Angeles.
(100) New CITE service offered by Engineering Index. Scientific Information Notes, 10:5 and 6 (October–November–December 1968) 7.
(101) New Clearinghouse Service [Clearinghouse Announcements in Science and Technology, CAST] Information Retrieval & Library Automation, 4:1/2 (June/July 1968) 6.
(102) New technologies and their impact. In: National Academy of Sciences. National Academy of Engineering. Committee on Scientific and Technical Communication (SATCOM). Scientific and technical communication. A pressing national problem and recommendations for its solution. National Academy of Sciences, Washington, D.C., 1969, p. 217–238.
(103) NUGENT, WILLIAM R. NELINET, the New England Library Information Network. Inforonics, Inc., Cambridge, Mass., 1968, 4 p. Presented at the IFIP Congress 68, Edinburgh, Scotland, 6 August 1968.
(104) OCKERMAN, LYNN; CACCIAPAGLIA, ANNA E.; WEINSTOCK, MELVIN. Selected mechanized scientific and technical information systems. First edition. Herner and Co., Washington, D.C., April 1968, 153 p. (PB-179 658) Prepared for Federal Council for Science and Technology, Committee on Scientific and Technical Information, Washington, D.C.
(105) PANDEX. New magnetic tape service from PANDEX. New York, 10 April 1968, 4 p.
(106) PANDEX. PANDEX spotcards. New York. (Brochure, 3 p.)
(107) PAXTON, E. A.; BODIE, E. K.; JACOB, M. E. Integrating major library functions into one computer-oriented system. In: American Society for Information Science Annual Meeting, Columbus, Ohio, 20–24 October 1968. Proceedings, vol. 5. Greenwood Publishing Corp., New York, 1968, p. 141–149.
(108) Phase I of CARDS in operation. Scientific Information Notes, 10:5 and 6 (October–November–December 1968) 12.
(109) PRESIDENT'S SCIENCE ADVISORY COMMITTEE. Science, government, and information: The responsibilites of the technical community and government in the transfer of information. U.S. Government Printing Office, Washington, D.C., January 1963.
(110) Requests for most "hard copies" subject to $3 charge in July. Defense Documentation Center Digest, 31 (6 May 1968) 1–3.
(111) RICHMOND, P. A. PANDEX. Book review. American Documentation, 19:3 (July 1968) 357–358.
(112) ROBERTS, A. HOOD; WOYNA, ADAM G. The management of small, special interest groups—some considerations. In: American Society for Information Science Annual Meeting, Columbus, Ohio, 20–24 October 1968. Proceedings, vol. 5. Greenwood Publishing Corp., New York, 1968, p. 233–237.
(113) SALTON, GERARD. Automatic information organization and retrieval. McGraw-Hill, New York, 1968, 480 p.
(114) SARETT, LEWIS H. The scientist and scientific data. American Documentation,

19:3 (July 1968) 299-304.
(115) SAVAGE, T. R. The interpretation of SDI data. American Documentation, 18:4 (October 1967) 242-246.
(116) SAVAGE, T. R. SDI bibliography 1. Share Research Corp., Santa Barbara, Calif., 15 February 1968, 26 p. (SRTP 1095)
(117) SCHATZ, SHARON. Facsimile transmission in libraries: a state of the art survey. Library Resources & Technical Services, 12:1 (Winter 1968) 5-15.
(118) SCHIEBER, WILLIAM D.; SHOFFNER, RALPH M. Telefacsimile in libraries: a report of an experiment in facsimile transmission and an analysis of implications for interlibrary loan systems. Institute of Library Research, University of California, [Berkeley] February 1968, 137 p.
(119) SCHLESS, ARTHUR P.; PURDY, MARIE E.; STEVENSON, ROBERT E. Reading guide and index to the cancer-virology literature. American Documentation, 19:2 (April 1968) 163-167.
(120) SCHNEIDER, JOHN H. A computerized system based on a hierarchical decimal classification: Use for selective dissemination of biomedical information (SDI). National Cancer Institute, Bethesda, Md., 1968. (Preprint, 9 p.) Presented at the Fifth Annual National Colloquium on Information Retrieval, Philadelphia, 3-4 May 1968.
(121) SCHNEIDER, JOHN H. Experimental trial of selective dissemination of biomedical information in an automated system based on a linear hierarchical decimal classification. In: American Society for Information Science Annual Meeting, Columbus, Ohio, 20-24 October 1968. Proceedings, vol. 5. Greenwood Publishing Corp., New York, 1968, p. 243-245.
(122) SCHNEIDER, JOHN H. Hierarchical decimal classification of information related to cancer research. National Cancer Institute, Bethesda, Md., 2 February 1968, 124 p. (PB-177 209)
(123) SCHULTZ, CLAIRE K., ed. H. P. Luhn: pioneer of information science; selected works. Spartan, New York, 1968, 320 p.
(124) SHANNON, ROBERT L. Atom agency's information falls out via microfiche. Data Systems News, 9:7 (15 April 1968) 8-10.
(125) SHARE RESEARCH CORPORATION. [Share Research Corporation literature] Santa Barbara, Calif., 1968.
(126) SIMONTON, WESLEY. Implications of the ERIC Clearinghouse for Library and Information Sciences. Special Libraries, 59:10 (December 1968) 769-774.
(127) SIMPSON, GUSTAVUS S., JR. The evolving U.S. national scientific and technical information system. Battelle Technical Review, (May-June 1968) 21-28.
(128) STEVENSON, CHRIS G. A librarian looks at the State Technical Services Act. Special Libraries, 59:3 (March 1968) 183-185.
(129) STUDER, WILLIAM J. Computer-based selective dissemination of information (SDI) service for faculty using Library of Congress Machine-Readable Catalog (MARC) Records. Aerospace Research Applications Center, Indiana University, Bloomington, September 1968, 253 p. Ph.D. Dissertation, Graduate Library School, Indiana University.
(130) SWANSON, ROWENA W. Information services for small-scale industry. [Brief communication on several papers presented at Puerto Rico Conference on Technology and Resources held in San Juan on 20-21 June 1968] American Documentation, 19:4 (October 1968) 412-413.
(131) TOLL, MARVIN G. Dissemination—choose it or lose. In: American Society for Information Science Annual Meeting, Columbus, Ohio, 20-24 October 1968. Proceedings, vol. 5. Greenwood Publishing Corp., New York, 1968, p. 239-241.
(132) TOWNSEND, LEROY B. Critical reviews—the author's point of view. Journal of Chemical Documentation, 8:4 (November 1968) 239-241. Presented before the Division of Chemical Literature Symposium on Critical Reviews, 155th National Meeting, ACS, San Francisco, 1 April 1968.
(133) TURNBULL, JAMES. Current Research Information System—USDA's newest development in information retrieval. Agricultural Science Review, 5 (Third Quarter

1967) 30–33.
(134) United States of America Standards Institute, Committee: Z39 Library Work and Documentation. Subcommittee SC2: Machine Input Records. American Society for Information Science Newsletter, 7:6 (November–December 1968) 8.
(135) UNIVERSITY OF CALIFORNIA, LOS ANGELES. INSTITUTE OF LIBRARY RESEARCH. Mechanized information services in the university library. Phase I: Planning. Los Angeles, 15 December 1967, 2 vols. (PB-178 441) (PB-178 442)
(136) URBACH, PETER F. User reaction as a system design tool at CFSTI. In: National Colloquium on Information Retrieval, 4th, 3–4 May 1967, Philadelphia. Proceedings, edited by Albert B. Tonik. International Information Incorporated, Philadelphia, 1967, p. 7–18, discussion, p. 18.
(137) WENTE, VAN A.; YOUNG, GIFFORD A. Operating experience with NASA/SCAN, a large scale selective announcement service. In: American Society for Information Science Annual Meeting, Columbus, Ohio, 20–24 October 1968. Proceedings, vol. 5. Greenwood Publishing Corp., New York, 1968, p. 217–223.
(138) WIXON, D. W.; HOUSMAN, E. M. Development and evaluation of a large-scale system for selective dissemination of information (SDI). Army Electronics Command, Fort Monmouth, N.J., August 1968, 38 p. (Research and development technical no. ECOM-3001) (AD-674 661)
(139) WYATT, H. V. Research newsletters in the biological sciences—a neglected literature service. Journal of Documentation, 23:4 (December 1967) 321–325.

III

Applications

From the planning and design of the system to the basic techniques and tools that are used, we turn to applications, with consideration of secondary products and services, automation in library operations, networks, and activities in the international exchange of information.

The first chapter in the section comments on the secondary services and products of scientific societies, governments, and a few commercial producers. Miss Keenan focuses on two kinds of articles—those that provide details of the total system, and those that describe cooperative projects and events leading toward compatibility and standardization of bibliographic formats for use in machine-based systems. She presents information in a manner that helps the reader relate trends in secondary services to trends in information science in general. Some of these trends—toward the standardization of machine-readable formats, for example—are much discussed in the literature. Less obvious are the concern for the information requirements of the individual user, as opposed to those of the library or information center, and concern for the need to build interfaces between discipline-oriented and mission-oriented networks.

The next chapter surveys the literature covering the theory and practice of computer applications to library processes, particularly in academic and special libraries, and notes some significant achievements in Canada and Great Britain. There is, Kilgour notes, an upward trend in the proportion of the literature reporting on operational systems, but he finds continuing scarcity of stimulating publications. The principal developments cited in the chapter are the proposal of the MARC II format as the standard for bibliographic interchange and the recommendation for establishing Federal agencies to assist the emergence of library automation. Several large-scale library automation projects are discussed, as are studies of methods and costs for converting bibliographic entries to machine-readable form and of book catalog production and off-line programs for acquisitions, circulation, and serials control. Kilgour comments on a number of significant unsolved problems, and he stresses the point that the major goal of library automation should be not cost reduction but innovation in library services to increase the productivity of both the librarian and the user.

Networks are the subject of the next chapter. While the number of network applications in classroom, library, medical, government, and business functions has greatly increased, Overhage finds that not much is really innovative in the field. He describes a number of interesting network applications, ranging from those featuring Computer-Aided Instruction to networks for multilibrary operations. There is, he notes, much discussion about national bibliographic networks and about the role of the Federal Government in such operations. The author describes several multiuniversity networks, as well as those operating for hospitals, airlines, railroads, manned space operations, and a number of other diverse applications. He stresses the need for file security and notes the increasing number of municipal information systems used for urban planning, fiscal management, and administration. Overhage feels that future large-scale investment in network development appears unlikely until convincing economic and cost/benefit studies supplement the available technological expertise.

In a chapter on international transfer—the first that has appeared in the *Annual Review* series—Lorenz traces the painfully slow development of philosophies and mechanisms of international exchange of publications and information and suggests that effective international information flow would do much to close economic, social, and educational gaps in underdeveloped countries. Among current international governmental efforts, a major planning study for a world science information program is being sponsored jointly by the International Council of Scientific Unions and UNESCO. Lorenz discusses this effort, as well as those of the OECD, the International Atomic Energy Agency, the International Federation for Documentation, and the International Federation of Library Associations. He notes that, in the United States, COSATI and NLM are promoting international information exchange. He discusses the efforts of the Communications Satellite Corporation and the International Telecommunication Satellite Consortium. He also discusses problems—cost, for example—that hinder progress toward efficient information transfer across national borders and states that the lack of standards for hardware and software may provide the greatest obstacle to the development of a worldwide information plan for many years to come.

9 Abstracting and Indexing Services in Science and Technology

STELLA KEENAN
National Federation of
Science Abstracting and
Indexing Services

INTRODUCTION

The purpose of this chapter is to update the section on secondary services written for the first volume of the *Annual Review of Information Science and Technology* by Simpson & Flanagan (86) and the section on secondary services prepared by the American Institute of Physics for Volume 2 (5). In Volume 3 of the *Annual Review,* published in October 1968, there was no specific section on secondary services. Secondary publications were mentioned in various chapters, but there was no conscious attempt to pull together all the relevant literature for 1967. This chapter, therefore, will attempt to review developments noted in the literature during 1967 and 1968. This chapter will overlap to some extent with other chapters, notably those by Berul, Landau, Overhage, Fairthorne, and Lorenz.

Scope

After an attempt to pinpoint trends observed in 1967 and 1968 and a review of surveys conducted during that period, the chapter will review developments in established services and the new services started in 1967 and 1968. This will be followed by an examination of cooperative activities and standardization. The reviewer is aware that the chapter emphasizes the developments of scientific society- and institution-produced products and services. These organizations are currently publicizing their programs, and there is a great deal of information available in the literature. Developments in commercial products do not seem to be as well documented, unless one turns to advertising blurbs, while an attempt to track down documentation on government developments sometimes feels like an exercise in "fugitive" literature retrieval.

Overview of 1967 and 1968

Looking back over 1967 and 1968, this reviewer notes that there have been several significant developments that have affected secondary publications. Secondary services are no longer able to regard themselves as separate entities in their own right—"no man is an island." In many areas of science and technology the concept of national networks is becoming more and more a reality. The scientific societies are taking their place as the focus for the development of a discipline-oriented information system. This is true for chemistry, physics, mathematics, engineering and psychology—to mention a few examples. In many cases, the society is actually the producer of the secondary service (for example, chemistry, mathematics, psychology) or works in close conjunction with this producer (physics, engineering). The secondary service publications that serve the scientific or technical disciplines are being included as an integral unit in the information networks.

Not only is the discipline-oriented network being developed, but the links between related networks are also being actively explored. This has led to careful consideration of relationships and links between networks for interfacing disciplines and between discipline- and mission-oriented services. Increased consideration is also being given to the requirements of the ultimate user, who may demand full text availability. The reference supplier (the abstracting and indexing service) and the document supplier (the library or clearinghouse) are being considered as connected units. Another significant change in the philosophy of several of the major discipline-oriented abstracting and indexing services seems to have occurred: After several attempts to develop custom-made services for individual users, secondary publishers now seem to be switching to the concept that they should confine themselves to "wholesaling" the information and making it available at an appropriate and economically viable price. "Retailers" may then develop packaged products for use by specialized groups of users. As more organizations are developing computer-based services, the investment required to develop such services, plus the cost of processing the rapidly increasing scientific literature, may be the cause of this shift in policy. Another development that has had significant impact is the advent of the machine-readable cataloging (MARC) system developed and maintained by the Library of Congress. As many of the major abstracting and indexing services are developing tape products, they are becoming increasingly aware that the community of users whom they serve includes many libraries, and industrial and academic organizations that will be using the MARC tapes. Therefore, increasing attention has been paid in the last two years to problems of standardization and compatibility of tape formats for the exchange of data. The standard recently developed by the United States of America Standards Institute (USASI) committee Z39 SC–2 on machine input records is particularly significant. This standard, which will probably be accepted as an international as well as a national standard, is the one used in the MARC system. While this standard does not, alone, provide a format for compatible exchange between secondary publishers, it provides one starting point for publishers to explore.

Compatibility of data exchange tapes and standardization of the bibliographic record are also concerns of the International Council of Scientific Unions/Abstracting Board (ICSU/AB), who are now studying these problems as part of the feasibility study for a world science information system in conjunction with UNESCO. The feasibility study is being conducted by a central committee jointly sponsored by ICSU and UNESCO under the name UNISIST. (It should be noted here that UNISIST is not an acronym.)

To sum up the overview, it seems to this reviewer that the development of major network systems in the United States has led to increasing concern among secondary service publishers about standardization, wholesaling of the data base, and the requirements of the direct user (the individual scientist) or the intermediary (the library or information service). This concern is also felt in terms of the rapidly increasing size of the data base required in many subject areas and the expense of developing machine-based information systems.

SURVEYS

The January 1968 issue of *Library Trends* (63) was devoted to developments in abstracting and indexing services. Foster Mohrhardt, in his editorial to this issue, states that

> although librarians have been major users of abstracting and indexing services, there has been all too little dialogue, feed-in or feedback between those who design and operate services and the librarians as users. In the past decade there is in evidence a recognition of librarians as primary users . . . and as a source of highly valuable critical information and advice to these services.

The articles in this issue vary considerably in level and specificity. The biological sciences are covered by Schultz (82) and the physical sciences by Keenan (52). Other articles deal with the interdependency of librarians and abstracting and indexing services (Tate & Wood, 96), national information systems (Aines, 2) and the Science Citation Index (Malin, 60). It is unfortunate that the quality of the lead article by Adams & Baker (1) on mission- and discipline-oriented scientific abstracting and indexing systems is not maintained throughout the issue.

Klempner (54) conducted a major survey of Government abstracting and indexing services in 1967. This study covered the distribution and use patterns of *Nuclear Science Abstracts (NSA), Scientific and Technical Aerospace Reports (STAR), Technical Abstracts Bulletin (TAB)*, and *United States Government Research and Development Reports (USGRDR)*. This detailed study establishes the concept of abstracting and indexing services as "diffusion media" for scientific and technical information. With data gathered by questionnaire, the study explores, in detail, the use of the above-named services by geographic, subject, and industry groups, among others. Characteristics of the questionnaire's recipient population are detailed at length, and qualitative comments on the abstracting and indexing services covered by the study are given. Especially interesting are the data on the use made of these services in Soviet-bloc countries.

In conclusion, Klempner states that "inadequate distribution of abstracting and indexing services and other federally-produced documents," coupled with the "parsimonious and generally sporadic support of the information dissemination function," and "information management decisions which often work at cross-purposes" result in the failure of Government to provide "a formalized national policy for information dissemination." His recommendations, if reviewed against the spectrum of organizational alternatives in the System Development Corporation (SDC) study of abstracting and indexing services published in 1966 (92), fall in the Government "capping" and "operating" end of the scale. He first recommends the formulation of a national policy that will aim at maximum utilization of the services in the study. He then goes on to suggest that Congressional policy should be vested in an already existing or a new agency that would implement "national policy decisions for the dissemination of scientific and technical information derived from publicly-expended funds." He further suggests that the Committee on Scientific and Technical Information (COSATI), with a strengthened and expanded position, might be the appropriate place for this activity.

The other major study conducted during 1966-68 and scheduled for publication in 1969 is the report from the National Academy of Sciences/National Academy of Engineering Committee on Scientific and Technical Communication (SATCOM). This report has had extensive review in draft form during the latter part of 1968. It is intended to parallel in part the reports prepared for COSATI on document-handling systems in 1965 (93) and on abstracting and indexing services in 1966 (92), both conducted by SDC. The SATCOM report has concentrated on a series of recommendations, with support chapters to back up these recommendations as necessary. Chapter 5 deals with the abstracting and indexing services (64). This chapter should prove of major interest to publishers of abstracting and indexing services, and the recommendations should be reviewed in conjunction with those in the SDC abstracting and indexing report.

The SDC report was prepared at the request of COSATI. The report from SATCOM is intended to represent the viewpoint of the private—as differentiated from the Government—sector of the information science community. The recommendations in the SATCOM report that are of particular importance to secondary publishers are that the Federal Government should fund the literature access services that are needed for the effective utilization of the knowledge resulting from Government-sponsored research and technical activities; "that the management of basic abstracting and indexing should be handled by the appropriate scientific and technical societies or federations thereof, though the use of for-profit services in special cases should not be precluded; management of other broad bibliographic services (e.g., title listings or citation indexes) [should be produced] by private for-profit organizations, national libraries, or societies." Other recommendations state that societies should play their part in the "basic abstracting process, forming federations where appropriate, learning to increase timeliness where necessary, and treating repackaging of their material by others as normal and desirable."

Showing a concern for standardization, the report urges that qualified organizations, with adequate guidance, undertake the "development and evaluation of a formal language for the specification of file formats." The report states that the "evaluation program should include, in particular, the testing of the language under development in the context of computer conversions from one format to another over an extensive set of samples."

The Division of Chemical Literature of the American Chemical Society held two meetings that could be regarded as surveys concentrating on areas related to secondary publications. In a symposium on the redesign of the technical literature, held in Atlantic City in September 1968, Bernier (16) makes a plea for "condensed" abstracts and adds to the adjectives used to describe abstracts—indicative, informative, critical, etc.—the concept of "aphorisms." He suggests that a collection of terse statements, prepared by competent authorities such as the author, editor, or reviewer, might provide an evaluative guide to the content of the original. Michaelson (62) suggests methods to increase the effectiveness of scientific papers at the time of writing. He suggests a form of structural abstract for which the author would be asked to answer a series of questions.

The other ACS symposium dealt with the subject of critical reviews at the Division of Chemical Literature meeting in San Francisco, April 1968. Herring went on record in 1968 (38) as saying that a review article should be regarded as a major publication, not a "tertiary" publication, i.e., something that evaluates the article after its primary publication and after the abstracting and indexing records have been carried in the appropriate secondary service. Herring repeats his argument in a detailed paper in which he describes some studies he made to determine the life of primary journal literature (37). Henderson (36) provides a good introduction to the symposium and a summary of many of the suggestions made for improving the review literature.

A survey of the secondary services covering food science is discussed by Lowry & Cocroft (59), who survey the coverage of major services, such as *Chemical Abstracts, Biological Abstracts,* and *Bibliography of Agriculture*; the comprehensive services, which cover a specific section of food technology; and the very specialized services.

Garfield (34) discusses several of the Institute for Scientific Information products in an unusual framework. Dealing specifically with citation indexing and the related products developed by his organization, he explores the concept of a bibliographic system. He discusses both the mechanical (hardware) and the intellectual (software) requirements in the design of a system for universal bibliographical control.

DEVELOPMENTS IN ESTABLISHED SERVICES

Scientific Society and Institution Services

It seems trite and obvious to begin a discussion of scientific secondary publications by looking at the growth of the literature and the increase in the coverage of major publications. The table, however, which is taken in part from Klempner's study (54) and from a statistical table prepared by the National Federation of Science Abstracting and Indexing Services (66), is useful in that it shows the significant proportional increase of certain Government, scientific society, and institutional publications.

Chemical Abstracts Service. Chemical Abstracts Service (CAS) has been working towards the development of an integrated chemical information system since 1959, with the aim of complete operation of the system by the 1970s. As stated by Vaughan (101), the aim of CAS has been

> ... not the computerization of the manual publishing system, but the development of a comprehensive, integrated information system. ... The goal of this work has been to eliminate redundant human intellectual and manipulative effort in processing information, and at the same time, to create a broader range of more responsive information services, only some of which will be the traditional publications.

Although there have been many articles in the literature discussing spe-

STATISTICS ON SELECTED ABSTRACTING AND INDEXING SERVICES SHOWING PERCENT OF GROWTH OVER A TEN-YEAR PERIOD.

†1955	†1965	†% Increase over 1965	Title of Service	†1957	†1962	†1965	†1967	†% Increase over 1957
3,280	6,865	100.15	Analytical Abstracts					
3,961	7,847	98.10	Applied Mech. Reviews	4,245	7,200	7,900	8,802	107%
30,058	110,119	266.35	Biological Abstracts	40,061*	100,858*	110,119*	125,026*	212
84,590	194,995	130.52	Chemical Abstracts	101,027*	169,465*	194,995*	240,000*	138
5,403	19,500	260.91	Electrical Engineering Abstracts					
25,600	49,000	91.40	Engineering Index	26,300*	45,000*	50,000*	56,560*	115
3,900[a]	26,851	588.48	Int. Aerospace Abstracts	6,770	10,000	26,850	33,116	389
			Mathematical Reviews	9,200	13,382	12,907	17,141	86
			Met. & Geoastr. Abstracts	5,000	12,000	9,000	9,000	80
8,020	48,118	499.75	Nuclear Science Abstracts					
10,160	34,000	234.64	Physics Abstracts					
9,103	16,619	82.56	Psychological Abstracts	9,074	8,776	16,619	17,202	90
7,463	13,214	77.06	Review of Metal Lit.**	8,219	11,542	13,214	23,800	190
26,720	59,238	121.69	Technical Abstract Bulletin					
3,500[a]	26,851	667.17	Scientific & Technical Aerospace Reports					

†*Acknowledgement*
This table has been derived in part from Klempner (54) in the left-hand columns, and NFSAIS (66) in the right-hand columns.
[a]Estimate

*Major publication only; does not include subsidiary publications such as *Chemical Titles; CBAC; Abstracts of Mycology; Plastics; Elect. Eng.*
**Metals Abstracts from January 1968.

cific aspects of CAS products and services, this reviewer has chosen to concentrate in detail on those that describe the total system, or cooperative projects with other organizations, both national and international. Other articles will be mentioned briefly at the end of the section.

Davenport (24) provides an excellent summary of the CAS system as it was originally conceived, and of its progress to date. "Single analysis/multiple use" is the basic concept of the system, together with the greatest flexibility of output. Another key concept is that computers should aid in the preparation of tools but should not completely replace manual search. Davenport's paper examines these three approaches from the viewpoint of preparation of services, retrieval methods, and integration with other scientific and technical information processors.

In summarizing the step-by-step conversion of CAS operations to a computer-based system, Davenport points out that each development has proceeded from pilot-scale to full-scale production. The system plan was originally developed in 1959 and the products from the computer-based operation have been available since 1961, when *Chemical Titles* was introduced. This was followed by *Chemical-Biological Activities* in 1965 and *Polymer Science and Technology* in 1967. Since 1965, CAS has operated the Chemical Compound Registry System based on a computer algorithm that normalizes a keyboarded record of the elements, bonds, and attachment symbols of molecular structural diagrams that define chemical substances. The latest product available from CAS is *Basic Journal Abstracts* (*BJA*), which was first issued in 1968 and contains abstracts selected from 33 core chemistry journals. One of the next developments from CAS will be the conversion of *Chemical Abstracts* (*CA*) issues and indexes to a computer base. All these services have a corresponding magnetic tape search service and are available on subscription in magnetic tape form. Davenport's paper also mentions cooperative activities with other organizations.

The newest CAS tape service began regular production in September 1968 as a derivative of the overall conversion of CAS processing to computer operations (20). *CA Condensates* provides weekly tapes containing the headings of all abstracts in the weekly issues of *CA*, plus the keyword issue index term appropriate to each abstract.

The coordination of information services in general and of CAS in particular is described by Baker et al. (14). A model of a coordinated international system for the transfer of chemical and chemical engineering information between primary published literature, secondary services, libraries, private information centers, and community information centers is discussed.

Moving from the theoretical model to practical reality, Rowlett et al. (78) describe the first step towards linking the primary and secondary products. In 1967 CAS, by arrangement with the editor, began on a pilot base to process manuscript text accepted for publication in the *Journal of Organic Chemistry* (*JOC*). CAS registry numbers are assigned and forwarded to the American Chemical Society for inclusion in the *JOC* issues. Using this pilot operation, CAS is hoping to link the primary publications in chemistry with the CAS operation; this link may, perhaps, lead to the coordination of subject-indexing procedures.

Another practical experiment, this time in linking CAS with another information network, resulted in the publication in December 1968 of *Desktop Analysis Tool* (*DAT*), available from the Clearinghouse for Federal Scientific and Technical Information. Based on the CAS Registry System, this computer-generated index of names, molecular formulas, CAS Registry numbers, and other data covers some 33,000 chemical substances of importance in foods, drugs, pesticides, cosmetics and related products. This publication venture is significant in that it has been set up as an experimental link between the CAS Registry and the information systems of the National Library of Medicine and the Food and Drug Administration (43).

In the international area, CAS is developing an active program in conjunction with the Organization for Economic Cooperation and Development (OECD). As described by Harris (35), this program has two complementary parts: information centers will be established in OECD countries, to provide users with information on the potential of the system. Once this "knowhow" has been established, experiments on processing the primary literature for input into the CAS system will be initiated.

Harris also describes the cooperative program developed between CAS and the Chemical Society in London. The latter has established an information unit jointly financed by the Office of Scientific and Technical Information (OSTI) of the U.K. and the Chemical Society. In Germany, CAS is working in cooperation with the Internationale Dokumentationsgesellschaft für Chemie (IDC), which has developed a joint program between *Chemische Zentralblatt, Gmelin Handbuch* and *Beilstein*.

The papers noted above on CAS have been selected because they indicate, in the opinion of this reviewer, an approach to computer-based information in a discipline that is taking significant steps to develop an operating network that relates to the other components of an information system. Links are also being established to other discipline- and mission-oriented networks on a national and international level.

To return to economic matters, CAS has developed a leasing system for tape services that may well be followed by other scientific societies. From 1967 on, CAS has had a leasing system for *CA* tapes that is tied to the purchase of the printed volumes of *CA*. A contract agreement drawn up between CAS and the lessee avoids many of the copyright problems faced by some secondary services publishers (4).

CAS is also attempting to serve the needs of specific groups of users with specialized products—notably *Chemical-Biological Activities* (*CBAC*), which commenced publication in 1965 and covers the biochemical literature. *Polymer Science and Technology* (*POST*) was established in 1967 to cover the polymer science literature. These services are both described in papers specially prepared for publication in the professional journals of the user community being served—the first by Ish & Terrant (50) and the second by Siegel et al. (85). The handling of agricultural and food science and technology in CAS publications is described by Dickman & O'Dette (27).

Details were published in 1968 of a tool that is long overdue to many in the publishing and library fields. The 1961 *Chemical Abstracts List of Periodicals* has been supplemented six times since initial publication. Publication of the *Comprehensive List of Periodicals for Chemistry and Chemical Engineering* (to be issued under the title *ACCESS*) is promised for 1969. This computer-based file of data on source journals in chemistry and chemical engineering will not be limited to *CA* coverage. As described by Wood (104), the list will include 24,000 entries for journals and 3,500 entries for monographs with holdings information from approximately 450 libraries.

Other papers in the literature describing specific aspects of the CAS were by Rule (80), who concentrated on the application of the IBM 2280 Film Recorder to CAS processes; and Tate (94, 95), who provides the most recent description of the Chemical Registry System developed by CAS. The Seventh CAS Open Forum in Miami Beach in 1967 focussed on the Registry System, with Park (75) providing a status report; in addition, Anzelmo (11) discussed error control in the CAS computing system, and Rush (81), the development of search guides and thesauri for computer-based services. Pinzelik & Howland studied the use of *Chemical Titles* as an alerting service at Purdue University (77).

BIOSIS. The main impetus of the BioSciences Information Service (BIOSIS) of *Biological Abstracts* program over the past two years has been the development of a machine-based service that becomes operational in 1969. At the Special Libraries Association (SLA) Conference in 1968, BIOSIS formally introduced the *Biological Abstracts* microfilm file (69,17). This file is available to subscribers of the printed edition of *BA*, who may lease the entire microfilm collection containing over two million research references from Volume 1 (1926) to date. As has been noted above for CAS publications, some of the best reviews of existing services have appeared in specialized journals. The Biological Abstracts Subjects in Context (BASIC) index is described for the pharmaceutical community of users by Zabriskie & Farren (106).

The special publication introduced in 1967 to cover the field of mycology (*Abstracts of Mycology*) underwent a reformatting in 1968 (49). It was changed from the style that allowed single abstracts to be cut and stored in a card file to the standard $8^{1}/_{2}'' \times 11''$ page size with abstracts printed on both sides of the page. BIOSIS makes second copies available on request at reduced rates for subscribers wishing to maintain individual card files. As a further development of special products, BIOSIS experimented in 1968 with the production of specialized bibliographies in a pilot program, similar to the one developed by the American Society for Metals (91). Three such bibliographies were prepared covering viral interference, chlorinated hydrocarbon pesticide effects on non-target organisms, and rubella (german measles).

In 1968, BIOSIS for the first time published as a separate item the list of serials covered in *BA*. According to Creps (23) the list contains about 7,500 entries. The entry consists of the American Society for Testing and Materials (ASTM) Coden, standard abbreviations according to the United States of America Standards Institute Standard (USASI)-Z39.5, and the full title of the journal.

An up-to-date review of the continuing cooperative program that commenced in 1965 with the Walter Reed Army Institute of Research (WRAIR) was provided by Rubinstein & Schultz (79). This is a study of the direct use of *BA* using an electro-writer and dataphone link between BIOSIS headquarters and WRAIR. Another activity aimed at serving a special group of users—in this case ichthyologists—is described by Schultz (83). This study is interesting in that it attempted to establish an interface between the abstracting and indexing service and the generator of the literature, rather than the user.

BIOSIS announced a tape service in 1968 that would become available in 1969 (13). To be called *BA-Previews*, the tape service contains the abstract number, title, index terms, authors' names, CROSS and biosystematic index codes, and the primary journal reference. A total of 220,000 records will be included in the first year. The development of *BA-Previews* is the result of a decade of research and development in the use of machine-based information records. This service is available on a leasing basis.

American Society for Metals. The American Society for Metals (ASM) has long been a pioneer in the information field. An up-to-date and candid critical review was published by Hyslop (40) documenting the successes and failures of the ASM information program since the *Review of Metal Literature* (*RML*) was established in 1944. The most significant recent achievement is the successful merger of *RML* and the British publication *Metallurgical Abstracts*, published by the Institute of Metals, which is regarded as a landmark in international cooperation. The new publication, as described by Hyslop (41), is published by Metals Abstracts Trust, a joint operation in which each society holds 50% interest. ASM is responsible for abstracting publications originating in the United States, Canada, and South America, while the Institute of Metals staff concentrate on United Kingdom and European publications. *Metals Abstracts (MA)* is printed in England by offset using typewritten composition. However, the monthly subject and author index is produced by computer in the same format as for *RML* but issued as a separate publication—*Metals Abstracts Index.* One unusual benefit of the merger was a reduction in subscription rates— *MA* is $120 per year less than the subscription to *RML.*

The ASM is also exploring ways of serving the special user groups by producing specialized "in-depth supplement" journals in specific fields of metallurgy (41). The first of these is the *Aluminum Technical Information Service*, prepared for The Aluminum Association, which commenced publication in March 1968. A series of special bibliographies was started in 1967 to cover practical topics dealing with operating and engineering metallurgy. ASM plans to issue about 75 titles in this series. By March 1969, 23 such bibliographies had appeared.

An important study on marketing was undertaken by the ASM in 1966 and 1967 with the need to take a hard look at the economics of running an information service. In discussing the economics of information systems, Hyslop (42) gives detailed information using the ASM as a case history. She suggests that there are four cost areas that can be identified:

1. transient start-up costs
2. operating costs
3. continuing developments and redesign costs
4. marketing costs.

She suggests that transient development cost should be subsidized, probably from Government funds, and that operating costs and marketing costs can be and should be recovered from the users. It is difficult to assess on-going development and redesign costs because of rapidly changing technological developments. She recommends careful and continuing study and examination of this area, because, as systems grow in size and in usage, this kind of cost should also be recovered in the marketplace, although subsidy may be required initially.

American Institute of Physics. An integrated information system for the physics community has been the basic aim of the American Institute of

Physics (AIP) information program for many years. The network concept currently being developed is described by Koch & Herschman (55) and details the relationship between primary and secondary publications. The AIP is in a particularly fortunate situation, in that its primary publications contain approximately 25% of the journal literature that is covered by *Physics Abstracts* (*Science Abstracts*, Section A), the main secondary service published by the Institution of Electrical Engineers (IEE) in London. This paper also relates the proposed physics network to the networks being developed in other disciplines.

A detailed statistical report on the content and coverage of *Physics Abstracts* for 1965 by Keenan & Brickwedde (53) updated an earlier statistical report prepared on *PA* in 1961. This report presents a comparison of two methods of identifying core journals in a scientific field. With the IEE developing a computer file for 1969 data, such statistical studies should be generated automatically as a by-product of the system.

The results of a joint AIP-IEE study on the effectiveness of the companion current awareness service to *PA*, *Current Papers in Physics (CPP)*, were published in 1967 and 1968. Slater & Keenan studied the current awareness methods used by physicists prior to the publication of *CPP* (88); the user response to coverage, arrangement, and format (87); and the actual use made of a specific issue of *CPP* by the user community (89). This latter study is of interest in that it attempts to develop, on a very small scale, a model of the use that might be made of an operating physics information system.

Institution of Electrical Engineers. As noted above, *Physics Abstracts* (*Science Abstracts*, Section A) is the main secondary service in physics, published by the IEE in London. Smith & East (90) review the development of *PA* and the relationship with the AIP primary publication program. They anticipate that the constituents of a basic store of information will include "basic bibliographic references, indexing terms, author's citations and abstracts." The services anticipated include "conventional" abstract journals and indexes (produced by computer-aided photo-composition methods), current-awareness journals, Selective Dissemination of Information (SDI) and on- and off-line searching of machine-stored indexes.

With the establishment of INSPEC (Information System for Physics, Electrotechnology & Control) in 1967, the IEE began to plan a computer-based service to cover all sections of *Science Abstracts*, of which *PA* forms Section A. Section B is *Electronic and Electrical Abstracts* (EEA), and Section C, which commenced publication in 1966, is *Computers and Control Abstracts* (CCA). Each section has a companion alerting service known as *Current Papers*. The INSPEC system, as described by Martin & Smith (61), employs the same basic concept as CAS—"single analysis/multiple use"—which is in this case expressed as a "once-and-for-all" intellectual effort. After a trial setting of *PA* published early in 1968, parallel operations between manual and mechanized production were established in August. Since January 1969, all INSPEC publications are produced by computer-controlled typesetting, using an ICL 1901 computer and a Lumitype 713 filmsetter.

In addition to the publication process and the joint research studies with AIP, mentioned above, Martin & Smith also review the SDI study being conducted in electronics, and the investigation of comparative efficiency in retrieval languages being undertaken by INSPEC. Further details of these studies are given by Aitchison et al. (3).

Originally conceived as an international system, INSPEC is already developing a program to obtain input from German organizations. Pilot projects are also being arranged with France and the USSR (61).

Engineering Index/Institute of Electrical and Electronics Engineers. In addition to the long-standing cooperative program between the AIP and the IEE, which dates back to the early 1960s, the IEE has more recently entered into cooperative programs with *Engineering Index (EI)* and the Institute of Electrical and Electronics Engineers (IEEE). The printed *EI* pilot publication, *Electrical/Electronics Section,* covering electrical/electronic engineering, was discontinued in December 1967, when the IEEE decided to develop part of its information program in conjunction with the IEE and become joint publishers of *Electrical and Electronics Abstracts (EEA) (Science Abstracts,* Section B). At the same time, IEEE agreed to provide direct input into this and *Computer and Control Abstracts (CCA) (Science Abstracts,* Section C) along much the same lines as the AIP/IEE program (71). *Engineering Index* has a contract with the IEEE to index the IEEE journals for input into *EEA; EI* also has agreements with the IEE to purchase abstracts from *EEA* in order to increase *EI* coverage, and with the IEEE to market *EEA* in the Western hemisphere. In 1969, this agreement will include the marketing of *CCA.*

Engineering Index inaugurated its tape service late in 1967 after experience with tape-generated monthly bulletins for plastics and electrical/electronics engineering. During 1968, the tape service was called the User Participation Program (UPP) and was regarded as experimental. This program, as described by Whaley et al. (103), offered the user three levels of service, as dictated by his needs, in-house capabilities, and facilities: a service for users with in-house processing capabilities and software; a service for users with in-house processing capabilities compatible with *EI* and who used *EI* software for searching; and a service for users with in-house capabilities and compatible equipment who wished to coordinate internal files with *EI*'s system.

As an experimental program, participation in UPP was necessarily limited. Starting in 1969, *EI* announced the development of CITE (*C*urrent *I*nformation on *T*apes for *E*ngineers) (71). This is an extension of the UPP program, covering the same fields of plastics and electrical/electronics engineering. Also announced for 1969 is a service that makes available on magnetic tape the more than 60,000 items that appear in the *Engineering Index Monthly* (28). Entitled COMPENDEX (*Com*puterized *E*ngineering In*dex*), the first tape is scheduled to be distributed in May 1969.

Woods conducted a management planning study for *EI* as the first phase of an information system development program (105). This study is an internal report dealing with the organizational structure, personnel assignments, and production flow at *EI*. The report contains a study on time lag between primary and secondary publication, or "coefficient of topicality," conducted by Bohnert. In addition to determining the public time lag (10.9 months for the *Monthly Bulletin* and 9.8 months for the *Plastics Section*), and the internal lag (8.26 months and 4.33 months respectively), suggestions for closing the gap to 1.25-2 months are made both by Bohnert and by Woods in an extension of the Bohnert study.

Battelle Memorial Institute. The major study being conducted for the engineering disciplines is by Battelle Memorial Institute, Columbus Laboratories (29). This is the latest development resulting from the Tripartite Committee report of 1966. The study is aimed at determining the technical feasibility and financial viability of a united engineering information and data system. As described by the Battelle staff, the system is expected to "collect, organize, analyze, evaluate, and disseminate information and data useful in engineering." The study has been designed in phases. The first phase identified topics to be explored by the Battelle team and was completed in 1968. The second phase, aimed at exploring these topics, is being conducted by interview during the early months of 1969.

American Petroleum Institute. The American Petroleum Institute (API) developed two new services in 1968. In April, *API Abstracts of Transportation and Storage Literature and Patents* appeared, and in July, *API Abstracts of Petroleum Substitutes Literature and Patents* commenced publication (10). One of the most interesting developments has been the use made of API's Central Abstracting and Indexing Service (CAIS) to produce a special publication for API's Committee on Air and Water Pollution, *Subject Index to Current Literature on Air and Water Conservation*. This publication, as described by Teitelbaum (97), makes use of the computer programs developed by CAIS and uses the subject authority list with additional terms added. This is an example of a small user group "riding piggyback" on a large system to produce an economical tool tailored to meet the users' special requirements.

American Mathematical Society. Following an investigation of improving information exchange in mathematics, started in 1965 by the Zelinisky Committee, the American Mathematical Society (AMS) set up the Committee to Monitor Problems in Communication, in 1967 (9). This Committee has established several pilot projects, which include the Mathematical Offprint Service (MOS) established in July 1968 (68) and a biweekly alerting journal in mathematics, *Contents of Contemporary Mathematical Journals,* slated for January 1969 (8). A special publication representing an attempt to meet the requirements of a specialized group of users, *Reviews of Algebraic Topology,* appeared early in 1969. This publication contains the material that appeared in *Mathematical Reviews* from 1940 to date in the subject area of algebraic and differential topology, topological groups, and homological algebra.

In network development, AMS initiated the formation of a Commission on a National Information System in Mathematics, which was established in August 1968. Eleven professional societies are represented on this Commission, which is due to issue a final report in June 1969 providing recommendations leading to the design of an information network in mathematics.

The AMS published a series of reports in 1967 and 1968 dealing with the development of computer aids for tape-control of photocomposing machines. One series deals with the mechanization of the *Mathematical Reviews* office procedures (6), and another covers the problem of preparing computer-processed tape to allow the setting of multiple-line equations (7).

Documentation Abstracts, Inc. A new kind of index has been proposed by Lipetz (58), editor of *Information Science Abstracts* (formerly *Documentation Abstracts*). This index appears in the final annual issue of the publication and is similar in concept to a citation index, with an added feature: it identifies the relationship between papers as analytic (inclusion of one paper in another), series continuation, review, affirmation, rebuttal, correction, etc., and shows the relationships by a series of codes designed for use in machine searching.

Government Services

The main source of information on government developments in secondary services is a Committee on Scientific and Technical Information (COSATI) report on progress in U.S. Government scientific and technical communication from 1967 (33). Because this is not exactly up-to-date information, this reviewer has selected only those topics that seem to indicate a trend of importance, such as cooperative input, development of networks, and studies whose results may affect the future of abstracting and indexing services.

Atomic Energy Commission. The Atomic Energy Commission (AEC) has inaugurated a program in which the developed countries process their literature for direct input into *Nuclear Science Abstracts (NSA)*. In 1967, approximately 70 articles a week were processed in the U.K. for *NSA*, and this increased to 85 per week in 1968 (72). Similar bilateral agreements have been made with Canada, Japan, and the Scandinavian countries.

These agreements are regarded by the AEC as one of the steps necessary to prepare for the International Nuclear Information System (INIS), which will handle nuclear science literature in a world system (12). The current plan for INIS is that each participating country will collect and analyze its own literature, abstract and index it in English, and store the information in compatible machine formats. National and regional computer centers will then provide output as required. The headquarters of the system will be located at the International Atomic Energy Agency in Vienna. A panel on descriptive cataloging, convened in December 1967, has drawn up rules for input to the INIS system (45).

It was reported in 1967 that the indexes to each issue of *NSA* (personal and corporate author, report number, and subject) are being machine arranged and composed (12). *Technical Briefs*, published jointly by the AEC and the National Aeronautics and Space Administration (NASA), expanded in coverage during 1967. The business-oriented summaries, which commenced publication in 1966, were limited initially to describing work at Argonne National Laboratory. During 1967, coverage expanded to include innovations developed at Sandia Laboratory and those developed as part of jointly sponsored AEC-NASA space nuclear systems programs.

Clearinghouse for Federal Scientific and Technical Information. This Clearinghouse is the main source for many of the specialized government publications—notably *Desktop Analysis Tool (DAT)* described earlier in the CAS section of this chapter and *Selected Water Resources Abstracts* (see the section, "New Products and Services"). The *Technical Abstract Bulletin (TAB)* issued by the Department of Defense ceased to carry duplicate announcements of reports contained in the *U.S. Government Research and Development Reports (USGRDR)*. The latter, from 1968 on, also listed all Government-sponsored technical translations following the termination of *Technical Translations* at the end of 1967 (21).

In 1968, the Clearinghouse introduced a new, rapid alerting tool to help scientists, engineers, and businessmen keep up with new technical information. *Clearinghouse Announcements in Science and Technology* appears in 46 sections and covers research in such fields as defense, space, education, and other national programs (22).

National Aeronautics and Space Administration. An agreement was announced in 1968 between NASA, the European Space Research Organization (ESRO), and European Launcher Development Organization (ELDO) Space Documentation Service (30). NASA is supplying magnetic tapes of the unclassified material in the NASA system, together with complete documentation on the system itself. In return, ESRO and ELDO are supplying direct input on European publications for inclusion in *Scientific and Technical Aerospace Reports (STAR)* and *International Aerospace Abstracts (IAA)*.

National Agricultural Library. The *Bibliography of Agriculture (B of A)* inaugurated detailed subject indexes with the monthly issues of *B of A* beginning in July 1967. A special computer-generated geographic index to *B of A* from 1966 to date has been prepared for use in the Library (65). In 1967, the Pesticides Information Center altered the format of the biweekly *Pesticides Documentation Bulletin* to produce a categorized citation file with author, and organizational, biographical, and subject indexes, all searchable by computer. A file that can locate over 18,000 abstracts published between 1930 and 1967 has been established by the center in conjunction with the U.S. Forest Service. This file, known as the International Tree Disease Register System for Literature Retrieval in Forest Pathology (INTREDIS), can be searched by subject, host, country, causal organism, and first author (26).

Two studies are being conducted under contract that may prove of particular significance in the future (65). The first of these is an attempt to determine the relationships of *B of A* with other abstracting and indexing services. The study is also looking at the indexing procedure and the machine record of the different services. The results of this study may lead to cooperative exchange arrangements between *B of A* and other services. The second study is aimed at determining the most efficient method of interfacing the Library's automated programs with other data banks available in machine-readable form. This study is one of the first steps being taken by the Library in the development of an information network in agriculture.

National Institutes of Health, National Institute of Neurological Diseases and Stroke. According to a report (67) that appeared in January 1969, the National Institute of Neurological Diseases and Stroke Neurological Information Network has had a steadily productive growth in services. The services include preparing and publishing biweekly abstract bulletins and monthly accession lists of select citations in many areas of interest; publishing compilations of current neurological and sensory research grant and contract programs; answering requests for specific information concerning neurosensory diseases; and preparing state-of-the-art reports, critical reviews, and related updated reviews of the literature.

Continuing service was rendered to the scientific community through the transmittal of copies of publications, bibliographies prepared on individual request, continuing bibliographies, and Xerox reproduction of material and tables of contents.

Secondary publications include the *Index to Current EEG Literature*, published quarterly by the Elsevier Publishing Company; the biweekly *Current Awareness Service Sleep Bulletin*; and the biweekly *Neuroendocrine Bulletin*, produced by the Brain Information Service. Brain Information Service also produces Section B of a monthly journal, *Communications in Behavioral Biology*. Section B is a listing of prepublication abstracts from cooperating journals that publish research articles in behavioral biology. The Parkinson Information Center (PIC) publishes a biweekly alerting bibliography, *Parkinson's Disease and Related Disorders: Citations from the Literature (PDRD:CL)*. The Parkinson Information Center function of indexing the neurological literature for incorporation into the National Library of Medicine's (NLM) computer-based MEDLARS (Medical Literature Analysis and Retrieval System) and announcements in *Index Medicus* has proven to be effective. This particular activity is serving as a model for the other information centers where decentralized indexing is being performed for NLM.

In 1968, a new current-awareness publication, *Communication Disorders*, was launched by the Information Center for Hearing, Speech, and Disorders of Human Communication. This new current-awareness service is designed to facilitate communication, integration of research efforts, and literature retrieval in the broad area of the communicative sciences.

National Library of Medicine. There has been a wealth of material on NLM programs during 1967 and 1968 with the establishment of the Biomedical Communication Network, the plans for MEDLARS II, and the publication of a major review of MEDLARS from 1963 to 1967 and a major evaluation study. In MEDLARS, the secondary publications—*Index Medicus* and the recurring bibliography series—are so completely integrated in the system that it becomes meaningless to review the secondary service as isolated from the system.

NEW PRODUCTS AND SERVICES

It is not possible to review in a comprehensive or detailed manner the new services developed in 1967 and 1968. Attention has therefore been paid to those services that are using a novel approach to abstracting and indexing (e.g., *Communications in Behavioral Biology*) or those that have received detailed descriptions in the information science literature (e.g., *Oral Research Abstracts*).

Communications in Behavioral Biology. In 1968, a novel approach to abstracting and indexing was launched by Academic Press. Bard (15) describes the new journal as one designed to simplify the scientists' literature problem. Part A of *Communications in Behavioral Biology (CBB)* consists of original articles, and Part B, published simultaneously, carries first the abstracts of the articles in *CBB*, followed by abstracts of papers to be published in the more than 20 journals cooperating with *CBB*. These abstracts are prepared by the Brain Information Service of NINDS (see above). An author and permuted term (PIT) index is published with each abstract section and cumulates quarterly. In addition, Academic Press sells reprints of articles appearing in *CBB*.

De Haen Service. Paul de Haen, Inc. has announced the construction of a comprehensive computerized data bank for the company's various drug information services. This data bank will add to their usual services by enabling them to offer detailed printed indices, specialized searches, as well as IBM cards and magnetic tape for use by subscribers. The first index, scheduled to be published early in 1969, will contain 300 pages with over 40,000 entries, permitting access to 5,700 new drugs reported on in the de Haen Drugs in Prospect Index card service during the years 1966, 1967, and 1968 (25).

Excerpta Medica. The Excerpta Medica Foundation, after several years of intensive study and development, announced early in 1969 that its biomedical computer-based information system is fully operational. Over 200,000 citations and 80,000 abstracts are processed and stored annually in the data bank. *Excerpta Medica* can store, retrieve, and provide on magnetic tape highly specific medical and chemical information on drugs and chemical compounds as reported in 3,000 of the world's leading biomedical journals.

The Foundation is in the process of establishing regional centers throughout the U.S. and in all countries of the world, so that its total information input can be processed by computer locally and made available to all U.S. medical scientists, medical institutions, and information centers. Negotiations are under way with European and Asian governments for the establishment of *Excerpta Medica*-based national information centers.

The Dutch Government has recently awarded a grant to the Foundation to develop the first on-line, real-time biomedical information network. It will comprise a four-terminal connection: *Excerpta Medica*'s Editorial Division, its Data Processing Center, Leyden University Academic Hospital, and Leyden University Data Processing Center. The contract includes programming for the system between *Excerpta Medica*'s NCR 315 RMC computer with a CRAM memory and Leyden University's IBM 360-50 with a Data Cell memory. Programming has begun and the terminals are expected to be operational by June 1969 (32).

A new weekly publication, *Drug Literature Computer Tape Service*, commenced early in 1969. Over 40,000 articles are included. A decimal classification scheme comprising 300 pharmacological and chemical categories is used to classify all drugs and chemical compounds, and the Wiswesser notation is used to record the chemical structure.

Institute for Scientific Information. The Institute for Scientific Information (ISI) announced in late 1968 two additions to the *Current Contents* series of current awareness journals. The first issue of *Current Contents, Education* was scheduled for January 1969, followed in March 1969 by *Current Contents in Behavioral, Social and Management Sciences*. The first annual volume of the *International Directory of Research & Development Scientists* covered the 1967 literature processed for inclusion in *Science Citation Index* for that year. It locates scientists by their institutional affiliation according to the information in the primary journal article.

Oral Research Abstracts. Published by the American Dental Association since 1966, *Oral Research Abstracts* is described by Koehler (56). Intended as a research tool to complement *Dental Abstracts*, a selective service directed at practicing dentists, *Oral Research Abstracts* covers journal articles and patent references. In addition, a demand search from the MEDLARS system is used to identify relevant articles. *MeSH* (*Medical Subject Headings*) are used as the base for the subject index.

PANDEX. The announced coverage of *PANDEX Current Index to Scientific and Technical Literature* beginning in 1968 is 1,900 journals, 6,000 books and 35,000 U.S. Government Reports (73). The biweekly bibliography claims interdisciplinary coverage and is completely computer-generated. As Siroonian points out (74), the annual cumulative index is only a few inches thick because it is produced on standard 4 x 6-inch microfiche. The subject index is a hybrid between a KWIC index and a manually produced index using subject headings. The full range of *PANDEX* service announced by CCM Information Sciences, Inc., late in 1968, includes the microfiche mentioned above, a microfilm edition, a weekly magnetic tape service, and an individualized search program. It will be interesting to see if this comprehensive service succeeds where others have failed (for example, *IOTA—Index of Technical Articles*), when demands are being made for increasingly specialized services.

Selected Water Resources Abstracts. *SWRA* provides an interesting example of the use of multiple input from several groups. This publication, which commenced in January 1968, has input furnished by Water Resources Scientific Information Center (WRSIC)-supported "centers of competence," 51 Water Resources Research Institutes administered under the Water Resources Research Act of 1964, and other Federal water resources agencies (102).

COOPERATION

In addition to the development of jointly produced or marketed products, the past year has seen an increase in intraservice cooperation. One indication of this was the reopening of a full-time secretariat for the National Federation of Science Abstracting and Indexing Services in July 1968 after a period of dormancy for two years. The members of this organization are scientific society and institutional publishers of abstracting and indexing services. The ultimate goal of the Federation is to improve communication among scientists through the documentation (abstracting, indexing, and analyzing) of the international scientific literature (66).

A parallel organization to serve the commercial publishers was established in 1968, the Information Industry Association (44). The purposes of IIA are:

> to serve as an independent association composed of organizations in the private sector involved in the creation, supply and distribution of information services of every type, to develop standards which will be of help to the field, [and] to develop policies which will be in the best interests of the orderly development of new techniques of the dissemination of information.

Another organization established with a rather different format is the Joint Agreement Group (JAG) (51). This organization was formed following the Spring Joint Computer Conference in May 1968, when representatives of several organizations such as the Association for Computing Machinery, the National Bureau of Standards, and the IEEE established an informal mutual-participation group for the purpose of arriving at common practices in the format of data elements and indexing and classification practices used in bibliographic data tapes. It was felt initially that the Group would be able to function more rapidly and more effectively if it maintained an informal structure and did not work within the confines of any existing organization such as USASI-Z39 or a solely Government, commercial, or nonprofit structure.

The main Government cooperative activity which has significance for the abstracting and indexing community is the National Serials Data Program (NSDP), which has been established by the Task Group of the Library of Congress, National Library of Agriculture, and National Library of Medicine (57). The Library of Congress acts as the executive agent and its Information Systems Office is responsible for the project. The Joint Committee on the Union List of Serials acts in an advisory capacity.

All abstracting and indexing services are concerned with information on the primary journal literature that they cover. Most of them print lists of journals covered, and in some cases these are available as separate publications. The CAS list has been a major reference tool for information on scientific literature since 1961, and an updated revision is due to be published under the name ACCESS (Wood, 104) in 1969. The relationship and the presumed overlap between this and similar publications and the NSDP need to be explored. A meeting between NSDP and selected secondary publishers was held in October 1968 and, according to Heumann (39), recommended that a further effort be made to improve communication between the Program and abstracting and indexing services.

International cooperation between abstracting and indexing services is possible for the major services represented by an International Scientific Union. Through its Abstracting Board, the International Council of Scientific Unions allows the major secondary service from each country and from each scientific discipline to participate in the activities of ICSU/AB. A recent study of the activities of ICSU/AB has led to a report recommending the broadening of its scope and activities (19).

ICSU/AB conducts a detailed survey of member service activities every odd year and publishes a resulting statistical report. Data on 1967 are currently being processed. In addition, ICSU/AB has conducted a detailed comparative study of *Physics Abstracts*, *Physikalische Berichte*, and the physics sections of *Bulletin Signalitique* for the year 1964. The results of these studies were published during 1967 and 1968 (46, 47, 48). A major activity of ICSU/AB at the present time is being done in conjunction with UNESCO: a Working Group of UNISIST to explore standards for the transfer of bibliographic information (Perez-Vitoria, 76).

A question that might be asked at this point is, "Why cooperate?" This reviewer feels strongly that the development of many of the cooperative programs described in this chapter have at their core a basic problem faced by the information community—the problem of standardization.

STANDARDIZATION

Standardization is a major concern to the services that will play a major role in a national or international information system. Of particular concern is standardization of data elements and tape formats.

In 1967, the Office of Science and Technology appointed a Task Group for the Interchange of Scientific and Technical Information in Machine Language (ISTIM). This Task Group, which was chaired by Sherwin (84), presented a final report in April 1968. In part, the objectives of the Group were: to define and recommend for adoption a specific, minimal set of basic standards and systemwide codes; and, using these standards and codes, to define and recommend one or more compatible formats for the purpose of representing in machine language the bibliographic descriptions of journal articles, reports, and monographs. The Task Group identified three subtask groups to cover common codes; basic standards; and record structure and content of standard, machine-readable bibliographic descriptions.

It was recommended that common codes for all units of the bibliographical record be developed and maintained by "an agency or organization having a functional operating need." On basic standards, the recommendation was that the USASI Standard X3.4-1967 ASCII code be specifically endorsed as the basic standard for information exchange. The debate over the use of an 8-bit system is outlined in the Group's report. The recommendations on record structure and content urged close cooperation with the USASI-Z39 Committee on Library Work, Documentation, and Related Publishing Practice, and the expansion of the latter to provide a staffed secretariat office.

The ISTIM report was not, in the opinion of this reviewer, well received in the abstracting and indexing field. One of the main objections was the first series of recommendations noted above, which suggested the establishment of codes for the units in the bibliographic record. It is interesting to note two developments that occurred later in 1968. Reference has already been made to the impact of MARC on secondary service publishers. A standard of prime concern to secondary publishers is the one developed by USASI-Z39 SC-2 on machine-input tape records (99). This standard, which was approved early in 1969, is currently being considered as an international standard. It represents the system in use at the Library of Congress in the MARC system. It has been stated that it is compatible with the INIS descriptive cataloging system already mentioned (45).

It was announced late in 1968 that USASI had received a grant to establish a full-time secretariat in the office of Jerrold Orne, chairman of USASI-Z39. Since Orne became chairman of Z39, there has been a great increase in the number of standards being developed and processed. At this time, it seems that there is much closer liaison between Z39 and other groups actively engaged in standardization work, both national and international. The best example of this is the revision of the Z39.5 *Standard on Journal Title Abbreviation*, which was undertaken in 1968. This standard represents close interaction with the British Standards Institute and is the first U.S. standard to carry notations on variant BSI practice in the text (100). However, this variation in practice does not imply permissiveness in the application of the standard in the United States.

If the ISTIM report foundered because of the emphasis on machine codes, the development of the Book Numbering Standard, in line with the system already used by the British National Bibliography and the R. R. Bowker Company, and the proposed parallel Periodical Numbering System that is currently being studied, are interesting developments. The latter holds particular significance in the development of the NSDP, who will have to select a machine code for periodical identification. As most abstracting and indexing services with a machine data base are using the ASTM Coden to identify journals, it seems to some services that the Coden has not been adequately considered as a candidate system.

Mention has already been made of the Joint Agreement Group (JAG), which was formed as an informal mutual participation group for the purpose of arriving at common practices in the format of data elements. This Group has attempted to maintain its informal structure because the participants felt that they could develop programs faster than USASI-Z39 or a similar formally structured organization. The best statement of the progress of this Group appears in a report given at the time of the 1968 FJCC Conference by Tompkins (98), which outlines the tentative common practices on formats for public bibliographic data tapes. He discusses criteria for transmission formats, character set delimiters, and string and access structures, and examines the consistency of the proposed format with formats used by CAS and the MARC II project in the Library of Congress.

Individual organizations are also working on the data element definition as required by their own organization. CAS, for example, has developed a detailed internal manual to meet its own requirements, and Blum (18) has concentrated on needs of the physics information system.

The National Federation of Science Abstracting and Indexing Services has attempted to coordinate the activities of member services through the Bibliographic Citation Committee, which was formed in September 1968. The purpose of this Committee is "to review the various bibliographic practices of abstracting and indexing services beginning with those of NFSAIS member services." Through this review, the Committee intends to "arrive at a set of NFSAIS recommendations for the content and order of the elements of data from printed and machine-readable bibliographic citations for use in abstracting and indexing publications and services" (70). It has already been noted that the recently formed Information Industry Association also intends to become involved in standardization activities.

On the international level, mention has already been made of the ICSU/AB and UNESCO Working Group on Bibliographic Descriptions as part of the UNISIST world science information system feasibility study. According to Perez-Vitoria (76), this Working Group is exploring standards for the transfer of basic bibliographic data, the structure and arrangement of elements, and the conversion of these elements into machine-readable form.

More abstracting and indexing organizations are becoming actively involved in the development of standards that affect their products and services, rather than waiting until after a standard is developed to complain about its inadequacies.

CONCLUSION

Perhaps the ultimate in store for secondary services is the situation of MEDLARS, in which the secondary product is completely integrated into the information system. When that occurs, it will no longer be necessary to have a chapter or section in the *Annual Review* devoted to this area of information science. Many of the developments reviewed in this chapter point to slow progress towards this millennium.

Many of the new services and networks have been brought about by cooperation, generally starting as a bilateral agreement between two organizations. Problems of standardization are of prime concern at this stage of development, and it seems that attempts at solutions are being made by many organizations operating practically in isolation from one another. A greater degree of communication and coordination of these activities might facilitate solutions. Agreement on a basic minimum set of data elements for the bibliographic record should be the first objective of concern to abstracting and indexing publishers.

REFERENCES

(1) ADAMS, SCOTT; BAKER, DALE B. Mission and discipline orientation in scientific abstracting and indexing services. Library Trends, 16:3 (January 1968) 307–322.
(2) AINES, ANDREW A. The promise of national information systems. Library Trends, 16:3 (January 1968) 410–418.
(3) AITCHISON, T. M.; MARTIN, M. D.; SMITH, J. R. Developments towards a computer-based information service in physics, electrotechnology and control. Information Storage and Retrieval, 4 (1968) 177–186.
(4) American Chemical Society Journal sold on film with license to copy. Information Retrieval & Library Automation, 4:3 (August 1968) 11.
(5) AMERICAN INSTITUTE OF PHYSICS. Techniques for publication and distribution of information. In: Annual review of information science and technology, vol. 2. Carlos A. Cuadra, ed. Wiley, Interscience, New York, 1967, p. 343–349.
(6) AMERICAN MATHEMATICAL SOCIETY. Development of computer aids for tape-control of photocomposing machines. Section A: Mechanization of Mathematical Reviews office procedures. Providence, R.I., Report no. 1, March 1967; Final report, August 1968, 56 p.
(7) AMERICAN MATHEMATICAL SOCIETY. Development of computer aids for tape-control of photocomposing machines. Section B: A system for computer-processed tape composition to include the setting of multiple line equations. Providence, R.I., Report no. 2, July 1967; Final report, August 1968, 50 p.
(8) American Mathematical Society. Contents of Contemporary Mathematical Journals. News from Science Abstracting and Indexing Services, 10:3 (August 1968) 3–4.
(9) American Mathematical Society [news]. News from Science Abstracting and Indexing Services, 10:4 (November 1968) 5–7.
(10) American Petroleum Institute [new publications]. News from Science Abstracting and Indexing Services, 10:4 (November 1968) 8.

(11) ANZELMO, FRANK D. Error control in the CAS computing system. In: Report of the Seventh Chemical Abstracts Services Open Forum, Miami Beach, Fla., 12 April 1967. Columbus, Ohio, May 1967, p. 11–15.
(12) ATOMIC ENERGY COMMISSION. In: Federal Council for Science and Technology. Committee on Scientific and Technical Information. Progress of the United States Government in scientific and technical communications, 1967. Washington, D.C., 1968, p. 17–20. (PB-180 867)
(13) BA–Previews: BIOSIS new machine language information service. Biological Abstracts, 50:5 (March 1 1969) [Editorial]
(14) BAKER, DALE B.; O'DETTE, RALPH E.; TATE, FRED A. Coordination of information services. In: American Society for Information Science Annual Meeting, Columbus, Ohio, 20–24 October 1968. Proceedings, vol. 5. Greenwood Publishing Corp., New York, 1968, p. 15–19.
(15) BARD, PHILIP. An introduction to Communications in Behavioral Biology. Communications in Behavioral Biology, 1:3 (March 1968).
(16) BERNIER, CHARLES L. Condensed technical literatures. Journal of Chemical Documentation, 8:4 (November 1968) 195–197. Presented before the Division of Chemical Literature, Symposium on Redesign of the Technical Literature, 156th Meeting, ACS, Atlantic City, September 1968.
(17) BioSciences Information Service of Biological Abstracts microfilm file containing 2,000,000 research references. Scientific Information Notes, 10:3 (June–July 1968) 24.
(18) BLUM, ARTHUR R. Data-element standardization as an aid in the transfer of physics information. In: American Society for Information Science Annual Meeting, Columbus, Ohio, 20–24 October 1968. Proceedings, vol. 5. Greenwood Publishing Corp., New York, 1968, p. 117–119.
(19) Broadening of scope, information standards considered at International Council of Scientific Unions Abstracting Board meeting. Scientific Information Notes, 10:4 (August–September 1968) 10.
(20) Chemical Abstracts Services; CA Condensates. News from Science Abstracting and Indexing Services, 10:4 (November 1968) 11.
(21) Clearinghouse for Federal Scientific and Technical Information. In: Federal Council for Science and Technology. Committee on Scientific and Technical Information. Progress of the United States Government in scientific and technical communications, 1967. Washington, D.C., 1968, p. 28–29. (PB-180 867)
(22) Clearinghouse offers new announcement service. [CAST—Clearinghouse Announcements in Science and Technology] Scientific Information Notes, 10:3 (June–July 1968) 23.
(23) CREPS, JOHN E. BA's List of Serials for 1968 to be published separately. Biological Abstracts, 48:24 (December 15 1968) [Editorial]
(24) DAVENPORT, W. C. CAS computer-based information services. Datamation, 14:3 (March 1968) 33–34, 37–39.
(25) De Haen Service. News from Science Abstracting and Indexing Services, 11:1 (February 1969) 9.
(26) Department of Agriculture. In: Federal Council for Science and Technology. Committee on Scientific and Technical Information. Progress of the United States Government in scientific and technical communications, 1967. Washington, D.C. 1968, p. 21–23. (PB-180 867)
(27) DICKMAN, JOHN T.; O'DETTE, RALPH E. Chemical Abstracts Service as a literature source for agricultural and food science and technology. Journal of Chemical Documentation, 8:2 (May 1968) 98–105.
(28) Engineering Index Inc. [news]. News from Science Abstracting and Indexing Services, 11:1 (February 1969) 6.
(29) Engineers to plan information and data system under National Science Foundation grant. Scientific Information Notes, 10:3 (June–July 1968) 6.
(30) ESRO/ELDO Space Documentation Service. News from Science Abstracting and In-

dexing Services, 10:4 (November 1968) 17.
(31) EXCERPTA MEDICA FOUNDATION. Excerpta Medica comprehensive drug literature computer tape service; a ten-point program. Amsterdam, October 1968, 6 p +.
(32) EXCERPTA MEDICA FOUNDATION. Excerpta Medica, the world-wide medical automated information networks. Amsterdam, 1969, 48 p.
(33) FEDERAL COUNCIL FOR SCIENCE AND TECHNOLOGY. COMMITTEE ON SCIENTIFIC AND TECHNICAL INFORMATION. Progress of the United States Government in scientific and technical communications, 1967. Washington, D.C. 1968, 91 + p. (PB-180 867).
(34) GARFIELD, EUGENE. "World Brain" or "Memex?" Mechanical and intellectual requirements for universal bibliographic control. In: The Foundations of Access to Knowledge. Syracuse University Press, Syracuse, N.Y., 1969, p. 169–196.
(35) HARRIS, MILTON. Presentation for panel on chemical information of OECD. Paris, 16–17 January 1968, 12 p. (Draft, unpublished)
(36) HENDERSON, MADELINE M. Critical reviews: introductory remarks. Journal of Chemical Documentation, 8:4 (November 1968) 231. Presented before the Division of Chemical Literature, 155th National Meeting, ACS, San Francisco, April 1968.
(37) HERRING, CONYERS. Critical reviews—the user's point of view. Journal of Chemical Documentation, 8:4 (November 1968) 232–236. Presented before the Division of Chemical Literature, 155th Meeting, ACS, San Francisco, April 1968.
(38) HERRING, CONYERS. Distill or drown: the need for reviews. Physics Today, 21:9 (September 1968) 27–33.
(39) HEUMANN, KARL. Notes of meeting on NSDP, October 9, 1968. (Private Communication); and NSDP [news]. News from Science Abstracting and Indexing Services, 10:4 (November 1968) 23.
(40) HYSLOP, MARJORIE R. American Society for Metals. In: Encyclopedia of Library and Information Science, vol. 1. Dekker, New York, 1968, p. 307–332.
(41) HYSLOP, MARJORIE R. ASM, Institute of Metals establish international abstracting journal. Materials Today, 151:3 (March 1968) 41–42.
(42) HYSLOP, MARJORIE R. The economics of information systems: observations of development costs and nature of the market. In: American Society for Information Science Annual Meeting, Columbus, Ohio, 20–24 October 1968. Proceedings, vol. 5. Greenwood Publishing Corp., New York, 1968, p. 301–306.
(43) Index to common data base linking information systems of Food and Drug Administration and National Library of Medicine with Chemical Abstracts Service Chemical Compound Registry System published. Scientific Information Notes, 10:4 (August–September 1968) 20.
(44) Information Industry Association (IIA) is formed. Scientific Information Notes, 10:5–6 (October–November–December 1968) 9.
(45) INTERNATIONAL ATOMIC ENERGY AGENCY. Rules recommended for input during the development of the International Nuclear Information System (INIS). Panel on descriptive cataloging for INIS input. Vienna, Austria, December 1967. (PL-273/1/Rev. 1)
(46) INTERNATIONAL COUNCIL OF SCIENTIFIC UNIONS/ABSTRACTING BOARD. World literature in physics; as seen through Bulletin Signalitique—1964 issues. Conseil International des Unions Scientifiques, Paris, 1967, 2 vols.
(47) INTERNATIONAL COUNCIL OF SCIENTIFIC UNIONS/ABSTRACTING BOARD. World literature in physics; as seen through Physics Abstracts—1964 issues. Conseil International des Unions Scientifiques, Paris, 1968, 2 vols.
(48) INTERNATIONAL COUNCIL OF SCIENTIFIC UNIONS/ABSTRACTING BOARD. World literature in physics; as seen through Physikalische Berichte—1964 issues. Conseil International des Unions Scientifiques, Paris, 1968, 2 vols.
(49) [Introduction] Abstracts of Mycology, 2:12 (December 1968).
(50) ISH, CARL J.; TERRANT, SHELDON W. JR. Chemical-Biological Activities: a specialized information service in biochemistry. American Journal of Pharmaceutical Education, 32 (May 1968) 201–210.

(51) Joint Agreement Group (JAG). News from Science Abstracting and Indexing Services, 11:1 (February 1969) 11.
(52) KEENAN, STELLA. Abstracting and indexing services in the physical sciences. Library Trends, 16:3 (January 1968) 329–336. Also published by Information Division, American Institute of Physics, New York, May 1968, 4 p. (ID 68-7)
(53) KEENAN, STELLA; BRICKWEDDE, F. G. Journal literature covered by Physics Abstracts in 1965. American Institute of Physics, Information Division, New York, February 1968, 1 vol. (various pagings) (ID 68-1)
(54) KLEMPNER, IRVING M. Diffusion of abstracting and indexing services for Government-sponsored research. Final report. Scarecrow, Metuchen, N.J., 1968, 336 p.
(55) KOCH, H. WILLIAM; HERSCHMAN, ARTHUR. A network for physics information. American Institute of Physics, Information Division, New York, October 1968, 16 p. (ID 68-13)
(56) KOEHLER, HENRY M. The development of "Oral Research Abstracts," a comprehensive abstracting service for dental researchers. In: American Documentation Institute. Annual Meeting, New York, 22–27 October 1967. Proceedings, vol. 4. Thompson, Washington, D.C., 1967, p. 213–217.
(57) LIBRARY OF CONGRESS, INFORMATION SYSTEMS OFFICE. Serials Data Program; progress reports to the Joint Committee on the Union List of Serials. Library of Congress, Washington, D.C., January 1969, 13 p. (Unpublished)
(58) LIPETZ, BEN-AMI. The continuity index of Documentation Abstracts. In: Congress of the International Federation for Information Processing (IFIP), 4th, Edinburgh, 5–10 August 1968. Proceedings. North-Holland Publishing Co., Amsterdam, 1968, G10–G12.
(59) LOWRY, CHARLES DOAK; COCROFT, ROBERT. Literature needs of food scientists. Journal of Chemical Documentation, 8:4 (November 1968) 228–230. Presented in Symposium on "Literature of Agricultural and Food Sciences—Problems and Some Solutions," Divisions of Chemical Literature and Agricultural and Food Chemistry, 155th Meeting, ACS, San Francisco, 2 April 1968.
(60) MALIN, MORTON V. The Science Citation Index: a new concept in indexing. Library Trends, 16:3 (January 1968) 374–387.
(61) MARTIN, M. D.; SMITH, J. R. INSPEC, a new concept in information services. Electronics & Power, (February 1969) 66–69.
(62) MICHAELSON, HERBERT B. Achieving a more disciplined R and D literature. Journal of Chemical Documentation, 8:4 (November 1968) 198–201. Presented before the Division of Chemical Literature, Symposium on Redesign of the Technical Literature, 156th Meeting ACS, Atlantic City, September 1968.
(63) MOHRHARDT, FOSTER E., ed. Science abstracting services—commercial, institutional and personal. Library Trends, 16:3 (January 1968) 303–418.
(64) NATIONAL ACADEMY OF SCIENCES/NATIONAL ACADEMY OF ENGINEERING. Committee on Scientific and Technical Communication. Scientific and technical communication: a pressing national problem and recommendations for its solution. NAS Publication 1707. Washington, D.C., 1969, 336 p.
(65) NATIONAL AGRICULTURAL LIBRARY [news]. News from Science Abstracting and Indexing Services, 10:4 (November 1968) 20.
(66) NATIONAL FEDERATION OF SCIENCE ABSTRACTING AND INDEXING SERVICES. 1958-1968 ten year progress report. Philadephia, Pa., 1968, 4 p.
(67) NATIONAL INSTITUTES OF HEALTH. NINDS neurological information network. Annual progress report. U.S. Public Health Service, National Institute of Neurological Diseases and Stroke, Bethesda, Md., 1969, 38 p.
(68) New American Mathematical Society Mathematical Offprint Service. Scientific Information Notes, 10:1 (February–March 1968) 23.
(69) New Biological Abstracts microfilm program. Biological Abstracts 49:11 (June 1 1968) [Editorial]
(70) NFSAIS Bibliographic Citation Committee. News from Science Abstracting and Indexing Services, 10:4 (November 1968) 1.

(71) NSF Grant proposals and future planning. Engineering Index Trustees Newsletter, 1:3 (December 1968) 1–2.
(72) Nuclear Science Abstracts. News from Science Abstracting and Indexing Services, 10:4 (November 1968) 24.
(73) PANDEX current index to scientific and technical literature. (Sample issue). CCM Information Services, Inc., New York, 1968.
(74) PANDEX. [Quarterly] Vol. 1, 1967. Pandex, Inc., New York. Reviewed by Harold A. Siroonian in: Special Libraries, 58:10 (December 1967) 729–730.
(75) PARK, MARGARET K. The Chemical Compound Registry: a status report. In: Report of the Seventh Chemical Abstracts Services Open Forum, Miami Beach, Fla., 12 April 1967. Columbus, Ohio, May 1967, p. 1–10.
(76) PEREZ-VITORIA, A. Towards a world science information system: An ICSU-UNESCO joint venture. Unesco Bulletin for Libraries, 23:1 (January–February 1969) 2–7.
(77) PINZELIK, J.; HOWLAND, L. A user study of Chemical Titles in a university setting. Paper presented at ACS, Division of Chemical Literature Meeting, Chicago, September 1967, 10 p. (Unpublished)
(78) ROWLETT, RUSSELL J.; TATE, FRED A.; WOOD, J. L. Relationships between primary publications and secondary information services. Columbus, Ohio, 1968, 17 p. (to be published)
(79) RUBINSTEIN, RICHARD I.; SCHULTZ, LOUISE. Evaluation of the usage of a custom biological literature search service—a three-year study. In: American Society for Information Science Annual Meeting, Columbus, Ohio, 20–24 October 1968. Proceedings, vol. 5. Greenwood Publishing Corp., New York, 1968, p. 317–322.
(80) RULE, DONALD F. The application of the 2280 film recorder to CAS processes. In: Report on the Eighth Chemical Abstracts Service Open Forum, Chicago, 12 September 1967. Columbus, Ohio, November 1967, p. 1–10.
(81) RUSH, JAMES E. Development of search guides and thesauri for CAS computer-based services. In: Report of the Seventh Chemical Abstracts Services Open Forum, Miami Beach, Fla., 12 April 1967. Columbus, Ohio, May 1967, p. 16–26.
(82) SCHULTZ, LOUISE. New developments in biological abstracting and indexing. Library Trends, 16:3 (January 1968) 337–352.
(83) SCHULTZ, LOUISE. Re-establishing the direct interface between an abstracting and indexing service and the generator of the literature. In: American Society for Information Science Annual Meeting, Columbus, Ohio, 20–24 October 1968. Proceedings, vol. 5. Greenwood Publishing Corp., New York, 1968, p. 101–105.
(84) SHERWIN, CHALMERS W. (Chairman) Final report of the Task Group for Interchange of Scientific and Technical Information in Machine Language (ISTIM), reporting to the Office of Science and Technology, Executive Office of the President. Washington, D.C., April 1968. 16 p. (Unpublished)
(85) SIEGEL, H.; VEAL, D. C.; McMULLEN, D. A. Polymer Science & Technology (POST): A computer-based information service. Journal of Polymer Science, Part C, no. 25 (1968) 191–196.
(86) SIMPSON, G. S., JR.; FLANAGAN, CAROLYN. Information centers and services. In: Annual review of information science and technology, vol. 1. Carlos A. Cuadra, ed. Wiley, Interscience, New York, 1966, p. 305–355.
(87) SLATER, MARGARET; KEENAN, STELLA. Current papers in physics user study—coverage, arrangement and format. Second report of CPP [Current Papers in Physics] study. Institution of Electrical Engineers, London; American Institute of Physics, New York, May 1968, 61 p. (Report nos. INSPEC/2 and AIP/CPP 2)
(88) SLATER, MARGARET; KEENAN, STELLA. Results of questionnaire on current awareness methods used by physicists prior to publication of "Current Papers in Physics." First report of CPP study. Institution of Electrical Engineers, London; American Institute of Physics, New York, September 1967, 35 p. (Report nos. INSPEC/1 and AIP/CPP1)
(89) SLATER, MARGARET; KEENAN, STELLA. Use made of "Current Papers in

Physics." Third report of CPP study. Institution of Electrical Engineers, London; American Institute of Physics, New York, July 1968, 67 p. (Report nos. INSPEC/3 and AIP/CPP 3)
(90) SMITH, J. R.; EAST, H. Information services in physics. In: De Reuck, Anthony; Knight, Julie, eds. Communication in science. Little, Brown, Boston, 1967, p. 134–143; discussion, p. 143–145.
(91) Special bibliographies: A new BIOSIS service. Biological Abstracts, 49:12 (15 June 1968) [Editorial]
(92) SYSTEM DEVELOPMENT CORPORATION. A system study of abstracting and indexing in the United States. Santa Monica, Calif., 16 December 1966, 228 p. (TM-WD-394) (PB-174 249)
(93) SYSTEM DEVELOPMENT CORPORATION. Recommendations for national document handling systems in science and technology: Appendix A; a background study. Santa Monica, Calif., 1965, 2 vols. (PB-168 267)
(94) TATE, FRED A. The Chemical Compound Registry System. In: De Reuck, Anthony; Knight, Julie, eds. Communication in science. Little, Brown, Boston, 1967, p. 158–162; discussion, p. 162–164.
(95) TATE, FRED A. A mechanized registry for chemical compounds. Chemistry, 41 (July–August 1968) 18–23.
(96) TATE, FRED A.; WOOD, JAMES L. Libraries and abstracting and indexing services—a study in interdependency. Library Trends, 16:3 (January 1968) 353–373.
(97) TEITELBAUM, PRISCILLA. A computer produced index for a small special library. In: National Colloquium on Information Retrieval, 5th, 3–4 May 1968, Philadelphia, Proceedings, edited by J. Ramey. Information Interscience Inc., Philadelphia, 1969, p. 71–76.
(98) TOMPKINS, HOWARD E. JAG report to the 1968 FJCC; tentative common practices on formats for public bibliographic data tapes. Oral presentation to the 1968 Fall Joint Computer Conference, San Francisco, 9–11 December 1968. (Unpublished)
(99) UNITED STATES OF AMERICA STANDARDS INSTITUTE. USA standard for a format for bibliographic information interchange on magnetic tape. USASI, New York, 1969. (USAS Z39.2–1969)
(100) UNITED STATES OF AMERICA STANDARDS INSTITUTE. USA standard for the abbreviation of titles of periodicals. USASI, New York, 1969, 14 p. (USAS-Z39.5–1969. Revision of Z39.5–1963)
(101) VAUGHAN, FREDERICK R. CAS unified processing for multiple services. In: Report on the Ninth Chemical Abstracts Service Open Forum, San Francisco, 2 April 1968. Columbus, Ohio, June 1968, 12 p.
(102) Water Resources Scientific Information Center. News from Science Abstracting and Indexing Services, 10:4 (November 1968) 27; 11:1 (February 1969) 15.
(103) WHALEY, FRED R.; CARRIGY, JOHN; HOHNECKER, WALTER. Computer-based services at Engineering Index. Engineering Index, New York, (24 April 1968) 6 p + (Unpublished) Paper presented in Moscow, September 1968, to selected VINITI personnel.
(104) WOOD, JAMES L. A comprehensive list of periodicals for chemistry and chemical engineering. Library Trends, 16:3 (January 1968) 398–409.
(105) WOODS, BILL M. Information system development. Phase I: Management planning. Engineering Index, New York, May 1968, 67 p. (PB-178 753)
(106) ZABRISKIE, K. H., JR.; FARREN, A. The BASIC index to Biological Abstracts. American Journal of Pharmaceutical Education, 32 (May 1968) 189–200.

10 Library Automation

FREDERICK G. KILGOUR
Ohio College Library Center

A major goal of library automation is adaptation of computer technology to become a continuously innovative library technology; application of computation to effect economies will not be enough. Only by development of an innovative technology that will continuously increase the productivity of the library staff will the soaring costs of libraries be brought into line with cost rises in the general economy. A rising living standard has long been forcing up library salaries at a rate well in excess of cost reduction achieved by economies. However, the conscious development of computation to achieve the economic goal of increasing productivity rather than the use of computers to effect economies holds the hope that library automation can eliminate the exponentiality of library cost rises and bring those increases into line with those of the economy as a whole.

Unhappily, some library economies effected in the past and in effect today have increased user costs by increasing the amount of time a user expends in obtaining information from a library. The user should, however, be considered an integral section of a library system, and his costs must be thought of as system costs. Library automation must also have the economic goal of increasing productivity for the user so that his costs do not continue to increase more rapidly than the general cost structure.

A perceptive view toward a library technology of the future can be gained from an imaginative reading of Salton's (121) excellent book, *Automatic Information Organization and Retrieval*, which appeared at the end of the year. This book presents a splendid discussion of experimental automatic text-handling methods and processing of large files, and it is stimulating and enjoyable reading. It provides a perspective and suggests avenues toward a truly innovative library technology that will include automatic subject indexing, classification, and descriptive cataloging.

The remainder of the first half of this chapter will comment on the literature of automation and then examine the countries and the types of libraries that are participating in automation. Next come interpretations of impact of technology on libraries, followed by an evaluation of principal developments. The first half concludes with reviews of contributions dealing with automation of use of libraries. Except for concluding "Reflections" the last half of the chapter treats of the familiar library processes of circulation, cataloging, serials control, and acquisitions.

LITERATURE

The literature of library automation is rapidly enlarging and acquiring a dynamic quality gratifying to behold, but it has yet to achieve the status of a mature corpus of publications emanating from an innovative technology. Lack of fullness is evidenced by the relatively few stimulating books appearing in the field. This year there were but three: Dolby et al. (48); Morse (93); and Salton (121). It is books that scholars, scientists, and technologists read for stimulating intellectual discussion of concepts and theories in their fields. Devotees of library automation will grow in sophistication with growth of book publication in the field.

Library automation now has a valuable retrospective bibliography, *Libraries and Automation* (Speer, 127), which contains some three thousand references, most of which appeared between 1958 and 1966. To keep up with current literature, one uses *Computing Reviews, Information Science Abstracts*, and *Library & Information Science Abstracts*.

There are now two journals available on subscription that are devoted to publishing papers on library automation. In March 1966, Kimber, of Queen's University School of Library Studies, put out the first issue of *Program; News of Computers in British University Libraries*. The first volume was available free, but its success led to its establishment on a subscription basis beginning with Volume 2, No. 1, for April 1968, and to a broadening of its scope, as shown by the omission of "University" from the subtitle. Further broadening will occur in Volume 3 when "British" will disappear. Volume 1, No. 1 of the American Library Association's quarterly *Journal of Library Automation* was dated March 1968. Its scope includes "all fields of research and development in library automation, including interlibrary communications; in research in information science directly related to library activities; and in the history and teaching of these subjects." Early issues of the *Journal* contained technical reports on library automation applications, but the last issue to appear in 1968 also had research papers on information science.

The four chapters containing library automation literature in this and previous volumes of the *Annual Review* do not have exactly the same scope, but their contents are sufficiently comparable to justify a search for trends. One trend is clearly apparent; there is an increasing number of papers appearing that report on operational library computerization. In the chapter in Volume 1, there were 19 such reports out of 66 references, or roughly 29%. In Volume 2, it was 12 out of 83, for 14%. Volume 3 had 17 out of 51, for one third; and this volume has 66 in 150, or two out of five. Clearly, both absolute and relative numbers of technical reports on library automation are rising.

WHICH LIBRARIES AUTOMATE?

The majority of library automation activities are in the United States. However, a half-dozen Canadian centers have development programs productive of publication. It is clear from articles in the British *Program* that, during the past three years, there has been a sharp increase in publication in Great Britain and that British public librarians are much more active in automation than are their American colleagues. German, Italian, Russian, and Swiss librarians are also developing computer applications, but publications emanating from these areas are few.

The major effort in library automation in the United States is in special and academic libraries. Cummings & Simmons (44) review history and current activity in medical libraries, which are distinguished from other types of libraries largely by the pioneering MEDLARS system, which the National Library of Medicine has developed and continues to evolve. Kershaw & Davis (68) report on mechanization in 27 libraries in the defense establishment. Their paper includes such details as types of equipment used, types of functions mechanized, and comparison of characteristics of storage and retrieval systems in 15 of the 27 libraries. Kilgour (72) describes the history of libraries that has led to the present crisis in academic libraries and reviews computer applications in college and university libraries.

TECHNICS AND LIBRARIES

Several authors undertook to assess the impact of new knowledge on libraries. System Development Corporation released an extensive report, *Technology and Libraries* (134), prepared for the National Advisory Commission on Libraries. This study analyzes reasons for library interest in technology, technologies that will effect library development, current application of those technologies, and the future direction those technologies will take. It also includes recommended programs of action for research and development. Somewhat the same material is summarized in a lucid paper by Cuadra & Mersel (40). *Technology and Libraries* contains an additional discussion of "procedural technology, and related equipment and materials technology." The most important finding of this study is that present research and development programs must be expanded at an accelerated rate if libraries are to improve their service.

Saracevic & Rees (122) confine their impact analysis to information science. They argue persuasively that librarianship must become applied information science, and conclude, "Paralyzed by decades of philosophical and literary argumentation, librarianship has much to gain from information science." But unfortunately, users, like death, will not wait.

Grose (55), at Newcastle, sees computation as an invading force that necessitates a reexamination of library principles and the shedding of present dogma. His article and those in the preceding two paragraphs are enjoyable reading, for they reveal a breaking of bonds and an influx of intellectuality.

Strieby (130) describes computerization of library activities within a single state—Indiana. Here, with the active participation of the faculty of the Graduate Library School at Indiana University and a group at Purdue, computerized techniques are evolving in public, academic, and special libraries. From a reading of Strieby's article it would appear that a few highly motivated groups can have considerable impact on a large number of libraries. Tanis (135) speaks of the impact of computerization on a single university library engaged in research and development. He discusses such problems as space, budget, and priorities, and observes that "to replace present procedures with machine procedures is expensive, but the valuable by-products are amazingly cheap. Unfortunately, one cannot just buy the by-products."

Bundy (28) reports on a study designed to determine the success or failure that libraries experience in adapting to innovative automation. She particularly emphasizes the human and social aspect of the introduction of automation. Especially demoralizing for the staff were unrealistic time schedules and pressures to start operation before testing of a system had been completed. The study of a successful automation project suggests that an ingredient of effective implementation is high motivation on the part of the chief of the organization, full-time development personnel, and staff participation in the planning stage. In contrast, a project conceived and introduced to the library by an outside group with external deadlines was unsuccessful, both technically and humanly. Such failures, which increase resistance to change, should be avoided and are certainly not typical of libraries alone. Bundy recommends that training for library management should include "more than ordinary sophistication with the computer and with the systems approach" and that training should be research oriented.

PRINCIPAL DEVELOPMENTS

Principal developments in 1968 included a recommendation for establishment of a national library agency, formulation of a standardized machine-readable format for communicating bibliographic data, and increased activity in investigations leading toward the design of a huge file of bibliographic records. The problem of how to organize extremely large files efficiently is the major of the most immediate intellectual challenges confronting designers of automated systems.

The President's National Advisory Commission on Libraries issued its report in October 1968 (96). Of its five recommendations, the two most important for future development of library automation are: one for the creation of a National Commission on Libraries and Information Science, a permanent Federal agency; and one for a Federal Institute of Library and Information Science, which would be a major center of research and development. There can be no doubt that both of these agencies would speed evolution of library automation.

MARC II

Under the able chairmanship of Henriette D. Avram, the Sub-Committee on Machine Input Records of the USASI Committee on Library Work and Documentation completed work on a proposed *USA Standard for a Format for Bibliographic Information Interchange on Magnetic Tape* (141). The Standard is concerned only with communication of bibliographic records, and not with record format in files. Furthermore, the Standard provides for all kinds of bibliographic information, is machine independent, accommodates each type of bibliographic data in a uniform structure, and is designed to facilitate conversion to other formats.

The first major application of the proposed Standard is the MARC II Format (10, 84), developed by the Information Systems Office of the Library of Congress. The Library of Congress has not used the MARC II format for its internal processing. Instead, it uses a record design that it calls MARC Processing Format (Avram & Droz, 9), and from which it generates the MARC II format for the MARC distribution service. This standard format for communication of bibliographic data will immensely speed and facilitate development of library automation. The standard MARC II format is comparable to a standard-size physical card containing a standard format of bibliographic data—one of the first achievements of the American Library Association 90 years ago. In exactly the same way that cards of a standard arrangement of data and size will fit in any library's catalog, housed in cabinets having standard-sized drawers, so MARC II records can be loaded into a local computer file using but one program, which may or may not involve transliteration. Similarly, the local system can be designed so that a bibliographic record can be copied out of the file and regenerated, if necessary, into MARC II for communication to other local computer files. In short, only one program will be needed to load a file, and only one to regenerate it for communication. The alternative to this happy procedure is a loading program for every style of bibliographic format, of which there are dozens already in existence. Moreover, it is impossible to achieve from dozens of formats a sufficient degree of uniformity to allow local manipulation with only one system of programs. MARC II has swept aside this frightful jungle, whose rapid growth was beginning to throttle library automation.

Obvious advantages of standardization have led to wide and rapid support for the proposed USA Standard in the United States and abroad. British librarians early perceived advantages of standardization and indeed contributed some data elements to the MARC II format. Coward (37, 38) and Kimber (75) describe MARC II as seen for British application.

File Organization

Increased activity in the study of efficient file organization for huge files of bibliographic records is gratifying, for an effective solution to this vexing problem must be found in the near future. The majority of work on file organization has involved relatively small files—certainly files containing fewer than a million entries. Moreover, investigators have concentrated on file design that would permit retrieval of groups of entries having one common characteristic or similar characteristics. The library automation designer needs a design for an enormous file of self-addressing entries from which each single entry can be retrieved uniquely and rapidly.

Nugent (97) and Ruecking (119) published highly interesting papers on compression coding to facilitate matching and retrieval. Both authors present algorithms for machine derivation of a code from a bibliographic entry. Ruecking emphasized diminution of effect of misspellings and, in an experimental test, achieved an overall retrieval accuracy of 98.67%. Kilgour (71) published results of an experiment in which simple truncation coding was employed. The highest percentage of correct replies produced by his trial runs was 97.3.

Techniques for producing physical addresses from derived codes are important for successful file design. Here, E. B. Parker (101) describes a hash code technique for scatter storage in a linear file as employed at Stanford in Project SPIRES. Kilgour (71) mentions a similar use of hash coding in a much smaller file at Yale and proposed use of hash codes to compute the position of a record in an n-dimensional array.

These findings suggest the concept of an on-line catalog divided into n small catalogs from which a score or fewer of entries would be displayed.

SYSTEM DESIGN

Authors continue to describe to librarians the new system approach and to urge its adoption. However, librarians are slow to look upon their libraries as other than conglomerates of procedures that, unfortunately, are also sometimes called systems. This year, Dews (47) and Waite (147) produced general discussions of the comprehensive approach to library system design that may be helpful in persuading librarians to look upon their institutions as a whole, rather than as a series of separate functions.

The year's most important publication in the field of library system design is Morse's *Library Effectiveness: A Systems Approach* (93), which is highly technical, in contrast to the two papers cited in the previous paragraph. Morse concentrates on development of techniques for measuring the extent to which a library satisfies user requirements. The book is addressed to librarians and systems analysts. The first half of the book discusses and presents mathematical models of library use; the second half contains specific applications of theory developed in the first half. Every librarian and library systems analyst who is prepared to make real efforts to meet the needs of library users should not only read and understand this book, but also apply its techniques.

Design of Networks

The comprehensive system approach to design and planning is a fruitful technique for network development. Indeed, it would be ridiculous not to use modern system design in library network planning. Bregzis (26) has written an excellent analysis of the library and technological components of networks. His paper will clarify, for the network designer, the goals to be attained and problems to be solved for some years to come.

Library network designers discussed three types of computer operations: (*1*) on-line access with the computer operating in a time-slicing mode; (*2*) on-line operation with the computer in an event-driven mode; and (*3*) batch processing.

Black (23) describes SDC's LISTS experiment, which involves a central computer operating in time-slicing mode. Seven libraries are remotely connected to the system. The experiment is to operate for six months, and its designers are seeking answers to various questions: Is a general-purpose data management system adequately efficient? Will libraries be able to afford such a system? At what values will the variables of on-line communication cause the system to be uneconomical? The findings of the LISTS experiment will be most useful to library network designers.

At the same meeting at which Black reported on LISTS, Kilgour (70) gave an account of an early system design for an on-line event-driven network to encompass 60-odd Ohio academic libraries. The system, which would require a half-dozen or more years to develop, includes a shared-cataloging operation, a remote catalog access and circulation procedure for users, remote bibliographic information retrieval by subject, serials control, and a technical processing system.

The first major library network to become operational was the New England Library Information Network—NELINET. Nugent (98) reports on the pilot operation, which employs batch processing to service requests from five New England university libraries via teletypewriter terminals for production of catalog card sets, book labels, and book pockets from a common catalog data file. This pilot operation simulates an on-line mode, which will be the next major development in NELINET. Staff members of Inforonics, Incorporated, which developed the NELINET system, produced a progress report (1), containing useful plans of and data related to catalog file searching and acquisition processing.

Bateman & Farris (14) describe an on-line network serving four small IBM libraries for technical processing. The system operates on an IBM 1460 computer. The data processing cost for acquisitions at the rate of 550 titles per month was $2.04 per title.

Other publications of interest in the field of library network development include articles by Cummings (41, 42, 43) on planning for a medical library network, and three publications (20, 21, 133) emanating from Syracuse University that report on the design and operation of a New York State film library network. This study found that a scheduling network for film libraries is workable, that it will be a necessity within a few years, and that it will not reduce operating costs. R. H. Parker (103) produced a study on the feasibility of a joint computer center for five university libraries in Washington, D.C. that is a model for this type of investigation. Moreover, it contains useful data, such as percentage of duplication of book and journal holdings among the libraries. Parker recommended a joint center, to be activated with a small or medium-sized computer operating in batch mode with basic records on tape; this system would be designed so that a larger on-line system could evolve from it.

Design of Individual Libraries

The year witnessed a comforting increase in publications discussing system design for individual libraries. In the past, library computerization has too often involved mere mechanization of existing procedures. However, the comprehensive system approach to planning the development of computerization holds the hope of invoking a powerful technology to improve information servicing as well as cost-benefit ratios of library operation and use. Shoffner (125) recounts the deliberation of representatives from nine university libraries on the issues involved in cooperative system design and development. No resolute judgment came out of the meeting on whether or not such cooperation is feasible, but the group recommended that a cooperative project be undertaken, because high potential benefits could be derived. The current cooperative activity among the University of Chicago, Columbia University, and Stanford University is such a project, from which there will surely be lessons to be learned.

The University of California Institute of Library Research studied the developmental program required to activate mechanized information services in a university library (142). Findings were that four years would be required to carry out detailed system design, programming and test, implementation, and initial operation. A further study (143) of the development and implementation of such a service yielded preliminary specifications for administrative and organizational factors, machine configuration and operation, and applications programming. De Gennaro (46), in a paper that attracted wide and favorable comment, discusses three general approaches to a library automation program and suggests that outside consultants will become increasingly useful. He makes the point that a library, to become successfully involved in automation, must build resources in staff, in equipment, in organization, and in administrative structure.

A half-dozen libraries published narratives of comprehensive computerization approaches, of which that at the University of Chicago Library (145), now in its third year, is the most extensive. The type of integrated bibliographic system that Chicago is developing is the avenue along which library automation for individual libraries as well as networks will proceed in the foreseeable future. To be sure, Chicago is not alone in this approach, but it is the major pioneer. De Gennaro (45) also narrated automation activities at the Harvard College Library, experience which furnished, in part, the basis of his general discussion reviewed in the previous paragraph. Parker describes the dedicated IBM 1440 computer system at the University of Missouri Library, including operation of an IBM 357 circulation system and acquisition system. Kimber (73) reviews various library computer applications, paying more than usual attention to British activities, and Evans & Wall (51) describe in detail the mechanization projects and plans at Britain's Loughborough University of Technology. Mackenzie (87) discusses the comprehensive system approach being taken at the University of Lancaster in a superior, scholarly article. An outstanding example of computerization in a special library is Chamis's article (33) on computers at the B. F. Goodrich Research Center Library. This library really uses computers, for its book catalog program formerly ran on an IBM 7090 and has been converted to an IBM System 360; information retrieval and serial control are on a GE 235, while circulation control uses an IBM 1130. Taylor (136) published a description of system plans for a most intriguing new library at recently established Hampshire College. Taylor's library will encompass an audio-visual section servicing tapes, records, TV tapes and films, a gallery, a bookstore, an experimental information transfer center, and a conventional library containing volumes and microforms. Taylor estimates that the library and information transfer center will be the heaviest users of Hampshire's computer facilities.

LIBRARY USE

Most publication in the field of library automation is concerned with mechanization of internal library operations. Of greater importance is the computerization of user activity because it holds the potential for huge improvement in cost/benefit ratios. This year, papers appeared on automation of reference services, selective dissemination of information, and library-related information storage and retrieval. Interestingly enough, the majority of publications are in the latter areas where, with the outstanding exception of the MEDLARS project, there is little operational activity.

Weil (149) reports results of an experiment in automation of a reference service to advise which biographical reference books should be used to answer a specific inquiry. Results were encouraging, for when the computer program and an experienced reference librarian were each challenged with the same 14 questions, the program responded with ten correct answers, and the librarian with eleven, which included one answer not located in a biographical reference work. Weil's finding is the type of positive result that, although not conclusive, demonstrates that to some extent computerization of reference services will facilitate library use.

Employing IBM's Report Program Generator and an IBM 360/75 at the University of Waterloo, Chen & Kingham (35) devised an operational system for production of subject reference lists or bibliographies on specific subjects. Whereas Weil's technique produces reference lists on demand, Chen & Kingham put out predefined lists. Cost to maintain information from which the lists are derived is less than half the manual cost. An inquiry by questionnaires, one third of which elicited replies, led to the conclusion that nearly all who purchased the lists found them useful.

Cooper (36) reviewed 17 current information services in science, medicine, and engineering, giving for each service valuable information on current status, data base, indexing, user population, user profile, profile/document matching, user notification and response form, equipment, and cost. Schneider (123) published results of a one-year test of a biomedical SDI system servicing 103 research scientists at the National Cancer Institute. The program is in FORTRAN IV and runs on an IBM 360/50, but preliminary trials indicate that PL/I with its substring and index built-in functions can perform matches more efficiently than can FORTRAN IV. However, the FORTRAN IV program performed matches at a cost of .088¢ per match. Preliminary tabulations of 5,205 evaluations revealed that 54% were either "very useful" or "of definite but limited use." A. M. Becker (16) describes an SDI system in operation at Sulzer Bros. Ltd., in Winterthur, Switzerland, that has been operational since March 1967, servicing 400 subscribers. Matches between profile and document are made on a UDC number. Becker reports that most of the 400 recipients are satisfied, and that expenses of the system are 25% less than for manual methods, whereas output has increased 40%. Jordan (65) published an untested model to evaluate SDI systems, an approach that could be useful for coping with some aspects of the complexities of those activities.

The SDI systems in the preceding paragraph concentrated on periodical and report literature, but Studer (132) conducted an experiment in SDI using monographs on MARC tapes. Results were good, and this suggests that SDI using books should be pursued.

Although the National Library of Medicine's MEDLARS system had precursors, MEDLARS is, nevertheless, the major pioneer in bibliographic information retrieval. This year, Austin (4) published what he called "the final chapter on the current MEDLARS system," in which he skillfully described the MEDLARS system design, operation, and products. This valuable publication also contains a bibliography of about 150 references to publications on the MEDLARS system. Rogers (116) produced another of his detailed, accurate, and useful cost analyses of the MEDLARS system. He found that "librarians working with machine aids accomplish 150% more than they would accomplish unaided."

Project INTREX puts out a *Semi-Annual Activity Report* as of 15 March and 15 September each year. These *Reports* contain much valuable information. The one for 15 September, 1968 (90), describes, in detail, storage and retrieval developments and the INTREX augmented catalog, which is to contain bibliographic descriptions of items in M.I.T.'s Engineering Library. During the period under review, a demonstration system was activated that possesses most of the planned-for retrieval functions, although the data base contains but 48 documents. This data base is to be expanded to a thousand documents for experimental purposes. The INTREX textaccess project moved forward during the year; the principal features of the system are described in the *Report* for 15 March 1968. This system will encompass the full text of some 10,000 documents in the Engineering Library whose bibliographic descriptions and indexes will be in the augmented catalog. It is expected that operational status will be attained in the first half of 1969.

E. B. Parker (101) likened the Stanford SPIRES project to the INTREX augmented catalog. SPIRES's first beneficiaries will be Stanford physicists. However, SPIRES is also being elaborated to provide internal processing of bibliographic information in the Stanford library, where remote terminals are being installed.

For the past half-dozen years, the Central Library and Documentation Branch of the International Labour Office at Geneva has been developing an Integrated Scientific Information Service (ISIS). Marthaler & McGurk (89) put out a description of procedures in the ISIS information retrieval and catalog production operation, and Thompson (137) describes more generally the systems wherein a Flexowriter is employed for input and processing is done on an IBM 360/30.

Bibliographic information retrieval depends heavily on cross-referencing, although little attention has been paid to this aspect of retrieval. However, Kochen & Tagliacozzo (79) published a descriptive paper in which they depicted properties and characteristics of cross-reference structure in indexes; the paper will furnish at least a partial base for further investigations in this field.

LIBRARY PROCESSES

Several publications (Boylan et al., 25; Chamis, 33; Pflug & Adams, 109) report essentially full computerization of library processes. Pflug, Adams, and their colleagues describe in detail the computerization of the Bochum University Library in Germany, a project initiated in 1963. Bochum, a new university, is the first to achieve full computerization. Close on its heels is Simon Fraser in Canada (Mather, 91), which has yet to automate its cataloging operations. At least two new universities in the United States have, for all practical purposes, failed in attempts to computerize, and others contemplating computerization will do well to study success achieved at these Canadian and German universities.

Circulation

The most important development during the year in library automation was activation of an on-line circulation system at the Bell Telephone Laboratories' Library (BELLREL) (Kennedy, 67), which possesses several features that are important departures from manual techniques. The most original components of the system are an on-line inquiry capability for status of a volume, and the inclusion in the data base of the entire catalogs of three libraries several miles distant from each other. BELLREL is the first circulation system to achieve instantaneousness between the moment of charging an item and capability of reply as to status of that item. No manual system can boast this quality, which is of the utmost importance for a circulation system in an academic library, where requests for a particular title often cluster within a few hours. Kennedy's description of the system is thorough and detailed and contains an account of its many products. BELLREL operates on a time-sharing IBM 360/40 in the comptroller's office. Kennedy's article contains detailed information as to machine and communication configuration, operating system, and application programs, which number 55 in all and are written in COBOL level F and basic assembly language.

BELLREL excites not only because it takes advantage of a computer to introduce a major improvement in library circulation systems, but also because it can well serve as a departure point for a new avenue of increased user services. As originally installed, BELLREL had two terminals for staff use in each of three libraries. However, the BELLREL system will certainly serve as a basis for development of remote access to catalogs to retrieve information other than the circulation status of a particular volume. A paper cited earlier (Kilgour, 70) reported a preliminary cost-benefit study at the Ohio State University Libraries of savings to be achieved by remote catalog access from a terminal in each of the University's buildings on its Columbus campus. The estimate employed the minimum wage rate for students and $10 an hour for faculty, and predicted an annual savings to users of nearly a million dollars.

Midwestern University has also activated an on-line circulation system (IBM, 63) that is somewhat less sophisticated than BELLREL; Midwestern's system is not based on a machine-readable converted catalog and does not supply information about recorded charges instantaneously. Rather, it employs a nightly printout of charges, thereby retaining the all-too-familiar delay between time of charge and information about the charge. Nevertheless, the system does incorporate advantages not possessed by the so-called 357 systems. The most interesting feature of Midwestern's application is that it operates remotely on an IBM 1401, which, like the BELLREL computer, is located in the business office.

A third on-line circulation system has been operating at the Illinois State Library since December 1966, but a detailed technical report has yet to appear. Still, one published description (Ruby, 118) may be sufficient to indicate to a designer whether or not more complete knowledge of the system might be helpful.

The library of the Lawrence Radiation Laboratory (Boylan et al., 25) has computerized its major processes. Like BELLREL, the Lawrence circulation system contains a machine-readable record for each title, but at Lawrence the record is on magnetic tape. There are two daily printouts, one arranged by call number and the other by borrower's name. The published description is thorough and well illustrated. Lawrence programs run on an IBM 1401, with 8K storage, and an IBM 7094 doing some sorting.

Ruecking (120) has published a fine description of the system approach, planning, and implementation of an IBM 357 circulation system at Rice University. His paper should be particularly helpful to a designer at initial stages of analysis of circulation activities. Kimber (74) estimated costs of an on-line circulation system for The Queen's University of Belfast and predicted that a computer system would be 15% more expensive but would effect a 45% reduction in staff time. Auld (3) published details of a 357 system that operates with an IBM 1620 computer at Oakland University. The principal innovation in the Oakland system is the use of trigger cards to control operation of the 357 and thereby increase flexibility of types of charges. The circulation system at Bochum (Pflug & Adams, 109) is similar to a 357 system, but it employs Siemens equipment. Simon Fraser uses an IBM 1030 system (Mather, 91). In Great Britain, Woods (151) reported on 18 months' experience with a circulation system based on a Friden Collectadata and an ICT computer. Printouts of the circulation record are produced in batches. An 80-column bookcard and the borrower's ID card are inserted into the Friden terminal to record a loan. Bearman (15), at the Chichester Library, describes a similar system operating with an IBM 360/40. Subsequently the printout was converted to an on-line interrogation file (Kimber, 76), the first in Britain. Kimber characterized the system as working "smoothly and efficiently and without fuss."

Catalogs

Many devotees of library automation are rightly convinced that the basic, major problems to be solved are in the area of catalog construction. Upstream from cataloging are acquisitions activities and serial control, and downstream lies circulation, while catalogs themselves are the bridge between the information store and the user. As might be expected, more worthwhile publications appear on computerization of cataloging processes than on any other area in library automation. Dolby et al. (48) make an outstanding contribution in their *Evaluation of the Utility and Cost of Computerized Library Catalogs*, a scholarly publication that takes full advantage of the published literature, which their analyses and interpretations exploit fully. Their major finding may provide the year's most quotable quote: "*The primary conclusion of this study is that mechanization of the cataloging function is not only necessary and desirable, but also inevitable.*" This two-hundred-page publication is a mine of important data and scholarly interpretation, one that every librarian and systems designer involved in any aspect of the computerization of cataloging processes for some years to come will use with profit.

Librarians have tacitly assumed that card catalogs would last forever, but personnel at the New York Public Library know differently. By 1965, their public catalog of eight million cards contained over two million that were worn out and needed replacement. The massive task of reconstruction has been under study for over a decade and a half and reached its culmination this year with a useful two-hundred-and-fifty-page publication, *Library Catalogs: Their Preservation and Maintenance by Photographic and Automated Techniques* (Henderson & Rosenthal, 61). Principal conclusions of the study are that the present public catalog should be reproduced photographically in book form from machine-readable data. Like the Dolby et al. (48) work, this report contains a host of useful factual material.

Vickery (146) published a theoretical consideration of the structure of bibliographic records with reference to machine manipulation. His analysis relates only to production of catalogs in conventional form. As was indicated in the discussion of file organization in a previous section of this chapter, "filing" in an on-line catalog is wholly unlike the arrangement of records in list form or on cards. Nevertheless, Vickery's analysis is a helpful disruption, as he calls it, of the conventional record into its elements.

New design for file organization of computerized catalogs must make it possible for the system to respond effectively to the user, and here it is necessary to know the information that the user employs to put a request to the system. Perrine (108) conducted a questionnaire investigation into the difficulties users experience with library card catalogs. Filing arrangements caused more difficulties than any other one factor, which suggests that the designer of a computerized catalog should eliminate user involvement in file organization. Lipetz & Stangl (85), in a preliminary report, relate findings that users of a university library catalog were searching for a specific document in four out of five searches. The remaining fifth of the searches were, in decreasing order of frequency: subject searches; document group searches, such as for books published by a given author; and a bibliographic data search that involved location of information in the card catalog itself. However, the authors warned that these are preliminary results and that relative percentages may change when all data have been analyzed.

A group at the University of Chicago Graduate Library School (144) completed an important study designed to determine—in part, at least— the requirements of a catalog based on what users remember about a book they have previously seen. Subject information proved to be the most memorable, and it was found to be potentially effective in retrieval of the book in more than 70% of cases, whereas only 16% of authors were recalled, and 23% of titles. Memorability of many other characteristics, such as translations, illustrations, type of binding, and so on, were also investigated and reported upon; indeed, the last section of the report discusses the possible usefulness of catalog access other than author, title and subject.

In a survey analogous to that by Lipetz & Stangl, Ayres and his colleagues at the British Atomic Weapons Research Establishment (12) found that less than 75% of author information with which users approached the catalog was correct, while their information about titles was over 90% correct.

To produce data to be employed in the evolving NELINET design, Nugent (99) investigated duplication of holdings among the six New England state university libraries. He found that a random title from any one of the libraries possessed a 40% chance of being duplicated in another randomly selected library. When he looked only at current imprints, this figure rose to 47%. Too little is known about duplication of holdings among libraries so these data of Nugent's, together with those of R. H. Parker (103) cited in an earlier section, are useful contributions to the literature.

Roberts (115), at the Washington University School of Medicine Library, examined 4,708 bibliographic records in machine-readable form to determine their overall size, as well as the size of various elements. Average character length of the full catalog record proved to be 227. This finding, together with those for the various entry elements in the record, is discussed and compared with similar findings from a previous half-dozen studies.

Benenfeld (19) describes in detail the data elements, structure, and coding of the machine-readable bibliographic record employed in the INTREX augmented catalog. INTREX employs 115 data elements, which provide for more information than is on a standard catalog card, such as control information concerning selection and processing of the document, as well as information about article citations and feedback from users. Benenfeld's report is sufficiently complete to be of use in design of a local, internal processing format.

Another study at Project INTREX (Lufkin, 86) investigated aspects of subject indexing. The learning period for librarians was three months, and for students, two months. This study also demonstrated that per-page indexing time and number of subject terms are dependent on document length. Moreover, consistency in indexing increased with increasing length of the document.

The City University Library in London (Cowburn & Enright, 39) produces a line-a-title, alphabetical subject index, as well as a classified index arranged by UDC. Hanson (57) describes the system and the programs that produce the indexes. Freeman (53) provides a thoughtful discussion of questions concerning classification that a system designer should consider. Freeman points out the importance of the relationship between the decision to reclassify a library and the decision to computerize a library catalog. In particular, existing distinctions among various library catalogs will lose significance, and the relative ability to employ a classification scheme in efficient search and retrieval will be enhanced. Although Freeman does not discuss relative merits of various classification schemes for use in machine searching, he does define questions to be answered, and any librarian contemplating reclassification should attempt to develop answers to Freeman's questions.

One indication of the advance of library automation is the increasing attention being paid to conversion of large files of catalog records. Krinos (81) ably analyzed cost factors in conversion processes and found that direct labor contributes nearly 90% to conversion costs; he warns that assumptions for labor cost and keying rate are critical. Krinos's analysis should be of assistance at the initiation of design of a conversion project. Dolby et al. (48) analyzed five studies of conversion costs and summarized their findings for convenient use. These authors suggest that costs may rise exponentially to the length of the record. Chapin & Pretzer (34) conducted a comparative investigation into costs of conversion by keypunching, paper-tape typewriting, and optical scanning by a service bureau while converting a truncated record from the shelf list into a machine-readable book card. There was no significant difference among the three techniques, except that paper-tape typewriting was slightly higher. Black (22) reports on conversion of full catalog records for more than 110,000 titles. Conversion maintained upper- and lower-case characters and diacriticals. A service bureau, using keypunching, carried out the initial conversion of 55,000 titles. Cost was approximately 60¢ per title.

Balfour (13) delineated an on-line conversion project employing IBM DATATEXT at the State University of New York at Buffalo. DATATEXT costs are sensitive to telephone-line charges, and, with inclusion of charges for a line between Buffalo and Cleveland, direct costs for conversion during the first six months of operation were 55¢ per title. P. E. Parker (102) published an article containing details of preparation of bibliographic data for conversion to MARC records, and Simmons (126) analyzed the cost to the Library of Congress, for one month, for conversion of catalog records to MARC format. Since Simmons did not employ a unit-cost technique, the overall cost was high—$1.57 per record.

Project INTREX (90) studied the economic feasibility of converting and communicating catalog records to a central file via an on-line teletypewriter terminal and an off-line paper-tape device. The study revealed an on-line operation cost of "$41.07 per file of ten records, whereas the cost of paper-tape input [was] $23.46 per file." Six files were used in each test. This investigation was really a study in conversion costs for the complex record employed in the INTREX augmented catalog system, and conversion costs of $2.35 and $4.11 per bibliographic record are high indeed.

The first section of this chapter discussed development for the MARC II distribution service to begin early in 1969. Experience with automation at the Library of Congress is covered in two articles (Reimers, 113, 114). Avram published a full report (6) on the original MARC project that is the major source of detailed information on that pilot effort. She also produced useful summaries (5, 7, 8) of the development and profitable experience with the original project. Other members of the Library of Congress produced a general description of the MARC system (Leach, 82), aspects of design problems from MARC magnetic tape formats (Knapp, 77), and a discussion of special characters and diacritical marks in Roman alphabets (Rather, 110).

J. P. Kennedy (66) portrayed use of MARC records at the Georgia Institute of Technology, where catalog cards are produced from MARC tapes. The system employs a Burroughs 5500 computer and a Flexowriter to print the cards. However, the Flexowriter proved an unreliable device at Georgia Tech, although it appears to have performed well elsewhere. Cost of production of catalog cards from a source file on tape is usually sensitive to size of the file and such is the case at Georgia Tech. However, during the latter part of the first half-year of operation, cards cost 9¢ each, and toward the end of the first year, Georgia Tech found that over half of all English language monographs cataloged were on the MARC file. Similarly, Bregzis (26) at the University of Toronto discovered that, in the early period of use of MARC tape, about one-half of Toronto's acquisitions of recently published books in English were represented by records on the tapes.

As most recently reported, the University of Chicago's on-line system (University of Chicago, 145; Payne, 106; Hecht, 60) employs keyboard operators to communicate bibliographic data prepared by catalogers to the central file. The complementary papers by Payne and Hecht contain the most detailed descriptions of the sophisticated Chicago system that have yet appeared. The off-line catalog card production is one of fewer than a half-dozen systems that produce cards in packs, alphabetized for filing in a specific catalog. Hecht's paper portrays the system concepts and some details of development of the computer programs, which now run on an IBM 360/50 having 512K bytes of core storage; the operating system under which the programs run is IBM-OS-MVT. Bregzis (27) depicted a query language for catalogers to use in on-line cataloging employing a CRT terminal.

As was indicated earlier, British public librarians have been more active in library computerization than have their colleagues in the United States. Maidment (88) elaborates on computer applications in public libraries, employing as a base of discussion his own library in the London Borough of Camden. He enticingly alludes to an inversion of work flow in technical processing, made possible by punch cards, whereby books go to the accessions department after they have been cataloged and classified; he reports that some of his *confrères* viewed this reversal as "almost immoral." Maidment's library has been putting out a book-form catalog for several years that is a union catalog for branches. The Dorset County Library (Carter, 32) has produced a book-form catalog of sets of plays, as well as a book-form subject catalog for the whole collection. The Atomic Weapons Research Establishment at Aldermaston (Ayres et al., 11) operates an integrated technical processing system based on an IBM 870 Document Writing System. Originally the 870 produced a book-form title list with UDC and author indexes, but, after two such catalogs were produced, the 870 became overburdened, so catalog production has been transferred to a computer.

The best paper on book catalogs to appear recently is Johnson's article on the highly successful book catalog for the Stanford undergraduate library (64). Perhaps the most important departure from classical librarianship is the abandonment of the main-entry concept in this catalog. Johnson also describes in useful detail solutions to various problems of alphabetizing entries and headings in a book-form catalog. Roberts (115) also published data helpful in sorting entries in book-form catalogs.

Another excellent description of book catalog production is in the Lawrence Radiation Laboratory report (Boylan et al., 25). The section of this report on catalogs contains useful detail and illuminating illustrations. The Naval Ship Missile Systems Engineering Station at Port Hueneme, California, has a book-form catalog encompassing a hundred thousand titles (Franke, 52). Kountz (80), at the County of Orange Public Library in California, studied comparative costs of computer and manual catalog maintenance. He demonstrated the extent to which cost per entry in a manual catalog is dependent upon number of files maintained. The Library maintains 26 files, and the cost of a computer-produced book-form catalog in 400 copies was much lower than that for manual maintenance. J. Becker (17) describes an interesting Italian project, which produced a 39-volume, computer-composed, book-form catalog containing 650,000 entries from the Italian national bibliography. This task was accomplished on an IBM 360/30 and an IBM 1403 printer. The author section of the book-form catalog at Bochum contains approximately 110,000 entries (Pflug & Adams, 109).

The Lorain County Community College in Lorain, Ohio, possesses an ingenious integrated technical processing system based on an IBM 1440 computer and on a Friden Flexowriter, which selectively drives an IBM

026 keypunch (Scott, 124). This system enabled a single cataloger to process 11,000 titles in a year. One of the system's various products is Flexowriter-produced catalog cards. Murrill (95) reports on a system producing catalog cards and an accession list for the Philip Morris Research Library that operates on an IBM 1620 computer and an IBM 870 Document Writing System. The programs are written in FORTRAN II. Kilgour (69) published a cost study of catalog card production during three years at the Yale Medical Library. An IBM 1401 manufactured the cards. With computer charges at $20 per hour, finished cards in packs destined for individual catalogs, but not alphabetized for filing, cost less than 10¢ per card. Weisbrod (150) published a description of the Yale Bibliographic System of card production that replaced the Medical Library system. The YBS programs are among the few sophisticated card production programs. Written in MAD, they run on an IBM 7094-7040 Direct Couple System.

Hirst (62) reports on an IBM MT/ST application for catalog card production at Mills College of Education in New York. He includes a gratifying amount of detail concerning the development and operation of his system. During the first year of operation, his library processed 52% more books than the previous year, but typist hours per week associated with card production were 36% less.

Acquisitions

Burgess & Ames (30), at the Washington State University Library, brought the first sophisticated on-line acquisition system to operational status in April 1968. Their extensive description contains full details of operation and product. Programs are written in PL/I and run on an IBM 360/67; the Library has two IBM 1050 terminals. The Oregon State University Library (Spigai & Taylor, 128) has operated a pilot on-line library acquisitions system, which it has been developing further. The publication describing this system appears to give enough detail necessary to allow one to duplicate it. On-line acquisitions activity at the University of Chicago (Payne, 106) was nearing operational status at the end of the year.

Muller & Thomson (94) review the development and operation of the University of Michigan Libraries' computer-based book-order system and evaluate its products and cost. The cost comparison had to be made in an environment of labile computer charges and system design. To the extent that cost could be included in the analysis, there was a 2% increase from the manual system of 1963–64 to the computer system of 1965–66. However, between 1965–66 and 1966–67, the cost per book order rose 23%. Costs as reported by Muller & Thomson reveal that data processing charges went up 10.8% and salaries 27.8%, which might argue for increased mechanization.

Lawrence Radiation Laboratory's system (Boylan et al., 25) contains an automated acquisitions system, which produces printouts of open orders alphabetized, closed orders also alphabetized, and a combined listing arranged by purchase order number. The programs also put out claim notices and statistical information.

Texas A&I University has an acquisition system that operates on an IBM 1620 with 40K core storage (Morris, 92). The system operated at a level of 10,000 orders in the first year and succeeded in clearing orders more rapidly, reducing unintentional duplication, and providing automatic accounting. Ayres et al. (11) and Scott (124) describe integrated processing systems that mechanized acquisitions and cataloging activities and were mentioned in the section on catalogs above. Wedgeworth (148) at Brown University and Stevenson & Cooper (129) of The City University Library in London describe computerized book-fund accounting systems. Auld (3) and Mather (91) recount problems that arise when newly automated acquisition systems are overloaded, and some solutions. Bochum is currently experimenting with a system that has been operational since April 1967 to determine what bibliographic information should be incorporated into the record at order time to make the record useful for cataloging (Pflug & Adams, 109).

Leonard et al. (83) published the extensive results of a study designed to determine the feasibility of establishing a book-processing center for academic libraries in Colorado. Their nearly four-hundred-page report contains a vast amount of data and information that surely would be useful or at least pertinent to design of similar book-processing centers. The study recommends some initial automation—including automation of the bookkeeping system, as well as production of spine labels, book card labels, book pocket labels, and shipping lists.

Serials

Colorado also produced an interesting study of the adaptation of an existing set of programs for production of a serials book catalog (Dougherty & Stephens, 49). The authors concluded that the automated serials listing system developed in one library could be adapted to the needs of a second library, but they were uncertain as to the circumstances that would make adoption of an existing system preferable to beginning afresh. They felt that their study suggested that libraries will not find it easy to use existing programs for some operations.

The University of Minnesota Biomedical Library (Grosch, 54; Strom, 131) has a batch-mode serials control system that attempts to avoid the problems generated by the prepunched arrival card system. The computer prints a daily check-in list containing computed predictions of the next issues to be received. The check-in clerk records receipt, or receipt and differences from prediction, on the list from which updating information is keypunched. The City University Library in London (Enright, 50) has developed a similar system. Roper (117) reports on application of a theory of publication of serial issues to a batch-computerized serials control system being tested at the University of California, Los Angeles, Biomedical Library.

COMPUTERS AND LIBRARIES

Machine-Readable Data Files in Libraries

In anticipation that libraries will be acquiring and servicing data in machine-readable forms in the foreseeable future, the Institute of Library Research at the University of California issued a series of five reports (Hayes, 59; Tompkins, 138; Troutman, 139, 140; Reilly, 112) investigating various problems directly related to such activity. Troutman (139) lists over two dozen such data files. Pearson (107) depicts problems that libraries must solve and procedures to be instituted in the acquisition, processing, and servicing of data files. Pearson's document will be useful to those librarians who are confronted with the acquisition, cataloging, and servicing of magnetic tapes.

Computation

In a typically perceptive paper, R. H. Parker (105), who has been using punch cards in library operations for a much longer time than anyone else, stated,

> Not every librarian is going to have to be a master of computer operations, but every administrator does need to know a great deal, in order to plan for and administer a bibliographic system based upon computer technology. Every librarian should, within five years from this date, know as much about how computers operate as he knows about how books are printed and bound.

But, it might be added, for different reasons; indeed, Parker goes on to say that a librarian in an executive position will need to be able to evaluate system design and equipment, so that he can decide among different proposals for an application. Parker then presents a guide that librarians would do well to follow in a program of self-renewal, a need for which now exists in some degree for every professional librarian.

Gull (56) published a brief but helpful manual on flow charts and work analysis that should prove a useful guide to those not already introduced to such procedures. Burkhalter (31) issued a book of a dozen case studies of detailed analysis of existing procedures that could prove an aid when analysis in depth is required. Palmer (100) introduces the librarian to computer programming in an intelligible and effective manner. The difficulty with most elementary introductions to programming is that they are based on examples, such as square root routines, that are of no interest to librarians. Palmer's paper deals entirely with bibliographic data processing.

As a result of the development of large, sophisticated library applications, increasing attention has been paid to programming languages, for it is quite possible that the cost of development of an integrated bibliographic system could equal or exceed the purchase cost of the computer. Therefore, it is necessary to analyze the relationship between reduced development cost and increased costs of operation resulting from the employment of a specific computer language. Burgess (29) has examined this problem of relative merits of programming languages and clearly describes for librarians the functions of programming languages, and operating systems as well. Dolby et al. (48) compared characteristics of ten computer languages, including relative processing speeds obtained from a few experiments in linguistic processing. The authors point out that there is no existing computer language that possesses all characteristics desirable for bibliographic data processing. Much more work needs to be done in this area of analysis of existing languages and, perhaps, in the construction of special languages for routine bibliographic data processing. Reilly (111) analyzed four generalized file management systems (CFSS, INFOL, MARK IV, and GIS), and suggested that GIS "offers satisfactory potential" for a bibliographic retrieval system.

Alanen (2) introduces a suggestion for production of a set of subroutines used extensively and repetitively in processing bibliographic data. In addition to I/O routines, she includes in her discussion procedures for hash coding, tag generation, search function, array searching, comparison, array initialization and transfers, data packing and unpacking in word machines, data mode conversion, and sort programs.

In a provocative paper, Kochen (78) describes and illustrates opportunities for the new types of bibliographic control that computation makes possible. What distinguishes Kochen's paper from general discussions on this topic is that, in using a programming language, he presents in detail how innovation can be developed. He employs SNOBOL in his exposition, thereby avoiding the type of purely rational presentation of future events that produces adverse reaction among librarians.

Various papers presented enough detail about programs for specific applications to be of use to designers. Avram & Droz (9) describe a COBOL program that processes MARC records on an IBM 360/30 to produce subject bibliographies. Among its other accomplishments, the paper puts to rest doubts that have been raised as to whether or not COBOL could be used to process MARC records. The paper also contains an interesting detailed comparison between the MARC II Communications Format and the MARC Processing Format as employed internally at the Library of Congress. Doubts also continued to be raised as to whether or not it is possible to sort Library of Congress call numbers in filing order for a shelf list, although several centers have accomplished this not-very-difficult feat. Boyd (24) depicts such a program designed at The Queen's University of Belfast. Hanson (57), of The City University in London, describes an analogous program that maintains a subject file in classified and alphabetical order. Harris (58) briefly reports on a program used in a pilot project for processing variable-length bibliographic records. Each of these various papers contains techniques that may suggest solutions to programmers working on similar problems.

J. Becker (18) reviews developments in technology that are of interest to librarians. His paper is useful not only in describing specific equipment in areas of printing and graphics, direct digital access, and mixed media presentation, but also in providing some appreciation of the direction of current technological development.

REFLECTIONS

Library computerization has begun with computerization of existing procedures. Indeed, it is difficult to see how the course could have been otherwise; technology advances from an existing base. Radio, for its first two decades following the turn of the century, mimicked point-to-point transmission of the semaphoric telegraph introduced at the end of the eighteenth century. Radio broadcasting—a wholly new development—began in 1919, but did not become a powerful social, political, and economic force until the end of its second decade. The make-and-break telegraphic spark that Marconi, the inventor of radio, had introduced could not transmit voice. However, during the first two decades of radio's existence, research, particularly by Lee de Forest, R. A. Fessenden, and E. H. Armstrong, produced continuous-wave transmission with high-reception sensitivity, thereby making broadcasting possible.

Just as early radio engineers used radio for telegraphy, library automators are using the computer during the first decade of its application to libraries to mimic classical library techniques. At the same time, research is underway on file organization, users' needs, subject indexing, subject classification, information retrieval, and document retrieval that will surely make possible a major expansion in library function similar to that which broadcasting contributed to communication. It is not yet altogether clear how the results of research will come together with the developments of library automation to produce a wholly new activity. However, the route should not be left to chance. Rather, the definition of new objectives to be achieved should be undertaken at the present time to improve effectiveness of directed research and library automation development.

Guidance for the definition of the new objectives can also be obtained from the history of technology. The history of electric power technology furnishes an effective analogy that suggests the course of library automation development. The principal objective of early electric power installations was furnishing illumination. The first installations of power systems consisted of steam boilers, steam engines, generators, and an illumination circuit. These installations were made in lighthouses, ships, stores, factories, and homes of the well-to-do. However, it was economically impossible for the homes of workers to have individual power plants, just as it is economically impossible for smaller libraries to possess their own computers. A solution to the economic and technical problems was found in the early 1880s with the establishment of a central power station that supplied power for illumination to a group of homes, stores, and factories. At first, small regions were carved out of large cities, and there was a power station for each region. With the acceptance of alternating current that could be transmitted over great distances, formation of networks became possible.

To bring electric power networks into being, it was necessary to standardize voltages, current flow, and cycle frequency. A similar problem of standardization confronts library automation.

An analogy with the development of electric power technologies suggests a central-station type of computerization, rather than local, dedicated, library computers. Central computers will supply computing power to local libraries for cooperative sharing of information and for communication. As subsequent decades of the electric power industry have seen power applications entirely unanticipated at the time central stations first went into operation, imaginative application of research results to automation of libraries will likely produce operations quite unanticipated at the present time.

The problem of standardization, well solved by the electric power industry, has had at least one triumphant solution in library automation, namely, development and acceptance of the MARC II format for communication of files of bibliographic information. However, it remains for the MARC standard to be elaborated to include communication of single bibliographic records.

To achieve a high degree of transferability analogous to that now existing in the electric power industries of North American and Western European countries, much remains to be done with hardware/software complements that will be processing MARC II records. Development of sophisticated hardware/software complements is expensive, and it will not be economically feasible to produce the equivalent of central power stations that require individual hardware/software development at each installation.

Some library automation centers attempt to weave transferability into their designs while others disregard it. The most useful suggestion in the literature reviewed in this chapter was that of Alanen (2) for design of logical program modules. This lead should be actively pursued, as should others, such as the goal of achieving transferability in dedicated or nondedicated machines by embedding compiler systems and parameterization of programs.

Responsibility for ensuring transferability is greater for library automation systems employing dedicated computers than for systems on nondedicated machines. Undoubtedly, solutions to the problem of transferability will involve several techniques, but for an automation system on a dedicated machine, it will be necessary to attain as complete assurance as possible that the system contains not only adequate compatibility, but also the flexibility and economic feasibility to serve all types of libraries.

To summarize, it appears that major efforts in the design of library automation should be in the direction of making information available to all information users when and where they require the information. There should also be deliberate efforts to define objectives involving imaginative use of computer power for library-like operations and services. Finally, but most urgently, solutions to problems of transferability should be vigorously sought.

REFERENCES

(1) AGENBROAD, JAMES E.; BUCKLAND, LAWRENCE F.; CURRAN, ANN T.; HODGINS, DONALD D.; NUGENT, WILLIAM R.; SIMMONS, ROBERT H. NELINET—New England library information network. Progress report, July 1, 1967 —March 30, 1968. Inforonics, Inc., Cambridge, Mass., 5 April 1968, 2 vols.
(2) ALANEN, SALLY S. A library of subroutines for bibliographic data processing. In: Congress of the International Federation for Information Processing (IFIP), 4th, Edinburgh, 5–10 August 1968. Proceedings. North-Holland Publishing Co., Amsterdam, 1968, p. G13–G17.
(3) AULD, LAWRENCE. Automated book order and circulation control procedures at the Oakland University Library. Journal of Library Automation, 1:2 (June 1968) 93–109.
(4) AUSTIN, CHARLES J. MEDLARS, 1963–1967. U.S. Dept. of Health, Education, and Welfare, Public Health Service, Washington, D.C., 1968, 76 p.
(5) AVRAM, HENRIETTE D. MARC is a four-letter word—a report on the first year and a half of LC's MAchine-Readable Cataloging pilot project. Library Journal, 93:13 (July 1968) 2601-2605.
(6) AVRAM, HENRIETTE D. The MARC pilot project. Library of Congress, Washington, DC., 1968, p. 183.

(7) AVRAM, HENRIETTE D. The MARC project of the Library of Congress. Drexel Library Quarterly, 4:4 (October 1968) 279–309.
(8) AVRAM, HENRIETTE D. MARC—the first two years. Library Resources & Technical Services, 12:3 (Summer 1968) 245–250.
(9) AVRAM, HENRIETTE D.; DROZ, JULIUS R. MARC II and COBOL. Journal of Library Automation, 1:4 (December 1968) 261–272.
(10) AVRAM, HENRIETTE D.; KNAPP, JOHN F.; RATHER, LUCIA J. The MARC II format: a communications format for bibliographic data. Information Systems Office, Library of Congress, Washington, D.C., January 1968, 167 p.; Supplement One, 1968, 7 p.
(11) AYRES, F. H.; GERMAN, JANICE; LOUKES, N.; SEARLE, R. H. AMCOS (Aldermaston Mechanized Cataloguing and Order System). 2nd report: stage one operational. AWRE Library Information Note, No. 68/10 (November 1968).
(12) AYRES, F. H.; GERMAN, JANICE; LOUKES, N.; SEARLE, R. H. Author versus title: a comparative survey of the accuracy of the information which the user brings to the library catalog. Journal of Documentation, 24:4 (December 1968) 266–272.
(13) BALFOUR, FREDERICK M. Conversion of bibliographic information to machine-readable form using on-line computer terminals. Journal of Library Automation, 1:4 (December 1968) 217–226.
(14) BATEMAN, BETTY B.; FARRIS, EUGENE H. Operating a multilibrary system by using long-distance communication to an on-line computer. In: American Society for Information Science Annual Meeting, Columbus, Ohio, 20–24 October 1968. Proceedings, vol. 5. Greenwood Publishing Corp., New York, 1968, p. 155–162.
(15) BEARMAN, H. K. GORDON. Library computerization in West Sussex. Program, 2:2 (July 1968) 53–58.
(16) BECKER, A. M. Documentation and electronic data processing. American Documentation, 19:3 (July 1968) 311–316.
(17) BECKER, JOSEPH. Automation activities at the Biblioteca Nazionale Centrale, Firenze. Bethesda, Md., 15 October 1968, 55 p.
(18) BECKER, JOSEPH. New technology of interest to librarians. Drexel Library Quarterly, 4:4 (October 1968) 310–316.
(19) BENENFELD, ALAN R. Generation and encoding of the Project INTREX augmented catalog data base. Catalog Data Input Group, Electronic Systems Laboratory, Department of Electrical Engineering, Massachusetts Institute of Technology, Cambridge, August 1968, 54 p. (ESL-R-360) (M.I.T. Project DSR 70054)
(20) BIDWELL, CHARLES M.; AURICCHIO, DOMINICK. A prototype system for a computer-based statewide film library network: a model for operation. Syracuse University, Center for Instructional Communications, Syracuse, N.Y., September 1968, 31 p.
(21) BIDWELL, CHARLES M.; DAY, MURIEL L. Statewide film library network: user's manual. Syracuse University, Center for Instructional Communications, September 1968, 53 p.
(22) BLACK, DONALD V. Creation of computer input in an expanded character set. Journal of Library Automation, 1:2 (June 1968) 110–120.
(23) BLACK, DONALD V. Library information system time-sharing on a large, general-purpose computer. In: Clinic on Library Applications of Data Processing, 6th, University of Illinois, Urbana, 5–8 May 1968. Proceedings [in press] (Preprint, 26 p.)
(24) BOYD, A. H. Computer processing of Library of Congress book numbers. Program, 1:4 (January 1967) 1–7.
(25) BOYLAN, MERLE N., JR.; CROCKER, ELIZABETH L.; VERITY, JOHN B.; BUGINAS, SCOTT J.; KING, JACK L.; WOINOWSK, ORRINE. Automated acquisition, cataloging, and circulation in a large research library. Lawrence Radiation Laboratory, University of California, Livermore, 1 May 1968, 94 p. (UCRL-50406) (TID-4500, UC-32, Mathematics and Computers)
(26) BREGZIS, RITVARS. Library networks of the future. Drexel Library Quarterly, 4:4 (October 1968) 261–270.

(27) BREGZIS, RITVARS. Query language for the reactive catalogue. In: National Colloquium on Information Retrieval, 4th, Philadelphia, 3–4 May 1967. Proceedings, edited by Albert B. Tonik. International Information Incorporated, Philadelphia, 1967, p. 77–90; discussion, p. 90–91.
(28) BUNDY, MARY LEE. Automation as innovation. Drexel Library Quarterly, 4:4 (October 1968) 317–328.
(29) BURGESS, THOMAS K. Computer operating systems and programming languages: a critical review of their features and limitations for processing bibliographic text. Oral presentation to the Stanford Conference on Collaborative Library Systems Design, 5 October 1968.
(30) BURGESS, THOMAS K.; AMES, L. LOLA: Library on-line acquisitions subsystem. Washington State University, Systems Office, Pullman, July 1968, 78 p.
(31) BURKHALTER, BARTON R. Case studies in systems analysis in a university library. Scarecrow Press, Metuchen, N.J., 1968, 186 p.
(32) CARTER, KENNETH. Dorset County Library: computers and cataloguing. Program, 2:2 (July 1968) 59–67.
(33) CHAMIS, ALICE YANOSKO. The application of computers at the B. F. Goodrich Research Center Library. Special Libraries, 59:1 (January 1968) 24–29.
(34) CHAPIN, RICHARD E.; PRETZER, DALE H. Comparative costs of converting shelf list records to machine readable form. Journal of Library Automation, 1:1 (March 1968) 66–74.
(35) CHEN, CHINGH-CHIH; KINGHAM, E. ROBERT. Subject reference lists produced by computer. Journal of Library Automation, 1:3 (September 1968) 178–197.
(36) COOPER, MARIANNE. Current information dissemination—ideas and practices. Journal of Chemical Documentation, 8:4 (November 1968) 207–218.
(37) COWARD, R. E. BNB [British National Bibliography] and computers. Library Association Record (August 1968) 198–202. Presented at Annual General Meeting of Cataloguing and Indexing Group of the Library Association, 10 May 1968.
(38) COWARD, R. E. MARC record service proposals. Council of the British National Bibliography, Ltd., London, July 1968.
(39) COWBURN, L. M.; ENRIGHT, B. J. Computerized UDC subject index in The City University Library. Program, 1:8 (January 1968) 1–5.
(40) CUADRA, CARLOS A.; MERSEL, JULES. Libraries and technological forces affecting them. Presented at Conference on The Library in Society—Towards the Year 2000, School of Library Science, University of Southern California, Los Angeles, 25–26 April 1968. (Preprint, 25 p.)
(41) CUMMINGS, MARTIN M. The biomedical communications problem. In: De Reuck, Anthony; Knight, Julie, eds. Ciba Foundation symposium on communication in science: Documentation and automation. J. & A. Churchill, London; Little, Brown, Boston, 1967, p. 110–122.
(42) CUMMINGS, MARTIN M. Plans for the development of a medical library network. Bulletin of the Cleveland Medical Library Association, 15:2 (April 1968) 68–79.
(43) CUMMINGS, MARTIN M. The role of the National Library of Medicine in the national biomedical library network. Annals of the New York Academy of Sciences, 142 (31 March 1967) 503–512.
(44) CUMMINGS, MARTIN M.; SIMMONS, RALPH A. Automation in medical libraries. In: Conference on the Use of Computers in Medical Education, University of Oklahoma Medical Center, Oklahoma City, 3–5 April 1968. Proceedings. Oklahoma City, 1968, p. 74–92.
(45) DE GENNARO, RICHARD. Automation in the Harvard College Library. Harvard Library Bulletin, 16:3 (July 1968) 217–236.
(46) DE GENNARO, RICHARD. The development and administration of automated systems in academic libraries. Journal of Library Automation, 1:1 (March 1968) 75–91.
(47) DEWS, J. DAVID. Computers and libraries. Program, 1:6 (July 1967) 25–34.
(48) DOLBY, J. L.; FORSYTH, V.; RESNIKOFF, H. L. An evaluation of the utility and

cost of computerized library catalogs. U.S. Office of Education, Washington, D.C., 1968, 205 p.
(49) DOUGHERTY, RICHARD M.; STEPHENS, JAMES G. Investigation concerning the modification of the University of Illinois computerized serials book catalog to achieve an operative system at the University of Colorado Libraries. University of Colorado Libraries, Boulder, April 1968, 65 p. (NSF-GN-641) (PB-178 216)
(50) ENRIGHT, B. J. An experimental periodicals checking list. Program, 1:7 (October 1967) 4–11.
(51) EVANS, A. J.; WALL, R. A. Library mechanisation projects at Loughborough University of Technology. Program, 1:6 (July 1967) 1–4.
(52) FRANKE, RICHARD D. Computerized library catalog. Datamation, 14:2 (February 1968) 45–52.
(53) FREEMAN, ROBERT R. Trends in bibliographic data processing in the context of reclassification of libraries. In: Conference on Reclassification, University of Maryland, College Park, 4–6 April 1968. Proceedings: Reclassification, rationale and problems. Edited by Jean M. Perrault. University of Maryland, School of Library and Information Services, College Park, 1968, p. 164–178.
(54) GROSCH, AUDREY N. University of Minnesota bio-medical library serials system. Oral presentation to the Special Libraries Association Conference, Los Angeles, 1968.
(55) GROSE, M. W. The place of the librarian in the computer age. Library Association Record (August 1968) 195–197.
(56) GULL, C. D. Logical flow charts and other new techniques for the administration of libraries and information centers. Library Resources & Technical Services, 12:1 (Winter 1968) 47–66.
(57) HANSON, D. G. A computer program to maintain a subject index on magnetic tape in alphabetical and classified order. Program, 1:8 (January 1968) 6–12.
(58) HARRIS, NEVILLE. Pilot projects using variable length library records. Program, 1:8 (January 1968) 13–16.
(59) HAYES, R. M. Mechanized information services in the university library—introduction and summary. University of California, Institute of Library Research, Los Angeles, 15 December 1967, 25 p.
(60) HECHT, KENNEY. The book processing system; program development. Oral presentation to the Stanford Conference on Collaborative Library Systems Development, 4 October 1968.
(61) HENDERSON, JAMES W.; ROSENTHAL, JOSEPH A., eds. Library catalogs: their preservation and maintenance by photographic and automated techniques. M.I.T. Press, Cambridge, 1968, 267 p.
(62) HIRST, ROBERT I. Adapting the IBM MT/ST [Magnetic Tape "Selectric" Typewriter] for library applications—a manual for planning. Special Libraries, 59:8 (October 1968) 626–633.
(63) IBM CORPORATION. DATA PROCESSING DIVISION. On-line library circulation control system: Moffet Library, Midwestern University, Wichita Falls, Texas. White Plains, N.Y., 1968, 16 p.
(64) JOHNSON, RICHARD D. A book catalog at Stanford. Journal of Library Automation, 1:1 (March 1968) 13–50.
(65) JORDAN, JOHN R. A framework for comparing SDI [Selective Dissemination of Information] Systems. American Documentation, 19:3 (July 1968) 221–222.
(66) KENNEDY, JOHN P. A local MARC Project: the Georgia Tech Library. In: Clinic on Library Applications of Data Processing, 6th, University of Illinois, Urbana, 5–8 May 1968. Proceedings [in press]. (Preprint, 19 p.)
(67) KENNEDY, R. A. Bell Laboratories' library real-time loan system (BELLREL). Journal of Library Automation, 1:2 (June 1968) 128–146.
(68) KERSHAW, GEORGE; DAVIS, J. EUGENE. Mechanization in defense libraries. Datamation, 14:1 (January 1968) 48–53.
(69) KILGOUR, FREDERICK G. Costs of library catalog cards produced by computer. Journal of Library Automation, 1:2 (June 1968) 121–127.

(70) KILGOUR, FREDERICK G. Initial system design for the Ohio College Library Center: a case history. In: Clinic on Library Applications of Data Processing, 6th, University of Illinois, Urbana, 5–8 May 1968. Proceedings [in press] (Preprint, 21 p.)
(71) KILGOUR, FREDERICK G. Retrieval of single entries from a computerized library catalog file. In: American Society for Information Science Annual Meeting, Columbus, Ohio, 20–24 October 1968. Proceedings, vol. 5. Greenwood Publishing Corp., New York, 1968, p. 133–136.
(72) KILGOUR, FREDERICK G. University libraries and computation. Drexel Library Quarterly, 4:3 (July 1968) 157–176.
(73) KIMBER, R. T. Computer applications in the fields of library housekeeping and information processing. Program, 1:6 (July 1967) 5–25.
(74) KIMBER, R. T. The cost of an on-line circulation system. Program, 2:3 (October 1968) 81–94.
(75) KIMBER, R. T. The MARC II format. Program, 2:1 (April 1968) 34–40.
(76) KIMBER, R. T. An operational computerised circulation system with on-line interrogation capability. Program, 2:3 (October 1968) 75–80.
(77) KNAPP, JOHN F. Design considerations for the MARC magnetic tape formats. Library Resources & Technical Services, 12:3 (Summer 1968) 275–285.
(78) KOCHEN, MANFRED. Newer techniques for processing bibliographic information. Drexel Library Quarterly, 4:3 (July 1968) 233–258.
(79) KOCHEN, MANFRED; TAGLIACOZZO, RENATA. A study of cross-referencing. Journal of Documentation, 24:3 (September 1968) 173–191.
(80) KOUNTZ, JOHN C. Cost comparison of computer versus manual catalog maintenance. Journal of Library Automation, 1:3 (September 1968) 159–177.
(81) KRINOS, J. D. Conversion of existing library catalogues to computer files. Hamilton Standard, Division of United Aircraft Corporation, Farmington, Conn., 12 January 1968, 11 p. (SP 01U68) Presented at the fifth National Colloquium on Information Retrieval, Philadelphia, 4 May 1968.
(82) LEACH, THEODORE EDWARD. A compendium of the MARC system. Library Resources & Technical Services, 12:3 (Summer 1968) 250–275.
(83) LEONARD, LAWRENCE E.; MAIER, JOAN M.; DOUGHERTY, RICHARD M. Colorado academic libraries book processing center study. Final report, 1 February 1967–30 April 1968, on phase 1 and 2. University of Colorado, Norlin Library, Boulder, 15 June 1968, 397 p. (PB-178 421)
(84) LIBRARY OF CONGRESS. INFORMATION SYSTEMS OFFICE. Subscribers' guide to the MARC distribution service. Library of Congress, Washington, D.C., August 1968, 68 p.
(85) LIPETZ, BEN-AMI; STANGL, PETER. User clues in initiating searches in a large library catalog. In: American Society for Information Science Annual Meeting, Columbus, Ohio, 20–24 October 1968. Proceedings, vol. 5. Greenwood Publishing Corp., New York, 1968, p. 137–139.
(86) LUFKIN, RICHARD C. Determination and analysis of some parameters affecting the subject indexing process. (Thesis—B.S.). Electronic Systems Laboratory, Department of Electrical Engineering, Massachusetts Institute of Technology, Cambridge, September 1968, 47 p. (Report ESL-R-364) (M.I.T. Project DSR 70054)
(87) MACKENZIE, A. GRAHAM. Systems analysis of a university library. Program, 2:1 (April 1968) 7–14.
(88) MAIDMENT, W. R. Computer methods in public libraries. Program, 2:1 (April 1968) 1–6.
(89) MARTHALER, M. P.; McGURK, A. K. Computerised IR and catalogue production within the ISIS [Integrated Scientific Information Service] System. International Labour Office, Central Library and Documentation Branch, Geneva, 1967, 15 p. (LD/Notes/27)
(90) MASSACHUSETTS INSTITUTE OF TECHNOLOGY. PROJECT INTREX. Semi-annual Activity Report, 15 March 1968 to 15 September 1968. Cambridge, Mass.,

1968.
(91) MATHER, DAN. Data processing in an academic library: some conclusions and observations. PNLA Quarterly, 32:4 (Summer 1968) 4–21.
(92) MORRIS, NED C. Computer based acquisitions system at Texas A & I University. Journal of Library Automation, 1:1 (March 1968) 1–12.
(93) MORSE, PHILIP M. Library effectiveness: a systems approach. M.I.T. Press, Cambridge, 1968. 207 p.
(94) MULLER, ROBERT H.; THOMSON, JAMES W. The computer-based book order system at the University of Michigan Library—a review and evaluation. In: Clinic on Library Applications of Data Processing, 6th, University of Illinois, Urbana, 5–8 May 1968. Proceedings [in press] (Preprint, 19 p.)
(95) MURRILL, DONALD P. Production of library catalog cards and bulletin using an IBM 1620 computer and an IBM 870 Document Writing System. Journal of Library Automation, 1:3 (September 1968) 198–212.
(96) NATIONAL ADVISORY COMMISSION ON LIBRARIES. Library services for the nation's needs: toward fulfillment of a national policy. ALA Bulletin, 63:1 (January 1969) 67–94.
(97) NUGENT, WILLIAM R. Compression word coding techniques for information retrieval. Journal of Library Automation, 1:4 (December 1968) 250–260.
(98) NUGENT, WILLIAM R. NELINET—the New England library information network. In: Congress of the International Federation for Information Processing (IFIP), 4th, Edinburgh, 5–10 August 1968. Proceedings. North-Holland Publishing Co., Amsterdam, 1968, p. G28–G32.
(99) NUGENT, WILLIAM R. Statistics of collection overlap at the libraries of the six New England state universities. Library Resources & Technical Services, 12:1 (Winter 1968) 31–36.
(100) PALMER, FOSTER M. Computer programming for the librarian. Drexel Library Quarterly, 4:3 (July 1968) 197–213.
(101) PARKER, EDWIN B. Developing a campus information retrieval system. Oral presentation to the Stanford Conference on Collaborative Library Systems Design, 5 October 1968.
(102) PARKER, PATRICIA E. The preparation of MARC bibliographic data for machine input. Library Resources & Technical Services, 12:3 (Summer 1968) 311–319.
(103) PARKER, RALPH H. A feasibility study for a joint computer center for five Washington, D.C., university libraries. Consortium of Universities of Metropolitan Washington, D.C., May 1968, 37 p.
(104) PARKER, RALPH H. Not a shared system: an account of a computer operation designed specifically—and solely—for library use at the University of Missouri. Library Journal, 92:19 (1 November 1967) 3967–3970.
(105) PARKER, RALPH H. What a university librarian should know about computation. Drexel Library Quarterly, 4:3 (July 1968) 177–184.
(106) PAYNE, CHARLES T. The University of Chicago's book processing system. Oral presentation to the Stanford Conference on Collaborative Library Systems Development, 4 October 1968.
(107) PEARSON, KARL M., JR. Providing for machine-readable statistical data sets in university research libraries. System Development Corp., Santa Monica, Calif., 17 May 1968, 157 p. (SP-3155)
(108) PERRINE, RICHARD H. Catalog use difficulties. RQ, 7:4 (Summer 1968) 169–174.
(109) PFLUG, GUNTHER; ADAMS, BERNHARD, ed. Elecktronische Datenverarbeitüng in der Universitätsbibliothek Bochum. Bochum, 1968, 147 p.
(110) RATHER, LUCIA J. Special characters and diacritical marks used in Roman alphabets. Library Resources & Technical Services, 12:3 (Summer 1968) 285–295.
(111) REILLY, KEVIN D. Evaluation of generalized file management systems. University of California, Institute of Library Research, Los Angeles, 15 December 1967, 46 p.
(112) REILLY, KEVIN D. Nature of typical data bases. University of California, Institute

of Library Research, Los Angeles, 15 December 1967, 51 p.
(113) REIMERS, PAUL R. Automation at the Library of Congress. Information Systems Office, Library of Congress, Washington, D.C., 19 p. Presented at 15th International Meeting of Institute of Management Sciences, Cleveland, Ohio, 11–13 September 1968.
(114) REIMERS, PAUL R. The effective use of bibliographic information and the role of automation in this process. Libri, 17:4 (1967) 305–313.
(115) ROBERTS, JUSTINE. Mechanization of library procedures in the medium-sized medical library. V: Alphabetization of the book catalog. Bulletin of the Medical Library Association, 56:1 (January 1968) 71–81.
(116) ROGERS, FRANK B. Costs of operating an information retrieval service. Drexel Library Quarterly, 4:4 (October 1968) 271–278.
(117) ROPER, FRED W. A computer-based serials control system for a large biomedical library. American Documentation, 19:2 (April 1968) 151–157.
(118) RUBY, HOMER V. Computerized circulation at Illinois State Library. Illinois Libraries, 50:2 (February 1968) 159–162.
(119) RUECKING, FREDERICK H., JR. Bibliographic retrieval from bibliographic input; the hypothesis and construction of a test. Journal of Library Automation, 1:4 (December 1968) 227–238.
(120) RUECKING, FREDERICK H., JR. The circulation system of the Fondren Library, Rice University. In: Texas Conference on Library Mechanization, 1st. Proceedings. Texas Library and Historical Commission, Austin, 1966, p. 21–30. (Monograph no. 6)
(121) SALTON, GERARD. Automatic information organization and retrieval. McGraw-Hill Book Co., New York, 1968, 514 p.
(122) SARACEVIC, TEFKO; REES, ALAN M. The impact of information science on library practice. Library Journal, 93:19 (1 November 1968) 4097–4101.
(123) SCHNEIDER, JOHN H. Experimental trial of selective dissemination of biomedical information in an automated system based on a linear hierarchical decimal classification. In: American Society for Information Science Annual Meeting, Columbus, Ohio, 20–24 October 1968. Proceedings, vol. 5. Greenwood Publishing Corp., New York, 1968, p. 243–245.
(124) SCOTT, JACK W. An integrated computer based technical processing system in a small college library. Journal of Library Automation, 1:3 (September 1968) 149–158.
(125) SHOFFNER, RALPH M. Joint design and development of library systems. University of California, Institute of Library Research, Los Angeles, 15 December 1967, 35 p.
(126) SIMMONS, P. A. An analysis of bibliographic data conversion costs. Library Resources & Technical Services, 12:3 (Summer 1968) 296–311.
(127) SPEER, JACK A. Libraries and automation: a bibliography with index. Kansas State Teachers College Press, Emporia, June 1967, 106 p.
(128) SPIGAI, FRANCES; TAYLOR, MARY. A pilot—an on-line library acquisition system. Programming support: Thomas Brantner, Mary Taylor, and Neil Tokerud. Project Director: Michael A. Jennings. Oregon State University, Computer Center, Corvallis, January 1968, 105 p. (CC-68-40)
(129) STEVENSON, C. L.; COOPER, J. A. A computerised accounts system at The City University. Program, 2:1 (April 1968) 15–29.
(130) STRIEBY, IRENE M. Impact of computerization on Indiana libraries. Hawaii Library Association Journal, 23 (June 1967) 8–15. Reprint in: SLANT (November 1967, March 1968, April 1968).
(131) STROM, KAREN D. Software design for bio-medical library serials control system. In: American Society for Information Science Annual Meeting, Columbus, Ohio, 20–24 October 1968. Proceedings, vol. 5. Greenwood Publishing Corp., New York, 1968, p. 267–275.
(132) STUDER, WILLIAM J. Computer-based selective dissemination of information (SDI) service for faculty using Library of Congress Machine-Readable Catalog (MARC) Records. Doctoral dissertation, Graduate Library School, Indiana University. Aerospace Research Applications Center, Indiana University, Bloomington, Septem-

ber 1968, 253 p.
(133) SULLIVAN, TODD. Statewide film library network: system-1, specifications-files. Syracuse University, Center for Instructional Communications, Syracuse, N.Y., June 30, 1968, 54 p.
(134) SYSTEM DEVELOPMENT CORPORATION. Technology and libraries. System Development Corp., Santa Monica, Calif., 15 November 1967, 167 p.
(135) TANIS, JAMES R. A university librarian looks at automation. Drexel Library Quarterly, 4:4 (October 1968) 329–334.
(136) TAYLOR, ROBERT S. Toward the design of a college library for the seventies. Wilson Library Bulletin, 43:1 (September 1968) 44–51.
(137) THOMPSON, G. K. Computerization of information retrieval and index production in the field of economic and social development. Unesco Bulletin for Libraries, 22:2 (March–April 1968) 66–72.
(138) TOMPKINS, MARY L. Summary of symposia on mechanized information services in the university library. University of California, Institute of Library Research, Los Angeles, 15 December 1967, 91 p.
(139) TROUTMAN, JOAN C. Inventory of available data bases. University of California, Institute of Library Research, Los Angeles, 15 December 1967, 55 p.
(140) TROUTMAN, JOAN C. Standards for cataloging of magnetic tape material. University of California, Institute of Library Research, Los Angeles, 15 December 1967, 34 p.
(141) UNITED STATES OF AMERICA STANDARDS INSTITUTE. COMMITTEE ON LIBRARY WORK AND DOCUMENTATION. SUB-COMMITTEE ON MACHINE INPUT RECORDS. USA standard for a format for bibliographic information interchange on magnetic tape. USASI, New York, 1969. (USAS Z39.2–1969)
(142) UNIVERSITY OF CALIFORNIA. INSTITUTE OF LIBRARY RESEARCH. Developmental program for a center for information services. University of California, Institute of Library Research, Los Angeles, 15 December 1967, 41 p.
(143) UNIVERSITY OF CALIFORNIA. INSTITUTE OF LIBRARY RESEARCH. Preliminary specifications (hardware and software) for a center for information services. University of California, Institute of Library Research, Los Angeles, 15 December 1967, 43 p.
(144) UNIVERSITY OF CHICAGO. GRADUATE LIBRARY SCHOOL. Requirements study for future catalogs. Progress report no. 2. Chicago, March 1968, 226 p. (NSF Grant GN-432)
(145) UNIVERSITY OF CHICAGO. LIBRARY. Development of an integrated, computer-based, bibliographical data system for a large university library. Chicago, 1968, 66 p. (PB-179 426)
(146) VICKERY, B. C. Bibliographic description, arrangement, and retrieval. Journal of Documentation, 24:1 (March 1968) 1–15.
(147) WAITE, DAVID P. Developing a library automation program. Wilson Library Bulletin, 43:1 (September 1968) 52–58.
(148) WEDGEWORTH, ROBERT. Brown University Library Fund accounting system. Journal of Library Automation, 1:1 (March 1968) 51–65.
(149) WEIL, CHERIE B. Automatic retrieval of biographical reference books. Journal of Library Automation, 1:4 (December 1968) 239–249.
(150) WEISBROD, DAVID L. An integrated computerized bibliographic system for libraries. Drexel Library Quarterly, 4:3 (July 1968) 214–232.
(151) WOODS, R. G. Use of an ICT 1907 computer in Southampton University Library. Report No. 3. Program, 2:1 (April 1968) 30–33.

11 Information Networks

CARL F. J. OVERHAGE[1]
Massachusetts Institute of Technology

BACKGROUND AND CONCEPTS

The rapidly growing rate at which information is produced and used in our complex society has presented us with major problems in information transfer. We encounter these problems not only in libraries, information centers, and schools, but also in many of the operations of government and business. The handling of large amounts of information is becoming a dominant theme in the management of our way of life. We are a technologically oriented society, and we have naturally turned to our communications technology to help us perform our enormous information transfer task. Beginning with the telegraph and continuing through the telephone, through radio and television to the communications satellite, the methods of electrical signal transmission have served to distribute information to its ultimate users.

It is characteristic of all these methods that the communications channels are geographically arranged in networks. When these channels are used for the transfer of certain categories of information, they are customarily said to constitute an *information network*. In this usage, to which the present chapter owes its title, the essential feature of an information network is the utilization of a set of communications channels through which the information is transferred by electrical signals. Most of the material to be reviewed

---

[1] The author is indebted to Mr. Joseph Becker, the senior author of last year's chapter on information networks, for valuable advice and useful citations. Dr. Jordan Baruch kindly made available a copy of the Educational Information Network (EIN) directory assembled by EDUCOM. Miss Rebecca Taggart, Head of the M.I.T. Engineering Libraries, and her resourceful staff responded cheerfully and effectively to numerous requests for documents from the bibliographic jungle of information science and technology.

in this chapter deals with advances in this kind of information network.

But our language is not controlled by communications engineers, and the word "network" is used in many other ways, even within the limited domain of information science and technology. To clarify, at the outset, what will be discussed in this chapter and what will be omitted, the table shows five clearly separable contexts in which the word "network" has been used. The present chapter will emphasize Networks D and E.

NETWORKS

Type	Context	Example
A	Science literature	Citation-linked papers
B	Organization structures	ERIC clearinghouses
C	Cooperative arrangements	Interlibrary loans
D	Communications systems	Press wire services
E	Computer-communications systems	NASA Recon system

Networks A: Science Literature

In discussing the literature of science, Price (109), in 1965, referred to "the total world network of scientific papers" and examined "the special relationship which is given by the citation of one paper by another in its footnotes or bibliography." More recently, the term has been used in a similar way by Garfield (58):

> The literature (of science) is a heavily crosslinked network. The clearly visible linkages are those ordinarily provided by authors in the forms of explicit citations.

Networks of this type are discussed in Chapter 1 of this review in the broader context of the problem of communications among scientists and engineers.

Networks B: Organization Structures

The view of a network as an organizational structure of functionally connected elements, without specific characterization of the communications links, is clearly reflected in the language used by the Educational Resources Information Center (ERIC) to describe its operations. ERIC is a national system for the widespread distribution of research results and research-related materials in the field of education. Its aim is to provide effective links between universities, professional organizations, school systems, and boards of education by making available all research results where they are needed and when they are needed by the users.

Sponsored and directed by the U.S. Office of Education, ERIC is based on the excellent concept that the research literature of education should be monitored, acquired, evaluated, abstracted, and indexed by a group of specialized centers or clearinghouses, each responsible for a specific subfield of education, and each staffed by a group of experts working in that subfield. Thus a group at Stanford University handles educational media and technology; a group at Ohio State University looks after science education; and there are 17 other such clearinghouses. Each clearinghouse generates its own reference materials (newsletters, bulletins, bibliographies, research reviews, and interpretive studies), besides contributing to common reference publications. In the world of scholarly communications, this system is one of the brightest advances of recent years. A concise description of the system is contained in a brochure (141) published by the Office of Education; a more detailed account has been given by Marron (88); and a critical evaluation of ERIC has been presented by Burchinal (25). The three papers refer to the system as a "network." A paper on the development of a thesaurus for ERIC by Eller & Panek (50) opens with the statement that ERIC "is a decentralized network of education subject-oriented clearinghouses . . . ."

Networks of this kind, however important their function and however superior their performance, are not the primary topic of this chapter. No discussion will be given of the important national information systems that are under development in chemistry by Chemical Abstracts Service, in physics by the American Institute of Physics, and in other fields of knowledge by other agencies.

Networks C: Interlibrary Cooperation

Cooperation through interlibrary loan arrangements has long been a tradition among librarians, and the pattern of these arrangements is often called a network. With the large increase in the flow of newly published materials, such arrangements have taken on greater importance than ever. The Federal Government has recognized the value of interlibrary cooperation and is providing financial assistance through the Library Services and Construction Act. In a broad survey of developments that currently affect the library's role in the dissemination of knowledge, Lorenz (85) has pointed out the potential significance of this contribution of the Federal Government. He explains that "interlibrary cooperation is defined as the establishment and operation of systems or networks of libraries, including State, school, college and university, public, and special libraries, working together to provide maximum effective use of funds in providing services to all library users."

Cooperative arrangements between libraries may or may not involve the utilization of communications networks for the transfer of information by electrical signals. In the absence of such communications facilities, the arrangements will be designated as networks C and excluded from review in this chapter. Interlibrary arrangements supported by electrical information transfer techniques will be considered as networks D or networks E, and advances in their operation will be reviewed.

Networks D: Communications Systems

Communications networks for information transfer differ among one another not only in the character of the signal (audio, video, digital data) and the method of transmission (wire, radio), but also in the structure of the network. We find, for example, that some systems (centralized networks) consist of a set of terminals clustered around a single central station, while others (distributed networks) consist of interconnected stations, each of which can communicate directly with each other station.

The private teletype networks that connect the head offices of many organizations with their branch offices are typical of centralized networks. Teletype links between libraries in an interlibrary loan network are also often centralized with respect to a State Library. In press wire services, a number of State and regional centers serve as secondary network nodes between local bureaus and national headquarters.

The telephone system of the United States is the great prototype of a distributed network. It is the ubiquitous communications facility, in which local centralized networks are interconnected by multiple paths. The network serves its subscribers in a great variety of functions. Many different information systems are embedded in the telephone network: we can obtain prompt information from directory services, weather bureaus, stock brokers, reference librarians, poison control centers, and countless others.

Wherever an information system functions by providing responses over a set of teletype or telephone channels without the intervention of computers, we are dealing with a network in the category of this section.

Networks E: Computer-Communications Systems

A major increase in the information transfer effectiveness of a communications network is achieved when a high-speed computer is used to store and process digitally encoded information. In fact, it is the combination of computers, data circuits, and user terminals that constitutes an information network in the modern sense, in which it has come to be recognized as a major resource in the operation of our society.

In the introduction to a paper that seeks to place the field of computer-communications systems in an overall perspective, Bauer (12) predicts:

Nearly all computers will be imbedded in and integrated with communications systems. As time goes on, these computer/communications systems will grow increasingly from relatively simple systems to larger, more complex and more comprehensive systems, with smaller systems integrated to form larger systems, and these used to form still larger systems in an ever-increasing interconnecting network.

The paper stresses the mutually supporting roles of the two technologies: communications techniques are essential to the internal operations of large computers, and computers are used to perform many tasks in the operation of communications networks.

The distinction between centralized and distributed networks applies to computer networks as it did to communications networks. Up to now, most computer networks have been centralized; a single computer facility has served a community of users at remote terminals. With the further development and proliferation of computer networks, we shall encounter networks of interconnected computers. Plans for such distributed computer networks have been formulated, and experimental systems are in operation. References will be included in subsequent sections. One of the most far-reaching schemes is the Advanced Research Projects Agency of the Department of Defense (ARPA) plan for a network of 35 interconnected computers at 16 locations. The EDUNET interuniversity network envisioned by the Interuniversity Communications Council (EDUCOM) is similar in its arrangements for the exchange of digital data and will include capabilities for handling video signals for educational television, personal video interchange, and facsimile. The Biomedical Communications Network planned by the National Library of Medicine will combine the characteristics of a network C and a network E.

In a review of communications techniques that are now under development for digital data networks, Simms (129) estimates that "there are today on the order of 1,000 computer systems providing access from remote terminals." The rate at which data can be transmitted over communications channels is a critical factor in the operation of information networks, and substantial progress is being made toward higher data rates. Kretzmer (78) describes the evolution of new data sets that will more effectively utilize the bandwidth of existing voice channels. A paper by Kaplan (75) on new communications technology considers the system aspects of computer networks and describes progress in transmission and multiplexing technology, in switching systems, and in store-and-forward systems.

Davies (38) has examined the characteristics of present and planned telephone systems and finds them in some respects less than ideally suited to real-time computer applications. He foresees a separate data network that takes care not only of these applications, but also of the signaling and control communications for the telephone network. A proposed design for such a network is discussed in a group of four papers (9, 39, 121, 143) by Davies and his collaborators at the National Physical Laboratory.

The time-shared use of a large computer by many persons at different terminals is being widely adopted for so many purposes that one can foresee regional and national networks of computers operated as general utilities. The organizational structure of such utilities is discussed in a fundamental paper by Dennis (43), in which he urges the development of public, message-switched communications services for internal traffic as an essential step in creating a free-enterprise information service industry.

Prospectus

Only Networks D and E involve information transfer by electrical communications, and only networks of these types will be discussed in the remainder of this chapter. The distinction between the two categories consists of the absence or presence of computers; this will almost everywhere be obvious without the explicit use of the letter designations.

Within the scope thus defined, the most useful classification of information networks will be obtained when we consider the nature of the information that is processed in the network. Educational information will be uppermost in the minds of most readers of this review and is the subject of the section entitled *Networks for Knowledge.* Classroom functions, library functions, and multipurpose networks are reviewed in separate subsections. The second major section deals with *Medical Networks.* What remains to be discussed is the large and important group of networks that serve the purposes of Government and business. The omission of this group would ignore the influence that these applications have had and will continue to have in shaping the technology of information transfer. In a brief section entitled *Government and Business Networks,* a few examples have been selected within an enormous range that extends from social security and law enforcement to fuel oil deliveries and menu planning.

There is one final matter with which we shall deal outside this subject-oriented classification of information networks. The rapidity with which information can be processed in a computer network has made it possible to design systems in which the input data consist of physical measurements of a changing situation, and the output data consist of control signals that operate on the same situation. This possibility has been exploited in the control of weapons and satellites. The discussion of the resulting rather special systems has been removed from the context of other government systems into a separate section on *Real-Time Information Networks.*

The chapter will conclude with a section on *Problems and Prospects.*

NETWORKS FOR KNOWLEDGE

When President Lyndon Johnson first used the felicitous phrase "networks for knowledge" in 1967, he was speaking in the context of broad social improvements. He urged that our new technology be used to bring the educational resources of a prosperous and successful society to the world of the poor and disadvantaged. His emphasis was on educational television broadcasting, but the concept is broad enough to cover the computer-communications networks of this section. No better term could be devised for networks that serve the purposes of education.

In 1968, the term was used by the 90th Congress in amending the Higher Education Act of 1965. A new part was inserted as "Title VIII — Networks for Knowledge." It is directed toward the sharing of resources through cooperative arrangements among colleges and universities, and it authorizes the Commissioner of Education to provide financial support for such arrangements. The Act (140) specifically refers to the joint use of classroom, library, and laboratory facilities, to interinstitutional catalogs and systems for electronic transmission of materials, to jointly operated closed-circuit television facilities, and to joint computer networks serving administrative and instructional purposes. The amounts authorized in the Act for the purposes of Title VIII are $340,000 for fiscal year 1969; $4,000,000 for fiscal year 1970; and $15,000,000 for fiscal year 1971, but no funds were appropriated by the 90th Congress prior to its adjournment.

Classroom Functions

Among the many purposes that are to be achieved by networks for knowledge, we first consider the improvement of those processes of teaching and learning that normally take place in a classroom. The persons who are physically present in a classroom at a given time represent the total range of the interaction between teacher and students in a conventional learning situation. The growing demands on education and the shortage of good teachers have given rise to many attempts to extend that interaction both in space and in time.

Most of the early efforts in this direction led to systems in which the student is a passive listener or viewer. A lecture may be transmitted to an overflow audience by closed-circuit television; it may be disseminated by video cables or microwave links through a school system; it may be sent into the homes connected by video cable to a community antenna television system (CATV); it may be publicly broadcast; it may be recorded on photographic film or magnetic tape so that prints can be used at different times and in different places. Some systems enable teachers or students to select the material they want at a given time. Dial-access systems have been designed for audio and video instruction in which any one of a large set of lectures can be reproduced for individual students on demand.

The first step toward systems in which the student can play a more active part has generally consisted of providing audio feedback from the student to the teacher over a voice line. A number of the better video diffusion systems provide this capability, and some educational television broadcasts encourage response by telephone.

A closed-circuit talk-back television network is used in Florida to disseminate extension courses from a center operated by the University of Florida to six remote locations. A two-way audio system with a limited graphic display capability is in operation among 15 high schools in Texas. Brief descriptions of both systems are contained in an EDUCOM article (56) on functioning media networks.

The next step has been the involvement of the computer. This offers a wholly new set of opportunities, not only for increased interaction by the student, but also for individualizing the sequence and the pace of the learning process. Computer-aided instruction (CAI) has become a large, active, and controversial field of endeavor. An excellent survey of its state in mid-1968 has been published by Zinn (145) who has also prepared a most valuable annotated bibliography (144) on the interactive use of computers for instruction. At the 1968 IFIPS Congress, a survey paper on the interaction of computer science and education was presented by Forsythe (52). He draws a clear distinction between computing for education (which includes computer-aided instruction) and education about computers, and he presents an overview, with 84 references, of all the ways in which computer science and education are now interacting.

A system of computer-aided instruction in which a number of student consoles are connected to a central computer is a computer-communication network of the type termed network E in this chapter. Such an information network acquires particular interest when the terminals are geographically spread over an extended area. A multicampus network of this type is in operation in New York State, where units of the State University and of the City University of New York are connected to a central computer by a network that extends from Buffalo to Long Island. The initial subjects of instruction, as listed in an early report by Lambe (79), included elementary German, French, and statistics.

Suppes (138) has reviewed the experience gained with programs developed at Stanford University in drill-and-practice mathematics, tutorial logic and algebra, tutorial Russian, and other subjects. In some of these programs, the computer in California was interactively connected with students in Kentucky and Mississippi.

A very interesting attempt to use computer-aided instruction in conjunction with a bibliographic data bank is in progress at the Vision Information

Center at Boston; it will be discussed in the section on Medical Networks.

The justly famous Dartmouth time-sharing computing system has provided on-line computer service to a number of secondary schools and colleges, but it is not a CAI system in the usual sense. As Kemeny & Kurtz (76) clearly point out in a 1967 report on this system, there is a distinction between two entirely different ways of using computers in instruction:

> One is to use them as teaching machines; to have the machine teach the student. . . . The other use is to have the students program the computer; in effect, here the student is the teacher and the machine learns.

The Dartmouth effort is concentrated on the second use; it stems from the belief that "learning to use a high-speed computer should be an essential part of a liberal education."

Many other regional networks have been created to make the services of a central computer available to a group of universities and colleges. The University of Iowa (69) and 10 area colleges have announced plans for an experimental computer network designed to stimulate computer use in research and teaching. A similar regional network in western Pennsylvania and West Virginia has been established by the Carnegie-Mellon University (29) at Pittsburgh for 10 colleges and universities and 7 secondary schools and school districts. Both networks are examples of a group of such projects sponsored by the National Science Foundation.

Classroom functions are also served by many of the multipurpose networks that will be discussed below. Bibliographic information in the whole area of instructional films, television, radio, programmed instruction, computer-aided instruction, and other audiovisual means of teaching is disseminated on a continuing basis by the ERIC Clearinghouse on Educational Media and Technology through the central ERIC publication *Research in Education* (114). The chapter by Silberman & Filep (127) in Volume 3 of this *Review* presents a comprehensive introduction.

Library Functions: Communications Networks

Nowhere has the impact of the recent acceleration of knowledge been stronger than in the operation of libraries where this knowledge must be made accessible to all who have a need for it. The first level on which new technology has been extensively applied toward the solution of this problem is the improvement of communications between libraries that participate in interlibrary loan arrangements. Thus, we find a great increase in the number of teletype links between libraries, and there is some experimentation with facsimile transmission. In the interest of strengthening service to all users, libraries in many States are grouped into multilevel organizations, with community libraries being backed up by area and regional reference centers, and ultimately by the State Library. Examples of States in which networks are in operation for more effective interlibrary cooperation are California, Florida, Idaho, Indiana, Kansas, Nebraska, New York, Oklahoma, Texas, and West Virginia. A library telecommunications directory (83), updated through July 1968, contains 416 listings of libraries in the United States and Canada using teletype for interlibrary communications.

In the State of New York, a pilot program in expanded interlibrary loan service is organized around the State Library, which serves as the referral agency and the hub and monitor of transactions supported by three major public libraries and nine of the largest subject resource libraries. All are interconnected by teletype; a set of facsimile links was used experimentally but discontinued in 1968. Local libraries wishing to use the network forward their loan requests by teletype or mail to the State Library. An evaluation of this pilot program was made in 1968 by Nelson Associates (96). The principal finding is that, while the operations have not established the inherent value of this particular interlibrary loan concept, the program is an important source of planning data and should be continued. Recent procedural changes have improved the performance of the network, and a follow-on report is to be issued in 1969. Notwithstanding their limitations, State networks have been of tremendous value in placing the total library resources of a large region at the disposal of users whose needs could not be fully met by their local libraries.

Although cooperative networks between university libraries serve a smaller clientele than the statewide or regional networks with which they may be integrated, the information demands of academic communities are substantial, and the network traffic may be heavy between cooperating universities. Several effective university networks are cited by Pizer (106): seven university medical libraries in Kentucky, North Carolina, and Virginia organized a network and found that interinstitutional library use increased 84%; eight colleges in the Finger Lakes region of New York organized a college center to provide common technical services and improved communications for member libraries; Five Associated University Libraries (FAUL) in New York and the Ohio College Library Center formulated plans for research on cooperative programs and centralized systems. [The State University of New York (SUNY) Biomedical Communication Network, which interconnects nine medical libraries, is built around a central computer at the SUNY Upstate Medical Center Library in Syracuse. Its operation will be discussed in the section on Medical Networks.]

To assist interlibrary loan activities among medical libraries in the metropolitan Detroit area, a serials automation project (90) centered at Wayne State University is preparing a union list of serials for more than 20 medical libraries. A regional reference and interlibrary loan service to non-profit institutional libraries in Pennsylvania, Delaware, and part of New Jersey was initiated in 1968 by the Library of the College of Physicians of Philadelphia (33) under a grant from the National Library of Medicine.

Regional access to scientific and technical information in the New York metropolitan area has been studied by a group under Shank (124), designated as the Science Library Project of the New York Metropolitan Reference and Research Library Agency, Inc. (METRO). The group recommends the creation of an organized network of libraries and information services with communications capabilities for technical data, bibliographic information, and visual images of library materials. Research and development is urged toward "a fully integrated system of information resources and information transfer facilities in the New York metropolitan region."

Library Functions: Computer-Communications Networks

Beyond the improvement of interlibrary communications, a more powerful attack on the information transfer problems of today's libraries is under way through the employment of high-speed digital computers. Computer-communications technology has been used primarily to construct bibliographic data networks that greatly extend the power of the reference librarian and enable many users to conduct effective searches directly from a computer terminal. One of the best features of such networks is their capability for combining the resources of different libraries. Such multi-library operations appear so promising that there has been a good deal of discussion on national bibliographic networks.

In the United States, the outstanding treatment of the problems of national information systems is still the System Development Corporation's 1965 report by Carter et al. (30). The need for a national document-handling system for science and technology has been reiterated by Borko (19) in the context of the larger vision of a World Science Information System. Simpson (130), in a searching analysis of trends, has predicted that the Federal Government's role will be dominant in the national information system of the future. The mechanism through which this pattern will evolve is standardization, first enforced within the Government, then adopted everywhere, of report formats and bibliographic data. The major producers of scientific and technical information (industry, universities, and research institutes), he says, "have been only remotely and casually concerned with the evolving U.S. information system."

The many circumstances that favor the growth of national information systems into "a coherent array" are reviewed by Aines (2) in a paper that calls on the library community to participate in this development. It is widely believed that the creation of an integrated national information system will be achieved through the coordinated further development of the existing systems in the various disciplines. Amey (5) has examined the structure and functions of coexisting information networks. Universal coding of data in machine-readable form will permit exchanges between systems, and interactive consoles will permit direct user access, but Amey believes that interrogation of the data banks will continue to remain primarily the responsibility of the information specialist. In discussing the relationship between an emerging regional network and a national plan for a Biomedical Communications Network, Davis (41) says:

> No national network can be created out of whole cloth. It must be constituted from vigorous, lively and progressive systems, networks, programs and institutions. Such regional and local projects ... should be highly visible entities surviving and viable because of the local freedom of initiative responsible for their very creation.

In a recent evaluation of prospects for a national information network in the United States, Becker (13) identifies the most important features in the design of such a network as formal organization, adequate provision for communications, bidirectional operation, and a directory and switching capability. "What we need most of all," he writes, "is a workable plan, not a rigid blueprint but a flexible framework for evolutionary network development, that will guide the growth of many emerging network programs." Becker believes that the Federal Government will provide the necessary leadership in planning the national network, and he urges combined action by the Government and the communications industry to bring about the technical integration of present and future information systems.

The National Advisory Commission on Libraries (93) has recommended the establishment of a Federal Institute of Library and Information Science, which "should have as one of its major responsibilities the system engineering and technical direction involved in the design and implementation of an integrated national library and information system."

In Great Britain, Dammers (36) presents the case for a national information network in which information would be digitally stored in mass memory devices, electrically transmitted to user terminals, and delivered as print through typographic output devices. He believes that such a network might become technically and economically feasible by 1972.

A worldwide science information system is under study by a joint ICSU-

UNESCO committee (51). The system is described in the committee's guidelines as "a flexible network based on the voluntary coordination of existing and future information services." Chapter 12 of this volume deals more comprehensively with international endeavors in the information field.

One of the most impressive component networks of an ultimate national system is the NASA Recon network, which consists of a number of remotely located consoles linked to a central computer by common-carrier telegraph lines. The user can search a file of 270,000 citations by subject terms, author, corporate source, and report or contract number. In an early evaluation conducted primarily at the Langley terminal of this network, Meister & Sullivan (89) found that the system, despite some faults, was accepted by its intended users as a significant improvement over conventional methods of information retrieval. Summit (137) describes later experiments in which the NASA bibliographic file was stored in an IBM-2321 data cell and interrogated from a remote terminal equipped with both screen display and printer. A new interactive information language (DIALOG) was used; it has special features to assist the user in the formulation and subsequent modification of his search requests.

In the field of textiles, the design of an on-line computer-based information retrieval system is described by Sheldon et al. (125). Simultaneous use of a central computer by 25 or 30 independent users will give access to document data by author or subject matter. During posting and updating, a structured thesaurus is employed as "an automatic filter for data input." Interstate and transatlantic experiments have been conducted to demonstrate the feasibility of this design.

Rice University (116) is developing a computer-based regional bibliographic reference service for 18 academic institutions in the Texas Gulf Coast region, while a long-range network plan for strengthening biological and agricultural information communications among land-grant universities and the National Agricultural Library is under study by the Interuniversity Communications Council, Inc. (EDUCOM).

To provide wholly effective library service to a user, the bibliographic access schemes that have been described must be accompanied by prompt access to the full text of any of the documents identified in the search. In most cases, this is accomplished by physical shipment of documents or photocopies. In the NASA system, full-text access is accomplished by providing, at each terminal location, a complete set of microfilm records of the documents in the system. The possibility of providing full text from a central location by means of facsimile transmission has often been discussed in planning information networks. Facsimile transmission has been proposed, for example, by Becker & Hayes (14) for implementation in the

Washington State library network by 1976. It is in limited use in existing networks, such as the Bay Area Reference Center described by Coenenberg (32). A facsimile network associated with the reference and research library resources program in New York State was abandoned during 1968 because of poor performance (97). Facsimile experiments in New York, Nevada, and Hawaii have been reviewed by Manning (87), who concludes that the promise and potential of facsimile transmission have not yet been realized. A major factor retarding the use of facsimile transmission has been its high cost under today's common-carrier tariffs.

In the networks that have been described, the purpose in transmitting bibliographic data is to assist the user in his search for information. In other networks, bibliographic data are manipulated by computers to support the operating functions of libraries (acquisition, circulation, etc.). NELINET is a network designed to provide technical processing services to a group of university libraries in New England. Nugent (100) describes the initial pilot operation, which involves batch processing of service requests, and the plans for a later time-sharing system. The functions are centered on a computer-stored catalog file and include file searches in support of cataloging operations and acquisitions, as well as the printing of cards, book pockets, and labels. Circulation control and other services may be added later. Bateman & Farris (11) describe the equipment, job functions, and procedures used to centralize procurement and cataloging for four IBM libraries. BELLREL is an on-line circulation system with a central computer connected to terminals in three libraries of Bell Telephone Laboratories. Kennedy (77) describes the system and reports on the first month's operating experience with roughly 1,500 transactions per day. Among the several objectives that are being achieved, the most important is improved service through computer pooling of dispersed library collections.

An experimental computer-communications network for scheduling the exchange of teaching films between three local film libraries and a central back-stopping library was established in New York State in 1967 by the Center for Instructional Communications of Syracuse University. As a prototype for a statewide film library network, this system has been thoroughly analyzed by Bidwell & Auricchio (17), who conclude that such a network is operable, that it will be a necessity within the next few years, and that it will not reduce operating costs.

Other Functions and Multipurpose Networks

Neither classroom instruction nor library automation were the original objectives of computer use at educational institutions. First and foremost, the computer served as a calculating machine. The manipulation of numerical data remains today the major assignment of most computer systems. The large computer facilities associated with our universities generally serve a variety of functions, and this trend toward diversity of application becomes particularly apparent as computers are connected to other computers in interuniversity networks.

Two plans for integrated multicomputer networks appear dominant in a survey of the activities of 1968: (*1*) the ARPA network, and (*2*) the Educational Information Network (EIN) of EDUCOM. The ARPA network, as described by Roberts (117), is planned as a combination of 35 computers at 16 locations from coast to coast. The number of consoles attached to these computers is estimated at 1,500. These computers are controlled by research groups that have agreed to accept a single network protocol in order to participate in network experiments. The initial interconnections will be by 2-KHz common-carrier lines.

The principal objectives in creating the ARPA network are to interchange and execute programs or data between computers. A program developed at one computer installation can operate on a data base kept at another computer. Conversely, data may be transmitted to a distant computer where a special program exists. In a given situation, one or the other procedure may be the more economical solution. Perhaps the most frequent case will be that in which only a problem statement is transmitted to a distant computer, where both the data base and the appropriate program are available. Scientific communication will derive major advantages from such connection between large computer centers. Roberts (117) says:

> The savings possible from non-duplication of effort are enormous. A network would foster the "community" use of computers. Cooperative programming would be stimulated, and in particular fields or disciplines it will be possible to achieve a "critical mass" of talent by allowing geographically separated people to work effectively in interaction with a system.

An even broader set of objectives was contemplated by EDUCOM in its 1966 Summer Study. Going beyond the integration of computer operations, the EDUCOM network is to facilitate the sharing of a wide set of educational resources among different colleges and universities. This will involve the transmission of bibliographic data and text between libraries, two-way interactive video communications between classrooms, direct access by students to large data banks and videotape libraries, rapid access to medical information in emergencies, the exchange of hospital records, programs of continuing education for persons outside the universities, and the handling of administrative information. This multimedia network concept and the evolutionary plan for its realization were reviewed by Becker & Olsen (15) in Volume 3 of this *Review*.

During 1968, EDUCOM initiated, as a first step in this comprehensive plan, an educational information network project (EIN), jointly sponsored by the Office of Education and the National Science Foundation. The purpose is to enable colleges and universities to share their computational resources with each other. The initial tasks have been described in the EDUCOM Bulletin (108). A catalog of existing computer networks is to be prepared. (More than eighty such networks have been identified.) A documentation format and techniques are to be developed so that a person in a distant college can select the computer resources that are appropriate to his problem and prepare his data in the form required for that combination of computer and program. Finally, a record-keeping system is to be established for the administration of interuniversity computer transactions.

While these large plans were under development, a number of less comprehensive multipurpose interuniversity networks were in actual operation in 1968 with considerable success. One of the most prominent of these is the Triangle Universities Computer Center (TUCC), which serves Duke University, the University of North Carolina, North Carolina State University, and some 35 smaller colleges. TUCC is geographically located at the center of a triangle formed by the three universities. With an IBM System/360 Model 75 computer at the Center and different computers at the three campus locations, the system handles computing loads of more than 1,000 jobs per day. Freeman & Pearson (55) have studied the relationship between efficiency and responsiveness in the operation of this multiprogrammed system. By offering a wide range of interactive and batch-operated services, and by running two job streams in parallel, the network has been able to satisfy its users while maintaining high efficiency. Brooks et al. (20) discuss the organizational, financial, and political factors that have been important to the success of TUCC. Location of the center on neutral ground—not on any of the campuses—is thought to be one of the chief factors, along with decentralization of customer consultation and service.

The North Carolina Computer Orientation Project (NCCOP), which is associated with TUCC, enables colleges throughout North Carolina to obtain computing service from the Center by teletype. This project, sponsored by the State Board of Higher Education, provides substantial technical assistance to participating colleges, in addition to the communications and computing services.

A multicampus regional computer center somewhat similar to TUCC has been implemented in the western part of New York State by the State University of New York. Initially it will serve four colleges of arts and science, and four community colleges. This network, of which the central facility is a CDC 6400 computer, is described by Lesser & Ralston (81), who devote particular attention to the economic factors involved in the operation. One of the most promising features of this experiment is a comprehensive plan for data-gathering and evaluation, which should yield valuable information for the rational design and operation of other networks.

The University of Georgia computer network, as described by Carmon (28), provides interesting illustrations of how far the range of problems handled on multipurpose networks may extend beyond classroom and library functions. A sawmill program, for example, takes data on the location, shapes, and sizes of knots in tree trunks and determines the way in which a trunk should be cut to yield a maximum amount of good lumber. A program called SCOUT takes data on this week's football-playing performance of next week's opponents and produces a report on the strengths and weaknesses of their offensive and defensive maneuvers.

A rather specialized but very heavy computing load in the atomic energy field is handled by remote-batch operations in a network centered on a CDC 6600 facility at the Courant Institute of Mathematical Science of New York University (35). Remote terminals are located at Dallas, Texas; Weston, Illinois; and Troy, New York.

Six land-grant universities in New England are cooperating in the development of a New England Center for Continuing Education. A six-state information network is contemplated for the transmission of voice, pictures, numerical data, teletypewriter messages, or directions for remote control of styli. In a preliminary report, Bardwell (7) surveys current network projects and facilities that are relevant to this plan.

Not all educational computer networks are centered on large universities. Bryn Mawr, Haverford, and Swarthmore Colleges have cooperated in the establishment of a computer center with a System/360 Model 44 computer at Haverford and terminals at the other two colleges (22). Franklin and Marshall College (53) formulated plans in 1967 for the organization of an Eastern Pennsylvania Information Center, which will make a large computing facility available to 50 or more small Middle-Atlantic colleges.

Space does not permit an exhaustive enumeration of the many multipurpose networks of this type that were being planned or actually operating in 1968. The network directory that is being assembled by EDUCOM, at this writing, shows over 50 university-based information networks, including the regional computer networks that are being sponsored by the National Science Foundation.

While the systems that have been presented here as networks for knowledge are, for the most part, university-oriented systems, it would be academic snobbery to overlook the important information networks that serve the needs of the press and of the intelligence agencies. What travels in those networks is more than administrative, financial, or operational information; it is substantive knowledge of a very real kind. But press and intelligence networks are not much in evidence in the professional literature of information science and technology, and this note concerning their existence is all that can be done for the present review.

MEDICAL NETWORKS

In the changing pattern of national goals, the improvement of medical care for all Americans is becoming one of the primary objectives of our society. The Federal Government is promoting the intensive involvement of science and technology in this effort and has shown a particular interest in information-handling and data processing. Medical networks serve a variety of functions. They are concerned with information about medical knowledge and also with data on patients and on hospital activities. In the former function they resemble the networks of the preceding section; in the latter function they must be able to process other types of data bases.

Medical Information Networks

During 1968, the National Library of Medicine put forward a comprehensive plan (94) for combining educational processes and information transfer operations in an integrated biomedical communications network (BCN). This network is to consist of five major functional components. The first is a library services component that will be, in essence, a computer-communications network for on-line access to the bibliographic data bases (MEDLARS and Current Catalog) of the National Library of Medicine. The hub of this service will be the Lister Hill Center for Biomedical Communications, which was established in 1968. The network will be controlled from this Center, which will be equipped with major computer and communications facilities. Here also, the input processing of the bibliographic data will be performed.

The Center for Biomedical Communications will be the first and highest level of a four-level hierarchy of access points. At the second level, where additional major computer facilities will be available, direct on-line access will be provided to the data bases at the highest level. At the third level, input/output devices and communications equipment will provide access to the files at the higher levels, while the local terminals at the fourth level are equipped only to communicate with the third-level centers but not directly with the files. The users of this network will include medical practitioners, researchers, teachers, students, and librarians. Access to full text, which must ultimately be provided in such a network with the same speed and reliability as the bibliographic citations, will be handled initially by conventional procedures at the libraries where the terminals are located. Experiments with telefacsimile, transient displays, and hard-copy printers are recommended in the plan.

The second major component of the BCN plan is designated "special information services." Rather than bibliographic data, this service will provide information itself from the professional literature, from unpublished documents, from industrial files, and from individual research scientists. The prototype of such a service is a toxicological information system. The network proposed in the BCN plan is an extension of earlier systems of a computer-operated poison information service, like the one discussed by Nodien & Rieders (99) in 1967. The technical features of this component of the network will resemble those of the library component, but the response must be more rapid and protection must be provided for proprietary information in the file. Specialized education services make up the third component of the network. This part of the plan will seek to apply new communications media to the continuing education of health workers at all levels and to the education of the medically uninformed. An audio and audiovisual service component will extend the current operations and plans of the National Medical Audiovisual Center at Atlanta. Audiovisual materials are to be disseminated by mail, teletype, telephone, data links, and television. A fifth component will provide the necessary support in data processing and data transmission facilities. Of special interest is a communications satellite pilot project, which is to operate as a three-year experiment in conjunction with the specialized education services component. The initial concentration will be on instructional television.

This ambitious plan, which is the subject of descriptive papers by Davis (41) and Simmons (128), rests on the solid foundation of the MEDLARS (Medical Literature Analysis and Retrieval System) operations of the National Library of Medicine. The initial step in BCN implementation is the new MEDLARS II computer configuration, which is to be selected in 1969 and will provide on-line access from remote terminals. Experiments with this type of operation have been going forward at the Remote Information Systems Center of the Library. Leiter & Gull (80) review the operating experience gained during five years of MEDLARS operation. They list the important features of the MEDLARS II configuration: (*1*) increased processing capability; (*2*) intermediate access storage; (*3*) time-sharing; (*4*) on-line access to data bases from remote terminals.

While the national network plan awaits approval and funding, regional efforts are going forward in similar directions. The State University of New York (SUNY) has started a biomedical communication network for nine medical libraries including the National Library of Medicine and other State and private institutions. The center of operations is at the

SUNY Upstate Medical Center Library in Syracuse. As described by Pizer (106, 107), this center will employ a staff of librarians, subject specialists, systems engineers, and programmers to supervise the operation of a computer facility with 600 million characters of data storage. The major components of the data base are: (*1*) the combined catalog records of three SUNY medical libraries from 1962 onward, plus the catalog records of the National Library of Medicine from 1966 onward; (*2*) five years' MEDLARS indexing data for more than one million journal articles; and (*3*) records showing holdings and location of more than 25,000 journal and serial titles among an important group of libraries in New York State. The user at a terminal in one of the participating libraries will be able to interrogate this file through a search request phrased in simple English, with the help of programmed instruction from the system. This regional system will provide important operating experience for the national network of which it is a precursor and of which it may become an important segment.

Under the designation "Telebiblios," a medical information system is being developed for a group of hospitals in the Chicago area. Ott (104) describes the planned operation of the system, which aims to provide at its terminals not only MEDLARS-derived bibliographic data but also the full text of the cited documents. The central computer facilities will also be made available for the voluntary filing of medical records.

The National Institute of Neurological Diseases and Blindness (NINDB) has addressed itself to the problem of disseminating specialized information that will be useful in the care and treatment of patients, in the teaching of medicine, and in medical research. The mechanism chosen for this purpose is the specialized information center. Bering (16) describes its function as "responding to appropriate questions in a substantive way using pertinent information in any form, as well as providing documents and bibliographies." The concept is in many respects similar to that which the Office of Education implemented in ERIC. Four core centers have been established in these fields: (*1*) basic neurological science, (*2*) clinical neurological problems, (*3*) vision and diseases of the eye, (*4*) speech, hearing, and communication. The application of computers is to be studied from the outset as an essential feature of these information systems. A particularly imaginative involvement of computer technology is under investigation at the Vision Information Center, (*3*) above, where the information transfer operation has been combined with instructional processes. In organizing the bibliographic access procedure for the Vision Information Center, Reinecke (113) decided to eliminate the need for an information specialist and provide direct user access without an intermediary, by programming the system for computer-aided instruction. The instructional material is taken from a programmed text on basic ophthalmology; its conversion to computer form has been described by Selig et al. (123). The bibliographic file contains literature relating to vision, from the year 1967; its indexing is controlled by a thesaurus that is fully compatible with the instructional material. Thus, a student interested in a specific subfield can go through the appropriate segment of the instructional program and follow this introduction by calling either for a list of selected references or for a display of the hierarchical arrangement of the thesaurus in the particular subfield. With this preparation, he engages in the direct use of the bibliographic data bank.

Hospital Networks

Computer-communications networks are used in medical work for the handling of many types of information other than the document stores and data banks that have been discussed. An excellent overview of medical information systems of all types is found in the chapter by Levy & Cammarn (82) in Volume 3 of this *Review*. Many hospital systems serve more than one of these functions. The discussion in the present review is limited to systems that have the characteristics of networks E, excluding those that are not planned to extend beyond the limits of a single hospital.

The largest medical-care network currently contemplated in the United States is the system that is to serve the Veterans Administration. The planning needs of this system are outlined by Rosen (118); a comprehensive planning document has been issued by the Department of Data Management of the Veterans Administration (142). With one national and seven regional data processing centers linked by telecommunications to each VA station, the network is to handle information related to a broad range of activities, including a direct patient care program that annually involves 600,000 hospital admissions, six million visits to outpatient clinics, and a budget of roughly one billion dollars. Feasibility studies are in progress on four major elements of this patient-care program: (*1*) automated hospital information systems, (*2*) clinical laboratory data systems, (*3*) pharmacy information systems, (*4*) patient treatment files. A linear programming system for dietetics has been put into experimental operation.

Repercussions of this type of planning are felt as far away as Sweden, where 15 hospitals in Stockholm County are reported (135) to be starting pilot experiments for an information network to deal with medical management, control, treatment, pharmacy operations, clinical laboratory, and inventory control.

Even the Papago Indians on their reservation in southern Arizona will be served by a medical information network. According to a news report (66), three clinics are to have terminals connected to a computer at Tucson, which will be used during off-time to provide community medical, environmental, and sociological data.

Siegel (126) describes THOMIS (Total Hospital Operating and Medical Information System), a network intended for the Downstate Medical Center of the State University of New York and its affiliated hospitals. A pilot project now working at the Center consists of an IBM 1410 computer and more than 50 IBM 1050 terminals. Among the operations included in this project are: admitting and discharging patients, ordering goods and services for hospitals and patients, billing and posting accounts, scheduling appointments, maintaining medical records for patients, and summarizing patient-care activities. Expansion is foreseen into preventive maintenance operations and dietary planning.

A computer network operated since 1967 by the Latter-Day Saints Hospital in Salt Lake City was originally used for research but has been increasingly applied to clinical programs, including heart catheterization, patient screening, and intensive care monitoring. The 20 terminals now in the system are located at distances up to 50 miles. A paper by Pryor et al. (110) gives details on the system and its uses.

Blue Cross of Central Ohio (102) has announced plans for a shared hospital accounting system that will process patient medical and financial records for hospitals extending through a 29-county area.

The hospital information service marketed by General Electric Company through its Medinet department is reported (59) to have become operational in two hospitals on administrative tasks. Later versions are to provide data processing for laboratory operations, medical records, automated mental status examinations, pharmacy operations, and other applications.

An interesting specialized use of medical information networks is the processing of analog signals. Caceres et al. (26) have studied the task of providing computer-aided interpretation of the 50 million electrocardiograms produced annually in the United States. They recommend small single-purpose computers at individual hospitals; regionally centralized large computers should serve as storage and retrieval centers for medical data pools. Abraham et al. (1) describe the use of a central computer by a group of neurophysiologists at the University of California in Los Angeles. Terminals in the investigators' laboratories transmit analog neurophysiological data to the computer, which provides statistical parameters and sequential analyses.

A number of factors that inhibit the successful use of medical information systems are discussed by Baruch (10), who points out that such systems often attempt to serve different user populations who have different conceptions of their information problems and different priorities with respect to system characteristics: "The direct patient-care population assigns first priority to speed of reliable access and training ease; the administrator assigns that rank to batch-processing ability and reliability of contents; while the researcher and educator require record continuity, batch-processing ability and modifiability." While this analysis leads to the specification of separate systems for different sets of users, there is a clear need for good communication among such separate systems, so that the system designer will be driven toward integration. Future technology may enable him to accomplish such integration without forcing unreasonable sacrifices on any one user group.

A computer-based national network in which the medical records of all persons in the United States would be made available to authorized users at remote terminals has been suggested as a way to secure important medical benefits. Full medical histories could be obtained by medical practitioners at all times, regardless of their previous knowledge of the patient. The early implementation of such a system appears unlikely; fears of possible abuses are widespread. Freed (54) discusses technical and legal protective measures applicable to such a network; he believes that adequate ways can be found to safeguard privacy and constitutional rights. Davis (40) considers the operation of a Universal Health Information Bank; he advocates the use of a Social Security number assigned at birth.

GOVERNMENT AND BUSINESS NETWORKS

The use of computers from remote terminals to accomplish administrative, financial, or operational tasks has become rather commonplace. In addition to the networks installed for their own use by many public and private organizations, a number of firms offer computer service over time-sharing networks with terminals on the premises of the clients. A 1968 directory of data centers (44) contains an estimate that more than 100 data centers offer such services. Typical of such operations is a Reaction Terminal Service (72) offered by ITT in four major cities. Central computers in California and New Jersey can each handle up to 50 customer-installed terminals simultaneously.

What is perhaps not so widely realized is that certain activities in our society are wholly dependent on the operation of information networks. Air transportation is an outstanding example. Without computer-aided reservations scheduling, no major airline could long continue to offer transportation at current fares, and without computer-communication facilities the air traffic control system would be unable to manage the utilization of the airspace. In the near future, many other activities are likely to develop similar dependence on information networks with on-line terminals: banking, trading in securities, theatre and hotel reservations, retail merchandising. The reader interested in the proliferation of information networks in this category is advised to follow the news reports in such publications as *EDP Weekly* and *Datamation*. A brief review can no longer hope to be exhaustive; it must limit itself to selected examples.

Government Networks

Many of the Federal Government's operations, such as internal revenue, social security, and military logistics, began some time ago to utilize computer-communications networks. Year by year, these networks have become more comprehensive, more powerful, and more efficient. Johnson (74) has examined the foreseeable needs of programs in health, education and welfare, and law enforcement. He cites the Government's Advanced Record System and the National Crime Information Center as illustrations of systems that involve close cooperation between Federal, State, and local authorities.

Spierer & Wills (132) give a comprehensive account of the operations of an experimental large-scale time-sharing system managed by the System Development Corporation (SDC). A modified Q-32 computer provides concurrent service to about 25 local and remote consoles. The main users are military organizations, but access is also available to other Government agencies, university groups, and industrial organizations.

A design for an integrated Federal statistical data center is discussed by Glaser et al. (60). Such a center would assemble and coordinate data from many originating agencies and would provide local or remote output of tabulations and statistical analyses in the form requested by the user. A thorough analysis of the technical and administrative problems encountered in the organization of such a center is presented.

A network created by the United States Geological Survey (95) consists of a central computer in Washington connected to four satellite computers at remote field offices. It serves both administrative and scientific needs.

The existing facilities of the Internal Revenue Service, as described by Armstrong (6), are arranged to combine all pertinent transactions for each taxpayer into a single consolidated account in a master file. Input data are converted to magnetic tapes at regional service centers; the tapes are then forwarded to a National Computer Center, which produces output tapes for return to the service centers. Bills, notices, and other documents are printed from these tapes. With the addition of communications links, this system will become a network E as defined in this review. In such an upgraded system, which is to be implemented within the next five years, field offices will have direct access to all files from display terminals distributed throughout the country.

The development of a National Crime Information Center (NCIC) was initiated by the FBI in 1965. A growing file of criminal information relating to vehicles, license plates, guns, wanted persons, etc. is under the control of an IBM360/50 computer in Washington. Access to this file is available from 64 terminals in 44 states. Local and state computers used in law enforcement are in many cases interfaced with the NCIC computer, so that over 700 law enforcement agencies now have direct access to the NCIC files. These figures are taken from a recent progress report (136), which also states that the system contained 586,000 active records in August 1968, and that a file relating to stolen, embezzled, counterfeited, or missing securities is being established. In mid-1968 the Center handled approximately 20,000 messages per day. Many spectacular instances of the success of real-time file interrogation have been reported, especially in connection with the apprehension of interstate fugitives.

Related efforts by individual States have been in the news. The Michigan State Police Department (91) is reported to be on-line with NCIC through its own B5500 computer, which handles data on suspects and on vehicles. New York State (98) has a comprehensive system for vehicle operators' license data; 70 terminals give access to an IBM 360/65 computer with 2321 data cell storage. The Ohio State Highway Patrol (101) has started a network to provide statewide access to files on vehicle registrations, operators' licenses, and stolen vehicles. The system will provide direct connection with NCIC.

State, regional, and local networks have been established for many functions other than law enforcement. Dueker (46) classifies such systems as being oriented primarily toward either management control or spatial planning. In their design, great emphasis should be placed on flexibility of use. Sawyer (120) discusses the functions of a planned regional system for the Southern California Association of Governments (six counties). These functions include fiscal, personnel, and planning administration for air pollution control, airports, parks and recreation, public works, and transportation.

The municipal information system now in operation in Los Angeles is described by Tamaru (139). In addition to payrolls, accounts payable, and inventory control, the system tackles such tasks as sanitation management and library technical services. Data on the operation of each of the city's four hundred refuse trucks is collected through six remote communication terminals. The library registration system maintains the records of more than 800,000 library users. Eleven cities in the San Gabriel Valley in California (49) plan to initiate a joint municipal data system for utility billing, financial planning, land-use management, general file management, and police statistics.

The problems of information networks for urban planning were discussed in a series of papers at a national planning conference (4) in Houston in April 1967. Of particular interest is a report by Peters & Kozik (105) on a data management demonstration study in the Lehigh-Northampton region of Pennsylvania, which aimed to develop data acquisition systems for planners and explore the use of data banks by school officials and tax assessors.

Stanley & Cranshaw (133) discuss the interesting problems involved in a management information system for Chicago's Department of Air Pollution Control. The computer will continuously receive data from a telemetered air-monitoring network and will correlate this information with meteorological and other data. This operation is expected to yield timely predictions of impending undesirable and hazardous levels of pollution.

Business Networks

The airlines reservation systems are among the largest and most prominent of the private information networks. The SABRE system of American Airlines has been in successful operation for a number of years and has grown to nearly 2,000 terminals. A new system of comparable size was put into operation in July 1968 by Eastern Airlines (48) after an expenditure of more than 2,000 man-years of effort in planning, designing, building, and testing. Another large system has been inaugurated by Continental Airlines (34). The airlines are also reported (3) to be planning a common automated reservation system for both travel agents and commercial accounts.

Operating information of a somewhat different character is needed to control the freight operations of a large railroad system. In 1968, the Southern Pacific (131) established a network extending from Texas to Oregon, with two IBM 360/65 computers, over 100 terminals, and more than 5,000 miles of private microwave lines. A smaller system for the Rio Grande is described by Day (42).

Stock quotation networks have been used by securities dealers for some time in connection with the major exchanges. Three electronics firms were reported in 1968 to be developing such services for the over-the-counter market (24). In the consumer credit field, the Household Finance Corporation (103) is connecting over 1,000 of its branch offices with an IBM 360/65 computer complex in Chicago through a nationwide interactive network. Two networks for hotel reservations were in the news in 1968: International Reservations Company (115), with computer facilities in Virginia, is initially providing services for Howard Johnson's 355 motor lodges; National Accommodations Reservations Service (67), with headquarters in Florida, has started with 25 operator centers, expects to have 100 by March 1969, and predicts 4,000 to 5,000 terminals in the system by 1971. Murphy (92) describes the file-updating performed by a central computer in a small-loan network in response to individual transactions entered at branch offices.

The Westinghouse Electric Corporation operates a private communications network, with more than 500 terminals throughout the United States linked to a UNIVAC 494 Computer at Pittsburgh. Cheek (31) describes the order processing and inventory control function of this system.

A management information system of substantial proportions has been established in the Bell System under the designation TELPORT. It uses a central GE M605 computer in a time-shared interactive mode to collect, edit, process, and retrieve data needed for reports and management decisions. Gould & Mosior (62) report that the system, as currently applied to toll network performance data, saves two months' preparation of reports and should eliminate about 300,000 pages of correspondence per year.

One of the most interesting networks for direct retrieval of factual technical data is a system developed by the Oak Ridge National Laboratory to provide data needed in evaluating the safety factors involved in nuclear power plant design. This CHORD-S (Computer Handling of Reactor Data-Safety) system became operational during 1968; it has been designed to include an impressive array of user-oriented features. There is, for example, a "lead-in" program that will guide the user to his information target without requiring him either to refer to code books or to know the structure of the data file. These user interactions are discussed by Cardwell (27) in a paper that also describes the process of building up the data file.

An on-line information service on product data in the fields of electronics, automation, and instrumentation is under study in Great Britain as an extension of a currently operating system described by Barlow (8), in which such data are selected by computer matches with a customer's interest profile and forwarded to him on printed cards.

REAL-TIME INFORMATION NETWORKS

The designation "real-time information system" has been used in the literature for two quite different purposes. Stimler & Brons (134) define a real-time data processing system as a combination of processor, communications, and terminals that provide simultaneous service to a specific number of customers, each receiving a reply to a message within a specified response time. "Real time" in this context means that the delay in a particular application is compatible with the objective. An airline reservation network is a typical real-time system under the above definition, from which the element of direct control is absent. In this review, such a system would be characterized by the terms "on-line" and "rapid response."

The second definition, to which this review adheres, states that real-time information systems continually sense and respond to selected changes in an object environment, in a manner and in a time period to enable regulation and control over events while they occur. This definition, in which direction and control are regarded as the essential features of real-time information systems, has been used by Sackman (119) in an essay concerning a public philosophy on the use of computers for the regulation and control of social affairs.

Large real-time computer-communications networks have been established for military command and control purposes, typically those of continental air defense (NORAD) and strategic air operations (SAC). The earliest important example was the Semi-Automatic Ground Environment (SAGE) system for air defense. In that nationwide network, aircraft could be continuously tracked and weapons could be directed against those that were identified as hostile. Hirsch (65) reports the release of preliminary specifications for a World Wide Military Command and Control System (WWMCCS), which will involve new data processing equipment estimated to cost $150 million at over one hundred processing centers. The specifications do not include the necessary communications subsystem, which is to be supplied by the Department of Defense.

The air traffic control system operated by the Federal Aviation Agency is in this same category. It is a rapidly evolving network of sensors (e.g., surveillance radars), communications links, and computers, all arranged to provide a data flow that gives maximum assistance to the pilots and the controllers who are responsible for flight operations.

For the control of manned space flight operations, the NASA Communications Network (NASCOM) has been established as a comprehensive real-time information system of truly global dimensions. As described by McLaughlin (86), it consists of a Real-Time Computer Center with two IBM 360/75 machines at Houston, connected through the Goddard Space Flight Center in Maryland to 18 remote communications sites, which track the spacecraft in its orbit around the earth. Fourteen of these sites are ground terminals; the remaining four are shipborne. Each site has local computers that act as message switchers and as tracking computers to position the antennas. Intermediate switching centers are operated at Canberra and Madrid.

The communications channels that make up this network exploit the full range of modern technology, from telegraph and teletype channels through conventional radio and microwave to satellite communications. Data from the spacecraft to the ground include a continuous sampling of two hundred parameters such as cabin pressure and temperature, attitude in space, heartbeat and body temperatures of crew members; these data are transmitted from the spacecraft at 51,200 bits per second. Each tracking site records, tests, and condenses these data before transmitting the information to the central communications processors (three Univac 494 machines each) at Goddard and Houston. The replies (control messages) produced by the Real-Time Computer Center are returned through the network to the local tracking stations which transmit the "up" data to the spacecraft overhead. The whole operation involves 33 Univac 1218 and 48 Univac 1230 computers, in addition to the central processors. The network is claimed to be the world's largest real-time communications system.

The use of real-time control systems has also been proposed for the monitoring of patients in hospitals, especially in intensive-care units. In the experiments performed up to now with such systems, the data supplied by the measuring instruments and processed by the computer have been presented (usually on a cathode-ray tube display) to a physician who controls the treatment of the patient. Thus the systems stop short of complete automation, just as flight control systems are designed to support rather than replace human decisions.

PROBLEMS AND PROSPECTS

Many of the obstacles that impede the flow of information in networks are restrictions that are encountered in all channels through which scientific and technical information may be transferred: access limitations based on national security or proprietary interests, considerations of privacy, copyright restrictions. The extremely fluid patterns in which information is distributed, displayed, and duplicated in information networks makes these problems rather acute in the operation of networks, but they are not unique to networks. There are, on the other hand, two problem areas that are specific to the computer-communications networks considered in this chapter. These are compatibility and regulation.

Compatibility

If the growth of computer communications networks is to lead ultimately to an integrated national information system, it will be necessary to secure agreement on a uniform manner of exchanging information among networks. This problem is generally labeled "compatibility and standardization," but this convenient tag should not obscure the need for specific problem definition. In a widely publicized letter to the Bureau of the Budget, Congressman Jack Brooks (23) points out:

> ... During our hearings, practically every witness agreed to the vital importance of "compatibility and standardization". Over the years, this term has achieved almost universal usage to describe a hazy, uncharted problem area in computer usage stemming from differences in data system design and manufacture. Within the perimeter

of this almost meaningless term lie countless problems of differing character and importance to which the term standardization has varying meaning and application . . .

A major effort to clarify this problem area is under way in the Automatic Data Processing Standards program (37) of the National Bureau of Standards. Little & Mooers (84) present a lucid statement of the rationale of this effort and the need for standardizing remote user control procedures and external data formats. Bhushan & Stotz (21) suggest specific procedures and formats that fit into the framework of existing United States standards.

A concrete step of considerable importance was the adoption, in March 1968, of the United States of America Standard Code for Information Interchange as a Federal standard (63). The use of this standard will greatly facilitate intercommunication between computer networks in the Federal establishment.

Recommendations to improve the flow of information within and among Federal, State, and local governments were made in April 1968 by an intergovernmental task force on information systems (68). Dr. Donald Hornig, President Johnson's Assistant for Science and Technology, established an *Ad Hoc* Task Group on the Interchange of Scientific and Technical Information in Machine Language (ISTIM) to review "the problem of improving the interchange of scientific and technical information." The United States Public Health Service (111) has undertaken a study on guidelines and standards for intercommunication among health facilities, regardless of the type of internal computer system they may have. Jacob (73) describes early operating experience with a standard data exchange format for cataloging descriptions used in the technical report literature. Blum (18) reports on data-element standardization work at the American Institute of Physics and its relationship to national and international standardization efforts.

Regulation

The growing interdependence of computers and communications service facilities has raised important problems of policy and regulation in the Federal Government. An inquiry into these problems was initiated late in 1966 by the Federal Communications Commission as Docket No. 16979. Irwin (71) and Scott (122) discuss the background events and examine the issues before the Commission; the first of these papers, published in 1967, forms an excellent introduction to this investigation. In a more recent paper, Irwin (70) deals with the question of options in the terminal market, with the control of communication lines, and with message-switching activities in data processing.

Because the operation of a time-sharing computer-communications network involves both data processing services and communications services, commercial service organizations of both types are interested in entering the new network market. For the common carriers, whose activities have been subject to regulation, this represents an extension into the non-regulated domain; for the data processing firms, who have operated in a free competitive market, it may mean the seeking of franchises and the filing of tariffs. A final point stressed by Irwin (71) is the difficulty of separately accounting for the costs of communications and data processing in an integrated network operation.

Greenberger (64), in reviewing these issues, concentrates on the distinction between transmission services and information services. Transmission services are subject to regulation; they are essential to the performance of information services. It does not follow, however, that information services must also be regulated; it may be possible to keep such services independent from the supporting transmission services.

Duggan (47) points out that free competition in the computer-communications field may be threatened by the proliferation of large digital computers in the nationwide telephone network. He suggests that the facilities employed in electronic switching stations (ESS) are computers that might be used to provide comprehensive data processing services to subscribers throughout the network.

The suitability of the communications services now supplied by the carriers for time-sharing computer services is itself the subject of some controversy. Quirk (112) reviews technological advances in adapting the telephone network to the needs of digital data transmission. He is optimistic about the results of cooperative planning for total computer communications systems: "Computers and communications will make beautiful music together for decades to come." Gold & Selwyn (61) take the view that the services provided by the common carriers are inadequate for the requirements of computer systems. They call for the application of existing technology to provide more specifically data-oriented communications services at lower cost, and they cite as an example the possible use of collection points to concentrate the long-distance traffic in remote real-time computer access.

The international implications of the FCC inquiry are discussed by Doyle (45), who points out that the formation of international information networks will involve communications systems that are controlled in different ways by the participating countries. The major task of coordination and standardization that will have to be performed before such networks can come into operation is further complicated by the language barriers that must be hurdled.

CONCLUSION

Critics of the information network concept have often pointed to the disparity between ambitious plans for the future and meagre results in the present. That gap has continued through 1968. Networks for knowledge have been in operation on a limited experimental scale that is small in relation to the bold plans for national systems. But experiments have generally confirmed the soundness of the network concept, and the underlying technology of computers and communications has advanced rapidly. The on-line interaction of users at remote terminals with large time-sharing computers has become almost commonplace, and we are on the threshold of network interconnections between large computers. Satellite communications are the most glamorous instance of broad progress in digital transmission techniques.

Against the brilliance of the technological outlook, the economic picture is decidedly bleak. The heroic funding that would permit information network experiments on a suitably large scale does not appear to be forthcoming. The reason is probably not just the fact that computer-communications systems are expensive. Where such systems can be justified by compelling analyses of costs vs. benefits, the necessary money has been found. The computers of the Internal Revenue Service and the network of the Federal Bureau of Investigation are illustrations in the Federal establishment; the airlines' reservation systems demonstrate the case in the private sector. But no such analyses can be made in the information field. While costs are known, benefits are not. As long ago as 1965, Fussler (57) warned the INTREX Planning Conference about this blank area on the map of information science and technology:

> There is a critical need for a sophisticated analysis of the economic values of information—broadly defined—to society. . . . What is likely to be the over-all effect upon society, measured by GNP, or whatever other measures are suitable, of increasing or diminishing the support of "informational activities"?

Until a substantial effort has been made to come to grips with this question, the arguments for support must be based on faith in intangible values. How effective that will be is shrouded in uncertainty. The pessimists will point to our school budgets; the optimists to our space program.

REFERENCES

(1) ABRAHAM, FREDERICK D.; BETYAR, LASZLO; JOHNSTON, RICHARD. An on-line multiprocessing interactive computer system for neurophysiological investigations. In: AFIPS conference proceedings, vol. 32; 1968 Spring Joint Computer Con-

ference. Thompson, Washington, D.C., p. 345–352.
(2) AINES, ANDREW A. The promise of national information systems. Library Trends, 16:3 (January 1968) 410–418.
(3) Airlines approach on-line agent system. Datamation, 14:7 (July 1968) 85–86.
(4) AMERICAN SOCIETY OF PLANNING OFFICIALS NATIONAL PLANNING CONFERENCE. Houston, Tex., April 1967. Threshold of planning information systems. Selected papers presented at the ADP workshops. American Society of Planning Officials, Chicago, 1967, 108 p.
(5) AMEY, GERALD X. Channel hierarchies for matching information sources to users' needs. In: American Society for Information Science Annual Meeting, Columbus, Ohio, 20–24 October 1968. Proceedings, vol. 5. Greenwood Publishing Corp., New York, 1968, p. 11–14.
(6) ARMSTRONG, LANCELOT W. The development and operation of the Internal Revenue Service network. In: Business Equipment Manufacturers Association. The computer: tool for management. Business Press, Elmhurst, Ill., 1968, p. 67–77.
(7) BARDWELL, JOHN D. New England land-grant network. A preliminary report. Educational Facilities Laboratories, June 1968, 94 p.
(8) BARLOW, D. H. Computer-based information service. Data Processing, 10:2 (March–April 1968) 102–110.
(9) BARTLETT, K. A. Transmission control in a local data network. In: Congress of the International Federation for Information Processing (IFIP), 4th, Edinburgh, 5–10 August 1968. Proceedings. North-Holland Publishing Co., Amsterdam, 1968.
(10) BARUCH, JORDAN J. The generalized medical information facility. In: Congress of the International Federation for Information Processing (IFIP), 4th, Edinburgh, 5–10 August 1968. Proceedings. North-Holland Publishing Co., Amsterdam, 1968, p. 19–23.
(11) BATEMAN, BETTY B.; FARRIS, EUGENE H. Operating a multilibrary system by using long-distance communications to an on-line computer. In: American Society for Information Science Annual Meeting, Columbus, Ohio, 20–24 October 1968. Proceedings, vol., 5. Greenwood Publishing Corp., New York, 1968, p. 155–162.
(12) BAUER, WALTER F. Computer/communications systems—patterns and prospects. In: Computer Communications Symposium, University of California at Los Angeles, 20–22 March 1967. Computers and communications—toward a computer utility, edited by Fred Gruenberger. Prentice-Hall, Englewood Cliffs, N.J., p. 13–37.
(13) BECKER, JOSEPH. Information network prospects in the United States. Library Trends, 17:3 (January 1969) 306–317.
(14) BECKER, JOSEPH; HAYES, ROBERT M. A proposed library network for Washington State: working paper for the Washington State Library. September 1967, 50 p.
(15) BECKER, JOSEPH; OLSEN, WALLACE C. Information networks. In: Annual review of information science and technology, vol. 3. Carlos A. Cuadra, ed. Encyclopaedia Britannica, Chicago, 1968.
(16) BERING, EDGAR A., JR. The neurological information network of the National Institute of Neurological Diseases and Blindness. Bulletin of the Medical Library Association, 55 (April 1967) 135–140.
(17) BIDWELL, CHARLES M.; AURICCHIO, DOMINICK. A prototype system for a computer-based statewide film library network. Center for Instructional Communications, Syracuse University, Syracuse, N.Y., September 1968, 53 p.
(18) BLUM, ARTHUR R. Data-element standardization as an aid in the transfer of physics information. In: American Society for Information Science Annual Meeting, Columbus, Ohio, 20–24 October 1968. Proceedings, vol. 5. Greenwood Publishing Corp., New York, 1968, p. 117–119.
(19) BORKO, HAROLD. National and international information networks in science and technology. In: AFIPS conference proceedings, vol. 33, part 2; 1968 Fall Joint Computer Conference. Thompson, Washington, D.C., p. 1469–1472.
(20) BROOKS, FREDERICK P., JR.; FERRELL, JAMES K.; GALLIE, THOMAS M. Organizational, financial, and political aspects of a three-university computing center. In: Congress of the International Federation for Information Processing (IFIP), 4th,

Edinburgh, 5–10 August 1968. Proceedings. North-Holland Publishing Co., Amsterdam, 1968.
(21) BHUSHAN, ABHAY K.; STOTZ, ROBERT H.   Procedures and standards for intercomputer communications. In: AFIPS conference proceedings, vol. 32; 1968 Spring Joint Computer Conference. Thompson, Washington, D.C., p. 95–104.
(22) Bryn Mawr, Haverford, and Swarthmore establish joint computer center. Communications of the ACM, 11:11   (November 1968) 793.
(23) Budget Director Schultze is advised of importance of standardization in DP usage by Rep. Brooks; "Optimum utilization of DP has strong unyielding support of the President and the mandate of Congress." [Correspondence] Communications of the ACM, 11:1   (January 1968) 55–56.
(24) Bunker-Ramo is victor in fight for NASD system. Datamation, 14:6   (June 1968) 105.
(25) BURCHINAL, LEE G.   Evaluation of ERIC. June 1968. U.S. Office of Education, Washington, D.C., 1968. (ED-202 449)
(26) CACERES, CESAR A.; KUSHNER, GABRIEL; WINER, DAVID E.; WEIHRER, ANNA LEA.   The key to a nationwide capability for computer analysis of medical signals: the dedicated medical signal processor. In: AFIPS conference proceedings, vol. 33, part 1; 1968 Fall Joint Computer Conference. Thompson, Washington, D.C., p. 381–385.
(27) CARDWELL, D. W.   Interactive telecommunications access by computer to design characteristics of the nation's nuclear power stations. In: AFIPS conference proceedings, vol. 33, part 1; 1968 Fall Joint Computer Conference. Thompson, Washington, D.C., p. 243–253.
(28) CARMON, JAMES L.   Education through remote terminals—The University of Georgia computer network. Computers and Automation, 17:3   (March 1968) 18–20.
(29) Carnegie-Mellon EDP Center set. EDP Weekly, 9:10   (24 June 1968) 4.
(30) CARTER, LAUNOR F.; CANTLEY, GORDON; et al.   National document-handling systems for science and technology. Wiley, New York, 1967, 344 p.
(31) CHEEK, ROBERT C.   TOPS: the Westinghouse teletype order processing and inventory control system. In: Business Equipment Manufacturers Association. The computer: tool for management. Business Press, Elmhurst, Ill., 1968, p. 78–90.
(32) COENENBERG, RICHARD.   Synergizing reference service in the San Francisco Bay region. ALA Bulletin, 62:11   (December 1968) 1379–1384.
(33) COLLEGE OF PHYSICIANS OF PHILADELPHIA.   Mid-eastern regional medical library service. [News release] Philadelphia, June 1968.
(34) Continental Airlines gets big reservation system. Datamation, 14:7   (July 1968) 106.
(35) Courant establishes 6600 network. EDP Weekly, 9:8   (10 June 1968) 3.
(36) DAMMERS, H. F.   Integrated information processing and the case for a national network. Information Storage and Retrieval, 4:2   (June 1968) 113–131. Presented at the First Cranfield International Conference on Mechanized Information Storage and Retrieval Systems, College of Aeronautics, Cranfield, England, 29–31 August 1967.
(37) Data formats in storage networks. Information Retrieval & Library Automation, 3 (1967) 3.
(38) DAVIES, D. W.   Communication networks to serve rapid-response computers. In: Congress of the International Federation for Information Processing (IFIP), 4th, Edinburgh, 5–10 August 1968. Proceedings. North-Holland Publishing Co., Amsterdam, 1968.
(39) DAVIES, D. W.   The principles of a data communication network for computers and remote peripherals. In: Congress of the International Federation for Information Processing (IFIP), 4th, Edinburgh, 5–10 August 1968. Proceedings. North-Holland Publishing Co., Amsterdam, 1968.
(40) DAVIS, RICHARD J.   Information transfer in a universal health information bank by use of the social security number. In: American Society for Information Science Annual Meeting, Columbus, Ohio, 20–24 October 1968. Proceedings, vol. 5. Greenwood Publishing Corp., New York, 1968, p. 249–253.
(41) DAVIS, RUTH M.   The relationship of regional networks to NLM's Biomedical

Communications Network. Oral presentation at the dedication exercises for the State University of New York Biomedical Communications Network, 18 October 1968. To be published.
(42) DAY, WILLIAM J. Rio Grande message switching/transportation system. In: National Conference of the Association for Computing Machinery, 23rd, Las Vegas, Nev., 27–29 August 1968. Proceedings. Brandon/Systems Press, Princeton, N.J., 1968, p. 307–319.
(43) DENNIS, JACK B. A position paper on computing and communications. In: ACM Symposium on Operating System Principles, Gatlinburg, Tenn., 1–4 October 1967. Proceedings. Communications of the ACM, 11:5 (May 1968) 370–377.
(44) Directory of data centers. Data Systems News, 9:13 (August 1968) 6, 10, 12–26, 29.
(45) DOYLE, STEPHEN E. Integration of computer research facilities with telecommunication systems: some legal problems. Law and Computer Technology, 1:4 (April 1968) 2–4.
(46) DUEKER, KENNETH J. A look at state and local information systems efforts. In: National Conference of the Association for Computing Machinery, 23rd, Las Vegas, Nev., 27–29 August 1968. Proceedings. Brandon/Systems Press, Princeton, N.J., 1968, p. 133–142.
(47) DUGGAN, MICHAEL A. Computer utilities and the ESS: accommodations or intimidations. In: National Conference of the Association for Computing Machinery, 23rd, Las Vegas, Nev., 27–29 August 1968. Proceedings. Brandon/Systems Press, Princeton, N.J., 1968, p. 201–210.
(48) Eastern implements new reservation system. Datamation, 14:9 (September 1968) 98.
(49) Eleven cities initiate joint EDO venture. Datamation, 14:9 (September 1968) 87.
(50) ELLER, JAMES L.; PANEK, ROBERT L. Thesaurus development for a decentralized information network. American Documentation, 19:3 (July 1968) 213–220.
(51) First meeting of Joint ICSU-UNESCO Committee on World-Wide Science Information System scheduled for December in Paris. Scientific Information Notes, 9 (October-November 1967) 9.
(52) FORSYTHE, G. E. Computer science and education. In: Congress of the International Federation for Information Processing (IFIP), 4th, Edinburgh, 5–10 August 1968. Proceedings. North-Holland Publishing Co., Amsterdam, 1968, p. 92–106.
(53) Franklin and Marshall College plans 50-college computer network. College Management, (January 1967).
(54) FREED, ROY N. A legal structure for a national medical center. In: AFIPS conference proceedings, vol. 33, part 1; 1968 Fall Joint Computer Conference. Thompson, Washington, D.C., p. 387–394.
(55) FREEMAN, DAVID N.; PEARSON, ROBERT R. Efficiency vs. responsiveness in a multiple-services computer facility. In: National Conference of the Association for Computing Machinery, 23rd, Las Vegas, Nev., 27–29 August 1968. Proceedings. Brandon/Systems Press, Princeton, N.J., 1968, p. 25–34B.
(56) Functioning media networks. EDUCOM, 3:3 (May 1968) 2–4.
(57) FUSSLER, H. H. Economics, libraries and Project INTREX. In: Planning Conference on Information Transfer Experiments (INTREX), Woods Hole, Mass., 2 August–3 September 1965. Report, edited by Carl F. J. Overhage and R. Joyce Harman. M.I.T. Press, Cambridge, Mass., 1965, p. 163–164.
(58) GARFIELD, EUGENE. Primordial concepts, citation indexing, and historio-bibliography. Journal of Library History, 2:3 (1967) 235–249.
(59) GE's Medinet on the air. Datamation, 14:11 (November 1968) 162.
(60) GLASER, E.; ROSENBLATT, D.; WOOD, M. K. The design of a federal statistical data center. American Statistician, 21 (February 1967) 12–20.
(61) GOLD, MICHAEL M.; SELWYN, LEE L. Real time computer communications and the public interest. In: AFIPS conference proceedings, vol. 33, part 2; 1968 Fall Joint Computer Conference. Thompson, Washington, D.C., p. 1473–1478.
(62) GOULD, E. P.; MOSIOR, J. W. TELPORT—time-shared information systems. Bell Laboratories Record, 46:6 (June 1968) 197–202.

(63) Government adopts standard code for information interchange. Scientific Information Notes, 10:2 (April–May 1968) 8.
(64) GREENBERGER, MARTIN. The border line between communications and data processing. Law and Computer Technology, 1:7 (July 1968) 7–9.
(65) HIRSCH, PHIL. Preliminary WWMCCS specs released; changes may be made to attract bids. Datamation, 14:11 (November 1968) 137, 139.
(66) Indian reservation to have medical information system. Datamation, 14:9 (September 1968) 104.
(67) Integration opens door to computers. Datamation, 14:9 (September 1968) 100.
(68) INTERGOVERNMENTAL TASK FORCE ON INFORMATION SYSTEMS. The dynamics of information flow: Recommendations to improve the flow of information within and among federal, state and local governments. Washington, D.C., April 1968, 37 p. (PB-178 307)
(69) Iowa colleges plan regional computer network. Communications of the ACM, 11:8 (August 1968) 584.
(70) IRWIN, MANLEY R. Government policy implications in data management. Datamation, 14:6 (June 1968) 37–40.
(71) IRWIN, MANLEY R. Time-shared information systems: market entry in search of a policy. In: AFIPS Conference Proceedings, vol. 31; 1967 Fall Joint Computer Conference, Anaheim, Calif. Thompson, Washington, D.C., 1967, p. 513–520.
(72) ITT's expanding network adds time-sharing service. Datamation, 14:6 (June 1968) 100, 105.
(73) JACOB, MARY ELLEN. Standard format for data exchange. Special Libraries, 59:4 (April 1968) 258–260.
(74) JOHNSON, H. R. Computers and the public welfare; law enforcement, social services and data banks. In: Computer Communications Symposium, University of California at Los Angeles, 20–22 March 1967. Computers and communications—toward a computer utility, edited by Fred Gruenberger. Prentice-Hall, Englewood Cliffs, N.J., p. 173–190.
(75) KAPLAN, SIDNEY J. The advancing communication technology and computer communication systems. In: AFIPS conference proceedings, vol. 32; 1968 Spring Joint Computer Conference. Thompson, Washington, D.C., p. 119–133.
(76) KEMENY, J. G.; KURTZ, T. E. The Darthmouth time-sharing computing system: final report. Hanover, N.H., June 1967.
(77) KENNEDY, R. A. Bell Laboratories' library real-time load system (BELLREL). Journal of Library Automation, 1:2 (June 1968) 128–146.
(78) KRETZMER, E. R. Modern techniques for data communication over telephone channels. In: Congress of the International Federation for Information Processing (IFIP), 4th, Edinburgh, 5–10 August 1968. Proceedings. North-Holland Publishing Co., Amsterdam, 1968.
(79) LAMBE, E. D. Computer-assisted instruction network. Progress report 1. Institute for Research in Learning and Instruction, New York, November 1967.
(80) LEITER, JOSEPH; GULL, C. D. The MEDLARS system in 1968. In: American Society for Information Science Annual Meeting, Columbus, Ohio, 20–24 October 1968. Proceedings, vol. 5. Greenwood Publishing Corp., New York, 1968, p. 255–262.
(81) LESSER, RICHARD C.; RALSTON, ANTHONY. The development of a multicampus regional computing center. In: Congress of the International Federation for Information Processing (IFIP), 4th, Edinburgh, 5–10 August 1968. Proceedings. North-Holland Publishing Co., Amsterdam, 1968.
(82) LEVY, RICHARD P.; CAMMARN, MAXINE R. Information systems applications in medicine. In: Annual review of information science and technology, vol. 3. Carlos A. Cuadra, ed. Encyclopaedia Britannica, Chicago, 1968.
(83) Library telecommunications directory: Canada-United States. 2d ed. Canadian Library Association, Library Mechanization Committee, London, Ont.; Duke University Medical Center, Durham, N. C., 1968.
(84) LITTLE, JOHN L.; MOOERS, CALVIN N. Standards for user procedures and data

formats in automated information systems and networks. In: AFIPS conference proceedings, vol. 32; 1968 Spring Joint Computer Conference. Thompson, Washington, D.C., p. 89-94.
(85) LORENZ, JOHN G. The communication network; the academic library and the dissemination of knowledge. In: Dedication of the University Library, Bowling Green State University, Ohio, February 1968, p. 19–27.
(86) McLAUGHLIN, R. A. NASCOM: NASA's communications network for Apollo. Datamation, 14:12 (December 1968) 42, 44, 45.
(87) MANNING, JOSEPHINE. Facsimile transmission—problems and potential. Library Journal, 93:19 (1 November 1968) 4102–4104.
(88) MARRON, HARVEY. ERIC . . . A national network to disseminate educational information. Special Libraries, 59:10 (December 1968) 775–782.
(89) MEISTER, D.; SULLIVAN, D. J. Evaluation of user reactions to a prototype on-line information retrieval system. Bunker-Ramo Corp., Canoga Park, Calif., October 1967, 62 p.
(90) Metropolitan Detroit's [medical library] network. Bulletin of the Medical Library Association, 56:3 (July 1968) 268–291. Contents: R. G. Cheshier: Introduction. H. A. Sullivan: ". . . informed by magic numbers." J. J. Engstrom: "The scattered and competing parts." B. C. Johnson: A step-by-step discard program. J. M. B. Smith: An analysis of the interlibrary loan in Metropolitan Detroit. G. S. Cruzat: Detroit Medical Library Group: Five year progress report. Presented at a Symposium at the Fall Meeting of the Midwest Regional Group of the Medical Library Association, Detroit, 20–21 October 1967.
(91) Michigan Police go on-line. Datamation, 14:8 (August 1968) 103.
(92) MURPHY, E. Communications-based MIS. Journal of Data Management, 6:2 (February 1968) 20–22, 24–25.
(93) NATIONAL ADVISORY COMMISSION ON LIBRARIES. Report. Reprinted in: Congressional Record, 114:173 (21 October 1968) E9355–E9373; also in: Special Libraries, 59:10 (December 1968) 813–839.
(94) NATIONAL LIBRARY OF MEDICINE. The biomedical communications network: technical development plan. Bethesda, Md., June 1968, 1 vol.
(95) Nationwide earth science computer network now operational. Communications of the ACM, 11:5 (May 1968) 383.
(96) NELSON ASSOCIATES, INCORPORATED. An evaluation of the New York State Library's NYSILL pilot program. New York, March 1968, 150 p.
(97) NELSON ASSOCIATES, INCORPORATED. The New York State Library's pilot program in the facsimile transmission of library materials. New York, June 1968, 85 p.
(98) New York has instant license replacement. Datamation, 14:9 (September 1968) 103.
(99) NODIEN, JOHN H.; RIEDERS, FREDERIC. Poison information by digital computer. American Journal of Public Health and the Nation's Health, 57 (June 1967) 1009–1014.
(100) NUGENT, WILLIAM R. NELINET, the New England Library Information Network. Inforonics, Inc., Cambridge, Mass., 1968, 4 p. Presented at the Congress of the International Federation for Information Processing (IFIP), 4th, Edinburgh, Scotland, 6 August 1968.
(101) Ohio highway patrol starts computer network. Datamation, 14:2 (February 1968) 79.
(102) Ohio hospital computer net planned. EDP Weekly, 8:44 (19 February 1968) 14.
(103) ORBIT is the name. EDUCOM, 3:4 (September 1968) 7.
(104) OTT, R. A. New medical communications system being introduced. Illinois Medical Journal, 133 (April 1968) 406–408.
(105) PETERS, CLAUDE; KOZIK, EUGENE. Time-sharing applications of regional data handling. In: American Society of Planning Officials National Planning Conference, Houston, Tex., April 1967. Threshold of Planning Information Systems. American Society of Planning Officials, Chicago, 1967, p. 76–108.
(106) PIZER, IRWIN H. Public and private university library networks. Oral presentation to the Syracuse University School of Library Science Colloquium, 1 August 1968.

(107) PIZER, IRWIN H. A regional medical library network. Bulletin of the Medical Library Association, 57: (April 1969) In press.
(108) Potential resources for EIN. EDUCOM, 3:5 (November 1968) 4–6.
(109) PRICE, DEREK J. DE SOLLA. Networks of scientific papers. Science, 149:3683 (30 July 1965) 510–515.
(110) PRYOR, T. ALLAN; GARDNER, REED M.; DAY, W. CLINTON. Computer system for research and clinical application to medicine. In: AFIPS conference proceedings, vol. 33, part 1; 1968 Fall Joint Computer Conference. Thompson, Washington, D.C., p. 809–816.
(111) Public Health Service and National Bureau of Standards to plan health communications network. Scientific Information Notes, 10:3 (June-July 1968) 2.
(112) QUIRK, W. B. Communications services—present and future. In: AFIPS Conference Proceedings, vol. 31; 1967 Fall Joint Computer Conference, Anaheim, Calif. Thompson, Washington, D.C., 1967, p. 520–522.
(113) REINECKE, ROBERT D. Vision information center—direct user access via computer-assisted instruction. In: American Society for Information Science Annual Meeting, Columbus, Ohio, 20–24 October 1968. Proceedings, vol. 5. Greenwood Publishing Corp., New York, 1968, p. 165–167.
(114) Research in Education. (A monthly abstract journal). Available from the U. S. Government Printing Office, Washington, D.C.
(115) Reservation system set for Howard Johnson's. Datamation, 14:12 (December 1968) 123.
(116) Rice University developing regional communication and information exchange connecting 18 gulf coast area academic institutions. Scientific Information Notes, 10:3 (June–July 1968) 1.
(117) ROBERTS, LAWRENCE G. Multiple computer networks and intercomputer communications. [Title only] In: ACM Symposium on Operating System Principles, Gatlinburg, Tenn., 1–4 October 1967. Proceedings. Communications of the ACM,11:5 (May 1968) 296.
(118) ROSEN, D. Medical care information system of the Veterans' Administration. Public Health Reports, 83 (May 1968) 363–371.
(119) SACKMAN, H. A public philosophy for real time information systems. System Development Corp., Santa Monica, Calif., 19 July 1968, 27 p. (SP-3126)
(120) SAWYER, THOMAS E. Preliminary design for a regional information system as an integral part of a statewide system. TRW Systems, Redondo Beach, Calif., August 1967, 43 p. Prepared for the Southern California Association of Governments.
(121) SCANTLEBURY, R. A.; WILKINSON, P. T.; BARTLETT, K. A. The design of a message switching centre for a digital communication network. In: Congress of the International Federation for Information Processing (IFIP), 4th, Edinburgh, 5–10 August 1968. Proceedings. North-Holland Publishing Co., Amsterdam, 1968.
(122) SCOTT, JAMES T. Economic and regulatory considerations in data networks. In: Business Equipment Manufacturers Association. The computer: tool for management. Business Press, Elmhurst, Ill., 1968, p. 91–102.
(123) SELIG, JUDITH A.; REINECKE, ROBERT D.; STOLUROW, LAWRENCE M. A computer-based system integrating instruction and information retrieval: a description of some methodological considerations. Technical report. Harvard Computing Center, Cambridge, Mass., February 1968, 44 p. (Report no. TR-5) (AD-672 187)
(124) SHANK, RUSSELL. Regional access to scientific and technical information. A program for action in the New York metropolitan area, supervised by Russell Shank. Report of the METRO Science Library Project 1966–1967. Metropolitan Reference and Research Library Agency, Inc., New York, 1968, 217 p. (METRO Misc. Publ. Series No. 1)
(125) SHELDON, R. C.; ROACH, R. A.; BACKER, S. Design of an on-line computer-based textile information retrieval system. Textile Research Journal, 38 (January 1968) 81–100.
(126) SIEGEL, S. J. Developing an information system for a hospital. Public Health Re-

ports, 83   (May 1968) 359–362.
(127) SILBERMAN, HARRY F.; FILEP, ROBERT T.   Information systems applications in education. In: Annual review of information science and technology, vol. 3. Carlos A. Cuadra, ed. Encyclopaedia Britannica, Chicago, 1968.
(128) SIMMONS, RALPH A.   The development of the national biomedical communications network. Oral presentation to the Stanford Conference on Collaborative Library System Development, Stanford University, Palo Alto, Calif., 4–5 October 1968. (To be published)
(129) SIMMS, R. L., JR.   Trends in computer/communication systems. Computers and Automation, 17:5   (May 1968) 22–25.
(130) SIMPSON, GUSTAVUS S., JR.   The evolving U.S. national scientific and technical information system. Battelle Technical Review, 17:5   (May-June 1968) 21–28.
(131) SP computer system goes on line. EDP Weekly, 9:30   (18 November 1968) 9.
(132) SPIERER, M.; WILLS, ROBERT D.   Applications of a large-scale time-sharing system. System Development Corp., Santa Monica, Calif., 30 August 1968, 32 p. (SP-3062)
(133) STANLEY, W. J.; CRANSHAW, D. D.   Use of a computer-based total management information system to support an air resource management program. Journal of the Air Pollution Control Association, 18   (March 1968) 158–159.
(134) STIMLER, S.; BRONS, K. A.   A methodology for calculating and optimizing real-time system performance. Communications of the ACM, 11:7   (July 1968) 509–516.
(135) Stockholm County, Sweden, plans. Datamation, 14:2   (February 1968) 88.
(136) Success of National Crime Information Center (NCIC) systems. FBI Law Enforcement Bulletin (October 1968).
(137) SUMMIT, ROGER K.   Remote information retrieval facility: Ames Research Center and NASA Headquarters. Lockheed Missiles and Space Co., Palo Alto, Calif., June 1968, 44 p. (N-07-68-1)
(138) SUPPES, PATRICK.   Computer-assisted instruction: an overview of operations and problems. In: Congress of the International Federation for Information Processing (IFIP), 4th, Edinburgh, 5–10 August 1968. Proceedings. North-Holland Publishing Co., Amsterdam, 1968.
(139) TAMARU, TAKUJI.   Prospects in municipal information systems: the example of Los Angeles. Computers and Automation, 17:1   (January 1968) 15–18.
(140) U.S. LAWS, STATUTES, ETC.   Public law 90–575. U.S. Government Printing Office, Washington, D.C., 16 October 1968. (Ninetieth Congress, second session. S. 3769)
(141) U.S. OFFICE OF EDUCATION.   How to use ERIC (Educational Resources Information Center). U.S. Government Printing Office, Washington, D.C., 1968, 16 p. (Superintendent of Documents Catalog No. FS 5. 212:12037)
(142) VETERANS ADMINISTRATION. DEPARTMENT OF DATA MANAGEMENT.   Long-range plan for a VA total information processing system. Proposed revision, January 1967. Washington, D.C., 1967 (LRP-no. 30-01-00)
(143) WILKINSON, P. T.; SCANTLEBURY, R. A.   The control functions in a local data network. In: Congress of the International Federation for Information Processing (IFIP), 4th, Edinburgh, 5–10 August 1968. Proceedings. North-Holland Publishing Co., Amsterdam, 1968.
(144) ZINN, KARL L.   A basic reference shelf on interactive use of computers for instruction. Stanford, Calif., September 1968. (A Series One paper from ERIC Clearinghouse on Educational Media and Technology)
(145) ZINN, KARL L.   Instructional uses of interactive computer systems. Datamation, 14:9   (September 1968) 22–27.

12 International Transfer of Information

JOHN G. LORENZ
Library of Congress

INTRODUCTION

Other than permanent peace and universal disarmament, it is possible that nothing could contribute more to making this world a better place to live than an effective worldwide system of information transfer. Upon such a system could be built educational progress, economic and social development, and scientific and technological advancement. There are many problems that need to be solved—problems of organization and administration, the development and acceptance of international standards, problems of language and technology. In addition, the costs of such a system or variety of systems would be very high, and whether or not there is the ability or willingness to provide support out of the present world economy is open to serious question. In the meantime, present efforts in diverse fields should certainly continue since these may eventually provide a base for a more comprehensive system.

Information is one of the most important and powerful resources existing in the world today. But there is great disparity in the quantity, quality, and degree of sophistication of information available in the many countries of the world. This is one of the basic reasons for the great disparity in economic, social, educational, scientific, and technological development between the developed and developing countries. If these disparities are to be reduced substantially and eventually minimized, international transfer of information will need to be greatly improved and developed.

A strong base of information and the ability to use it can contribute importantly to the prosperity of a nation. For example, information on economics can help produce economic stability; the availability of technological information is one of the characteristics of the technologically advanced countries; the dissemination of health information provides a great assist to preventive medicine programs in countries with longer life expectancies.

As Borko (5) says:

> Information is seen as a means by which a developing nation can increase its gross national product, raise the standard of living for its citizens and narrow the gap between the have and the have-not nations of the world. In short, information is seen as a very valuable commodity which should flow freely across national boundaries to the mutual benefit of all.

This chapter will describe briefly the history of international transfer of information, to provide a perspective for present efforts and to illustrate that their objectives are by no means new or unique. It will then examine the activities of informational governmental and nongovernmental organizations and United States Government agencies and professional societies involved in international transfer activities.

The working definition of "international transfer" that will be used for this chapter is:

> The physical or electronic transmission of information in recorded form from individuals and groups as parts of organizations and agencies in one nation to those in another on a formalized bilateral or multilateral basis.

HISTORICAL OVERVIEW

One of the oldest objectives of civilization has been the transfer of information across geographic distances. The famed libraries of Alexandria represent one of the earliest recorded successful efforts toward this objective. According to Wormann (55), the policy of these libraries was " . . . to collect manuscripts from all over the world as the nucleus of a great international research library, to prepare them for use by bibliographical control, and to preserve them for posterity." They also included a translation center where the literature of the Mediterranean, the Middle East, and India were translated into Greek. All through history since "the grandeur that was Greece and the glory that was Rome," there has been an ebb and flow toward the goal of international organization and transfer of information.

In comparison to Alexandria, no major universal libraries existed in the medieval and Renaissance periods even though there is evidence in the correspondence of scholars that the interest in, need for, and willingness to exchange and provide access to sources of recorded knowledge persisted.

According to UNESCO (51), it was not until 1817 that exchanges of publications became more organized and systematized on an international basis, on the initiative of the University of Marburg in Germany. By 1885 the Marburger Tauschverein consisted of 68 members, including Oxford, Cambridge, the British Museum, the Academia dei Lincei, the Smithsonian Institution, the Royal Society in Sydney, and the University of Melbourne.

Historically, the first individual to make recorded impact in dramatizing the need for international exchange of publications and the transfer of information was the colorful French citizen, courtier, magician, and ventriloquist, M. Alexandre Vattemare [1796–1864].

According to Stevens (35), Vattemare, in his travels to the theatres and courts of Europe, visits to libraries and observations of their duplicate treasures, developed his real mission in life:

> . . . to open a channel of communication between the PEOPLE of the various nations of the world, which shall bring them together upon the neutral ground of letters, and by making them better acquainted with each other's laws, manners and customs and intellectual wealth, by acts of mutual kindness and courtesy, to cultivate the spirit of peace and of reciprocal respect and good feeling. (54)

M. Vattemare sailed to the United States in 1839, bearing letters of endorsement from M. Guizot, Minister of Public Instruction in France, the Duc de Broglie, Washington Irving, and Samuel F. B. Morse. As reported by the Joint Committee on the Library of Congress (11), he proposed to Congress a system for the international exchange of library duplicates, saying that "America will have the most to gain," since the "libraries of Europe, splendid, copious, rich, have been the slow accumulation of four centuries." He proposed that the Library of Congress act as a central exchange agency for the United States, and that the Librarian be authorized to obtain lists of material available for exchange from the executives of the States and receive the lists of exchange materials sent from foreign countries. He also suggested that, as a beginning, copies of copyright works deposited in the Department of State and Congressional documents be made available to the Library Committee for use on exchange. The Committee on the Library felt that the United States might "to a limited extent, advantageously enter into the proposed arrangement," making clear, at the same time, that their primary interest was in disseminating abroad current information on our own country and receiving current information in return. The viewpoint of the Committee on the Library is expressed in their Report of June 5, 1840 (12). This motivation has remained a key element in the international transfer of information down to the present day.

According to Kipp (32), for the next fifteen years no satisfactory method of obtaining foreign documents was discovered until Congress, in 1857, assigned the responsibility for such exchanges to the Department of State. By 1867, the pattern which was to continue to the present was established by a joint resolution. This provided 50 copies of all documents for the Joint Committee on the Library to be exchanged through the Smithsonian Institution for materials published in foreign countries and especially by foreign governments. These materials were to be deposited in the Library of Congress.

In 1875 an international geographical congress held in Paris recommended the adoption of a uniform system of exchanging the literary and scientific publications of all nations. Following discussions at three other international conferences in Brussels in 1877, 1880, and 1883, the delegates formulated the Brussels Conventions providing for the establishment of international exchange bureaus in each country. The conventions were formally adopted in 1886.

In the decades that followed, some governments responded well and some indifferently. By 1914 the number of depositories abroad increased to 92, but the Library of Congress, the United States depository, was receiving fewer than 8,000 volumes. As a result of an aggressive development program including considerable travel by Library of Congress representatives to foreign government officials and libraries, this increased to 35,000 per year by 1930. The principal problem was the lack of centralization of responsibility in many countries of the world for document distribution and exchange. A series of bilateral agreements between the United States and foreign governments beginning in 1936 resulted in further improvement, but World War II brought a sharp reduction. In 1943, the Librarian of Congress, Archibald MacLeish, reported (33):

> The requirements for all kinds of government print had multiplied, yet a threatened world-wide paper shortage has greatly reduced the size of the editions. Organizations for the centralized control and distribution of official publications has become ineffective, sometimes inoperative altogether, so that it is extremely difficult to ascertain the nature and extent of current materials. Countries jealously guard from one another a knowledge of their publications.

The Librarian of Congress further pointed up the importance of the continuing international transfer and exchange of information in his 1944

Report (34) in referring to an Interdepartmental Committee for the Acquisition of Foreign Publications and its "job of securing from foreign countries materials necessary, first, to the prosecution of the war, second, to the studies which must now be made in preparation for the peace which is to follow the war, and third, to the general collections of the Library—that is, to this country's store of books and materials of scholarship."

The creation of the United Nations in 1945, and subsequently of UNESCO, with the objective of bringing about a freer flow of information among nations, gave particular encouragement to the concept of international exchange and transfer. One of the first international meetings called by UNESCO was a meeting of experts in 1948 to discuss the problems of international exchange.

It was not until 1958, however, that specific progress was made through UNESCO. This was the adoption of a Convention concerning the International Exchange of Publications at the tenth session of the UNESCO General Conference. The convention stated their conviction (50) "that development of the international exchange of publications is essential to the free exchange of ideas and knowledge among the peoples of the world."

The scope of the exchange convention includes publications of an educational, legal, scientific and technical, cultural, and informational nature, such as books, newspapers and periodicals, maps and plans, prints, photographs, microcopies, musical works, Braille publications, and other graphic material. Responsibility for costs and conditions of transport are specified in considerable detail.

Many of the problems and limitations of international transfer still exist today; i.e., lack of a central responsibility and of an adequately supported mechanism in many countries, publication in insufficient quantity for international distribution, imbalance between quantity sent and quantity received, delay in transmitting materials, limitations in staff, space and funds to acquire and distribute on the one hand and receive, catalog and make available on the other. Since the exchange of documents, a basic and relatively inexpensive means of international transfer of information, is still being done so imperfectly, it could provide a basis for pessimism that more sophisticated, infinitely more expensive systems (involving more information, analyzed in greater depth, with the added costs of abstracting, indexing, translating, computer storage and manipulation and electronic transmission) will soon be developed and available.

There has been a growing concern for improved international transfer of information over the past decade. In 1958, an International Conference on Science Information, held in Washington, D.C., was sponsored by the National Science Foundation, the National Academy of Sciences-National Research Council, and the American Documentation Institute (now

American Society for Information Science). A paper on "International Cooperation in Physics Abstracting" by Crowther (14) reported on the activities of the International Council of Scientific Unions Abstracting Board. The most fruitful activities of the Board up to that time had been in the location and acquisition of material for abstracting. At a UNESCO Conference on Scientific Abstracting held in Paris in 1949, a plan for a single universal international abstracting service was rejected as impracticable. A more modest proposal, for the formation of a single international physics abstracting journal by the amalgamation of the only two journals dealing with this subject then existing, was referred to a committee of the International Union of Physics. This committee reached the important conclusion that, however attractive might be the idea of a single international abstracting organization for physics, it was necessary, for the present, that abstracting journals be available in three or four different languages, to serve the interests of different language groups.

A paper by Chamberlin (9), of New York University, recommended an International Institute for Scientific Information within the framework of UNESCO with an annual budget at that time of $283,350,000. Six areas of responsibility and interest were suggested: abstracting, indexing and cataloging, status of science, translation, library and information centers, devices.

Another paper, by Boquet (4), of the Institut Pasteur in Paris, proposed the creation of an International Center of Scientific Information with the following goals:

1. To assure close cooperation between all documentation centers (national and regional centers, centers operating under state control, as well as private centers).
2. To collect, classify, select, preserve, translate, and reproduce scientific information by modern methods.
3. To facilitate the dissemination of periodicals and selected monographs by publishing them in the officially adopted languages.
4. To organize symposia and conferences and to publish their reports.
5. To publish at regular intervals indexes, tables of contents, and journals devoted to summaries of periodicals.
6. To carry out bibliographical work for scientific institutions, laboratories, and offices of various industries.
7. To organize research services for unifying and improving documentation methods.
8. To aid relations between all scientists by publishing a directory of research centers and lists of specialists.

These goals were much too broad and extensive at that time and probably still are today when costs are substantially greater.

The problems and present status of international transfer are well summarized and brought up to date by Day (16). He points out that strong international systems can be built only on a foundation of strong national systems, and very few of these yet exist. Language remains a key problem since a large proportion of technical information is produced in languages not readable by many segments of the technical community. Existing laws and national policies inhibit the transfer of information. National telecommunications systems are not ready for the volume and complexity of the job to be done. There are critical problems of organization and provision of resources to implement joint international programs. The problem of developing criteria, processes, and techniques to reduce duplication of holdings, indexing, abstracting, translating and keyboarding remains unsolved. The need for international standards for indexing and classification as well as standards for hardware and software is still largely unmet. And lastly, there is the shortage of trained manpower to operate computer-based systems.

Despite these problems, however, some progress is being made and following are some of the programs and plans of international and national organizations as reflected in recent publications.

INTERNATIONAL GOVERNMENTAL ORGANIZATIONS

The most important plan now being developed is the jointly sponsored investigation of the International Council of Scientific Unions (ICSU) and UNESCO. According to a National Science Foundation publication (24), the purpose of the investigation is to promote compatibility among the science information systems being created in many countries and in several disciplines in response to the exponential growth of science information. To prevent the development of barriers between disciplines, languages, differing computer technologies, and even to some extent nations, effective means of interchange among existing and planned systems are to be developed before they become too rigidly established to permit effective interchange.

The joint committee will follow these guidelines: (*1*) The proposed worldwide science information system should be a flexible network based on the voluntary coordination of existing and future information services; (*2*) Initially the system should be restricted to the natural sciences as represented by the disciplines covered by ICSU and its constituent unions; (*3*) The study should concern itself with questions of standardization to facilitate the transferability of information and with ways to increase selectivity within the system, both before publication and after; and (*4*) Special attention should be paid to the growing needs of scientists in the developing countries.

Pérez-Vitoria (42) indicates the establishment of working groups in the following areas: evaluation, compression, and organization of scientific information; standards for the transfer of basic bibliographical data; indexing and classification; research needs; language problems; developing countries and the problems of their access to the system.

An Advisory Group composed of representatives of international and national organizations already well advanced in computerized systems has been established to act as a liaison between the Committee and the organizations involved.

At the July 23-25, 1968, meeting (27), the various working groups suggested, and it was agreed, that a feasibility study be prepared for submission to member states, competent scientific, academic and professional institutions and organizations, and individual specialists for comments and suggestions, which will be taken into consideration in the preparation of the final text of the study.

ICSU is also active in the establishment and acceptance of international standards. As reported by the National Science Foundation (7), the ICSU Abstracting Board at its annual meeting in July 1968 adopted a common system for periodical title abbreviations. The system comprises the common elements of the International Standards Organization and the United States of America Standards Institute systems, which form the basis of the joint Anglo-American standard.

A second major international effort on transfer of information is being carried on by the Organization for Economic Cooperation and Development (OECD) in its Feasibility Study on an International Network of Information Systems. Members of this organization include Austria, Belgium, Canada, Denmark, Finland, France, Germany, Italy, Japan, the Netherlands, Spain, Sweden, Switzerland, the United Kingdom, and the United States, with Yugoslavia as an observer. Currently the OECD information policy group is considering the technical information needs of its member countries, with its frame of reference primarily oriented toward information systems that would support technological and economic growth in industrialized countries.

Although the representative makeup of OECD and the primary area of interest appear to be more limited than the UNESCO-ICSU effort, it is an active organization and already can show material progress in two areas.

Under the aegis of the OECD, MEDLARS began development as an international medical information system, and the framework of an international chemical information system is now being planned. A number of member countries are already committed to this latter undertaking. As

Day has pointed out, a prime requirement for international systems is a base of strong national systems. In this case, the chemical information system of the American Chemical Society, and particularly the ACS's Chemical Abstracts Service, would presumably be a keystone in the international system.

A publication of OECD (46) reports that the Council of Mutual Economic Assistance (COMECON), which is an Eastern European intergovernmental organization with about the same functions as those of OECD, has set up a coordinating agency through which the member countries have developed principles of free information exchange and rules to be followed for indexing and abstracting. This source indicated that over 8.5 million items of information were supplied by USSR information agencies, and Soviet agencies received more than 1.5 million items in return.

A fourth major international effort is the International Nuclear Information System sponsored by the International Atomic Energy Agency (IAEA). According to Day (16, p. 8–9), the objective is to create a centralized information system using modern computer technology. Each country or group of countries would scan its own literature, identify items relevant to nuclear science and its applications, write standardized machine-readable bibliographic descriptions, and assign subject-indexing terms. These records would be collected in Vienna at the IAEA and would be put on a master tape that could be copied and made available to all participants for their own national nuclear information systems. As a first step, the IAEA is drafting standards for machine-readable bibliographic descriptions. In 1968 it planned to carry out experiments based on voluntary inputs from a small number of member states, and it also plans to make a detailed systems study with the object of drawing up a first design of a total reference system. Using this work as a basis, the IAEA plans to make a definitive proposal to its member states and, if this is accepted, to begin implementation of the project in 1970.

There are several other efforts being made by international organizations in specific fields of information. One of the most significant is the Committee on Data for Science and Technology (CODATA), which has been established by ICSU (Day, 16, p. 10) to promote communications and voluntary coordination among compilers of standard reference tables of scientific data. CODATA has members from eleven international unions and the following six countries: France, Germany, Japan, United Kingdom, United States, and Russia. The participating unions are active in astronomy, biological sciences, geodesy, physics, and chemistry.

A CODATA Newsletter (30) began publication in 1968 with the purpose of improving international communication. The first issue reported on the first international conference of the group and the organization and activities of CODATA, including its objective of making worldwide distribution of data compilations.

Other representative ICSU-related organizations concerned with international transfer of information include the International Astronomical Union (IAU), the International Union of Biological Sciences (IUBS), the International Union of Geological Sciences (IUGS), the International Union of Pure and Applied Physics (IUPAP), and the International Union of Pure and Applied Chemistry (IUPAC). However, no 1968 publications reporting specific progress in international transfer by these organizations have been located.

The United Nations and many of its member organizations, such as the Economic and Social Council (ECOSOC), the Food and Agriculture Organization (FAO), the Educational, Scientific and Cultural Organization (UNESCO), the World Health Organization (WHO), the International Telecommunication Unit (ITU), and the World Meteorological Organization (WMO), all have, either implicitly or explicitly, as one of their principal objectives the international transfer of information in their particular fields of responsibility and interest.

In terms of general responsibility and continuing effort in the development of international information transfer, UNESCO is probably the most important international governmental agency. The Constitution of UNESCO provides that it is to assure the conservation and protection of the world's inheritance of books and give the people of all countries access to the printed and published material produced by any one of them. UNESCO has the specific objective under its mass communications responsibilities of improving the free flow of information among countries; maintaining, increasing, and diffusing knowledge by the exchange of publications; and fostering the development of libraries and documentation and archives programs. This organization also has a broad publication program. One of its principal publications is the *UNESCO Bulletin for Libraries*. A 1968 article (Słabczynski, 47) in this publication gives a good general overview of international information transfer. It traces its background to the beginning of recorded history. For current practice, based on the importance of exchange to international understanding, the article recommends: a more liberal attitude toward reciprocity, particularly for the developing countries, and as wide a geographical extension of exchange as possible; the addition of summaries in foreign languages at the end of every scientific work published in a less well-known language; publication by every nation of lists of materials for exchange; and speedier circulation of exchange material. The last step could be accomplished by the elimination of bulk transport where possible and the direct forwarding of exchange material by individual institutions, with the international exchange services having a coordinating informational and bibliographical function.

UNESCO has also been the instrument for developing international agreements on the importation of educational, scientific, and cultural materials. The Beirut Agreement adopted in 1948 facilitates the international circulation of visual and auditory materials, and the Florence Agreement of 1950 reduced the tariff and trade barriers, not only of audiovisual materials, but also of books and other publications, works of art, scientific equipment, and articles for the blind. In November 1967, a meeting was held in Geneva to review these agreements. The report (52), published in May 1968, found that the agreements were working well and should be made better known and acceded to by more governments.

UNESCO also assists developing countries in establishing libraries and documentation centers through which they are able to receive and exchange information with other countries of the world. A meeting on National Planning of Library Services in Asia was held by UNESCO and the Government of Ceylon in Colombo in December 1967 and reported in several sources in 1968 publications (Lorenz, 36, 44; Evans, 21). UNESCO also provides leadership and coordination in establishing book development programs for the production and distribution of informational and educational materials so that the worldwide flow of books is increased. A Conference on Book Development in Africa was held in Accra, Ghana, in February 1968 and was also reported by UNESCO (49).

INTERNATIONAL NONGOVERNMENTAL ORGANIZATIONS

The International Federation for Documentation (FID), supported partially by UNESCO funds, is one of the leading international nongovernmental organizations that has as one of its main objectives the improvement of the international transfer of information. The proceedings of its International Congress on Documentation, held in September 1967 in Tokyo, included several papers pertinent to the subject, e.g., "Information Systems and Copyright—An International Solution" by Howard J. Hilton of Pennsylvania State University; and "A World-Wide Chemical and Chemical Engineering Information System" by Dale B. Baker, Fred A. Tate, and Ralph E. Odette, Chemical Abstracts Service (10).

The Federation is also the center for the Universal Decimal Classification. It is a truism to say that standards, conformity, and compatibility in the classification of information are important elements in international and, in fact, in any efficient transfer of recorded information. In 1968 the Federation held a Seminar on UDC in a Mechanized Retrieval System. The seminar was conducted by Pauline Atherton and Robert Freeman and was attended by 61 people from 14 countries. This seminar was reported by Angell (2) and at greater length by Corbett (13).

The Federation also has a publishing program to assist in the international transfer of information, e.g., *Directories of Science Information Sources: International Bibliography*, published in 1967; and *FID News Bulletin*, a monthly publication including a calendar of important meetings, reports on international conferences, and announcements of publications and other activities important to information transfer.

The International Federation of Library Associations (IFLA) is another nongovernmental organization that has as one of its objectives the improvement of international transfer of information, especially through its committees on Union Catalogs and International Loans, Exchange of Publications, and the Exchange of Official Publications. In 1954 the Federation developed an agreement on interlibrary loan principles. It has also worked toward international agreement on cataloging principles. Its Committee on Statistics and Standards has been developing international standards for statistics relating to libraries so that statistics reported from various nations can be compared. As the result of two international conferences involving representatives of IFLA, the International Federation for Documentation (FID), and the International Standards Organization, a publication was produced in 1968 entitled *The International Standardisation of Library Statistics* (31).

Proposals for specialized information centers abound among international organizations. One example is a proposed World Institute for Documentation of Housing, Building, and Planning which grew out of a Committee of the Economic and Social Council of the United Nations (ECOSOC). The Institute is to be located in New Delhi and supported by funds from member states. When it is operational, the Institute plans to acquire, abstract, synthesize, and disseminate the relevant literature in the field in four languages to agencies at national levels.

The International Road Research Documentation project was established in 1965 under the auspices of the Organization for Economic Cooperation and Development. It involves selecting and disseminating information in the form of abstracts of research reports and published articles and summaries of current road research projects in the United Kingdom and many other countries. The Technical Information and Library Group at the Road Research Laboratory, Crowthorne, Berkshire, England, is one of three coordinating centers for this work, the other two being the Laboratoire Central des Ponts et Chaussées in Paris and the Forschungsgesellschaft für das Strassenwesen in Cologne, supported by the Büdesanstalt für das Strassenwesen. The member countries are Austria, Belgium, Canada, Denmark, Ireland, the Netherlands, Norway, Portugal, Spain and Sweden, and in addition there is an arrangement between the Road Research Laboratory and the Highway Research Board in the United States for the exchange of material. Each member is responsible for analyzing and indexing its own literature, and material from nonmember countries is shared. Information is therefore analyzed and indexed once only. Abstracts are prepared in one of the three official languages, French, English, and German, and are indexed using key words selected from a trilingual thesaurus of terms in the field of road and road-traffic research and related subjects. Each abstract is sent to the coordinating center that deals with the language in which it is written, and the center then allocates an IRRD number, processes the information, and distributes the abstracts to all member countries (23).

Also assisting nations in overcoming language barriers is the European Translation Centre (ETC) at Delft in the Netherlands. In 1968, this center completed the first annual cumulative volume of its *World Index* (20) citing translations from non-Western languages relating to science and technology. According to a National Science Foundation description (19), the Index is composed of two parts:

1. An alphabetical listing of journal articles and patents translated at a great variety of places (e.g., government agencies, universities, industry, translating bureaus) that have been reported to ETC either directly or via existing announcement lists;
2. A list of periodicals translated cover-to-cover, abstracted publications, and periodicals of which selected articles are translated.

The annual cumulation contains approximately 2,000 titles—a relatively small number—of journals, monographs, and report series from Eastern Europe, Southwest Asia, and the Orient. For most of these, several translations are cited. Translations in progress are also listed. The *World Index* provides access to about 50,000 translated articles.

Some international organizations are quite informal, being based on voluntary cooperation among and contributions from their members. An example is ICIREPAT, an acronym for International Cooperation in Information Retrieval among Examining Patent Offices. Its program of shared use and development of mechanized IR systems for various technical fields is slowly coming into effect and was described at the FID/IFIP Joint Conference in Rome, Italy, and the subsequent proceedings (17).

UNITED STATES GOVERNMENT AGENCIES

In addition to the contribution of international organizations to the international transfer of information, many United States Governmental agencies participate in such transfer on both a bilateral and multilateral basis. The "hot line" between the White House and the Kremlin is probably one of the most dramatic developments in bilateral information transfer. In 1968 a widely read newspaper supplement (25) had an open letter that proposed a similar transfer link between Washington and Peking. Subsequently, in early 1969, the same publication (1) reported that Peking cut the only existing direct telephone line between it and the United States but, not long after, reopened the Warsaw diplomatic channel.

A measure of the importance of international transfer in the Federal establishment is the fact that the Committee on Scientific and Technical Information (COSATI) of the Federal Council for Science and Technology (FCST) in the Executive Office of the President has a Panel on International Information Activities. Some of the Federal agencies represented on this panel are: Department of Agriculture; Atomic Energy Commission; Department of Commerce; Department of Defense; Department of Health, Education, and Welfare (National Library of Medicine); Department of Interior; Library of Congress; National Aeronautics and Space Administration; National Science Foundation; Department of State; and Department of Transportation.

A COSATI report (22, p. 8) released in 1968 refers to the preparation of a new Federal policy governing the foreign dissemination of scientific and technical information by the agencies of the United States Government. This policy was issued in January 1969. The fundamental objectives are to ensure that there exists within the United States at least one accessible copy of each significant publication of the worldwide scientific and technical literature; to establish international scientific and technical information systems through which the worldwide scientific and technical literature will flow routinely into the United States elements of the systems; to influence and encourage the establishment of standards so that foreign information systems and those of the United States are compatible; and to utilize scientific and technical information effectively in support of agency missions, and in support of overall United States objectives in raising the economic and industrial standards of other nations. Policies include seeking the widest possible dissemination of knowledge and, in particular, the open exchange of scientific and technical information; and seeking reasonable return for information sent, taking into account the capability of other countries to make a return. In addition, the United States agencies are expected to give first consideration to cooperation with multilateral organizations if they provide means that are at least as effective as bilateral agreements in meeting the United States objectives.

The publication also highlights the specific activities of several agencies. Some of the major examples follow.

The United States Patent Office of the Department of Commerce (22,

p. 31), has been working in the field of mechanical information retrieval under ICIREPAT, and indexing of patents has been virtually completed in the field of analog-digital converters. The National Bureau of Standards, Office of Standard Reference Data (22, p. 29), has participated in the activities of CODATA. Preliminary discussions on the development of an international program with European countries, including the USSR, have continued, but as yet only a few cooperative projects have been initiated. Some examples of these are cited in the National Bureau of Standards *Technical News Bulletin* (29).

Also under the Department of Commerce, the Bureau of the Census (18, p. 98) maintains arrangements involving the exchange of technical and statistical materials with approximately 250 national organizations and institutions located in 130 countries and approximately 50 international organizations.

In the same Department, the Environmental Science Service Administration is engaged with other countries in data exchange, cooperative research, international weather station agreements, satellite services, observatory operations, and oceanographic studies.

The Department of Defense maintains a Bilateral Information Exchange, under which the United States exchanges scientific and technical data with allied nations on research projects of common interest. Under these programs, United States personnel are at present working with their counterparts in 16 countries on 380 different research projects. As reported (18, p. 45–46), an important area of information exchange is exercised through international organizations such as the Advisory Group for Aerospace Research and Development (AGARD), the NATO Air Force Armaments Group Program (TTCP), and the von Kármán Institute (VKI). The United States furnishes both financial and personnel support to these organizations.

In the Department of Health, Education, and Welfare, the National Library of Medicine has taken action (22, p. 51–52) toward the further extension of MEDLARS under the auspices of the OECD. Through the Department of State, the United States proposed the establishment of a consortium of interested European member countries of OECD to introduce MEDLARS search technology in their countries. Following approval of the OECD Science Information Policy Group in January 1967, an international working party developed proposals that called for the training of searchers from member countries. The present plan calls for the development of bilateral agreements at the rate of one per year. Computer operations are presently being conducted by three existing overseas MEDLARS Stations at the Karolinska Institut in Stockholm, Sweden, at the National Lending Library for Science and Technology and the University of Newcastle-upon-Tyne in the United Kingdom, both OECD member countries. As part of the cooperative international effort, the member countries will provide the NLM with 50,000 indexed citations derived from their own national biomedical journal literature.

In addition, WHO accepted an invitation from NLM to enter into an agreement whereby MEDLARS search services can be provided for members of WHO expert committees throughout the world, and for WHO headquarters staff. The Library assisted the Medical Research Council of Australia in its planning to establish a MEDLARS search center. An agreement is being developed with the National Library in Canberra with computing services to be done at the University of Sydney. Preliminary negotiations with Japanese and Canadian interests are also going on, leading toward further bilateral agreements. A report on MEDLARS (Austin, 3) including a discussion on the Decentralization Program appeared in 1968. A technical description on how the National Lending Library in the United Kingdom uses MEDLARS in searching for medical information was also published (Harley, 26).

The Library of Congress (LC) made significant progress in its contribution to international information transfer in 1968 by its further development of the international Shared Cataloging Program. As described by the Librarian of Congress (Mumford, 39), this program is acquiring, to the extent possible and with funds available under Title II of the Higher Education Act of 1965, all library materials currently published throughout the world that are of value to scholarship; the program is providing catalog information for these materials promptly and distributing such bibliographic information. Under the program, by the end of 1968, acquisitions and cataloging offices had been established in Belgrade, Florence, London, The Hague, Oslo, Paris, Rio de Janeiro, Tokyo, Vienna, and Wiesbaden. They cover the publications of Austria, Belgium, Brazil, Denmark, England, East Germany, Finland, France, Italy, Japan, the Netherlands, Norway, Sweden, Switzerland, West Germany, and Yugoslavia. In order to speed up cataloging for American libraries, LC utilizes the cataloging done in these countries. One regional acquisitions office—in Nairobi, Kenya, for the acquisition of East African publications—is operating in an area where the book trade is not yet developed and no national bibliography is available. In addition, five countries were sending bibliographic information directly to LC and shared cataloging procedures were being applied at the Library of Congress to the publications of Canada, New Zealand, Australia, South Africa, and the USSR. By the end of 1968, a total of 21 countries were receiving shared cataloging coverage as part of NPAC. The results of this cooperative program of shared cataloging are embodied not only in Library of Congress catalog cards, but also in the Library's published *National Union Catalog*, which is more and more becoming a guide to important scholarly materials published around the world. The program, therefore, is one of mutual benefit to libraries and scholarship everywhere. As means of payment for the bibliographic services provided by some of the national libraries involved, credit accounts have been established in the United States against which they can purchase United States publications —a further enhancement of international transfer.

The continuing significance of the international exchange program, which is operated jointly by the Library of Congress and the Smithsonian Institution and handles the millions of pieces of material each year, should not be overlooked in any discussion of international transfer. In 1968, for example, the Library of Congress received 472,844 items from foreign governments and institutions and sent out 1,052,277 items, including United States Government publications, through the Smithsonian International Exchange Service.

A recent Library of Congress achievement that has great importance for information transfer is the development of a Machine-Readable Cataloging (MARC) communications format. The format was developed in cooperation with major libraries and library associations and has been approved by the key committees of the U.S. American Standards Institute; the format is also being used by the British National Bibliography. A weekly MARC Distribution Service including, at first, Library of Congress American imprint monograph cataloging on magnetic tape, began in March 1969 and is available to all subscribers at an initial rate of $600 per year (38). The catalog information included will expand first to all English-language monographs and then later to French- and German-language materials.

The National Aeronautics and Space Administration (NASA) has an active program (22, p. 69–70) for the international exchange of aerospace and aerospace-related information; the program has been refined and expanded, reaching a total of 298 organizations in 48 countries in 1967. Documents received through these exchanges are announced in companion abstract journals (*Scientific and Technical Aerospace Reports* and *International Aerospace Abstracts*) and copies are made available for public sale through the Clearinghouse for Federal Scientific and Technical Information (CFSTI). In addition to specific exchange arrangements with foreign government organizations, universities, colleges, observatories, societies, and institutes, NASA also maintains an agreement with the European Space Research Organization (ESRO). Under this agreement, NASA receives aerospace documents from European space-research activities in a form that permits their announcement and dissemination without reprocessing. These reports are available to other nations, large and small, by purchase from CFSTI. There are approximately 400,000 documents (Day,

15), of which 90,000 resulted from exchange arrangements with organizations outside the United States. All have been abstracted, indexed, microfilmed, and placed under computer control for rapid servicing.

The activities of the National Science Foundation and its Office of Science Information Services in the field of international information transfer (40) include a wide variety of science information projects, such as acquisition of foreign publications; support and publication of announcement media (translation indexes, guides, directories); international travel for science information purposes; the support of committees and secretariats, e.g., U.S. National Committee for the International Federation for Documentation (USNCFID), the Secretariat of the International Association of Technological University Libraries (IATUL), and the International Council of Scientific Unions Abstracting Board; and staff support for review and monitorship of science information activities of various international organizations. The Foundation also provides support for reference and information aids, e.g., *International Directory of Psychologists*, and arranges for the translation of 78,000 pages of foreign literature (41).

QUASI-PUBLIC ORGANIZATIONS

One of the most recent developments in international transfer is the International Telecommunication Satellite Consortium (INTELSAT). According to an early 1969 news item (Unna, 53), a conference was to be held in Washington, D.C., beginning on February 24, 1969, on the establishment of a permanent communications system. INTELSAT has 63 members, and the USSR, not a member, will have a delegation at the conference. On February 5, 1969, an internationally owned satellite was launched by the INTELSAT Consortium. This is one of four and will link ground stations on the United States mainland, Hawaii, Thailand, Australia, Japan and the Philippines (28). It is capable of handling 1,200 two-way telephone conversations or four television programs.

Another example of quasi-public organization activity in international transfer of information is the Communications Satellite Corporation (COMSAT). Under this organization, satellites are launched by NASA, which relinquishes control to COMSAT after they are in their presumed orbit. This organization is under the review of the Office of Telecommunications Management in the Executive Office of the President, which is charged (22, p. 78–79) with fostering a national program of commercial communications satellite service and with coordinating the activities of Governmental agencies to ensure full and effective compliance with the policies set forth in the Communications Satellite Act of 1962. Considerable progress has been achieved by COMSAT in creating a global communications satellite system:

1. Communications satellite service is now available in both the Atlantic and Pacific Ocean Basins.
2. During the past year, three new satellites were positioned successfully in synchronous orbit and placed in operational service, extending full-time service to the Pacific region and expanding the existing capability between the United States and Europe.
3. Highly reliable wideband service capable of carrying voice, data, and video is now available among the United States, Europe, Africa, South America, and Asia, extending along a perimeter of Japan, Thailand, and Australia.

The global communications satellite system has opened an entire new range of communications potential for high speed information exchange among the nations of the world.

Also in the quasi-public field, there is the National Academy of Sciences-National Academy of Engineering-National Research Council complex, which is supported by public and private funds and has as one of its objectives the improvement of international information transfer; for example, the Academy supports ICSU and FID in their efforts. A specific example of an Academy activity in the international transfer field is the World Data Center A for Rockets and Satellites, which exchanges geophysical observations in accordance with principles set forth by ICSU. There is also a World Center for Geophysics related to the International Geophysical Union, which exchanges geophysical, weather, and space data at a high level of international cooperation. The United States, the USSR and other countries are included.

U.S. PROFESSIONAL ASSOCIATIONS

Many professional associations are also involved in international transfer of information. The American Chemical Society has been previously mentioned. According to a summary of Board and Committee actions at the 1968 national meeting (Riegel, 45), the Society is actively considering (*1*) establishment of an international information system based on the CAS computer-based system, under the auspices of the OECD; (*2*) cooperation with the ICSU-UNESCO Committee on the Feasibility Study for a Worldwide Chemical Information System; (*3*) formalization of relationships with The Chemical Society (London) and a consortium of societies in the United Kingdom; and (*4*) development of agreements with the Gesellschaft Deutscher Chemiker and Internationale Dokumentationsgesellschaft für Chemie, GmbH, of Germany. In a speech to the Society at the national meeting, the President, Dr. Robert W. Cairns, said specifically (*8*):

ACS has made an offer to member countries of the Organization for Economic Cooperation and Development (the countries of western Europe, Canada, Japan, Turkey, and the U.S.) to work cooperatively toward the development of local chemical information centers over the world. *Chemical Abstracts* would receive input from the literature of the countries involved and, in return, would arrange for output through each of the centers. It is now thought that the ideal system would encompass five to six major centers with a large number of related and more specialized distribution centers.

CONCLUDING COMMENTS

A review of the literature of 1968 on international transfer of information leads to the conclusion that this field is still in a relatively primitive state of development, both in organization and the application of information science. Considerable ferment and planning is going on, based on the recognized need for accomplishment, particularly to assist the developing nations of the world. But many difficult problems have not been fully considered or resolved—problems of defining specific objectives, developing standards, agreeing on the content and the technology of the information systems, analyzing costs as related to benefits, and determining the source of funding, which is certain to be substantial.

In his keynote address at the FID/IFIP 1967 conference, Pietsch (43), in reviewing the current state and future prospects of information and automatic documentation, concluded: ". . . we are left with misgivings on viewing the entire electronic undertaking. Hardware/software seem in many cases unable to provide expected results, above all in the international sphere."

With so much information being produced in the developed countries, why is more not being transferred internationally, more fully, more efficiently, and more quickly? In 1968, *The Economist* (48) took a look at the problem and found: "One important reason is that there is just too much information to take in. The Western World is probably now spending $1,000 million a year merely on filing and indexing scientific information from 30,000 major journals, whose number is increasing by 1,500 annually." The writer sees the possibility that information, instead of passing freely across national frontiers, could become locked in separate national computer repositories. He also points to the proliferation of languages that the different computers speak as one of the problems requiring solution.

As a result of the many unresolved problems in more sophisticated international information transfer, it is probably fair to say that more is still being accomplished and will continue to be accomplished for some time in the future in the use of traditional methods in the international interchange of hard copy. The breakthroughs that have been made in using the new technology are principally in the transfer of bibliographic citations and, in some cases, abstracts of information. For the use of information in depth, access to complete documents is still frequently necessary. In the developing countries, particularly, such access will probably continue to be for some time to come a missing ingredient in the information transfer process.

As difficult as the problem is, the search for solutions must continue because they are still basic to worldwide progress. A former president of FID (Lowry, 37) summed up the situation in 1968 and predicted that international information systems will take many years to evolve, and that in the meantime bilateral systems will tend to stabilize, and conversion to meet international system requirements will become more difficult.

But to make the world a better place to live, we must continue to work for improvement. We tend to forget how much accomplishments in the present are based on much of the international transfer of information which has gone on in the past. We had a good reminder recently in the speech made by Astronaut Frank Borman (6) when he stood before the Congress of the United States on January 9, 1969, after his return from orbiting the moon and said: ". . . we stood on the shoulders of giants, because how can anyone think of Apollo 8 without thinking of Galileo, or Copernicus, or Keppler, or Jules Verne, or Oberth, or Tsiolkovskiy, or Goddard . . . ?"

If information over the ages had been confined to its country of origin and not been transferred, we should be not only far from the moon, but also far from many other achievements. A perfected system of international information transfer may be just as difficult and costly as getting to the moon, but it is no less important, and its benefits to our civilization may be greater.

REFERENCES

(1) ANDERSON, JACK. Russia blasts Parade's proposal for hot line to China. Parade, Washington Post, (5 January 1969) 4.
(2) ANGELL, RICHARD S. Report on the Seminar on the Universal Decimal Classification in a Mechanized Retrieval System, Copenhagen, September 2-6, 1968. In: Library of Congress Information Bulletin, 27:42 (17 October 1968) Appendix, p. 635-636.
(3) AUSTIN, CHARLES J. MEDLARS, 1963-1967. National Library of Medicine, Bethesda, Md., 1968.
(4) BOQUET, PAUL. Creation of an international center of scientific information. In: International Conference on Scientific Information, Washington, D.C., 1958. Proceedings. National Academy of Sciences, National Research Council, Washington, D.C.,

1959, v. 2, p. 1517–1521.
(5) BORKO, H. National and international information networks in science and technology. In: AFIPS conference proceedings, vol. 33, part 2; 1968 Fall Joint Computer Conference. Thompson, Washington, D.C., p. 1469–1472.
(6) BORMAN, FRANK. [Address to Joint Session of Congress] Congressional Record, (91st Congress, 1st Session), 115:5 (9 January 1969) H168.
(7) Broadening of scope, information standards considered at International Council of Scientific Unions Abstracting Board meeting. Scientific Information Notes, 10:4 (August–September 1968) 10.
(8) CAIRNS, ROBERT W. ACS responsibilities for communication. Chemical and Engineering News, 46:48 (11 November 1968) 52.
(9) CHAMBERLIN, WALDO. An international institute for scientific information. In: International Conference on Scientific Information, Washington, D.C., 1958. Proceedings. National Academy of Sciences, National Research Council, Washington, D.C., 1959, v. 2, p. 1523–1534.
(10) CONFERENCE OF FID, 33rd; and INTERNATIONAL CONGRESS ON DOCUMENTATION, Tokyo, 12–22 September 1967. Proceedings. Science Council of Japan, Tokyo, 1968, 842 p.
(11) CONGRESS. JOINT COMMITTEE ON THE LIBRARY. Memorial of Alexandre Vattemare. February 5, 1840. [Washington, D.C., 1840] (26th Congress, 1st Session. House. Doc. no. 50) p. 2.
(12) CONGRESS. JOINT COMMITTEE ON THE LIBRARY. Report . . . [on] the Memorial of Mr. Alexandre Vattemare . . . [on international literary exchanges.] Blair & Rives, Washington, D.C., 1840. (26th Congress, 1st Session. Senate. Doc. no. 521) p. 2.
(13) CORBETT, LINDSAY. Report on the FID Seminar on UDC in a Mechanized Retrieval System, Copenhagen, September 2–6, 1968. AWRE Library Information Note, 68:9 (7 October 1968) 32 p.
(14) CROWTHER, B. M. International cooperation in physics abstracting. In: International Conference on Scientific Information, Washington, D.C., 16–21 November 1958. Proceedings. National Academy of Sciences, National Research Council, Washington, D.C., 1959, v. 1, p. 481–489.
(15) DAY, MELVIN S. Cooperation through the exchange of scientific and technical information. Presented at United Nations Space Conference, Vienna, Austria, August 1968.
(16) DAY, MELVIN S. The development of international scientific and technical information systems. In: International Technical Communications Conference, 15th, Los Angeles, 8–11 May 1968. Proceedings. Society of Technical Writers and Publishers, Washington, D.C., 1968, paper I-1 (4 p.).
(17) DEKKER, J. Shared use and development of mechanized IR systems in patent offices. In: FID/IFIP Joint Conference, Rome, Italy, 14–17 June 1967. Proceedings: Mechanized information storage, retrieval and dissemination. Edited by Kjell Samuelson. North-Holland Publishing Co., Amsterdam, 1968, p. 269–279.
(18) DEPARTMENT OF STATE. BUREAU OF EDUCATIONAL AND CULTURAL AFFAIRS. A guide to U.S. Government agencies involved in international educational and cultural activities. Washington, D.C., 1968, 188 p.
(19) European Translation Centre issues first world index of scientific translations, 1967. Scientific Information Notes, 10:3 (June–July 1968) 12.
(20) EUROPEAN TRANSLATION CENTRE. World index of scientific translations, 1967. Delft, The Netherlands, 1968.
(21) EVANS, EVELYN J. A. Meeting of experts on national planning of library services in Asia. UNESCO Bulletin for Libraries, 22:3 (May–June 1968) 114–118.
(22) FEDERAL COUNCIL FOR SCIENCE AND TECHNOLOGY. COMMITTEE ON SCIENTIFIC AND TECHNICAL INFORMATION. Progress of the United States Government in scientific and technical communications. Washington, D.C., 1967, 91 p.
(23) FEDERAL COUNCIL FOR SCIENCE AND TECHNOLOGY. COMMITTEE ON

SCIENTIFIC AND TECHNICAL INFORMATION. PANEL ON INTERNATIONAL INFORMATION ACTIVITIES. International road research documentation. News Briefs, 14 (14 February 1968).
(24) First meeting of Joint ICSU-UNESCO Committee on World-Wide Science Information System scheduled for December in Paris. Scientific Information Notes, 9 (October–November 1967) 9.
(25) GORKIN, JESS. An open letter to the American people. Parade, Washington Post (29 September 1968) 4–5.
(26) HARLEY, A. J. MEDLARS and the flow of scientific information. Medical and Biological Illustration, 18 (January 1968) 38–42.
(27) ICSU-UNESCO CENTRAL COMMITTEE TO STUDY THE FEASIBILITY OF A WORLD SCIENCE INFORMATION SYSTEM. Report of the second session, 23–25 July 1968. Paris, 30 September 1968, 10 p. (ICSU-UNESCO/CSI/3.9)
(28) INTELSAT's Pacific link launched. Washington Post (6 February 1969) A7.
(29) International cooperation in standard reference data projects. National Bureau of Standards Technical News Bulletin, 52:4 (April 1968) 88.
(30) INTERNATIONAL COUNCIL OF SCIENTIFIC UNIONS. Committee on Data for Science and Technology. CODATA Newsletter, vol. 1 (October 1968).
(31) The international standardisation of library statistics; a progress report. La normalisation internationale des statistiques relatives aux bibliothèques; état des travaux. International Federation of Library Associations, International Organization for Standardization, London, 1968, 216 p.
(32) KIPP, LAURENCE J. The international exchange of publications; a report of programs within the United States Government for exchange with Latin America, based upon a survey made for the Interdepartmental Committee on Scientific and Cultural Cooperation, under direction of the Library of Congress. Wakefield, Mass., 1950?, 116 p.
(33) LIBRARY OF CONGRESS. LIBRARIAN OF CONGRESS. Report of the Librarian of Congress for the fiscal year ended June 30, 1943 [by Archibald MacLeish, Librarian of Congress]. Library of Congress, Washington, D.C., 1944, 279 p.
(34) LIBRARY OF CONGRESS. LIBRARIAN OF CONGRESS. Report of the Librarian of Congress for the fiscal year ended June 30, 1944 [by Archibald MacLeish, Librarian of Congress]. Library of Congress, Washington, D.C., 1945, 204 p.
(35) LIBRARY OF CONGRESS. PROCESSING DEPARTMENT. The role of the Library of Congress in the international exchange of official publications; a brief history, by Robert D. Stevens. Washington, D.C., 1953, 85 p.
(36) LORENZ, JOHN G. Report on a meeting on national planning of library services in Asia, Colombo, Ceylon, 11–19 December 1967. In: Library of Congress Information Bulletin, 26:52 (28 December 1967) 855–857.
(37) LOWRY, W. KENNETH. Science information problems needing solution. [Opinion paper] American Documentation, 19:3 (July 1968) 352–354.
(38) MARC subscriptions. In: Library of Congress Information Bulletin, 27:39 (26 September 1968) 581.
(39) MUMFORD, L. QUINCY. International co-operation in shared cataloguing. UNESCO Bulletin for Libraries, 22:1 (January-February 1968) 9–12.
(40) NATIONAL SCIENCE FOUNDATION. Seventeenth annual report for the fiscal year ended June 30, 1967. Washington, D.C., 1968, 219 p. (NSF-68-1)
(41) NATIONAL SCIENCE FOUNDATION. OFFICE OF SCIENCE INFORMATION SERVICE. Annual report, fiscal year 1968. National Science Foundation, Washington, D.C., 1968, 16 p.+ appendices.
(42) PÉREZ-VITORIA, A. Towards a world science information system: an ICSU-UNESCO joint venture. UNESCO Bulletin for Libraries, 23:1 (January–February 1969) 5.
(43) PIETSCH, E. Information and automatic documentation, current state and future prospects. In: FID/IFIP Joint Conference, Rome, Italy, 14–17 June 1967. Proceedings: Mechanized information storage, retrieval and dissemination. Edited by Kjell Samuel-

son. North-Holland Publishing Co., Amsterdam, 1968, p. 11.
(44) Planning of Asian library services and pilot project in Ceylon. Scientific Information Notes, 10:1 (February–March 1968) 7.
(45) RIEGEL, BYRON. Board Committee reports—Chemical Abstracts Service. Chemical & Engineering News, 46:47 (4 November 1968) 57.
(46) A scientific and technical information policy to facilitate and accelerate the dissemination of knowledge. OECD Observer, no. 33 (April 1968) 37–38.
(47) SŁABCZYNSKI, W. New trends in the international exchange of publications. UNESCO Bulletin for Libraries, 12:5 (September–October 1968) 218–224.
(48) The technological gap. The Economist, 226:6499 (16 March 1968) 75.
(49) UNESCO meeting on book development in Africa. UNESCO Bulletin for Libraries, 22:4 (July–August 1968) 206–207.
(50) UNITED NATIONS EDUCATIONAL, SCIENTIFIC AND CULTURAL ORGANIZATION. Convention concerning the international exchange of publications. Adopted by the General Conference at its Tenth Session, Paris, 3 December 1958.
(51) UNITED NATIONS EDUCATIONAL, SCIENTIFIC AND CULTURAL ORGANIZATION. Handbook of international exchanges of publications. 3d ed. UNESCO, Paris, 1964, 767 p.
(52) UNITED NATIONS EDUCATIONAL, SCIENTIFIC AND CULTURAL ORGANIZATION. Report on meeting of government experts to review the application of the agreements on the importation of educational, scientific and cultural materials, Geneva, 20–29 November 1967. Paris, May 1968. (COM/CS/184/10)
(53) UNNA, WARREN. Russians to attend INTELSAT Conference. Washington Post (23 January 1969) F12.
(54) VATTEMARE, ALEXANDRE. Report on the subject of international exchanges. J. & G. S. Gideon, Washington, D.C., 1848, p. 23.
(55) WORMANN, CURT D. Aspects of international library cooperation. Library Quarterly, 38:4 (October 1968) 338.

IV

The Profession

The final two chapters in this volume deal with the management of the information center and with other professional aspects of the field. Despite their opening statement in Chapter 13, "Library and Information Center Management," that the management function is almost impossible to isolate from the milieu and processes of the organization being managed, Wasserman and Daniel delineate and define most of the important issues of management. They emphasize the behavioral approach and discuss the literature that they review in terms of some of the classical considerations of management: organization structure, objectives and goals, education and training of the manager, planning, human relations, measurement and evaluation of performance, and reporting. While Wasserman and Daniel display strong feelings about the importance of "human factors" in management, they present a balanced overview of the topic, covering such diverse subjects as the value of a library advisory committee and the problems of establishing a sound cost-accounting system for technical information systems.

Chapter 14 begins with a report on the continuing struggle toward definition of the field of information science and on the increasing concern with the growth and bibliographic control of the literature in the field. Shera and McFarland find that most literature that deals with professional aspects is concerned with the world of librarianship rather than of information science, information technology, or science information. They examine the professional organization of the field, the professional education of the information scientist, support for research and development in information science, and manpower resources.

Shera and McFarland note that trends identified in earlier volumes toward a convergence of views and concerns among librarians, information scientists, and others involved with information transfer have continued and strengthened, but they warn that, at the same time, there is an unfortunate tendency to press for inadequately conceived, planned, and staffed programs of education and training, both for nonprofessional personnel and for information scientists and technologists.

13 Library and Information Center Management

PAUL WASSERMAN and
EVELYN DANIEL[1]
University of Maryland

INTRODUCTION

The management function of libraries and information centers nearly defies isolation. It is inextricably interwoven with the fabric and the processes of the organization managed. Its measure is the sum of the contribution of all the parts, a number of which are treated as full-scale chapters in this and earlier volumes of the *Annual Review*. Much of the literature dealing with management is repetitive and hortatory. There is a plethora of generally pedestrian how-to-do-it tracts and a paucity of analytical and research contributions. Since the fare is meager and there is little of substance to digest, this chapter will be less a review and more a prescriptive overview than are most chapters in this series.

A survey of the literature in the field shows three main classes. These might be categorized as the pragmatic type, the systems approach, and the external view. The pragmatic type is not as much in vogue today as in past years. This is the how-to-do-it school, well represented by such works as those of Lock (55) and Johns (49). A subset of this group is the how-we-did-it article, examples of which abound in the current library journals. Unfortunately, without an overall framework, these examples have limited application.

The systems approach is the newest innovative technique to invade the library management field. In a recent, first-rate contribution, Morse (69) proposes a strategy for applying the analytic methods of operations research to the library operation. Adelson (1) and Gordon (38) note the close

---

[1]Credit and appreciation are expressed to Sarah M. Thomas, from whom the authors have received assistance in the preparation of this chapter.

relationship between the development of computer techniques in information centers and the systems approach for managers. Currently, there is a vast increase in the literature applying systems analysis techniques to a wide variety of fields. Dougherty & Heinritz (28) and Kemper (50) outline ways of applying these techniques to library work.

The third kind of management literature in the information field is that generated for use by top management—the external view. Ironically, some of the most useful and interesting materials fall into this category, much of it concerned with whether or not the establishment of an information center is feasible and practical from a cost benefit standpoint. Toan (106), Heany (44), and Limberg (54) discuss the uses of information, alternative ways of handling it, and a method of evaluating current information systems, not necessarily limited to libraries and/or information centers. Meltzer (66), manager of the Technical Information Center at Martin Marietta, presents an excellent discussion of the values accruing to management from an information center.

Some notice should also be taken of what might constitute a fourth kind of library management literature. The textbooks written for administration classes in library schools could be considered another subdivision of the how-to-do-it pattern. Stebbins & Mohrhardt (98) and the Indian librarian Gujrati (42) break the administrator's world up into chunks concerned with acquisitions, cataloging, personnel problems, budgeting, etc. A case-study approach is proposed by Lowell (56). The principal value of her work, however, is in the excellent bibliographic summary introducing each chapter.

SCOPE OF THIS REVIEW

The purpose of this chapter is to detail certain key elements of management from a behavioral standpoint, considering predominantly human concerns rather than formal or structural ones. It is in this area that there is little in the writings on library management to support some of the contentions. And it is here that this chapter will, on occasion, depart from the review format and assume tutorial overtones. The intention is not to preach, but to present a framework for a more complete picture of administrative behavior, and to call attention to the gaps in the literature where issues have not been identified and fully delineated.

The focus will be upon the department within the organization concerned with library, retrieval, and documentation functions, but not with data generated in and by the organization for its own decision-making processes, such as economic, marketing, or financial intelligence compiled internally. While it is patently true that such intelligence is essential to contemporary corporate or public management, responsibility for it by libraries and information centers is, as yet, relatively uncommon. To generalize from such limited present experience might risk erroneous conclusions.

Management functions may legitimately be viewed as a mélange of every organizational concern. Thus, it is necessary to delimit so that we may concentrate on what is most crucial. This account will cover the following topical areas: the purpose of establishment and the formulation of objectives, the organizational structure, the administration of the library, and the measurement and evaluation of performance. To unify and organize the total picture of management in the information center, it has been necessary to select fleeting references to current work, concepts from other disciplines, and even some older material usually outside the purview of an *Annual Review*.

Currently, there is a degree of semantic ambiguity between the terms "library" and "information center." Long and tendentious opinions surround this distinction in nomenclature. Darby (24), Bourne et al. (14), and Kertesz (52) all attempt to differentiate among libraries, information centers, and information analysis centers. While it is true that libraries have been historically known as book collections, and information and analysis centers are more concerned with data transmission and repackaging, all three actually represent points on a continuum. It seems that the distinction between the terms is more in print than in practice, at least where special libraries are concerned. For the balance of this chapter, the terms will be used more or less interchangeably.

PURPOSES AND OBJECTIVES

The existence of a library or information center in a corporate milieu is less to be expected than in an academic one; yet, a research-oriented corporation is more likely to have an information center than is a mercantile business. And, in a context in which information is a concomitant of basic organizational production and services—as in research and development, economic analysis, government and clientele services—the existence of a library is most certain of all. Bedsole (10) notes that the existence of an information center is not a function of organizational size, but is correlated more closely with the clientele served.

Nowhere in the literature is there documentation to suggest at what stage an organization can no longer perform effectively without its own information center. Doubtless, such decisions deserve the same kind of methodological analysis as managements apply to determinations about whether or not to embark upon establishing other in-house facilities. DiSalvo (27) discusses the "make or buy" judgment, which is now more significant than ever before in the light of all the available alternatives in today's culture to the company's own library. Yet, even when external forces are seen to be highly relevant to the organization's needs, and information can be purchased from various sources, Counts (23) calls attention to the fact that the organization's own library may contribute invaluably as the organizational link to these external sources. Without this link, such contacts would perhaps be unknown or little exploited. Wilhelmy & Brown (117) report that the primary indicator of need for a library may be viewed most realistically as a function of the number of problems to which the organization is susceptible where information is seen as a dramatic requisite.

During the twentieth century, there has been a phenomenal increase in the number of American special libraries and information centers. Dr. A. T. Kruzas,[2] compiler of the *Directory of Special Libraries and Information Centers*, states that their number exceeded 12,000 in 1966. Of these, he estimates that 25% are departmental and professional libraries in colleges and universities, 25% are company libraries, 15% are Government libraries, 5% subject departments within public library systems, and the balance of 30% comprise libraries maintained by nonprofit organizations and institutions in all subject fields. Kruzas reports that of the approximately 3,000 company libraries in operation in 1966, about one-half were founded after 1950. This trend gives no sign of abating.

The crucial factor relating to development of a library or information center is that it must satisfy the recurrent demands for information from a specific group of individuals—usually within the organization; occasionally, within a specific department or division of the organization; and at times, even outside the organization. Such a facility may offer access in great depth to material in a specialized area; it may provide more shallow coverage in a very wide range of activities; or it may do both. Holm (46) comments on the trend toward more specialized collections and access via network techniques to other sources. Rosenbloom & Wolek (86) found that the central consideration affecting the library's program and dimensions is that established by the organization in which the special library performs.

Graham et al. (41) have written an article on the establishment of a technical information center in a chemical corporation. They report that contemporary management, more typically than not, recognizes the need for, and strives within the limits of organizational constraints to achieve, efficient, well-planned, and well-coordinated functional units built around the specialization of task and staff. It is exactly here that the *raison d'être* of the library or information center is to be found—with the information

---

[2]Dr. A. T. Kruzas, University of Michigan School of Library Science, in a letter to the author dated January 8, 1969.

gathering and dissemination function of the complex organization placed in the hands of those who are expert in its management. In design, this is the essence of simplicity—information specialists concentrate on their specialty, saving time and effort for those who have neither the time nor, frequently, the training, skill, or interest to control this function themselves. In the process, there is provided a central organizational reservoir of materials, fact-gathering skills, and information-distributing procedures. Program details vary, based upon organizational demands, resources, staff allocations, and subject expertise—from service as an information bureau prepared to supply quickly one or two apt references, to the undertaking of thorough research into the state of the art on any subject under investigation. But in concept, as Myatt (70) points out, the harnessing of information, wherever and in whatever form it is to be found, departs from the stereotype of the more conventional library, oriented predominantly to book collecting.

The services proffered by an information center will, in large measure, be determined by the purposes for which it is initially established. Dyke (31) lists the following six reasons for instituting a technical information center: to enhance communication, to improve the quality of decision making, to reduce duplication, to increase creativity, to reduce paperwork, and to improve customer service. Thus, a coordinated plan for resolving the organization's information problems and for providing research material and technical skills to aid in the decision-making processes constitutes a potentially powerful organizational tool. The necessity of eliminating costly duplication is also noted by Bourne et al. (14). Frequently, in organizations without library programs, books, journals, and research reports are acquired in abundance for specific individuals. Elsewhere in the organization, the availability of the material is unknown. Documents are received and not retained. Similar materials are ordered at different times in different places. They must be paid for, handled, and stored, and if lost, reordered. Where a library exists, these processes are orderly, efficient, and centralized under professional management. Centralization of acquisitions reduces paperwork and, consequently, accounting costs, as well as enabling the organization to realize discount opportunities not otherwise available.

Two additional contributions of the information center have not been fully explored in the current literature. One is the public relations value. The existence of a library or information center demonstrates that organizational decisions can be based upon reliable and current information. There is a contact point between the organization and other libraries and like institutions, making possible the exchange of information, pooling of resources, and sharing of programs of common interest and value. Perhaps the most salient contribution of an information center is the creation and designation of a specific department committed to organizational information support. Personnel are thus put on notice that information is a highly valued commodity and, as a consequence, the organizational decision-making process is, or may be, very subtly enlarged.

Not infrequently, at the point of serious attention to crystalizing the scope, structure, and other requisites relating to the start-up of the library or information center, outside consultants have been known to bring clarity and detachment to the process. Berry (26) has compiled a directory of library consultants, which includes an introduction by Ralph Blasingame detailing the nature of the service performed and specifying when it is advisable to seek help from a consultant. Wasserman & Greer (115) have provided a more universal guide to consultants for business, industry, and government, which also includes specialized information-oriented firms. The Special Libraries Association (91) concentrates on such problems through its Consultation Service, which maintains a roster of carefully screened experts available for assignment according to their subject competence and geographic proximity.

As the professional charged with responsibility for the information center, the administrator naturally assumes a responsible role in the formulation of its goals. Lowry (57) emphasizes that the environment of the center's operations must be understood before information objectives can be set. Consistency between the library's goals and the overall organizational goals is an essential component. Unfortunately, the larger organization's objectives may not be defined. The decisions, plans, and forecasts required by the library administrator for coordination of his efforts may be nonexistent. Demands for more concrete plans from an aggressive administrator may distress his supervisor. On the other hand, these demands may catalyze a much-needed analysis at higher levels. Doubtless, organizational life is more tranquil with a library administrator who does not strain to blend his efforts with the broader design, but remains content in his own role. Perhaps this is one subtle reason for the predominance of the more passive strain of library administrator. Taking another viewpoint, Galin (37) asserts that it is not essential that higher-level objectives be clearly defined; it is necessary only that the objectives of the information center do not materially contradict important company or research objectives.

Goal formulation is a complex and vital topic for library administrators, but little is being written about it. Perhaps this is a reflection of practice. However, some of the subtleties of goal formulation bear discussion. The library committee is a device employed to facilitate the process. It is less common, perhaps, in the more typical corporation than in the research-oriented organization only one step removed from academia, where many tend to view themselves really as displaced academics. Informal devices are employed frequently. Whatever the procedure, the more widespread the involvement of interested personnel, the more acceptance and understanding of library purposes result. Olsson (75) presents the theory of management by objective. In his approach, an organization's goals are identified and defined, interpreted and communicated to personnel at all levels so that all efforts and activities are directed to a central purpose. This method is a means of combating the ambiguity of goals within large organizations as observed by Presthus (83).

To be meaningful, goals must help to shape the library's internal processing and to match library performance with clientele requirements. The widest range of objectives is possible in any special library; hence the need to derive priorities and to translate them into resource allocation terms. Since it may not be possible to achieve every goal simultaneously, such ranking and relative weighting is the only rational course. The rank order necessarily fluctuates as circumstances within the overall organization and in the library change—with shifts in resources, advances in technology, improved physical arrangements, staff modifications, new overall organizational efforts, etc.

A distinction must be made here between policies and objectives. Steiner (99), in his comprehensive study of top management planning, carefully demarcates the boundaries that exist between policies, objectives, goals, plans, and so on. He defines a policy as a guide to action to achieve an objective. Often, the term "policy formulation" is confused and is used to connote both the development of organizational objectives and their implementation through the formulation of general rules of action. Policies determine how resources are to be allocated to satisfy the ultimate aims of the organization. It is fruitless to talk about policy formulation within a vacuum, for policies are shaped only out of the need for implements designed for larger purposes. The selection of objectives or goals and the assignment of relative importance to them—priorities and values that are then translated into resource allocation terms for each of the goals—are the essential first order of effective library management.

An integral part of policy making is the planning of activities that will achieve aims most expeditiously. Policies are designed to help channel effort and to simplify daily decisions. Because policies are set up as guides to operation, they are seldom specific, and it is frequently necessary for the library manager to interpret policy. Steiner (99) establishes a hierarchical relationship that leads downward from objectives to policies, and then to procedures, standard operating plans, and rules which are the methods or techniques by and through which policies are achieved. The library manager might wish to consider the feasibility of interpreting some policies by written procedures, keeping in mind that he could thus lose a certain amount of flexibility.

One important reason for differentiating objectives from policies is to reduce the prospect that policies might become objectives by evolving from practice rather than being formulated by library management. In a now-classic article, Merton (67) expands on this idea, showing the process whereby a rigid or sacred institutional policy soon becomes an objective. Once a policy has lost its rationale, even though it is still offered as a final authority by anyone anywhere in the library, it has become an objective and a highly questionable one.

Often, the goals of an organization cannot be achieved within a limited period of time. Consequently, the policies and programs established have to be directed primarily toward one goal and only secondarily toward others. One purpose of sound administrative policy is to seek to resolve any conflict there may be between objectives. Policies guide organizational action and represent the best thinking by library management about how objectives may be most effectively achieved under the conditions facing the library. An important point in the discussion of objectives and policies is that all the responsible staff members be given a clear understanding of the basic aims of the library within the larger enterprise, so that the policies of the library may be logically formulated to achieve these ends.

ORGANIZATIONAL STRUCTURE

Placement

Perhaps the greatest organizational intrigue connected with library and information centers, particularly at the point of their inspiration, is the decision about where the library is to be subsumed in the organization. Put another way, who shall control the information function, and where in the organizational hierarchy should the responsibility for it reside? Typically, the choice of where the information center is to be fixed in the hierarchy is made only once. Too frequently, perhaps, this is found to be but an accident of local history. Once the organization is fixed, shifts of location are uncommon, though they are not impossible.

Bourne et al. (14) suggest that the information center should report to a high level of management, to one that has general responsibility for major groups. They warn against assigning the library to a department with more limited responsibility. In organizations that maintain research departments, the information center frequently functions as a subunit. Yet, once its own identity has been forged—particularly if it provides a service to the entire organization—elevation of the center to independent department status as a staff unit under the supervision of a senior official may not be unthinkable. The original location of a special library may serve as an inhibiting factor in its use by others in the organization, for example, when it exists as an adjunct to research and is viewed by others as supportive of this activity only. Here, the political and organizational costs of relocation, the consequences of disengagement, the psychological self-assurance, and the administrative dexterity of the information center manager will all be factors to be considered.

The intriguing problem of the placement of the library in the political hierarchy has been largely ignored by the writers on library planning. Some of the intangibles that will vitally affect the library's value to the organization are only cursorily considered, if at all. A partial listing of some factors that need thoughtful consideration by library managers would include the significance of a sympathetic managerial attitude in the acceptance and full use of library service; the degree to which this sympathetic frame of mind is endangered when the library is affiliated with the research department; the importance of sponsorship by an information-conscious, high-level officer; the organizational perils involved in subordination of the library to another department; and the necessity of achieving the highest possible bureaucratic sanctuary within the organization. Each of these factors could be developed at some length, and it is tempting to do so in the light of the lacunae in the literature.

The physical placement of the library has received a little more consideration in the writings on library management. Anthony (7) discusses in detail some of the considerations affecting the selection of the site for the planned center. He points out that dilution of the library's resources may be avoided by careful site selection and recommends that the library be placed centrally in an area to which people go regularly for other purposes; for example, to use computer services, document reproduction facilities, or administration and personnel departments. Central placement is certainly the most obvious answer to the question of where to fit a library in an organization. Skolnik (89) says the two important parameters affecting the design of an information center are the groups being served and the technical operations necessary to serve them. He would seem to opt for placing the library close to its primary user clientele, rather than to the center of the entire organization. Boaz (12) rather matter of factly sums it up by stating that the position of the library within an organization should be determined by its ultimate service goals.

Against diverse backgrounds of opinion about where to fit a library in a given organization, it would be useful to be able to draw upon empirical evidence in a sizable sample of organizations about where the library does fit and why. Unfortunately, such data do not exist. Bedsole (10) offers data for only 21 libraries in which he conducted personal interviews. He does not provide details for his larger mail sample of 117 corporations. In a recent study of special library personnel, the Special Libraries Association (93) offers the following disclaimer:

> Some use was made of all the data received in the 1,137 usable responses with the exception of that furnished in answer to the query on the title of the librarian's supervisor. The wide diversity of replies to this question precluded any meaningful classifications.

In 1952, Strieby (103) made a study of the position of selected corporation libraries according to the organization charts of their parent organizations. She observed that special libraries were as diverse as the firms they served and that the libraries fell into any number of organizational patterns. Strauss et al. (102) made a similar study in 1964 with similar results.

Several factors that have influenced the physical placement of a special library or information center in the past may become nonexistent in the future. Thus, the growing insistence on library networks points to a possible division between collections of resource materials and the access point of the user. Increasing utilization of telephone, teletype, and similar developments reduces the necessity for geographic proximity of library facilities. These factors may seem obvious, but there are ramifications of such changes that need research and exploration.

All administrators would certainly agree that the overriding consideration in the organizational placement of the special library is the need to do justice to the information requirements of the organization of which it is a part. No special library exists for its own purposes or in its own right. Where it exists, it exists as a service auxiliary of the parent organization. The blend of needs, personalities, data requirements, and other factors of different organizations makes it impossible to generalize about the most appropriate location for a library in any given institutional setting. Perhaps the only guidance possible is the suggestion that original placement be given considerable attention and that a judgment, once made, need not fix the place inexorably.

Centralization or Decentralization

One problem that concerns libraries and other service departments in large organizations, particularly those in which there may be more than one plant or office location, is whether or not to decentralize the library service. A survey (2) of the advantages of centralized management operations versus those of decentralized ones was conducted ten years ago. Some of these findings are still valid today. The chief advantage of centralization (in addition to the manifest dividends of greater economy, efficiency, etc.) was found to be the companywide service feature, while the chief advantage of a decentralized system was considered to be the closeness of the center to the operations and the personalized contact possible.

In a more recent work, Kent et al. (51) pursue the centralization-decentralization problem from a different tack. They analyze the cost of indexing and analyzing reports and attempt to show how the advantages of a centralized information processing agency may be offset by physical queuing problems, service delays, and the lack of subject specialists to structure queries. (The latter is an intellectual queuing problem.) Friedman (36) attempts to prove that a centrally organized library requires a decentralized computer information processing system, and vice versa.

Of course, the degree of centralization or decentralization is another factor. Cooper (22) describes the pattern that typifies the university library system and can be applied to other organizations as well. The library system is a loose confederation that combines some of the elements of both centralization and decentralization. The librarian controls systemwide library policy, participates in the selection of the heads of individual libraries, and generally administers acquisitions programs. Under such a design, the central library is often a coordinating unit, housing the central union catalog of all books and journals in the various libraries and even serving as acquisitions and catalog center for the system. Under these terms, each library has its own staff, which is usually appointed by the chief librarian in collaboration with the representative of the department in which the library is located. Such a system provides for a pattern of centralized planning and control, with a highly decentralized administration of operations. As Lowry & Kennedy (58) show, coordination may be centralized while operations are decentralized. This "bottoms-up" management frequently encourages initiative and creative suggestions from lower levels of the organization and is a managerial style that has come into use in other than library situations, as well as in a limited number of library situations in recent years.

Relations with Management and with Users

A special library or information center is in the somewhat uncomfortable position of serving two masters—management and the individual users. Channels of communication must be maintained in all directions.

One method of communication that is touted as useful is use of the library committee. Advisory committees, formal or informal, often serve several purposes in this regard. They relate the information center to the several organizational components, they provide a useful internal political mechanism for gaining organizational budgetary support, and they help delineate subject areas to be developed in the information program. Extension of the committee's powers into unwarranted jurisdictional zones that usurp the administrative prerogative of the librarian may be disastrous. Success or failure will be determined by the administrative acumen of the librarian, the nature of local personalities, and the methods of their choice to serve, as well as the exercise of strategic judgment about how to exploit their potential contribution effectively.

Emory (32) theorizes that information has value to the extent that it contributes to an organization's goals. He presents a mathematical formula for assigning a utility value to a given piece of information. Successful managerial relations may be gauged, at least in one respect, by the degree to which organizational decision processes show the influence of information gained through the information center. To the extent that the manager of the information center is an interested party in organizational decision processes, the expertise and intelligence with which he is charged can be drawn into focus to enlarge the information base of decisions.

Boaz (12) points out that the company or organization has a responsibility to keep the librarian informed of new plans and developments. The information center has sometimes been found to be an isolated segment of the organization, out of touch and not considered in the major decision processes. This should not be the case today. Meltzer (66) demonstrates that, in contemporary organizations with their great reliance upon factual evidence as the basis of decision making, information service enjoys an extraordinary potential. Thus, library committees may be considered a means of lateral communication, and the interconnections with management in the decision-making process, means of communication upward.

The most necessary relationship is that with the user. Maizell (63) outlines an informal method of systems analysis in ascertaining user characteristics. Links may be forged through the imagination and dexterity of the administrator in correlating with other units and with individuals. They are fashioned out of the products and services derived from the information center. Wilhelmy & Brown (117) assert that the use of the information is the real payoff of any center. The capacity of the information center to relate is tied squarely to the level of activity that it generates in the form of clientele programs and services.

Size and Cost Considerations

The size of an information center or library is strikingly variable. Myatt (70) reports that some organizations prefer a small information center with highly experienced information personnel who depend heavily on external resources. As might be expected, these organizations are most frequently found in metropolitan centers, where other collections and other experts are readily available. Other organizations, he notes, develop large libraries in which a high proportion of fact-finding is done on the premises. The location of the organization is a determinant of where this fact-finding is done because the isolated organization must rely on its own resources to a far greater extent than the library located in a highly developed center of bibliographic activity. In essence, the salient contribution of the information program is seen, not in the extent and range of library collections, but rather, in the rapid and efficient identification and drawing in of information wherever it is found.

The costs of information service have been a relatively unexplored area until recently; now, more and more attempts are being made to place the marketing of information on a more rational basis. Emory (32) designates some of the factors governing the cost of information, such as the volume of data handled, response time, accuracy, and flexibility. He makes an important distinction between the cost of information and its value.

Meltzer (66) suggests the difficulty of providing accurate figures on the costs of a library or information center. The United States Office of Education (74) concluded an extensive survey of a select group of special libraries serving the Federal Government. The study is of nominal utility in comparison with special libraries outside the category. The Special Libraries Association's (94) compilation of six profiles of representative special libraries in terms of staff, space, and money gives some indication of the probable level of support required for an information center. An early survey from the chemical industry (2) details some factors of information service and translates them into cost and budget dimensions.

The two principal classes of cost most often discussed are the start-up cost and the periodic budget or maintenance charges. Hyslop (48) adds an additional cost, that of system refinement and redesign as a continuing element in operation. Little guidance is available for the calculation of these nonstandard costs, because the literature in this area is shallow. Many of the calculations are a function of tradeoff between, on the one hand, services and technology, and on the other, the financial drain on the organization. Interestingly, very little documentation exists that details clearly and precisely the actual costs of system changes, modifications and installation of new programs, automation of technical procedures and processes, application and utility of machines to information retrieval processes, and so on. Much managerial decision making in the information context is taken on faith. The paucity of the literature illustrates the stark need for more clear and precise cost intelligence.

Hyslop (48) contends that development costs of an information center should be Government-subsidized and that operating costs should be recovered from the users. This introduction of the marketplace as an element in the dissemination of information might be a way of forcing centers to develop more realistic cost figures. Peters (79) outlines a complicated cost-control system for a technical information center. One recent contribution of importance is Helmkamp's (45) study, which is designed as an operating manual to aid managers of technical information centers in the establishment of a sound cost-accounting system. While oriented particularly to NASA search and dissemination systems, the methodology has generalized pertinence.

Kyle (53) stresses the advantages for the special library in development of an annual budget as the basis for efficient planning, and as a tool with which to demonstrate needed variations from year to year to the organization's management. Meltzer (66) comments on the high proportion of expenditures for staff compared to other resources of the library or information center. Not uncommonly, salaries for the professional staff and other personnel will range from 60 to 80% of library budget charges, he says. [Kyle (53) estimates 65 to 85% compared to an average of 50% for a general library.] Wages and salaries will, of course, be based upon geographic location, level of responsibility, size and magnitude of the program, scope of assignment, and subject expertise. The Special Libraries Association (93) conducted a survey of salaries in 1959, which was updated in 1967 (95). Frarey & Rosenstein (35) report salaries for new library school graduates as an annual feature of *Library Journal*. These provide some indications of salary trends by region and by type of library.

THE ADMINISTRATION OF THE LIBRARY

To recapitulate, we have established the library or information center, formulated objectives for it based on company direction, placed it within its parent organization, considered whether to centralize it or not, related it to its environment, and discussed its size and cost. Now, we introduce the leading character: the administrator. This section will be a discourse on the administrator, the planning function, human relations, and scientific management. The predominant emphasis will be placed on the human element.

The Administrator

The theme of change is the dominant motif for a discussion of the administrator. As we examine his background, his educational accomplishments, the nature of his position, and some of the role conflicts he will face, we will constantly be comparing what used to be with what is today and with what will be in the future. Management at its core is seen in the capacity of the human being who performs the administrative role. The problem, in essence, is one of attracting and stimulating individuals with the cast of mind, the commitment, the knowledge, the experience, and the imagination to develop the library at a time when talent is zealously competed for, and when more rewarding incentives may be obtained in other pursuits.

Furthermore, as demonstrated in the most recent Special Libraries Association (SLA) Salary Survey (95), the decision base, the scale of magnitude of managerial responsibility, and the relative prestige accorded to those engaged in information center management tend to be seriously limited. The corporate or government context delimits the organizational options of the library manager. One would expect the organization's tolerance for growth, or lack of it, to condition its choice of a library manager. Conversely, the sophisticated library manager will probably attempt to match his capacities to the propensities of the organization he seeks to serve.

Some few inquiries have been made in the past into the personality of the librarian. The ones most frequently cited are the Douglass study (29) based on library school students, published in 1957, and an earlier one by Bryan (17) on the public librarian. A recent contribution to this field is the master's study by DeWeese (25), a student in the Purdue University Library Operations Research Group, on the psychological strivings of members of one library culture.

An interesting area that cries out for exploration is that of the psychological propensity of those drawn to the special library situation in comparison with that of individuals drawn to the more secure academic and public library berths. The likelihood that more senior administrative responsibility would be unavailable to library staff members may even have influenced the sex composition of library staff personnel. As the rising sense of the importance of information, combined with the advent of a technology capable of transferring information rapidly and efficiently, has made a dramatic change in the promotional opportunities available, it has probably also changed the type of person attracted to the role. Still, the limited availability of senior posts in the information center milieu, when contrasted, for example, with the academic or the public library, is a deterrent.

Because of the limited amount of data, we must speculate on the personality characteristics of the administrator. For example, we might speculate that the professionals in the information center field tend to be more mobile than their traditional library counterparts. They may be, at least in part, conditioned by the need to be "where the action is," at least as the action is defined by those in the special library or information center movement. Information center professionals also seem to be attracted to settings in which they can practice a degree of entrepreneurial freedom, certainly not a commonly held desire of the traditional librarian.

Unfortunately, few details about the backgrounds or characteristics of the special library and information center administrator are now available, as the Battelle report (8) points out. Anderson (6) notes the difficulty of listing general qualifications for technical librarians. Apparently, many managers have been drawn from traditional librarianship. With the increased technical requisites and broader administrative responsibility more recently implied in the role, there has been an influx of people from technical pursuits, including subject indexing and abstracting, as well as from other managerial roles. As the newer information science forges its way, with the technological base of information activity becoming a clearer requisite, a higher premium may be expected to be placed upon those who master the technical side of the information function. Still, Gordon (38) and Moon (68) agree that the managerial role in the information center resides in the twilight zone between technological expertise and administrative effectiveness; neither alone suffices.

To fit this prescription precisely, the administrator is seen to be the product of both library and information science education, with a disciplinary base and with management insights. Galin (37) summarizes, as the three principal areas in which personal competence is required: management of information systems, understanding of the technical operations of information systems functions, and a substantive knowledge of science and technology.

One key influence upon the ability of a field to generate appropriate leadership is its process of educational acculturation. On the theory that administrators are developed through experience rather than in the university, library education has, until very recently, played only a modest role, as Stone (101) points out. Some developments may be worthy of note, however. The need for training having been identified, the first developments were *ex post facto* programs. An institute for supervisory training at the School of Library Science at UCLA in 1960 was probably the beginning. A Seminar on Middle Manager Development in Libraries was held at the Catholic University in 1964 as a result of an ALA Committee recommendation. The program, considered a pilot project, is discussed in a review by Stone (101).

A more recent development is the University of Maryland Library Administrators Development Program (107). This annual two-week summer institute is designed to meet the needs of those who assume senior responsibilities in large and complex agencies. The emphasis is upon such issues as organization theory and organizational processes, the human dimension of organizations, and managerial problems of innovation and change. As outlined in the schedule, topics are developed in sessions on theories of administration and management, the characteristics of complex organizations, interorganizational relationships, problem solving, leadership, motivation, communication, objective formulation, personnel relations, decision making, financial planning and control, performance appraisal, the impact of technology on information organizations, and the implementation of change, in seminar, case study, and role playing.

The University of Washington Graduate School of Librarianship (108), in conjunction with the Graduate School of Business at the same university, offered a comparable program under Office of Education sponsorship in the spring of 1969. The pattern is also seen to be taking hold in the State of Ohio (97), where specialized programs for administrators—in this instance, public library administrators—have begun.

Special programs to meet the particular need of middle-management personnel in libraries have been more uncommon. Maizell (61) suggests a program of continuing education adaptable to the individual. A number of libraries have taken advantage of internal company programs or industrywide programs, but the evidence of special programs oriented to the needs of middle-management personnel in libraries is limited. The American Management Association has, from time to time, sponsored workshops for those managerially concerned with special libraries. Two examples are the September 1968 workshop (4) and the 15th annual EDP conference (5). Under sponsorship of the U.S. Office of Education, a number of universities have offered or plan to offer institutes oriented to the needs of middle-management personnel in libraries in Denver, Maryland, Michigan, Miami of Ohio and other areas. Government concern with managerial problems of libraries is reflected in some of the activities of the Committee on Scientific and Technical Information (COSATI) (34), especially in its Special Committee on Management.

The educational programs listed above are geared to the man in the field. Yet Stone (101) sees the necessity for preparation for administrative roles through formal education of the library student. She stigmatizes many of the library schools for their pedestrian curricular concerns, which scarcely touch the more sophisticated issues surrounding management behavior. An attempt to modify library administration courses is made in the recently published volume edited by Wasserman & Bundy (114).

White (116) examines library education from another viewpoint. His concern is in measuring the capacity of library schools to change the role perception of new entrants to the library field, from that of functionaries performing at relatively low organizational levels to a role of more ambitious commitment and aspiration, via the professional acculturation process. To strive for enhanced professional status implies a clearer understanding of the characteristics and attributes as well as the image and the status of those who play such roles. Bundy & Wasserman (20) emphasize the need to strive for an organizational culture more compatible with achievement of the goals and values of professionalism than of the culture of the employee. Two studies by Walters (109) and Segal (88) that relate directly or tangentially to these issues are currently in progress.

One way in which the role of the administrator in the special library context differs, Wasserman (112) sees, is in the degree of economic responsibility imposed by cost-conscious organizations, which constantly force tradeoffs between the ideal and the possible. For, while his academic counterpart may continue to function under the possible misapprehension that feverish collection-building is preferable to discriminating choice, the special library administrator enjoys no such luxury. He is forced to choose carefully to ensure a close and precise match between the requirements of his clientele and the physical collection. Rippon & Francis (85) underline the necessity of closely diagnosing the patterns of information need of the manager's constituency, determining whether they relate to broad, general lines of inquiry or to narrow, specific ones. Thus, the manager's function, in part, is to understand clearly how his program and services are to be most strategically exploited. The sophistication of the administrator will be reflected in his perception of the nature of his organization, and this, in turn, will condition his contribution.

The development of information centers, with their emphasis and insistence on information *per se*, has drastically changed the role of the administrator of a special library or information center. As an illustration, the traditional library stresses subject access to the book collection through a card catalog. Client service is a one-to-one response to individual need, with the card catalog seen as the library's primary substantive contribution. The special library reorients its concentration from reader to material. The entire information store—periodicals, serials, records, documents, etc., not only the books—may then be analyzed. The personal service, one question at a time, is not neglected, but the library adds the tasks of screening and reviewing indexes and, perhaps, abstracting nonbook acquisitions. Access to nonbooks may thus be similar to that provided for books. The strategy for such access, and the case for its implementation, is thus seen as the responsibility of the library manager, who has ascertained its relevance to organizational requirements.

The need for a level of sophistication on the part of the library manager about the subject matter of the field in which the information center is concentrated is a hotly debated issue. There are two conflicting views. McGowan (59) holds that the professional function of information management based upon systems analysis and the capacity to exploit the technology to advantage is the sole stock-in-trade of the information manager. For the other view, Kertesz (52), Darby (24) and Wasserman (111) see the special librarian's competence linked directly with his sophistication in the substantive field in which the organization performs. Perhaps professional information handling and subject specialization may both be seen, not as unique, but as part of the increasing specialization of roles in modern organizations of large size and complexity. As the mandate of the information center shifts from a traditional custodial function to one related to the dynamics of the organization of which it is a part, each responsibility may be accentuated. Kertesz (52) makes the point that the output of the information is not the same as its input. Subject analysis and repackaging of information play a crucial role, for the information manager not only selects, but also synthesizes and evaluates, to offer screened access to pertinent, relevant information. And the process is enlarged and rationalized by the growing importance of the application of electronic data processing to information center activity, according to Galin (37). Traditional librarianship is thus modified in two ways—in the increased extent to which judgment in the evaluation and appropriateness of information is exercised, and in the more sophisticated means for storing and retrieving it.

The transition from more conventional library practice to advanced information center routine varies markedly from field to field and from organization to organization. In science information centers, propelled perhaps by the Weinberg (81) committee recommendations and the vitality of the American response to the exigencies of science and technology, this transition has been most rapid. Corporate endeavor in fields outside of science and technology has shown a far lower rate of acceptance of the need to develop more refined mechanisms for information control. Perhaps this is due in part to the lack of precision in the information itself or, perhaps, to the lesser utility accorded its use in decision making in nontechnical fields. One consequence of the decreased demand for top-flight information centers in the nontechnical areas may be seen in the lesser prestige, status, and responsibility accorded library managers in these areas.

For the information manager to carry out his role effectively, he must be sensitive to the potential uses and applications of modern technology to information requirements. The subtleties surrounding the exploitation of this technology rationally and economically are explored in Wasserman (110). Mann & Williams (64) detail the perils and pitfalls of applying machine technology in a public utility, an institutional base that is somewhat parallel to a library. Both the attractions and the deterrents in library automation are explored, from a behavioral viewpoint, in a recent article by Bundy (18).

The organizational framework within which the library administrator functions requires certain capacities and a considerable amount of sophistication. To perform in a staff role to the organization and in a line role as information center administrator requires an inordinate tolerance for ambiguity not often demanded in organizations. Etzioni (33) sees the role of expert and the concept of administrator as frequently disjoint, with each function independent of the other. The background and preparation of the director of the information center are more typically in information service rather than in management. The director's lack of administrative sophistication may explain why there is often confusion in his role perception, his understanding of the nature of his authority, and his ability to orient his performance within such a framework. To specify the problem is not to solve it, nor is the confusion of role characteristic solely of the library administrator. Marcson (65) describes the role of the research administrator who faces similar problems. Perhaps in a limited way, this issue illuminates the need for enhanced administrative sophistication and the corresponding understanding of organizational relationships with their political consequences among those who make up the information team. To perceive the intrinsic ambivalence of such role performance is the beginning of understanding.

In the midst of these unsettling considerations a clamor arises for a new style of manager, one who will relinquish some of his authority to his subordinates. Nyren (73) claims that the position of head librarian is being magnified, with inhibiting effects on line librarians. Thompson (105) also discusses this "ancient problem of freedom vs. control." The shift from the more authoritarian form of management now prevalent, to one in which the decision base is shared among the professional group through the entire range of decisions, is the focus of a recent article by Smith (90). He perceives a change in management to a concern centered more on knowledge and technical capacity than on authority. And, as an active voice is conferred on other than administrative personnel, the status of other personnel is increased, leading ultimately to an information organization more genuinely professional in its composition and personality than appears now to be the case.

Moreover, the variability of organizational views of the library, from the concept of a static collection at one extreme to the dynamic hub of corporate information transfer at the other, requires of the administrator a psychological capacity to engender universal acceptance for his department at both extremes, an acceptance perhaps impossible to achieve fully. The capacity of the library administrator to function as an agent for change when technology, the organization of information, and client need are all dramatically changing, and in a bureaucratic form that, by its nature, resists innovation, constitutes probably the most important challenge to managerial ingenuity. Presthus (82) assesses the tolerance of library bureaucracies to change in one study of the Maryland Manpower Research Program. Another study (107) deals with the propensity of the administrator of the special library and information center to serve as change agent.

Williams (118) concerns himself with the capacity of the library environment to tolerate change, with emphasis on the receptivity or resistance to such change on the part of library personnel.

The management posture involves other inherent role-conflicts as well. The administrator's expertise is legitimately oriented toward the goal aspirations of the organization in which he finds himself. Yet, as a professional, he relates to a peer group who perform by a set of standards and goals determined and delineated by the professional group, such as ALA (3) and SLA (92). Gouldner (39 and 40) depicts the conflict between local and cosmopolitan orientation in two articles that are old, but still worthy of thoughtful consideration. Nimer (71) has recently reviewed professionalism in a bibliographic summary, oriented to librarianship and information science. She highlights this dichotomy between the professional role and the administrative role of the information center manager. This "schizophrenic" condition is accentuated as library personnel aspire upward organizationally, tending more and more to lay aside their expert plumage as they assume the coloration of the administrative breed. While this condition may be equally true in other fields, it may be more pronounced in libraries and information centers because of the way in which they are organizationally structured. The combination of this duality of roles, coupled with the limited conceptual and theoretical base of practice, and the very modest demands for subject competence put upon information service personnel, may contribute to the higher value placed upon administration. Scott (87) has effectively detailed these and other stresses inherent in the role of the professional in organizations seeking other ends.

Boaz (11) places possible elements of an ethical code for professional librarians in three categories: the relationship of the librarian to society, to his client, and to his colleagues. The propriety of keeping corporate secrets is a clear moral duty for the administrative officer of the library. Other issues of corporate loyalty—for example, the uses to which information is put—may come into conflict with the librarian's moral duty to society. Although no one seems yet to have explored this question, perhaps it is reasonable to surmise that the librarian has most typically played a value-neutral role, refusing to be concerned with where, how, and to what end use the information he stores or delivers is put. Ridgeway (84) relates the story of the involvement of library personnel in activities related to allegedly questionable ends in the account of the General Motors Corporation's legal library in connection with an attempt to gather incriminating data on Ralph Nader. Evidence of such activity would certainly be difficult to document, but the story does point up another role conflict of which the individual administrator must be conscious.

Hope (47) outlines some of the requisite characteristics for the library manager of the future. Along with more training and greater versatility, he foresees that librarians will have to learn much more about the psychology of working in close proximity with other people. Staats (96) in speaking of the Government manager of the future, says that he must possess qualities of restlessness, research, drive, and dissatisfaction—a collection of alliterative qualities equally apt for library managers of the future, both in and out of the Government.

Planning

Stone (101) states that one of the library executive's primary duties is to plan. Yet, many administrators seek to solve problems only when they are actually faced with them. Library administrators employing this strategy rely principally upon experience and intuition to resolve problems. Such an approach has the advantage of being simple and flexible, but it fails to take into account anticipated developments. As a consequence, the result is often opportunistic, even haphazard, problem solution. Obviously, this is in conflict with the tenets of contemporary administrative philosophy.

Planning is a continuous process. Steiner (99) tells us that planning involves choosing from among alternative courses of action. For planning to be successful, the librarian requires a sense of direction and a perspective that, hopefully, he has gained from a thoughtful determination of the objectives he has previously set for himself and his library.

Much of the literature on planning for libraries and information centers concentrates on physical planning, involving such matters as equipment and layout. Lock (55), Anthony (7), and Skolnik (89) all concern themselves with this indisputably vital area of library planning. But the scope of an administrator's planning activities should be more comprehensive. He must visualize the range of services the library is to provide, who is to be served, what techniques are to be employed, and the projected changes to be made in the library's parent organization that may require modification of the library's program. In addition, there is the question of how far ahead planning should be done, and in how much detail. It is obvious that effective progress and order depend upon a careful blueprint and anticipation of future requirements and activities.

Kyle (53) emphasizes that the ideal is a written program and plan of action that states clearly the purpose of the library, its terms of reference, and the methods of achieving desired results. This plan should be formulated through consultation with every organizational entity that is to be strategic to library resource attainment and clientele service. The very process of formulation often brings with it clarity about what it is the library seeks to achieve, why it exists, whom it serves, and in what ways.

Logically, the program of the information center will work out its arrangements to make goals, rules, and staff concepts of programs and norms generally consistent. Yet, it is not always clearly understood what parties have an interest in decision processes of a library or information center. Galin (37) enumerates the parties who have a stake in development planning as the staff; the management personnel of the parent organization; and the clientele, both within and without the organization, who may be present or potential users. A key function of the library administrator is to evaluate the needs of the situation and to strike a balance between the often-conflicting demands of the various interests so that his unit may survive and thrive. It is in the adroit handling of these multiple factors that the manager ensures the clearest prospects of achieving his own ends and those of the department in his charge.

Generally, it can be said that the special library is concerned fundamentally with the goals of the organization of which it is a part, and it would logically follow that the program in, say, a research laboratory would differ sharply from that in a Federal reserve bank. Yet, as Steiner (99) concludes, even though the precise type of planning may vary enormously among companies, there are a number of characteristics of administration that have universal application. In well-administered libraries, operations are forecast as far ahead as practicable, so that there is sufficient time for analysis to determine the best way of handling anticipated problems. Galin (37) found that an overwhelming proportion of information center planning is in the short-time range. Even in the most sophisticated systems he analyzed, he approximated that only 20% of the development planning could be considered long-range. Of course, the difficulty of divining the advance plans of the parent organization is a key factor. This requirement relates back to the need for effective communication with other divisions of the institution. Obviously, it will be easier to predict some types of future problems than others. But, unless the special library is in the position of receiving facts in time to modify its program thoughtfully, eleventh-hour judgments and adjustments become its inevitable operating style.

In planning considerations, a recent development is program budgeting, which evolved as a strategy to aid in governmental long-range planning, and which might usefully be explored for possible application to the management of libraries and information centers. Bradley's (15) statement on program budgeting defines the relationship between budget action and the achievement of policy objectives. He emphasizes the necessity of careful analysis in the preplanning stage. Novick (72) outlines the basic concepts of program budgeting for long-range planning purposes. Thompson (104), taking an opposing position, warns that the PPB ("planning-programming-budgeting") approach underestimates human capacities and may end up as the scientific administration of all things, including people. He pillories the advocates of this approach, calling them "new Taylorites"[3] who have seized upon the PPB method as a ploy to gain political power.

Human Relations

According to McGregor (60), most people who speak of employee roles in organizations discuss questions of employee participation in management, job satisfaction, and productivity, and base their ideas upon what is commonly termed the "Human Relations School." It was this movement that first identified the correlation of productivity with job satisfaction and employee adjustment. The need for informing the staff about what is transpiring in the organization, particularly under conditions of change, is stressed by Williams (118), who says that participation can give individuals a sense of belonging and a sense of commitment that increase the probability of success of the change. More recently, Carey (21) has criticized the traditional human relations concepts and characterized them as oversimplified, unrealistic, perhaps unscientific, and even empirically unsound. Yet, to question is not completely to dismiss.

Advocates of the interpersonal method of the study of management, such as Presthus (83) and Dubin (30), identify several issues relating to the interpersonal relationships in an organization, such as personality conflicts, the need to preserve freedom of action while maintaining control, the means of dealing with conflict, and the necessity for coordination.

Personality problems arise in many ways. A frequent mistake made is that of building organizations around individuals. When this happens, as it so frequently does in library settings, the disadvantages are felt in the difficulty of training understudies, in overemphasis upon personalities, in a reduction in the possibilities for coordination, and in an increase of possible friction. One subtle problem is the way in which information may sometimes be guarded to deter others from sharing control over procedures. As long as one and only one person knows a procedure, a fact, or a program element, he remains its sole custodian and must be depended upon by the organization. To the extent that one person builds up a store of such information, he becomes less vulnerable to replacement, sometimes even building a personal following among those who must rely on him for what he alone knows. The ultimate effect of this problem is considerable turmoil in the organization upon his retirement or resignation.

Brophy & Gazda (16) suggest ways to handle a staff member who has poor interpersonal relations with supervisors, co-workers, or clientele. The

---

[3] After Frederick Taylor, considered by many the father of the scientific management school.

essential is to recognize that any administrative job must be carried out by individuals, and the results can be no better than the human beings who do the work.

The prospects for greatest effectiveness and enthusiasm are enhanced when organizational lines and position descriptions are not so sharply drawn that they unduly diminish individual freedom of action. Nyren (73) sees a climate of permissiveness for individual initiative and role enlargement as a powerful motivational factor. Clarity of responsibility and authority in a position are not incongruent with personal freedom. It is usually only when the authority structure is rigid and narrowly confining that constraint on freedom of action may diminish the effectiveness of people. Skill in administration calls for obtaining a fine balance between the needs of the individual and the plan of action.

Superficial harmony in an organizational setting does not necessarily signify an effective, smooth organization. Bundy (19) observes that conflict is an inevitable concomitant of the formal organization, although the issues are often played down because of the tendency for people to avoid conflict. She notes that libraries are frequently the scene of personality conflicts, as well as conflicts related to functional responsibility and clashes in striving for resources. While acute conflict can never be easily resolved, concealment of conflict does not remove it either.

Coordination is a dynamic aspect of relationships. Stone (101) defines it as "the interrelating of all the parts of an organization to ensure harmonious operation." Coordination calls for actions by people—indoctrination, training, meetings, supervision. Perhaps it is best achieved when those working together clearly understand common goals, when they understand the methods designed to attain them, and when provision is made for an adequate exchange of information and ideas through proper direction and group deliberation.

Scientific Management

Little has been said here of the technical side of information center administration because the emphasis has been primarily upon behavioral considerations. However, there is an abundance of literature in the field of special librarianship and information science on such issues as efficiency measures, time and motion studies, charting and diagramming, work flow and processes, methods analysis, and other procedural elements of management as evidenced by the review chapters of this and past volumes of the *Annual Review*. A good example of these articles is that by Gull (43), who has adapted logical flow charts for administrators of libraries and information centers, probably a useful device for planning purposes. Dougherty & Heinritz (28) are an inclusive source for studies of this type.

MEASUREMENT AND EVALUATION OF PERFORMANCE

The development of standards, methods of measurement, evaluation of results, and reporting to management and clientele will comprise the final section of this chapter. Although there is a logical basis for proceeding in an orderly manner from standards development, to measurement, to evaluation, and finally, to reporting results, it must be recognized that there is much interaction among these subtopics. A graphic representation might present an array of symbiotic relationships, but, constrained by print and paper, we will present them in oversimplified, straight-line fashion.

Development of Standards

The American Library Association (3) has developed a set of minimum standards for public library systems. These standards, while perhaps vague and general, appear to have many points of local applicability. One important utility for any set of standards is to demonstrate to trustees and other officials that professional guidelines do exist, so that local efforts may be patterned after recommendations. Because of the range in the kinds and types of special libraries, the standards advanced by the Special Libraries Association (92) are rather indefinite and intended only to sketch some of the elements that should be present in a successful special library. The professional standards set for the librarian are more explicit than are the other criteria in the latter document.

In measuring performance within the organization and the library or information center, the manager may discover that standards are essential and that he himself must take the lead in setting them. Stokes (100) provides a straightforward analysis of standards development in a plain, expository manner, outlining the how, where, and when of it and briefly mentioning some of the human problems involved.

Methods of Measurement

There are two questions that relate to measuring the effectiveness of a library or information center. The first relates to its adequacy of performance: How do the information program and its results match up with the organization's requirements? The second is related to the matter of efficiency: How do its results compare with the most effective possible use of the available resources? The test of adequacy becomes the absolute measure of accomplishment; the efficiency is the accomplishment relative to the available resources.

In 1965, Battelle (9) sponsored a forum for managers of information analysis centers. One of the major issues discussed was the problem of how to measure the effectiveness of analysis centers. Maizell (62) also treats this problem, pointing out that in a time when cost/effectiveness analysis is becoming a pervasive phenomenon, each organizational subdivision must be subject to the same economic scrutiny until reasonable measures are derived by which to evaluate its distinct contribution.

One very promising line of research oriented toward devising more rigorous performance measurement tools in libraries has been the work by Orr et al. (76, 77, 78), under way at the Institute for the Advancement of Medical Communication, under National Library of Medicine sponsorship. The project addresses itself to developing methods for collecting objective data suitable for planning and guiding biomedical library programs. While the experience has centered upon the medical library, the method and the process are broadly applicable and offer the first tangible, generally useful library performance measure yet devised. The work, in the first stages in a broad-scale design of specific performance-gauging instruments, deserves careful scrutiny by students of library and information center administration.

Evaluation of Results

Until new measurement methods have been more fully developed and applied, the basis for evaluation is limited to intangibles or to the statistical records traditionally kept by libraries. The development of new information services has made many of these statistics meaningless. For example, Pings et al. (80) analyzed the statistics compiled by medical school libraries and found that they were highly redundant, of questionable reliability, of little use for predictive purposes, and of minimal utility generally.

The basis of evaluation should be the comparison between what a library achieves and the purpose for which it is intended. It is extremely difficult to determine precisely the return on an investment in a service function such as a library. The same problem is seen as one attempts to evaluate such service functions as public relations or advertising. One measure of the information center is reflected in the qualifications and credentials of its manager. While his leadership is a crucial ingredient, it is only one factor that contributes toward attainment of the library goals. Moreover, the administrator's contribution is relevant only insofar as it contributes to those goals. The real concern is the total effort, and it is this total effort that stands in need of detached periodic review and assessment.

Reporting to Management and Clientele

The services of a special library must be used and enjoyed to be valued and respected. As Stone (101) indicates, publications are one of the most important means of building a public relations program. From this, it should follow that the periodic report to management by the library manager, describing openly the operation of the library, may do far more than is at first obvious. Therefore, Boodson (13) cautions that care should be expended in preparing the report to ensure that it is readable and agreeable in appearance, that any statements made in it are clearly supported, and that any statistics used are consistent over time.

The problem of what to report to management and how often may be resolved by directives from above. Yet, in cases in which no reports are explicitly required, Kyle (53) reminds us that this does not necessarily make such reporting unnecessary or undesirable. There is something to be gained, she notes, in demonstrating to top management improvements in service or savings in funds. In addition, she warns that institutional managements change their minds and may begin asking for reports. The problem of collecting and compiling data and organizing them into an adequate report on short notice, when such data have not been collected regularly, can be frustrating and wasteful; data collection for the periodic report can help to anticipate such difficulty.

CONCLUSION

This chapter has sought to define and to discuss the major issues and responsibilities facing the manager of a library or information center. Because the selection of issues to be covered, and their definition, is a personal process, there will doubtless be differences that individual readers will have about such choices. Some worthwhile writings have undoubtedly been omitted thereby, while other contributions that, perhaps, fail to reach the high standards for inclusion set by other *Annual Review* chapters, have been cited as a consequence of the limited quality of the extant literature. Ideally, the overall impact of this chapter will be to underscore the crucial need for more research, both basic and applied, as well as for new theoretical, conceptual, and philosophical contributions to the literature of information center administration. For one can argue plausibly that, in an increasingly complex organizational milieu, it is precisely through the enhanced sophistication which stems from deeper understanding of the behavioral aspects of bureaucratic existence that information center administrators will succeed or fail. To suggest that the present state of the art is more in the realm of art than science, that principles of special library administration are few or nonexistent, is only to confirm that present managerial performance and effectiveness are more a matter of striving than attainment. Perhaps this may be the lure to attract those who will study and speculate further about the issues that were drawn into focus here.

REFERENCES

(1) ADELSON, MARVIN. The system approach: a perspective. Wilson Library Bulletin, 42:7 (March 1968) 711–715.

(2) Administration of technical information groups. Industrial and Engineering Chemistry, 51 (March 1959) 48A–61A.
(3) AMERICAN LIBRARY ASSOCIATION. Minimum standards for public library systems, 1966. Chicago, 1967, 69 p.
(4) AMERICAN MANAGEMENT ASSOCIATION. Developing the common data base for operating a management information system. New York, 1968.
(5) AMERICAN MANAGEMENT ASSOCIATION. EDP management in the 1970's. New York, 1969.
(6) ANDERSON, ALICE G. The company library—information center plus. Information and Records Management, 2:3 (February-March 1968) 21–22.
(7) ANTHONY, L. J. Library planning. In: Ashworth, Wilfred, ed. Handbook of special librarianship and information work. 3rd ed., rev. and enlarged. ASLIB, London, 1967, p. 309–364.
(8) BATTELLE MEMORIAL INSTITUTE. Final report on a survey of science-information manpower in engineering and the natural sciences. Project leader: Robert S. Kohn. Columbus, Ohio, 1966, 86 p. (PB-174 439)
(9) BATTELLE MEMORIAL INSTITUTE. Proceedings of 1st *Ad-Hoc* Forum of Scientific and Technical Information Analysis Center Managers, Directors, and Professional Analysts. Columbus, Ohio, November 7–11, 1965.
(10) BEDSOLE, D. T. Library services in large industrial corporations. Doctoral dissertation. University of Michigan, Ann Arbor, 1961.
(11) BOAZ, MARTHA. Does the library profession really have a code of ethics? Special Libraries, 59:5 (May-June 1968) 353–354.
(12) BOAZ, MARTHA. Evaluation of special library service for upper management. Special Libraries, 59:10 (December 1968) 789–791.
(13) BOODSON, K. Publications of the library and information department. In: Ashworth, Wilfred, ed. Handbook of special librarianship and information work. 3rd ed., rev. and enlarged. ASLIB, London, 1967, p. 482–523.
(14) BOURNE, CHARLES P.; WORTH, JEANNE B.; NELSON, JEAN W. The corporate library/information center. Stanford Research Institute, Menlo Park, Calif. December, 1968. (Long Range Planning Service. Report 363) Note: This report is for the sole and private use of clients of the Long Range Planning Service.
(15) BRADLEY, BRENT D. Some views on program budgeting. RAND Corp. Santa Monica, Calif., November 1967.
(16) BROPHY, ALFRED L.; GAZDA, GEORGE M. Handling the problem staff member. Illinois Libraries (December 1961) 760–763.
(17) BRYAN, ALICE I. The public librarian. Columbia University Press, New York, 1952.
(18) BUNDY, MARY LEE. Automation as innovation. Drexel Library Quarterly, 4:1 (January 1968) 100.
(19) BUNDY, MARY LEE. Conflict in libraries. College and Research Libraries, 27 (July 1966) 253–262.
(20) BUNDY, MARY LEE; WASSERMAN, PAUL. Professionalism reconsidered. College and Research Libraries, 29:1 (January 1968) 5–26.
(21) CAREY, ALEX. The Hawthorne studies: A radical criticism. American Sociological Review, 32:3 (June 1967) 403–416.
(22) COOPER, MARIANNE. Organizational patterns of academic science libraries. College and Research Libraries, 29:5 (November 1968) 357–363.
(23) COUNTS, RICHARD W. Marketing aspects of the user interface problem in information centers. In: American Society for Information Science Annual Meeting, Columbus, Ohio, 20–24 October 1968. Proceedings, vol. 5. Greenwood Publishing Corp., New York, 1968, p. 307–309.
(24) DARBY, RALPH L. Information analysis centers as a source for information and data. Special Libraries, 59:2 (February 1968) 91–97.
(25) DeWEESE, LEMUEL C. Status concerns and professionalization among librarians. M.S. thesis. Purdue University, Lafayette, Ind., January 1969.

(26) Directory of library consultants. Editor: John Berry III. Bowker, New York. (In preparation)
(27) DiSALVO, JOSEPH. Experiment to transfer technology from a university-based center. Final report. Indiana University Foundation, Aerospace Research Applications Center, Bloomington, February 1968. (NASA-CR-93482)
(28) DOUGHERTY, RICHARD M.; HEINRITZ, F. J. Scientific management of library operations. Scarecrow Press, Metuchen, N.J., 1966.
(29) DOUGLASS, R. R. The personality of the librarian. Doctoral dissertation. University of Chicago, 1957.
(30) DUBIN, ROBERT. Human relations in administration; the sociology of organizations. Prentice-Hall, Englewood Cliffs, N.J., 1961.
(31) DYKE, FREEMAN H., JR. How to manage and use technical information. Industrial Education Institute, Boston, 1968.
(32) EMORY, JAMES C. Economics of information. In: American Management Association, Ideas for management. New York, 1968, p. 158–167.
(33) ETZIONI, AMITAI. Authority structure and organizational effectiveness. Administrative Science Quarterly, 4:1 (June 1959) 43–67.
(34) FEDERAL COUNCIL FOR SCIENCE AND TECHNOLOGY. COMMITTEE ON SCIENTIFIC AND TECHNICAL INFORMATION. Progress of the United States Government in scientific and technical communication, 1966. Washington, D.C., 1966, p. 5–6.
(35) FRAREY, CARLYLE J.; ROSENSTEIN, RICHARDS. Placements and salaries in 1968: the same tune—in a higher key. Library Journal, 93:12 (15 June 1968) 2444–2449.
(36) FRIEDMAN, LEE A. Designing for management functions in man/computer systems. Oral presentation to the Symposium on Management: Man's Role in Complex Systems, Human Factors Society Convention, 25 September 1967, Boston.
(37) GALIN, MELVIN PHILIP. The management of scientific and technical information systems in industry. Doctoral dissertation. Indiana University, Bloomington, 1967.
(38) GORDON, PAUL J. All very well in practice! But how does it work out in theory? Wilson Library Bulletin, 42:7 (March 1968) 676–685.
(39) GOULDNER, ALVIN W. Cosmopolitan locals: toward an analysis of latent social roles. Part I. Administrative Science Quarterly, 2:3 (December 1957) 281–306.
(40) GOULDNER, ALVIN W. Cosmopolitan locals: toward an analysis of latent social roles. Part II. Administrative Science Quarterly, 2:4 (March 1958) 444–480.
(41) GRAHAM, RONALD A.; LEE, ARTHUR E.; MEYER, ROGER L. The creation of a new technical information center for a diversified chemical corporation. Journal of Chemical Documentation, 8:2 (May 1968) 60–66.
(42) GUJRATI, B. S. Library administration. 2d ed. Indian Book Co., Kashmere Gate, Delhi, India, 1966.
(43) GULL, C. D. Logical flow charts and other new techniques for the administration of libraries and information centers. Library Resources and Technical Services, 12:1 (Winter 1961) 47–66.
(44) HEANY, DONALD F. Development of information systems: what management needs to know. Ronald Press, New York, 1968.
(45) HELMKAMP, JOHN G. Managerial cost accounting for a technical information center. Aerospace Research Applications Center, Indiana University Foundation, Bloomington, 1968.
(46) HOLM, BART E. How to manage your information. Reinhold, New York, 1968.
(47) HOPE, NELSON W. The role of the small special library in tomorrow's world. Sci-Tech News (Fall 1968) 60–62.
(48) HYSLOP, MARJORIE R. The economics of information systems: observations of development costs and nature of the market. In: American Society for Information Science Annual Meeting, Columbus, Ohio, 20–24 October 1968. Proceedings, vol. 5. Greenwood Publishing Corp., New York, 1968. p. 301–306.
(49) JOHNS, ADA WINIFRED. Special libraries; development of the concept, their or-

ganization and their services. Scarecrow Press, Metuchen, N.J., 1968.
(50) KEMPER, ROBERT EUGENE. Strategic planning for library systems. Doctoral dissertation. University of Washington, Seattle, 1968.
(51) KENT, ALLEN; TAULBEE, ORRIN E.; BELZER, JACK. Electronic handling of information: testing and evaluation. Thompson, Washington, D.C., 1967.
(52) KERTESZ, FRANÇOIS. The information center concept. Oak Ridge National Laboratory, Oak Ridge, Tenn., 2 July 1968. (ORNL-TM-2281)
(53) KYLE, BARBARA R. F. Administration. In: Ashworth, Wilfred, ed. Handbook of special librarianship and information work. 3rd ed., rev. and enlarged, ASLIB, London, 1967, p. 12–34.
(54) LIMBERG, HERMAN. How to meet management's information needs. In: American Management Association. Ideas for management. New York, 1968, p. 188–198.
(55) LOCK, REGINALD NORTHWOOD. Library administration. Crosby Lockwood and Son, London, 1965.
(56) LOWELL, MILDRED (HAWKSWORTH). The management of libraries and information centers. Scarecrow Press, Metuchen, N.J., 1968.
(57) LOWRY, W. KENNETH. The goals of information center administration. In: Conference on Technical Information Center Administration (TICA), Drexel Institute of Technology, Philadelphia, 15–17 June 1964. Spartan Books, Washington, D.C., 1964.
(58) LOWRY, W. KENNETH; KENNEDY, ROBERT A. Bell Telephone Laboratories technical information services. Bell Telephone Laboratories, Murray Hill, N.Y., September 1968, 17 p. (P-856-1048) To be published in Polish in: Aktualne Problemy Informacji i Dokumentacji.
(59) McGOWAN, J. The library and the technical information center. In: Conference on Technical Information Center Administration, 2d (TICA 2), St. David's, 14–17 June 1965. Proceedings, edited by Arthur W. Elias. Spartan Books, Washington, D.C.; Macmillan, London, 1965.
(60) McGREGOR, DOUGLAS M. The human side of enterprise. In: Leadership and motivation, M.I.T. Press, Cambridge, Mass., 1966, p. 3–20.
(61) MAIZELL, ROBERT E. Continuing education in technical information services. Journal of Chemical Documentation, 7 (May 1967) 115–119.
(62) MAIZELL, ROBERT E. Standards for measuring the effectiveness of technical library performance. IRE Transactions on Engineering Management, PGEM-7 (June 1960) 69–73.
(63) MAIZELL, ROBERT E. The user and systems analysis. Southern Connecticut State College, New Haven, 1968. (Papers in Library Information Science. Library Science paper No. 11)
(64) MANN, FLOYD C.; WILLIAMS, LAWRENCE K. Observations on the dynamics of a change to electronic data processing equipment. Administrative Science Quarterly, 5:2 (September 1960) 217–256.
(65) MARCSON, SIMON. The scientist in American industry; some organizational determinants in manpower utilization. Industrial Relations Section, Department of Economics, Princeton University, Princeton, N.J., 1960.
(66) MELTZER, MORTON F. The information center: management's hidden asset. American Management Association, New York, 1967.
(67) MERTON, ROBERT K. Bureaucratic structure and personality. Social Forces, 18 (May 1940) 560–568.
(68) MOON, E. E. Administrative indigestion? (Editorial) Library Journal, 93:5 (March 1968) 931.
(69) MORSE, PHILIP M. Library effectiveness: a systems approach. M.I.T. Press, Cambridge, Mass., 1968.
(70) MYATT, DEWITT O. Special design considerations for information services supporting the small firm. Presented at the Conference on Technical Information Services for Puerto Rico Industry, San Juan, Puerto Rico, 20–21 June 1968 (Preprint, 14 p.)
(71) NIMER, GILDA. Professions and professionalism: a bibliographic overview. University of Maryland, School of Library and Information Services, Manpower Research

Project, Newsletter Issue No. 2, July 1968.
(72) NOVICK, DAVID. Long-range planning through program budgeting. RAND Corp., Santa Monica, Calif., 1968.
(73) NYREN, J. Transfer of authority. (Editorial) Library Journal, 93 (June 1968) 2189.
(74) OFFICE OF EDUCATION. Survey of special libraries serving the federal government. Washington, D.C., 1968. (OE-15067)
(75) OLSSON, DAVID E. Management by objective. Pacific Books, Palo Alto, Calif., 1968.
(76) ORR, RICHARD H.; PINGS, VERN M.; PIZER, IRWIN H.; OLSON, EDWIN E. Development of methodologic tools for planning and managing library services. In: Project goals and approach. Bulletin of the Medical Library Association, 56:3 (July 1968) 235–240.
(77) ORR, RICHARD H.; PINGS, VERN M.; PIZER, IRWIN H.; OLSON, EDWIN E.; SPENCER, CAROL C. Development of methodologic tools for planning and managing library services. II: Measuring a library's capability for providing documents. Bulletin of the Medical Library Association, 56:3 (July 1968) 241–267.
(78) ORR, RICHARD H.; PINGS, VERN M.; OLSON, EDWIN E.; PIZER, IRWIN H. Development of methodologic tools for planning and managing library services. III: Standardized inventories of library services. Bulletin of the Medical Library Association, 56:4 (October 1968) 380–403.
(79) PETERS, ALEC. Controlling costs in technical information centers. In: Conference on Technical Information Center Administration (TICA), Drexel Institute of Technology, Philadelphia, 15–17 June 1964. Spartan Books, Washington, D.C., 1964.
(80) PINGS, VERN M.; OLSON, EDWIN E.; ORR, RICHARD H. Summary report of a study of academic medical library statistics. To be published in the July 1969, or October 1969 issue of the Bulletin of the Medical Library Association.
(81) PRESIDENT'S SCIENCE ADVISORY COMMITTEE. Science, government and information: the responsibilities of the technical community and the government in the transfer of information. U.S. Government Printing Office, Washington, D.C., 1963.
(82) PRESTHUS, ROBERT V. Librarian's role in a changing organization. In: Progress research; discussed in: Wasserman, Paul; Bundy, Mary Lee. A program of research into the identification of manpower requirements, the educational preparation and the utilization of manpower in the library and information professions. Final report, Phase I. University of Maryland, School of Library and Information Services, College Park, January 1969. (Project No. 7-1084)
(83) PRESTHUS, ROBERT V. The organizational society; an analysis and a theory. Knopf, New York, 1962.
(84) RIDGEWAY, JAMES. GM comes clean. New Republic, 154:14 (April 1966) 8–9.
(85) RIPPON, J. S.; FRANCIS, S. Selection and acquisition of library materials. In: Ashworth, Wilfred, ed. Handbook of special librarianship and information work. 3d ed., rev. and enlarged. ASLIB, London, 1967.
(86) ROSENBLOOM, RICHARD S.; WOLEK, FRANCIS W. Technology, information, and organization. Information transfer in industrial R and D. Harvard University, Graduate School of Business Administration, Boston, June 1967, 252 p. (PB-175 959)
(87) SCOTT, W. RICHARD. Professionals in bureaucracies—areas in conflict. In: Vollmer, Howard H.; Mills, Donald L., eds. Professionalization. Prentice-Hall, Englewood Cliffs, N.J., 1966.
(88) SEGAL, STANLEY J. Personality and ability patterns of librarians and information service workers related to work roles and work settings. In: Progress research; discussed in Wasserman, Paul; Bundy, Mary Lee. A program of research into the identification of manpower requirements, the educational preparation and the utilization of manpower in the library and information professions. Final report, Phase I. University of Maryland, School of Library and Information Services, College Park, January 1969. (Project No. 7-1084)
(89) SKOLNIK, HERMAN. Information center design. In: Conference on Technical Information Center Administration (TICA), Drexel Institute of Technology, Phila-

delphia, 15–17 June, 1964. Spartan Books, Washington, D.C., 1964.
(90) SMITH, ELDRED. Do libraries need managers? Library Journal, 94:3 (February 1969) 501–506.
(91) SPECIAL LIBRARIES ASSOCIATION. Activities and organization. New York, [n.d.], p. 14.
(92) SPECIAL LIBRARIES ASSOCIATION. Objectives and standards for special libraries. Special Libraries Association, New York, December 1964.
(93) SPECIAL LIBRARIES ASSOCIATION. Personnel survey, 1959. Special Libraries 51:3 (March 1960) 133–159.
(94) SPECIAL LIBRARIES ASSOCIATION. Profiles of special libraries, compiled by Ruth S. Leonard. Special Libraries Association, New York, Spring, 1966.
(95) SPECIAL LIBRARIES ASSOCIATION. PERSONNEL COMMITTEE. A study of 1967 annual salaries of members of the Special Libraries Association. Special Libraries, 58:4 (April 1967) 217–254.
(96) STAATS, ELMER B. The government manager in 2000 A.D. Wilson Library Bulletin 42:7 (March 1968) 701–710.
(97) STATE LIBRARY OF OHIO. Library executive development program. News from the State Library, No. 84 (20 August 1968) 4; No. 86 (31 October 1968) 2.
(98) STEBBINS, KATHLEEN B.; MOHRHARDT, FOSTER E. Personnel administration in libraries. 2d ed. Scarecrow Press, Metuchen, N.J., 1966.
(99) STEINER, GEORGE A. Top management planning. Macmillan, London, 1969.
(100) STOKES, PAUL M. A total systems approach to management control. American Management Association, New York, 1968.
(101) STONE, ELIZABETH. Training for the improvement of library administration. University of Illinois, Graduate School of Library Science, Champaign, 1967.
(102) STRAUSS, LUCILLE J.; STRIEBY, IRENE M.; BROWN, ALBERTA L. Scientific and technical libraries; their organization and administration. Wiley, Interscience, New York, 1964, p. 6–14.
(103) STRIEBY, IRENE M. Organizational relations of special librarians. Library Trends, 1:2 (October 1952) 173–188.
(104) THOMPSON, VICTOR A. How scientific management thwarts innovation. Trans-Action (June 1968) 51–55.
(105) THOMPSON, VICTOR A. The organizational dimension. Wilson Library Bulletin, 42:7 (March 1968) 693–700.
(106) TOAN, ARTHUR B., JR. Using information to manage. Ronald Press, New York, 1968.
(107) UNIVERSITY OF MARYLAND. Library administrators development program. School of Library and Information Services, College Park, 1969. (Brochure)
(108) UNIVERSITY OF WASHINGTON. Library executive development program; an institute for advanced study for librarians. Graduate School of Librarianship, Seattle, 1969. (Brochure)
(109) WALTERS, J. HART, JR. Image and status of the library and information service field. In: Progress research; discussed in: Wasserman, Paul; Bundy, Mary Lee. A program of research into the identification of manpower requirements, the educational preparation and the utilization of manpower in the library and information professions. Final report, Phase I. University of Maryland, School of Library and Information Services, College Park, January 1969. (Project No. 7-1084)
(110) WASSERMAN, PAUL. The librarian and the machine; observations on the applications of machines in administration of college and university libraries. Gale Research, Detroit, 1965, p. 121–132.
(111) WASSERMAN, PAUL. The library and information professions in a time of change. PNLA Quarterly, 31:2 (January 1967) 134–145.
(112) WASSERMAN, PAUL. The role of the information specialist in industry. In: Symposium on Management Information Systems and the Information Specialist, Purdue University, Lafayette, Ind., 12–13 July 1965. Proceedings, edited by John M. Houkes. Sponsored by the Krannert Graduate School of Industrial Administration and the Uni-

versity Libraries. Lafayette, 1966, p. 104–122.
(113) WASSERMAN, PAUL; BUNDY, MARY LEE. Leadership for change. In: Progress research; discussed in: Wasserman, Paul; Bundy, Mary Lee. A program of research into the identification of manpower requirements, the educational preparation and the utilization of manpower in the library and information professions. Final report, Phase I. University of Maryland, School of Library and Information Services, College Park, January 1969. (Project No. 7-1084)
(114) WASSERMAN, PAUL; BUNDY, MARY LEE, eds. Reader in library administration. Microcard Editions, Washington, D.C., 1968.
(115) WASSERMAN, PAUL; GREER, WILLIS R., JR. Consultants and consulting organizations; a reference source and directory of concerns engaged in consultation for business and industry. Graduate School of Business and Public Administration, Cornell Univ., Ithaca, N.Y., 1966.
(116) WHITE, RODNEY F. Education, careers and professionalization in library and information science. In: Progress research; discussed in: Wasserman, Paul; Bundy, Mary Lee. A program of research into the identification of manpower requirements, the educational preparation and the utilization of manpower in the library and information professions. Final report, Phase I. University of Maryland, School of Library and Information Services, College Park, January 1969. (Project No. 7-1084)
(117) WILHELMY, ODIN, JR.; BROWN, PATRICIA L. The information analysis center —key to better use of the information resource. Journal of Chemical Documentation, 8:2 (May 1968) 106–109.
(118) WILLIAMS, LAWRENCE K. Managing change: a test of the administration. Wilson Library Bulletin, 42:7 (March 1968) 686–692.

14 Professional Aspects of Information Science and Technology

JESSE H. SHERA and
ANNE S. McFARLAND
Case Western Reserve University

INTRODUCTION

It was our experience in reviewing the 1968 literature, as it was of Atherton & Greer (10) in 1967, that most of the material, even that with implications for information science, had been drawn from the traditionally oriented literature on librarianship. The present treatment will be divided into five sections: Dimensions of the Field; Professional Organization of the Field; The Professional Education of the Information Scientist; Support for Research and Development; and Manpower Resources. The material that falls within this chapter will include relatively little that is related solely to information science *per se*; however, much that relates to librarianship is applicable by implication, extrapolation, and deduction to information science.

DIMENSIONS OF THE FIELD

The old acrimony that for so many years characterized debate over definitions of information science, and particularly over its relations to librarianship, now seems to be yielding to a less argumentative point of view. A true consensus has not yet been reached, but an atmosphere of agreement is being achieved in which polemics are being replaced by at least a measure of objectivity, and in which information scientists and librarians are able to communicate. During 1968, several individuals proposed definitions of the field. The number of such definitions certainly indicates dissatisfaction with existing definitions, yet we have found that this year's literature shows far greater agreement than has been achieved prior to this time.

At the Albany Conference on Bibliographic Control of Library Science

Literature, held in April 1968, Corrigan (26), of the College of Librarianship, Wales, took the view that library science is an all-inclusive, or parent, term that encompasses all knowledge "concerned with creation, recording, transmission, storage, retrieval and use of information." He summarizes his position by saying that "if one wanted a two-word definition, perhaps storage and retrieval best covers the core of library science."

Borko (16), after reviewing the several definitions of information science that have been advanced in the past, has attempted to formulate a definition that would synthesize his findings. Information science, he suggests, is:

> an interdisciplinary science that investigates the properties and behavior of information, the forces that govern the flow and use of information, and the techniques, both manual and mechanical, of processing information for optimal storage, retrieval, and dissemination.

According to Borko, then, information science is investigative rather than operational; and it is distinct from documentation, which is an application of the findings of the information scientists to actual situations. Documentation, "which is one of many applied components of information science," is concerned with "acquiring, storing, retrieving, and disseminating recorded documentary information primarily in the form of report and journal literature." He adds that documentation has "tended to emphasize the use of data processing equipment, reprography and microforms as techniques of information handling."

In response to Borko's essay, Hoshovsky & Massey (54) presented to the 1968 convention of the American Society for Information Science a definition of the field which emphasizes output:

> Information science is that *body of knowledge*, consisting of descriptions, theories, and techniques, which provides *understanding* of the *means* through which society's *information needs* are met and which provides understanding required to improve capabilities to define and meet such needs. (Italics theirs)

The editors of the *International Encyclopedia of the Social Sciences* would seem to have taken much this same view, at least by implication, for they subsumed the article on information services, libraries, reference materials, and bibliographic issues under the general rubric of "Information Storage and Retrieval" (57). Becker (12), who wrote the article on the general field for this encyclopedia, uses the phrase "information storage and retrieval" as a generic term to include the totality of operations, systems, and research involved in making available the intellectual content of recorded knowledge. He does not draw a sharp line of demarcation, as Borko does, between the operational and the research activities, and his treatment is heavily weighted on the side of mechanization. He does, however, say that the field of information storage and retrieval is interdisciplinary and must draw from many areas of expertise.

To Shera (92), however, librarianship is the generic term; and information science is an area of research that draws its substance, methods, and techniques from a variety of disciplines to achieve an understanding of the properties, behavior, and flow of information. It is not "souped-up" librarianship or information retrieval, nor is it antithetical to either. Rather, information science provides the intellectual and theoretical base for the librarian's operations. The two fields are halves of a whole. In his understanding of the meaning of the term "information science," Shera is very close to Borko; and Borko, consciously or unconsciously, has drawn from the basic distinctions made by the 1962 and 1963 conferences at the Georgia Institute of Technology, which were following the leadership of Robert Hayes. Clearly, a reasonably consistent pattern is beginning to emerge.

Saracevic & Rees (87), in a paper presented before the 1968 convention of the Special Libraries Association in Los Angeles, address themselves to the question of the extent to which information science qualifies as a true science, and in so doing have listed seven conditions that should be met: (*1*) a community of interests in a given set of phenomena; (*2*) a number of persons working in the area who possess accepted qualifications, commitment, and interest, and who are usually, though not necessarily, affiliated with academic or research institutions; (*3*) a body of techniques, tools, and methods for purposes of research; (*4*) a theoretical base, which may be either nascent or mature; (*5*) a formalized education structure, or system, that will provide entry into the field; (*6*) a formal, or informal, communication system that channels information to those participating in the work; (*7*) a professional association and a scholarly journal for the dissemination of professional, and professionally related, knowledge.

The authors conclude that information science "meets most, if not all" of these conditions. Furthermore, they observe that information science can provide the theoretical base that will not only qualify librarianship as a true profession, but also, and far more importantly, will improve the operations of the librarian, enabling him to strengthen his services. They conclude their paper with a plea for improved interaction between the information scientists and the librarians, better communication and understanding between the two groups, and a stronger and better-structured educational system than either profession has exhibited to the present time.

Fuellhart & Weeks (47) conducted a particularly extensive study, including tabulation and analysis of lexical resources in information science, in which they sought to identify individuals and organizations that have compiled lexical aids in information science. They then analyzed these aids for the identification of commonly, frequently, or rarely used terms, and provided the sources from which further inferences might be drawn regarding the characteristics of the topical universe and its application to the discipline of information science. They have made a number of observations that are relevant to the definition of information science. Their most important conclusion is that there is no formal structure for the discipline of information science, as determined from an examination of these lexical aids. They attribute this lack of structure to the interdisciplinary character of the science in its present state of development. Many of the terms in their lexical sources have originated in other disciplines and have been taken over by the information scientists with little change in their original meanings. Thus, the boundaries of the science are particularly difficult to delineate and, without such delineation, "the development of a structured representation of the topical universe is a formidable task." The authors further observe that each resource examined reflects the point of view of its author or compiler, even in those classification schemes and structured authority files that attempt to represent the topical universe of the discipline of information science. The influence of the authors' individualities explains, in large measure, the low percentage of terminological agreement among the materials studied. The authors believe that the structure of a discipline should present

> a balance between general and specific concepts. The establishment of this balance ... is requisite to the design of a systematic vocabulary and in the development of standards for lexical resources which purport to accurately represent the structure of a discipline.

The variety of disciplines that can contribute to the development of information science is apparent in Kochen's compilation of readings in the organization and retrieval of information (63). This compilation and the study of Fuellhart & Weeks (47) support Fairthorne's view (43) that there is no single discipline of information science, but rather that it is "more a federation of technologies than a set of specialist activities developed from common principles." These principles, he holds, are not even recognized, much less developed; but in the information sciences and technologies, "the fundamental topic is that of language, its physical, social, referential, and intensional aspects." The only unity that the field possesses, apart from this "essential common origin in the uses of language," has come from "overlapping techniques and technologies. It has not come from application of common principles." In his position, Fairthorne is much closer to the contemporary American view than to that of his associates on the other side of the Atlantic. The extent to which American usage of the term "information science" differs from that in Europe is clearly evident from the proceedings of the FID International Conference on Education for Scientific Information Work (59), held at Queen Elizabeth College, London, under the sponsorship of ASLIB, in the spring of 1967. At this series of meetings, all participants except those from the United States used the term "information science" to represent, not research and development in the information field, but a highly specialized form of bibliographic service to scientific and scholarly research. In Europe especially, the use of the term seems closer to "documentation" than to the investigatory activities that characterize it in the United States.

Nitecki (77) attempts to hypothesize a model for a science of librarianship through a construct that coordinates a triadic relationship among books, users, and "the relative aspect of knowledge." But library science remains "a broad, flexible, and consistent theoretical framework for adapting library operations to expanding knowledge."

Francis (46), in an address delivered at Senate House, University of London, argues for a holistic approach to the problem of information and rejects the trend toward excessive specialization in libraries and information centers.

Graziano (50) argues that, since documentalists are engaged in manipulating physical phenomena, the application of phenomenology in conjunction with the methods of speculative philosophy would be of value in describing what is observed in the most basic way possible. Orne (80) describes the system by which standards are formulated, reviewed, and approved, and appeals for their application to information science.

Thus, after a protracted period of varying degrees of discord between the librarians and the information scientists, the two fields are beginning to recognize their interrelationships. This trend is evidenced not only by the formation of the Information Science and Automation Division in the ALA, but also by the launching, in January 1968, of the Division's new quarterly publication, *Journal of Library Automation.* The contents of the publication are not very different from those of *American Documentation.*

The attitude of the information scientists seems to differ sharply from that of the librarians concerning the professionalization of their activities. For years the librarians have been relentlessly searching for those elements in their practice that qualify them as being professional. Bundy & Wasserman (20) have been the latest to plough this well-cultivated field, but their only mention of information science appears obliquely as a warning that:

if librarianship does not move much more rapidly forward toward enhanced professionalism, the field will not only decline rapidly, but ultimately face obsolescence. Already, traditional and conventional libraries are being replaced as new agencies and new practitioners respond more appropriately to changing requirements for information and professional service.

But it is not the failure of librarianship to qualify as a profession that is the cause for alarm; the danger arises from the inability of the librarians to meet the challenge of changing social needs. If librarians become occupationally obsolete, it will not be because, as Bundy & Wasserman state, "librarianship can be seen to have made only slow and gradual evolution as a profession and exists now as only a marginal entry in the competitive race for professional status," but because librarians have done poorly the job that society has demanded of them.

In contrast to the librarians, the information scientists have wasted little time or ink and paper over their credentials as a profession. This indifference is doubtless due to the fact that most of them have come from academic disciplines, the professionalism of which had long since been established. Moreover, information science, whatever its dimensions, is — at least in the United States — basically research oriented, whereas librarianship is not. Because information science is only incidentally service-directed, its practitioners are not concerned with proving that such service as they might render meets the standards of professionalism set by the lawyer, the doctor, or the minister; the information scientist takes his professionalism for granted.

Ferguson (44) studied the responses of selected staff members from some 650 organizations providing information services to social sciences. His results seem to indicate that there is a definite split between the librarians and those who have entered the information field from other disciplines:

> There appears to be a split between the two groups; the librarians resisting technical innovation involving computer applications, and the information specialists not only eagerly adopting these techniques but attempting to force them upon the rest of the information profession.

Thus, Ferguson is one of the few to conclude that there really may be "two cultures" in the information world.

A growing awareness of the need to relate information science to current social developments and problems is suggested by a grant made by

Encyclopaedia Britannica, Inc. (56) to the University of Chicago, on the occasion of the Britannica's bicentennial celebration. This grant will make possible the designation of outstanding leaders in information science as Britannica Scholars. They will "exchange views with the University faculty and other scholars" in "an interdisciplinary effort within the University to explore the social implications of information sciences." A conference on the results of this research program is planned to follow the completion of this year-long effort.

Finally, information science and librarianship are both represented in the recommendations of the National Advisory Commission on Libraries (72). After a period of intensive study extending over more than a year, and the accumulation of volumes of transcribed testimony and special studies and reports, the Commission made five basic recommendations: (*1*) that a National Commission on Libraries and Information Science be established as a permanent Federal planning agency; (*2*) that the role of the Library of Congress as the National Library of the United States be recognized and its position strengthened; (*3*) that a Federal Institute of Library and Information Science be established as "a principal center for basic and applied research in all relevant areas"; (*4*) that the critically important role of the United States Office of Education in meeting needs for library service be recognized and fully accepted; and (*5*) that the library agencies of the several States be strengthened to "overcome deficiencies in fulfilling their current functions." Legislation is being prepared to implement the Commission's recommendations.

PROFESSIONAL ORGANIZATION OF THE FIELD

Perhaps the most significant event of 1968 with regard to the bibliographic control of library and information science literature was the conference held at the State University of New York at Albany in April. Formally known as the Conference on the Bibliographic Control of Library Science Literature, the conference was attended by representatives from the commercial and noncommercial indexing and abstracting services in library and information science, representatives from library school faculties, personnel engaged in information systems work, and an impressive number of the librarians who work with library science collections, mainly those connected with schools of library science. Although the term "information science" was not part of the conference title, it definitely was in use throughout the conference sessions. Nyren (78) reports the following exchange between Gerald Lazorick and David Batty: " 'I think library science is a subset of information science,' said Lazorick, to which Batty promptly replied, 'Information science is a part of library science.' " It seems to have been universally accepted by those participants managing library science collections that all of the material in both fields is relevant and must be collected.

The conference—funded by the H. W. Wilson Foundation, coordinated by the University Library at the State University of New York at Albany, and sponsored by the Library Education Division of the American Library Association—was the brainchild of David L. Mitchell, then Librarian of the School of Library Science, SUNYA, who hoped that with such an assemblage the pressing problems of control of the literature of the field could be approached most advantageously. Ten individuals presented papers to serve as background for the general discussion sessions. These papers now exist only in preprint form and are being edited by Mr. Mitchell for formal publication.

In an article aptly titled "The Shoemaker's Children," Nyren (78) succinctly summarizes the proceedings of the conference. It became painfully obvious to the participants that indexing and abstracting services in the field are badly outdated in vocabulary, that they are slow to appear, and that they do not cite all of the relevant documents.

The recommendations produced by the discussion sessions of the conference (25) include idealistic projects as well as more hardheaded, practical programs that can be implemented easily. The conference had no formal mechanism for channeling its recommendations, but sent them to every organization mentioned, such as the H. W. Wilson Company, the Library and Information Sciences Research Branch of the Office of Education, the American Library Association, and editors of various journals. The primary recommendations are directed at *Library Literature*, since it is the central, continuing indexing tool for the American library profession. It was suggested that it significantly broaden its coverage, not only of periodicals indexed, but also of monographs listed, that it continually revise and publish its list of subject headings, and that subscription rates be made adequate to provide for the increased coverage.

An additional recommendation is that the three major English-language services, *Library Literature*, *Library Science Abstracts*, and *Documentation Abstracts*, cooperate with ERIC Clearinghouse for Library and Information Sciences (CLIS) to determine agreements on the scope and policy of each service. Simonton (95) states that ERIC/CLIS is most interested in cooperation with the other bibliographic services.

Library school librarians were exhorted to develop cooperative acquisition arrangements (perhaps even to develop their own fast announcement service, until such a service could be absorbed by one of the commercial organizations), to become active in gathering historical material on a depository basis (preferably by region), and to develop a definite membership organization. There was great enthusiasm for a reviewing journal, since it had been pointed out that two of the greatest drawbacks to quality acquisitions work are, first, the limited number of reviews and, second, the fact that the same books are usually reviewed over and over again. In the same vein, an annual review of the year's work in librarianship was recommended, a suggestion which held a certain irony in view of advertisements for *Advances in Librarianship* (2) which appeared soon after the conference but had no relation to it.

Events that may have had direct relationship to the Albany conference were announcements late in 1968 that *Library Science Abstracts, Library Literature,* and *Documentation Abstracts* would all make significant changes in coverage and frequency of publication. *Library Science Abstracts* will be renamed *Library and Information Science Abstracts,* to appear bimonthly as of January 1969. *Library Literature* also announced its intent to become bimonthly in 1969, while *Documentation Abstracts* began 1969 with a new title: *Information Science Abstracts.* It has been stated that "The new title will reflect more accurately the scope of the journal. It will also reflect changes in word usage. The term 'documentation' is confusing and uncommunicative, especially for readers in the United States, and is losing favor" (34).

A decision resulting from a meeting of the *Library Literature* staff with Ben-Ami Lipetz of *Documentation Abstracts* and Wesley Simonton of ERIC/CLIS was that the three organizations represented would concentrate upon unification of vocabulary. Some of the problems involved in such an endeavor have already been mentioned in reference to the monograph by Fuellhart & Weeks (47). Efforts toward unification of vocabulary are progressing on the Continent, as reported in a recent article by Coates (23) explaining work being done in construction of an "Intermediate Lexicon" that would aid in conversion from one indexing system to another. Coates states that there are about 30 indexing systems in existence for the field of documentation. In early 1969, French and English versions of the lexicon should appear; these will serve as the basis for further work among the cooperating groups, which include the Classification Research Group, the French Groupe d'Etude sur l'Information Scientifique, and the Deutschegesellschaft für Dokumentation.

A major outgrowth of the Albany conference was the impetus that it gave to the Discussion Group for Library Science Librarians. This organization, a part of the ALA structure, has membership open to any person having responsibility for a library science collection and welcomes contributions from any individual interested in the problems of library science collections. The Group began in 1966 as the Committee on Relations of Library Science Librarians and attained its present designation at the 1968 annual meeting of ALA. The immediate aims of the Group have been modest, but there has already been positive action in planning for the encouragement of regional discussion groups; initiating a survey designed to give profiles of the major library and information science collections as well as to indicate problems common to such collections; identifying and encouraging cooperation among the larger library school collections with the ALA Headquarters Library, the Library of Congress, and the ERIC Clearinghouse for Library and Information Sciences; and providing support for the project of exchange and analysis of acquisitions lists to be coordinated by the Library Science Library, Case Western Reserve University.

The Albany conference was directly responsible for the formation of another group, loosely designated as the International Study Group, which is to be mainly concerned with research into the problems of information patterns within library and information science, and with work toward establishing various services for which a need is indicated (25).

The concern for research into user needs may have been due primarily to the paper by Little entitled "Use and Users of Library Literature" (66), which outlines the lack of knowledge of the use patterns of library literature. There was general agreement that such knowledge would logically have to precede efficient mechanisms for bibliographic control. To our knowledge, no definite project has yet been undertaken. The lack of a central organization to direct the work of this specific group will probably ensure its passage into oblivion.

Although earlier *Annual Review* chapters corresponding to this one have indicated a number of organizations interested in the library and information science fields, the groups mentioned above are the only ones at present primarily concerned with more effective bibliographic organization of the field.

One piece of work directed toward a specific item, the *Annual Review* itself and its users, is the study by Cuadra et al. (29) on the impact of the *Annual Review*. The 121-page report describes the exhaustive analysis that was made of the survey questionnaires and indicates ways in which its users differ from its nonusers. The survey also solicited opinions on how to improve the *Annual Review*. Although the major conclusions are few and hardly revolutionary, such a study could serve as a model for future attempts to define the users and the use made of the literature. It is worth mentioning that both this study and Little's paper (66) commend the work of the American Psychological Association's Project on Scientific Information Exchange in Psychology.

To the authors' knowledge, there are only two noteworthy items concerning professional information centers in library and information science. The first item refers to an established organization, the Bibliographic Systems Center (BSC) at Case Western Reserve University. Under recent grants from UNESCO, the staff at the Center has computerized the handling of requests from the profession, thus providing more efficient service as well as the capacity to produce book catalogs of the collection. UNESCO's interest in the problems of scientific and technical information, and in the problems of organizing that information, has been the impetus for expansion of the BSC's facilities and holdings so that it could act as a clearinghouse for classification schemes, subject heading lists, descriptors, thesauri, etc., in the English language. A companion clearinghouse for non-English-language material has been established in Warsaw at the Central Institute for Scientific, Technical and Economic Information (21).

Of far broader interest to the profession in general is the establishment of a Clearinghouse for Library and Information Sciences (CLIS) at the University of Minnesota, as part of the ERIC network. This Clearinghouse has two major functions. The first of these is to gather fugitive literature on library and information science, and, if such material is unavailable directly from its issuing agency, to see that it may be obtained from the ERIC Document Reproduction Center (42). Since ERIC/CLIS was one of the later clearinghouses established, evidence of its activities does not show positively until the 1968 issues of *Research in Education*. This official ERIC monthly publication carries abstracts of material chosen by each clearinghouse for inclusion, together with résumés of research projects currently in progress. In a paper originally presented in June 1968, Simonton (95) states that only 105 documents had appeared since the April 1968 issue of *Research in Education*, the first issue in which ERIC/CLIS documents appeared. The maximum number of items that any one Clearinghouse can list per month is 50.

The second major function is to issue state-of-the-art reports; two such reports have already been published. Since the Clearinghouse lacks the staff to answer all individual requests, it attempts to anticipate user demand and to prepare reports in areas in which coverage has been weak. Also, the Clearinghouse has begun issuing a Newsletter (41) that will appear irregularly and that will carry news of future developments. ERIC/CLIS has repeatedly announced its desire for the contribution of material from those in the field, and, in fact, Simonton (see above) stresses the point heavily; but it is the opinion of the authors, who have been engaged in collecting fugitive material themselves, that this material will not come to light readily.

In addition to the expanded work of the information centers and the abstracting and indexing services, there are new professional information sources. In spite of what may already seem to be an inordinate number of periodicals in the field, perhaps ten more have appeared or have been announced during 1968. Some of these are oriented toward more traditional library services or are directly concerned with public libraries, but there are a number of them that bear directly upon information science and technology. In addition to the ERIC/CLIS Newsletter mentioned above, the Clearinghouse for Federal Scientific and Technical Information has begun issuing *CAST (Clearinghouse Announcements in Science and Technology)* Category 17, Information Science. Appearing biweekly, *CAST* (76), usually four to six pages in length, abstracts technical reports of concern to the field and provides full bibliographic data. This publication is an adjunct to the United States Government Research and Development Reports and is intended to be a fast announcement service.

Three full-format journals have appeared. The first, mentioned earlier, is the *Journal of Library Automation*, published by the Information Science and Automation Division of the American Library Association. *The Information Scientist*, the new official publication of the British Institute of Information Scientists, has replaced its former bulletin. Beginning in January 1969, the British Library Association will publish a *Journal of Librarianship* to appear quarterly and to "publish longer review and research articles, and the longer critical book reviews which rarely find space in the Record." (39) A promotional flyer for this journal indicates that it will deal with library and information work both in the United Kingdom and abroad.

During 1968 there have been a few other publications of note to those concerned with retrospective control of the field's work. The most important of these is the *Bibliography on Information Science and Technology* issued by the Defense Documentation Center (32). This two-volume bibliography covers AD reports cataloged by the Center from 1953 through September 1967 and provides abstracts for most of the material. In view of the changing vocabulary of the field, it is interesting to note that this title duplicates that of the bibliography issued by the System Development Corporation beginning in 1965. Another major event is the appearance of the first volume of *Encyclopedia of Library and Information Science* edited by Kent et al. (40). The present publication schedule calls for two volumes per year to be issued until the set of 18 volumes is complete.

THE PROFESSIONAL EDUCATION OF THE INFORMATION SCIENTIST

The tripartite division of programs for the professional education of information scientists (library-school based, engineering-school based, and departmental based) devised by Saracevic & Rees (87) seems a practicable classification for a review of the literature. Asheim (9), in surveying the state of the accredited library schools, found that for the year 1966–67, 22 of the schools added 85 new courses, of which 16 were in information science, and in addition two schools added entirely new programs in that field. Eleven schools, according to Asheim, are "definitely planning the addition of courses or programs in Information Science." He is careful to note, however, that his statistics were derived solely from questionnaires, and that he made no attempt at evaluation of the courses or programs.

Asheim's findings are basically in agreement with the results of a study of the curricula of the accredited library schools made by Rees & Riccio (81) for the FID London conference of 1967. Their survey, which covered the same academic period as that of Asheim, showed that 17 schools offered a total of 25 courses in data processing and library automation; 19 schools offered a total of 39 courses in documentation and information storage, retrieval, and dissemination; six schools offered a total of 13 courses in information science research methodology; and a few schools, such as the University of Chicago, Case Western Reserve University, the University of Pittsburgh, and Florida State University, have formalized specialized subcurricular sequences in this field. The Drexel Institute of Technology and the University of California at Los Angeles offer a degree in information science at the master's level.

At the FID conference, Hayes (53) described the program at UCLA, while Bracken & Shilling (18) surveyed the offerings in "practical, or on-the-job," training in information science. It is not possible to equate these findings with those of Asheim and Rees & Riccio, but the tabulations do indicate that the length of such training varies greatly from institution to institution; it can be as short as five days or extend to over one year. Moreover, a substantial amount of such training is carried on intramurally by individual industries, though a few corporations indicated a willingness to support trainees at universities where appropriate educational facilities are available. Also, like the others, Bracken & Shilling end their full report on a note of accelerated change: "The need for more practical training programs is apparent and certainly in the next several years, there will be a major increase in the availability of practical training programs in information science." In the face of this optimism, however, it may be relevant to note that of almost 120 conferences, workshops, and short courses for the continuing education of librarians, listed in the 1968–69 directory issued by the Office of Library Education of the American Library Association (4), only 17 (if one can judge from the titles) relate specifically to information science, storage and retrieval, or library automation. Nevertheless, Asheim (7), looking into the future against a background of statistics on all library school programs compiled by Schick (89), believes that there will be a steady increase in experimentation with new curricula.

Descriptions of a limited number of specific curricula in information-related areas, either in operation or projected for the near future, have appeared in recent months. Slamecka (96) sets forth the underlying philosophy as well as the structure of the graduate program in information science at the Georgia Institute of Technology. The program was predicated on the assumption that the study of information and information-based processes and their applications is not restricted to librarianship, but rather that it is a new field which does not owe allegiance to any single profession or field of knowledge. The program that leads both to the Master of Science and Doctor of Philosophy degrees offers these "options": The first is based on the abstract theories of information process and general systems, the objectives of information science as a metascience, and the development and application of a set of general techniques and devices for problem solving in science, subsuming such problems as the methodology of science and scientific research, the codification of knowledge, scientific and technological forecasting, and the optimization of cognitive processes. The second, which is professionally oriented in the direction of information engineering, emphasizes the design and study of information processing systems; it is concerned with the engineering foundations, techniques, and devices pertaining to the study, design, and operation of social and corporate information systems, science information systems, and the application of information processing techniques and devices for a large variety of purposes. The third is focused on the design and operation of computer systems and utilities, treating not only the advanced design of programming and operating systems, but also, and with particular emphasis, the interaction of both hardware and software with the objectives and needs of users.

The ACM Curriculum Committee on Computer Science (1) has advanced recommendations for courses in computer science. The report includes discussion of the various advanced programs but makes no specific recommendations. There is no linkage of these programs with any programs of an information science nature.

Bromberg (19) has hypothesized an ideal master's program for the professional education of science librarians serving industry and government. He contends that the student should be equipped in his undergraduate course with two years each of college mathematics, chemistry, physics, and biology, together with a good general education in the humanities and social sciences, including economics and foreign languages. Some training in public speaking is also recommended. Bromberg holds that librarians should not be trained alike and should not be interchangeable. For the professional degree for science librarians he suggests some 11 required courses.

The National Library of Medicine has evinced growing concern for the improvement of specialized education for medical librarians. As a result, the NLM has received support from the United States Public Health Service, through the Extramural Program of the National Library of Medicine, for exploration and experimentation leading to the design of new graduate curricula in this area. In September 1967, the School of Librarianship of the University of Washington sponsored an invitational conference (60) that brought together a limited number of highly qualified and knowledgeable people in the health sciences in general and medical librarianship in particular. The purpose of the conference was to consider the current needs and requirements of health science librarians and to develop, through working papers and discussions, a graduate program that would terminate in a health sciences librarianship degree. A comparable conference on a far smaller scale was held in Cleveland in November 1966 (24).

The absence of adequate facilities for continuing professional education for librarians is considered by Klempner (62) to be largely responsible for the inability of librarians, even special librarians, to satisfy the rising demand of users for information in depth. Thus, he urges the profession to exert every possible pressure on library associations, library schools, business and industrial management, Government agencies, and instrumentalities at all levels to provide and support "formal courses, meetings, seminars, and workshops essential to keep us abreast of current developments. Thus we may truly become disseminators of information rather than keepers of the collections."

A model for the development of curricula in information science was defined by a group of library educators concerned with information science programs in their respective schools, according to a press release from the American Society for Information Science (55). The work was done at a workshop held in September at the University of Pittsburgh's School of Library and Information Science. Published proceedings are not yet available.

Jahoda (61) finds widespread dissatisfaction with current education for librarianship, resulting in large measure from the absence of a theoretical framework for what is being taught, the small amount of research in library schools, and a critical shortage of qualified library school faculty. He finds as sources of optimism: increasing availability of funds for research and student aid; improvement in entrance-level salary scales for both beginning librarians and library school faculty; the initiation of "a critical review journal in our field, the *Annual Review of Information Science and Technology*" and, perhaps most important of all, a growing dialogue between librarians and professionals in other disciplines who are concerned about improved information services.

Cuadra & Katter (30) suggest that the kind of experiment they conducted at the University of Syracuse, in which they had students make relevance judgments of selected documents and subsequently discuss both the judgments and, still later, the experimental findings, may have substantial educational value. The students were encouraged to think critically about the judgment process involved in appraising documents and information requirements. Such a procedure might well make an important addition to the conventional teaching techniques in library school curricula.

At the School of Library Science of Case Western Reserve University, a laboratory course was developed on the basis of, and in conjunction with, a research project designed to test and evaluate a variety of retrieval systems. Saracevic (86) has described the approach, methodology, problems, and solutions in developing and teaching such a course. Further experimentation will follow as the course continues.

Rothstein (84) sees the truly professional librarian as approaching the skills and abilities of the information specialist. Thus, one of the responsibilities of the librarian in special fields is to "act as a 'literature specialist'."

The May 1, 1968, issue of *Library Journal* contained a brief essay by Harlow of Rutgers (52) on the character and responsibilities of a graduate library school, followed by short comments from eight library-school faculty members. However, neither the original statement nor any of the commentaries upon it are anything but conventional. No issues were joined, no innovations proposed, and everyone was strongly in favor of education and research.

Developments Abroad

Of the foreign materials relating to the fields of this chapter, the most comprehensive are the published proceedings of the International Conference on Education for Scientific Information Work, held at Queen Elizabeth College, London, in April 1967 (59); certain of the American papers presented have been mentioned earlier. The conference brought together some 50 delegates from 15 countries; the United States was represented by six delegates.

The program of the conference was divided into five areas, of which the third area was subdivided as follows: I. Future Needs of Education in Information Science; II. Educational Background for Entry to Courses and their Ultimate Aim; IIIa. Syllabus and Structure of Courses (theoretical papers); IIIb. Syllabus and Structure of Courses (practical papers); IV. Collaboration; V. The Provision of Teachers and Research Work. Those interested in education for librarianship and information science on this side of the Atlantic will probably find subdivisions I and III the most useful, though, again, the reader must be warned that the use of the term "information scientist" carries a quite different connotation in Europe than it does in America.

The collected papers of the conference are most valuable for the individual contributions rather than for any generalized conclusions or recommendations. Saunders (88) of the library school of the University of Sheffield tries heroically, but without conspicuous success, to draw some valid conclusions. There may be some comfort in knowing that the problems of professional education for librarianship and information science are as slippery in Queen Elizabeth College as they are in the council chambers of Berkeley or Ann Arbor.

In 1966, the Office of Scientific and Technical Information of the United Kingdom contracted with the School of Librarianship and Information Science of the University of Sheffield to prepare a study of the content of technical and educational requirements for work at all levels in scientific and technical libraries and information departments. Schur & Saunders (90) produced a study involving interviews with some 1,000 workers in this field. The inquiry emphasized the characteristics of scientific information personnel, educational and training programs presently available in the United Kingdom, the nature of the curricula, the institutions providing such training, and the need for an increased supply of trained workers.

In Dembowska's general survey on the state of documentation throughout the world (33), a short section is devoted to the situation respecting professional education. The report begins with the activities of UNESCO and devotes particular attention to the programs in Eastern Europe. She concludes that "the notion of a documentalist as a representative of a separate profession begins successively to take shape . . . side by side with the training of candidates for the profession of documentalists, the training of potential users of information in various fields is a matter gaining an ever increasing importance." A more detailed presentation of the educational programs in Latin America, continental Europe, Great Britain, and Mexico is to be found in the proceedings of the 1967 conference on library education held at the University of Illinois (58). But in the presentations in these proceedings, the education of information scientists is overshadowed by an emphasis on education for conventional library practice.

SUPPORT FOR RESEARCH AND DEVELOPMENT IN INFORMATION SCIENCE

The area of support can most easily be treated by dividing the subject into three broad categories: support for education for library and information science; Federal support for information activities in general; and non-Federal support for library and information programs.

After surveying the statistics of Federal support for library education for the years 1966–1968, Shera (91) concludes that there has been a steady rise in contributions of the United States Government to library school programs, and that not all of these contributions are derived from the *Higher Education Act of 1965*. A variety of laws passed by the Congress provide opportunities for assistance to library education. The National Science Foundation, the National Institutes of Health (mainly through the National Library of Medicine), and many of the public welfare agencies, as well as the United States Office of Education, have made provision for library schools to profit from cooperation in their grants programs.

Shera's study of statistical projections also shows that library schools expect to share in a steadily growing support for higher education generally, but he points out that little of this largesse is related to the realities of actual need. The demand for student fellowships and scholarships is still substantially in excess of the resources, while the library schools have not taken sufficient advantage of assistance to library research. Moreover, the sums allotted in the field of research in librarianship and information science have gone more frequently to independent research organizations and universities without library education programs than they have to the library schools. There can be no doubt that library education is now paying the penalty for its long neglect of research. Such neglect is, perhaps, to be expected in a profession like librarianship that is predominantly service-oriented. But the entire blame is not to be placed at the doors of the library schools. As Shera (91) says:

> The administrative machinery of the Federal support programs needs thorough revision: expansion of deadlines to permit adequate preparation of proposals; reduction in elaborate accounting procedures; improved channels of communication between the schools and the Federal agencies involved; and improved awareness on the part of government personnel of the real needs of library education.

The major source of Federal funding for information science projects, the National Science Foundation, has increased its contribution from Fiscal Year 1967 to Fiscal Year 1968. NSF support for Fiscal Year 1967 was $10.7 million for 146 grants and contracts (74), while in 1968, 154 grants and contracts received $14.5 million. In light of certain statements made earlier regarding funding for research by agencies outside formal library and information science education programs, it is significant to note the following statement from the OSIS report (75).

> NSF channels its support for discipline-oriented information primarily through the scientific societies because: (1) A scientific society usually includes the majority of active research personnel in a

given scientific field; (2) societies have traditionally provided information products for the scientific community; (3) the society can respond to the expressed information requirements of its members; and (4) active scientists and engineers become involved in the development of a science information system(s) which serves their needs through their respective professional societies.

NSF also channels support into two other major areas: Federal and general science information activities. The breakdown given by NSF of its 1968 expenditures is indicative of how little of the funding has gone to traditionally library-oriented institutions: "These awards were distributed among 32 scientific societies, 26 academic institutions, eight research institutes, eight commercial organizations, four museums, five Federal agencies, seven foreign organizations . . . and to one individual" (75). For a detailed breakdown of awards, amounts, duration of projects, etc., refer to the National Science Foundation *Grants and Awards* volume (73).

Another Federal agency, the Office of Education, has been active in funding library research. For a list of research projects supported by OE in Fiscal 1968, see the listing in the LED *Newsletter* for September 1968 (64).

The State Technical Services Act is another source of funding for information technology projects. In an article summarizing the purposes and projections of the Act, Stevenson (98) says: "States are being asked to devise new, imaginative, forward-looking programs to bring useful technical information to local industry. These programs will be financed with state funds and matching Federal funds. In Fiscal Year 1968, 6.5 million dollars was allocated by the federal government for the purposes of the Act." The latest annual report, Fiscal Year 1967 (79), provides details on the programs that were funded, many of them involving information systems and services.

As examples of reports issued by military establishments cataloging the projects funded by each, refer to the publication *Information Sciences, 1967* (3) and to the projection contained in *U.S. Army Research & Development Information Program, FY 1968-FY 1972* (101). The former report covers projects active in FY 1967 but also includes "efforts funded with FY 66, 67 and 68 funds." In addition, extensive bibliographies accompany the project listings. The format of the latter report does not make it easy to tabulate the number of such contracts. Another difficulty is that the funding section has been extracted and must be obtained separately—an inconvenience and annoyance, especially since a need-to-know must be established and a Facility Clearance furnished! The first-mentioned report indicates approximately one million dollars in spending but does not give specific financial information by contract.

With regard to non-Federally funded research, McCrossan's article (67) is quite valuable. In addition to studying announcements of projects included in the American Library Association's Library Research Clearinghouse, McCrossan scanned journals for announcements and checked various directories for information about funding organizations. He found that library research had been funded by an extremely varied group, that information science and automation have been the most heavily funded areas, and that organizations generally not related to the library field seem to be interested if the projects fit into their broadest aims and goals. McCrossan has compiled a table of areas and selected projects that have been funded.

Although McCrossan takes an optimistic stance, a comparison of the 1967 and 1968 *Bowker Annual* (17) sections entitled "Grants to Libraries or for Library Purposes" shows that the amount of money given by the independent organizations has fallen drastically, though the total number of organizations funding projects remains almost the same. The information in this section to the *Bowker Annual* is compiled from *Foundation News*, the bulletin of the Foundation Library Center, which reports only grants of $10,000 or above. In 1966, 92 foundations contributed a total of approximately $24.5 million; and in 1967, 93 foundations contributed a total of approximately $12 million, less than half the amount listed for the previous year.

At the international level, UNESCO has continued to fund library and information science projects. In 1967, a Department of Documentation, Libraries, and Archives was established and will continue to work closely with three other international organizations coordinating library and information science work: the International Federation of Library Associations, the International Federation for Documentation, and the International Council on Archives (100). UNESCO's aim is to promote library development and cooperation rather than to fund individual projects, but its relevance to the profession as a funding agency should not be overlooked.

MANPOWER RESOURCES OF THE FIELD

As one might expect, the writings in the area of manpower during 1968 show a tremendous amount of disagreement and few "hard" conclusions. It is interesting, as will be noted more fully later, that those who contend there is *not* a serious manpower shortage are economists rather than librarians. As was the case with the 1967 literature, very little of the discussion is directly concerned with the field of information science. A notable exception is a paper by Borko (15), who advocates that with the aid of systems analysts, the library manpower problem could be more easily identified. He outlines some of the basic processes of systems analysis and indicates the general application of these procedures to library routines.

An area that has received a tremendous amount of attention has been that of the library technician. A useful survey and review of the development and growth of technician programs in the 1960s has recently been issued as the first of the ERIC/CLIS state-of-the-art series (13). Another bibliography, appearing early in 1968 (102), indicated that interest in library technician programs extends back into the late 1940s, although the bulk of the material appeared during the 1960s.

The American Library Association has issued a sequence of position papers and official policy statements, largely involving the question of the library technician in the manpower problem. The first ALA item is the published report of the March 1967 Conference on Manpower Needs and Utilization (8). This conference was mentioned in the Atherton & Greer article (10) in the preceding volume of the *Annual Review*, but apparently the published report was not available at that time. In addition to containing some exceedingly bland recommendations, the report includes two valuable articles by individuals concerned with manpower problems in comparable fields.

An article entitled "Library Manpower Problems" (65), a report presented at the second Council Meeting at the Kansas City Conference of ALA, delineates general lines of progress and planning since the 1967 conference in San Francisco. The report recommends "the establishment of a unit within headquarters responsible for gathering library manpower data and information on all types of library personnel . . . " This statement shows clearly the lack of manpower data at present. The report is unequivocal that "although there are many myths current about details, the library manpower crisis *is* a reality."

A far more meaningful paper is that by Asheim (6) appearing in the ALA Bulletin for October 1968. The author, in his official capacity as director of the Office of Library Education of the ALA, has prepared a "position paper" that he hopes will promote discussion and eventually lead to an official statement of policy clarifying the present confused situation respecting levels of performance for all workers in libraries. Asheim defines five levels of library personnel, two levels being considered professional and three nonprofessional, although the highest of the three would involve "preprofessional responsibilities at a high level" and would require a bachelor's degree. He believes that although upward movement can occur in the upper three positions of the career ladder, those employed on the bottom two levels cannot or should not want to choose to move into the professional positions. (This position is challenged by Ginzberg, as will be noted later.) In defining the three nonprofessional levels, Asheim disagrees with the recommendations of another ALA Committee (see below) that two technical positions are sufficient. Fifteen reactions from librarians in the field to the paper are printed; although there are a few minor disagreements, consensus with Asheim's view is generally established.

The statement on definition of library technical personnel with which Asheim disagrees was prepared by the Interdivisional *Ad Hoc* Committee of the Library Education Division and the Library Administration Division of the ALA. This statement, the so-called Deininger report, was approved by the executive boards of both divisions at the ALA Midwinter meeting in January 1968, and therefore represents official policy of the divisions. In an article entitled "The Subprofessional or Technical Assistant—a Statement of Definition" (5) the Committee proposes two position titles— library clerk and library technical assistant—and delineates examples of typical duties to accompany the positions. Following the report of this Committee, LED appointed an Interdivisional Committee on Training Programs for Supportive Library Staff to prepare guidelines for establishment and evaluation of such training programs.

The Draft of Guidelines for Training Programs for Library Technical Assistants, a working document prepared by the Interdivisional Committee, appeared in LED's May *Newsletter* (37). The draft reiterates some of the definitions prepared by the earlier Committee but then concentrates on planning training programs.

Of course, many libraries have already begun tackling the staffing problem through their own programs, and it is questionable what effect the ultimate ALA recommendations will have on such established programs. An example of such independent action is the recommendation of the Maryland Library Association's Legislative and Planning Committee (70). The proposal receives explication, dissent, defense, and agreement in a series of articles by Finkler (45), Taylor (99), Duchac (38), Slocum (97), and Robinson (83).

In contrast to the elaborate statements of policy being prepared by ALA, none of the other library or information science organizations have taken formal positions. However, individual members of the Special Libraries Association (SLA) have written with regard to the role of the technician to the special library. In one such article, Meyer (69) defines three characteristics of special libraries that have a bearing on the training of library technicians. His main point is the need for competence, especially in a subject area, and he argues that performance is the key to higher salaries and promotions. He encourages the involvement of SLA members in local training and argues that course content should be based on liberal arts and should include training in technical skills. He also recommends that SLA's Employment Committee, which has heretofore been concerned only with professional librarians, help with technician placement.

Three publications stress heavily the idea that library technician training belongs in the community colleges. Shores (93) states:

> The junior college is in an advantageous position to assume a major responsibility for library technician education. By 1970, more than half of all college freshmen and sophomores in the U.S. will be enrolled in junior colleges.

He feels that enough weight has been thrown behind the programs to make them successful and that the Martinson report, the GS-1411 series and the ALA *Ad Hoc* Committee's Report sustain his feelings. Shores and Garloch (48), who share his general sentiments, both outline briefly the type of course they would like to see given in technician training programs. For an extremely detailed program, nothing can match the TEX-TEC syllabi (94), which further articulate what a middle-level library technology program should contain.

On the other side of the fence, those directly concerned with the training of library technicians are working through the Council on Library Technology to deal with the problems facing directors of library technology programs. Some of the main points made in the proceedings of the second annual conference of this group (28) are that with the loose personnel classifications that now exist, graduates of library technology programs might not be able to find jobs at suitable levels and at suitable pay, that the profession fears technicians will be hired as "cheap substitutes" for jobs that demand professional skills, and that librarians are therefore often hostile to such programs. Although most programs are now connected with junior and community colleges, Booth, in the conference proceedings, states that the Association of Research Libraries wants to set up its own training programs for technicians. He does not indicate what the nature of the programs would be.

The existence of another organization may be noted here. The Society of Library and Information Technicians (SOLIT), which was originally limited to students and graduates of the Department of Agriculture's Seminar in Library Techniques, is now open to anyone employed as a library or information technician. This organization will soon begin publication of a newsletter.

The Council on Library Technology has recently issued *A Directory of Institutions in the United States and Canada Offering or Developing Courses in Library Technology* (27). In the introduction to this factual compendium, editor John B. Nicholson, Jr. states: "In mid-1967 there were known to be approximately 45 Library Technology programs in existence. At the time of this writing, there are nearly ninety such programs. Because of this, the current directory will doubtless be outdated within a matter of months."

At this time, the only in-depth research program on library and information science manpower is that being conducted at the University of Maryland under the direction of Wasserman & Bundy. In a progress report (103), the authors indicate that the first phase of the program has been to develop a research design integrating the knowledge of the specialists on the study team into an approach to library problems. Since the study group is made up primarily of nonlibrarians drawn from such fields as political science, psychology, economics, business and public administration, and sociology, some of the early sessions have involved orienting them to library problems.

In an article for the November 1968 *Wilson Library Bulletin*, Bolino (14) has prepared a summary of "some important trends that have not yet been reported sufficiently in the literature." He begins with a scathing statement about the "very unsophisticated nature of the data and the cavalier approach to the presentation of tabular information" practiced by librarians. He makes four points that are of relevance to the manpower hassle, but the last of these—concerned with library shortages—is really the most important and the freshest. He states that librarians are confusing *real* vacancies with the need for additional personnel. A real vacancy, as an economist would define it, is a position for which there is actually money available. Perhaps his most valuable observation is:

> Although the *number* of professional vacancies has risen, the *rate* has declined. . . . The overriding conclusion suggested by these statistics is that the shortages are exaggerated. The vacancy rates are tolerable, and it is very possible that they can be reduced with more effective use of existing manpower.

In substantial agreement with Bolino are Ginzberg & Brown (49), who state: "These data indicate that with respect to *effective* demand, that is, with respect to the budgeted funds available for hiring personnel, the shortages are within tolerance limits." In their 59-page monograph, they summarize all points of view on the manpower problem, stress the lack of hard data about the field (which encourages disagreement ad infinitum), present a succinct manpower profile of the field, and devote seven pages to findings and recommendations, which are well worth reading. To us, the most startling point made here is the disagreement with a carefully drawn career ladder, such as that of Asheim, based primarily on formal educational qualifications. Ginzberg & Brown claim that relations between educational preparation and the occupational structure are loose, in the sense that many library positions are filled by individuals who do not have the training recommended by the official organizations in the field. It is their contention that there is a need for a more open career ladder:

> We have seen that a serious deterrent to both recruitment and utilization of librarian manpower is the absence of an orderly system of progression in which more emphasis is placed on experience and performance and less on attendance at formal classroom instruction.

There have been two reports linking the manpower problem to specific areas. Dougherty (35) concentrates on technical services, and a report prepared under the direction of Kohn at Battelle (11) examines science-information manpower in engineering and the natural sciences. The latter is an exciting and yet perplexing report. Written for the National Science Foundation, it purports to be a survey of the field and is the report that bears most directly upon information scientists. It has an almost overwhelming number of charts, tables, and graphs, but the summary of findings is disappointingly poor. The lengthy section titled "Results" is confusing to read, possibly as a result of being poorly formatted typographically. For most readers, the most valuable section is the initial nine-page "Discussion and Observations" portion, which is well written and does attempt to summarize both findings and feelings of the investigators. A serious omission is a copy of the questionnaire from which the vast number of tables are compiled. An additional omission is a description of the questions used in the various personal interviews and the relation of these to the main questionnaire. Nonetheless, data do exist and are now available to the person willing to contend with this report.

This year saw the publication of a number of reports that span the areas of manpower and education. Library education does not emerge with any great degree of credit from Hall's attempt (51) to relate the training offered by a selected sample of accredited library schools to the actual performance of specified tasks believed by administrators and professional librarians to be necessary to the operation of a public library. In the Hall study, an inventory of 231 "knowledges, skills, and abilities" was developed. She organizes these "behaviors" into a "Taxonomy of Educational Objectives for Public Service Librarians," using the method developed by Bloom and his associates. The comparison of this taxonomy with an analysis of the offerings of selected graduate library schools reveals, according to the investigator, that:

> Although objectives as stated in school catalogs, and as defined by instructors, indicated an intention to develop the more complex intel-

lectual skills, the emphasis in actual teaching . . . was largely upon factual information to the relative neglect of other desirable levels of achievement.

Clayton (22) studied the personality traits and biographical data of 150 full-time students enrolled in the library school of the University of Oklahoma to determine whether distinct personality traits could be found. Specifically, he sought to discover whether statistically significant differences would appear on various scales of the California Psychological Inventory when the accumulated data thus obtained were matched against biographical information obtained from specially designed questionnaires. The results of this inquiry are not impressive, nor even very clear. The author concludes that:

> If the field of librarianship does need men and women who possess dynamic qualities commonly associated with being progressive, mature, intelligent, forceful and articulate, it would appear from these data that more care should be given to recruiting potential librarians who place a high premium on academic matters and who are not exhausted from several years of unsatisfying work.

Mr. Clayton would seem to have used a vast array of statistical heavy artillery to batter down an open door.

The personality characteristics of librarians have also been investigated by McMahon (68). Her locale was Tasmania, and the subjects were 30 librarians employed in public, university, or special libraries. The investigator regards her findings as being in essential agreement with those of Douglass (36) for American librarians, and with the belief of Morrison (71) that librarians lack the traits most closely associated with forceful leadership. The year's studies indicate that "little old ladies" of both sexes still seem to be too much with us.

Ryan (85) analyzed questionnaires sent to random samples of academic and special librarians in Los Angeles County, California, and Cook County, Illinois, in an attempt to determine librarians' "perceptions" of librarianship. Analysis of her data led the author to conclude that: an affinity for books and reading and a close identification with library use are important factors in the choice of librarianship as a career; the choice of librarianship is most likely to be made after graduation from college; librarianship appeals more to the "idealistically-oriented" than to the "materially-oriented" person; librarians with a professional library degree tend to be more satisfied with their careers than do those who have no such degree; and librarianship does not have to be the primary occupational choice of those who are most successful in the profession or derive the greatest satisfaction from its practice.

In general, the year's work indicates a great amount of attention to the areas of education and manpower. While it may well be true that there is not a manpower *shortage*, it does seem that there is a manpower *problem*. The constant reference to the need for redefinition—and sometimes *initial* definition—of job categories, classification, and levels indicates a concern for the probable misuse of librarians and the possibility that adequate definition of positions and realistic assignment of personnel could ease the problem. It is our hope that, especially in light of the Maryland project, with its dialogue between librarians and social scientists, the former will be able to assess more accurately the nature of the problems of the field.

SUMMARY AND CONCLUSIONS

One year's accumulation of the published literature is much too short a time to identify tendencies, much less trends. The phenomena noted by Atherton & Greer (10) in the 1967 *Annual Review* would seem to be valid for 1968: convergent forces within and among the various professional associations and educational institutions; improved communication and coordinated planning of information systems; progress in the study of manpower needs; precise definition of job descriptions and position classification; elevation of salaries; and a growing awareness of the need for improving research with financial support for it.

Although funds continue to be available for the promotion of research, the amount of research being done is still disproportionate to other activities. It seems clear, however, that information scientists have been far more concerned with research, both theoretical and practical, than the librarians. As indicated in the OSIS report (75), traditionally oriented librarians may often stand very little chance of receiving research funds.

Though the 1968 literature produced a number of definitions of the field and sometimes appeared contradictory with regard to the ability of information scientists and librarians to join forces, the authors found that the extremes were represented by only a few individuals. The majority of writing seems to indicate that definitions of the relationship between information science and traditional librarianship are approaching consensus.

If there was any major achievement during 1968, it was the realization by both librarians and information scientists that the problems of controlling their own information are neither simple nor solved. The rapid response by the field's bibliographical services to the needs demonstrated at the Albany conference indicates the beginnings of interest in and work toward solutions in this area.

A great amount of work in the field this year has centered on manpower and on education. It is our conclusion that the studies involving personality characteristics, though scarcely inspiring, may be indicative of problems underlying both educational curricula as well as the oft-discussed need for manpower realignments. Awareness of two potential dangers emerges from the reading of the year's literature in manpower and in education. The first is the growing encroachment of low-level training which could threaten the profession with an invasion of mediocrity; such a horde of semiskilled personnel, under an assumed professionalism, can discredit the levels of ability required for adequate performance of professional responsibilities.

Second, there is an apparent rush on the part of academic institutions to plunge into courses, training programs, degree programs, and even research in information sciences without adequate faculty resources for sound educational offerings. One hears much too often the plaintive, not to say anguished, cry, "We are inaugurating a course in information science in our school; please send us your syllabi, outlines, and other materials that will help us to determine what we should teach." Listings in a catalog do not a program make. Nevertheless, there may still be a kind of comfort to be derived from the knowledge that even the most progressive and pioneering schools are plagued by the same stubborn problems that confront all of us, from the hills of Berkeley to 114th Street and Amsterdam Avenue.

REFERENCES

(1) ACM CURRICULUM COMMITTEE ON COMPUTER SCIENCE. Curriculum 68; recommendations for academic programs in computer science. Communications of the ACM, 11:3 (March 1968) 151–197.
(2) Advances in Librarianship. Edited by Melvin J. Voight. Academic Press, New York. V. 1 advertised in preparation in: Journal of Library Automation, 1:1 (March 1968).
(3) AIR FORCE. DIRECTORATE OF INFORMATION SCIENCES. Information sciences—1967; a summary report of the FY 1967 active contracts and grants of the Directorate of Information Sciences. Air Force Office of Scientific Research, Arlington, Va., 1968, 190 p. (AFOSR 68-0006) (AD 675 992)
(4) AMERICAN LIBRARY ASSOCIATION. Continuing education for librarians—conferences, workshops, and short courses, 1968–69. Office for Library Education, American Library Association, Chicago, December 1967.
(5) AMERICAN LIBRARY ASSOCIATION. The subprofessional or technical assistant—a statement of definitions. A report developed by the Interdivisional *Ad Hoc* Committee of the Library Education Division and the Library Administration Division. ALA Bulletin, 62:4 (April 1968) 387–397.
(6) ASHEIM, LESTER E. Education and manpower for librarianship; first steps toward a statement of policy. ALA Bulletin, 62:9 (October 1968) 1096–1106.
(7) ASHEIM, LESTER. The future of library education in the U.S. In: Schick, Frank L., ed. North American library education directory and statistics, 1966–68. American Library Association, Chicago, 1968, p. 41–43.
(8) ASHEIM, LESTER, ed. Library manpower and utilization. A conference sponsored by the Office for Library Education and the Library Administration Division with the

cooperation of the National Book Committee, Washington, D.C., 9–11 March 1967. American Library Association, Chicago, 1967, 39 p.
(9) ASHEIM, LESTER. The state of the accredited library schools, 1966–67. Library Quarterly, 38:4 (October 1968) 323–337.
(10) ATHERTON, PAULINE; GREER, ROGER. Professional aspects of information science and technology. In: Annual review of information science and technology, vol. 3. Carlos A. Cuadra, ed. Encyclopaedia Britannica, Chicago, 1968, p. 329–355.
(11) BATTELLE MEMORIAL INSTITUTE. Final report on a survey of science-information manpower in engineering and the natural sciences. Project leader: Robert S. Kohn. Columbus, Ohio, 1966, 86 p. (PB 174 439)
(12) BECKER, JOSEPH. Information storage and retrieval: the field. In: International encyclopedia of the social sciences. David L. Sills, ed. Macmillan Co. and Free Press, New York, 1968, v.7, p. 301–304.
(13) BOELKE, JOANNE. Library technicians; a survey of current developments. ERIC Clearinghouse for Library and Information Sciences, Minneapolis, Minn., 1968, 9 p.
(14) BOLINO, AUGUST C. Trends in library manpower. Wilson Library Bulletin, 43:3 (November 1968) 269–278.
(15) BORKO, HAROLD. The contribution of system analysis procedures toward the solution of the library manpower crisis. Southern California Chapter, Special Libraries Association Bulletin, 29:4 (Summer 1968) 145–148.
(16) BORKO, HAROLD. Information science: what is it? American Documentation, 19:1 (January 1968) 3–5.
(17) The Bowker Annual of library and book trade information. Phyllis B. Steckler, ed. Wyllis E. Wright, consulting ed. 12th edition. Sponsored by the Council of National Library Associations. Bowker, New York, 1967, 454 p.
(18) BRACKEN, MARILYN C.; SHILLING, CHARLES W. Survey of practical training in information science. American Documentation, 19:2 (April 1968) 113–119.
(19) BROMBERG, ERIK. Education for special librarianship—a curriculum proposal. Special Libraries, 59:8 (October 1968) 646–647.
(20) BUNDY, MARY LEE; WASSERMAN, PAUL. Professionalism reconsidered. College & Research Libraries, 29:1 (January 1968) 5–26.
(21) CIINTE, Warsaw, Poland. News from Science Abstracting and Indexing Services, 10:4 (November 1968) p. 15.
(22) CLAYTON, HOWARD. An investigation of personality characteristics among library students at one midwestern university. U.S. Office of Education, Bureau of Research, Washington, D.C., 1968.
(23) COATES, E. J. Library science and documentation literature; a new development in international cooperation. Library Association Record, 70:7 (July 1968) 178–179.
(24) CONFERENCE ON REGIONAL MEDICAL LIBRARY SERVICES, Bratenahl, Ohio, 4 November 1966. Proceedings. Robert G. Cheshier, Chairman. Editors: Barbara Denison, Robert G. Cheshier, and Alan M. Rees, Cleveland Health Sciences Library, Cleveland, Ohio, 1967, 90 p.
(25) CONFERENCE ON THE BIBLIOGRAPHIC CONTROL OF LIBRARY SCIENCE LITERATURE. Summary of recommendations [prepared by the Conference Editorial Committee]. Albany, N.Y., 1968, 8 p.
(26) CORRIGAN, PHILIP R. D. A model system of bibliographic organization for library science literature. College of Librarianship, Aberystwyth, Wales, 1968, 48 p. Preprint available from David L. Mitchell, School of Library Science, State University of New York at Albany.
(27) COUNCIL ON LIBRARY TECHNOLOGY. A directory of institutions in the United States and Canada offering or developing courses in library technology. John B. Nicholson, Jr., ed. University of Maryland, Baltimore, 1968, 48 p.
(28) COUNCIL ON LIBRARY TECHNOLOGY. CONFERENCE, 2d, Toledo, 1968. Progress and prospect; a summary of the proceedings. Toledo, Ohio, 1968, 16 p.
(29) CUADRA, CARLOS; HARRIS, LINDA; KATTER, ROBERT. Impact study of

the "Annual review of information science and technology." Final report. System Development Corp., Santa Monica, Calif., 15 November 1968. 114 p. (TM 4125)
(30) CUADRA, CARLOS A.; KATTER, ROBERT V. Implications of relevance research for library operations and training. Special Libraries, 59:7 (September 1968) 503–507.
(31) DALY, DOROTHY B. The manpower crisis in social welfare: its relevance for the field of library science. In: Asheim, Lester, ed. Library manpower and utilization. A conference sponsored by the Office for Library Education and the Library Administration Division with the cooperation of the National Book Committee, March 9–11, 1967, Washington, D.C. American Library Association, Chicago, 1967, p. 26–30.
(32) DEFENSE DOCUMENTATION CENTER FOR SCIENTIFIC AND TECHNICAL INFORMATION. Bibliography on information sciences—a scheduled bibliography. Cameron Station, Alexandria, Va., February 1968, 2 vols. (vol. 1: AD 829 001; vol. 2: AD 829 002).
(33) DEMBOWSKA, MARIA. Documentation and scientific information—outline of problems and trends. Translated by Halina Dunin. National Science Foundation, Special Foreign Currency Science Information Program, Washington, D.C., 1968, 155 p. (TT 67-56000) Translation of monograph: Dokumentacja i Informacja Naukowa: Zarys Problematyki i Kierunki Rozwoju, Warsaw, 1965, 146 p.
(34) DOCUMENTATION ABSTRACTS, INC. News from Science Abstracting and Indexing Services, 10:4 (November 1968), 11.
(35) DOUGHERTY, RICHARD M. Manpower utilization in technical services. Library Resources & Technical Services, 12:1 (Winter 1968) 77–82.
(36) DOUGLASS, R. R. The personality of the librarian. Doctoral thesis. University of Chicago, Chicago, 1957.
(37) Draft of guidelines for training programs for library technical assistants. LED Newsletter, no. 65 (May 1968) 14–20.
(38) DUCHAC, KENNETH F. The target is up; Maryland's standards: interpretation and justification. Library Journal, 93:18 (15 October 1968) 3752–3753.
(39) DUDLEY, E. P. New professional journal. Library Association Record, 70:3 (March 1968) 57.
(40) Encyclopedia of library and information science, vol. 1. Editors: Allen Kent; Harold Lancour; William Z. Nasri. Dekker, New York, 1968, 676 p.
(41) ERIC Clearinghouse for Library and Information Sciences. Newsletter, no. 1. University of Minnesota, Minneapolis, September 1968, 4 p.
(42) ERIC Reproduction Service [now being operated by The National Cash Register Company] Information Retrieval & Library Automation, 4:1/2 (June–July 1968) 7–8.
(43) FAIRTHORNE, ROBERT A. The scope and aims of the information sciences and technologies. (Preprint) Prepared for presentation at the International Congress of Scientific Information, Moscow, September 1968. To be published in a volume of the Congress papers, by VINITI.
(44) FERGUSON, JOHN DUNCAN ALEXANDER. The sociology of information organizations. Thesis—Columbia University. University Microfilms, Ann Arbor, Mich., 1967, 227 p.
(45) FINKLER, NORMAN. Maryland's manpower shortage; an introduction to a revolutionary proposal for professional personnel and staffing standards. Library Journal, 93:18 (15 October 1968) 3745–3746.
(46) FRANCIS, Sir FRANK. The two cultures in information work. The second ASLIB Annual Lecture. ASLIB Proceedings, 20:6 (June 1968) 266–278.
(47) FUELLHART, PATRICIA O.; WEEKS, DAVID C. Compilation and analysis of lexical resources in information science. Biological Sciences Communication Project, George Washington University, Washington, D.C., 15 June 1968, 39 p. (BSCP Communique 29-68)
(48) GARLOCH, LORENA A. The community colleges and the library technician program. Stechert-Hafner Book News, 22:6 (February 1968) 81–83.
(49) GINZBERG, ELI; BROWN, CAROL A. Manpower for library services. Conserva-

tion of Human Resources Project, Columbia University, New York 1967, 59 p.
(50) GRAZIANO, EUGENE E. On a theory of documentation. American Documentation, 19:1 (January 1968) 85–89.
(51) HALL, ANNA C. Selected educational objectives. University of Pittsburgh, Pittsburgh, Pa., 1968.
(52) HARLOW, NEAL. The character and responsibility of a graduate [library] school. With comments by R. B. Land, G. A. Marco, A. H. Horn, P. D. Morrison, K. R. Shaffer, P. Wasserman, H. Goldstein, and L. A. Allen. Library Journal, 93:9 (1 May 1968) 1869–1875.
(53) HAYES, R. M. Education for information systems analysis. In: International Conference on Education for Scientific Information Work, London, 3–7 April 1967. Proceedings. Fédération Internationale de Documentation (FID), The Hague, 1967, p. 105–114.
(54) HOSHOVSKY, G.; MASSEY, ROBERT J. Information science—its ends, means, and opportunities. In: American Society for Information Science Annual Meeting, Columbus, Ohio, 20–24 October 1968. Proceedings, vol. 5. Greenwood Publishing Corp., New York, 1968, p. 47–55.
(55) Information science workshop. Library Journal, 93:21 (1 December 1968) 4483.
(56) Information Sciences Year [began at the University of Chicago on January 1, 1968] Special Libraries, 59:2 (February 1968) 114.
(57) Information Storage and Retrieval. In: International encyclopedia of the social sciences. David L. Sills, ed. Macmillan Co. & Free Press, New York, 1968, v. 7, p. 301–331.
(58) INTERNATIONAL CONFERENCE ON EDUCATION FOR LIBRARIANSHIP, University of Illinois, 1967. Library education: an international survey; [Papers] edited by Larry Earl Bone. University of Illinois Graduate School of Library Science, Urbana; 388 p. distributed by the Illini Union Bookstore, Champaign, 1968.
(59) INTERNATIONAL CONFERENCE ON EDUCATION FOR SCIENTIFIC INFORMATION WORK, London, 3–7 April 1967. Proceedings. Organised on behalf of the International Federation for Documentation by ASLIB, the Institute of Information Scientists, and the Office for Scientific and Technical Information. Fédération Internationale de Documentation (FID) The Hague, September 1967, 270 p. (FID 422)
(60) INVITATIONAL CONFERENCE ON EDUCATION FOR HEALTH SCIENCES LIBRARIANSHIP, University of Washington, Seattle, 10–12 September 1967. Proceedings, edited by Irving Lieberman. School of Librarianship, University of Washington, Seattle, 1968, 216 p.
(61) JAHODA, GERALD. Evolving educational objectives of library schools. Bulletin of the Medical Library Association, 56:2 (April 1968) 138–140.
(62) KLEMPNER, IRVING M. Information centers and continuing education for librarianship. Special Libraries, 59:9 (November 1968) 729–732. Based on his talk presented at the Annual Meeting of SLA's Upstate New York Chapter on 6 April 1968.
(63) KOCHEN, MANFRED, ed. The growth of knowledge; readings on organization and retrieval of information. Wiley, New York, 1968, 394 p.
(64) Library and Information Sciences Research Branch Projects supported in Fiscal Year 1968. LED Newsletter, no. 66 (September 1968) 11–13.
(65) Library manpower problems; a committee report. ALA Bulletin, 62:8 (September 1968) 995–1000.
(66) LITTLE, THOMPSON M. Use and users of library literature. Hofstra University, Hempstead, N.Y., 1968, 34 p. Preprint available from David L. Mitchell, School of Library Science, State University of New York at Albany.
(67) McCROSSAN, JOHN. How to get a grant for library research. ALA Bulletin, 62:6 (June 1968) 722–732.
(68) McMAHON, ANNE. The personality of the librarian; prevalent social values and attitudes towards the profession. Libraries Board of South Australia, Adelaide, 1967, 127 p. Occasional papers in librarianship, no. 5.
(69) MEYER, ROBERT S. Library technician training programs and special libraries.

Index

Aagard, James S., 86
Abate, J., 128
Abraham, Frederick, 360
Abrams, R. A., 26
Abstracting and indexing services, 273–303
  distribution patterns, 231, 276
Abstracts, as document surrogates, 80
Abstracts of Mycology, 283
Abstracts of Petroleum Substitutes Literature and Patents, 287
Abstracts of Transportation and Storage Literature and Patents, 287
Academic libraries, automation, 307, 308, 312–314
  networks, 348–349
ACCESS chemistry and chemical engineering periodicals list, 282, 295
Accessibility of information, 7
Ackermann, H. J., 99
ACM (*see* Association for Computing Machinery)
Acquisitions systems, automated, 324–325
Acton, Forman S., 114
Adams, Bernhard, 316, 318, 323, 325
Adams, Scott, 275
Adams, T. W., 44
Adelson, Marvin, 405
Administrative roles in libraries and information centers, 422–426
Advanced Research Projects Agency (ARPA), 343, 353
Advances in Librarianship, 447
AEGIS data management system, 219
Aerospace Research Application Center, 252
Afanassiev, V. N., 128, 211
AFESP (Air Force English Syntax Project), 156
Africa, book development conference, 389
Agenbroad, James E., 330
Agnew, I., 170
Agricultural information, study of diffusion and use, 16–17
Agricultural information services, 282
Aines, Andrew A., 47, 275, 371
AIP (*see* American Institute of Physics)
Air and water pollution literature, 287, 293
Air Force Avionics Laboratory, 232
Air Force Directorate of Information Sciences, 466
Air Force SDI system, 245, 253
Air pollution information system, 364
Aitchison, T. M., 47, 248, 249, 256, 258, 286
Alanen, Sally S., 327, 330
Allais, Christiane, 167
Allais, Claude, 167
Allen, R. P., 115, 123, 125, 133
Allen, Thomas J., 3–29, 5, 6, 7, 8, 9, 10, 20, 26
ALPAC report, 164
Alsop, John R., 170
ALTAC programming language, 254
Aluminum Technical Information Service, 284
AMACUS (Automated Microfilm Aperture Card Update System), 183–184, 196
American Chemical Society (ACS), 242, 397–398
  Division of Chemical Literature, 277
American Dental Association, 293
American Institute of Physics (AIP), 93, 96, 204, 220, 256, 284–285, 368
American Library Association, 193, 242, 425, 430, 446, 451, 459, 460
American Management Association, 421
American Mathematical Society, information services, 256, 288
American Petroleum Institute (API), 215, 287
American Psychological Association, 242
  Project on Information Exchange in Psychology, 12, 13, 16, 18, 25
American Society for Information

474 INDEX

Science (ASIS), 453
American Society for Metals (ASM), 283–284
American Society of Planning Officials, 35, 371
Ames, L., 324
Amey, Gerald X., 261, 350
Analog signals, computerized analysis, 360
Anderson, Alice G., 419
Anderson, Jack, 399
Anderson, Stanford, 35
Anderson, Ronald R., 69
Andrews, F. M., 4
Andreyewsky, A., 172
Andrien, M., 26
Angell, Richard S., 93, 96, 389
Announcement media, user studies, 45, 233
Annual Review of Information Science and Technology, 23, 241, 448
Annual reviews, role in dissemination of information, 241
Anthony, L. J., 243, 244, 248, 254, 258, 413, 426
Anzelmo, Frank, 282
Aperture card systems, 183–184, 189, 207
Archard, T. N. J., 195
Armitage, Janet E., 95
Armstrong, Lancelot W., 362
Army Electronics Command, SDI system, 245, 253
Army Materiel Command, 183
Army Technical Library Improvement Studies (*see* ATLIS)
Artandi, Susan, 76, 77, 86, 244, 247
Asheim, Lester, 450, 451, 459, 466
Asia, library services, 389
ASIS (*see* American Society for Information Science)
ASI-ST data management system, 219
ASLIB (Association of Special Libraries and Information Bureaus), Coordinate Indexing Group, 92
ASM (*see* American Society for Metals)
Association for Computing Machinery (ACM), 93, 452
Association of Research Libraries, 194
Association of Special Libraries and Information Bureaus (*see* ASLIB)
Associative memories, 125
Associative techniques, document retrieval, 86, 159, 213
Atherton, Pauline, 56, 96, 204, 208, 209, 439, 459, 465

ATLIS workshop on automation in libraries, 100
Atomic Energy Commission, information services, 245, 253, 289
Atomic Weapons Research Establishment, 323
AUDACIOUS reference retrieval system, 56, 96, 209
Auerbach Corp., 59, 219
Auld, Lawrence, 318, 325
Auricchio, Dominick, 331, 351
Austin, Charles, 234, 315, 394
Automated language processing, 145–174
Automated Microfilm Aperture Card Update System (*see* AMACUS)
Automatic content analysis, 154–163
Automatic indexing, 86
Automatic Information Organization and Retrieval, 205–206, 305–306
Automation of library technical processes, 316–326, 352
Automation Instrument Data Service, 257
Avram, Henriette D., 233, 261, 262, 309, 322, 327
Axner, David H., 259
Ayres, F. H., 320, 323, 325

Bach, Emmon, 148, 149
Bachman, C. W., 132
Back, K., 26
Backer, Paul O., 162
Backer, S., 125, 376
Baille, A., 100
Baker, Dale B., 275, 280
Baker, Norman R., 5, 7, 43
Baker, Walter S., 207
Bakewell, K. G. B., 89
Balfour, Frederick M., 321
Ballou, Hubbard W., 181
BA-Previews, 283
Bard, Philip, 291
Bardez, Joan N., 173
Bardwell, John D., 355
Bar-Hillel, Yehoshua, 78, 150
Barhydt, G. C., 92
Barlow, D. H., 257, 365
Barnett, A. J., 116, 123, 133
Barnhill, E. A., 41
Barrett, William, 192
Bartlett, K. A., 371, 376
Baruch, Jordan J., 113, 360
BASIC (Biological Abstracts Subjects in Context), 282–283
Basic Journal Abstracts, 280

Batch-processing retrieval systems, 208
Bateman, Betty B., 312, 352
Battelle Memorial Institute, 287, 419, 430, 463
Batten, W. E., 100
Bauer, Walter F., 342
Baumanis, G. J., 54
Baxendale, Stanley, 86
Bay Area Reference Center, 352
Bayes' theorem, 45
Baykushev, B. P., 142
Bearman, H. K. Gordon, 318
Becker, A. M., 250, 252, 315
Becker, Joseph, 323, 328, 350, 351, 354, 440
Bedsole, D. T., 407, 413
Behavioral aspects, library and information center management, 410–411, 418–429
Behavioral studies, information transfer and use, 5–25
Beiser, Leo, 186
Bell, Colin J., 100, 216
Bell Telephone Laboratories, library automation, 316–317, 352
BELLREL (*see* Bell Telephone Laboratories)
Belok, A., 186
Belzer, Jack, 435
Benenfeld, Alan R., 320
Bennett, John L., 210
Bennigson, L. A., 69, 142
Bergman, S., 226
Bering, Edgar A., Jr., 241, 358
Bernier, Charles L., 77, 80, 95, 239, 241, 277
Bernshtein, E. S., 105
Berry, John, 410
Berul, Lawrence H., 59, 203–227, 207, 235, 259
BEST data management system, 219
Betyar, Laszlo, 370
Bever, Thomas G., 151, 152
B. F. Goodrich Co., Research Center Library, 313
  SDI system, 250
Bhimani, B. L., 102
Bhushan, Abhay K., 368
Bibliographic standards, 261–262
Bibliography of Agriculture, 234, 290
Bibliography on Information Science and Technology, 450
Bidwell, Charles M., 331, 352
Bill, Edward S., 43
Billups, Roderick C., 41
Biological Abstracts, 282

Biological Abstracts Subjects in Context (*see* BASIC)
Biological sciences, abstracting and indexing services, 275, 282–283, 290–293
Biomedical Communications Network, 350, 356–358
Biosciences Information Service (*see* BIOSIS)
BIOSIS (Biosciences Information Service), 282–283
Bird, R., 116
Birnbaum, Henrik, 165
Bjorge, S. E., 45, 233, 267
Black, Donald V., 311, 321
Black, H., 115
Blair, Fred, 156
Blankenship, D. A., 62, 135
Blee, Michael, 256
Bleir, R. E., 123, 125, 134
Bloch, U., 244, 246, 248, 254
Blum, Arthur R., 299, 368
Boaz, Martha, 413, 416, 425
Bobrow, Daniel G., 154, 157, 169
Bochum University Library, 316, 318
Bodie, E. K., 268
Boelke, Joanne, 467
Bohnert, Herbert G., 162
Bohnert, Lea M., 75, 77, 79
Bolino, August C., 462
Bond, Selah Jr., 239
Boodson, K., 432
Book catalogs, computer-produced, 313, 323, 325
Book numbering standard, 296
Book processing center, feasibility study, 325
Bookchin, Beatrice, 157
Book-fund accounting systems, 325
Boquet, Paul, 384
Borko, Harold, 31, 55, 127, 209, 349, 380, 440, 458
Borman, Frank, 399
Borov, G. I., 142
Borsei, A. A., 123, 128, 132
Bos, A. C., 123, 128, 132
Boucher, W., 39
Bourne, Charles P., 31, 407, 409, 412
Bowles, Edmund, 169
Bowman, S., 119
Boyd, A. H., 328
Boylan, Merle N., Jr., 316, 317, 323, 325
Boylan, Nancy, 233
Bracken, Marilyn C., 451
Bradley, Brent D., 427

Brain Information Service, 292
Bregzis, Ritvars, 100, 211, 311, 322
Brenner, Everett H., 215
Brewer, Jocelyn, 103
Brewer, S., 122
Brickwedde, F. G., 285
Briner, L. L., 157, 216, 217
British National Reprographic Centre for Documentation, 178, 191
Bromberg, Erik, 452
Brons, K. A., 365
Brookes, B. C., 51, 52
Brooks, Frederick P., Jr., 354
Brophy, Alfred L., 428
Brown, Alberta L., 437
Brown, Carol A., 462
Brown, Marilyn T., 243, 248, 249, 250, 255
Brown, Patricia L., 206, 229, 242, 408, 416
Brown, R. R., 116, 123
Brown University Library, 325
Bryan, Alice I., 419
Bryant, J. H., 135
BTSS data management system, 219
Buckerfield, P. S. T., 133
Buckland, Lawrence F., 330
Buckley, Clay W., 192, 197
Budington, W. S., 232
Buginas, Scott J., 331
Building design, effect on communication patterns, 10–11
Bundy, Mary Lee, 308, 421, 423, 429, 438, 443, 462
Burchinal, Lee G., 194, 341
Burger, John F., 171, 173
Burgess, Thomas K., 324, 327
Burket, R. C., 62, 135
Burkhalter, Barton R., 326
Burroughs 5500 computer, 253, 322, 363
Burton, Dolores M., 167
Business information systems, 115–116
Buttelmann, H. William, 173
Buzawa, M. John, 188

CA Condensates, 280
Cacciapaglia, Anna E., 268
Caceres, Cesar A., 360
Cairns, Robert W., 397
California, Los Angeles, municipal information system, 363
California, San Gabriel Valley, municipal information system, 363
California Education Information System, 114

Cammarn, Maxine R., 113, 359
Canada, library automation activities, 316
Cantley, Gordon, 497
Caras, Gus J., 38, 80, 130, 264
Carbonell, Jaime R., 58, 67
Card Automated Reproduction and Distribution System (*see* CARDS Project)
Card catalogs, user studies, 319-320
CARD microstorage device, 190
CARDS Project, 234
Cardwell, D. W., 372
Carey, Alex, 428
Carlson, C. O., 186
Carmon, James L., 355
Carnegie-Mellon University, regional computer network, 347
Carney, G. J., 169, 216, 217
Carrigy, John, 303
Carroll, John B., 78
Carter, Kenneth, 323
Carter, L. F., 42, 349
Case Western Reserve University.
  Bibliographic Systems Center, 448–449
  Center for Documentation and Communication Research, 54, 56, 75, 81, 82, 454
CAST (Clearinghouse Announcements in Science and Technology), 233, 253, 289, 450
Castore, C. H., 54
Catalog cards, computer-produced, 322, 324
Cataloging processes, automation, 318–324
CATALOGS data management system, 219
Cathode ray tubes (*see* CRT displays)
Catholic University, 420
Cautin, Harvey, 210, 211, 226
Cavara, L., 54
CCA 103 on-line retrieval system, 219, 221
CDC 3300 computer, 250
  3400/3600 computer, 251
  6400 computer, 355
Ceccato, Silvio, 100
Center for Research in Scientific Communication (*see* Johns Hopkins University. Center for Research in Scientific Communication)

Cetron, M. G., 35
CFSS (Combined File Search System), 125, 208, 220
CFSTI (see Clearinghouse for Federal Scientific and Technical Information)
Chai, D. T., 165
Chained access to files, 121–125
Chamberlin, Waldo, 384
Chamis, Alice Yanosko, 313, 316
Chapin, N., 130
Chapin, Paul G., 148
Chapin, Richard E., 321
Charney, Elinor, 100
Chartrand, Robert L., 47, 115
Cheek, Robert C., 116, 365
Chemical Abstracts Service, 234, 278, 279, 280–282, 297
  SDI services, 244, 245, 250, 255
Chemical Compound Registry System, 280, 281, 282
Chemical information systems and services, 86, 212, 278, 280–282
Chemical Society (London), 281
Chemical Titles, 282
Chen, Chingh-Chih, 314
Cheney, A. G., 263
Chernyi, A. I., 101
Chestnut, Harold, 38
Childs, D. L., 125
Chinese-English machine translation, 165
Chomsky, Noam, 146, 147, 148, 150, 152, 156
Chonez, Nicole, 86
CHORD-S (Computer Handling of Reactor Data-Safety), 365
Chow, D. K., 123
Chu, C. K., 93
Churchman, C. West, 33
Circulation systems, automated, 316–318
Citation patterns, 17, 18
CITE (Current Information Tapes for Engineers), 255, 287
Civil disorder information system, 207
City University (London) Library, 325, 326, 328
Clancy, K. P., 132
Clapp, Verner W., 45
Clark, R. L., 114, 129
Classification, 84–85
Classification Research Group (London), 88, 90, 93
Classification systems, 86–92
  in machine searching, 56, 96–97, 204, 208, 250, 252–253, 315, 389
Clayton, Howard, 464
Clearinghouse for Federal Scientific and Technical Information (CFSTI), 45, 232–233, 289
Clearinghouse for Library and Information Sciences (see ERIC Clearinghouse for Library and Information Sciences)
Climenson, W. D., 55, 119, 205
Cloot, P. L., 41, 118, 119
Clumping techniques, 86, 159
Clustering techniques, 56, 86, 126–127
Coates, E. J., 93, 447
COBOL programming language, 327, 328
Cochrane, James, 219
Cocke algorithm, 157–158, 164, 165
Cocroft, Robert, 278
CODATA (Committee for Data on Science and Technology), 387–388, 393
Code compression systems, 310
Coding systems, 123–124
Coe, R. M., 41
Coenenberg, Richard, 352
COGENT II data management system, 219
Cohan, Leonard, 260
Cohen, H. M., 116, 129
Cohen, S. I., 7, 9, 10
Colby, Kenneth Mark, 101
Coles, L. Stephen, 162
College and university libraries, automation, 307, 308, 312–314
  networks, 348–389
College of Physicians (Philadelphia) Library, 349
Colleges and universities, information networks, 352, 353–355
Collen, M. F., 136
Combinatorial Syntactic Analysis system, 164
Combined File Search System (see CFSS)
Commission on a National Information System in Mathematics, 288
Committee on National Library Information Systems (see CONLIS)
Committee on Scientific and Technical Communication (see SATCOM)
Committee on Scientific and Technical Information (see COSATI)
Commodities, classification scheme, 97

478 INDEX

Communication Disorders, 291
Communications in Behavioral Biology, 291–292
Communications networks, 347–349
Communications patterns, effect of building design, 10–11
  in research and development organizations, 9–10
Communications technology, 343–344, 355
COMPENDEX (Computerized Engineering Index), 287
Comprehensive List of Periodicals for Chemistry and Chemical Engineering, 282, 295
Computational linguistics, 146
Computational stylistics, 167
Computer and Control Abstracts, 286
Computer-assisted instruction, 346–347, 358–359
Computer-assisted medical diagnosis, 114
Computer-communications networks, 342–344, 349–352
Computer graphics, 119, 158
Computer hardware, 59
Computer input devices, 119, 156, 322
Computer output microfilm recorders, 183
Computer software, 59–60, 218–222
Computer Software and Management Information Center (*see* COSMIC)
Computer utilities, 344
Computers and privacy, 46
Computers and the Humanities, 167
COMSAT (Communications Satellite Corp.), 396
Conference on Machine-Readable Cataloging Copy, 234
Conference on Regional Medical Library Services, 467
Conference on the Bibliographic Control of Library Science Literature, 445–446
CONLIS (Committee on National Library Information Systems), 47
Conrath, D. W., 10
Consad Research Corp., 47, 115, 130
Consultants, directories, 410
  role in innovative processes, 8, 20
Content analysis, specification and control, 73–109, 154, 161
Contextual mapping, forecasting technique, 34
Continental Airlines, reservations system, 364

Conventions and meetings, contributions to journal literature, 13–14
  information exchange, 12–15
Conway, Benjamin, 40
Conway, Edward F., 189, 190, 207
Cooke, J. E., 41
Cooper, J. A., 325
Cooper, Marianne, 240, 242, 249, 250, 251, 252, 255, 256, 257, 314, 415
Cooper, W. S., 52
Coordinate indexing, 91–92, 93, 207
Copeland, B. R., 37
Copyright law, 45–46
Corbett, Lindsay, 389
Cornell University, Department of Computer Science, 55, 216, 223
Cornew, Ronald W., 165
Correlational grammar, 160–161
Corrigan, Philip, 88, 440
COSATI, 45, 93, 231, 237, 238, 276, 277, 288, 392, 421
  Panel on Information Analysis Centers, 236
  Task Group on Dissemination of Information, 232
COSMIC (Computer Software and Management Information Center), 231
Cost-effectiveness analysis, 47–51, 222, 243–246, 284, 417
Costs of libraries and information centers, 416–418
Cottrell, William B., 238
Couger, J. Daniel, 40
Council on Library Technology, 461
Counts, Richard W., 252, 408
Coward, R. E., 310
Cowburn, L. M., 320
Coyaud, M., 101
Craig, Dwin R., 182
Crane, Diana, 16, 17
Cranfield International Conference on Mechanized Information Storage and Retrieval Systems, 101
Cranshaw, D. D., 115, 130, 364
Creager, William A., 69
Creps, John E., 283
Crime information systems (*see* Law enforcement information systems)
Criminal justice information systems (*see* Law enforcement information systems)
Critical reviews, role in dissemination of information, 241, 277–278
Crocker, Elizabeth L., 331

Croghan, A., 97
Cronkhite, L. W., Jr., 113, 117
Cropper, Ann G., 58
Cross-referencing structures, 85, 316
Crowther, B. M., 384
CRT displays, 59, 119, 156, 162, 322
Cuadra, Carlos A., 23, 81, 241, 307, 448, 453
Cummings, Martin M., 307, 312
Curran, Ann T., 330
Current-awareness services (*see also* Abstracting and indexing services; *see also* SDI systems), 42, 96, 242–258
Current Contents series, 293
Current Information Tapes for Engineers (*see* CITE)
Current Papers in Physics, 22–23, 285
Curry, William C., 58
Curtice, Robert M., 86, 171, 215

Dale, Alfred G., 101
Daly, Dorothy B., 468
Dammers, H. F., 47, 86, 92, 205, 235, 250, 350
Daniel, Evelyn, 405–438
Danielson, T., 138
Darby, Ralph L., 237, 238, 407, 422
Dartmouth College, time-sharing computer system, 347
DATA CENTRAL information system, 216, 220–221
Data Corp., 220
Data File Two storage and retrieval system, 123, 125, 134
Data management software, 218–222
DATAPLUS retrieval language, 211
DATATEXT time-sharing language, 210
Dattola, R. T., 102
Davenport, W. C., 280
Davies, D. W., 343, 372
Davis, Arthur I., 191
Davis, Charles H., 94
Davis, J. Eugene, 237, 307
Davis, L. S., 114
Davis, Richard J., 114, 361
Davis, Ruth M., 350, 357
Davison, P. S., 257
Day, A. M., 172
Day, Melvin S., 246, 248, 251, 385, 387, 396
Day, Muriel L., 331
Day, W. Clinton, 376
Day, William J., 116, 132, 364

Decauville, N. Siot, 101
DeCecco, John P., 151
Decision tables for system analysis, 49
Decision theory, 36–38, 41, 45, 51, 52
Deese, James, 80
Defense Documentation Center, 181, 450
Defense Intelligence Agency, 118
Defense libraries, automation, 307
DeGennaro, Richard, 313
DeGrolier, Eric, 90, 91
DeHaen drug information services, 292
Dekker, J., 400
Delany, D. P., 91
Delphi technique, as a planning tool, 34–35
Demboska, Maria, 455
Denning, Peter J., 58
Dennis, Jack B., 344
Denstman, Harold, 176
Department of Agriculture, Current Research Information System, 238
Department of Commerce, international information projects, 392–393
Department of Defense, information projects, 393, 457
Department of State. Bureau of Educational and Cultural Affairs, 400
Desk Top Analysis Tool, 234, 281, 289
Detroit medical library network, 349
DeWeese, Lemuel C., 419
Dewey, H., 95
Dewey Decimal Classification, 91, 96
Dews, J. David, 311
DIALOG on-line retrieval system, 219, 221, 351
Dickman, John T., 282
Dickson, Paul A., 44, 233
Dictionary construction, 86, 158–159
Diesing, Arthur C., 244, 250, 255
Digital plotting, 119
Direct access to files, 120, 123
Directory of Computerized Information in Science and Technology, 260
DiSalvo, Joseph, 407
Discussion Group for Library Science Librarians, 447–448
Display devices, 58–59, 119
Dittrich, Wolfgang, 102
DL-1 (*see* IMS)
DM-1 data management system, 132, 134, 219
Document analysis, 78–83
Document dissemination, 229–270

480 INDEX

Document retrieval, file organization, 124
  linguistic aspects, 79–80
  systems, 203–227
  Systems evaluation, 49-50
Document surrogates, 206, 234–235, 260–262
Documentation Abstracts (*see* Information Science Abstracts)
Documentation literature, indexing system, 94
Documentation standards, 97, 261, 275, 295–298, 368
Doebler, Paul D., 36
Dolby, J. L., 167, 306, 318, 319, 321, 327
Doran, Thomas, 198
Dostert, Bozena H., 161
Dougherty, Richard M., 325, 334, 406, 429, 463
Douglass, R. R., 419, 463
Dow Chemical Corp. SDI system, 245, 250, 255
Dowkont, A. G., 133
Downie, C. S., 244, 247, 253
Doyle, Stephen E., 369
DPS (Document Processing System), 216, 220
Droz, Julius R., 309, 327
Drug information systems, 86, 292–293
Dubin, Robert, 428
Dubner, H., 135
Duchac, Kenneth F., 460
Dudley, E. P., 468
Dueker, Kenneth J., 115, 363
Duggan, Michael A., 369
Duncan, Sheila, 171
Dunn, R. G., 113, 117
Du Pont Co., chemical structure search system, 212
Dutton, Brian, 161
Dyke, Freeman H., Jr., 409

Earl, L. L., 102
Earl, P. H., 62, 264
East, H., 285
Eastern Airlines, reservation system, 364
Eastern Pennsylvania Information Center, 355
Eastman Kodak Co., 181
  MIRACODE system (*see* MIRACODE microfilm retrieval system)
Easy English retrieval language, 210–211

Education for information science, 450–455
Education for library administrators, 420–422
Education information systems and networks, 114, 340–341, 345–347, 353–356
Education thesaurus, 92, 341
Educational Information Network (EIN), 353–354
Educational research, information needs compared with physical science research, 14–15
Educational researchers, participation in invisible colleges, 20–21
Educational Resources Information Center (*see* ERIC)
Educational television, 345–346
EDUCOM (Interuniversity Communications Council), 259, 351, 353–354
EDUNET, 343
EJC (*see* Engineers' Joint Council)
Electrocardiograms, computerized analysis, 360
Electronics and instrumentation data network, 365
Elkind, Jerome I., 62, 67
Eller, James L., 341
Emory, James C., 416, 417
Enea, Horace, 101
Encyclopaedia Britannica, Inc., 444–445
Encyclopedia of Library and Information Science, 450
Engineering drawings, storage and dissemination, 180, 183–184, 190–193
Engineering Index Inc., information services, 220, 245, 255, 286–287
Engineering information systems, 255, 287
Engineering societies, role in information transfer, 15
Engineers, information-gathering patterns, 6–7
Engineers' Joint Council (EJC), 93
English Grammar I, 156
English Grammar II, 156–157
Enright, B. J., 320, 326
Erat, K., 113
Ergonomics, application to computer display design, 58
ERIC, 340–341, 449
  Clearinghouse for Library and

Information Sciences, 238, 242, 449
Clearinghouse for Linguistics, 238
Clearinghouse on Educational Media and Technology, 347
Erskine, R., 123, 133
Etzioni, A., 423
EURATOM (*see* European Atomic Energy Community)
European Atomic Energy Community (EURATOM), 205
European Launcher Development Organization (ELDO), 290
European Space Research Organization (ESRO), 289–290, 395
European Translation Centre, 391
Evaluation of SDI systems, 243–249
Evaluation of the Utility and Cost of Computerized Library Catalogs, 318
Evans, A. J., 312
Evans, D., 119, 123, 125
Evans, Evelyn J. A., 389
Evans, S. J. W., 58
Excerpta Medica Foundation, 257, 292–293

Faceted classification, 89, 97
Facsimile transmission, 259, 351–352
  cost effectiveness study, 51
Fairthorne, Robert A., 73–109, 79, 102, 442
Fano, R. M., 132
Farkas, Irene S., 251
Farradane, J., 90
Farren, A., 283
Farris, Eugene H., 312, 352
Federal Communications Commission, 368, 369
Federal Council for Science and Technology, 45, 93, 421
  Committee on Scientific and Technical Innovation, 396, 400
Federal libraries, survey, 417
Federal regulation of computer and communication services, 268–269
Federal role in information science, 44, 230–234, 277, 309, 341, 349–350, 391–392, 455–457
Federally Supported Information Analysis Centers, 237–238
Feigenbaum, Donald S., 40
Feldman, Jerome, 158
Ferguson, John, 444
Ferrell, James K 371

Festinger, L., 11
FID (*see* International Federation for Documentation)
File-accessing techniques, 120–127
File design, 127–129
File management software, 218–222
File organization, 111–143, 212, 310–311
  card catalogs, 319
File security, 46, 132, 361
File structures, for geographic retrieval, 115, 127
Filep, Robert T., 114, 347
Fillmore, Charles, 148, 149, 157
Film libraries, 312, 352
Finkler, Norman, 460
Finkler, R., 115
Fiscal constraints, system analysis, 43–45
Fischer, Margaret, 224
Fishburn, P. C., 37
Fisher, C. H., 33
Fishman, G. S., 38
Fitzroy, Peter T., 64
Flanagan, Carolyn, 273
Fleming, Ilah, 170
Fodor, Jerry A., 148, 149, 151, 152
Fontana, J. M., 113
Food and Drug Administration (FDA), 220, 234, 281
Food science abstracting and indexing services, 278, 282
Forecasting techniques, 34–36
FOREM (File Organization Evaluation Model), 129
FORGE data management system, 219
Formatted File System, 118
Forsyth, V., 332
Forsythe, G. E., 114, 346
FORTRAN IV programming language, 252, 314
Foskett, D. J., 87
Francis, Frank, 443
Francis, S., 422
Francis, W. Nelson, 167
Franke, Richard D., 323
Franklin and Marshall College, 355
Frarey, Carlyle J., 418
Fraser, Bruce, 151
Fraser, J. Bruce, 157, 169
Freed, Roy N., 46, 114, 361
Freeman, David N., 354
Freeman, Robert R., 56, 61, 96, 99, 153, 204, 208, 209, 226, 320
Friedberg, L. M., 118, 123, 133

Friedlander, Gordon D., 260
Friedman, Joyce, 155
Friedman, Lee A., 46, 415
Frischmuth, D. S., 5
Frohman, A., 11
Fry, J. P., 219
Fuellhart, Patricia O., 442, 447
Full-text storage and retrieval, digital form, 259–260
Functional overlap of systems, 46–47
Furth, Stephen E., 260
Fussler, Herman H., 370

Galin, Melvin Philip, 410, 420, 423, 427
Gallagher, P. J., 86
Gallie, Thomas M., 371
Gardner, Reed M., 376
Garfield, Eugene, 159, 278, 340
Garloch, Lorena A., 461
Garrett, Merrill, 151, 152
Garvey, W. D., 14, 15
Garvin, Paul L., 78, 165, 166
Gass, S. I., 115
Gazda, George M., 428
GE 235 computer, 250, 313
 265 computer, 211
 M605 computer, 365
Gelblat, M., 113, 125
General Electric Co., (see also GE) Medinet system, 360
General Precision Systems, Advanced Products Division, 198
Generalized Information System (see GIS)
Geo-coding, 115, 127
Geometric coding method, 123
Georgia Institute of Technology, 322, 452
Gerdel, J. K., 118
German, Janice, 331
Germany, library automation activities, 316
Gerstberger, P. G., 6, 7, 8, 10, 26
Gerstenfeld, A., 8, 10, 26
Ghosh, S. P., 125
Gifford, G., 54
GIM (Generalized Information Management), 221
Ginsberg, Helen F., 86
Ginzberg, Eli, 462
GIS (Generalized Information System), 125, 126, 134, 219, 327
Giuliano, Vincent E., 101, 171, 224
Glaser, E., 362

Gleason, Edward Michael, 41
Glinski, B. C., 139
Gloege, W. P., 27
Godel, Robert F., 152
Gold, Michael M., 57, 58, 369
Goldhammer, Donald, 103
Goodenough, John B., 158
Gopinath, M. A., 88
Gordin, Jess, 401
Gordon, B. L., 93
Gordon, Louis, 41
Gordon, Paul J., 405, 420
Gotlieb, C. C., 86, 159
Gould, E. P., 134, 365
Gouldner, Alvin W., 425
Gourio, H., 130
Graham, Robert M., 46
Graham, Ronald A., 408
Graham, W. R., 21
Grammar testers, 155–157
Grant, C. B. S., 44, 47
Graphical input-output devices, 119
Grau, Albert A., 227
Grauer, Robert T., 137
Gray, S. B., 184, 190
Graziano, Eugene E., 41, 76, 443
Great Britain. Interdepartmental Group in Microcopying, 180–181
 library automation activities, 306, 313, 318, 322–323
 Ministry of Technology, commodities classification, 97
 National Reprographic Centre for Documentation, 178, 191
Green, Claude Cordell, 170, 211
Green, Paul E., 45
Greenberger, Martin, 369
Greer, Roger, 439, 459, 465
Greer, Willis R., Jr., 410
Gregg, H. R., 49
GREMAS search system, 212
Gries, David, 158
Griffel, D., 134
Grimes, Joseph, 166
Grogan, Paul J., 231
Gronemann, U. F., 199
Grosch, Audrey N., 325
Grose, M. W., 308
Grosse, Louis N., 156
Grossman, A., 114
Group size, effect on communication patterns, 17
Gruber, Jeffrey, 150
Gujrati, B. S., 406
Gull, C. D., 38, 326, 357, 429
Gullahorn, J. T., 11

INDEX 483

Gummere, Richard M., Jr., 42
Grunwald, Wilhelm, 103
Guilford, J. P., 90

Hagerty, Katherine, 80
Haglind, J. B., 99
Haibt, Luther, 216, 217
Hall, A. D., Jr., 114
Hall, Anna C., 463
Hall, Michael D., 103
Hall, P., 113, 117
Halle, Morris, 146, 147
Halsey, Richard S., 189
Hamblen, John W., 44
Hammersmith, Alan G., 60
Hampshire College Library, automation activities, 314
Hanel, R. S., 127
Hanson, D. G., 320, 328
Harbeck, Rudolf, 77
Hare, Van Court, Jr., 39
Harley, A. J., 394
Harlow, Neal, 454
Harms, Robert T., 149
Harris, Jessica L., 194
Harris, Linda, 26, 241, 265, 468
Harris, Milton, 281
Harris, Neville, 328
Harris, Zellig, 146
Harrison, Annette, 46
Hart, Harold, 241
Harvard College Library, automation activities, 313
Harway, Norman, 104
Hash coding, 310
Hawken, William R., 176, 181, 189
Hayashi, Hideyuki, 166
Hayes, Robert M., 326, 351, 451
Hayes International Corp., 103
Haygarth Jackson, A. R., 215
Hays, David G., 35, 78, 171, 186
Head, Robert V., 60, 111
Headly, P., 113
Heald, J. Heston, 93
Heany, Donald F., 38, 116, 406
Heath, F. R., 116
Hecht, Kenney, 322
Hedley, W. W., 116
Heilprin, Laurence B., 45, 186
Heinritz, F. J., 406, 429
Heintz, H. F., 231
Helander, Donald P., 105
Held, Stuart, 188
Helmer, Olaf, 34
Helmkamp, John G., 418

Henderson, James W., 319
Henderson, Madeline M., 82, 241, 278
Henisz-Dostert, Bozena, 171
Herman, D. J., 129
Herner, Saul, 42, 103
Herring, Conyers, 240, 241, 277, 278
Herschel, J. F. W., 186
Herschman, Arthur, 65, 257, 285
Heumann, Karl, 295
Heuristic approaches to language processing, 166
Hickok, William G., 173
Hierarchical indexing structures, 90, 91, 96, 159
High Polymer Science and Technology Center, 238
High-reduction microform systems, 185–189
Higher Education Act of 1965. Title VIII, 345
Hill, D. R., 126
Hill, S. R., Jr., 137
Hillman, Donald J., 103, 210, 215, 216, 217
Hirsch, Phil, 366
Hirst, Caroline Perkins, 104
Hirst, Norman F., 104
Hirst, Robert I., 324
Hisley, B. L., 142
Hiz, Henry, 149
Hoadley, Howard W., 199
Hockett, Charles F., 146
Hodgins, Donald D., 330
Hoffer, Joe R., 238
Hoffman, Warren S., 212
Hohnecker, Walter, 303
Holm, Bart E., 408
Holman, K., 103
Holst, Wilhelm, 104
Holt, Arthur Lee, 39
Holt, R. B., 174
Holzbauer, Herbert, 230, 251
Homer, Eugene D., 38, 130
Honeywell H-200 computer, 256
Hope, Nelson W., 425
Horwood, E. M., 127, 130
Hoshovsky, A. G., 207, 247, 440
Hospital information systems, 113, 359–361
Housman, Edward M., 47, 244, 246, 248, 253
Houston, Jean I., 171
Howell, J. T., 113, 117
Howland, L., 282
Hsiao, D. K-M., 125
Hudson, G. R., 70

Hudson, S., 97
Hugo, Michael, 62
Human factors, in analysis of document contents, 78–81
    man-system interface, 57–58
Human relations, libraries and information centers, 428–429
Humphrey, John A., 44
Hutton, Fred C., 212
H. W. Wilson Co., 446
Hyslop, Marjorie R., 44, 283, 284, 417

IBM Corp., library automation project, 352
IBM 347 data collector, 313, 318
    360 computers, 211, 220, 221, 252, 255, 257, 292, 313, 314, 316, 317, 318, 322, 323, 327, 355, 363, 364
    360/67 computer, 324
    360/75 computer, 314, 354, 366
    870 document writer, 323, 324
    1360 photodigital storage device, 197
    1401 computer, 255, 317
    1410 computer, 360
    1440 computer, 313, 323
    1460 computer, 312
    1620 computer, 318, 324, 325
    2280 film recorder, 282
    2741 communications terminal, 210
    7094–7040 direct couple system, 324
IBM DATATEXT system, 321
IBM Technical Information Retrieval Center (ITIRC), 216, 217
IBM transformational grammar project, 156
ICIREPAT (International Cooperation in Information Retrieval among Examining Patent Offices), 391, 392
ICL 1901 computer, 286
ICS data management system, 219
ICSU, 275, 295, 297, 384, 385, 386, 387, 397
ICT 1901 computer, 256
Icthyology information, 283
Idea generation (*see* Innovative processes)
IDS (Integrated Data Store), 119, 125, 132
IEEE (*see* Institute of Electrical and Electronics Engineers)
Iker, Howard F., 104
Illinois State Library, automation activities, 317

Illumination for document copying, 192–193
IMRADS (Information Management, Retrieval and Dissemination System), 219
IMS data management system, 219
Index compatibility, 96
Indexed sequential access to files, 122, 123, 125
Indexer consistency, 81, 320
Indexing, by word choosing, 85
    computer-assisted, 210, 218
    from abstracts, 80
    principles and theory, 77–78, 91–92
    techniques, 95, 288
Indiana, library automation activities, 308
Indiana University, SDI system, 245, 246, 247, 250–251
Industrial and Engineering Chemistry, 242
InfoData Systems, Inc., 221
INFOL (Information Oriented Language), 118, 134, 219
Informatics Inc., 133
Information analysis centers, 235–239
Information Center for Hearing, Speech, and Disorders of Human Communication, 291
Information centers, management, 405–438
Information Dynamics Corp., 47, 130
Information Exchange Group. National Institutes of Health, 240–241
Information-gathering patterns, scientists and technologists, 5–8, 21, 240
Information Industry Association, 294
Information networks, 339–377
    overlap and decentralization studies, 47
Information science, definitions and parameters, 407, 439–445
    education, 450–455
    professional literature, 445–450
Information Science Abstracts, 288, 447
Information systems, design and evaluation, 31–70, 205, 243–249, 312–314, 315
    documentation and implementation, 40–42
    funding studies, 43–45
    retrieval effectiveness, 51–55
Information transfer, conventions and meetings, 12–15

INDEX 485

social and behavioral studies, 5–25
Information Usage, 242
Information user and use studies, 3–29, 42–43
Inforonics Inc., 312
INIS (*see* International Nuclear Information System)
Innovative processes, information use patterns, 5–9, 16–17, 41–42
INQUIRE on-line retrieval system, 221
INSCAN compiler, 134
INSPEC (Information Service in Physics, Electrotechnology, and Control), 256–257, 285–286
Institute for Scientific Information, 251, 278, 293
Institute for the Advancement of Medical Communication, 431
Institute of Electrical and Electronics Engineers (IEEE), 242, 286–287
Institute of Reprographic Technology, 181
Institution of Electrical Engineers, information services, 256, 285–286
Integrated Data Store (*see* IDS)
Integrated Science Information Service, 316
INTELSAT (International Telecommunication Satellite Consortium), 396
Interactive retrieval systems, 208–212
Intergovernmental Task Force on Information Systems, 231–232
Interlibrary loan networks, 347–349
Internal Revenue Service, information network, 362
International Conference on Education for Librarianship, 469
International Conference on Education for Scientific Information Work, 443, 454
International Conference on Science Information, 383–384
International Congress of Psychology, 12, 15
International Congress on Reprography, 176
International Council of Scientific Unions (*see* ICSU)
International Directory of Research and Development Scientists, 293
International Federation for Documentation (FID), 96, 97, 389–390

International Federation of Library Associations (IFLA), 390
International information projects, 97, 281, 284, 286, 289, 290, 292, 295, 392–395, 454–455, 458
International Labour Office, Integrated Science Information Service, 316
International Nuclear Information System (INIS), 289, 296, 387
International Road Research Documentation Project, 390–391
International Standardization of Library Statistics, 390
International standards, 97, 386, 390
International Standards Organization, 97
International Symposium on Relational Factors in Classification, 89–90
International transfer of information, 12–13, 379–402
International Tree Disease Register System, 290
International Union of Pure and Applied Chemistry (IUPAC), 86
Internationale Dokumentationgesellschaft für Chemie, 281
Interpersonal communication, relation to scientific productivity, 5, 7–8, 16–22
Interuniversity Communications Council (*see* EDUCOM)
INTIPS data management system, 219
Inventory control systems, 116, 129, 365
Invisible colleges, 16–22, 240
Invitational Conference on Education for Health Sciences Librarianship, 469
Irwin, Manley R., 368, 369
Ish, Carl J., 282
Israel, Ministry of Defense, SDI systems, 248, 254
ISTIM (*see* Task Group for the Interchange of Scientific and Technical Information in Machine Language)
ITIRC (*see* IBM Technical Information Retrieval Center)
Ito, Y., 140
IUPAC (*see* International Union of Pure and Applied Chemistry)
Ives, H. D., 186

Jackman, Chester, 191
Jackson, B. F., 183, 184

Lister Hill Center for Biomedical Communications (*see* Biomedical Communications Network)
List-processing languages, 119
List-processing systems, 121–122, 123, 125–126
LISTS (Library Information System Time-Sharing), 311
Little, John L., 368
Little, Thompson M., 448
Liu, H., 131, 132, 133
Lochak, K., 156
Lock, Reginald Northwood, 405, 426
Lockemann, Peter C., 169
Lockheed Missiles and Space Company, 221
 Electronic Sciences Laboratory, 105
LogEtronic SP 10/70 contact printer, 182
Londe, Dave L., 156
London, Gertrude, 239
Lorain County (Ohio) Community College, 323–324
Lorenz, John G., 341, 377–402, 389
Lougborough University of Technology, 313
Loukes, N., 331
Lowe, T. C., 128
Lowell, Mildred H., 406
Lowry, Charles Doak, 278
Lowry, W. Kenneth, 230, 232, 254, 256, 398, 410, 415
LUCID on-line retrieval system, 119, 219
Lufkin, Richard C., 320
Luginbyhl, T. T., 244, 253
Lum, V. Y., 127, 128, 141
Lumitype 713 filmsetter, 286
Lutterback, Ernst, 77
Lynch, Michael F., 86, 95
Lyons, John, 147

Machine-aided translation, 164–166
Machine-readable bibliographic records, 315, 320–321, 326
Machine-Readable Cataloging (*see* MARC Project)
Machine-Readable records, distribution, 234, 255, 260–262, 280, 281–282, 283, 286, 292, 295–297
 in automated language processing, 167
Mackenzie, A. Graham, 313
MADAM data management system, 219

Magnetic tape distribution services, 255, 260–262, 280, 281–282, 283, 287, 290, 293, 322
Magnino, Joseph J., Jr., 216, 217
Maidment, W. R., 322
Maier, Joan M., 334
Maissoneuve, J., 11
Maizell, Robert E., 99, 416, 421, 430
Malin, Morton V., 275
MANAGE data management system, 219, 220
Management information systems, 365
 analysis and design, 40, 111–143
Management of libraries and information centers, 405–438
Management of system design efforts, 39–42
Man-machine communication (*see also* User-system interface), 163–164, 213–214
Mann, Floyd C., 423
Manning, Josephine, 259, 352
Man-system interface, 57–58, 213–314
Manuscript announcement services, 242
MARC Project, 233–234, 296, 307, 309–310, 322, 327–328, 395
 applications, 250, 315
Marcson, Simon, 424
MARK IV file management system, 123, 134, 219
Maron, M. E., 163
Marquis, D. G., 9
Marron, Harvey, 341
Marschak, Jacob, 37
Marthaler, M. P., 316
Martin, M. D., 61, 263, 285, 298
Martins, Gary R., 157, 165
Martinez, Samuel J., 105
Martz, P., 139
Massachusetts Institute of Technology, 315
Massey, Robert J., 440
Mathematical models, in information systems analysis, 36–38, 50, 54, 213
 of library use, 311
Mathematical Offprint Service, 245, 288
Mathematics information services, 288
Mather, Dan, 316, 318, 325
Mathews, F. W., 215
Mathews, S. K., 192
Mathiot, Madeleine, 103
Mattson, R. L., 128
Maurer, W. D., 121

INDEX 489

Mayne, A. J., 87
McCamy, C. S., 195, 196
McCawley, James D., 148, 149, 150
McCrossan, John, 458
McDaniel, J., 165
McFarland, Anne S., 438–471
McGee, W. C., 125
McGowan, J., 422
McGregor, Douglas M., 428
McGurk, A. K., 316
McIntosh, S., 134
McKenney, James L., 35
McLamore, Hilliard, 60
McLaughlin, R. A., 366
McLaurin, M. J., 118, 123
McLean, J. B., 125, 131
McLuhan, Marshall, 229
McMahon, Anne, 464
McMullen, D. A., 302
Media networks, 345–347, 357
Medical information systems, 41, 93, 96, 113–114, 117, 207, 290–291, 292, 314, 358–361
Medical library education, 452–453
 networks, 312, 348–349
 planning, 431
Medical records systems, 113–114, 251
MEDLARS (Medical Literature Analysis and Retrieval System), 50, 55–56, 81, 234, 291, 307, 315, 357, 386, 393–394
Meetings and conventions, contributions to journal literature, 13–14
 information exchange, 12–15
Meiser, D., 209, 351
Melcher, Daniel, 59
Mellner, C., 138
Meltzer, Morton F., 406, 416, 417, 418
Menden, Werner, 105
Menkhaus, E. J., 116, 129
Menzel, Herbert, 21
Mersel, Jules, 307
Merton, Robert K., 22, 412
Messier, Michel, 137
Metallurgical Abstracts, 284
Metallurgical information, 96, 283–287
Metals Abstracts, 284
Metals Abstracts Trust, 284
METRO (*see* New York Metropolitan Reference and Research Library, Inc.)
Meyer, E., 212
Meyer, Robert S., 460
Meyer, Roger L., 434
Michaelson, Herbert B., 277

MICRODOC, 199
Microfiche dissemination systems, 259, 293
Microfilm Association of Great Britain, 181
Microfilm dissemination systems, 282, 293, 351
 cartridge systems, 194–195
 input to optical character recognition devices, 184
Microform dissemination systems, 259
 storage and retrieval systems, 189–190
 technology, 175–201, 207
Microphotography, 180, 191
Micropublishing, 193–195
Midwestern University, library automation activities, 317
Military command and control systems, 366–367
Miller, W., 158
Mills, J., 87
Mills College of Education, automated catalog card production, 324
Milne, Gordon G., 197
Milsum, J. H., 33
Minker, J., 119, 128
MIRACODE microfilm retrieval system, 207
Miron, Murray S., 171
Mitchell, H. S., 97
Mitchell, M. B., 58
Mitchell, R. P., 102
MITRE transformational grammar, 156
Modeling, 35, 36–38, 41, 50–51, 53
Mohrhardt, Foster E., 44, 275, 406
Molgaard-Hansen, Rasmus, 96
Montgomery, Christine A., 145–174, 158, 159, 160, 170
Montijo, R. E., Jr., 114, 132
Montreal General Hospital, nephrology information system, 207
Mooers, Calvin N., 46, 212, 368
Moon, E. E., 420
Moore, Michael R., 40
Moreland, George B., 44
Morenoff, E., 125, 131
Morgan, Robert A., 192
Morris, Ned C., 325
Morris, R., 121
Morrison, D. R., 124
Morrison, P. D., 463
Morse, Philip M., 306, 311, 405
Morton, M. S. S., 119
Mosior, J. W., 134, 365

Mosler Selectriever system, 189, 190
Motor vehicle information systems, 114–115, 132
Mount, Ellis, 237
Moys, Elizabeth M., 97
Muller, Robert H., 324
Multicomputer networks, 353
MULTICS data management system, 219
Multistage search techniques, 212–215
Mulvihill, John G., 94, 215
Mumford, L. Quincy, 394
Municipal information systems, 115, 364
Murphy, E., 364
Murray, D. M., 102
Murrill, Donald P., 324
Myatt, Dewitt O., 409, 416

Nadler, E. B., 4, 16
Nakanishi, T., 116
NAL (*see* National Agricultural Library)
Namian, P., 130
Nance, J. W., 221
Nance, Richard E., 43
NASA Communications Network (NASCOM), 366–367
  information systems and services, 44–45, 209, 231, 245, 246, 251–252, 253, 289, 290, 351
  international information projects, 395–396
National Academy of Sciences, Automatic Language Processing Advisory Committee, 164
National Research Council, 397
National Advisory Commission on Libraries, 45, 307, 309, 350, 445
National Aeronautics and Space Administration (*see* NASA)
National Agricultural Library (NAL), 233–234, 260, 291, 351
National Bureau of Standards, 179
  Automatic Data Processing Program, 368
National Cancer Institute, information services, 242, 245, 252, 314
National Conference on Content Analysis, 106
National Crime Information Center, 115, 362–363
National Federation of Science Abstracting and Indexing Services (NFSAIS), 278, 294, 297

National information networks, 47, 349–350, 356–358, 361
National Institute of Neurological Diseases and Blindness, information centers, 358–359
National Institute of Neurological Diseases and Stroke, 290–291, 292
National Institutes of Health, Information Exchange Group, 240–241
National libraries, document dissemination, 233–234
  serials data program, 294
National Library of Medicine (NLM), 233–234, 281, 291, 350, 356–358, 452–453
National Medical Audiovisual Center, 357
National Microfilm Association, 181
National Physical Laboratory, 165
National Science Foundation (NSF), 96, 347, 354, 385, 386, 391, 396, 456–457
National Serials Data Program, 294, 295
NATO (*see* North Atlantic Treaty Organization)
Natural language information processing, 153–167
  text searching, 216–218, 220
Navarro, J., 115
NCR 315 computer, 292
Needham, Roger M., 86, 159
Neelameghan, A., 88
NELINET (*see* New England Library Network)
Nelson, C., 27
Nelson, Carl E., 180, 191
Nelson, Donald B., 221, 268
Nelson, Edward A., 60
Nelson, Jean W., 433
Nelson Associates, Inc., 348
Neurological Information Network, 290–291, 358–359
Neurophysiology information, 360
Neville, H. H., 91
New England Center for Continuing Education, 355
New England Library Network (NELINET), 234, 312, 320, 352
New York Metropolitan Reference and Research Library Agency, Inc. (METRO), 349
New York State Library, interlibrary loan service, 348

INDEX 491

New York University. Courant Institute of Mathematical Science, 355
Newsletters, role in dissemination of information, 241–242
NFSAIS (*see* National Federation of Science Abstracting and Indexing Services)
Nichols, Owen D., 93
Nickerson, Raymond S., 57, 62
Nieset, Robert T., 179
Nimer, Gilda, 425
Ninke, W. H., 119
NIPS data management system, 220
Nitecki, Joseph Z., 443
NLM (*see* National Library of Medicine)
Noble, A. S., 118, 130
Nodien, John H., 357
Non-Impact Printing Project, 183
Nordyke, P., Jr., 116, 123
North, D. W., 37
North Atlantic Treaty Organization (NATO), 97
North Carolina Computer Orientation Project, 354
Notamarco, Brunella, 161
Novick, David, 427
NSF (*see* National Science Foundation)
Nuclear Safety Information Center, 238
Nuclear science information, 96, 253, 289, 355, 365
Nugent, William R., 47, 234, 310, 312, 320, 330, 352
Nyeky, R., 207
Nyren, J., 424, 429
Nyren, Karl, 445, 446

Oak Ridge National Laboratory, 365
Oakland University, library automation, 318
Ockerman, Lynn, 231
O'Connor, John, 74, 78, 79, 82
O'Dette, Ralph E., 282, 299
OECD (*see* Organization for Economic Cooperation and Development)
Offer, K. D., 244, 246, 248, 254
Office of Naval Research, 75, 93
O'Gara, P. W., 11
Ogg, Jay, 224
Ohio State University, lexicography project, 148
  library automation activities, 317
Olle, T. W., 118, 123, 134
Ollerenshaw, R., 192
Olsen, Wallace, 354

Olson, Edwin E., 67, 436
Olsson, David E., 411
OMNIBUS data base management system, 126, 133
On-line acquisitions system, 324
On-line information systems, 208–212, 351, 352, 356–365
On-line library cataloging, 322
  interface problems, 57–58
On-line transformational grammar testers, 155–157
Operational constraints, system analysis, 45–47
Oppenheimer, G., 132
Optical character recognition, 158, 184
Optical coincidence systems, 91, 93, 207
Oral Research Abstracts, 293
Orange County (California) Public Library, 323
ORBIT on-line retrieval system, 221
Orchard-Hays, W., 129
Oregon State University Library, 324
Organization for Economic Cooperation and Development (OECD), 281, 385, 386, 390, 393–394, 397
Organization policy and structure, effect on information transfer and use, 7–11, 43
  effect on role of libraries and information centers, 412–415, 419
Orne, Jerrold, 443
Orr, Richard H., 43, 431, 436
Ott, R. A., 358
Overhage, Carl F. J., 338–377
Owens, P. J., 141

Packer, A. H., 50
Paisley, William J., 4, 5, 12, 19, 25, 26, 28
Palmer, Foster M., 327
PANDEX, 245, 250, 257, 293
Panek, Robert L., 341
Paperback books, use in county library, 44
Pariser, Bertram, 93
Park, Margaret K., 282
Parker, Edwin B., 19, 20, 23, 310, 315
Parker, Patricia E., 321
Parker, Ralph H., 312, 320, 326, 335
Parkinson Information Center, 291
Pascalev, T. G., 142
PATRICIA text-string retrieval system, 124
Pattern recognition, 158
Patterson, Miles, 11

Paxton, E. A., 250
Payne, Charles T., 322, 324
Pearson, Karl M., Jr., 326
Pearson, Robert R., 354
PEEKABIT search system, 212
Pelz, D. C., 4, 28
Pendergraft, Eugene D., 106
Perez-Vitoria, A., 295, 386
Performing arts, classification scheme, 97
Perreault, Jean M., 87, 90, 91, 106
Perrine, Richard H., 319
Perry, Peter, 91
Personality characteristics, library and information center personnel, 419–420, 425–426
PERT (Program Evaluation and Review Technique), 118, 119
Peters, Alec, 417
Peters, Claude, 364
Peters, Joan, 173
Pflug, Gunther, 316, 318, 323, 325
Philco 212 computer, 254
Philip Morris Research Library, 324
Phonology, 146, 157, 166
Photo Chromic Micro Image system, 259
Photodigital storage devices, 197
Physical sciences, abstracting and indexing services, 275, 280, 285–286
Physical sciences information, compared with social sciences, 14–15
Physics Abstracts, 22, 285
Physics information network, 285
Physics information sources, users and uses, 22–23
Pietransanta, Alfred M., 60
Pietrzyk, Alfred, 170, 219
Pietsch, E., 398
Piette, J., 205, 222
Pings, Vern M., 67, 431, 436
Pinzelik, J., 282
Pizer, Irwin H., 67, 348, 358, 436
PL/1 programming language, 221, 314–315, 324
Planning and forecasting techniques, 34–36, 39
Planning-information systems, 35
Plath, Warren J., 164
Poland. Central Institute for Scientific, Technical and Economic Information, 449
Poliski, I. M., 113

Political factors in system planning, 44–45
Pollock, S. M., 51
Polton, D. J., 86
Polymer science information services, 238, 282
Porter, J. D., 50
Postal, Paul M., 146, 148, 157
Postley, J. A., 123, 134
Powell, H. W., 116
Pratt, Allan D., 106
Preprints, 13, 14
Presthus, Robert V., 411, 424, 428
Pretzer, Dale H., 321
Price, Derek J. De Solla, 340
Price, Nancy, 56, 106
Price, W. L., 172
Problem-solving, information use patterns, 5–8
Production control systems, 116
Professional societies, role in information transfer, 12–15, 242, 254–257, 277–298, 397–398, 456–457
Program budgeting, libraries and information centers, 427–428
Program Evaluation and Review Technique (*see* PERT)
Programming languages, comparison, 158, 327
  for bibliographic processing, 327–328
Project INTREX, 315, 320, 321
Project Medico, 86
Pryor, T. Allan, 360
Psycholinguistics, 151–152
Psychological Abstracts, 18
Psychologists, communications patterns, 18
  publication habits, 15
Public libraries, automation, 322–323
Publishing industry, impact of technology, 36, 260
Purdy, Marie E., 226, 269
Putnam, Arnold O., 41
Pyle, J. L., 119

Quade, E. S., 39
Queen's University (Belfast), library automation, 318, 328
Query formulation, 56
Query languages, 210–212
Queueing analysis, in file design, 128
Question-answering systems, 161–164
QUICKTRAN time-sharing language, 210

INDEX   493

Quillian, M. R., 169
Quirk, W. B., 369
QWICK QUERY data management system, 219

Railroad freight operations networks, 264
Ralston, Anthony, 355
RAND tablet, 166
Random access to files, 128
Ranganathan, S. R., 77, 87
Raphael, Bertram, 163, 170, 211
RAPID data management system, 219
Rapp, F., 226
Rather, Lucia J., 263, 322, 331
Rayward, W. B., 107
Reactive Catalogue query language, 211
Reading Guide to Cancer Virology Literature, 242
Real English retrieval language, 210–211
Real-time information networks, 365–367
Recall and precision studies, 53, 55, 247–249
Record-keeping systems, 117–118
Rees, Alan M., 31, 53, 308, 441, 450, 451
Reference retrieval systems, 316, 351, 352
Reference services, automation studies, 314
Regan, Edward, 70, 210, 211
Regulation of computer and communication services, 368–369
Reilly, Kevin D., 219, 326, 327
Reimers, Paul R., 322
Reinecke, Robert D., 358, 376
Reintjes, J. F., 199
Reitz, Conrad, 47
Reitz, G., 172
Relevance studies, retrieval effectiveness, 52, 53–54, 82–83, 213, 216, 247–249, 256
Remote storage and access devices, microforms, 189–190
Report program generators, 118, 123, 133
Reprography and microform technology, 175–201
Rescher, Nicholas, 34
Research in Education, 347
Reservation systems, 364
Resnick, M., 134
Resnikoff, H. L., 167, 332

Retrieval effectiveness measures, 51–55, 82–83, 310, 314–315
Review of Metal Literature, 283
RFMS file management system, 219
Riccio, Dorothy, 451
Rice University, 351
  library automation, 318
  regional bibliographic service, 351
Richmond, P. A., 257
Richter, A. C., 115, 127
Ridgeway, James, 425
Rieders, Frederic, 357
Riegel, Byron, 397
Rippon, J. S., 422
Ritti, Richard, 28
Roach, R. A., 376
Roberts, A. Hood, 170, 238
Roberts, Justine, 320, 323
Roberts, Laurence G., 353
Robinson, Charles W., 460
Robinson, Jane J., 157
Robinson, Patrick J., 64
Rocchio, J. J., Jr., 126
Rogers, E. M., 16
Rogers, Frank B., 315
Rolling, L., 205, 222
Romerio, G. F., 54
Romney, A., Kimball, 107
Root, R. T., 49
Roper, Fred W., 326
Rosen, D., 114, 359
Rosenbaum, C. P., 113
Rosenbaum, Peter S., 148, 155, 156, 157, 164
Rosenblatt, D., 373
Rosenbloom, Richard S., 408
Rosenburg, Victor, 6
Rosenstein, Richard S., 418
Rosenthal, Joseph A., 319
Rosove, Perry E., 34
Rostron, R. M., 107
Rothenberg, Douglas H., 50
Rothery, Brian, 60
Rothman, H., 85
Rothstein, Samuel, 454
Rouault, J., 100
Rovner, P. D., 119, 123, 125
Rowlett, Russel J., 280
Rubenstein, A. H., 26
Rubenstein, Herbert, 78, 159
Rubin, Jack, 181
Rubin, L., 136
Rubinoff, Morris, 95, 158, 210
Rubinstein, Richard I., 283
Ruby, Homer V., 317

Rudwick, B. H., 50
Ruecking, Frederick H., Jr., 310, 318
Ruffels, W. R., 116, 129
Ruggles, Terry, 173
Rule, Donald F., 282
Runck, Howard, 41
Rush, James E., 77, 282
Russell, Bertrand, 173, 174
Russell, W. S., 139
Russian-English machine translation, 165
Ryan, Mary Jane, 464

Sabezynski, W., 388
Sable, J., 119, 128, 134, 219
Sackman, Harold, 33, 39, 57, 366
Sadacca, Robert, 49
St. Laurent, M. C., 81
Sakai, Itiroo, 146
Salmon, Stephen R., 200
Salton, Gerard, 46, 53, 55, 77, 83, 107, 124, 126, 157, 159, 160, 205, 208, 212, 214, 216, 217, 222, 235, 237, 305, 306
Samuelson, Kjell, 57
Sandia Corp. SDI system, 250
Santiago, Antony, 90
Saporta, Sol, 173
Saracevic, Tefko, 56, 308, 441, 450, 454
Sarett, Lewis H., 240
SATCOM, 235, 260, 276–277
Satellite communications, 396–397
Sato, A., 140
Saunders, W. L., 455
Savage, T. R., 246, 247, 257
Sawyer, Thomas E., 363
Saxton, D. R., 116
SC 4020 COM recorder, 183
Scantleburg, R. A., 376, 377
SCERT computer evaluation tool, 129
Schachter, D., 26
Schank, Roger, 107
Schatz, Sharon, 259
Scheduling by computer, 113, 114, 129
Schick, Frank I., 451
Schieber, William D., 51, 259
Schiminovich, Samuel, 56, 106
Schless, Arthur P., 207, 240, 242
Schlesinger, J. R., 44
Schmidt, C. T., 92
Schmitz, Richard F., 103
Schneider, John H., 96, 248, 249, 252, 314
Schneider, Klaus, 96
Schoene, William J., 156

Schriever, G. A., 49
Schultz, Claire K., 258
Schultz, Louise, 275, 283
Schultz, Morton J., 176
Schumacher, Anne W., 40, 47
Schur, H., 455, 470
Schwarcz, Robert M., 161, 173
Schwartz, E. S., 59
Science Citation Index, 18, 275
Scientific Documentation Centre, 257
Scientists and technologists,
  information-gathering patterns, 5–8, 21, 240
  information needs and uses, 4
Scientists in Organizations, 4
Scott, Jack W., 324, 325
Scott, James T., 368
Scott, Peter R., 197
Scott, W. Richard, 425
SDI systems, 42, 96, 217, 242–258, 286, 314–315
  operating costs and charges, 245
Search accuracy studies, 55–56
Search strategies, 206, 212–216, 252, 253, 255, 256
Searle, R. H., 331
Secondary-key access to files, 123–125
Secondary publications services, 231, 234–235, 273–303
Security of computer files, 46, 132, 361
Sedelow, Sally Y., 166
Sedelow, Walter A., 173
See, Richard, 165
Segal, Stanley J., 421
Selected Water Resources Abstracts, 293
Selective Dissemination of Information (*see* SDI systems)
Selectriever system, 189, 190
Selig, Judith A., 359
Selwyn, Lee W., 369
Semantic analysis, automatic, 158–161
Semantic theory, 147–151
Semple, P., Jr., 135
Senko, Michael, 111–143, 127, 129
Sequential access to files, 120, 123
Serials acquisition and control systems, 325–326
Service Bureau Corp., 226
Shank, Russell, 207, 349
Shannon, Robert L., 259
Share Research Corp., 257
Sharma, R. L., 128
Shaw, A., 158
Shaw, E., 115

Shaw, T. N., 85
Sheldon, R. C., 125, 351
Shell Research Ltd., information system, 205, 250
Shepard, R. B., 137
Shera, Jesse H., 438–471, 441, 455, 456
Sherry, Murray E., 101, 171, 224
Sherwin, Chalmers W., 295
Shilling, Charles W., 451
Shoffner, Ralph M., 51, 119, 129, 219, 259, 312
Shores, Louis, 461, 471
Sibson, R., 86
Siegel, H., 282
Siegel, S. J., 113, 360
Siegmann, J., 26
Silberman, Harry F., 114, 347
Silkiner, M. D., 184
Simmons, P. A., 321
Simmons, Ralph A., 307, 357
Simmons, Robert F., 161, 171
Simmons, Robert H., 330
Simms, Daniel M., 42
Simms, R. L., Jr., 343
Simon, Herbert A., 36
Simon Fraser University, library automation, 316, 318
Simonton, Wesley, 238, 446, 449
Simpson, Gustavus S., Jr., 230, 236, 273, 349
Simulation models, 35, 38, 43, 115, 116, 130, 186
Sinowitz, Norman R., 134, 211
Skolnik, Herman, 413, 426
Slack, W., 114
Slamecka, Vladimir, 452
Slater, Margaret, 22, 28, 29, 285
Slivinski, T. A., 127, 128
Slocum, Grace, 460
SMART system, 55, 157, 159, 160, 212, 214, 215, 216
Smith, Abbott M., 197
Smith, B. N., 174
Smith, Eldred, 424
Smith, Foster D., Jr., 47
Smith, J. R., 61, 263, 285, 298
Smith, L. H., 55
Smith, Steven B., 157, 165, 170
Smith, Walter L., 173
Smith, William A., Jr., 57
Smithsonian Institution, International Exchange Service, 395
Smitzer, L. A., 195
SNOBOL programming language, 327

Social and behavioral studies, information transfer and use, 5–25
Social and cultural effects of system analysis, 33–34, 39
Social effects of automation, 308, 366
Social interaction, spatial determinants, 10–11
Social sciences information, compared with physical sciences, 14–15
Social sciences information systems and services, 238, 293
Society of Library and Information Technicians, 461
Sociologists, publication habits, 15
Soergel, Dagobert, 90
Southern California Association of Governments (SCAG), regional information system, 363
SPAN data management system, 219
Sparck-Jones, Karen, 86, 107, 127, 159
Special Libraries Association, 282, 410, 414, 417, 418, 419, 425, 430
Speech Communications Research Laboratory, 167
Speer, Jack A., 306
Spencer, Carol C., 67, 436
Spierer, M., 362
Spigai, Frances, 324
SPIRES (Stanford Physics Information Retrieval System), 310, 315–316
Staats, Elmer B., 426
Standard Code for Information Exchange, 368
Standard Telecommunications, Ltd., 249
Standardization, 46, 97, 367–368
  bibliographic data elements, 261–262, 275, 295–298, 309–310, 368
Standards for engineering drawings, 191
Standards for libraries, 430
Standards for periodicals titles, 296–297
Stanfel, Larry E., 53, 213
Stanford University, 323
  Institute for Communication Research, 16
Stangl, Peter, 319
Stanley, W. J., 115, 130, 364
Starkweather, John, 108
State and local information systems, 115, 363
State Technical Services Act, 231, 238, 457
State University of New York.
  biomedical network, 357–358
  regional computer center, 354

Technical Information Dissemination Bureau, 245, 251
State University of New York at Albany, 445–446
State University of New York at Buffalo, 321
Statistical aids to vocabulary building, 158–159
Statistical decision theory, 36–38
Statistical measures of retrieval effectiveness, 51–52, 55
Statistical methods of thesaurus construction, 95
Statistical word association, 86, 158–159
Stebbins, Kathleen B., 406
Stefferud, Einar A., 219
Steiner, George A., 411, 426, 427
Stephens, J. A., 119
Stephens, James G., 325
Stevens, G. W., 180
Stevens, S. S., 83
Stevenson, C. L., 325
Stevenson, Chris G., 231, 457
Stevenson, Robert E., 226, 269
Stewart, J., 114, 129
Stimler, S., 365
Stinnett, B. R., 115
Stock quotation networks, 364
Stogniy, A. A., 128, 211
Stokes, Paul M., 430
Stolurow, Lawrence M., 376
Stone, Don Charles, 86, 95, 158
Stone, Elizabeth, 420, 421, 426, 429, 431
Stone, Philip J., 108
Storage organization, 128
Stotz, Robert H., 368
Straight, D. M., 9
Strauss, Lucille, 414
Streufert, Siegfried, 54
Strieby, Irene M., 308, 414, 437
String analysis, 157
Strom, Karen D., 325
Strom, R. E., 172
Studer, William J., 243, 244, 246, 247, 248, 250, 252, 257, 315
Stylistic analysis, 166–167
Subject indexing, libraries, 320, 328
Suga, T., 108
SULIS SDI system, 250
Sullivan, D. J., 209, 351
Sullivan, Todd, 337
Summit, Roger K., 221, 351
Sundeen, Donald H., 133, 218, 219
Suppes, Patrick, 346

Sutherland, William H., 48
Sutton-Smith, C. N., 118, 119
Svenonius, Elaine, 107
Sviridov, F. A., 97
Swanson, Rowena W., 227, 231, 238
Sweden. Stockholm County, hospital information network, 359
Swets, John A., 51
Symbolic logic, in linguistic theory, 150–151
Syntactic analysis, automatic, 155–158, 164
Syntactic theory, 147–151
SYNTOL (Syntagmatic Organization Language), 90
SYNTRAN natural language processing system, 157, 216, 217
Syracuse University, Center for Instructional Communications, 312, 352
System analysis, education applications, 42
  fiscal constraints, 43–45
  libraries, 43–44, 48, 311, 326–327, 405–406, 429
  operational constraints, 45–47
  place and value for society, 33–34
System Development Corp., 167, 219, 221, 236, 237, 241, 276, 277, 307, 311, 349, 362
Systems design and evaluation, 31–70, 205, 243–249, 312–314, 315
Szanser, A. J. M., 165, 172

Tagliacosso, Renata, 85, 316
Tague, Jean Mary, 86
Tamaru, Takuji, 363
Tancredi, Samuel A., 93
Tanis, James R., 308
Task Group for the Interchange of Scientific and Technical Information in Machine Language (ISTIM), 295–297, 368
Tate, Fred A., 265, 275, 282, 299, 302
Taulbee, Orrin E., 108, 435
Taylor, J. G., 115
Taylor, Mary, 324
Taylor, Nettie B., 460
Taylor, Robert S., 57, 314
TDMS (Time-Shared Data Management System), (see also TS/CDMS), 126, 234
Technical libraries, contrasted with information analysis centers, 236–237, 238

Technical progress, planning and forecasting, 34–36
Technical reports, use in educational research, 14
Technology and Libraries, 307–308
Technology in libraries, 328
Teicher, S. N., 199
Teitelbaum, Priscilla, 287
Telebiblios medical information system, 358
TELPORT management information system, 365
Teplitz, Arthur, 186, 188
TERMATREX system, 207
Terminological impediments to content analysis, 74–76
Terrant, Sheldon W., Jr., 265, 282
TEST (*see* Thesaurus of Engineering and Scientific Terms)
Tewlow, Jules S., 36
Texas A and I University, 325
TEX-TEC syllabi, 461
Textile information system, 351
Text-processing, 85–86
Text-processing systems, 216–218, 220
Thayer, G. N., 117
The Double Helix, as a comment on the invisible college, 21–22
Thesauri, construction and use, 92–94, 158–159, 166
Thesaurus of Engineering and Scientific Terms, 75, 93
THOMIS (Total Hospital Operating and Medical Information System), 360
Thompson, D. A., 57, 128
Thompson, Frederick B., 169
Thompson, G. K., 316
Thompson, James W., 324
Thompson, K. C., 116, 127
Thompson, Victor A., 424, 427
Tibbetts, Raymond E., 188
Time lag, secondary publications, 287
Time-shared Data Management System (*see* TDMS)
Time-sharing services, 361, 362, 369
Tinker, John F., 81
Titus, James P., 44
Toan, Arthur B., Jr., 406
Toll, Marvin, 232, 234
Tompkins, Howard E., 297
Tompkins, Mary L., 326
Tondow, M., 114
Townsend, Leroy B., 241
Toxicology information system, 357

Trade off analysis (*see* Cost effectiveness analysis)
Traister, W. A., 118, 123
Transformation techniques, file access, 120–121
Transformational grammars, 147, 155–158
Translator-writing systems, 158
Trew, Siegfried, 213
Triangle Universities Computer Center, 354
Troutman, Joan C., 326
TRW Systems, 221
TS/CDMS data management system, 219, 220
Turnbull, James, 238
Turoff, Murray, 41
Tversky, Amos, 54

Uber, G. T., 119
Ullman, Stephen, 108
Ultrafiche, 186–189
UNESCO, 97, 275, 381, 383, 384, 385, 388–389, 397, 455, 458
UNISIST science information system feasibility study, 275, 295, 297, 350–351
United Kingdom. Atomic Energy Authority, SDI system, 254
United Nations Educational, Scientific, and Cultural Organization (*see* UNESCO)
UNIVAC 494 computer, 365, 367
  1218 computer, 367
  1230 computer, 367
Universal Decimal Classification (UDC), 89, 91, 96, 320, 323
  use in machine search systems, 56, 96–97, 204, 208, 250, 315, 389
University of Alabama Medical Center, 113
University of California. Institute of Library Research, 261, 313, 326
University of California at Los Angeles, 113, 451
  Biomedical Library, 326
University of Chicago, SDI system, 251
University of Chicago Library, automation activities, 313, 322, 324
University of Florida, 346
University of Georgia, 231
  computer network, 355
University of Iowa, regional computer network, 347
University of Lancaster, 313

University of Leicester, 242
University of Maryland, 420, 424
  School of Library and Information Services, 96, 420
University of Michigan Library, 324
University of Minnesota Biomedical Library, 325–326
  ERIC Clearinghouse (see ERIC Clearinghouse for Library and Information Sciences)
University of Missouri Library, automation activities, 313
University of Pennsylvania. Moore School of Electrical Engineering, 210
University of Sheffield. School of Librarianship and Information Science, 455
University of Texas, 219
University of Toronto, 211, 322
University of Washington. Graduate School of Librarianship, 421
Unna, Warren, 396
Urbach, Peter F., 62, 233, 264, 267
Urban planning information systems, 25, 130, 363–364
U. S. Coast Guard Personnel Office, information system, 207
U. S. Congress Joint Committee on the Library, 381, 400
U. S. Geological Survey, information system, 362
U. S. Government Research and Development Reports, 289
U. S. National Libraries Task Force, 234
U. S. Office of Education, 194, 354, 417, 421, 446, 457
U. S. Public Health Service, health communication network, 368
U. S. A. Standards Institute, 46, 193, 261, 275, 296, 297, 309
User Participation Program, Engineering Index Inc., 286–287
User profiling, 250, 252, 253, 257
User studies, 5–29, 44–45, 51, 233, 319–320
User-system interface, 57–58, 358–359, 365
Utility theory, 37
Utterback, J. M., 5, 6

Vallee, Jacques F., 211
Van Brunt, E. E., 136
Van Cura, L. J., 114

Varden, Lloyd E., 192
Vattemare, Alexandre, 381
Vaughan, Frederick R., 278
Veal, D. C., 302
Veaner, Allen B., 175–201, 180, 181, 193
Ver Hulst, T., 186
Verity, John B., 331
Verry, H. R., 180
Veterans Administration, medical information system, 114, 359
Vickery, B. C., 77, 78, 206, 319
Vincent, Dale L., 471
Vision Information Center, 358–359
Vocabulary construction, automatic, 158–159
Von Glasersfeld, Ernst, 161
Voos, Henry, 43
Vorhaus, A. H., 123, 125, 134
Vransky, V. K., 114

Wagner, C. P., 27
Waite, David P., 311
Waite, Stephen V. F., 167
Walker, Donald E., 156
Walker, G. L., 165
Wall, Eugene, 47
Wall, R. A., 312
Walter Reed Army Institute of Research (WRAIR), 283
Walters, J. Hart, Jr., 421
Wares, Alan, 170
Warheit, I. A., 125, 208, 220
Warren, M. E. E., 133
Washington State library network, 352
Washington State University, Center for the Development of Community College Education, 471
Washington State University Library, 324
Washington University, medical library, 320
Wasserman, Paul, 405–438, 410, 421, 422, 423, 438, 443, 462
Water Resources Scientific Information Center, 293
Watkins, W. J., 253, 257
Watt, W. C., 78, 79, 163
Way, William, 86
Weeks, David C., 442, 447
Weighting of search terms, 215–216
Weihrer, Anna Lea, 372
Weil, Cherie B., 314
Weinberg, S. B., 135
Weinberg Report, 235–236, 423

INDEX   499

Weingarten, A., 128
Weinreich, Uriel, 149, 150
Weinstock, Melvin, 268
Weisbrod, David L., 324
Weksel, W., 151, 152
Welch, Noreen O., 58, 219, 221
Wellisch, Jean B., 45
Wente, Van A., 243, 246, 248, 251, 253
Werner, Heinz, 78
Wessel, Andrew E., 108, 217
Wesseling, J. C. G., 91, 106
West, G. P., 60
WESTAR (Westinghouse Telephone Aperture Retrieval), 207
Westat Research, Inc., 49, 52, 55
Whaley, Fred R., 286
Whelan, E. K., 263
Whelan, S., 172
White, C., 116, 129
White, Rodney F., 421
Whitehead, Alfred N., 174
Whitley, Richard, 17
Whitman, D., 69, 142
Whittenburg, John A., 40
Wiederkehr, R. R. V., 62, 264, 267
Wilczynski, Janusz S., 188
Wilde, Daniel U., 213
Wilhelmy, Odin, Jr., 408, 416
Wilkinson, P. T., 376, 377
Wilks, Yorick, 160
Williams, J. H., Jr., 77, 86, 126
Williams, Lawrence K., 423, 425, 428
Williams, P. E., 142
Williams, S. B., 132
Willis, B. H., 115, 130
Wills, Robert D., 362
Wilshire, Bruce, 78
Winer, David E., 372
Wixon, Darvey W., 47, 244, 246, 248, 253
Wofsey, Marvin M., 60
Woinowsk, Orrine, 331
Wolfenden, K., 114, 129
Wolek, Francis W., 408
Wolk, Stuart, 41

Wood, James L., 275, 282, 295, 302
Wood, M. K., 373
Woods, Bill M., 287
Woods, R. G., 318
Woods, W. A., 162, 164
Woolley, Jon H., 224
Wooster, Harold, 43, 195
World Congress of Sociology, 12, 15
World Index of Scientific Translations, 391
World Institute for Documentation of Housing, Building and Planning, 390
World science information projects, historical survey, 384–385
Worldwide Chemical Information System, feasibility, 397
Worldwide Military Command and Control System, 366
Worldwide science information systems, 275, 295, 297, 350–351
Wormann, Curt D., 380
Worth, Jeanne B., 433
Worthy, R. M., 170, 172
Woyna, Adam G., 238
Wuelfing, Ron A., 41
Wyatt, H. W., 241

Yale University, bibliographic system, 324
Yates, D. N., 172
Yngve, Victor H., 166
Young, Gifford A., 243, 246, 248, 251, 253
Young, Stanley, 40

Zabriskie, K. H., Jr., 283
Zatocoding, 212
Zavala, Albert, 27
Zenner, Philip, 201
Zhogolev, E. A., 109
Ziegler, J. R., 133
Ziehe, Theodore W., 133, 219
Zinn, Karl L., 346

Combined Index to Volumes 1–3

Boldface numerals refer to volume numbers.

ABC storage and retrieval system, **2**:107; **3**:81
Abdian, A.G., **1**:310
A. B. Dick Co., **1**:199
Abelson, Philip H., **2**:247, 368; **3**:419
Abraham, C. T., **1**:93, 94
Abraham, Sidney, **3**:427
Abramson, J. H., **2**:317
Abstracting and indexing studies, **1**:309–320; **2**:402, 403; **3**:115, 343–349
Abstracting publications, use of, **1**:79; **2**:22
Abstracting services, **1**:309–320; **2**:112–114, 343
Abstracts of Mycology, **2**:346
Abstracts of the Institute of Paper Chemistry, **2**:349
ABT Associates, Inc., **3**:370
Accessibility of information, **3**:9, 65–66
Accola, F. A., **1**:301
Acerenza, Ermelinda, **1**:31
Acheson, E. D., **3**:406
Ackerman, H. J., **2**:141
Ackerman, William B., **3**:232
ACM (*see* Association for Computing Machinery)
Acme Visible Records, Inc., **1**:204
Acoustic couplers, **2**:194
Acoustically-coupled teletypes, **2**:233
Acquisitions systems, automated, **1**:282; **2**:264; **3**:250–253
ACS (*see* American Chemical Society)
ACSI-MATIC Project, **2**:134
Acton, Forman S., **3**:369
ADAM (Advanced Data Management), **1**:124, **2**:142, 143, 240; **3**:155–156
Adams (Charles W.) Associates, Inc., **2**:198, 212
Adams, E. N., **2**:237; **3**:358
Adams, Scott, **1**:182, 296; **2**:262, 344
Adams, William Mansfield, **1**:45, 47; **3**:91, 122
Adaptive teaching systems, **3**:386

ADEPT time-sharing supervisor, **3**:206, 218–219, 381
Adey, W. R., **3**:427
ADI (*see* American Society for Information Science)
Adkinson, Burton W., **1**:310; **3**:170, 244
Administrative planning, computer-assisted, **3**:369–370
ADMINS data base program, **2**:240, 241; **3**:219
Advanced Data Management (*see* ADAM)
Advanced Research Projects Agency (ARPA), **2**:161; **3**:300, 308, 316
Advances in Biomedical Computer Applications, **2**:315
AEC (*see* Atomic Energy Commission)
AED free storage package, **3**:148–149
Aerospace Materials Information Center, **2**:96, 98; **3**:274
AESOP (An Evolutionary System for Online Processing), **2**:52, 137; **3**:156, 218
Afflerbach, Lois, **1**:84
AFIPS (*see* American Federation of Information Processing Societies)
Agarwal, R. K, **1**:201
Agricultural scientists, information sources, **2**:19
AIAA (*see* American Institute of Aeronautics and Astronautics)
AID (Automatic Information Distribution), **3**:277
AIDS (Aero-Space Intelligence Data System), **1**:124
AIDS (Automated Information Dissemination System), **3**:278
AIMS (Auerbach Information Management System) **1**:125–126
AIP (*see* American Institute of Physics)
Air Force Aero Propulsion Laboratory, **3**:64, 270
Air Force Decision Sciences Laboratory, **3**:215

COMBINED INDEX 501

Air Force Flight Dynamics Laboratory, 2:47
Air Force Foreign Technology Division, 1:138
Air Force Materials Laboratory, 2:49
Air Force Office of Scientific Research, Information Science Directorate, 2:36
Air Force Systems Command, 1:127; 2:137
Aitchison, T. M., 3:129
Akron Children's Hospital, 1:257
ALA Bulletin, 3:243
Albritton, Errett C., 2:368
Album, H. H., 1:347
Alden Electronic and Impulse Recording Co., 2:200; 3:53
Alexander, David, 3:425
Alexander, Robert W., 3:319
Alexander, Samuel N., 3:298
Alger, I., 3:415
ALGOL programming language, 3:152, 380
Algorithms for natural language processing, 2:172–174
Allderige, J. M., 2:52
Allen, Dwight W., 3:320, 342, 357, 368, 369
Allen, Layman, 1:262, 323
Allen, Scott I., 1:266; 2:108; 3:409
Allen, Thomas J., 1:59, 61, 64; 2:25, 26; 3:9, 10, 11, 13, 14, 25, 65
Allen-Babcock Computing, Inc., 2:209–212
Almendinger, Vladimir V., 2:148
Alouche, F., 3:192
ALPAC report, 2:178; 3:180, 190
Alpert, Daniel, 3:232
ALPHA system, 3:250, 269–270
Alphanumeric compression (*see* Code-compression systems)
Alphanumeric input/output consoles, 2:195
Altman, Berthold, 1:173, 175, 182; 2:107; 3:73, 81
Ambiguous sentence processing, 2:171
American Anthropologist, 1:146
American Association for Public Opinion Research, 3:16
American Association of Law Libraries, 2:260
American Association of School Administrators, 3:368
American Chemical Society (ACS), 2:342, 349; 3:43, 52
American Chemical Society, Chemical Abstracts Service (*see* Chemical Abstracts Service)
American Chemical Society, *Handbook for Authors*, 3:38
American College of Surgeons, 2:312
American Documentation, 3:122
American Documentation Institute (*see* American Society for Information Science)
American Federation of Information Processing Societies (AFIPS), 1:139
American Institute of Aeronautics and Astronautics (AIAA), 3:283
American Institute of Physics (AIP), 1:50, 67, 82, 83, 349; 2:100, 110, 342, 350; 3:274
American Institutes for Research, 3:364
American Library Association (ALA), 2:260, 276; 3:241, 246
 Information Sciences and Automation Division, 2:256, 260; 3:241, 243
 Library Research Clearinghouse, 2:256
 Library Technology Program, 1:291; 3:242
American Library Directory, 1:305, 306
American Management Association, 3:220, 383
American Mathematical Society, 1:315; 2:350; 3:43
American Petroleum Institute (API), 1:93; 3:271
American Psychological Association (APA), 1:4, 8, 41, 44, 49, 53, 54, 55, 60, 65, 66, 67; 2:15; 3:5, 17–18
American Society for Information Science (*formerly* American Documentation Institute), 1:1–9, 18, 20, 26; 2:31, 45, 65, 360; 3:242
 Special Interest Group on Library Automation, 2:256, 260
American Society for Metals (ASM), 1:315, 316; 2:72, 128, 348; 3:26
American Society for Testing and Materials, CODEN list (*see* *CODEN for Periodical Titles*)
American Standard Code for Information Interchange (ASCII), 1:213; 3:143, 246
American Stock Exchange, 2:193
American University, 1:197
Amico, Anthony F., 3:162
Amminger, Ottilie, 2:112
Ampex Corp., 1:201, 202
Ampex Videofile system, 1:204; 2:203
Amreich, M., 3:274

AN/FSQ-32 computer (see Q-32 computer)
Analog signals, computerized analysis, 2:324; 3:400, 413–415
Anastasio, Ernest, 3:367
Anchev, N., 3:420
Anderson, Alan A., 2:65, 77
Anderson, B. R., 3:233
Anderson, F., 2:13; 3:422
Anderson, M. D., 2:109
Anderson, Margaret R., 2:111, 366
Anderson, Ronald R., 3:86, 159, 162, 189, 192, 273
Anderson, Ruth, 2:51, 140
Andiron, M. P., Jr., 1:68
Andrews, Frank M., 3:2, 10, 11, 14
Andrews, M. C., 1:212
Anelex 80 disc storage, 2:206
Angell, Richard S., 1:84, 91; 3:129
Anglo-American cataloging rules, 3:251
Annual Review of Psychology, 1:4, 8
Annual Reviews, Inc., 1:8
ANPAK code-compression system, 3:144–145
Antarctic Bibliography, 1:317
APA (see American Psychological Association)
Aperture card systems, 1:204
Aperture cards, use in DARE retrieval system, 3:268
API (see American Petroleum Institute)
APL programming language, 2:126; 3:223, 381
Applied Mechanics Reviews, 1:315; 2:348
ARCS (see Automated Ring Code System)
Ardman, Harvey, 3:267, 279, 283
ARDS display console, 3:211
Argonne National Laboratory, 3:245–246
Armenti, A. W., 1:123
Armitage, J. D., 1:195
Armitage, Janet E., 3:51, 121, 146, 148
Armitage, Peter, 3:370
Armstrong, Frances T., 3:103, 167
Armstrong, J. A., 1:207
Army Biological Laboratory, 1:295
Army Chemical Information and Data Systems Organization, 2:140, 287; 3:159
Army Engineers Research and Development Laboratories, 3:271
Army Materiel Command, 2:200
Army Missile Command, 2:202
Army Natick Laboratories, 3:89, 278, 280
Army Research Office (ARO), 2:140
Army technical libraries, SDI system, 2:112

Arnold, Richard F., 2:38
Arora, B. M., 3:211
ARPA (see Advanced Research Projects Agency)
Artandi, Susan, 1:83, 89, 91, 173, 183; 2:91; 3:129
Arthur D. Little, Inc., 1:246; 3:250, 307
Artificial intelligence, 2:37, 129
Asbury, W. C., 1:332
ASCA (Automatic Subject Citation Alert), 3:279
Asheim, Lester E., 3:341
Asher, J. W., 1:255
Ashworth, Wilfred, 3:129
Asian countries, education for information science, 1:29–30
ASLIB (Association of Special Libraries and Information Bureaus), 2:31
Aslib-Cranfield project, 1:81, 172, 182; 2:54, 64, 65–70, 87, 89, 90, 92, 97, 99, 101; 3:191
ASM (see American Society for Metals)
ASP (Association String Processor), 2:139
Association for Computing Machinery (ACM), 1:20, 139, 161; 2:198; 3:138
Association for Educational Data Processing, 3:299
Association of Research Libraries (ARL), 2:261, 272
Association of Special Libraries and Information Bureaus (see ASLIB)
Association-Storing Processor, 2:103
Associative memories, 1:114–116, 207–208, 210, 211; 2:129, 131
Associative Parallel Processor (APP), 1:211
Associative techniques, document retrieval, 2:70–71; 3:75, 86, 127–128, 140–141, 151–152, 188–189, 273
Atherton, Pauline, 1:50, 51, 67, 72, 82, 83, 90, 91, 175, 182, 183; 2:110, 340, 342, 343; 3:67, 124, 141, 274, 329–355
Atkinson, Richard C., 3:358, 374
ATLIS Workshop on Automation in Libraries, 3:250
Atomic Energy Commission (AEC), 1:294, 311, 342; 2:205
  Division of Technical Information, 2:273, 343; 3:248, 269
Atomic Weapons Research Establishment (AWRE), 3:279
Atwood, Ruth, 3:418
Audio input/output, 1:197; 2:193, 194, 233; 3:379
Audio Magnetic Data Transceiver, 2:194

COMBINED INDEX   503

Audiovisual Instruction, **3**:304
Auerbach Corp., **1**:44, 63, 116, 126, 128; **2**:27, 130, 193, 198, 340, 390; **3**:3, 13, 208
Augustin, Donald C., **3**:239
Ausman, Robert K., **3**:408, 420
Austin, Charles J., **1**:119, 316; **2**:355; **3**:309
Author abstracting and indexing, **1**:83–84, 175; **3**:51, 67, 106
Author languages, in computer-assisted instruction, **3**:379–382
Authors League of America, Inc., **2**:412
AUTODIN (Automatic Digital Network), **3**:317
AUTODOC document production program, **3**:208
Automated diagnostic screening, **3**:411–413
Automated Information Dissemination System (*see* AIDS project)
Automated language processing, **1**:137–169; **2**:161–186, **3**:169–199
Automated Literature Processing Handling and Analysis (*see* ALPHA system)
Automated medical history system, **3**:407, 410
Automated Ring Code System (ARCS), **3**:268
Automatic abstracting, **1**:162; **2**:89; **3**:51, 117–118, 170
Automatic classification, **1**:175, 182; **2**:103–112, 141
Automatic indexing, **1**:86–88, 175–182; **2**:103–112; **3**:51–52, 109, 119–121, 170
Automatic Language Processing Advisory Committee Report (*see* ALPAC Report)
Automatic Media Systems, Inc., **1**:198
Automatic Subject Citation Alert (*see* ASCA system)
Automatic text analysis and classification, **2**:88; **3**:189
Automatic text processing systems, **3**:169–199
Automation activities in large bibliographic centers, **2**:261–264
Automation and the Library of Congress, **2**:274
Automation in pathology, **2**:324
Automation of library technical processes, **1**:278–279, 280, 282–288; **3**:241–262
Autopsy information, **3**:404
AUTOVON (Automatic Voice Network), **3**:314
Avery, K., **2**:187

Avram, Henriette D., **2**:268, 269; **3**:248
Ayers, F. H., **3**:129
Azaroff, Leonid V., **2**:369

Babbott, David, **3**:416
Babcock, James D., **3**:229
Bachman, Charles W., **2**:126, 127
Bachrach, J. A., **3**:182, 192
Backer, Paul O., **2**:176
Backer, Stanley, **1**:265
Bailey, Catherine A., **1**:44; **2**:340
Baker, C. L., **2**:225
Baker, Charles E., **3**:212
Baker, Dale B., **2**:339; **3**:326
Baker, F. T., **2**:130, 131
Baker, J. D., **1**:239
Baker, Norman R., **3**:64
Baker, W. O., **1**:341
Ball, N. A., **2**:196
Ballou, Hubbard, **2**:202
Balson, M., **3**:420
Baltimore County (Md.) Public Library, **2**:258; **3**:254–255
Balz, Charles F., **1**:86; **2**:107, 277
Bancroft, W. N., **3**:233
Banking and credit information systems, **3**:315
Banks, D. G., **2**:92
Banzhaf, John, III, **2**:141
Baran, Paul, **3**:229
Barber, Bernard, **1**:16
Barden, W. A., **1**:276
Bare, Carole E., **2**:340
Bar-Hillel, Y., **1**:2, 137, 145, 154, 159; **3**:129
Barhydt, Gordon C., **1**:173, 264; **2**:79
Barlow, A. E., **1**:125, 271
Barlow, John S., **3**:420
Barnard, F. T., **2**:141
Barnes, R. C. M., **2**:340
Barnes, Robert F., Jr., **2**:37, 90
Barnett, C. C., Jr., **3**:233
Barnett, G. O., **1**:130, 257, 258; **2**:147, 243; **3**:409
Barnett, J. W., **3**:421
Barnett, Michael P., **1**:197, 198, 266; **2**:278, 349
Barnhard, Howard J., **3**:133, 165
Barnum, Alan R., **2**:142
Barraclough, Elizabeth, D., **2**:330
Barrett, Raymond P., **1**:72, 244
Barron, D. W., **3**:149
Bartlett, J. M., **2**:173
Barton, H. A., **2**:341
Bartram, Philip R., **2**:137; **3**:154, 240
Baruch, J. J., **1**:255–271, 257

BASEBALL, 3:225
BASIC (Beginners' All Purpose Symbolic Instruction Code), 3:362
BASIC (Biological Abstracts Subjects in Context), 1:313
Basic Indexing and Retrieval System (*see* BIRS)
BATCH number organic compound code, 2:141
Batchlor, Charles D., 3:420
Bates, Frank, 3:259
Battelle Memorial Institute, 1:17, 308, 310
Batts, Nathalie C., 2:267
Batty, C. D., 2:102; 3:344, 349
Bauer, Charles K., 2:256
Bauer, Gerd, 3:129
Baum, C., 3:233
Bauman, Milton, 2:352
Baumanis, George J., 3:84, 189
Baust, Roger T., 2:214
Baxendale, Phyllis B., 1:9, 71–106, 86, 129; 2:88, 104; 3:110, 185, 186, 188, 192, 195
Bayes' theorem, 2:320
Baylor University, 1:257
Bayroff, A. G., 3:366
Beatty, J., 1:118
Beaver, Donald D., 2:367, 3:15
Bechtold, Henry P., 3:319
Becker, Joseph, 1:112, 296; 2:42, 276; 3:289–327, 306, 310, 311
Beckett, Peter G. S., 3:408
Beckman, Margaret, 2:273
Bednarek, A. R., 3:76
Behavioral studies, information transfer and use, 1:41–68; 3:1–31, 79
Belfour, A. J., 1:326, 327, 329
Bell Telephone Laboratories, 1:196, 197, 200, 229; 3:34, 268, 280
Beller, R. J., 3:163, 193, 208
Bellville, J. Weldon, 3:406
Belth, Marc, 1:26
Bely, N., 3:192
Belzer, Jack, 2:434; 3:76, 96, 297, 423
Bemer, R. W., 3:144
Benjamin, Curtis G., 1:348; 2:410
Benner, Frank H., 3:145
Bennett, Edward M., 2:52; 3:156, 199, 239
Bennett, Ian C., 3:425
Bennett, James H., 3:359
Bennett, John L., 1:102; 3:110, 188, 195
Bennett, Lowry M., 3:319
Bennett, Walter L., 3:420
Bennigson, Lawrence, 3:135, 166
Benschoter, Reba Ann, 3:420
Benson, R. A., 1:289, 290

Benson-Lehner Co., 1:196, 199; 2:192
Berezner, Susan C., 3:193
Bergen, Daniel Patrick, 2:344
Bergman, Samuel, 3:100, 197, 287
Bering, Edgar A., Jr., 1:329; 3:420
Berkeley, Edmund C., 2:215, 234; 3:233
Berkner, Dimity S., 3:342
Berlyne, Daniel E., 2:165
Berman, M. L., 3:193, 213
Bernard, Jessie, 1:56, 58, 61, 67, 175; 3:13
Bernays, Peter M., 1:314
Bernberg, R. E., 1:238
Bernick, M. D., 1:184
Bernier, Charles L., 1:83; 3:129
Bernshtein, E. S., 2:64
Bernstein, Alex, 1:105
Bernstein, L., 2:126
Berson, Alan S., 3:420
Berul, Lawrence, 2:390
Berztiss, A. T., 1:114
BEST data management system, 1:125
Beum, C. O., Jr., 3:95
Bever, T. G., 1:162
B. F. Goodrich Co., 3:248, 277–278
Bhimani, B. V., 2:234
Bibliographic access to published information, 2:344, 345
Bibliographic data analysis, 2:274–275
Bibliographic data centers, 2:359
Bibliographic search systems (*see* Reference retrieval systems)
Bibliography of Agriculture, 2:20, 349
Bichel, R. L., 1:117
Bickert, C. E., 3:94
Bigelow, Julian, 1:75, 76
Biggs, Homer G., 3:400
Biggs, J. M., 1:230
Binder, Sidney, 3:406
Binford, R. L., 1:85, 175, 182
Bingham, H. W., 1:227
Biological Abstracts, 1:312–313, 349; 2:20, 345
Biological scientists, information needs and uses, 1:50, 56–58, 61, 67; 3:19
Biomedical scientists, literature use study, 2:10
BioResearch Titles, 1:313; 2:346
BioSciences Information Service (BIOSIS), 1:312–313, 349; 2:345
BIOSIS (*see* BioSciences Information Service)
Bird, Jack, 3:340, 349
Bird, R. M., 1:195, 211; 2:130
BIRS (Basic Indexing and Retrieval System), 3:157–158
Bisco, Ralph L., 3:313, 319

COMBINED INDEX 505

Bitzer, Donald L., **2**:198, 237; **3**:211, 233, 319, 382
Bitzer, Maryann, **3**:379, 387
Bivona, William A., **2**:112; **3**:89
Black, Donald V., **1**:8, 273–303; **2**:258
Black, F. S., **1**:156
Black, G., **3**:316
Blackwell, Frederick W., **3**:152
Blagden, J. F., **2**:90, 98; **3**:82, 129
Blanchard, J. Richard, **2**:397
Blandy, Richard, **3**:353
Blankenship, Donald A., **2**:106
Bleier, Robert E., **3**:153, 233
Bliss, H. E., **2**:102
Bliss, Warren H., **3**:52
Blizard, E. P., **2**:343
Bloomfield, Masse, **1**:84, 85; **2**:89, 96, 108, 439
Bloomquist, C. E., **2**:47
Blose, W. F., **1**:271
Blum, Joseph, **3**:233
Blunt, Charles R., **2**:55, 57, 64; **3**:68
Bobka, Marilyn E., **3**:142
Bobrow, Daniel G., **1**:76, 150; **2**:88, 129, 136, 161–186, 173, 175, 176, 177, 236; **3**:49, 129, 134, 149, 169, 177, 192, 196, 209, 224, 225, 233
Boehm, Barry W., **3**:92
Boggs, S. T., **1**:323
Bohnert, Herbert G., **2**:126
BOLD (Bibliographic On-Line Display), **1**:290; **2**:52, 134, 197, 239; **3**:208
Bolinger, Dwight, **2**:165
Bolles, S. W., **1**:335
Bolotsky, G. R., **1**:267
Bolt, Richard A., **2**:108, 134, 243
Bolt, Beranek and Newman, Inc. (BBN), **1**:125, 248, 265; **2**:161, 173, 199, 212; **3**:215
Boman, Mogens, **3**:279
Bonn, George, **1**:18; **2**:407
Bonner, Raymond E., **3**:425
Bonnett, H. T., **2**:286, 291
Bonneville Power Administration, **3**:90, 277, 280
Book acquisition systems, automated, **3**:250–253
Book catalogs, computer-produced, **1**:276, 278, 283–286; **2**:258; **3**:253–256, 265, 283
Book indexing, **1**:83; **2**:109
Book retrieval from library stacks, **2**:275
Booth, J. B., **1**:213
Booz-Allen Applied Research, Inc., **2**:53, 258, 277; **3**:306
Boozer, Robert F., **3**:364

Bordaz, Victoria, **3**:428
Borillo, A., **3**:192
Borko, Harold, **1**:15, 51, 90, 91, 138, 150, 173, 175, 182, 290; **2**:35–61, 42, 52, 106, 134, 239, 434; **3**:62, 120, 129, 170, 190, 192, 349
Borkowski, Casimir, **2**:106; **3**:116, 188
Borov, Ivan, **3**:420
Bose, Anindya, **3**:423
Bottle, R. T., **2**:436; **3**:340
Bouman, H., **1**:117
Bourne, Charles P., **1**:9, 80, 117, 171–190, 173; **2**:27; **3**:62, 144, 353
Bowden, Drummond H., **3**:420
Bowers, D. M., **2**:134
Bowles, Edmund A., **3**:170
Bowman, Carlos M., **2**:293, 294, 300, 367; **3**:142
Boyer, Ernest Leroy, **2**:408
Bozman, William R., **2**:356
Bracken, Marilyn C., **2**:432, 435; **3**:339, 343, 348
Brackett, John W., **3**:209
Braddock, J. V., **3**:268
Bradstreet, S. W., **1**:326, 329
Brady, Edward L., **2**:361
Brady, R. T., **3**:233
Braille print-outs, **1**:255
Braine, M. D. S., **1**:146
Brandeis, E. P., **1**:202
Brandhorst, W. T., **1**:311; **2**:99, 128; **3**:130, 150
Brandon, G. L., **3**:358, 371, 373, 374, 375, 376
Branscomb, Lewis C., **3**:320
Brasenose Conference on the Automation of Libraries, **2**:258, 261, 264, 269; **3**:309
Bratten, J. E., **3**:391
Bregzis, Ritvars, **1**:284; **3**:246, 309
Brenner, Everett H., **1**:73, 81, 92; **2**:90, 95
Brewer, Jocelyn, **1**:99, 152, 162
Briggs, G. E., **1**:243, 271
Brigham Young University, **1**:326
Bright, Frank F., **3**:260
Brillouin, L., **3**:332
Brinberg, Louis, **3**:420
British Museum Library, **2**:258, 261, 268
British National Bibliography, **2**:263
British National Health Service, **3**:424
Broadbent, Derek, **3**:421
Broadbent, James C., **3**:421
BRO-DART, Inc., **3**:254
Brodman, Estelle, **1**:302
Brodman, Keeve, **2**:318; **3**:411
Bromberg, Erik, **1**:30; **3**:90, 277, 281, 341

Brotherton, Dale E., 2:130
Brown, Betty Martin, 3:354
Brown, Bobby, 3:379
Brown, George H., 3:301
Brown, George W., 3:66, 226, 297, 387
Brown, James Duff, 2:101
Brown, Norman, 3:257
Brown, Patricia L., 3:263–288
Brown, Roger, 1:146, 276; 2:172
Brown, Sanborn, 3:233
Brown, W. S., 3:33, 34, 280
Brown, William F., 3:151
Browne, T. C., 3:163, 193, 208
Browne, T. D., 3:94
Brownson, Helen L., 1:183; 2:64
Brownstein, Cy, 3:283
Broxis, P. F., 2:101
Bruce, Robert A., 2:320, 323
Brunenkant, E. J., 1:311
Brunner, R. Gordon, 3:67
Bry, Ilse, 1:84
Bryan, G. E., 2:225; 3:205
Bryan, Glenn L., 3:362
Bryan, Harrison, 2:256
Bryant, Edward C., 2:64; 3:64, 66, 92, 128, 141
Bryant, J. H., 1:261; 2:143, 239
Bryon, John, 2:109
Buck, E. R., 3:275
Buckland, Lawrence F., 1:192, 199, 288; 2:348, 351, 357
Buetell, T. D., 1:124
Buhl, Norma A., 3:250, 257
Bunderson, C. V., 3:359, 362, 371, 373
Bundy, Mary Lee, 2:278, 440; 3:341, 342, 346, 355
Bunker-Ramo Corp., 1:151, 196, 318
Bunker-Ramo 340 computer, 3:152
Burch, George E., 3:404
Burchinal, Lee G., 2:405; 3:21, 324, 336, 388
Bureau of Labor Statistics data bank, 3:314
Bureau of Reclamation, 3:278
Bureau of Ships, 1:83, 278–279
Bureau of the Budget, 1:345
Burger, J. B., 1:120, 135; 2:299
Burger, John F., 3:111, 176, 183, 209, 233
Burgis, D. R., 1:101
Burkholder, David F., 3:402
Burnaugh, Howard P., 1:290; 2:52, 134, 239; 3:190, 208
Burroughs B8500 computer, 1:208; 2:210
Burroughs Corp., 1:208; 2:212
Buscher, William, 1:187
Bush, George P., 2:353

Bush, Vannevar, 1:16; 2:187, 197
Busha, Charles H., 3:320
Bushnell, Don D., 1:243; 3:342, 357, 368, 371, 388
Buswell, D. L., 1:124
Buxbaum, R. C., 2:318

C-10 Data Management System, 3:156–157
Caceres, Cesar A., 1:258; 3:413, 423
CADET programming language, 1:230
CADRE (Current Awareness and Document Retrieval for Engineers), 1:316
Caffrey, John, 1:264; 3:368, 371
Cahill, Charles A., 3:421
Cahn, R. S., 2:295
CAI (*see* Computer-assisted instruction)
Caie, Harriet B., 3:421
Cain, Alexander M., 2:268; 3:320, 418
CAL programming language (University of California), 3:223, 381
Calatayud, Juan B., 3:413, 427
CALCULAID algebraic computation system, 1:234
Calder, G., 3:421
Caldwell, Linda, 3:320
Caless, T. W., 3:124, 141, 274
California Automated Management Information System (AMIS), 3:314
California Computer Products, 2:192
California Educational Information System, 3:368
California State Library, 2:270; 3:307
Calingaert, Peter, 3:93, 234
Call number display system, 2:276
Callahan, John A., 3:421
Callahan, Michael D., 3:208
Cambridge Language Research Unit, 1:141, 142–144, 151; 2:165, 167, 168; 3:147
Cambridge University Library, 2:261
Cambridge University Mathematical Laboratory, 3:149
Cammack, Floyd, 2:106, 3:256
Cammarn, Maxine R., 3:397–428, 425
Campbell, C. M., 1:257
Campbell, H. C., 2:265
CAMPUS simulation model for educational planning, 3:370
Canada, Food and Drug Directorate, 1:259
Canada, National Research Council Library, 1:277
Canada, Province of Ontario, libraries, 2:265
Canadian Industries, Ltd., 2:294, 299; 3:142

Canning, Richard G., 2:52
Cantley, Gordon, 3:27
Capell, L. T., 2:289
Caras, Gus J., 3:120
Card catalogs, 2:18, 29, 268
Carey, W. N., Jr., 1:323
Carlson, Arthur R., 3:130
Carlson, C. O., 1:205
Carlson, Walter, 1:310, 327, 329
Carnegie Commission on Educational Television, 3:301
Carnegie Institute of Technology (*see* Carnegie-Mellon University)
Carnegie-Mellon University, 1:196; 2:233
 time-sharing system, 3:207
Carnegie Review, 3:232
Carney, Gerard J., 2:109
Carney, Homer C., 3:193
Carr, J. W., III, 3:153
Carr, William F., 3:426·
Carrington, David K., 2:265
Carroll, John M., 3:343
Carroll, Robert F., 3:194, 286
Carson, R. W., 1:207, 323
Carson Laboratories, 3:53
Carstensen, F. V., 1:150
Carter, Brice, Jr., 2:128
Carter, Launor F., 1:341; 2:364, 386, 392; 3:21, 24, 193
Cartwright, Kelley L., 2:270
CAS (*see* Chemical Abstracts Service)
Case Institute of Technology (*see* Case Western Reserve University)
Case Western Reserve University, 1:16, 17, 20, 22, 183; 2:37, 71, 77, 78
 Center for Documentation and Communication Research, 3:77–79, 90, 142–143
CASSIS (Communications and Social Science Information Service), 3:311
Castleman, Paul, 2:324; 3:409
Catalog cards, automated production system, 2:267, 270; 3:247
Catalog cards, conversion to machine-readable records, 1:286–289
Cataloging backlog reduction, 2:267
Catassi, C. A., 3:402
Cathode-ray tube (*see* CRT)
CATO programming language, 3:380
Cattley, J. M., 1:72, 80; 2:92
Cautin, Harvey, 3:87, 100, 151, 193, 287
Cavanaugh, Joseph M., 3:66
Cayless, C. F., 3:129
CBS Laboratories, 3:302
CDC (*see also* Control Data Corp.)
 449 portable computer, 2:214

915 variable-format page reader, 1:193
1604-A computer, 2:196
1640 computer, 2:199
3300 computer, 2:263
3600 computer, 2:147; 3:158, 279
8090 computer, 2:267
Cease, D. R., 1:125, 271
Cederlund, C. 3:421
Center for Applied Linguistics, 3:220
Center for Research in Scientific Communication, Johns Hopkins University, 3:17, 65
Centre d'Etudes pour la Traduction Automatique, 3:220
Cestac, Françoise, 1:29
CFSS (Combined File Search System), 3:157, 278
CFSTI (*see* Clearinghouse for Federal Scientific and Technical Information)
Chafe, H. David, 2:72, 348; 3:26
Chalouka, B., 1:194
Chamis, Alice Yanosko, 3:194, 286
Chapanis, Alphonse, 2:40
Chapin, P. G., 2:165; 3:163, 183, 208
Chapin, W. E., 1:322
Char, Beverly F., 3:155
Character coding, 2:214, 3:143
Charp, Sylvia, 3:341, 342, 358, 368, 371
Chatman, S., 1:160
Chatterson, Lynne A., 3:369
Check, Thomas B., 2:198, 231; 3:211, 213
Chemical Abstracts, 1:314; 2:17, 22, 105, 111–113, 285, 287, 291, 298, 339; 3:122, 146
Chemical Abstracts Service (CAS), 1:264, 309, 313, 348; 2:111, 140, 285, 293–295, 299, 330, 342, 346, 403; 3:44, 47, 56, 142, 159, 212, 220
Chemical and Engineering News, 1:47
Chemical-Biological Activities (CBAC), 1:314
Chemical-Biological Coordination Center (CBCC), 3:159
Chemical information systems, 1:120–121, 263–264, 314; 2:51, 139–141, 285–309, 403; 3:142–143, 158–159, 220
Chemical nomenclature, 2:288–290
Chemical Titles, 1:314; 3:279
Chemisches Zentralblatt, 2:291
Chemists, information needs, 2:16–17, 22
Cherniavskii, V. S., 2:64
Chernyi, A. I., 3:332
Cheshier, Robert, 3:418
Chesky, Kenneth, 3:425
Chess-playing computer program, 3:201

508 COMBINED INDEX

Cheydleur, Benjamin F., 1:27, 114; 3:93
Chien, R. T., 3:128, 130, 147, 166
Childers, Thomas, 3:254
Chinese Ideographic Composer, 1:200
Chinese language, semiautomatic text input system, 3:181
Chipman, Mary L., 3:417
Chomsky, C., 3:235
Chomsky, Noam, 1:139, 140, 142, 153; 2:162, 170
Chow, C. K., 1:195
Chu, J. T., 1:195
Churchill, N. C., 2:37
CIDS (*see* Army Chemical Information and Data Systems Organization)
CIRC (Central Information Reference and Control), 1:117, 244, 3:81
Circulation and stack management automation, 1:291–294; 2:275; 3:256–258
Citation graphing, 3:147
Citation indexing, 1:51–52, 84–85; 2:110; 3:10, 36, 121–123, 279
Citations, use in grouping of records, 3:147
City University of New York, 1:320
Clague, P., 3:129
Clampett, H. A., Jr., 1:119
Clancey, John J., 3:239
Clapp, Verner W., 2:274
Clark, W. A., 3:234
Clarke, D. C., 1:83, 147, 149, 297; 3:186, 192
Clarke, Victoria C., 3:40
CLASS instructional system, 3:372
Classification, 2:99–103, 106–107
Classification systems, in machine searching, 3:67, 124, 141–143, 157, 274
  in SDI user profiling, 3:280
  in thesauri-building, 2:95–96; 3:182
  maintenance and revision, 3:124–125
Classification theory, 1:88–95, 142–143; 3:85, 126
Claus, C. J., 1:206
Clearinghouse for Federal Scientific and Technical Information (CFSTI), 1:309, 317, 343–344; 2:13, 201; 3:22, 65, 68, 70, 90
Cleveland Medical Library, 1:50
Cleverdon, Cyril, 1:81, 91, 172, 173, 182, 183; 2:67, 68, 70, 87, 89, 90, 92, 97, 99, 101; 3:193
Cliffe, Percy, 3:421
Climax Molybdenum Co., optical coincidence system, 3:95
Climenson, W. Douglas, 1:9, 109–135; 2:123; 3:157, 158

Clinical laboratory data processing, 2:322–323; 3:400–402
Clippinger, R. F., 1:211
CLUE extracting technique, 2:17
Clumping of semantic categories, 3:147, 189, 273
Clustering techniques, 1:143; 2:168; 3:126, 147, 189, 273
CMI (*see* computer-managed instruction)
Coates, E. J., 2:91
Coblans, Herbert, 2:276, 344
COBOL programming language, 2:126, 145; 3:380
Cocroft, Robert, 2:113
Coddington, D. C., 3:94
Code for identification of recorded knowledge, 3:124
Code-compression systems, 3:143–145
CODEN for Periodical Titles, 2:273, 342; 3:252–253
Coding systems, 1:117–118; 2:50; 3:141–146
  chemical compounds, 2:290–293; 3:142–143, 147–148, 158–159
  linguistic data, 2:268; 3:116
  medical data, 3:401, 410
Coe, Kenneth L., 1:266
Cognitronic "speechmaker," 2:193
COGO programming language, 1:231
Cogswell, J. F., 1:269; 3:93, 99, 367
Cohan, Leonard, 1:18; 2:422, 435
Cohen, G., 1:302
Cohen, Jacques, 3:149
Cohen, S. M., 1:92, 182
Cohen, Stephen I., 2:25
Cohn, R., 3:424
Cohrssen, B. A., 3:62
Cole, Jonathan R., 3:23
Cole, Stephen, 3:23
Coleman, James S., 3:14
Coles, L. Stephen, 3:190, 234
COLINGO programming language, 1:125, 155; 2:136, 142, 144, 145
COLLECT program for retrieval of grammatical information, 3:116
Colleges and universities, educational uses of computers, 3:358–359, 362, 366, 371–372
  information networks, 3:299–300, 301, 302
Collen, Morris F., 2:317; 3:406, 412
Columbia University, 1:16
  Bureau of Applied Social Research, 2:7
  Library, 2:7
Colvin, Laura C., 3:344
Combined File Search System (*see* CFSS)

COMIT list-processing language, 1:153; 2:126; 3:152, 224, 280
Command languages, 1:125; 3:222–223
Commercial information networks, 3:293–294
Committee on National Library Information Systems (*see* CONLIS)
Committee on Scientific and Technical Communication (*see* SATCOM)
Committee on Scientific and Technical Information (*see* COSATI)
Communication patterns of scientists, 1:52–64; 3:11–15, 17
Compiler languages, 2:126
  in computer-assisted instruction, 3:380
COMPOSE/PRODUCE report generator, 3:154
Composition Information Services, 1:198
Compton, Bertita E., 2:371, 426; 3:22, 40, 41, 333
Computational linguistics, 1:139–150; 2:236; 3:111, 170
Computer and the Library, 2:257
Computer-assisted counseling, 3:367–368
Computer-Assisted Explanation, 3:232
Computer-assisted instruction, 1:243–244, 264–265; 2:198–199, 237–238; 3:303, 358–362, 371, 372, 385–387
  author languages, 3:379–382
  costs, 3:382–385
  design considerations, 3:374–376
  in medical education, 3:415–416
  user evaluations, 3:373–374
Computer-assisted medical diagnosis, 1:248–265; 2:318–321; 3:411–413
Computer-assisted patient data collection and processing, 1:248; 2:316–318; 3:403–410
Computer-assisted testing, 3:366–367, 407
Computer Associates, Inc., 2:142
Computer-based employment system, 3:369
Computer-based information systems, survey, 3:265
Computer Command and Control Co., 1:116
Computer Communications, Inc., 2:196
Computer Display Review, 2:198
Computer graphics, 2:198, 230; 3:47, 210–217
Computer input devices, 1:193–197; 2:188–191; 3:44–47
Computer interrogation of humans, 2:236
Computer-managed instruction, 3:362–365
Computer-mobile, 3:299
Computer networks, 3:226–227

Computer printout equipment, 1:200; 2:191, 278
Computer Research Corp., 1:208, 225; 2:229; 3:317, 371
Computer scheduling, 3:369, 403
Computer simulation, in retrieval system evaluation, 2:64
Computer Usage Co., 1:278, 295
Computer utilities, 1:225; 2:228; 3:228–229, 293–313
Computerized driving simulator, 3:361
Computerized inventory control, 3:402
Computerized typesetting, 1:197–200, 317–318; 2:263, 278, 352–358; 3:43–44, 47–48
Computers and Education, 3:298
Computers and privacy, 3:229, 295
Computers on Campus, 3:368
COMPUTEST compiler, 3:416
Conference of Biological Editors, committee on form and style, 2:342
Conference on computers in American education, 3:299
Conference on World Education, 3:292
Confrey, Eugene A., 2:368
CONLIS (Committee on National Library Information Systems), 2:260, 396; 3:294
Conner, Arthur N., Jr., 1:204; 2:95
Connor, John M., 3:341
Connor, Judith Holt, 3:276
Connors, Thomas L., 2:240; 3:155
Conrad, Carleton, 1:326, 327
Conrad, G. M., 1:312
Conrow, K., 2:292
Content-addressable memories, 1:114–116, 210–211; 2:207–208; 3:129, 131
Content analysis, specification and control, 1:71–106; 2:47–50, 87–122; 3:105–136
Control Abstracts, 2:347
Control Data Corp. (*see also* CDC), 1:193, 202, 238; 3:211
Conventions and meetings, effect on journal publication, 3:18, 40
  information exchange patterns, 1:54-55, 66; 3:16–17, 22, 40–41, 65
CONVERSE system, 2:52; 3:111, 151, 360
Cook, C. J., 2:27
Cooley, Stephen G. E., 3:417
Coons, Steven A., 2:241
Cooper, W. S., 1:76, 78, 156
Cooperative library programs, 2:264–265
Coordinate indexing systems, 1:319, 2:71, 75, 3:266–267
COPAK code—compression system, 3:144–145

Copper Development Association, 1:323
Copyright law, 1:346–347; 2:408–412; 3:54
Corbato, F. J., 1:226; 2:212, 225; 3:240
Corbett, Lindsay, 3:279
Corbin, Harold S., 2:197
Corey, Lewis, 3:336
Corin, Judith, 2:111, 366
Cornell Medical Index, 2:316–317
Cornell University, 1:24
  Department of Computer Science, 2:69; 3:114, 161, 273
Cornog, D. Y., 3:45
Corrado, Victor M., 2:356
Correa, Hector, 3:370
Correlation grammars, 2:175
Corrigan, J. J., 3:95
Corrigan, Phillip, 3:344
Corrigan, Robert E., 2:40
COSATI, 1:3, 32, 33, 212, 279, 324, 338, 339–343, 347, 348; 2:96, 260, 261, 286, 343, 361, 391, 402, 403, 412; 3:24, 294
  Task Group on National Systems 1:341–343
Cossum, W. E., 1:120; 2:297
Cost-effectiveness models, education applications, 3:370
Cotten, I., 2:187
Cottrell, Norman E., 1:349; 2:45; 3:326
Coull, Dorothy C., 3:421
Coulson, John E., 3:363
Council of National Library Associations, 2:260
Council of Social Science Data Archives, 3:313
Council on Library Resources (CLR), 1:201, 213, 286, 297, 298; 2:276, 405; 3:308
Counseling, computer-assisted, 3:367–368
COURSEWRITER programming language, 3:381
Couture de Troismonts, R., 1:31
Covey, Marvin L., 3:320
Cox, Carl R., 1:282
Cox, James, 1:293
Cox, N. S. M., 2:257; 3:247, 282
Coyaud, Maurice, 1:90; 3:170, 192
Cozan, Lee W., 3:100
Cozier, W. A., 2:138
Craig, James A., 2:177, 235; 3:190, 193
Crandall, R. Gordon, 3:408
Crane, Diana, 3:15
Crane, E. M., 2:296, 298
Cranefield, Paul F., 3:419
Craven, Kenneth, 1:18; 2:423, 435
Cravens, David W., 2:366
Craver, John S., 2:206
Crawford, D. J., 1:211
Crawford, J. H., 1:341
Creative Research Services, Inc., 2:276
Creelman, Marjorie, 2:170
Cremer, Martin, 1:29
Crime information systems, 1:262; 3:201, 314
Critical incident techniques, 1:62–65; 2:27; 3:12
Crocker, Stephen D., 3:235
Cronin, John W., 2:264, 404
Cronkhite, Leonard W., Jr., 3:421
Crooks, J., 3:403
Cros, R. C., 1:90; 3:192
CROSS (Computerized Rearrangements of Special Subjects), 1:313
Crow, James E., 3:53, 282
Crowder, D., 2:53
Crowe, J. E., 3:162
Croxton, Fred E., 3:262
CRT displays, 1:196, 200, 235, 237–238, 290; 2:294–299; 3:47–49, 117, 156, 181, 211–212, 214, 254, 259, 372, 374, 378–379, 382, 407
CTSS (Compatible Time-Sharing System), 1:225–226; 2:212, 225, 226, 227; 3:50, 202, 206–208, 210, 219–220
Cuadra, Carlos A., 1:1–14, 173, 183; 2:78, 420, 421, 431, 439; 3:7, 36, 70, 77, 88, 108, 336
Cuff, Renata, 2:10
Culler, Glen J., 1:226, 235, 236; 2:199
Culliton, E. H., III, 3:420
Cultural and political systems, effect on information transfer, 3:4, 22–23
Cummings, Martin M., 1:316; 3:69, 312, 417
Cunningham, Jay L., 3:320
Cunningham, Joseph A., 1:196
Curran, Ann T., 2:272; 3:248
Current Awareness and Document Retrieval for Engineers (see Project CADRE)
Current-awareness systems, 2:28, 364; 3:275–281 (see also Indexing and Abstracting Services; SDI systems)
Current Chemical Papers, 2:22
Current Medical Terminology, 2:323
Current Papers in Physics, 2:347
Currier, Donald R., 2:45
Curtice, Robert M., 1:120, 182; 2:128; 3:75, 96, 120, 127, 132, 140, 164, 187, 188, 189, 193
Cutrona, L. J., 1:206
Cypress photodigital storage device, 2:202–204; 3:221–222

DAC display systems, 2:195
Dahlberg, Ingetraut, 1:82
Daily, Jay E., 3:343
Dale, Alfred G., 1:91, 182
Dale, Bruce, 2:234
Dale, N., 1:91, 152, 182
Daley, R. C., 1:229; 3:234
Dalton, Phyllis I., 2:407
Damerau, F. J., 1:87, 94, 175, 182
Dammann, J. E., 1:195
D'Andrade, R. G., 1:168
Danielson, Rosamond, 2:276
Danielson, T., 3:408
Dannatt, R. J., 3:321
Danner, H., 1:81
DARE (Documentation Automated Retrieval Equipment), 2:202; 3:267–268, 279
Darley, D. Lucille, 3:224
Darley, J. G., 1:323
Darling, Louise, 3:417
Darlington, J. L., 1:159
Dartmouth College, 3:359, 362, 371
DASA (see Defense Atomic Support Agency)
Data banks, statewide remote access systems, 3:313
Data centers, 2:360–362
Data Communications Report, 2:198
DATA 620I computer, 2:213, 214
Data Corporation of Los Angeles, 1:193
Data description languages, 2:144
Data Disc Corp., 1:202
Data distribution, 2:358–362
Data Equipment Corp., 1:196
Data Machines, Inc., 2:214
Data management systems, 1:123–128; 2:123–160, 239; 3:153–161
Data processing, education applications, 3:368–370
 in clinical laboratories, 3:400–402
 in Title III ESEA projects, 3:368
 libraries, 1:281; 3:242–243, 265, 269–272
Data Processing for Education, 3:357
Data Products Corp., 1:200
Data Trend Corp., 1:195
DATATEXT, 2:213
Datatrol Corp., 1:122
Datta, S., 3:94
Davenport, William C., 1:267, 314; 2:350
Davenport, William P., 1:213; 2:229
David, Edward E., Jr., 2:225
Davies, D. W., 3:316
Davis, B. G., 3:195
Davis, Bobby, 3:426

Davis, Charles H., 3:193, 280
Davis, Daniel, 3:357
Davis, D. R., 1:110
Davis, J. E., 2:53
Davis, M. R., 3:234
Davis, Richard A., 1:44; 2:340; 3:340, 341
Davis, Ruth M., 1:9, 221–254, 232, 236; 2:196, 212, 223, 235; 3:66, 93, 201
Davis, William G., 3:388
Davison, Keith, 2:101
Day, Melvin S., 1:311; 2:111, 366, 370, 431; 3:67
DDC (see Defense Documentation Center)
DDP 516 computer, 2:213
DEACON Project, 1:159; 2:139, 177, 235
Dean, Averil J., 2:80; 3:132
Dear, Robert E., 3:374, 375
Dearden, J., 1:263; 2:39
Dearing, V. A., 1:160
DeBacker, M., 2:296, 298
Debons, Anthony, 1:239
DEC 338 computer, 2:196; 3:204, 211, 213, 214
DEC 340 CRT, 2:196
Decauville, N. Siot, 3:192, 193
DEDUCOM (DEDUctive COMmunicator), 1:156
Deese, J., 1:146
Defense Atomic Support Agency (DASA), 1:325
Defense Documentation Center (DDC), 1:276–277, 309; 2:95, 102, 135; 3:279
Defense Intelligence Agency (DIA), 2:142, 148
Defense Metals Information Center, 1:321, 325
Definitors, 2:105
De Gennaro, Richard, 1:285; 3:247
De Grazia, Alfred, 1:82
De Grolier, Eric, 1:89
Deighton, Lee C., 2:363, 410
Dekonsky, K., 1:194
de Laclemandiere, Jean, 1:29
De Laet, F. C. R., 2:98
Delbigio, G., 3:157
Dell, R. B., 3:422
De Maine, P. A. D., 2:294; 3:163, 165, 208
Denning, Peter J., 2:134
Dennis, Jack B., 1:225, 227; 3:234
Dennis, Sally F., 3:85, 188, 193
Dennis, W. C., 1:164; 2:138
Denz, Ronald F., 3:229
Department of Agriculture, 2:399
 Graduate School, 1:32
 information requirements survey, 2:19

research information system, 3:314
Department of Commerce, 1:309, 344; 2:13
Department of Defense (DOD), 1:348
 Engineering Data Systems Project, 2:200
 libraries and information centers mechanization, 2:53, 258, 277
 user studies, 1:63; 3:12-13, 21-22
Department of the Interior, computer network, 3:316
De Pasquale, Nicholas P., 3:404
Dertouzos, M. L., 2:232
Derwent's Ringdoc service, 3:268
de Saussure, Ferdinand, 1:90
Deschambeau, George L., 3:422
Descriptor control, 2:94, 95, 97
Deskalov, I., 3:420
Detwiller, L. T., 3:422
Deutsch, K. W., 1:323; 2:89, 103
Deutsch, L. Peter, 1:253; 3:193, 224
Deutsche Bibliothek, 2:263, 278
Dewey Decimal Classification, use in SDI user profiling, 3:280
Dews, J. D., 2:257; 3:247
DIA (*see* Defense Intelligence Agency)
Diagnosis of diseases (*see* Computer-assisted medical diagnosis)
Dial-access information retrieval systems, 3:303-304
Diary studies, 2:5-6
DiBello, Frank A., 2:47
Dick, Walter, 3:357, 358, 366, 373, 376, 388
Dickman, John T., 2:350
Dickson, William C., 3:299
Dictionaries, in syntactic analysis, 3:187
Dictionary construction, automatic procedures for, 2:69; 3:182
Dictionary lookup with associative memories, 2:130
Dictionary semantic networks, 2:172
DIDS 4000 display console, 2:197
Diebold, A. R., Jr., 1:76
Diebold, John, and Associates, 1:291
Digital-analog devices, in medical analyses, 3:412, 413
Digital Equipment Corp., 1:196
Digital storage systems, 1:201-202; 2:204-210; 3:221-222, 268
 comparison with document storage, 3:301
Dijkstra, E. W., 1:231
Dimsdale, B., 3:116
Direct-access storage media, 2:128
Direct view storage tubes, 2:198

Directed graphs, 2:127
Display Oriented Computer Usage Systems (*see* DOCUS)
Display systems, 1:196-197, 236-241; 2:194-198, 230-232, 239, 276; 3:47-49, 55, 89, 181, 185, 211-212, 254, 267, 272, 378-379
Dixon, P. J., 3:154
Dixon, W. J., 3:209
Dixon Industries, Inc., 1:212
Dlugos, Joyce, 3:194, 286
DM-1 data management system, 2:127, 134, 137, 142, 144, 145; 3:154-155
Dobbs, G. H., 1:128; 2:238
Dobrowolski, Zygmunt, 1:72, 73
Document analysis (*see* Content analysis, specification, and control)
Document dissemination systems, 1:308-309; 3:263-288
Document distribution, 2:358-359
Document representation techniques, 1:79; 2:65, 92-93; 3:75-76, 88, 105-106, 114-123
Document retrieval, associative techniques, 2:70-71; 3:75, 86, 127-128, 140-141, 151-152, 188-189, 273
 syntactic procedures, 3:183-187
Document retrieval systems, 1:122-123, 244-246, 276-277; 2:42-46, 55, 64, 134; 3:139, 263-288
 file organization, 2:50-51
Document transmission systems, 2:200-201
Documentation Abstracts, 2:101, 3:51, 147
Documentation Automated Retrieval Equipment (*see* DARE system)
Documentation, Inc., 1:16, 172; 2:128
DOCUS (Display Oriented Computer Usage System), 2:52, 137
DOD (*see* Department of Defense)
Dodd, George G., 2:126
Dodson, Ann T., 3:98, 270
Doebler, Paul D., 3:43
Doermann, August H., 2:368
Dolby, James L., 2:257, 3:197
Domabyl, H. P., 1:195
Donahue, C. P., Jr., 3:93, 99, 388
Donohue, Joseph C., 1:22; 2:437; 3:21
Dorian, G. H., 1:206, 210
Dorn, William S., 3:381
Dorward, Donald L., 2:91, 139
Doudnikoff, Basil, 1:204; 2:95
Dougherty, Richard M., 1:201; 3:125
Douglas, Mary L., 3:259
Douglas Aircraft Co., mechanized information system, 2:267; 3:266, 283

Doumani, George A., 1:317
Dove Data Storage and Retrieval System, 3:268
Dovel, J. A., Jr., 2:97
Dow Chemical Co., 2:294–299; 3:142
Downs, George E., 3:403
Doyle, L. B., 1:91, 94, 143, 173; 2:106; 3:189
DP 4000 drum printer, 2:299
Dray, Sheldon, 2:368
Drefus, Hubert L., 2:88
Drew, D. L., 2:52, 134
Drexel Institute of Technology, 1:22; 2:42
Drug Information Handling by the American Medical Association, 2:329
Drug information systems, 1:259; 2:128, 329; 3:268, 402–403
Dual dictionaries, 3:266
Dubinski, George A., 3:92, 285
Duchac, Kenneth F., 3:321
Duda, Richard O., 3:82, 93
Dugan, James A., 2:130, 208
Duggan, Hector E., 3:401
Duggar, B. C., 1:240
Dugger, Edward, 1:326, 327, 239; 3:76
Duke, Martin, 3:405
Duke University, 3:300
Dulin, James Thomas, 3:369
Dumey, A. I., 1:202
Dunham, J. L., 3:359, 362, 371, 373
Dunlap, Connie, 3:250
Dunn, E. S., Jr., 1:323; 2:406
Dunning, A. W., 1:213
Dunphy, Dexter C., 1:105; 3:135, 198
DuPont Co., 2:94
  chemical structure search system, 3:158
  microfiche report system, 3:53
  Savannah River Laboratory, book acquisition and circulation system, 2:294; 3:250
Duquet, Robert T., 2:55, 64; 3:92
Dura Mach 10 input device, 3:45
Dutton, Brian, 2:175
Dye, H. E., 2:47
Dykeman, Alice, 3:399
Dym, Eleanor D., 3:75, 88, 96, 423
DYNAMOD II, educational planning model, 3:370
Dyson, G. M., 3:51, 130
Dzubak, B. J., 1:109

Earl, P. H., 3:90
Easley, J. A., Jr., 2:237
East, H., 2:350
Eastern Pennsylvania Information Center, 3:372
Eastlake, Donald E., III, 3:235
Eastman Kodak Co., 1:203; 3:301, 368
Eastman Kodak MIRACODE (*see* MIRACODE microfilm retrieval system)
Easton, William B., 3:387
Easy English command language, 3:151, 272
Ebersole, J. L., 2:394
Eckert, Phillip F., 1:311; 2:99, 128
Eckles, James E., 3:375
ECS 100 communication system, 2:201
Edgewood Arsenal, chemical notation system, 2:299–300
  Toxicological Information Center, 3:159
EDIT-LAYOUT display system, 3:48
Edmundson, H. P., 1:87, 94
EDP Analyzer, 2:142
EDS on-line editor, 3:208
Education for information science, 2:15–35
Education information systems, 1:264–265; 3:296, 357–395
  operational examples, 3:371–372
Educational Communications System project, 3:302
Educational Facilities Laboratories, Inc., 3:244, 312
Educational Resources Information Center (*see* ERIC)
Educational Technology, 3:357
Educational television networks, 3:301
Educational Testing Service, 2:318
EDUCOM (Interuniversity Communications Council), 2:261, 331, 395–396; 3:66, 226, 227, 296–297, 298, 301, 303, 306
EDUNET study on information networks, 3:171, 226, 296–297
Edwards, Judith B., 3:320
Edwards, W., 1:243
EIN (Electronic Information Network), 3:227
Eisman, S. H., 2:292
EJC (*see* Engineers Joint Council)
Eldridge, Arthur J., Jr., 2:232
Electrical and Electronics Abstracts, 2:347
Electrocardiograms, computerized analysis, 1:255, 258; 2:320–321, 322; 3:413–414
Electroencephalograms, computerized analysis, 3:413–414
Electroluminescent displays, 2:198; 3:211
Electron beam recording, 1:206; 2:192; 3:221, 268
Electronic information handling, conference, 3:297

Electronic printing, 3:48
Electronic Video Recording (EVR), 3:302
Elementary and Secondary Education Act (see ESEA)
Eli Lilly and Co., 2:299
Elias, Arthur W., 3:130, 336
ELIZA program, 2:103, 177, 236; 3:225, 380
Elkin, Milton, 3:428
Elkington, J. R., 3:418
Elliott, Roger W., 1:157; 2:169
Ellis, T. O., 1:250; 3:213, 234
Ellsworth, Ralph, 2:435
Elsinore Conference on Classification Research, 1:89
Elsom, Katharine O., 3:412
Ember, G. Diapas, 3:418
Emerson, William G., 1:335
Emery, James, 3:76
Ende, Asher H., 2:400
Engel, Gerald L., 3:357
Engel, Jan M., 2:198, 232
Engel, K., 3:422
Engineering drawings, retrieval, 2:200; 3:268
Engineering Index, 1:315–316; 2:347; 3:278
Engineering information networks, 1:316; 2:398
Engineering thesauri, 2:67, 93
Engineers, information-gathering patterns, 1:60, 62–63; 2:20; 3:9, 12
Engineers Joint Council (EJC), 1:82, 83, 93, 316, 349; 2:67, 93, 110, 398; 3:125, 312
Englebart, D. C., 2:196, 197; 3:193, 213
Engleman, C., 1:234
English, W. K., 3:213, 181
English as a programming language, 2:235–236
English Electric KDF9 computer, 3:149
Entelek, Inc., 2:238; 3:357
Enumerative classification schemes, 2:100
EPAM models for semantic categorization, 2:168
Epstein, Marion, 3:367
Epstein, Martin N., 2:109
ERIC, 2:404–405; 3:270, 298–299
ERIC Clearinghouse on Educational Media and Technology, 3:357
Ericson, R. Peter, 3:425
Erikson, Warren J., 3:70
Eriksson, Ann M., 3:269
Ernst, M. L., 1:183
Ernst, R. L., 3:103

Error-control systems, 1:212
Ervin-Tripp, S. M., 1:145, 146; 2:170, 172
ESEA (Title III) computer projects, 3:299, 368, 371
Esso Research and Engineering Co., 1:308, 322, 325
Estavan, Donald P., 3:93, 99, 374, 388
Estrin, G., 3:229
EURATOM (see European Atomic Energy Community)
European Atomic Energy Community (EURATOM), 1:151; 2:75, 96
European countries, education for information science, 1:29–30
Evans, Alfred S., 3:401
Evans, Arthur, Jr., 3:224, 235
Evans, David, 3:145
Evans, George J., Jr., 3:321
Evans, Mary R., 3:414
Evans, P. N., 3:162
Evans, T. G., 1:247
Eyman, Eleanor G., 2:272

Fabens, W., 3:195
Fabrizio, Ralph, 3:46, 57
Facet analysis, 2:97, 100–101
  in thesaurus building, 2:90, 95
Facsimile transmission, 1:213; 2:200–201, 397; 3:55, 272, 311
Fact retrieval and inferential systems, 1:157; 2:137–139
Factor analysis, in automatic classification systems, 2:106
FAIR (Fast Access Information Retrieval), 3:274
Fairchild-Hiller Corp., Republic Aviation Div., 2:204
Fairthorne, Robert A., 1:73, 75, 76, 90, 91, 173, 175, 181; 3:63, 74, 80
Falkoff, A. D., 3:235
Fall, James E., 3:70
Fallon, Frances, 2:345
Fallout ratio, 2:89
Fano, Robert M., 1:224, 225, 226; 2:225; 3:50, 57, 229, 389
Fanwick, Charles, 1:193; 2:204; 3:63
Farell, Jules, 1:95
Farley, Earl A., 1:8, 273–303; 2:258
Farradane, J. E. L., 1:72, 90, 92; 2:425; 3:74, 80
Farris, B. K., 3:92
Farris, Eugene H., 2:52, 266; 3:308
Fasana, Paul J., 3:62, 69, 70, 249
FASEB (see Federation of American Societies for Experimental Biology)
FASTRAND drum storage, 3:214

COMBINED INDEX 515

Faust, Richard, 3:100
FDA (see Food and Drug Administration)
Federal Communications Commission (FCC), 2:228; 3:227, 291, 293, 316
Federal Council for Science and Technology, 1:338, 339
Federal Library Committee, 1:338, 345; 2:405
Federal role in information science, 1:327–328, 337–346; 2:431–432
Federation of American Societies for Experimental Biology (FASEB), 1:67
Federman, Philip J., 3:89, 101
Feeman, James F., 2:141
Feiblmann, J. K., 1:89
Feigenbaum, Edward A., 3:237
Fein, Louis, 3:65, 333
Feingold, Samuel, 3:359, 362
Feinler, E. J., 1:322; 2:27
Feinstein, Alvan R., 3:398
Feldhausen, John, 3:379
Feldman, A., 2:296, 299
Feldman, J. A., 1:115; 2:129
Feldman, Myra S., 3:250, 257
Ferguson, J., 1:306; 3:353
Fernbach, S., 2:204
Fetter, William A., 2:198
Feurzeig, Wallace, 1:264, 265; 3:239, 360, 389
FID (see International Federation for Documentation)
Field encoding, 3:145
File organization and management, 1:107–135; 2:37, 50–52, 102, 123–160; 3:137–167, 247
File structures, 1:109–110; 3:148–150
Filep, Robert T., 3:357–395, 358, 362, 373, 374, 378
Files, J. B., 3:424
Filing rules for machine sorting, 2:270
Fill, K., 1:29
Fillmore, Charles J., 2:163
Film chip memories, 2:205
Fineberg, Mark F., 3:239
Finley, Paul R., 3:422
Fischer, Marguerite, 2:107, 331
Fishenden, R. M., 2:340
Fisher, Stanley, 1:95
Fishman, Elizabeth Jane, 3:358
Fitzpatrick, W. H., 1:345
Flack, Herbert L., 3:403
Flanagan, Carolyn, 1:9, 305–325, 333
Flanagan, John 3:364
Flannery, Anne, 2:275
Fleisher, A., 1:211
Flood, Barbara, 3:83

Flood, Merrill M., 3:293
Flood, Paul K., 3:359
Florida Atlantic University, 1:280, 288, 292
Florida State University, 2:9
    Computer Assisted Instruction Center, 3:358, 366, 373
Flynn, J. M., 3:376
FOCAL programming language, 3:381
Focke, Helen, 1:16; 2:435
Fodor, Jerry A., 1:76, 140, 141; 2:166, 170
Fogel, Marc, 3:85
FOIL programming language, 3:380
Fonkalsrud, Eric W., 3:358, 416
Food and Drug Administration (FDA), 2:287, 329
Ford, Donald F., 3:92, 162
Ford, J. D., Jr., 1:160
Ford Foundation, 3:301
    Educational Facilities Laboratories, Inc., 3:244, 312
Forecasting Institute, Swedish Central Bureau of Statistics, 3:370
Foreman, Alling C., 3:155
Forman, Barry, 2:103
Formatted File System, 2:145, 148
Forrest, William H., Jr., 3:406
Forsyth, D. M., 3:235
Fort Monmouth (N.J.), SDI system, 3:279
Forte, Allen, 3:235
FORTRAN programming language, 2:55, 242; 3:208, 380
FORTRAN IV programming language, 3:157
Foskett, D. J., 1:90; 3:130
Fossum, Earl G., 2:50, 95, 102, 135
Foster, D. R., 1:162
Foster, J. M., 3:152
Foster, W. R., 1:84, 2:73
Fox, L., 2:126
Franco, A. G., 1:212
Frank, W. L., 1:237, 238
Franklin, R. H., 2:229
Franklin and Marshall College, 3:372
Franklin Institute Research Laboratories, Metal Powder Technical Information Center, 3:313
Franks, Emory W., 2:108, 146, 148, 164; 3:157
Franks, Winifred, 3:100, 134, 197
Frarey, Carlyle J., 3:345
Fraser, A. G., 3:162
Fraser, B., 2:164
Fraser, C., 1:146

Fraser, J. Bruce, 1:148; 2:161–186; 3:129, 169, 177, 192, 209
Freeman, Monroe E., 1:310, 345; 3:69
Freeman, Robert R., 1:92, 332; 2:81, 100, 339–384; 3:67, 121, 124, 141, 157, 274
French, J. L., 3:366
Fried, B. D., 1:226, 235, 236
Friedberg, Charles K., 3:425
Friedman, Joyce, 2:173, 174
Friedman, Sandor A., 3:426
Frijda, Nico H., 2:168
Frome, Julius, 3:90, 275
Fromer, R., 3:362
Frost system of xerography, 1:206
Frutiger, Adrian, 3:46, 57
Fry, Bernard M., 1:311
Fry, George, and Associates, 1:291
Frye, C. H., 3:358, 359, 362, 377, 380
Fugmann, Robert, 1:91, 92
Fukunaga, K., 1:195
Fuller, H. W., 2:198
Fuller, R. H., 1:195, 211
Fundamentals of Display Systems, 2:198
Funderburk, B. J., 3:282
Fussler, Herman H., 3:255

Gable, Martha A., 3:321
Gabrieli, E. R., 3:401
Gabrini, Philippe J., 3:148
Gagliardi, U. O., 1:183
Gaifman, H., 1:141
Gainen, L., 3:95
Gaines, R. S., 1:211
Galentine, Paul, 1:128
Galford, Robert R., 2:9
Gall, Russell G., 2:130
Gallagher, Joan L, 2:99, 111, 367
Gallenson, L., 1:225, 227; 3:211, 235
Galli, E. J., 1:117, 3:182
Gani, J., 3:370
Gannett, E. K., 3:33
Gardin, J. C., 1:72, 90, 91, 92, 123, 185; 3:191, 192
Gardin, Natacha, 3:130
Gardner, Arthur E., 2:356
Gardner, Elmer A., 3:422
Gardner, R. C., 3:130
Garfield, Eugene, 2:111, 293; 3:279
Garfinkel, J. J., 3:193
Garfunkel, J. M., 1:270
Garner, Harvey L., 2:57
Garner, Ralph, 3:85
Garrett, Roger, 3:16, 134
Garvey, William D., 1:53; 2:15, 362, 363, 368, 370, 371, 426; 3:17, 18, 22, 40, 41

Garvin, David, 2:361
Garvin, Paul L., 1:76, 139, 141, 162; 3:131, 190
Garvis, Francis J., 2:405
Gasking, E. B., 1:16
Gasper, Max R., 3:423
Gasser, E. B., 1:131, 267
Gastaut, H., 3:416
Gaster, Kathleen, 3:125
GE 225 computer, 2:275; 3:160, 205
GE 235 computer, 3:278
GE 645 computer, 2:197, 224; 3:203
Geddes, Andrew, 2:265; 3:243
Geddes, L. A., 1:271
Geis, George R., 3:416
Gelberg, Alan, 2:141
Gelman, M., 3:371, 389
General Dynamics Corp., 1:289
General Electric Co., 1:125, 159, 202, 206; 2:126; 3:303 (*see also* GE)
General Inquirer, mechanized content analysis system, 3:113
General Motors Corp., 2:195
General Precision, Inc., PARD system, 3:267
General-Purpose Display System, 2:195, 239
General Services Administration, Advanced Record System (ARS), 3:316–317
Generalized data management systems, 2:123–160; 3:153–158
Generalized Information Processing System (*see* GIPSY)
Generalized Information System (*see* GIS)
Generalized Random Extract Device (GRED), 2:144, 145, 147
Generic posting, 2:94
GENIE time-sharing system, 3:225
Gentile, J. Ronald, 3:344, 373, 378
Genung, Harriett, 3:344
Genzlinger, Vance, 1:247
George, A. L., 1:76
George, Virginia, 1:303; 3:254
George Washington University, 1:67, 257
Georgetown University, 1:151
Georgia Institute of Technology, 1:18, 19, 22, 32; 3:246
Geoscience Abstracts, 1:315
Gerard, Ralph, 3:321, 348, 357
Gerber, L. S., 2:330
Gerbner, G., 3:170
German, Janice A., 3:129
Germany, library automation, 2:276
National Library, 2:263
Gerstberger, Peter G., 3:9, 65

Gertsma, Robert H., 3:415
Gibson, Charles T., 2:211
Gilman, David Alan, 3:376, 389
Gilmore, John S., 3:21, 22, 66
Gilyarevskii, R. S., 3:332
Ginsberg, Helen F., 3:131
Ginsburg, Seymour, 3:131
Ginzberg, Eli, 3:350
GIPSY (Generalized Information Processing System), 3:156-157
GIRLS (Generalized Information Retrieval and Listing System), 1:124
GIS (Generalized Information System), 1:126, 127; 2:125, 133, 136, 142-145, 149, 239; 3:153
Giuliani, Emilio R., 3:421
Giuliano, Vincent E., 1:154; 2:65, 70, 77, 104; 3:72, 96, 132, 164, 187, 189, 194
Givon, Talmy, 3:111, 178, 179, 194
Glaser, Edward L., 1:225, 227; 3:95, 229
Glaser, Robert, 3:378, 379
Glaser, William A., 3:313
Glasersfeld, Ernst von, 1:162; 2:175
Glinski, Bernice C., 3:399
Gluck, D. J., 1:120, 121; 2:293
Gluck, S. E., 1:210
Glueck, B. C., Jr., 3:409
Goffman, E. G., 1:227
Goffman, William, 1:173; 2:72
Goldberg, J., 1:131
Goldberg, Murray D., 2:361
Goldblum, Edward J., 2:112
Goldhor, Herbert, 1:276
Goldman, Abraham, 2:411
Goldstein, Gordon D., 3:323
Goldstein, Harold, 3:344, 350
Goldstein, Leo S., 3:421
Goldwyn, A. J., 1:22, 326; 3:418
Good, I. J., 3:76
Goodenough, J. B., 1:94
Goodgold, Albert, 3:408
Goodlad, John I., 1:264; 3:368
Goodman, A. F., 3:62, 65
Goodman, F. L., 1:26, 77
Goodyear Associative Processor, 2:130
Gopinath, M. A., 3:340
Gordon, Burgess L., 2:323
Gordon, Maxwell, 2:297
Gorman, Patrick A., 3:427
Gorn, Saul, 1:20, 27; 3:329, 331, 341
Gosin, Robert F., 3:423
Gosnell, Charles F., 2:409, 411
Gott, Alan H., 2:190
Gotterer, Malcolm H., 1:238; 3:64, 76
Gottshall, David B., 3:236
Goudsmit, Samuel A., 2:389

Gould, David, 1:120
Gould, I. H., 1:82
Gould, Laura, 3:131
Gould, W. S., 3:94
Government documents, library processing, 2:273
Grabbe, E. M., 3:322
Grace, Gloria Lauer, 3:208
GRACE (Graphic Arts Composing Equipment), 1:296-297
Graham, H. L., 2:232
Graham, R. M., 3:240
Graham, T., 3:424
Graham, Warren R., 3:65
Grammars, 1:139-140, 146; 2:162-165, 173, 175; 3:172-175, 179, 183, 186, 201
Grand Valley State College, dial-access information system, 3:303
Granito, Charles E., 1:82; 2:141
Grant, Charles M., Jr., 2:111, 366
Grant, E. E., 3:95, 235
Grant, Joan, 2:8, 28
Graph properties, 2:127, 168
Graphic data coding, 1:235; 3:145-146
Graphical input/output devices, 1:196-197, 237- 240; 2:195, 232; 3:211-212
  applications, 1:197; 3:215-217
Graphical interaction techniques, 1:230, 240-241; 3:212-213
Grauer, Robert T., 3:131, 164
Graves, Patricia A., 2:357; 3:235
Graves, R.W., 3:286
Gravitz, Melvin A., 3:407
Gray, Dwight E., 2:339-384
Gray, H. J., 1:133; 2:125, 135; 3:153
Gray, J. C., 3:148
Gray, Stephen, 2:196
Great Britain, Advisory Council on Scientific Policy, 2:16, 20, 340
  educational planning models, 3:370
  National Lending Library for Science and Technology, 2:22
Green, B. F., 3:225
Green, David, 2:368; 3:42
Green, James S., 3:88, 162
Green, Robert S., 2:130, 131
Green, Sterling, 1:83
Greenberg, Murray, 3:412
Greenberger, Martin, 1:226, 227; 2:243
Greenblatt, Richard D., 3:235
Greene, James A., Jr., 3:416
Greene, Marjorie, 3:122, 131
Greer, F. L., 2:96
Greer, Roger, 3:329-355
Grems, Mandalay, 1:95

Grenias, E. C., 1:248
Grieb, William E., Jr., 3:355
Griebach, Sheila, 3:131
Griffel, David, 3:237
Griffin, Hillis L., 3:241-262
Griffith, Belver C., 1:53; 2:15, 340, 348, 351, 363, 368, 371, 426, 427; 3:18
Griffith, J. R., 1:259
Griffiths, T. V., 1:150
GRINS program for on-line communication, 3:88
Grisell, James, 3:408
Grissom, G., 3:274
Groeben, J. Von Der, 3:423
Groen, Guy, 3:358
Groom, Dale, 2:328
Grose, Michael N., 3:282
Gross, L. N., 3:163, 183, 193, 208
Gross, W., 2:187
Grossman, Alvin, 3:299, 368
Grossman, Fred, 3:44, 212
Grubb, Ralph, 3:362
Gruenberger, Fred, 2:215; 3:235
Guard, James R., 3:387
Gudobba, Roger, 3:408
Guide to Microreproduction Equipment, 2:202
Guiles, Kay D., 3:260
Gull, C. D., 1:172; 2:278, 436, 441; 3:350
Gummere, Richard M., Jr., 3:350
Gunderson, D. C., 2:131
Gysbers, Jack C., 3:213

Hackett, E., 3:424
Haddon, B. K., 3:149
Haefner, R. R., 1:294
Hager, George P., 2:139, 330, 393
Hagerty, Katherine, 3:88, 115
Hakansson, B., 3:421
Hale, John, 1:79
Hall, Andrew D., Jr., 3:369
Hall, Michael D., 3:131
Hall, P., 3:408
Hall, R. M. S., 2:361
Hall, V. E., 3:37, 415
Halnan, K. E., 3:413
Halpern, Mark, 3:235
Hamilton, M. L., 1:197
Hammer, Donald P., 1:280; 2:269, 385-417; 3:270, 289
Hammidi, I. B., 3:358, 389, 416
Hammond, William, 3:125
Handling Toxicological Information, 2:329
Hanlon, Alfred G., 1:205; 2:129, 131, 208
Hansen, D. L., 3:233

Hansen, Duncan N., 3:357, 358, 366, 373, 376
Harasymin, S. J., 3:367
Hardegg, W., 2:17
Hardway, C. L., 3:212
Haring, D. R., 1:196, 238
Harley, A. J., 2:330
Harman, R. Joyce, 1:38, 274; 3:237
Harmon, Glynn, 3:338
Harnack, Robert S., 3:364
Harper, Kenneth E., 1:88
Harris, Eleanor T., 1:83
Harris, Fred R., 3:338
Harris, Jerome J., 2:329
Harris, Jessica L., 2:270
Harris, Michael H., 1:292
Harris, Zellig S., 1:139; 2:175
Harris Intertype phototypesetters, 1:199
Harrison, Annette, 3:236, 322
Harrison, Sylvia, 3:97
Harry Diamond Laboratories, Army Materiel Command, 1:182
Hart, Gary L., 3:100
Hartley, D. F., 3:162
Hartman, Thomas F., 3:358
Harvard-NEEDS-Newton Information System for Vocational Decisions, 3:368
Harvard University, 1:19, 151, 182, 285, 291; 2:174; 3:303, 358
   Baker Library, 2:272
   Center for Cognitive Studies, 1:145; 2:170
   Cruft Laboratory, 3:204, 215-216
   Graduate School of Business Administration, 1:62
   Widener Library, 2:269
Harvey, John F., 2:419-444; 3:330, 351
Harway, Norman I., 1:76
Hash addressing, definition, 3:214
Haskell, R. J., Jr., 3:374
Hassler, Frank L., 1:260
Haswell, Harold A., 2:405
Hatch, Lucille, 2:436
Hattersley, Paul G., 3:423
Hattery, Lowell H., 1:28; 2:353, 356
Havlik, Robert J., 1:346
Havron, M. Dean, 2:55, 76
Hawkridge, David G., 3:415
Hayashi, H., 3:183
Hayes, Robert M., 1:19, 21, 26, 86, 93, 112, 280; 2:42, 266, 434; 3:131, 139, 236, 271, 306, 340, 348
Hayes International Corp., 3:269
Hays, David G., 1:141, 161; 2:236; 3:111, 112, 170, 230, 236

Hayward notation for chemical compounds, 2:140, 294
Hazelton, Irene, 3:198
Head, Robert V., 1:128; 2:243
Heald, J. Heston, 2:48, 93, 97; 3:125
Heaps, Doreen, 3:351
Hedgpeth, J. W., 1:323
Hedman, Lorraine L., 3:322, 423
Hefner Ronald G., 3:44
Heidelberg University, periodicals usage survey, 2:17
Heilprin, Laurence B., 1:4, 26, 172
Heiner, Joseph A., Jr., 2:147
Heinz, O., 2:27
Helander, Donald P., 3:286
Hell, Rudolf, 1:198, 199
Heller, Robert, 2:344
Hellerman, H., 1:226
Helm, C. E., 3:367
Hemphill, J. K., 1:323
Henderson, Madeline M., 1:183; 3:61
Henisz-Dostert, Bozena, 3:131, 194
Herbert, Evan, 2:392; 3:302
Herbert, J., 2:205
Herman, Donald J., 3:95
Herner, Mary, 1:79; 2:1–34; 3:27, 103
Herner, Saul, 1:79, 81, 108, 182; 2:1–34, 8, 331, 394; 3:1, 2, 7, 9, 89, 103, 280, 281
Herner and Co., 1:173; 2:397
Heron, David W., 2:397
Herriat, R. G., 3:195
Herrmann, William W., 1:269; 3:95
Herschman, Arthur, 2:339–384; 3:131
Hersey, David F., 1:84, 310; 3:125
Hertz, D. B., 3:62
Herzog, W. T., 1:323
Hewer, David J., 3:84, 95
Hickey, Albert E., 3:322, 357, 373
Hicks, B. L., 3:319
Hicks, G. Philip, 2:323
Hieber, Caroline E., 2:22, 24
Hierarchical indexing structures, 2:94
Hierarchy linkage, 2:125
Higher Education Act of 1965; Title II-B, 1:32; 2:264; 3:306
Higher Education Act of 1968; Title IX—Networks for Knowledge, 3:298
Highway Research Information Service, 1:323
Hillman, Donald J., 1:24, 26, 77, 78, 89, 90; 2:37, 64, 104, 105; 3:110, 184
Hilton, Howard J., 3:124
Hilton, W. Ralph, 2:64, 105
Hindson, R., 2:366
Hines, Theodore C., 1:73, 81, 92, 93; 2:270, 438; 3:351

Hinman, Kendall A., 1:131
Hirayama, Kenzo, 1:84, 86; 2:65; 3:166
Hirschberg, L., 3:192
Hirschowitz, Basil I., 3:416
Hirshleifer, Jack, 3:76
Hitch, Charles J., 3:370
Hitt, W. D., 1:17
Hittel, L. A., 2:201, 229
Hiz, H., 1:162; 2:291
Ho, C. Y., 1:195
Hoagland, A. S., 1:209
Hoban, Charles F., 3:17
Hobbs, L. S., 2:198, 207; 3:379, 390
Hochberg, Howard M., 3:413
Hoffer, Joe R., 1:323
Hoffman, A., 2:297
Hoffman, John M., 1:173, 183
Hoffman, Warren S., 3:164
Hogan, Douglas L., 2:234
Hogan, P., 3:415
Hogan, Richard C., 3:399
Hohnecker, Walter, 3:124
Holland, Harold E., 3:336
Hollander, G. L., 2:204
Hollander, Matthias, 3:37, 106
Holm, Bart E., 1:92; 2:110
Holman, Wendell K., 3:131
Holmes, Emory H., 3:30, 135, 355
Holmgren, A., 3:421
Holographic techniques, 1:206–207; 3:53–54
Holsti, Ole R., 1:76, 160; 3:114
Holt, A. L., 1:322
Holt, Anatol W., 1:127
Holtzman, W. H., 3:359, 362, 371, 373
Holzbauer, Herbert, 2:344; 3:336, 341, 342
Holzbaur, Frederick W., 2:52, 112, 266; 3:308
Honeywell Corp., 1:202, 211, 295; 3:372, 385
Honeywell 200 computer, 3:372
Hooper, Robert S., 1:81, 84, 171; 2:65, 80, 101; 3:75, 95
Hope, C. S., 3:413
Horn, L., 3:179
Horowitz, Paul, 2:296, 298
Horty, John F., 1:95
Horvath, Paul J., 3:194, 266, 277
Hoshovsky, Alexander G., 1:347, 2:97, 110, 113, 343
Hospital information systems, 2:242–243, 324–327; 3:315–316, 399–403
Houldin, Russell J., 2:231
Houston Fearless Corp., 2:202
Howard, James H., 2:198

Howard, Paul, 2:405
HRB-Singer, Inc., 2:55
Huang, Theodore S., 1:212
Huber, Melvin L., 2:286, 289, 291
Human Resources Information System (*see* HUMARIS)
Human Sciences Research, Inc., 1:183; 2:43, 55
HUMARIS (Human Resources Information System), 3:405
Humphrey, Roger A., 3:212
Humphries, D. E., 1:219
Hungarian Scientific Institute for Technical Documentation for Machine Industry, 1:84, 85
Hunka, S., 3:381
Hunt, James R., 2:408
Huntress, E. M., 2:289
Huskey, H. D., 1:233
Hutchins, Ronald D., 2:5, 9
Hutchisson, Elmer, 1:349
Hyams, H., 2:345
Hyde, E., 3:164, 166
Hypertext, 2:197
Hypothesis-testing studies, computer-assisted instruction, 3:373–376
Hyslop, Marjorie R., 1:86, 93, 315; 2:72, 93, 94, 96, 97, 348, 399; 3:25

Iberall, A. S., 2:36
IBM (*see also* International Business Machines Corp.)
  ATS (Administrative Terminal System), 1:195, 286; 3:308
  Business information network, 3:315
  Cambridge Scientific Center, time-sharing monitor, 3:207
  CIS (Current Information Selection) system, 2:111; 3:276
  Combined File Search System (*see* CFSS)
  Cypress storage device, 2:202–204; 3:221–222
  MT/ST typewriter, 3:255
  SDI systems, 3:276–277
  Technical Information Retrieval Center (ITIRC), 3:266
  TSS (time-sharing supervisor), 3:202
  Watson Research Center, 3:216–217
  Yorktown Heights laboratory, 3:358, 372
357 Data Collector, 1:292; 2:275; 3:256
360 computers, 1:110; 2:134, 144, 189, 206, 273; 3:157, 204, 205, 206, 207, 218, 245, 255, 258, 275, 276, 277, 280, 364, 418
360/67 computer, 2:210, 224; 3:202, 206, 207, 252
870 document writer, 1:284; 3:271, 275
1030 data collector, 1:294
1130 computer, 2:213; 3:204, 211, 216–217, 299
1230 optical scanner, 2:318
1232 optical scanner, 3:364
1287 optical character reader, 2:189
1301 disc storage device, 1:110; 3:158, 160
1350 storage device, 2:205
1400 file management system, 3:157
1401 computer, 1:122, 277, 278, 285, 315; 2:209, 273; 3:245, 253, 277, 280
1403 printer, 1:284, 285
1404 printer, 1:283
1410 computer, 2:148; 3:159, 277, 371
1440 data network, 3:371, 399
1460 computer, 1:280; 2:263; 3:276
1500 instructional system, 2:199; 3:205, 303, 371, 372, 384, 385
1620 computer, 2:55, 272; 3:416
1710 computer, 2:193; 3:257
1800 computer, 3:205
1800/1500 instructional system, 3:371
1975 optical scanner, 2:189
2250 display, 2:196, 231; 3:204, 211, 216, 217, 299
2260 display, 2:197
2280 CRT, 3:47
2314 storage device, 2:206
2321 data cell, 1:202
7010 computer, 3:158
7030 computer, 1:234; 3:155, 156
7040 computer, 3:145, 160, 280
7090 computer, 1:110, 279; 3:144
7044 computer, 1:278; 3:149
7094 computer, 1:285, 296; 2:108, 126, 173, 209, 267; 3:159, 276
7094 CTSS, 3:206, 207
7404 graphic output unit, 1:196
7770 audio response unit, 2:193
7772 audio response unit, 2:193
IC 6000 computer, 2:209
ICSU (International Council of Scientific Unions), 2:341, 361; 3:294
ICT 1900 computer, 1:213
Idaho library teletype network, 3:311
Ide, Eleanor, 3:1, 132, 164, 273, 274
IDEA data analysis program, 3:209
IDEEA (Information Data Exchange Experimental Activity), 3:314
IDS (Integrated Data Store), 1:125; 2:126, 134; 3:153

COMBINED INDEX   521

IEEE (*see* Institute of Electrical and Electronics Engineers)
IEEE Transactions on Electronic Computers, 2:191
IEEE Transactions on Human Factors in Electronics, 3:210, 303
Ieri, Aldo, 3:412
IFIPS (*see* International Federation of Information Processing Societies)
Iker, H. P., 1:76
ILLIAC IV computer, 2:212
ILLINET, 3:300
Illinois State Library, real-time circulation system, 3:257
IMP (Interface Message Processor), 3:227
IMRADS (Information Management, Retrieval and Dissemination System), 2:144, 147
IMS instructional management system, 3:363, 264
Independence Foundation of Philadelphia, 1:274
Index maintenance, 2:133
Index Medicus, 1:316; 2:315, 349; 3:122
Index term extraction, 2:104–106
Index term frequency, 1:87; 3:146
Index term weighting, 2:99; 3:140–141, 150–151, 159, 277–278
Index terms, chaining systems, 2:50
Indexer consistency, 1:84, 171; 2:69, 80; 3:82, 84–85, 119
Indexer training techniques, 3:274
Indexing and abstracting services, 1:79, 309–320; 2:343–345; 3:115
Indexing depth, relation to retrieval effectiveness, 1:80–81; 2:80; 3:82
Indexing languages, 1:90, 91, 174–181; 2:66–67, 91, 93–103
 control, 2:48–50, 87, 93–103; 3:118, 123
Indexing principles and theory, 1:80–95; 2:90–93
Indexing techniques, efficiency, 1:175–179; 3:122
India. Documentation Research & Training Center, 1:30
 National Scientific Documentation Center (INSDOC), 1:30
Indiana library communications network, 3:311
Indiana State Library, 3:280
Industrial and Engineering Chemistry, 1:46–47
INFO-COM message network, 3:317
INFOL (Information Oriented Language), 2:145, 147; 3:153

INFORM programming language, 3:381
Informatics, Inc., 1:125; 2:137
Information Centers, automation, 2:255–284
 DOD-sponsored, 2:53
 establishment by user needs analysis, 1:322–323; 2:46–47
 in South Africa, 2:28
Information centers and services, 1:305–335
Information Displays, Inc., 1:196
Information Exchange Group, National Institutes of Health, 3:15, 42
Information-gathering patterns, scientists, 1:49, 53–57, 59–60; 2:20–21, 28; 3:4, 11–12, 15, 19, 42, 65
Information Management, Inc., 2:403; 3:312
Information networks, 2:391–396; 3:289–327
 colleges and universities, 3:299-300, 301, 302
 Federal role, 3:294–295
Information Oriented Language (*see* INFOL)
Information Processing Code (IPC), 3:143
Information retrieval, behavioral studies, 2:77; 3:1–31, 79
Information Retrieval and Library Automation Newsletter, 3:241
Information science, definitions, 2:420–422
 education, 1:15–35; 2:432–439
Information Service in Physics, Electronics and Control (*see* INSPEC)
Information systems, design and evaluation, 1:171–190; 2:35–57, 63–82; 2:92; 3:61–103, 139
 dial-access, 3:303–304
 on-line, 2:52–53, 134, 197; 3:48–50, 55, 87–88, 154–160, 180–183, 190, 255, 267, 269–272
 request interpretation studies, 3:83–85
Information transfer, behavioral studies, 3:11, 14, 24
 conventions and meetings, 3:16–17, 22, 40–41, 65
 effect of cultural and political systems, 3:4, 22–23
 effect of organization policy and structure, 3:6, 13–14
Infronics, Inc., 2:351
Infosearch project, 3:18
Ingold, C. K., 2:295
Inktronic process, 3:48, 378
Inman, C. L., 3:131

522 COMBINED INDEX

INSDOC (see Indian National Scientific Documentation Center)
INSPEC (Information Service in Physics, Electronics and Control), 2:347
Institute for Scientific Information, 1:16; 3:279
Institute for the Advancement of Medical Communication, 1:67
Institute of Electrical and Electronics Engineers (IEEE), 1:62; 2:110; 3:12
Instructional management systems, 3:362–365
Instructional materials, computer-generated, 3:377–378
Integrated Data Store (see IDS)
Intelligence Information Processing System (see INTIPS)
INTELSAT, 3:302
Interdata Model 3 computer, 2:213
Interemic Equivalence Classes (IEC), 1:152–153
Interface devices, instructional systems, 3:378–379
Interface hardware, 2:230–236
International Atomic Energy Agency, 3:157, 312–313
International Business Machines Corp., 1:110, 125; 2:52, 130, 212, 213; 3:160 (see also IBM)
International Council of Scientific Unions (see ICSU)
International Federation for Documentation (FID), 1:20, 22, 29, 73
International Federation of Information Processing Societies (IFIPS), 1:139, 191, 193
International Labour Office, 2:29, 94, 113
International Micrographic Congress, 2:202
International Telephone and Telegraph Corp. (see ITT)
International Union of Pure and Applied Chemistry (IUPAC), 2:294
International Union of Pure and Applied Physics, 2:342
Interuniversity Communications Council (see EDUCOM)
INTIPS (Intelligence Information Processing System), 2:150
Invisible colleges, 2:367; 3:5, 14–15, 65
IOPAK code-compression system, 3:144
IPI instructional management system, 3:364
IPL-V programming language, 2:38; 3:152–153

Ipsen, Johannes, 3:412
Irick, P. E., 1:323
Irons, E., 2:174
Irwin, Manley R., 2:228; 3:228, 322
Isaac, A. M., 2:97, 100
Isaacs, Herbert H., 1:95, 262; 3:236
Isakov, P., 3:73
Isard, S., 1:145
ISI (see Institute for Scientific Information)
Itek Corp., 1:112, 204, 207; 2:208
Iterative search processes, 1:119–120; 2:71, 106; 3:141
Ithaca College, dial-access information system, 3:304
ITIRC (see IBM Technical Information Retrieval Center)
Ito, T., 1:195
ITT ADX 7300 computer, 3:278
ITTS graphical interaction system, 3:206
IUPAC (see International Union of Pure and Applied Chemistry)
Ivanov, M. V., 3:323
Iverson, K. E., 3:235
Ivie, Evan L., 2:240

Jackson, Betty S., 2:370
Jackson, David M., 3:135, 147, 166, 198
Jackson, Eugene B., 3:243, 265
Jackson, Ivan F., 3:249
Jackson, Larry K., 3:426
Jacobs, Charles R., 2:95
Jacobsen, William H., Jr., 3:164
Jacobus, David P., 2:330, 346
Jacoby, J. E., 1:84
Jaffe, Janet P., 3:336
Jaffee, Harry, 3:425
Jahoda, Gerald, 1:281; 2:5, 9, 30, 80, 436; 3:132
Jakobovits, Leon A., 3:7, 20
James, Richard T., 2:229
Janda, Kenneth, 3:275, 279
Janeway, Elizabeth, 2:412
Janke, N. C., 3:132
Janning, Edward A., 1:84; 2:49, 96, 98
Jenkins, J. E., 1:323
Jensen, Paul A., 2:127, 168
Jerman, Max, 3:358, 393
Jernigan, Elizabeth Thorne, 3:344
Jewett, Paul, 3:406
Johanningsmeir, Walter F., 1:100, 186
Johns Hopkins University, 1:287, 293
  Center for Research in Scientific Communication, 3:17, 65
Johnson, Bruce B., 3:239
Johnson, Harold R., 3:293, 295
Johnson, Howard W., 3:340

Johnson, J. Burlin, 2:359
Johnson, Katherine, 2:400
Johnson, Lyndon B., 3:289, 292
Johnson, Nicholas, 3:291
Johnson, Roger L., 3:319, 358, 362
Johnson, Thayne, 1:326, 329
Johnston, David A., 3:269
Joint Publications Research Service (JPRS), 1:162
Jolkovsky, A., 3:194
Jolliffe, J. W., 2:268
Jones, Arthur E., 2:228
Jones, James M., 3:97, 101
Jones, Malcolm M., 3:236
Jones, Paul E., 2:70, 77; 3:72, 75, 86, 120, 127, 140, 141, 187, 188, 189, 193
Jones, R. D., 3:87, 229, 313, 323
Jones, Robert C., 3:261
Jones, Robert G., 3:343
Jones, Shirli O., 2:267, 366; 3:51, 52, 57, 106, 254, 263–288, 266, 283
Jonker Business Machines Co., 1:204
Joshi, A. K., 1:162
JOSS (Johnniac Open Shop System), 1:264; 2:147, 225, 233; 3:205, 223, 381
Journal literature, 2:339; 3:15–16, 20, 32–35, 41–42
Journal of Biological Chemistry, 2:23
Journal of Typographic Research, 3:46
Journal of Verbal Learning and Verbal Behavior, 2:170
Jover, S. I., 3:92
JOVIAL programming language, 1:117; 2:146; 3:380
Judd, D. R., 3:316
Judy, Richard W., 3:370
Juhasz, Stephen, 1:82, 86; 2:112
Jukes, Thomas H., 2:368
Justice, Ben, 3:212

Kado, R. T., 3:427
Kain, R. Y., 3:49
Kaminstein, Abraham L., 2:411
Kamp, M., 3:426
Kango, Kiyoshi, 1:86
Kaplan, Ira T., 3:57
Kaplow, Roy, 1:233; 3:209
Karel, Leonard, 1:296, 316
Karp, Richard M., 2:38
Karush, W., 3:375
Kasarda, Andrew J., 3:92, 162, 192, 194, 273
Kasher, Asa, 1:159; 2:88, 137; 3:129, 191, 194
Kaskey, Gilbert, 2:50, 95, 102, 135

Katke, B. J., 3:195
Katter, Robert V., 2:65, 78, 79, 92; 3:7, 36, 70, 75, 77, 85, 88, 108, 114
Katz, Elihu, 3:14
Katz, Jerrold J., 1:76, 139, 140, 141, 142; 2:165–167
Katzenmeyer, William J., 3:323
Katz-Fodor theory, 1:141, 142
Kaufman, Roger A., 2:40
Kaula, P. N., 1:30; 3:344
Kavet, Joel, 3:423
Kawin, B., 3:423
Kay, Martin, 1:111, 141; 2:357; 3:111, 115, 116, 132, 183, 220, 236
Keen, Michael, 2:67, 87, 89, 90, 92, 97, 99, 101; 3:84, 85, 134, 193
Keenan, Stella, 2:339–384, 340; 3:20
Keenan, Thomas A., 3:226, 387
Keesecker, P. M., 3:44
Keller, Leo, 3:358
Kelley, K. L., 3:111
Kellogg, Charles H., 1:159; 2:138, 236; 3:111, 151, 164, 190, 236, 360
Kelman, G. S., 3:423
Kemeny, John G., 2:227; 3:236, 362, 371
Kemp, D. Alasdair, 2:369
Kennedy, Daniel N., 3:212
Kennedy, Edward M., 3:295
Kenney, Laraine, 2:29
Kenny, K., 3:58
Kent, Allen, 1:84, 305, 329; 2:41, 87, 330, 396, 434; 3:66, 67, 88, 297, 300, 317, 323, 423
Kentesc, Francis, 2:426
Kerby, H. R., 2:226
Kernel sentences, 1:162; 2:105, 177; 3:111
Kerr-Waller, R. D., 3:278
Kershaw, G. A., 2:53
Kertesz, Francois, 1:311, 326; 2:55
Kessler, M. M., 1:22, 246; 2:52, 241; 3:33, 159, 201, 236, 323
Keyword indexing, 1:82, 84, 86
Kiefer, Ferenc, 2:167
Kieffer, Paula, 2:258; 3:260
Kiersky, Loretta J., 2:364
Kikuchi, T., 3:166
Kilburn, T., 1:111
Kilgour, Frederick G., 1:276, 283, 284; 2:10, 262, 270, 362; 3:62, 249, 306
Kincade, Robert G., 3:19
King, Donald W., 1:85, 182; 2:75; 3:61–103, 65, 68, 73, 75, 81, 82, 94
King, G. W., 1:112, 154, 167
King, Harold B., 3:323
Kinney, Thomas D., 3:400

Kiriyama, Iwao, 1:203
Kirk, D. B., 3:124, 141, 274
Kirschner, Stanley, 2:141
Kittredge, R., 3:188
Klein, Sheldon, 1:141, 149; 3:181, 185
Kleinmuntz, B., 1:141, 149
Kleinrock, L., 3:229
Klempner, Irving M., 3:97
Klerer, Melvin, 3:44, 212
Kline, Nathan S., 3:424
Klingbiel, Paul H., 2:95
Klinger, R. F., 3:76
Klingman, J., 3:423
Klooster, A., Jr., 1:219
Kloss, G., 3:412
Kloss, K., 3:163
Knoke, P. J., 2:52
Knowlton, Kenneth C., 2:126
Knox, William T., 1:322, 324, 329, 339; 2:392
Knueven, P., 2:187
Knutson, Jack, 3:358
Knutti, Sarah H., 3:404
Kochen, Manfred, 1:26, 75, 78, 92, 121, 265; 3:132, 133, 170, 225
Koestler, Arthur, 3:12
Koford, J. S., 2:242
Kohlers, Paul A., 2:170
Kohn, Giuliano, 1:211
Kohn, R. S., 1:37
Kolb, Margaret C., 3:267, 423
Kolbe, Helen, 2:272
Kolk, A. J., Jr., 1:210
Koller, H. R., 1:26; 2:286
Kolstad, Per, 3:406
Konecci, Eugene B., 2:287, 288
Kooi, Beverly Y., 3:363
Kopstein, Felix F., 3:376, 382, 391
Korein, Julius, 1:270; 2:321; 3:408
Korfhage, Robert, 3:379
Korn, Henry, 3:400
Kornblum, R. D., 1:203
Körner, H. G., 1:92
Kornfeld, Leo L., 3:399
Korotkin, Arthur L., 1:92
Kosakoff, Martin, 1:124
Kosonocky, Walter F., 1:207
Köster, Kurt, 2:263
Kotani, Masao, 1:30
Kouris, M., 1:83; 2:348
Kovalevsky, V. A., 1:195
Kozak, Andrew S., 3:236
Kozma, A., 1:217
Kozumplik, William A., 3:254, 283
Kraft, Donald H., 1:175; 3:62, 97
Krakiwsky, M. L., 1:131, 266
Krasteva, Zorka, 3:420
Krebs, L. T., 3:369
Kreider, D. L., 3:359
Kreysa, Frank, 1:310, 327; 2:65, 73
Kriebel, C. H., 2:37
Krollman, F., 1:161
Kronenberg, R. A., 3:323
Kronick, David A., 1:50
Kronmal, Richard A., 2:132
Krug, Judith F., 3:338
Kudlaty, W. J., 1:82
Kuebler, Wolf, 2:369
Kuehler, J. D., 2:226
Kuehn, R. L., 3:89
Kuehne, C., 3:130
Kuhn, Thomas S., 3:28
Kulagina, O. S., 3:190
Kulkarni, J. M., 2:101
Kumar, Kalish, 2:369
Kuney, Joseph H., 1:46; 2:299, 350, 352, 356; 3:31–59, 43
Kuno, Susumu, 1:147, 150, 162; 2:162, 173, 174, 175; 3:172, 174, 181
Kuppin, M. A., 3:195
Kurfeerst, Marvin, 1:255, 269; 3:88, 96, 423
Kuroda, Sige-Yuki, 3:179
Kurtz, Thomas E., 2:227; 3:236, 358, 359, 362, 371
Kurtzke, J. F., 3:413
Kvalnes, F. H., 2:75
KWIC indexes, 1:45–46, 82, 85, 86, 277, 289; 2:20, 107, 108, 331
KWOC indexes, 2:267

L^6 list language, 2:126; 3:224
Ladenson, Alen, 3:338
Lakhut, D. G., 2:64
Lakoff, George, 2:163, 164
Lamb, Sidney M., 1:139; 3:131, 164
Lamkin, Burton E., 3:63, 249
Lampson, B. W., 1:231; 2:211; 3:193
Lamson, Baldwin G., 3:116, 399
Lancaster, F. W., 1:79, 80, 81, 85, 92, 173, 182; 2:54, 64, 65; 3:75, 81, 83, 84
Lance, G. N., 3:85, 126, 195
Landee, Franc A., 3:162
Landis, Daniel, 3:89, 97, 101
Landrum, John H., 3:320
Landwehr, J. B., 1:255
Landy, B., 3:162
Lang, C. A., 1:197, 230
Lang, W. Y., 3:48, 58
Lange, R. T., 3:254, 283
Langefors, B., 1:197
Langendoen, Terence, 2:164; 3:133

COMBINED INDEX 525

Langner, Mildred Crowe, 3:270, 417
Lanning, Lawrence E., 3:403
Large Capacity Storage (LCS), 2:206
Large-Scale Integration (LSI), 2:209-210
Larntz, F. Kinley, Jr., 3:358, 359
Laser displays, 1:206–207; 3:212
Laska, Eugene, 3:409
Lathey, Charles E., 3:293
Lathrup, J., 1:327, 329
Laucus, Carol A., 2:272
Lauer, Carol M., 1:98, 185
Lauer, Hugh C., 3:237
Laughery, K., 3:235
Laurie, Jean, 3:413
Law, H. B., 2:229
Law Enforcement Automated Data System (LEADS), 3:314
Lawler, Eugene L., 2:38
Lawson, Harold W., Jr., 3:152
Laymon, Richard S., 3:82
LC^2 programming language, 3:224
Leach, Theodore E., 3:320
Leader, Harrold, 3:424, 426
LEAP programming language, 3:214
Lebow, Irving, 3:269
Lebowitz, Abraham S., 2:273; 3:251, 252
Lederberg, Joshua, 3:237
Ledley, Robert S., 1:108; 2:297, 319
Lee, C. Y., 1:211
Lee, David, 3:426
Lee, Richard M., 3:424
Leech, P. C., 3:133
Lees, R. B., 1:139
Lefkovitz, David, 1:91; 2:128, 134, 136, 140; 3:142, 167
Lefkowitz, B., 3:92
Legal information, full-text storage and retrieval, 3:269
Legal Information Thru Electronics (see LITE system)
Legibility Project, National Bureau of Standards, 3:45
Legibility studies, 3:45–46, 89
Lehigh University, 1:32, 53, 201
  Center for the Information Sciences, 1:22; 2:37, 64, 275; 3:159–160, 273
Lehrer, Norman H., 2:198
Leimkuhler, Ferdinand F., 2:38; 3:63, 68, 97, 98, 150
Leinbach, Robert C., 3:426
Leishman, Reed O., 2:147
Leith, E. N., 1:195, 206
Leland, W. H., 3:420
Lendvayova, Olga, 3:133
Leonard, Faye, 3:260
Leonard, Jimmer M., 3:374

Leondar, Judith C., 3:129
Lerner, Rita G., 2:339-384; 3:131
Lesk, M. E., 1:80, 134, 160, 182; 2:69, 88, 90, 94, 96, 99, 107; 3:134, 189
Levery, Francis, 1:81
Levien, Roger E., 1:115, 2:88, 89, 103, 136, 138; 3:147, 191
Levine, Jack B., 3:370
Levine, P. H., 3:424
Levinthal, C., 2:295
Levitt, Donald G., 2:128, 329
Levy, Francis, 1:90, 185; 3:130, 192
Levy, Gertrude C., 3:133, 165
Levy, Richard P., 3:397–428, 425
Lewin, Morton H., 1:196, 210; 2:209
Lewis, Brian N., 3:375, 386
Lewis, John R., 2:329
Lewis, P. A. W., 1:94, 210; 3:110, 176, 188
Lewis, Robert F., 2:405
Libbey, Miles A., 2:105, 339-384; 3:15, 26, 133, 195
Libraries of the Future, 1:297–298
Library automation, 1:246, 273–303; 2:255–284; 3:269–272, 306
  and building planning, 3:311–312
  bibliography, 3:244
  current-awareness systems, 3:275–281
  SLA-ALA survey, 3:242–243, 258
  technical processes, 1:278–279, 280, 282–288; 3:241–262
Library buildings, impact of technology, 3:244
Library communication networks, 1:298; 3:310–312
Library cooperation, 3:306–308
Library education, 2:15–35
Library networks, 3:304–312
Library of Congress, 1:172, 286, 288, 289, 317, 345; 2:264, 266, 268, 269, 272, 278; 3:242–243, 305
  Automation Techniques Exchange (see LOCATE)
  National Referral Center for Science and Technology (see National Referral Center for Science and Technology)
  Project MARC (see Project MARC)
Library Services and Construction Act., 3:306
Library Technology Reports, 3:256
Librascope Division. General Precision, Inc., 1:202, 211; 2:130
Licklider, J. C. R., 1:222, 223, 228, 232, 241, 297; 2:52, 237, 386, 387, 388; 3:18, 43, 49, 201–240, 213, 237, 348
Lieberman, D. V., 1:147, 148, 162

Liebhold, K., 1:325
Lieblich, I., 3:131
Liebold, F. B., Jr., 3:212
Light, I., 1:325, 329
Limberg, Herman, 3:98
Lin, A. D., 1:110, 118
Lin, Thomas T., 2:95
LINC (Laboratory Instrument Computer), 2:317, 323; 3:204
Lincoln WAND, 2:197, 232
Lindberg, D. A. B., 1:257; 2:330; 3:400
Lindgren, Nilo, 2:230, 440
Lindquist, A. B., 2:211
Line, Maurice B., 2:18
Line drawings, encoding and manipulation, 3:145–146
Line printers, 1:200
Linebarger, Robert N., 3:239
Linguistic analysis programs, 2:162; 3:209
Linkage of data elements, 2:124–125, 135; 3:146–148
Links and roles, 1:92; 2:75, 90, 92, 97, 98
Lipetz, Ben-Ami, 1:43, 51, 85; 2:23, 88, 279, 330
Lipson, Joseph I., 3:378
LISP programming language, 1:156; 2:129, 136, 172, 234; 3:152–153, 205, 224, 380
List-organized files, 2:135; 3:148–150
List-processing, 1:114–116; 2:135, 199; 3:149, 152–153
List-processing languages, 2:126; 3:152–153, 224
List processors, 2:130
Liston, David M., Jr., 2:46; 3:24, 68
LITE system. 3:269
Littauer, S. V., 3:95
Little, John L., 3:47, 59
Liu, C. N., 3:58
LLMPS batch-processing system, 3:208
Lloyd, D. B., 1:125
Lloyd, G. A., 1:84
LOCATE, 2:256; 3:244
Lochak, D., 1:148; 2:164, 165
Lock, K., 1:209, 211
Lockheed Missiles and Space Co., 3:254, 283
Lockley, Lawrence C., 1:45
Loeber, Thomas S., 3:261
Logcher, R. D., 1:250
Loges, E. G., 2:53
Logical data elements, 2:124; 3:141–143
Lohmann, A. W., 1:195
LOLITA programming system, 3:152–153
Loman, D., 1:72
Londe, David L., 2:173; 3:177, 183

London, Gertrude, 1:88, 93; 2:95; 3:133, 183
London University, 1:197
Long, B. L., 1:310
Long, H. S., 3:373, 374
Long, John M., 3:133, 146
Long, Robert E., 3:130, 192, 209
Long Distance Xerography (LDX), 1:213; 2:191, 201
Long Island College Hospital, Hoagland Library, 3:309
Longyear, Christopher R., 3:193
Loomba, J. K., 1:100, 166
Lorch, Stephen, 3:225
Lorenz, John G., 3:305
Los Angeles County Hospital, 1:248
Los Angeles Police Department, 1:262
Love, H. H., Jr., 1:114; 2:103, 139
Lowe, Thomas C., 3:87, 93, 149, 163, 193, 272
Lowe, Thomas L., 3:87
Lowry, Charles D., 2:113
Lowry, W. K., 2:425
Lowry-Cocraft Abstracts, 1:319
Lucas, F. V., 3:424
LUCID programming language, 1:125, 155; 2:138, 145, 240; 3:153, 218
Luckie, Peter, 2:55, 64; 3:92
Ludman, Harold, 3:405
Lueck, Antoinette L., 3:64, 270
Luhn, H. P., 1:4; 2:88, 365
Luke, Ann, 3:333
Lulich, L., 1:323
Lundstedt, Sven, 2:91
Lustig, H. A., 1:203
Luxenberg, H. R., 3:89
Lykken, Louis, 2:370
Lyman, Elisabeth R., 3:319, 359
Lynch, Michael F., 1:131, 266; 2:89, 330; 3:51, 121, 146, 162
Lyon, Cathryn C., 3:282
LYRIC programming language, 3:381

Ma, R., 1:165
Maass, W. G., 1:213
MAC (*see* Project MAC)
MacDonald, H. R., 3:426
Machine-aided translation, 1:151–154; 3:87, 180, 182, 190
Machine-readable bibliographic records, 1:284–285, 286–289; 2:268–269; 3:245–248, 256–257, 271
MAchine-Readable Cataloging (*see* Project MARC)
Mack, James D., 2:275
MacKay, D. G., 2:171

MacLean, Roderick, 3:424
MacLennan, Hector, 3:424
Macy, Josiah, 3:428
MAD programming language, 3:227; 3:381
MADAM (Moderately Advanced DAta Management), 1:126; 2:149; 3:156–157
Maddock, Jerome T., 3:286, 423
Magee, Marguerite, 2:23
MAGIC (Machine for Automatic Graphics Interface to a Computer), 1:196
Magnafax Telecopier, 2:200
Magnavox DARE system, 2:202–203; 3:267–268
Magnino, Joseph J., Jr., 1:156; 2:111, 366; 3:160, 165, 190
Magnis, N. E., 1:226
Magnuski, H. S., 2:197
Maher, J. J., 1:86
Maizell, Robert E., 3:341, 342
Majewski, Zygmunt, 1:29
Makris, Constantine J., 2:356
Mallen, G. L., 3:375
Maloney, Clifford J., 1:83; 2:109
Maloney, James V., Jr., 2:312; 3:358, 422
Maloney, William F., 3:416
Management information systems, 1:247, 262–263; 2:243; 3:267
Man-computer communication, 1:221–254; 2:40–41, 197, 223–254; 3:160, 201–240, 272–273
 in computer-assisted instruction, 1:243–244; 3:358–360, 377, 378–379, 381, 386
 in counseling systems, 3:367–368
 in libraries and information centers, 1:246; 3:266
 on-line retrieval systems, 3:87–88, 180–182, 190, 266
Manfield, Elaine, 3:322, 423
Mann, Donald, 3:256
Mann, William C., 2:127, 168
Manning, R. T., 2:320
Mantell, LeRoy H., 2:387
Manual for Building a Technical Thesaurus, 2:93
Manual information systems, 3:265, 270
Manzone, M. G., 3:267
MAP mathematical analysis system, 1:233–234
Mapleson, W. W., 2:95, 331
MAPTEXT stylistic analysis program, 3:113
Maranchik, John, Jr., 1:322
MARC (*see* Project MARC)

Marchand, N., 1:216
Marden, Ethel C., 1:120; 2:51, 293
Margaritis, Paul G., 1:262
Margolis, J., 3:36, 122
Marill, Thomas, 3:300
Marine Midland Corp., 3:315
MARK III file management system, 1:125
Marks, Leonard H., 3:302
Marks, Melvin R., 2:77
Marks, S., 1:167
Markus, John, 2:344, 353, 354, 356
Markuson, Barbara Evans, 1:84; 2:88, 225–284, 269; 3:243, 324
Maron, M. E., 1:9, 115, 121, 191; 2:88, 89, 103, 104, 136, 138; 3:84, 147, 191
Marquis, Donald G., 1:59; 3:25
Marron, Beatrice A., 2:51, 140; 3:144, 163, 209
Marron, H., 3:70, 324, 336
Marsh, G. N., 3:424
Marthaler, Marc P., 2:94, 99, 107, 113
Martin, Eric W., 2:329
Martin, Miles, 3:65
Martin, William A., 3:237
Martinez, Samuel J., 3:271
Martins, Gary R., 1:152; 3:133
Martinson, John L., 3:352
Martyn, John, 1:58, 79, 85; 2:110; 3:67
Martz, Patricia, 3:399
Maryland, public library development, 3:307
Massachusetts General Hospital, computer project, 1:248, 257; 2:144, 147, 242, 324; 3:409
Massachusetts Institute of Technology, 1:59, 61, 64, 151, 196, 197, 229, 231, 234; 2:194, 235; 3:10, 33, 50, 159, 271–272
 Computer-Aided Design Project, 2:242
 CTSS system (*see* CTSS)
 Lincoln Laboratory, 1:241; 3:207, 208, 214–215, 300
 Project MAC (*see* Project MAC)
 Project TIP (*see* Project TIP)
Masterman, Margaret, 1:144, 3:182
Mathematical analysis systems, 1:233–234
Mathematical models, in classification studies, 1:90; 3:126
 in educational planning, 3:370
 in information systems analysis, 1:81, 86; 2:37, 38, 90, 102–103; 3:67–68
Mathers, Boyd L., 3:323
Matheson, James E., 3:375
Mathew, William D., 2:241

528 COMBINED INDEX

Mathews, Max V., 1:85, 160, 197, 200; 2:353; 3:39
Mathews, William D., 3:133, 190, 237
Mathiot, Madeline, 1:99, 165
MATHLAB symbolic computation program, 1:234
Matlack, R. C., Jr., 3:133
Matthew effect, in scientific research, 3:23
Matthews, F. W., 2:99; 3:159, 164, 166
Matthews, Geraldine, 1:197
Mattingly, Don, 1:124
Mattson, R. L., 1:195
May, Kenneth O., 3:133
Mayeda, T., 3:353
Mayer, S., 1:244
Mayer, S. R., 3:344
Mayer, Steven E., 2:43, 60, 86
Mayne, John G., 3:407
McCabe, John, 1:112
McCabe, LeRoy B., 3:98
McCandless, Nan P., 1:82, 86
McCarn, Davis B., 3:74, 75
McCarrick, Helen, 3:424
McCarthy, John, 1:225
McClelland, R. M. A., 2:95, 331
McConlogue, Keren L., 1:83, 147, 149
McCormick, Bruce H., 1:195
McCracken, Daniel, 2:237; 3:380
McCullough, J. D., 1:208
McCune, Lois C., 3:244
McDonald, D. F., 3:285
McDonnell, Patricia M., 1:120; 2:75, 292; 3:81, 82
McDonough, A. M., 2:39
McEachen, John C., 3:82
McFarlan, F. W., 2:39
McFarlane, R. E., 2:75
McGarvey, Alan R., 2:345
McGrath, William E., 2:272
McGrew, Elizabeth A., 3:427
McGuire, Christine H., 3:416
McGuire, Michael T., 3:225
McGuirk, J. A., 3:162
McIntosh, Stuart, 3:237
McJenkin, V., 3:342, 352
McKean, K. O., 1:145
McKnight, W. J., 3:316
McLaughlin, Curtis P., 1:69
McLean, John B., 2:150; 3:143, 149
McMullen, D. A., 2:140
McNab, J. W., 3:421
McNamara, J., 2:89
MDS 1101-DPC magnetic-tape encoder, 2:189
Meada, H., 1:219

Meade, Guthrie T., 3:260
Meadow, Charles T., 2:236; 3:165, 170
Meadow, H. R., 1:246
Mechanical-Chemical Code (MCC) for chemical compounds, 3:142
Medical Coding System (MCS), 3:142
Medical Data Screen (MDS), 2:318; 3:411
Medical education, 2:327; 3:415–417
Medical electronics, 2:325
Medical information systems, 1:248, 256–259; 2:311–338; 3:397–428
Medical libraries, bibliographic networks, 2:330–331; 3:309
Medical Library Assistance Act of 1965, 2:262, 265
Medical literature searching, 3:417–419
Medical records, recording and reporting systems, 2:316–318; 3:403–410
Medical scientists, information needs, 2:5, 8; 3:14, 18–19
Medi-data, Inc., 3:315
MEDLARS (MEDical Literature Analysis and Retrieval System), 1:119, 197, 295–297, 316; 2:73–75, 275, 314, 330, 405; 3:69, 81, 417–418
Meeker, Robert J., 3:135, 166, 208
Meetings and conventions, effect on journal publication, 2:15; 3:18, 40
information exchange patterns, 1:54–55, 66; 2:21, 370; 3:16–17, 22, 40–41, 65
Meighan, S. S., 3:342, 424
Meise, Norman, R., 2:393; 3:67, 306, 324
Meister, David, 3:87, 101
Melaragno, R., 3:375, 377
Mel'chuk, I. A., 3:190, 194
Mellner, C., 3:408
Melton, Jessica S., 1:183; 2:90, 105, 112; 3:185
Melville, Robert S., 3:400
Melvin, David Skene, 3:324
Memory Centered Processor (MCP), 2:112
Memory construction and design, 1:206, 209–211
Menden, Werner H., 3:80
Menne, Albert, 1:78
MENTOR programming language, 3:380
Menzel, Herbert, 1:8, 41–69, 42, 44, 45, 49; 2:1, 7, 27, 328; 3:2, 7, 9, 10, 12, 14
Merck, Sharp and Dohme information system, 3:267
Merendine, E., 2:53
Merritt, C. Allen, 1:95; 3:133, 266, 276
Mersel, Jules, 3:21
Merton, Robert, 3:23, 24
Messick, D. M., 3:366
Messier, M., 3:131, 164

Metal Powder Technical Information Center, 3:313
Metcalf, E. A., 1:82
Metcalfe, John, 1:91
Meteorological and Geoastrophysical Abstracts, 1:315
Meyer, E., 2:297
Meyer-Uhlenried, K. H., 1:92
Miami-Dade County serials systems, 2:272
Michael, G., 2:190
Michel, M., 2:187
Michelson, D., 3:274
Michener, James C., 2:187–222; 3:281
Michigan State University, 2:277; 3:158
MICRO document retrieval system, 2:52, 134
Microelectronics Abstracts, 1:319
Microfiche storage and retrieval, 1:204; 2:201–204; 3:53, 55, 272, 282–283
Microfilm book catalogs, 3:254
Microfilm storage and retrieval, 1:203–205, 293; 2:322; 3:52–53, 55, 267–268, 275, 282–283, 404
Microforms, publication and distribution, 3:52–53
 role in document retrieval, 3:282–283
Microprogramming, 2:208–209
Microthesauri, 2:97
Microwave networks for multimedia transmission, 3:310
Mikhailov, A. E., 3:196, 294, 332
Military communications systems, 3:314, 317
Military information systems, 1:259–261
Miller, Arthur R., 3:295
Miller, D. M., 2:32
Miller, Don K., 3:417
Miller, G. A., 1:145, 146
Miller, J. E., 1:160, 197, 200; 2:353
Miller, James G., 2:331, 395; 3:226, 312, 357, 387, 415
Miller, W. R., 1:146
Milliken, J. G., 3:94
Milliman, Gordon, 3:324
Mills, Jack, 1:81, 88, 183, 187; 2:83, 116; 3:193
Mills, R. G., 1:213, 229; 2:223–254; 3:201
MIMO input-output terminal, 1:195
Minckler, T. M., 3:424
Minder, Thomas, 2:278, 422; 3:307
Minker, Jack, 2:123–160; 3:153
Minnesota Hospital Service Association, 2:326
Minnesota Mining and Manufacturing Co., 1:196; 2:192
Minsky, Marvin L., 2:88

MIRACODE microfilm retrieval system, 1:314; 2:200; 3:53, 275, 283
Mission Bay Research Foundation, 1:319
M.I.T. (*see* Massachusetts Institute of Technology)
Mitchell, David S., 3:415
Mitchell, J. H., 3:404
MITRE Corp., 1:125, 147, 148; 2:137, 173, 174; 3:155–156, 161, 218
 Analysis Procedure for Transformational Grammars, 1:147–148; 2:165
Mitzel, Harold E., 3:358, 371, 373, 374, 375, 376
Moderately Advanced Data Management System (*see* MADAM)
Mohrhardt, Foster E., 3:306
Moise, J. E., 1:332
MOLDS management information system, 2:52
Molgaard-Hansen, R., 3:133
Molineux, James E., 3:366
Molnar, C. E., 3:234
Monroe, Margaret E., 3:338
Montague, Barbara A., 1:182
Montgomery, Christine, 1:83, 175
Montgomery, Edison, 3:66, 297
Montgomery, Edwin, 2:421
Montijo, R. E., Jr., 3:314, 325
Montillon, George D., 1:124
Monto, A., 3:426
Moody, L. A., 3:95
Mooers, Calvin N., 1:90, 117, 239, 240
Moore, Edythe, 3:62
Moore, Frederick J., 2:324
Moore, J. E., 2:92
Moore, William H., Jr., 3:135, 166, 208, 239
Moravcsik, Michael J., 2:369
Morchand, Charles A., 3:310
Morehouse, H. G., 2:277, 397
Morenoff, Edward, 2:150; 3:143, 149
Morgan, H. L., 1:263, 314; 2:140, 293
Morgan, R., 1:244
Morrill, Charles S., 3:386
Morrill, D., 3:424
Morris, William A., 3:21
Morrison, H. W., 3:387
Moser, C. A., 3:370
Moses, Joel, 3:201
Mosler Safe Company, 1:204; 2:202
 Selectriever system, 3:283
Mosmann, Charles J., 3:368, 371
Moss, R., 2:94; 3:118
Mota, Miguel, 3:418
Motherwell, George M., 2:102
Motorola Co., 1:200

530 COMBINED INDEX

Motorola TP-4000 printer, 1:200; 3:378
Mott, Thomas H., Jr., 3:387
Mountbatten, Earl, 2:387
Muckler, F., 1:236
Muerzeig, W., 1:243, 244
Muhlbach, Robert P., 2:356
Mullen, J. M., 2:297; 3:45, 58, 237
Muller, Robert H., 3:338
Mullins, Nicholas C., 2:367; 3:14
Multi-access computer systems, 2:228; 3:205–208
MULTICS time-sharing system, 2:197, 212, 224, 226; 3:203, 219–220, 229
MULTILANG coding system, 3:146
Multi-list file system, 3:148
Multimedia techniques in medical education, 3:416–417
Multiphasic Health Checkup, 2:317
Multiple Instantaneous Response File (MIRF), 1:114
Multiprocessing, 2:212
Mulvihil, John G., 2:90, 95
Mumford, L. Quincy, 2:404
Munger, Sara, 1:103
Munson, J. H., 3:82
Murdock, John W., 1:322; 3:24, 68, 330, 334
Muroga, S., 1:118
Murphy, D., 3:359, 373, 374
Murphy, Daniel L., 2:129, 136; 3:149, 224
Murray, Hubert, Jr., 2:45, 387
Murray, Joseph, 2:370
Murtha, J. C., 2:212, 226
Myatt, D. O., 1:322; 3:92
Myers, W. C., 1:216

Nance, Richard E., 3:64
NAS (*see* National Academy of Sciences)
NAS/NRC (*see* National Academy of Sciences—National Research Council)
NASA information services, 3:21–22
  SCAN system, 3:277
  Scientific and Technical Information Facility, 1:309, 318; 2:128, 278
  SDI system, 1:318; 2:111; 3:90, 277
  Tech Briefs, 3:22
  Technical Thesaurus, 2:97
  videotape document storage system, 2:203
Nassau County Library System, 2:265
Nathan, Gad, 3:74
National Academy of Sciences (NAS), 1:67, 68, 120, 348
  report on copyright problems, 3:54
  Task Group for Interchange of Scientific and Technical Information in Machine Language, 3:293
National Academy of Sciences—National Research Council. ALPAC report, 3:180, 190
  Committee on Information in the Behavioral Sciences, 3:24
  Committee on Modern Methods for Handling Chemical Information, 2:294
National Advisory Commission on Libraries, 2:401; 3:304
National Aeronautics and Space Administration (*see* NASA)
National Agricultural Library, 1:321; 2:19; 3:306
National Air Pollution Technical Information Center (NAPTIC), 1:46, 48
National Association of Educational Broadcasters, 3:302
National Bureau of Standards (NBS), 1:151, 196, 197, 344; 2:51, 140, 287, 297
  Legibility Project, 3:45
  program for digital data system standards, 3:293
National Cancer Institute, 3:280
National Cash Register Co., 1:125, 205; 2:204 (*see also* NCR)
National Clearinghouse for Mental Health Information (NCMHI), 3:90, 275
National Commission on Technology, Automation and Economic Progress, 3:293
National Crime Information Center (NCIC), 3:314
National Data Center proposal, 2:406–407
National Education Association, 3:369
National Electronics Research Council, 2:366
National Federation of Science Abstracting and Indexing Services (NFSAIS), 1:309
National Institutes of Health (NIH), 1:258, 348; 2:287
  Child Health and Human Development Information Center, 1:323
  Information Exchange Group, 3:15, 42
National Lending Library for Science and Technology (*see* Great Britain, National Lending Library for Science and Technology)
National Library of Medicine (NLM), 2:73, 262, 287, 330; 3:256, 270, 305–306, 417

MEDLARS project (*see* MEDLARS)
National Microfilm Association, 1:203; 2:201
National Military Command System (NMCS), 1:260
National Program for Acquisitions and Cataloging, 2:264
National Referral Center for Science and Technology, 1:309, 317, 343–344; 2:359
National Reprographic Centre for Documentation, 3:282
National Research Council Library (Canada), 1:277
National Science Foundation (NSF), 1:4, 68, 172, 173, 183, 293, 309, 317, 329, 348; 2:36, 76, 272, 286, 349, 359; 3:107, 255, 294, 308, 312
  Chemical Information Unit, 2:287
  information systems compendium, 3:265
  Office of Science Information Service (OSIS), 1:341, 345; 2:339
National science information networks, 3:312
National serials data program, 2:272
National Union Catalog, 1:286–287
NATO (*see* North Atlantic Treaty Organization)
Natural language processing, 1:297; 2:161–186; 3:169–199, 377, 410
Natural language processor, components, 3:176
Natural language programming, 3:225
Natural language retrieval systems, 1:155–159; 3:266, 269, 271–273
Natural language search strategies, 3:151
Natural language systems, code-compression techniques, 3:144
Natural language text-processing, 2:89, 103; 3:115–117, 160, 220
Naturmann, Louis I., 1:74
Naval, I. Alzona, 3:420
Naval Medical Research Institute, 3:359
Naval Weapons Laboratory, 3:282
Navy Training Research Laboratory, 3:359, 377
Naylor, W. C., 1:195
Naznitsky, I., 3:167
NBS (*see* National Bureau of Standards)
NCMHI (*see* National Clearinghouse for Mental Health Information)
NCR (*see also* National Cash Register Co.)
  315 Rod Memory Computer, 1:209
  735 Magnetic Tape Encoder, 2:189

Photo Chromic Micro Image microfiche system, 3:52
Neal, James P., 3:38
Nebel, B. E., 2:356
Needham, R. M., 1:91, 94, 143, 144; 3:162, 189
NEEDS (New England Educational Data System), 3:368
Neelameghan, A., 1:91, 175; 3:338, 340, 350
Neeland, Frances, 3:196, 237, 353, 424
Neese, R., 3:422
Nelson, Bryce, 3:196
Nelson, Edward A., 3:70
Nelson, Paul J., 3:160, 190, 276
Nelson, Theodore H., 1:95, 204; 2:197; 3:225
Netherlands, Technological University Library (Delft), 2:275
Neumann, P. G., 1:250; 3:234
Neurological information network, 3:418
Neuroscience information, 3:39–40, 415
Neuse, Durwood H., 1:134, 168
New England Library Network (NELINET), 3:310
New England Telephone and Telegraph Co., 2:233
New Era Data Systems, Inc., 1:193
New York Academy of Medicine, 2:329
New York Academy of Science, 1:259; 2:315
New York City Planning Commission, 1:320
New York Institute of Technology, 3:364
New York Metropolitan Reference and Research Library Agency, Inc., (METRO), 3:310
New York Public Library, 2:262
New York State, film library network, 3:308–309
New York State Library, industry information needs survey, 3:307
New York Times, 2:408
New York University. Linguistic String Project, 2:175
Newell, A., 1:242
Newell, G. R., 3:424
Newill, Vaun A., 1:173; 2:72; 3:76
Newmark, G., 3:377
Newmark, Mark, 3:124
Newton, John M., 3:322, 357, 373
NFSAIS (*see* National Federation of Science Abstracting and Indexing Services)
Nicolaus, John J., 1:278
N. I. H. (*see* National Institutes of Health)

Nike-X computer, 2:226
Ninke, W. H., 1:196
Nixi display tube, 2:276
NLM (see National Library of Medicine)
Nobbs, Peter M., 3:124
Nodien, John H., 3:424
Nolan, J. F., 1:123
Nordbye, Kjell, 3:406
Norman, Jacque B., 2:326
North, A. Frederick, Jr., 3:416
North, J., 3:353
North, R. C., 1:100, 166
North American Aviation, 2:193; 3:3, 13, 282, 283
North Atlantic Treaty Organization (NATO). Institute on the Evaluation of Information Retrieval Systems, 2:65
North Carolina State University, 3:300
Northern Virginia Community College, 3:372
Northwestern University, 1:18; 2:322; 3:279
Norton, A. C., 3:39, 415
Norton, L. M., 3:163, 193, 208
Noto, Thomas A., 3:400
Novak, Joseph D., 3:425
Novikov, I. I., 2:361
NSF (see National Science Foundation)
Nuclear Magnetic Resonance Abstracts, 1:319
Nuclear Physics, 2:343
Nuclear Safety Information Center, 1:321
Nuclear Science Abstracts, 2:27; 3:248
Nugent, William R., 3:255
NUPAK code-compression system, 3:144
Nursing, computer-assisted instruction, 2:199
Nyquist, E. B., 2:408

Oak Ridge National Laboratory (ORNL), 1:325
Oakford, Robert V., 3:369
Oatfield, Harold, 3:268
Obermayer, R., 1:236
Obukhova, O. I., 2:361
Oceanic Index, 1:319-320
Ochel, K. A., 1:166
O'Connor, Joel S., 3:269
O'Connor, John, 1:82, 175, 182; 2:79; 3:83, 108, 353
Odeh, Anna, 3:358
Odette, R. E., 3:326
OECD (see Organization for Economic Cooperation and Development)

Oettinger, Anthony G., 1:16, 137, 154; 2:242
Office of Naval Research, 2:36, 55, 359; 3:359
Office of Science and Technology (OST), 1:338, 339, 343; 2:286, 331
Office of Technical Services (OTS), 1:72
Official Airline Guide, 2:176
Ogilvie, Daniel M., 3:135, 198
Ohio Bell Telephone Co., business information system, 3:315
Ohio College Library Center, 3:310
Ohio State University, 1:151
  dial-access information system, 3:303
Ohlman, Herbert, 1:26
Ohringer, Lee, 2:351
Oklahoma Christian College, dial-access information system, 3:303
Oklahoma State University, 3:368
O'Leary, P. T., 2:92
Oliva, John J., 2:80; 3:132
Oliver, Lawrence H., 1:92, 101; 2:91
Oliveri, Blanche L., 3:306
Olle, T. William, 2:147; 3:153
Olney, John, 2:172; 3:177, 182
Olsen, Wallace C., 3:289-327
Olsson, David E., 3:425
Ommaya, A. K., 3:410
On-line bibliographic networks, 1:283-284; 3:308-310
On-line book ordering systems, 3:251
On-line information systems, 1:257-258; 2:52-53, 134, 197; 3:48-50, 55, 87-88, 154-160, 180-183, 190, 205-210, 217-220, 227, 255, 267, 269-272
On-line mathematical assistance programs, comparison, 3:209
On-line programming and debugging languages, 1:229-232; 3:223-225
On-line text editing, 1:160-161; 2:197; 3:45, 48-49, 51, 117
On-line text processing, 1:195; 3:49, 180-183, 208
Ontario (Canada) Province libraries, 2:265
OPL programming language, 1:230; 3:380
Opler, Ascher, 1:111; 2:209, 299
OPS programming language, 3:224
OPS-3 computation and simulation system, 1:234
Optical character recognition, 1:193-195, 287, 298; 2:188-191, 233; 3:46-47
  chemical structures, 2:297
Optical coincidence systems, 1:259; 2:95, 98; 3:267, 270, 275
Optical data storage, 1:207
Optner, Stanford L., 2:39

COMBINED INDEX 533

Oral Roberts University, dial-access information system, 3:304
Oregon State Library, 3:254
Organization for Economic Cooperation and Development (OECD), 3:370
Organization policy and structure effect on information transfer and use, 1:57; 2:25; 3:5-6, 13-14
ORNL (*see* Oak Ridge National Laboratory)
Orr, D. B., 3:190
Orr, J. S., 3:413
Orr, Richard H., 1:65, 84, 175; 2:65, 73, 80; 3:25
Osgood, Charles E., 1:146; 2:165; 3:7, 16, 20
Ossorio, Peter G., 1:90, 91
OST (*see* Office of Science and Technology)
O'Sullivan, Thomas C., 3:209
O'Toole, John F., Jr., 3:368
O'Toole, Richard, 2:327; 3:406
Otten, Klaus W., 2:234
Overhage, Carl F. J., 1:274; 3:35, 237
Overlap of abstracting and indexing services, 1:79
Owens, Donald H., 1:325, 329
Oxford University. Bodleian Library, 2:261
Oxhandler, Eugene K., 3:309, 325
Ozark Pioneer Library System, 3:311

Pacific Aerospace Library, 1:82
Packer, Rod E., 1:264
Page, E. B., 3:367, 392
Page, Irvine H., 2:363
Paige, Jeffry M., 2:171
Painter, Ann F., 1:72; 2:436
Paisley, William J., 1:26, 44, 80; 2:31, 340, 363, 367; 3:1-30, 2, 7, 16, 19, 21, 134
PAL programming language, 3:224
Palmer, Foster M., 2:262, 269
Palmer, P. E. S., 3:410
Palmer, R. R., 3:401
PANDEX, 3:260
Panning, Ida J., 1:306
Papier, Lawrence S., 1:173, 183; 2:95
PARD (Precision Annotated Retrieval Display), 3:267
Park, M. K., 3:45
Parker, D. B., 1:238; 2:198
Parker, Edward K., 2:112
Parker, Edwin B., 2:363, 364, 367; 3:16, 25, 26, 29, 121, 196
Parker, Ralph H., 2:266; 3:204

Parkhi, R. S., 3:340
Parkhouse, James, 3:425
Parkins, Phyllis V., 1:349; 2:330, 346
Parks, W., 3:333, 353
Pasek, Robert L., 2:113
Pask, Gordon, 1:27; 3:375, 386
Pasternack, R. F., 1:120, 267; 2:292
Pasternack, S., 2:343, 367, 369, 403
Patent information systems, 1:261
Patient data systems, computer-assisted, 2:317; 3:403-410
Patrick, Robert L., 3:261
Pattern Congruity Method, 2:80, 92
Pattern recognition, radiographs and radio-isotope scans, 3:401, 414-415
Payne, Aubrey H., 2:53
Payne, Charles T., 3:255
Payne, Dan, 1:79
Payne, Lawrence Charles, 3:425
PDP-1 computer, 1:248; 2:194; 3:149, 204-205, 214, 215
PDP-4 computer, 2:196
PDP-6 computer, 2:225; 3:206
PDP-8 computer, 2:213; 3:160, 204
PDP-8S computer, 3:204
PDP-10 computer, 2:210
Pearson, J. S., 3:394
Peckham, Ben M., 3:426
Pellegrino, J. A., 3:211
Pelz, Donald C., 3:2, 10, 11, 14
PENCIL graphic encoding language, 3:145-146
Pendergraft, E. D., 1:152
Pennsylvania State University, 1:19, 24; 3:358, 359, 368, 371, 373-374
Perreault, Jean M., 1:90, 91, 92; 2:101; 3:134, 192
Perry Publications, 1:193
Personal indexes, 2:9-10
Perstein, M. H., 3:380
Pessin, V., 3:401
Pesticides Information Center, 1:323
Peters, Bernard, 3:229
Peters, Stanley, 2:164
Petersen, Harold E., 3:229
Peterson, E. L., 3:402
Peterson, G. D., 3:92
Peterson, Norman, 3:92, 285
Petrick, S. R., 1:147, 148, 150, 165; 2:173
Pfaff, W. A., 1:203
Pfeffer, Harold, 2:64
Pfizer Medical Research Laboratories, 3:246
Pflug, Gunther, 2:268, 276
Pharmaceutical information (*see* Drug information)

Pharmacy management, computer-assisted, 3:403
Phelps, Ralph H., 3:70
Philco Corp., 1:193, 199, 296; 2:189, 190
Philco 102 computer, 3:372
2000 CPU, 3:372
Philco-Ford instructional system, 3:303, 372
Philipson, Herman, 2:190
Phillips, A. H., 2:352
Phonetic coding, 2:108, 243
Photocharge system, 1:206
Photochromic glass display device, 3:212
Photochromic Microimage System (PCMI), 2:204
Photochromic recording techniques, 1:205-206, 210
Photocomposition, 1:199-200, 296-297, 317-318; 2:349, 352-358; 3:47-48, 263, 278
Photodigital storage devices, 2:202-204, 226; 3:221-222
Photointerpretation systems, 2:236
Photon phototypesetters, 1:199, 296; 2:278, 299, 355; 3:214
Photostore, 1:112, 118
Phrase-indexing systems, 3:51, 121, 146, 273
Phrase-structure grammars, 3:172, 175, 178, 182
Physical Review, 2:341
Physical sciences abstracting services, 2:112
Physicists, information-exchange patterns, 2:16, 27; 3:15, 20
Physics abstracts, 2:22, 27, 28, 340, 347
Physics journals, 2:341
Physiological measurements, computer-assisted analysis, 1:258; 3:413-415
Pickford, A. G. A., 3:274
Picture transmission, 1:212
Pierce, John R., 2:228; 3:33, 285
Pierce, K., 3:420
Pietsch, E. H., 1:22, 29
Piez, Gladys T., 1:291
PIL programming language, 3:208, 223
Pilloton, R. L., 1:325
Pings, Vern M., 2:13; 3:65, 418
Pipberger, Hubert V., 3:420, 423
Piróg, Wojciech, 1:29
Pittsburgh Regional Library Center, 3:307-308
Pizer, Irwin H., 3:309, 320, 418
PL/1 programming language, 2:126, 209; 3:152, 247, 252, 258-259

PLAN (Program for Learning in Accordance with Needs), 3:364
PLANIT (Programmed LANguage for Interactive Teaching), 3:362, 381
Planning Research Corp., 1:296
Plasma display panels, 2:198; 3:211, 379
Platnick, Phyllis, 2:268
PLATO system, 2:199, 238; 3:359
Platt, John R., 1:297
Plummer, William W., 3:232
Poindron, Paul, 1:29
Poland, C. B., 1:110
Polansky, R. B., 1:217
Political and cultural systems, effect on information transfer, 3:4, 22-23
Pollack, Seymour V., 2:314
Pollock, Stephen, 3:72, 73, 139
Polymer Science and Technology (POST), 2:347
Pool, Ithiel D., 2:240
Poole, Harry H., 2:198
Popecki, Joseph T., 2:270
Popov, Ivan, 3:420
Poppelbaum, W. J., 2:204
Pordy, Leon, 3:425
Postal, Paul M., 1:139, 140, 141, 142; 2:164, 165, 166
Postlethwait, S. N., 3:425
Postley, John A., 1:124; 2:51
Poterack, James, 3:285
Potter, Bob, 3:425
Poulton, R. K., 3:94
Powers, Dan, 3:325
Powers, Ruth V., 2:128; 3:167
Pratt, Peyton, 3:406
Precision Annotated Retrieval Display (*see* PARD)
Precision Instrument Co., 2:205
Predictive parsers, 2:174, 178
Prelog, V., 2:295
Prentice, Donald D., 1:109, 113
Preparata, F. P., 3:128, 130, 147
Preprints, 2:368; 3:33
President's Committee on Libraries, 2:259, 401
President's Science Advisory Committee (PSAC), 1:338, 341; 2:329
President's Task Force on Communications Policy, 3:292-293
Press, Laurence I., 3:209
Presto, Andrew J., 3:426
Price, Derek De Solla, 2:367; 3:4, 5, 12, 14, 15
Prince, M. David, 2:198
Prince, Thomas R., 2:39
Prisendorf, Anthony, 2:406

Privacy and security in computer systems, 3:229, 295
Probabilistic techniques for key address assignment, 2:132
Problem-oriented programming languages, 1:230–231; 3:224
Problem solving, 1:241–243
computer interaction, 2:223–254
Proctor and Gamble Co., 1:124
Professional societies, role in information science, 1:347–349; 2:423–431
Program budgeting for educational planning, 3:370
Program Management System (PMS), 2:126
Program packages, 3:208–210
Programmed texts, use in medical education, 3:415–416
Project CADRE, 3:278
Project GROW, 3:385
Project INTREX, 1:18, 265, 274–276; 2:187, 261, 280; 3:55, 160, 220, 271–272, 282, 308
Project LEX, 2:48, 93, 97, 107, 399
Project LOCAL (Laboratory for Computer-Assisted Learning), 3:362
Project MAC, 1:123, 196, 225, 226, 229; 2:212, 231; 3:159, 206, 371
Project MARC, 2:258, 269; 3:242–243, 245–248, 251, 310
Project SHARP, 1:278–279
Project TIP, 1:246; 3:159, 219, 308
Pronko, Eugene, 1:173; 2:349
Proppe, Albin, 3:425
Protosynthex I, 1:160
Protosynthex II, 1:158
Prywes, Noah S., 1:245, 246; 2:89, 106, 125, 135
PSAC (see President's Science Advisory Committee)
Psycholinguistics, 1:145–146; 2:170–171
Psychological Abstracts, 2:340, 349
Public Broadcasting Act of 1967, 3:292
Public Health Service, 1:46
Division of Air Pollution, 1:322
Office of Pesticides, 3:280, 281
Public school systems, use of instructional management systems, 3:363–364
Publication and distribution of information, 2:339–372; 3:31–59
Purdue University, 1:18; 2:38
Pye, Ltd., 1:213

Q-32 Computer, 1:234; 2:227; 3:151, 154, 206, 218
Quade, E. S., 2:40; 3:99

Quarton, Gardner C., 2:236; 3:225
Quatze, Jesse, 2:233
Query formulation, 2:136, 143–144; 3:110–111, 151, 179, 363
Question-answering systems, 1:154–160; 2:177; 3:177–181, 183, 190–191, 221, 360–361
QUIKTRAN programming language, 2:212; 3:381
Quillian, M. R., 1:76, 141, 144; 2:161–186; 3:129, 134, 169, 192, 220
Quinn, E. M., 3:358
Quirk, Randolph, 1:76
Quirk, W. B., 3:228, 238, 322
QUUP query language, 3:363

Rabinow Engineering Co., 1:193, 287 (see also Control Data Corp.)
RADC (see Rome Air Development Center)
Rader, Gary, 3:279
Radio Corp. of America, 1:196, 199, 200, 208, 210, 211; 3:302, 303, 372, 385 (see also RCA)
Radov, Karl B., 3:358
Ragan, Lawrence, 3:325
Ragusa, Dorothy, 3:423
Rahman, Abdul, 3:340
Raisig, L. Miles, 2:10, 111
Rajchman, T. A., 1:209
Ramage, William W., 3:378, 379
Ramgren, O., 3:402
RAND Corp., 1:141, 151, 162, 196, 228, 238; 2:138, 233; 3:220, 295
RAND tablet, 1:196, 238; 2:195, 196; 3:181, 204, 211, 213
Random-access storage device, 1:202; 2:226
Randomatic Data Systems, 1:203
Randomizing search techniques, 2:132
Randt, Clark T., 1:270; 3:408
Ranganathan, S. R., 1:89, 91; 3:338, 340
Rapaport, A., 3:366
Raphael, A., 3:353
Raphael, Bertram, 1:156; 3:49
Rapp, Fredericka, 3:93, 100, 163, 193, 287
Rapp, Marjorie L., 3:131, 194
Rardin, Thomas E., 2:323
Rath, Gustave J., 2:29; 3:18, 325
Rational Data File, 2:138–139
Raver, N., 1:134
Rawski, Conrad H., 2:344
Raytheon Corp., DIDS 400 display console, 2:197
Space and Information Systems Division, 3:209

Rayward, W. Boyd, 3:82, 119
Razar, Michael, 1:121
RCA (*see also* Radio Corp. of America)
  Spectra 70 computers, 2:209; 3:372
READ (Real-time Electronic Access and Display), 1:196
Read-only storage, 2:208–209
Reagan, F. H., Jr., 2:228
Recall and precision studies, 2:67; 3:74–75, 80, 81, 88
Recognition Equipment, Inc., 1:193; 2:190
Recordak Corp., 1:204 (*see also* Eastman-Kodak Co.)
Recursive graph structures for semantic representation, 2:168
Reddy, J. M., 3:387
Redfern, P., 3:370
Redman, Helen F., 2:370
Redstone Arsenal, library automation project, 3:250, 269
Reed, David M., 2:64, 104, 105; 3:92, 162, 192, 273
Reed, J. B., 2:112
Reed, Sarah R., 1:20
Rees, Alan M., 1:22, 173, 182, 183; 2:63–86, 260, 340; 3:7, 70, 77, 99, 107, 191
Reference retrieval systems, 1:289–290; 3:159–160, 201, 204, 219
Reference services, automation studies, 1:279; 2:274–275
  user studies, 2:23, 29
Reich, A., 1:206, 210
Reich, D. L., 1:114
Reichertz, P., 3:412
Reid, J. Christopher, 3:379
Reimann, O. A., 1:210
Reisman, Arnold, 3:375
Reisner, Phyllis, 1:88, 93, 2:48
Reitman, Walter R., 1:242; 2:103
Reitz, Gerhard, 1:152; 3:48, 197
Relational structure manipulation, 2:127
Relevance studies, 1:91, 173–174, 183; 2:65, 69, 74, 77–80; 3:7–9, 36, 70–74, 76–79, 81, 84, 87, 88, 107–109, 115, 161, 185
  interpretation of requests, 2:79; 3:83, 273–274
Remsen, Douglas B., 2:345
Report generators, 3:154
Report literature, characteristics, 2:369–370
Representation of semantic information, 2:168–169
Request processing, by telephone, 3:18–19
Request stacking model for document access, 2:134

Research in Education, 3:270
Research-in-progress information systems, 3:314
Research laboratories, information flow 2:25; 3:10–11, 13
Reservation systems, 2:197; 3:314–315
Reslock, Mary H., 3:162
Resnikoff, H. L., 3:197
Retrieval systems, request interpretation studies, 3:83–85
Revard, Carter, 3:196
Review of Metal Literature, 2:348
Reynolds, A. G., 3:130
Reznikoff, Marvin, 3:425
Rhode Island. Dept. of State Library Services, 3:307
Rhodes, J. M., 3:427
Rhorbacker, Donald L., 2:131
Rian, John F., 1:131, 267
Rice University, 3:246
Rich, Robert P., 1:20
Richard, O. W., 3:342
Richardson, Charles A., 3:402
Richardson, Jesse O., 2:238
Richardson, Robert J., 3:364
Richmond, Phyllis A., 1:76, 84, 89, 91, 92; 2:54, 64, 99
Riddles, A. J., 1:95, 182, 261
Rieders, Frederic, 3:424
Riester, A. W., 2:75
Rigby, Malcom, 1:72, 315
Rigby, Perry, 3:406
Rigney, Joseph W., 3:362
Riley, Wallace B., 2:367
Ring, Otto, 1:92
Ripperger, E. A., 2:348
Rippy, D. E., 1:196
Ritchie, R. W., 3:359
Rivest, E. L., 3:385
Roberts, A. Hood, 3:270
Roberts, Lawrence G., 1:115, 237; 2:137, 197, 232; 3:211, 226, 238, 300, 325
Robertson, George J., 3:425
Robertson, Joseph G., 1:134
Robinson, J., 1:141
Robinson, Jane J., 1:83; 3:179
Robinson, M. C., 3:426
Rocappi Service Center, 1:197
Rocchio, Joseph J., Jr., 1:119, 173, 182; 2:64, 131; 3:197
Rochester Conference on Data Acquisition and Processing in Biology and Medicine, 2:315
Rockwell, M. A., Jr., 3:426
Rodgers, Theodore S., 3:358
Rogers, Bruce G., 3:366

COMBINED INDEX   537

Rogers, Frank B., 2:275, 405
Rogers, Miles S., 3:209
Rohlf, Robert H., 3:311
Rolling, Loll N., 1:76; 2:75, 96, 111
Romano, Michael T., 3:417, 425
Rome, H. P., 3:394
Rome Air Development Center (RADC), 1:116, 194; 2:130, 137, 150
Rosa, J., 1:196, 239
Rose, Charles A., 3:345, 425
Rose, F. C., 3:45, 57
Rosen, Charles A., 3:415
Rosenbaum, Joseph, 2:237; 3:358, 377, 380
Rosenbaum, Peter S., 2:164, 165; 3:134, 180, 238
Rosenberg, Art, 2:225
Rosenberg, Mervin, 3:409, 410
Rosenberg, Ronald D., 3:212
Rosenberg, Victor, 1:120; 2:21, 29; 3:9, 65
Rosenblatt, D., 3:95
Rosenbloom, Richard S., 1:62, 64, 323; 2:390; 3:10, 12, 13, 14, 65
Rosenblum, Marcus, 1:323; 3:418
Rosenquist, B. A., 3:93, 99, 388
Rosenstock, Henry M., 2:361
Rosenthal, Ethel, 3:427
Rosner, Stuart W., 3:426
Ross, Douglas T., 1:197; 2:242; 3:148
Ross, John Robert, 1:162; 2:164
Rossini, Frederick D., 2:360
Rossmassler, S. A., 2:361
Rostow, Eugene, 3:292
Rothenberg, L., 2:72; 3:198, 343
Rothman, John, 2:110
Rothstein, Samuel, 1:30
Rotz, F. B., 1:219
Roudabush, Glen E., 1:160, 161, 197, 201; 2:351
Rovner, Paul D., 2:129
Rowell, John T., 3:27
Rowland, George E., 3:65
Rowland, T. J., 2:369
Rubenstein, A. H., 2:33
Rubenstein, Herbert, 1:95, 145; 2:171
Rubin, J., 2:187
Rubinoff, Elayne R., 3:79, 80, 100, 197
Rubinoff, Morris, 1:83; 2:96, 97, 110; 3:84, 87, 93, 111, 134, 163, 183, 272
Rudin, Bernard D., 2:104, 108; 3:121
Rudin, Irving S., 3:106
Ruecking, Frederick, Jr., 3:246, 251
Rugari, Anthony D., 3:212
Ruhl, Mary Jane, 1:82, 175
Rule, D. F., 3:44
Rush, J. E., 3:167
RUSH time-sharing system, 2:212; 3:229

Russell, Bertrand, 2:94
Russell, Martin, 1:315; 3:121
Russell, Susan J., 2:272
Russell, William S., 3:399
Russell Soundex Alphabet, 2:134
Russian text indexing, 2:108–109
Rutgers University, 1:22, 91, 326
Ruyle, Adrian, 3:209
Rydell, L. H., 3:425

Sable, Jerome, 1:125, 128; 2:123–160, 135, 142; 3:153, 154, 163
SABRE reservation system, 2:197, 213
Sackman, H., 3:95, 100
Sadowsky, D., 3:410
SAFARI text-processing program, 3:49, 116–117, 161, 175, 208
Sage, C. R., 2:99, 112, 365
SAGE (Semi Automated Ground Environment), 2:195
Sager, Donald, 3:344
Sager, Naomi, 2:175; 3:187
Saha, J., 1:30
St. Laurent, M. C., 3:82, 119
St. Louis Junior College District, book catalog, 3:254
St. Ville, Joseph M., 3:426
Sakai-Cocke, Itiro, 2:174
Saki, T., 1:193
Salkoff, M., 3:187
Salmon, Stephen R., 3:243, 333
Salton, Gerard, 1:26, 29, 80, 119, 121, 155, 160, 161, 182, 245, 329; 2:52, 65, 69, 88, 90, 94, 96, 99, 126, 127, 131, 364; 3:80, 85, 109, 134, 140, 147, 151, 169–199, 185, 197, 273
Saltzer, Jerome H., 1:226; 2:225
Salzman, Roy M., 2:126
Sammet, Jean E., 2:235
Samuel, A. L., 1:226
Sanders 720 display console, 2:197
Sandia Corp., 3:270
Sansom, F. John, 3:239
Saporta, L. J., 1:216
Saporta, S., 1:139
Sapru, R. P., 3:426
Saracevic, Tefko, 1:22; 2:65, 72, 77; 3:81, 191, 343
Sasaki, Sharon, 3:260
Sass, Margo A., 3:238
Sastri, Madagula I., 2:112; 3:87
SATCOM (Committee on Scientific and Technical Communications), 1:348; 2:261, 401–402
Satellite communications, 2:399–400; 3:301–302

Satterthwait, A. C., **1**:153
Saunders, W. L., **3**:354
Savage, Terry L., **1**:113; **2**:104
SAVIS audiovisual interface units, **3**:385
Savitt, Donald A., **1**:114; **2**:103, 139
Sayer, J., **2**:390
Sayers, B. M., **3**:426
SCAN current-awareness system, **3**:277
Scansistor optical scanning device, **1**:194
Scarrott, G. G., **1**:110, 209, 210
SCC 650 computer, **2**:213
Schafer, Emil, **1**:84, 85
Schaffir, K. H., **3**:95
Schane, Jean E., **2**:164, 173
Schatz, Sharon, **3**:325
Schatzoff, M., **1**:247; **3**:100
Schay, G., Jr., **1**:118
Schecter, George, **3**:166, 170
Scheduling by computer, **3**:369, 403
Scheele, Martin, **1**:92
Scheffler, F. L., **3**:82, 274
Scherr, A. L., **1**:227
Schirmer, Robert F., **1**:83; **2**:94, 96, 109
Schmidt, Dean A., **2**:315
Schmitz, Richard F., **3**:131
Schneider, John H., **3**:90, 190, 280
Schneidewind, Norman F., **3**:100, 362
Schoene, W. J., **3**:195
Schoenfeld, Robert L., **3**:426
Schon, D. A., **1**:311
Schoonard, J. W., **3**:358
Schorow, Mitchell, **3**:426
Schreider, Y. A., **1**:75, 76
Schuchmann, Martin, **1**:84, 92
Schuck, H. J., **1**:166
Schultheiss, Louis, **2**:42, 266
Schultz, Claire K., **1**:84, 175; **2**:65, 80, 370, 434; **3**:333
Schultz, Douglas G., **2**:78; **3**:7, 70, 77, 107
Schultz, J. L., **2**:86
Schultz, Jan R., **3**:377
Schultz, Louise, **3**:27
Schultz, Wallace L., **1**:105, 189
Schum, David A., **1**:243, 271
Schumacher, Anne W., **2**:55, 76
Schur, Herbert, **1**:30; **3**:354
Schurdak, John, J., **3**:392
Schure, Alexander, **3**:364
Schwartz, Bettina C., **1**:98, 185
Schwartz, H. A., **3**:373, 374
Schwartz, Jules, **1**:227, 264, **3**:100, 206, 371
Schwetman, Herbert D., **3**:425
Science, **2**:400
Science Citation Index, **2**:111, **3**:122

Science Information Exchange (SIE), **1**:84, 309, 344–345; **2**:73; **3**:69
Science information networks, **3**:294, 312
Scientific and Technical Aerospace Reports (STAR), **1**:318
Scientific Data Systems Co., **3**:381 (*see also* SDS)
Scientists, as authors, **3**:35–36
 information-gathering patterns, **2**:5–8, 10–11, 16–28; **3**:4, 11–12, 15, 19, 42, 65–66
Scientists and technologists, information needs and uses, **1**:45–56; **3**:1, 10–11, 17, 31, 65
Scoones, M., **3**:252
Scott, Christopher, **3**:12
Scott, R. W., **1**:325, 329
Scratchpad memories, **1**:210–211
SCRIBE, case history system, **3**:410
SDC (*see* System Development Corp.)
SDI Systems, **1**:295; **2**:99, 111–112, 365–367; **3**:89–90, 160–161, 190, 276–281, 418
SDS 940 computer, **3**:205, 224
SDS Sigma 2 computer, **2**:213
SDS Sigma 7 computer, **2**:210
Sea-Launched Information Analysis Center, **2**:47
Search strategies, **1**:112–113, 118–122; **2**:128, 131–136; **3**:84–85, 140–141, 150–152, 155, 157–160, 251, 266, 273, 277–279
Searle, Victor C., **1**:46, 48, 322
Searls, Donald T., **3**:130, 163
Secondary Key Retrieval, **1**:110
Secondary publications, **2**:343; **3**:67
Securities and Exchange Commission. Financial Library, **3**:282
Sedelow, Sally Yeates, **1**:159, 160; **3**:113, 183, 188
Sedelow, Walter A., Jr., **1**:159, 160; **3**:188
Sedgwick Printout Systems, **3**:254
See, Richard, **1**:151; **3**:101
Seeley, L. C., **3**:366
Segarra, Carlos O., **3**:70, 271
Segel, Ronald R., **3**:331
Seibert, Warren F., **1**:26
Seidel, R. I., **3**:376, 382, 391
Seiden, Herbert R., **3**:27
Seismological Society of America, **1**:45
Selected Current Aerospace Notices (*see* SCAN current-awareness system)
Selective Dissemination of Information (*see* SDI systems)
Selectriever system, **2**:202; **3**:283
Selfridge, Oliver, **3**:226

Semantic analysis, 1:141–146; 2:105, 165–170; 3:51, 87, 111, 175–180, 273, 360
Semantic dictionaries, 3:176
Semantic memories, 1:144–145, 3:220–221
Semple, Parlan, Jr., 2:143, 239
Senett, W. P., 3:131
Sentence analysis, 2:161, 164; 3:111
SEPOL programming language, 1:231
Sequencing linkage, 2:125
Serials acquisitions systems, automated, 1:282–283; 2:271; 3:252
Shank, Russell, 1:74, 85; 2:367; 3:270, 341
Shapiro, R. M., 1:127
Shared Memory Computer Display System, 2:196
Sharmir, E., 3:129
Sharp, John R., 1:73, 74, 75; 2:48, 87–122, 108; 3:135, 170, 191
SHARP (*see* Project SHARP)
Shaw, Christopher J., 2:243
Shaw, J. C., 1:264; 3:239
Shaw, Ralph R., 1:42, 296, 297; 2:6, 103; 3:253
Shaw, T. N., 3:275
Shelf lists, 1:285, 287, 293
Shelton, G. L., Jr., 3:58
Shenderov, V. Z., 3:75
Sher, Irving H., 3:279
Shera, Jesse H., 1:22; 2:273, 274, 344, 435; 3:331
Sherrington, Andrew M., 2:65, 73
Sherrod, John, 1:9, 33, 327, 329, 337–351, 340; 2:403, 407
Shiff, Robert, 3:282
Shillan, D., 1:144; 2:104
Shilling, Charles W., 1:56, 58, 61, 67, 175, 184; 2:432, 435; 3:13, 354
Shindell, Sidney, 2:327
Shipman, Joseph C., 2:274, 344
Ships Analysis and Retrieval Project (*see* Project SHARP)
Shirey, Donald L., 3:88
Shively, R., 1:209
Shoffner, Ralph M., 1:112; 2:270, 277, 397; 3:137–167
Sholtz, Paul N., 3:407
Shubin, H., 3:426
Shuford, E. H., 1:243
Shumway, R. H., 3:85, 128
Shure, Gerald H., 3:135, 154, 208
Sibley, W. L., 3:213
Siders, R. A., 2:198
SIE (*see* Scientific Information Exchange)
Siegel, Arthur S., 3:89
Siegmann, Philip J., 2:340, 348, 351, 426

Siekevitz, Philip, 2:368
Silberman, Harry F., 3:357–395, 360, 363, 374, 377
Siler, William, 3:400
Sillers, S. J., 1:120
Silveira, H. M., 1:197
Silver, Carl A., 3:89, 97
Silvern, Gloria, 1:244; 3:326, 358
Silvern, Leonard C., 3:326, 358
Simek, J. G., 3:46
Simmons, Earl M., 1:322; 3:420, 426
Simmons, H., 3:233
Simmons, Robert F., 1:9, 76, 83, 129, 137–169, 137, 147, 149, 154, 158, 159; 2:138, 139, 162, 169, 177; 3:130, 135, 176, 185, 209, 239, 360, 377
Simmons, Walt R., 3:406
Simon, Herbert A., 1:156, 242, 2:171
Simons, M. E., 3:424
Simonson, W. E., 3:228, 293
Simpson, G. S., Jr., 1:305–335, 322, 329
Simpson, George M., 3:424
Simulation models, for educational planning, 3:370
  instructional uses, 3:361–362
Siroonian, Harold A., 3:282
Skelton, Margaret W., 1:294
Sketchpad graphical communication system, 1:237
Skinner, B. F., 2:169
Skipper, James E., 3:338
Skolnik, Herman, 3:340
Skulski, M., 1:259
Slack, Warner V., 2:317; 3:407
Slagle, J. R., 1:156
Slamecka, Vladimir, 1:23, 26, 82, 84; 3:68, 118
Slater, Margaret, 1:79; 3:20
Slavin, Morton, 3:403
SLIC (Selective Listing in Combination), 2:108
SLIP programming language, 2:126; 3:51
Slivka, Robert M., 3:97
Sloane, Margaret N., 3:341, 342
Slobin, D. I., 1:145; 2:170, 172
Slojowski, F. E., 2:126
Slotlow, H. G., 3:211, 379, 382
Small, V. H., 3:190
Small computers, 2:213–214; 3:204–206
Smallwood, Richard D., 3:375
Smart, Charles R., 2:328
SMART system, 1:119, 120, 122, 155–156, 160; 2:69–70, 94, 126; 3:85–86, 90, 109, 161, 185, 190–191, 381
Smith, Alfred G., 3:13
Smith, Charles P., 3:98, 326

Smith, Clagett G., 2:20, 26, 27
Smith, Cyril, 3:370
Smith, F. R., 2:267, 366; 3:254, 266, 283
Smith, J. Chandler, 2:323
Smith, J. L., 1:117; 2:52, 134
Smith, Jack W., 3:299
Smith, Joan M. B., 2:24
Smith, John Miles, 3:87
Smith, Marshall S., 3:135, 198
Smith, Meredith, 2:10
Smith, O. D., 3:213
Smith, R. E., 3:366
Smith, Steven B., 1:152; 3:133
Smithsonian Institution, 1:344
Snediker, James M., 2:37
SNOBOL programming language, 2:126, 173; 3:208, 224
Snyder, D. C., 3:233
Snyder, Monroe B., 2:55, 76; 3:79
Snyder, William R., 3:359
Snyderman, M., 3:70
Social science information systems, 1:320; 3:275, 311, 313
Social scientists, information exchange patterns, 2:11; 3:17–18, 22
Society for Information Display, 2:198; 3:210
Society of Automotive Engineers (SAE), 1:318
Socioeconomic data base systems, 2:148
Socratic-type teaching system, 1:243–244
Soergel, Dagobert, 1:86; 3:68, 126, 198
Software-simulated associative memories, 2:129–130
Sokoloff, Leon, 1:82
Sokolov, A. V., 2:64
SOLID file organization and search system, 3:208
SOLOMON processing concept, 2:226
Solomonoff, R. J., 3:190
Soltis, Steve J., 3:404
Solution Development Record, 1:64–65; 2:26; 3:9, 10
South Africa, management information survey, 2:9, 12, 28
South America, education for information science, 2:31
Southern Methodist University. Regional Technical Information Center, 2:265
Southhampton University, student library use study, 2:18
Southwest Regional Laboratory, 3:363
Spagnuolo, Mario, 3:412
Spain, R. J., 2:198
SPAN data base system, 2:148, 149

Sparck Jones, Karen, 1:94, 141, 142, 143, 144; 2:89; 3:111, 135, 147, 166, 177
Sparks, David E., 2:355
Special Libraries, 3:249
Special Libraries Association (SLA), 2:260, 276, 359; 3:241, 242, 243
Speech synthesis and recognition, 2:194, 234
Speierman, K. H., 1:218
Speight, Frank Y., 1:349; 2:361; 3:106, 326
Spencer, Carol C., 3:122
Spencer, W. A., 1:257, 271
Spiegel, Allen D., 3:426
Spiegel, J., 2:52, 239
Spiegler, Donna, 1:326, 329
Spiekerman, Ralph E., 3:421
Spitzer, J. F., 1:155
Spivak, Alfred P., 3:417
SPLAN school planning system, 3:369
Spolsky, Bernard, 3:360, 393
Spraberry, Mary N., 3:400
Spring, William C., Jr., 2:311–338
Springer, Doris V., 3:386
Springman, Mary Adele, 3:336, 354
Spruth, W. G., 1:134
Standard Computer Corp., 2:209
Standard Telecommunication Laboratories, Ltd., 3:278
Standardization, bibliographic data elements, 2:263; 3:248
  digital information systems, 2:357; 3:293
Stanford University, 1:197, 288; 3:303
  ERIC Clearinghouse on Educational Media and Technology, 3:357
  Physics Information Retrieval System (SPIRES), 3:26
  School of Education, 3:299
  School Planning Laboratory, 3:369
Stanwood, Richard H., 1:86; 2:107, 277, 366
STAR (see *Scientific and Technical Aerospace Reports*)
Starkweather, J. A., 3:416
State education information networks, 3:299
State library planning, 2:407–408; 3:306
State Technical Services Act of 1965 (P.L. 89–182), 1:346; 2:265; 3:313
State University of New York (SUNY) biomedical information system, 3:309, 418
  computer network, 3:300, 303
  Library Processing Center, 3:250–251
State University of New York. Downstate

Medical Center. Medical Research Library, 3:309
Statistical aids to vocabulary building, 1:247–248; 2:94; 3:110
Statistical methods, document retrieval, 2:70–71; 3:75, 86, 127–128, 140–141, 187–189, 273
Statistical modeling, 1:247
Statistical word association, 2:70; 3:273
Stauffer, William M., 3:413, 426
Stearns, Charles M., 3:192, 243
Stearns, Jack, 1:310, 327
Stedry, A. C., 2:37
Stegmaier, R. B., Jr., 1:310
Steil, Gilbert P., Jr., 3:157
Stein, Charles R., 3:74, 75
Steinberger, N., 3:131
Steiner, Jan W., 3:417, 421
Stepp, Robert E., 3:426
Sterling, Theodore, 2:314, 320
Stern, Michael M., 2:354
Stevens, Mary Elizabeth, 1:74, 75, 81, 86, 87, 173, 175, 183; 2:104; 3:47
Stevenson, C. G., 3:62
Stewart, Bruce W., 1:283; 2:271
Stewart, G. T., 2:330
Stickley, G. F., 3:426
Stiefel, Rudy C., 2:214
Stockwell, Robert, 2:165
Stolurow, Lawrence M., 3:326, 357, 358
Stolz, W. S., 1:150
Stone, C. Walter, 3:263, 305
Stone, Don C., 2:89; 3:100, 111, 134, 197
Stone, Phillip J., 1:76, 160; 3:113, 170, 176, 180
Stone, Walter C., 1:298
Storage organization, 1:109–112, 201–207; 2:127–131; 3:149–150, 217–218
Storer, Norman W., 2:362
Stotler, Donald, 3:364
Stotz, Robert H., 1:230; 3:213
Stowe, Arthur N., 2:137
Strain, Paula M., 3:257
Strange, J. G., 2:348
Stratton, William D., 2:232
Straumfjord, Jon V., 3:400
Strauss, Jon C., 3:239
STRESS programming language, 1:230; 3:224
Stretch, Terrance T., 3:103, 167
String analysis, 3:86, 110, 121, 186–187
String-processing languages, 2:126; 3:224
Stroebel, Charles F., 3:409
Stromberg-Carlson SC 1100 display unit, 1:196
  4020 microfilm printer, 2:191; 3:254
Strong, S., 1:252
STRUDL programming language, 2:235; 3:224
Stuart, Michael, 3:359
Stuart, Walter J., 1:26
STUDENT question answering program, 2:171
Stylistic analysis, 1:159–160; 3:113–114
Stylus-input tablets 3:212
Subramaniam, J. B., 3:162
Sullivan, Dennis J., 3:87, 101
Sullivan, W. A., 1:206
Summers, J. K., 2:52; 3:156, 181, 239
Summit, Roger K., 2:52; 3:239
Suppes, Patrick, 2:199; 3:358, 393
SURF (Support of User Records and Files), 2:149
Survey of automation activities in libraries, 3:242, 243, 258, 265
Survey of Chemical Notation Systems, 2:286, 291
Sussenguth, Edward H., Jr., 1:119, 121
Sutherland, Georgia, 3:239
Sutherland, Ivan E., 1:221, 226, 229, 233; 2:230
Sutherland, W. P., 1:229
Sutherland, William R., 1:235; 3:180, 215
Svenonius, Elaine, 3:82, 119
Swallow, Ronald, 3:379
Swank, Raynard C., 3:340, 341
Swanson, Don R., 1:16, 21, 81, 83, 90, 172, 174, 183; 2:80, 363, 389, 390, 433; 3:18, 82
Swanson, Rowena W., 2:36, 39, 393; 3:48, 59, 61, 294, 331, 341
Swartzentruber, P. E., 3:58
Sweden. Royal Library (Stockholm), 2:263
Sweeney, James W., 3:414
Swenson, W. M., 3:366
Swets, John A., 1:173, 265; 3:73, 139, 239
SWIFT (Significant Words in the Full Title), 2:141
Sylvania Corp., 1:194; 2:100, 201
Symbiont I system, 3:49
Symbol representation standards, 2:357–358
Symbolic integration program, 3:201
Symposium for Systems Under Development for Vocational Guidance—IBM, 3:368
Symposium on Computer Augmentation of Human Reasoning, 3:232
Symposium on Computer-Centered Data Base Systems, 2:238
Synonym classes, 3:116

Syntactic analysis, 1:147–150, 152–153; 2:104, 173–174; 3:110–111, 170, 179, 360
  in document retrieval systems, 2:106; 3:183–187, 273
Syntactic theory, 2:162–165
SYNTOL (Syntagmatic Organization Language), 1:90, 91, 123; 3:186
Syracuse University, 3:385
  film library, 3:308–309
System analysis, in design and evaluation of information systems, 2:35–41; 3:62–70
  in libraries, 2:266–267; 3:249
System Development Corporation (SDC), 1:4, 72, 125, 183, 228, 234, 265, 279, 290, 341, 342; 2:77, 172, 173, 223, 227, 402; 3:77–78, 90, 151, 153–154, 202, 206, 218, 304, 363, 367, 371, 372
Systems evaluation, 1:327; 2:64–82; 3:61–103, 107, 139

Tabuchi, Toshiaki, 1:84
Taft, Martin Israel, 3:375
Taft, Terril D., 3:115, 132, 236
TAG (Teacher's Automated Guide), 3:364
Tagliacozzo, Renata, 3:133
Tague, Jean, 1:182; 2:89, 90, 94
Takashima, M., 1:210
Takle, Karen G., 3:266, 276
Talerico, Linda, 3:412
Tanaka, R. I., 2:52
Tannenbaum, P. H., 1:150
Taranta, Angelo, 3:412
Tarter, Michael E., 2:132
Tasker Instruments Corp., 1:196
Tate, Fred A., 1:314; 2:285–309, 346; 3:47, 142, 199, 240, 326
Taube, Mortimer, 1:16, 81, 90, 93, 172, 173, 183; 2:88, 435
Tauber, Alfred S., 3:76, 282
Tauber, S. J., 1:267
Tauber, Stephen L., 1:120
Taulbee, Orrin E., 1:90; 2:40, 42; 3:75, 81, 105–136, 297
Tavares, J. F. C., 1:86
Taylor, Robert S., 1:8, 15–40, 17, 26; 2:419–421, 435; 3:9, 18, 62, 135, 266, 340, 341
Taylor, Robert W., 3:210
Taylor, S. H., 3:414
TDMS (Time-Shared Data Management System), 2:137, 144, 146, 148, 240; 3:153–155, 218–219
Te Nuyl, Th. W., 1:117; 2:65
TEACH programming language, 3:224

Teal, Gilbert E., 3:57
Technical information systems, U.S.S.R., 3:171
Technical reports, mechanized processing, 3:271
Technique to Retrieve Information from Abstracts of Literature (see TRIAL program)
Teitelman, Warren, 2:173; 3:181, 224
TEKTRONIX display scope, 3:55, 211
Telecommunications, as a developing technology, 3:293, 316
TELECOMP programming language, 2:212; 3:223, 381
Teleputer system, 2:199
Teletypewriters, in library communications networks, 1:240; 3:310–311
Television outputs, 1:213; 2:196, 328; 3:267, 302
Tell, Björn V., 1:30, 91, 173, 183; 2:65
Teltsch, Kathleen, 3:326
Tennehouse, A. B., 1:268
Teplitz, Arthur, 1:203
Terragno, P. J., 1:184, 187
Tervila, L., 3:412
Testing, computer-assisted, 3:366–367, 407
Tewlow, Jules S., 3:43
Texas A & M University, 1:282, 283; 2:271
Texas Council of Health Science Libraries, 3:308
Texas Gulf Coast libraries, Regional Information and Communication Exchange, 3:311
Texas Institute for Rehabilitation and Research, clinical data system, 2:324–325
Texas Regional Technical Information Center, 2:265
Texas State Library, communications network study, 3:310
Textbook on Mechanized Information Retrieval, 2:287
Thatcher, R. A., 3:427
Thesauri, construction and use, 1:92–95, 316; 2:48–49, 93–97, 102, 399; 3:124, 125, 182
Thiesmayer, L. R., 2:348
Thin film memories, 1:209; 2:207
Thiokol Chemical Corp., 2:147
Thomas, W., 3:412
Thomas Publishing Co., 2:201
Thompson, David A., 3:126, 135, 150
Thompson, Fredrick B., 1:231; 2:139, 177, 235
Thompson, Gerald L., 3:359

COMBINED INDEX 543

Thompson, H., 1:222
Thompson, John D., 3:423
Thompson, L., 2:99
Thompson-Ramo-Wooldridge, 1:176
Thomson, Lucille H., 3:159, 164, 166
Thonstad, Tore, 3:370
Thorne, J. P., 2:174
Thorne, R. G., 1:172
Thornhill, D. E., 3:211
Thorpe, J., 3:401
Three-dimensional drawing simulation, 2:198
Tideman, David, 3:367
Tidmarsh, Mavis, 2:18
Tierney, James M., 3:98, 270
Time-shared Data Management System (*see* TDMS)
Time-shared Routines for Analysis, Classification and Evaluation (*see* TRACE)
Time-sharing systems, 1:224–229, 290; 2:210–213, 225, 246; 3:50, 151, 153–156, 202–203, 205–210, 217–220, 227
 comparisons, 3:209–210
 directory, 3:317
 educational applications, 2:199; 3:371
 FCC investigation, 3:227
 hospital applications, 1:248; 3:409
 in colleges and universities, 3:300
 mathematical and computational applications, 1:233–234
Timonen, S., 3:412
Tinker, John F., 1:81; 2:96
TINT programming language, 3:381
Title, Irwin, 3:402
Title indexing, 2:67, 69; 3:147
Titus, James P., 3:229, 337
Todd, M. A., 1:271
Tolles, Walter E., 3:427
Toman, J., 1:29, 91
Tomeski, Edward A., 3:102
Tompkins, C. B., 1:235
Tompkins, Howard E., 3:67
Tompkins, Mary L., 2:275
Tonge, Fred M., 3:151, 180
Tootill, G. C., 1:82
Torkelson, Leif O., 3:417
Tosh, L. W., 1:152
Towster, A. E., 3:195
Toxicology information, 2:329
Toyoda, Junichi, 2:132
TRAC text-handling language, 1:239–240
TRACE (Time-shared Routines for Analysis, Classification and Evaluation), 3:154, 208
Transformational grammars, 1:139–140, 147; 2:163–165, 173–174; 3:174–176, 183, 201
Translation systems, machine-aided, 2:176; 3:182, 190
Traub, J. F., 1:72, 85; 3:33, 285
Travelers Insurance Co., 3:316
Tree-structured files, 2:106, 134, 145, 166, 167
Treseder, Anne, 3:342, 424
Tretiak, O. J., 1:212
Treu, Siegfried, 3:62, 79
TRIAL System, 3:279
Triangle Universities' Computation Center (TUCC), 3:300
Trocchi, Robert F., 3:348
Trueswell, R. W., 2:29
Tsao, R., 3:100
Tschirgi, Robert D., 3:298
Tukey, John W., 2:275; 3:75
Tulane University, 1:257
Tunis, C. J., 3:46
Tuohy, John H., 3:427
Tupac, J. D., 3:70
Turn, Rein, 3:229
Turnbull, James, 3:327
Turner, Arch H., 2:315
Twelker, Paul, 3:361
TX-O computer, 2:194
TX-2 computer, 1:116; 3:214
Tyler, Louise L., 3:368
Tymshare Corp., 2:194
Typesetting, 1:197–200; 2:278, 352–358; 3:43–44, 47–48
Tyson, Joseph W., 1:56, 58, 61, 67; 3:13

Uchida, H., 3:147
UCLA (*see* University of California at Los Angeles)
Uhr, Leonard, 1:265; 3:377
Uhrenholdt, A., 3:427
Ullman, S., 1:141
Ullmann, Hans C., 2:91, 97
Umstead, Charles R., 3:257
UNESCO, 2:345; 3:294
UNICON system, 2:205
Unilever Research Laboratory, 3:275
United Nations Educational, Scientific, and Cultural Organization (*see* UNESCO)
UNIVAC 494 computer, 1:208
 1004 computer, 2:265
 1107 computer, 1:277
 1108-II computer, 2:210
Universal Decimal Classification (UDC), use in automatic indexing, 1:315; 3:121

use in machine search systems, 2:81, 96, 100; 3:67, 124, 141–142, 157, 274
University of California, 1:22
　at Berkeley, 1:151
　at Irvine, 3:298, 358
　at Los Angeles (UCLA), 1:21, 288, 291, 293, 294, 296; 2:165, 328; 3:358
　at Santa Cruz, 1:278, 287
　Institute of Library Research, 2:277, 279; 3:271, 272
　Lawrence Radiation Laboratory, 3:221–222
　School of Medicine, 3:416
University of Chicago, 1:18, 19, 21, 25; 3:255
University of Colorado, 1:296
University of Dayton Research Institute, 2:96; 3:274
University of Edinburgh, 2:174
University of Guelph, Library Documentation Center, 2:273
University of Illinois, 1:32, 195, 276; 2:199, 238; 3:300, 359, 362, 382
University of Maryland, 1:22, 292
University of Miami, 3:300
University of Michigan, 1:19, 24
　Center for Research on Learning and Teaching, 3:357
　Library, 3:250
　Systems Engineering Laboratory, 2:38
University of Missouri, 1:257; 2:315, 323
University of Nevada, 1:213
University of North Carolina, 1:18, 24; 3:300
University of Pennsylvania, 1:162; 2:175, 294, 299
　Moore School of Electrical Engineering, 3:87, 148, 151, 153, 160, 272
University of Pittsburgh, 1:198, 201; 2:351; 3:300
University of Rochester, 1:284
　Medical Library, 3:309
University of Southern California, School of Medicine, 1:248
University of Texas, Laboratory for Computer-Assisted Instruction, 3:303, 362, 371, 373
　Linguistic Research Center, 1:141, 151, 152, 157
University of Toronto, 1:284; 3:370
University of Tulsa, Department of Information Services, 3:271
University of Wisconsin, 2:317, 318, 323
　Library, 3:255
Upatnieks, J., 1:217
Urbach, Peter, 3:69, 90, 97

Urban, G. H., 1:175
URBANDOC, 1:320
Urdang Laurence, 2:352
Urquhart, A. B., 1:197
Urquhart, D. J., 1:79; 2:22, 340
U.S.A. Standards Institute, 2:264, 342; 3:248
U.S. Congress, House of Representatives, Committee on the Judiciary, 1:346, 347
U.S. Congress, Senate, Committee on Government Operations, 1:337
U.S. Government Research and Development Reports (USGRDR), 1:317
U.S. Information Agency, 3:302
U.S. Naval Academy, 3:359
U.S. Office of Education, 3:299, 370
　ERIC program (*see* ERIC)
U.S. Patent Office, 2:75, 287
User languages, 2:136, 143, 144, 236; 3:151
User profiling, 3:160–161, 276–280
　by hierarchical subject classification, 3:280
User studies, 1:41–68, 322–323; 2:1–31; 3:2–3, 21, 25–26
　Department of Defense, 3:12–13
User-system interaction studies, 2:74, 137; 3:83–85, 87–88
U.S.S.R., technical information systems, 3:171, 294
Uspenskii, V. A., 2:88
Utterschaut, L., 2:11
Uzeta, Carlos B., 3:285

Vallbona, Carlos, 1:258; 2:324; 3:400
Van Buskirk, R. C., 1:37
Van Cott, Harold P., 2:106; 3:19
Van Cura, Lawrence J., 3:426
Van Dam, Andries, 1:196; 2:47, 187–222, 198, 231; 3:281
Van Den Bogaerde, Mary Louise, 3:136
Vander Lugt, A., 1:195
Vander Stouw, G. G., 3:142, 167
Van Horn, R. K., 1:194
Van Houten, R., 2:12
Van Luik, James, 1:82, 85, 102, 264
Van Meter, Clarence T., 2:128, 134; 3:158
Van Oot, J. G., 2:75, 92, 98
Van Peenen, Hubert J., 1:270; 2:330; 3:424
Van Riper, Paul P., 3:355
Van Woerkom, Andriann J., 2:318
Vasarhelyi, P. E., 1:84; 3:136
Vauquois, B., 3:199

COMBINED INDEX 545

Vcherashni, R. P., 3:75
Veaner, Allen B., 1:203
Veillon, G., 3:175
VELA Seismic Information Analysis Center (VESIAC), 3:141–142, 274
Venner, Frank H., 3:167
Verbally-Indexed-Associations (VIA), 3:113
Ver Hoef, E. W., 2:150
Verhoeff, J., 2:276
Vermont, library planning, 3:307
VESIAC (*see* VELA Seismic Information Analysis Center)
Vesser, W. C., 3:212
Vickery, B. C., 2:100, 364
VIDEO-IR transmission system, 1:212–213
Video technology, in educational networks, 2:328; 3:301, 302
Videofile system, 1:204; 2:203
Viil, Heino, 2:47
Vilentschuk, Lydia, 1:30
Vinsonhaler, John F., 2:113; 3:157, 366
VIP (Variable Information Processing), 1:124
Virbel, Jacques, 3:192
Virginia State College, dial-access information system, 3:303
Vitagliano, V. J., 1:332
VITAL compiler-compiler, 3:224
Vocabulary control, 1:88–95; 2:48–50, 87, 93–103; 3:118, 123
Voress, Hugh E., 1:86, 311
Vorhaus, Alfred H., 2:239; 3:167, 240
Vyssotsky, V. A., 1:250; 2:212; 3:240

Waddington, Guy, 2:360
WADEX (Word and author index), 1:315; 2:344
Waggoner, Cecil L., 3:402
Wagner, Frank S., Jr., 2:98
Wagner, G., 2:17
Wagner, Henry N., 3:427
Wagner, John G., 3:427
Wahlin, Ejnar S., 2:101; 3:136
Wainio, Elizabeth, 3:278
Waite, W. M., 3:149
Waks, David J., 3:240
Waldo, W. H., 2:296, 298
Walker, Clyde M., 3:119
Walker, Donald E., 2;173; 3:49, 102, 116, 167, 175, 183, 240
Walker, J. F., 1:83, 147; 2:109
Walker, J. R. A., 3:275
Walker, Weldon J., 3:413
Wall, Eugene, 1:80, 83; 3:63

Wall, R. E., 1:98, 147, 149
Wallace, Everett M., 1:191; 2:106, 3:27, 30, 135, 342, 355
Wallen, Carl, 3:361
Wallenstein, M. B., 1:350
WALNUT microfilm retrieval system, 2:203
Walter, D. O., 3:427
Walter Reed Army Institute of Research, 2:287, 299, 346
WAND ultrasonic input device, 2:197
Wantman, M. E., 1:234
Warburton, C. R., 1:109
Ward, J. E., 1:230; 3:211
Ware, Willis H., 1:192, 200, 209; 2:247; 3:229, 240, 295
Warheit, I. A., 3:244
Wascak, M. L., 1:332
Washington State, library programs, 2:269; 3:246, 306
Washington State University, Library, 3:251
Wasserman, Paul, 2:435, 440; 3:341, 342, 346, 355
Waterhouse, William T., 3:278
WATFOR compiler, 3:208
Watson, James D., 3:26
Watson, Richard, 3:27
Watts, S. P., 3:406
Waugh, Douglas W., 2:236
Way, Katharine, 1:80; 2:343
Wayne State University, 1:151; 2:13
Weaver, Barbara N., 3:286, 423
Weaver, Vance, 2:342
Webb, Eugene J., 3:25
Webb, Jesse, 3:367
Webb, John W., 1:266; 2:108
Webster, E., 1:199, 200
Wechsler, D., 3:233
Weed, Lawrence L., 3:405
Weighting of search terms, 2:99; 3:140–141, 150–151, 159, 277–278
Weihrer, Anna Lea, 3:413, 426, 427
Weil, Ben H., 1:314
Weil, Janet Whalen, 3:403
Weil, M. H., 1:248; 3:426
Weil, Thomas P., 3:403
Weinberg report, 1:83, 321, 341
Weinman, David G., 3:130, 163
Weinreich, U., 1:142; 2:165, 166
Weinstein, Edward A., 3:254
Weinstein, Iram, 3:375
Weinstein, S. Jane, 1:259; 2:94
Weinstock, Melvin, 3:304, 305
Weinwurm, George F., 3:70
Weir, R. D., 3:421

Weis, R. L., 3:88, 114
Weisberg, D., 2:297
Weisman, Herman M., 2:361; 3:331
Weiss, A. D., 1:197
Weiss, Irvin J., 3:256
Weissman, Clark, 1:225, 227; 3:100, 206, 371, 380
Weizenbaum, Joseph, 1:229, 230, 231; 2:103, 177, 236; 3:181, 225, 240, 380, 394
Weksel, William, 3:407
Welch, John T., Jr., 2:292; 3:68, 102
Weller, John M., 3:416
Welles, J. G., 3:94
Wells, A. J., 2:263
Welt, Isaac D., 1:82, 321; 3:136
Wendler, Charles C., 2:39
Wente, Van A., 1:80, 311; 3:90, 277, 281
Werner, David J., 2:5, 29; 3:18
Wesley, James P., 2:369
Wessel, C. J., 3:62
West, M., 3:353
Western Electric Co., Inktronic process, 3:48
Western Michigan University, dial-access information system, 3:304
Western Reserve University (*see* Case Western Reserve University)
Western Union Telegraph Co., 1:213
Westervelt, F. H., 3:240
Westin, Alan F., 3:229
Westinghouse Electric Corp., 1:197; 2:243
Westinghouse Learning Corp., 3:364
Westrate, J. Lee, 1:345
Wetsel, F. R., 1:314
Weyerhaeuser Corp., management information system, 3:315
Weyl, F. Joachim, 2:402
Weyman, A., 2:350
Weymouth, William, 3:428
Whaley, Fred R., 1:333; 3:278
White, R. H., 1:267
White, Wade L., 3:48, 58, 197
Whiteley, R. B., 2:52
Whiteman, John R., 3:413, 427
Whiting, R., 3:423
Whitman, David, 3:135, 166
Whittingham, D. J., 2:330
Wied, George, 3:427
Wiederkehr, R. R. V., 3:68, 69, 73, 94, 97, 102
Wiggington, Ronald L., 2:232; 3:213
Wiggins, Emilie V., 3:256
Wiig, R., 3:100
Wilcox, J. L., 3:233
Wilcox, Richard H., 1:241; 2:36

Wilds, Preston Lea, 3:415
Wilkes, M. V., 1:210, 211
Wilkes, Mary Allen, 3:240
Wilkins, Donald, 3:65
Wilkinson, William A., 3:252
Wilkinson, William D., 3:238
Wilks, Yorick, 3:87, 176
Willenbrock, F. Karl, 2:387
Willey, Edward N., 3:404
Williams, Ann S., 1:82, 303
Williams, Bernard J. S., 3:282
Williams, J. H., 1:87, 91, 175, 182; 2:107; 3:85
Williams, K. J., 2:327
Williams, S. B., 1:130
Williams, Thomas L., 3:378
Williams, T. M., 1:78
Williams, Van Zandt, 1:349; 2:362, 398
Williams, William D., 2:137; 3:154, 240
Williams, W. F., 2:48; 3:85, 97, 126, 195
Williamson, D., 3:132, 164
Williamson, R., 3:132, 164
Williamsport (Pa.) Area Community College, 3:371
Wills, Robert D., 3:167, 240
Willson, R. H., 3:211
Wilmer, Harry A., 3:416
Wilmot, C. A., 2:47
Wilson, H. A., 3:358
Wilson, Ira G., 2:39
Wilson, Leslie, 3:333
Wilson, Marthann E., 2:39
Wilson, William J., 1:120
Winckler, Paul A., 3:336
Wing, Paul, 3:428
Wing, Richard L., 1:243; 3:361, 374
Winiecki, Kenneth B., 2:242
Winkler, C., 3:412
Winkler, U., 1:166
Winsberg, Fred, 3:428
Winsor, Travis, 3:426
Winters, R. W., 3:422
Wirth, Bradford P., 3:428
Wise, F. H., 1:244
Wiswesser, W. J., 2:141, 291; 3:164
Wiswesser line notation for chemical compounds, 2:141, 294, 300; 3:142
Witherspoon, John P., 3:327
Wodtke, Kenneth H., 3:378
Wolek, Francis W., 1:62; 2:390; 3:10, 12, 13, 14, 65
Wolf, A. W., 3:235
Wolfe, Hugh C., 1:349; 2:339-384
Wolfe, Molly A., 3:89, 280, 281
Wolfe, W. L., 1:326
Wood, James L., 1:266

Wood, M. K., 3:95
Wood, N. W., 2:113
Woodford, F. Peter, 3:36–37
Woods, William A., 2:176; 3:136, 177–179, 240
Woodward, P. M., 2:126
Wooster, Harold, 1:18; 3:66
Worth, Dean S., 3:236
Wuest, F. J., 1:49, 53, 55
Wurtele, Zivia S., 3:370, 394
Wyatt, H. V., 3:340
Wyllys, Ronald E., 1:15, 87, 162; 2:45; 3:27, 118
Wynn, W. H., 2:168
Wynne, B. E., Jr., 3:95

Xerographic systems, 1:206, 213; 2:232
Xerox Corp., 1:204; 2:200, 277; 3:311
Xhignesse, Louis V., 3:16, 20

Yale University, 1:276, 283; 2:10, 262; 3:246
Yamada, H., 3:182
Yanagawa, Niroshi, 3:412
Yang, Chao-Chih, 2:131
Yarnall, Stephen R., 2:320, 323
Yeakel, Allen E., 3:405
Yeats, J. C. R., 1:82
Yerke, Theodore B., 1:85; 3:119
Yershov, A. P., 1:231–232

Yett, F. A., 3:391
Yngve, V. H., 1:153
Yoder, Richard D., 3:408, 414
Youden, William W., 2:277
Young, Gifford A., 1:311; 3:90, 277, 281
Yovits, M. C., 3:103

Zabriskie, Kenneth H., Jr., 1:264, 314; 2:330
Zachert, Martha Jane K., 3:341
Zachert, Virginia, 3:415
Zajac, E. E., 3:213
Zaltman, Gerald, 3:15
Zatocoding, 1:117
Zator Co., 1:16
Zavala, Albert, 2:106
Zeiger, Marion, 2:359
Zell, Hans M., 2:277
Zieke, Theodore W., 1:111; 2:357; 3:235
Ziff, Paul, 3:196
Ziman, J. M., 2:369
Zinn, Karl L., 3:303, 327, 342, 357, 371, 379, 381, 384, 395
Zipf, E. M., 1:313
Zuckerman, Harriet, 3:23
Zull, Carolyn G., 3:84, 189
Zurcher, F. W., 1:218
Zunde, Pranas, 1:82; 3:67, 68, 103, 118, 146
Zwicky, Arnold M., 1:147, 148